D1190949

Texts in Computer Science

Series Editors

David Gries, Department of Computer Science, Cornell University, Ithaca, NY, USA

Orit Hazzan, Faculty of Education in Technology and Science, Technion—Israel Institute of Technology, Haifa, Israel

Titles in this series now included in the Thomson Reuters Book Citation Index!

'Texts in Computer Science' (TCS) delivers high-quality instructional content for undergraduates and graduates in all areas of computing and information science, with a strong emphasis on core foundational and theoretical material but inclusive of some prominent applications-related content. TCS books should be reasonably self-contained and aim to provide students with modern and clear accounts of topics ranging across the computing curriculum. As a result, the books are ideal for semester courses or for individual self-study in cases where people need to expand their knowledge. All texts are authored by established experts in their fields, reviewed internally and by the series editors, and provide numerous examples, problems, and other pedagogical tools; many contain fully worked solutions.

The TCS series is comprised of high-quality, self-contained books that have broad and comprehensive coverage and are generally in hardback format and sometimes contain color. For undergraduate textbooks that are likely to be more brief and modular in their approach, require only black and white, and are under 275 pages, Springer offers the flexibly designed Undergraduate Topics in Computer Science series, to which we refer potential authors.

More information about this series at https://link.springer.com/bookseries/3191

Marco T. Morazán

Animated Problem Solving

An Introduction to Program Design
Using Video Game Development

 Springer

Marco T. Morazán
Department of Computer Science
Seton Hall University
South Orange, NJ, USA

ISSN 1868-0941   ISSN 1868-095X   (electronic)
Texts in Computer Science
ISBN 978-3-030-85090-6   ISBN 978-3-030-85091-3   (eBook)
https://doi.org/10.1007/978-3-030-85091-3

This Springer imprint is published by the registered company Springer Nature Switzerland AG.
The registered company address is: Gewerbestrasse 11, 6330 Cham, Switzerland

To my parents, Doris and Marco, who taught me to love teaching and to realize that having an education is not a privilege but a responsibility.

Preface

Everybody engages in problem solving. It is a natural and inevitable part of life. Historically, the link between problem solving and programming has been less emphasized. When you write an essay, you are programming—at different levels many times. You make sure ideas flow and arguments make use of the data you are analyzing. You write several drafts of the essay. Each draft represents a refinement. Every paragraph has a point and you avoid repeating yourself. All this is part of programming, including computer programming. Programmers, people who solve problems using a computer, go through the exact same steps to write a program. The same steps are taken by a psychologist analyzing a patient and by a chemist experimenting in a laboratory. Even a painter engages in programming. No? Does a painter not want to elicit an outcome or an emotion in you? Indeed, how to achieve this is a problem that must be solved by the artist. Consider the painting *Sorrowing Old Man (At Eternity's Gate)* by Vincent van Gogh (search for it on the internet). Can you see the old man's sorrow? Can you imagine the weight of the years on him? If so, we can say that the painter successfully solved the problem. This brings us to another important component of problem solving: testing. It is not only important to solve a problem. It is equally important to test the solution to make sure it works and in many cases to make sure that the solution is efficient.

This book is about systematic problem solving or if you like about systematic reasoning. Unlike most textbooks about programming, this textbook is not about tinkering with or hacking code. This book is about making a plan to solve a problem and then implementing the solution. As we shall discover, it turns out that the solutions to many problems are similar. This should not come as a surprise because we often solve many problems using similar data. How do you do grocery shopping? You make a list of items and check them off as you put them in your cart. How do you manage your chores today? You make a list of chores and check them off as you get them done. Pretty similar, no? Similarities give rise to abstraction to avoid repetitions—or reinventing the proverbial wheel. This book, therefore, is also about abstraction. Thinking abstractly is a powerful tool in problem solving.

In this textbook, all the solutions to problems are expressed as programs. It is important to be somewhat precise about what a program is. A program is much more than just code written using a programming language. Remember that a program is a solution to a problem. Therefore, a program has a design, code, examples of how it works, and tests. That is, it communicates how the problem is solved and illustrates that the solution works. If any of the mentioned components are missing, then we have an incomplete program. Would you believe someone who simply told you that n^2, where n is a nonnegative integer, is the sum of the first n odd numbers? Many readers would be skeptical. What if they also provided the following examples:

$$0^2 = 0$$
$$2^2 = 1 + 3$$
$$4^2 = 1 + 3 + 5 + 7$$

It is very likely that most readers would now feel more confident that the claim is true. It is the same in programming. We cannot simply say that here is a function that does this or that. We need to explain how the function computes its value, and we need to have examples that show how it works. The steps taken to design a program in a systematic manner is called a *design recipe*. In this textbook, you shall study many different design recipes. Each design recipe shall become a tool in your problem-solving toolbox.

There are two problem-solving techniques that are emphasized throughout the book: *divide and conquer* and *iterative refinement*. Divide and conquer is the process by which a large problem is broken into two or more smaller problems that are easier to solve and then the solutions for the smaller pieces are combined to create an answer to the problem. Iterative refinement is the process by which a solution to a problem is gradually made better—like the drafts of an essay. Mastering these techniques is essential to becoming a good problem solver and programmer.

Finally, problem solving ought to be fun. To this end, this book promises that by the end of it you will have designed and implemented a multiplayer video game that you can play with your friends over the internet. To achieve this, however, there is a lot about problem solving and programming that you must first learn. The game is developed using iterative refinement. As we learn about programming, we shall apply our new knowledge to develop increasingly better versions of the video game. In fact, every skill you develop for problem solving and program design is transferable to other (non-programming) domains and to other programming languages.

1 The Languages and the Parts of the Book

The book uses the Racket student languages to write programs. These languages are chosen for several reasons. The first is that they have an error-messaging system specifically designed for beginners. This means that unlike common programming languages the error messages are likely to make sense to beginners. If you do not understand an error message, do not hesitate to ask your professor or search for help online. The second is that the syntax is simple and easy to understand. This is important because the emphasis is always on problem solving and not on how to correctly write expressions. The third is that the student languages progressively become richer. At the beginning, you have fewer features at your disposal and, therefore, the possible errors are fewer. The fourth reason is that the student languages come with powerful libraries to create graphics, animations, and video games. These libraries allow students to inject their own personalities in the development of games and animations. You are strongly encouraged to be creative. Finally, the fifth reason is that the Racket student languages are likely to put all students on the same playing field. Most students will be learning the syntax of the programming language together for the first time.

The book is divided into five parts. Part I focuses on the basics. It starts with how to write expressions. Once expressions are mastered, the first abstraction lesson introduces us to functions. In addition, this part introduces you to conditional expressions that allow you to write programs that make decisions. Just this much knowledge allows us to write interactive programs and puts us on our way to a multiplayer video game. As you shall discover, decision-making is fundamental to solving problems that involve information that has many varieties. For example, the whole numbers may be positive or negative—two varieties—and how a whole number is processed depends on which variety a given number belongs to. Think about how to compute the absolute value of a whole number.

Part II introduces you to compound data of finite size. Compound data has multiple values associated. For example, a point on the Cartesian plane is compound data of finite size. There are two values: an x coordinate and a y coordinate. Being able to define compound data of finite size to represent elements in the real or an imaginary world is a powerful skill to develop.

Part III introduces you to compound data of arbitrary size. This is data that has multiple values, but the number of values is not fixed. Once again, think about a grocery list. Sometimes there are no items in the list and at other times there may be 10, 6, or 17 items in the list. This is where you are introduced to *structural recursion*—a powerful data-processing strategy that uses divide and conquer to process data whose size is not fixed. The types of data that are introduced are lists, intervals, natural numbers, and binary trees. The knowledge developed is used to develop a video game that is more challenging for the player.

Part IV delves into abstraction. This section is where we learn how to eliminate repetitions in our solutions to problems. In fact, we learn how different data can be processed and different problems can be solved in exactly the same way. You are introduced to generic programming, which is abstraction over the type of data processed. This leads to the realization that functions are data and, perhaps more surprising, that data are functions. In other words, the line between data and functions is artificial—a fact that is not emphasized enough in Computer Science textbooks. This realization naturally leads to object-oriented programming—a topic that you are likely to study extensively.

Part V introduces you to distributed programming—using multiple computers to solve a problem. This is a topic that until now has never been addressed in a textbook for beginning programmers. The fact that you develop proficiency in program design makes it possible for this topic, common in modern computer applications, to be discussed. If you have ever sent a text message or have ever played a game online, then you have benefitted from and have used a distributed program. It is impossible, of course, to discuss all the nuances of distributed programming in this textbook. Nonetheless, you are introduced to a modern trend that is likely to be common throughout your professional career and beyond.

2 Acknowledgments

This book is the product of over ten years of work at Seton Hall University building on the shoulders of giants in Computer Science. There are many persons and groups who deserve credit for informing my work. The `Racket` community has been unequivocal in its support for the techniques that I have developed. There is an unpayable debt of gratitude owed to Matthias Felleisen from Northeastern University for our discussions over the years about Computer Science education, Liberal Arts education, and program design. My students and I have greatly benefitted from his support. Other Racketeers who have deeply influenced me are Shriram Krishnamurthi, Matthew Flatt, Robert Bruce Findler, and Kathi Fisler. This textbook is a tribute to our debates and their published work.

I would also like to thank the Trends in Functional Programming (TFP) and the Trends in Functional Programming in Education (TFPIE) communities. These communities provided (and continue to provide) a venue to discuss and present work advancing Computer Science education. I am grateful to many individuals including Peter Achten, Jurriaan Hage, Pieter Koopman, Simon Thompson, and Marko van Eekelen. Their insightful feedback has informed much of the material in this textbook.

Finally, I would like to thank Seton Hall University and its Department of Computer Science for supporting the development of the work presented in this textbook. In particular, the support of John T. Saccoman, Manfred Minimair, and Daniel Gross is appreciated. Most of all, I am grateful to all my CS1 students over the past decade who have informed my Computer Science education efforts. It is likely true that my students have learned a great deal in my courses, but it is an absolute certainty that I have learned more from them. They have refined the delivery of every idea found in this textbook. I am especially grateful to all my undergraduate tutors and teaching assistants, including Shamil Dzhatdoyev, Josie Des Rosiers, Nicholas Olson, Nicholas Nelson, Lindsey Reams, Craig Pelling, Barbara Mucha, Joshua Schappel, Sachin Mahashabde, Rositsa Abrasheva, Isabella Felix, and Sena Karsavran. Without my dedicated students at Seton Hall University and their insight into what students understood, this textbook would have been impossible.

Contents

Part I
The Basics of Problem Solving
with a Computer

Chapter 1
The Science of Problem Solving

We all solve problems every day. Have you ever thought about how you go about problem solving? Do you randomly go about trying potential solutions to a problem or do you think about how to solve the problem? Most of the time you probably think about the problem to find a solution. A natural question that arises is how do we think about a problem to find a solution. In other words, what steps do we take to arrive to a plausible solution? The solution is plausible until we test it and feel confident that it works. If it does not work, of course, we go back to thinking about the problem to obtain a refined solution. Understanding how to think about problems and solutions is where Computer Science and programming are beneficial to everyone.

Computer Science is not the study of computers just like Chemistry is not the study of test tubes nor Astronomy is the study of telescopes. So, why is it called Computer Science? Although there is no clear answer to this question, the best guess is that Computer Science is an umbrella term for many disciplines whose primary tool is the computer, such as programming language theory, algorithmics, software engineering, data mining, robotics, and artificial intelligence. If Computer Science is not the study of the computer, then what is Computer Science and what do computer scientists do? Computer scientists solve problems. Unlike biologists who solve problems in Biology or diplomats who solve problems in Diplomacy, computer scientists solve problems that are relevant to all fields of study and to all facets of human life. Stated simply, Computer Science is multidisciplinary. Therefore, the best way to describe Computer Science is to say that it is the science of problem solving. Programming is how computer scientists express solutions to problems. Although Computer Science is a relatively young discipline,[1] it has developed many effective techniques to solve problems. This is why everyone ought to learn to design programs. Problem solving is an *essential* skill just like reading, writing, and doing arithmetic. Your journey through this book will help you learn effective problem solving techniques.

---

[1] The first Computer Science Program was established in 1953 at the University of Cambridge in the United Kingdom. The first Computer Science Department in the United States was established at Purdue University in 1962.

© The Author(s), under exclusive license to Springer Nature Switzerland AG 2022
M. T. Morazán, *Animated Problem Solving*, Texts in Computer Science,
https://doi.org/10.1007/978-3-030-85091-3_1

Two of the best-known problem solving techniques are *divide and conquer* and *iterative refinement*. Problem solvers use divide and conquer when a larger problem is decomposable into smaller problems. Instead of solving an entire problem in one huge step, the problem is divided into a set of smaller problems. These subproblems are all solved independently, and then their solutions are combined to formulate the answer to the large problem. For example, consider computing your quiz average. You can divide this problem into two smaller problems: sum the quiz grades and count the number of quizzes. Once these subproblems are solved, the results are combined by dividing the former by the latter to formulate the quiz average.

Iterative refinement is used to develop a solution in steps. This is particularly useful to manage the complexity of a problem. Instead of developing a full answer at once, you solve a simpler version of the problem. Once that is done, you add complexity to the problem and re-solve it. This process continues until you have a full answer. For instance, consider the problem of developing a video game like Pacman. You may first create a game that only has Pacman. Then you create a game that has Pacman and food. The next version of the game has Pacman, the food, and one ghost. Finally, the last version of the game has Pacman, the food, and multiple ghosts.

You have been taught to solve problems most of your life. This means that you have been taught to compute. For example, you have been taught to compute meaning from English expressions. You know that *Thelma is that pig* has a different meaning from *That is Thelma's pig*. Other languages that you have been trained to do computations with are Arithmetic and Algebra. For example, you know how to compute the value of the following expression: 5 * (8 + 2). In essence, we use expressions to describe computations and we evaluate expressions to derive meaning. You may have never thought explicitly about divide and conquer or about iterative refinement, but you have been taught to use these techniques. Consider writing an essay. The first step is to create an outline. This is where you decompose your argument into different points. Perhaps, every point is implemented as a different section. You combine the different sections into an essay by making sure that your argument easily flows from one section to the next. As you can observe, you are using divide and conquer. Staying with essay development, you first write a rough draft and then repeatedly make improvements until you are happy with the result. In other words, you are using iterative refinement.

If we are going to express solutions to problems using a computer, we need to use a *programming language* much like we use English to communicate. A programming language allows us to communicate to the computer what we want it to do. There are many programming languages. Each has its strengths and weaknesses. You will learn many programming languages as you explore the world of Computer Science. We will start with a programming language called *Beginning Student Language* (BSL). BSL is a programming language specifically designed to teach beginners like yourself how to design and implement solutions to problems. A solution to a problem written in BSL (or any other programming language) is called a *program*. When a program is evaluated, we obtain its meaning. That is, we obtain the solution to an instance of a problem.

Fig. 1 DrRacket's language menu

3 Getting Started

In order to write programs, we need a programming development environment.[2]
A programming development environment is to programs what a text editor is to
essays. Just like you write an essay using a text editor, we write programs using
a programming development environment. There is, however, a major difference
between a programming development environment and a text editor. You can do
more than write programs with a programming development environment. You can
also evaluate programs.

The first step you need to take is to download and install the programming
development environment called DrRacket using the following link:

> https://download.racket-lang.org/

After installing DrRacket, run it and go to the Language menu. Click on Choose
Language.... A pop-up menu will appear and you need to click on Beginning
Student. Figure 1 illustrates what the language menu ought to look like. Click on
OK and then click on the RUN button toward the top right corner of DrRacket.

You are now ready to program! Figure 2 displays DrRacket's interface (the colors
on your computer may vary). The top half is called the *definitions area* and the bottom
half is called the *interactions area*. We type programs in the definitions area and we
interact with our programs in the interactions area. After typing a program in the

---

[2] A programming development environment is commonly called an integrated development environment (IDE).

Fig. 2 DrRacket's interface

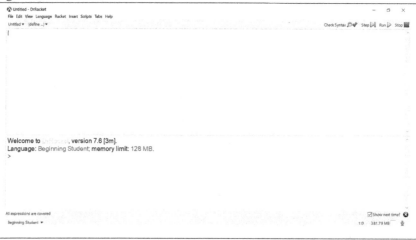

definitions area, you may click the RUN button to evaluate your program. Let us try this out. Type the following string[3] in the definitions area:

```
"Hello World! I am DrRacket."
```

Now click on RUN. In the interactions window you will see the string printed. Congratulations! You just wrote your first program. When you clicked on the RUN button, you told DrRacket to evaluate your program. The value of a string is just the string itself. Once DrRacket knows the value of a program, it is printed in the interactions area.

---

* **Ex. 1** — Write and run a program that prints your name.

** **Ex. 2** — Write and run a program that prints your age.

** **Ex. 3** — Write and run a program that prints your name and your age.

So, what is a program? A program is similar to an essay. In an essay, you express an argument in favor of or against a point of view. In a program, you express the solution to a problem. They both have in common the use of *expressions*. In English, your expressions are words that may be used to construct larger expressions like sentences and paragraphs. In programming, your basic expressions are values (for now), like strings and numbers, that may be used to create larger useful expressions. We will start by studying expressions and discover how expressions lead us to functions—the sentences of Algebra and programming.

---

[3] A string is anything inside,"", double quotes.

Fig. 3 Initial grammar for expressions

```
          expr ::= string
               ::= number
        string::= "<character>*"
        number ::= positive
               ::= negative
      positive ::= mag
      negative ::= -mag
           mag ::= int
               ::= real
               ::= fraction
           int ::= digit⁺
         digit ::= 0|1|2|3|4|5|6|7|8|9
          real ::= digit*.digit⁺
      fraction ::= int/nonzero-int
  nonzero-int ::= <1|2|3|4|5|6|7|8|9>int
       program ::= expr*
```

To do so, we need to know how to write valid expressions. That is, we need a mechanism to describe how to write expressions. We will use a *grammar* to describe expressions. A grammar consists of a series of production rules. A production rule tells a programmer, for example, how to type valid expressions.

Figure 3 displays our initial grammar for expressions. Each production rule consists of three parts. The leftmost part is the syntactic category being defined. If this is missing, it means that it is the same syntactic category as the production rule above it. The middle part is always the symbol ::=. The symbol ::= may be read as *is* or as *may be substituted by*. The rightmost part is the definition of the syntactic category. The first two rules state that an expression, expr, is either a string or a number. The next rule states that a string starts and ends with ". In between, you may have 0 or more characters. The * means 0 or more.[4] Observe that character is in a different font and surrounded by < and >. This indicates that it is a syntactic category we only describe verbally. You may think of a character as anything that is produced by a keystroke such as letters, spaces, and punctuation marks.[5] The next rule states that a number is either a positive or negative. A positive is a mag (magnitude) and a negative is a – followed by a mag.

There are three rules for mag. These state that a mag may be an integer, a real, or a fraction. An int is 1 or more digits (the ⁺ means 1 or more and is called *Kleene plus*). A digit is an integer in [0..9]. A real is 0 or more digits followed by a . followed by 1 or more digits. Finally, a fraction is an int followed by a followed by a nonzero integer. In the grammar, the | means or. Therefore, a nonzero-int is any digit from 1 to 9 followed by an integer.

---

[4] In a grammar, a * is called *Kleene star*, named after the American mathematician Stephen Cole Kleene.

[5] Characters inside a computer are represented by an ASCII code. For example, the ASCII code for a is 97. You will learn more about ASCII codes in a Computer Architecture course.

We are now ready for our initial grammatical definition of a program. The last rule in Fig. 3 states that a program is 0 or more expressions. Why do we need 0 or more expressions? Given that a program may compute an arbitrary number of values, a program may have 0 or more expressions.

Let us try to write a new program. To write a new program, open a new tab in DrRacket by using `Ctrl-T`. `Ctrl-T` means pressing the `Ctrl` and the T keys at the same time. Now write a program in the definitions area to compute the name of this textbook, the number one million, and negative 8.7 as follows:

```
"Program By Design"
1000000
-8.7
```

The result in the interactions area after clicking RUN is

```
"Program by Design"
1000000
-8.7
```

---

* **Ex. 4** — Write and run a program that prints your year of birth and your age.

** **Ex. 5** — Write and run a program that prints your favorite color, your lucky number, and the largest prime number less than 25.

---

4 Computing New Values

So far, all our programs have computed constant values, that is, values that we wrote before running the program. In order for programs to be truly useful, we need to be able to compute new values. That is, we need to be able to combine values to create new values. Fortunately, BSL provides us with application expressions. An application expression applies a function to one or more arguments. The function, in essence, combines its inputs to create a new value and returns this new value. Therefore, an application expression evaluates to the value returned by the function.

We extend the `expr`'s production rules in Fig. 3 to include application expressions as follows:

expr ::= (<function> expr⁺)

This production rule states that an application expression starts with an opening parenthesis, followed by a function (the operator), followed by 1 or more expressions (the operands), followed by a closing parenthesis. The function and each of its arguments must be separated from each other by one or more spaces. BSL provides us with many functions, for example, to combine numbers and to combine strings. Table 1 lists some of the functions BSL provides along with sample uses.

At this point, you may feel that the syntax notation is a bit awkward. In your Mathematics textbooks, for example, the basic operations (i.e., +, -, *, and /) are

Function	Sample application expression	Value
+	(+ 1 2 3 4 5)	15
–	(– 5 8 2)	–5
*	(* 39 45 29 2)	101790
/	(/ 20 4 2)	2.5
expt	(expt 64 1/2)	8
string-length	(string-length "Program By Design")	17
string-append	(string-append "Hello " "World")	"Hello World"

Table 1: Some numerical and string BSL functions

written using *infix* notation. This means that the operator is written in the middle of the operands. For example, the sum of 1, 2, 3, 4, and 5 is written as 1 + 2 + 3 + 4 + 5. A function application, on the other hand, is written operator first and then in parentheses the operands. For example, applying f to 3 is written as f(3). In contrast, BSL uses *prefix* notation. That is, inside parentheses we first write the operator and then the operands. Observe that the basic operations are functions, and therefore, BSL treats them no differently than other functions (i.e., they are written using prefix notation). Thus, the sum of 1, 2, 3, 4, and 5 is written as (+ 1 2 3 4 5) and applying f to 3 is written as (f 3). Always remember that when you want to apply a function to some arguments, you must put in parentheses the function first and then the arguments. As you can see, the translation from the syntax used in Mathematics textbooks to BSL syntax is straightforward. One of the advantages of BSL syntax is that it may be less typing as is the case for the sum of 1, 2, 3, 4, and 5. More importantly, however, is that ambiguity cannot arise. For example, in Mathematics syntax what is the value of 10 + 4 * 5? It depends if you add or you multiply first. You probably remember operator precedence and believe the correct value is 30. In BSL, we do not rely on remembering operator precedence. Prefix notation and the use of parentheses always make it clear what arguments a function is applied to. If the value of 10 + 4 * 5 is 30, then we write (+ 10 (* 4 5)) in BSL. Observe that BSL syntax clearly communicates to the readers of our code that the arguments to * are 4 and 5 and that the arguments to + are 10 and the value of (* 4 5).

This last example explicitly shows us that application expressions may be nested. In (+ 10 (* 4 5)), (* 4 5) is nested. There is no limit to the number or the depth of nested expressions as subtly suggested by the above production rule for application expressions. Always keep in mind that in an application expression for every opening parenthesis, there must be a matching closing parenthesis. Furthermore, remember that a closing parenthesis cannot simply be written anywhere in an application expression. A closing parenthesis must appear after the last argument to a function. Otherwise, the *meaning* of the application expression (i.e., what it evaluates to) changes. For example, the following two expressions have different meanings:

(* (+ 4 1) 7 (– 15 5))   (* (+ 4 1 7) (– 15 5))

Fig. 4 Accessing DrRacket's Help Desk

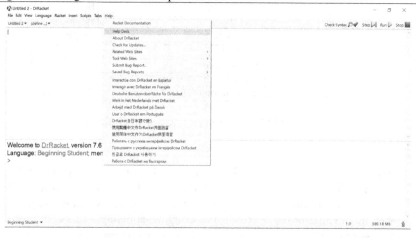

In the first, the last argument to + is 1 and 7 is an argument for ∗. It evaluates to 25. In the second, the last argument to + is 7 and 7 is not an argument for ∗. It evaluates to 120. As you can see, the meaning of the above expressions is different. Always be careful about where you close your parentheses.

There is one more thing you may be wondering. Do all functions take as input an arbitrary number of expressions like + and ∗? The answer to this is no. It depends on the function that is being applied. For example, `string-length` only takes one input. If you are not sure if a function accepts an arbitrary number of arguments, you have two options. You can try using it in a program or in the interactions area. Consider `string-append` from Table 1. Can we give it more than two arguments? Let us try it by typing after the prompt, >, in the interactions area the following:

```
(string-append "Hello" " " "World" "!" " " "I am DrRacket.")
```

After hitting `Enter`, the following value is printed:

```
"Hello World! I am DrRacket."
```

The answer to our question is that we can give `string-append` more than two arguments. Below the output string, you get the `DrRacket` prompt again. `DrRacket` is ready to evaluate another expression for you.

The second option is to consult `DrRacket`'s `Help Desk` as illustrated in Fig. 4. A browser pops up and you can type BSL in the search box. After clicking on BSL,

you are taken to the documentation page for the BSL language. On this page a search
for `string-append` yields

```
(string-append s t z ...) → string

    s : string
    t : string
    z : string

Concatenates the characters of several strings.

> (string-append "hello" " " "world" " " "good bye")
"hello world good bye"
```

The ... means that the function takes as input an arbitrary number of arguments.
The arrow means returns. After the arrow, we find the *type* of value returned. Further
down, we see the *type* of each input: all are `string` type. The types of the inputs and
the type of the output define the *signature* of the function. It clearly informs anyone
who wishes to use `string-append` that if they provide strings as input, the function
returns a string as its value. In terms of high school Mathematics, you may think of
the input types as the domain of the function and the return type is the range of the
function. Finally, at the bottom we see a brief description of the function's *purpose*
and an example of its use. Whenever you are unsure if BSL has a function or you are
unsure of how to use a BSL function, you may look for it in DrRacket's `Help Desk`
to determine if it exists and, if so, the signature tells you the expected inputs and the
expected output.

5 Definitions and Interactions Areas Differences

As you have seen, expressions written in both the definitions and the interactions
areas can be evaluated. In the definitions area you need to click RUN. In the interactions
area you need to hit `Enter`. So, why are there two areas?

As stated before, the two areas are used for different purposes. In the definitions
area, we write programs. These are solutions to problems that we may save and
run multiple times. In the interactions area, we ask DrRacket to evaluate one-time
expressions, that is, expressions that we are not interested in running multiple times.
The difference may seem subtle, but as you advance through the first few chapters
of this book, the differences will become better delineated.

A good rule of thumb to follow is that if you wish to save the expressions you
write to solve a problem, then you write them in the definitions area. If you only
want to quickly have DrRacket evaluate an expressions for you, then write it in the
interactions window.

Fig. 5 Saving your work

6 Saving Your Work

It is an unfortunate fact that computers may crash. When this happens your unsaved work is likely to be lost. Therefore, it is important that you regularly save your work. It is a good idea for you to create a directory for the programs you will develop as you read this book. You may even want to create subdirectories for each chapter. This is an effective way to keep your files organized.

To save your work go the `File` menu. If it is the first time saving your current program, click on `Save Definitions As...` as illustrated in Fig. 5. After this, find the directory you wish to save your work in and enter a filename. If you choose the filename `Exercise-2-Chapter-4`, your work is saved in a file named `Exercise-2-Chapter-4.rkt`. The `.rkt` extension is automatically added to indicate that it is a `Racket` file. In reality, it is a BSL file, but it is saved as a `Racket` file given that BSL is a subset of `Racket`. If it is not the first time saving the current program, click on `Save Definitions` inside the `File` menu. Alternatively, you may simply use `Ctrl+S`.

7 Error Messages

Errors are part of the problem solving process and even the most experienced problem solvers write programs with errors in them. Do not panic when you get an error message. Remember the famous saying *errāre hūmānum est* (to err is human[6]). The error message is `DrRacket`'s attempt to help you diagnose the error.

---

[6] The complete saying, coined by Alexander Pope in his *Essay on Criticism*, is *to err is human; to forgive, divine.*

An important lesson to absorb is that error messages help us diagnose and correct *bugs*[7] in our programs. An error message itself does not diagnose the bug nor does it tell us how to fix the bug. That is left to us as program developers, because only the program developers really know the intended meaning of expressions in a program. DrRacket approximates where an error occurs, but the programmer must diagnose and remedy the bug.

7.1 Grammatical Errors

As you now know, essays and programs are both written following the production rules of a grammar. The English grammar tells you how to write a valid English expression. Similarly, the BSL grammar tells you how to write valid BSL programs. When you write a valid BSL program and click on RUN, DrRacket evaluates your program and prints the answer.

If you fail to write a valid BSL program and click on RUN, DrRacket prints an error message. When DrRacket detects a grammatical error, an informative error message is printed in the interactions window. The message details the grammatical error. For example, type the following in the definitions area:

```
"Hello World! I am DrRacket.
```

After clicking RUN, the following error message appears in the interactions window:

```
read-syntax: expected a closing '"'
```

The error message states that it was expecting to find a closing double quote. As you have probably already observed, the opening double quote does not have a matching closing double quote. Always make sure to read error messages, because they are usually helpful in determining the cause of errors.

Grammatical errors may also occur writing application expressions. Type the following program:

```
(sting-append "I'm done" " " "and going home!")
```

After clicking RUN, the following error message is displayed:

```
sting-append: this function is not defined
```

DrRacket is telling us that it does not know the function sting-append. We can clearly see that the name of the function is misspelled and we correct it as follows:

```
(string-append "I'm done" " " "and going home!")
```

---

[7] The term *computer bug* stems from a moth found trapped in a computer relay in 1947. The bug was removed and taped to the log book. The log book along with the moth are part of the Smithsonian National Museum of American History collection in Washington D.C.

Fig. 6 Grammatical Error

Another common grammatical error is failing to properly write an application expression with balanced parentheses. For instance, type the following program in the definitions area to compute (4 * 5) + (50 / 10):

```
(+ (* 4 5 (/ 50 10))
```

After clicking RUN, the following error message is displayed:

```
read-syntax: expected a ')' to close '('
```

DrRacket is informing us that there is a missing closing parenthesis. Observe that in the definitions window, the opening parenthesis before + is highlighted as displayed in Fig. 6. DrRacket is letting us know which opening parenthesis it could not match. If we do not think carefully about the error, we may be tempted to fix the bug by adding a closing parenthesis at the end as follows:

```
(+ (* 4 5 (/ 50 10)))
```

After clicking RUN, the following error message is displayed:

```
+: expects at least 2 arguments, but found only 1
```

This is a type error. We will discuss type errors in the next subsection. After some thought, we realize that we placed the missing closing parenthesis in the wrong place. DrRacket could not find a closing parenthesis for the first opening parenthesis. The bug, however, is that the parenthesis before * was not properly closed. We fix the problem as follows:

```
(+ (* 4 5) (/ 50 10))
```

After clicking RUN, the correct value for (4 * 5) + (50 / 10), 25, is printed in the interactions area.

Fig. 7 Runtime error

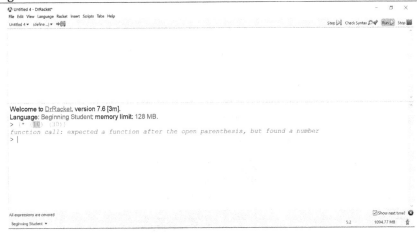

Another common grammatical mistake is to place an expression inside parentheses when a function is not applied. This mistake is common among beginners and it is one you need to be careful about. For instance, consider typing after the DrRacket's prompt:

```
(* (10) (30))
```

Figure 7 displays the error message after hitting Enter. Observe that 10 is highlighted in pink. DrRacket is telling us that it did not find a function after the opening parenthesis for the first operand. Instead, it found 10. 10 is not a function and, therefore, should not be in the operator position. In fact, 10 is a number and a number by itself is not written inside parenthesis when it is intended as an argument to a function.

---

* **Ex. 6 —** Type and fix the following buggy expressions:

1.(+ (* 1 2)) 7 (* 5 10))
2.((* 9 6 4))
3.(string-len "Isa and Sena")
4.(sine (/ pi 2))
5.(squareroot (str-length "Yes!"))

7.2 Type Errors

Another kind of error that we may make is called a *type error*. Type errors mostly occur in two ways. The first is when the wrong number of arguments are provided to a function. Let us revisit a program from the previous subsection.

```
(+ (* 4 5 (/ 50 10)))
```

After clicking RUN, the following error message is displayed:

```
+: expects at least 2 arguments, but found only 1
```

DrRacket is telling us that it believes that we are not correctly using +. We are not providing the right number of arguments to +. This is a very common mistake done by beginners and it is important that we keep this in mind as we implement solutions to problems.

The second is when the wrong type of argument is given to a function. For example, type the following after the prompt in the interactions area:

```
(string-append "My lucky number is: " 8)
```

After clicking RUN, the following error message is displayed:

```
string-append: expects a string as 2nd argument, given 8
```

The `string-append` function expects all its inputs to be strings. In this example, the second argument is a number. To fix this bug, we must make the second argument a string as follows:

```
(string-append "My lucky number is: " "8")
```

After clicking RUN, the string is printed in the interactions area. It is worth highlighting that "8" is not the same as 8. The former is a string and the latter is a number, that is, they are different types of data.

Providing a function with the wrong type of input is a very common mistake. Therefore, *type theory* is an important and growing discipline within Computer Science. As we progress through this textbook, we will learn design techniques to help us avoid type errors. Furthermore, we will learn how to exploit the type of data being processed to design solutions (and programs) to problems.

---

* **Ex. 7** — Type and fix the following buggy expressions:

1. (string-length 9865)
2. (number->string "7615461")
3. (sqr "20")
4. (add1 (add1 (add1 "7"))))
5. (sub1 (add1 (string->number (string-length "100"))))
6. (string-append 'Animating "Programs" 'Textbook)

Fig. 8 Runtime error

7.3 Runtime Errors

You need to be aware of a third kind of error called a runtime error. Unlike grammatical and type errors, runtime errors are not detected until after an evaluation has started. For example, type the following program in the definitions area:

```
(* 5 0)
(+ 5 0)
(/ 5 0)
(- 5 0)
```

The results after clicking RUN are displayed in Fig. 8. We can observe that the first two expressions are evaluated and their results are printed. The third expression is highlighted in pink signalling that an error has been detected during its evaluation. The error message in the interactions window informs us that there has been an attempt to divide by 0. The fourth expression is highlighted in black signalling that it has not been evaluated.

Our programs may also contain runtime errors that do not generate an error message. For example, write the following program to compute $f(4)$, where $f(x) = 2x^2 + 10x + 3$:[8]

```
(+ (* 2 (sqr 4)) (* 10 4) 4)
```

After clicking RUN, no error message is generated and 76 is printed in the interactions window. Observe, however, that 76 is not the value of $f(4)$. These are probably the hardest errors to fix, because no error message is generated. In this example, the bug is rather easy to spot. The last 4 in the expression is a typo and should be 3.

---

[8] sqr is a BSL function that squares its input. Look it up in the Help Desk!

Fig. 9 Testing in BSL

(a) A Failed Test.   (b) A Successful Test.

To help protect ourselves against this type of error, most programming languages, including BSL, allow programmers to write *unit tests*. A unit test validates that two different expressions evaluate to the same value. In order to write unit tests, we need to expand our grammar as follows:

```
program ::= {expr | test}*
    test ::= (check-expect expr expr)
```

Now, a program is 0 or more expressions or tests. The curly braces are used to delimit the scope of the Kleene star and should not be typed as part of any program. In BSL, we write a unit test by typing inside parentheses check-expect and two expressions. The first expression is the one that we wish to test and it provides what is called the *actual value*. The second expression provides what is called the *expected value* of the first expression.

We can now rewrite our buggy program as follows:

```
(+ (* 2 (sqr 4)) (* 10 4) 4)

(check-expect (+ (* 2 (sqr 4)) (* 10 4) 4) 75)
```

Figure 9a displays DrRacket after clicking run. When tests fail, you get a pop-up window indicating the number of tests evaluated and the number that passed. For each failed test, the actual and expected values are displayed. In addition, the line number of the error in your program is reported.[9] In Fig. 9a, we see that 1 test was evaluated and 0 tests passed. The only failed test is at line 3. We correct our program as follows:

```
(+ (* 2 (sqr 4)) (* 10 4) 3)

(check-expect (+ (* 2 (sqr 4)) (* 10 4) 3) 75)
```

Figure 9b displays the result after pressing RUN. There is no pop-up window with failed tests and DrRacket in the interactions area indicates that all tests pass.

It may or may not have bothered you that we had to type the same expression twice. This may be tolerable when you only need to type one expression twice. Most programmers, however, would find it extremely annoying and, more importantly,

---

[9] You may configure DrRacket to display line numbers in the View menu.

Fig. 10 Rectangle of width 3 and height 4

4

3

error-prone to have to retype multiple expressions multiple times. Furthermore, evaluating the same expression multiple times (i.e., once for every time it is typed) may make programs slower. In the next chapter, we will learn techniques to avoid the repeated typing of the same expression to write tests.

** **Ex. 8** — Fix the runtime errors in the following program:
```
"I have square with a perimeter of 20"
"The length of a side is: "
(/ 20 0)
"The area is:"
(+ 20 20)

(check-expect (* 4 (/ 20 0)) 20)
(check-expect (+ 20 20) (sqr (/ 20 0)))
```

** **Ex. 9** — For a rectangle displayed in Fig. 10, write a program that computes

1. The rectangle's area
2. The rectangle's perimeter
3. The rectangle's diagonal distance from the lower left corner to the top right corner

Make sure you write unit tests to validate your computed values.

---

8 What Have We Learned in This Chapter?

The important lessons of Chap. 1 are summarized as follows:

- We write programs using a programming development environment.

Fig. 11 Chapter 1 BSL grammar

```
      program ::= {expr | test}*
         test ::= (check-expect expr  expr)
         expr ::= string
              ::= number
              ::= (<function>expr⁺)
       string ::= "<character>*"
       number ::= positive
              ::= negative
     positive ::= mag
     negative ::= -mag
          mag ::= int
              ::= real
              ::= fraction
          int ::= digit⁺
        digit ::= 0|1|2|3|4|5|6|7|8|9
        real::=digit* digit⁺
     fraction ::= int/nonzero-int
  nonzero-int ::= <1|2|3|4|5|6|7|8|9> int
```

- DrRacket is the IDE used in this textbook.

  - The definitions area is where programs are written.
  - The interactions area is where one-time expressions are evaluated and where error messages are printed.
  - To evaluate a program, click on RUN.

- A programming language is used to write solutions to problems. We call such a solution a program.
- The syntax of a programming language may be described using a grammar. The BSL syntax developed so far is displayed in Fig. 11.

  - A program is 0 or more expressions.
  - An expression can either be a number, a string, or an application expression.
  - Strings are written inside double quotes.
  - A number is a positive or negative integer, real, or fraction.
  - An application expression is used to apply a function to its arguments. Inside parentheses you first write the function name and then its arguments all separated by 1 or more spaces.

- Use DrRacket's Help Desk to determine if a function exists or to learn how to use a function.
- In order to minimize the danger of loss, frequently save your work.
- Error messages help us determine where a bug occurs but are unable to tell us how to fix the bug.
- Unit testing helps us find runtime errors by validating that an actual value is the same as an expected value.

Chapter 2
Expressions and Data Types

You have learned to write expressions using numbers, strings, and applications. Although this has enabled you to write programs, we need a richer set of data types to make problem solving easier. This chapter introduces a broader set of data types that are part of BSL. These are divided into two broad categories: *primitive* and *compound*. A primitive data type is any type of data that is indivisible. For example, numbers are a primitive data type. A compound data type is one that contains multiple pieces of data. A piece of compound data can be divided into its component parts. For example, a coordinate on the two-dimensional Cartesian plane is compound data. Every coordinate is composed of an x and a *y* value. The new data types introduced in this chapter are Boolean, symbol, character, and image. This chapter also revisits the number and string data types to present them in more detail. In addition, this chapter introduces how to define constants to avoid having to type the same expression multiple times in programs.

Consider computing the area and the perimeter of the rectangles in Fig. 12. Thinking about the problem leads us to conclude that area is computed by multiplying the width and the length of a rectangle and perimeter is computed by adding the doubling of the width and the doubling of the length. Based on this analysis, Fig. 13 displays a solution in the form of a program. The first thing you notice is that comments are used to document a program. Anything after a ; is a comment in BSL. Specifically, comments are used to document how area and perimeter are computed. This helps the programmer and anyone else who reads the program to understand the solution to the problem. Comments are also used to identify the computation performed for each rectangle. Finally, unit tests are written to make sure that the computations yield the correct values. Observe that there is one test for each computation.

The program in Fig. 13 contains many repeated expressions. This is considered poor programming, because repetitions are boring and lead to errors. Quite frankly, no one wants to do the same thing over and over again. Therefore, we need a mechanism to avoid repetitions in our programs. One idea that is promising is to compute a value once. Instead of (typing and) evaluating each expression multiple

© The Author(s), under exclusive license to Springer Nature Switzerland AG 2022
M. T. Morazán, *Animated Problem Solving*, Texts in Computer Science,
https://doi.org/10.1007/978-3-030-85091-3_2

Fig. 12 Three rectangles

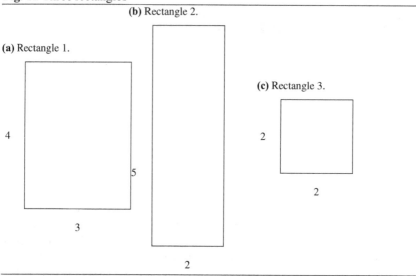

(b) Rectangle 2.

(a) Rectangle 1.

(c) Rectangle 3.

4

2

5

2

3

2

2

times, use the value of the expression multiple times. For this we need to learn a little more BSL syntax to define variables. Variables are used to store the values of expressions.

9 Definitions

To define and use variables, the BSL syntax is extended as follows:

```
program ::= {expr | test | def}*
    def ::= (define <variable name> expr)
    expr ::= <variable name>
```

A program consists of 0 or more expressions, tests, and definitions. A definition starts with an opening parenthesis, followed by the keyword `define`, followed by a variable name, followed by an expression, and ends with a closing parenthesis. A variable name consists of a number of characters without spaces.[10] An expression may be a variable name. This is how variables are used.

A definition binds the variable to the value of the expression. For example, type the following in the definitions area:

```
(define DELTA-X 5)
```

```
(define i (* 4 25))
```

---

[10] Some characters are not allowed such as #.

Fig. 13 Version 1 of the area and perimeter program for the rectangles in Fig. 12

```
;; Area = width * height
;; Perimeter = (2 * width) + (2 * height)

;; Area for rectangle 1
"The area for rectangle 1 is: "
(* 3 4)
(check-expect (* 3 4) 12)

;; Perimeter for rectangle 1
"The perimeter for rectangle 1 is: "
(+ (* 2 3) (* 2 4))
(check-expect (+ (* 2 3) (* 2 4)) 14)

;; Area for rectangle 2
"The area for rectangle 2 is: "
(* 2 5)
(check-expect (* 2 5) 10)

;; Perimeter for rectangle 2
"The perimeter for rectangle 2 is: "
(+ (* 2 2) (* 2 5))
(check-expect (+ (* 2 2) (* 2 5)) 14)

;; Area for rectangle 3
"The area for rectangle 3 is: "
(* 2 2)
(check-expect (* 2 2) 4)

;; Perimeter for rectangle 3
"The perimeter for rectangle 3 is: "
(+ (* 2 2) (* 2 2))
(check-expect (+ (* 2 2) (* 2 2)) 8)
```

These two definitions bind DELTA-X to 5 and bind i to 100. After clicking RUN, typing the expression and pressing Enter at the prompt in the interactions area returns 5 and typing the expression i and Enter at the prompt returns 100. Defining variables is how typing and evaluating the same expression more than once is avoided. They store the value of an expression allowing programmers to avoid multiple evaluations of the same expression. Instead, the defined variable is used multiple times.

By convention, two types of variables are distinguished: those whose value may change and those whose value may not change. The latter are called *constants*. Both are defined using the def syntax. The convention in this textbook is to use uppercase letters for constants and lowercase letters otherwise. In the above example, DELTA-X is considered a constant and i is not considered a constant. In BSL, there is no such convention and it is up to the programmers to use this convention.

Armed with the def syntax, the program in Fig. 13 may be rewritten as displayed in Fig. 14. Observe that for each value computed a constant is defined. Instead of using generic variable names like x and i, the constants are given names that inform

Fig. 14 Version 2 of the area and perimeter program for the rectangles in Fig. 12

```
;; Area = width * height
;; Perimeter = (2 * width) + (2 * height)

;; Area for rectangle 1
(define AREA1 (* 3 4))

(check-expect AREA1 12)

;; Perimeter for rectangle 1
(define PERIM1 (+ (* 2 3) (* 2 4)))

(check-expect PERIM1 14)

;; Area for rectangle 2
(define AREA2 (* 2 5))

(check-expect AREA2 10)

;; Perimeter for rectangle 2
(define PERIM2 (+ (* 2 2) (* 2 5)))

(check-expect PERIM2 14)

;; Area for rectangle 3
(define AREA3 (* 2 2))

(check-expect AREA3 4)

;; Perimeter for rectangle 3
(define PERIM3 (+ (* 2 2) (* 2 2)))

(check-expect PERIM3 8)
```

any reader what they represent. This is a good practice and it is a practice that is followed in this textbook. It is a habit that every programmer is encouraged to follow. The value of each constant is defined by an expression. Subsequently, the variable is used to refer to the value of the expression instead of reevaluating the same expression again. For instance, in the unit tests the constants are used. Observe also that it is no longer necessary for the program to return each area and perimeter value, which eliminates the need to clutter the interactions area with printed values. If a value needs to be examined, type the name of the variable at the prompt and hit Enter.

Which version of the program is clearer? Most people will argue that the program in Fig. 14 is clearer. Any interested reader can see what the constants represent. Furthermore, they can easily see that the tests are there to make sure that the values of the constants are correct. Admittedly, for this rather small and simple program, it may not seem significant. Nonetheless, it is important for you to realize now that as the size of programs grows, it is harder for a programmer (and a reader) to remember

Fig. 15 An error in unit testing using `check-expect` with real numbers

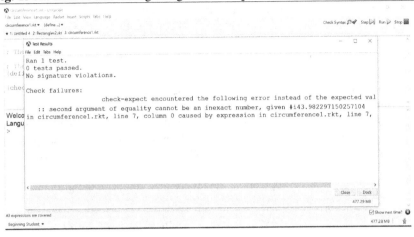

all the details. Therefore, the goal of a program is twofold. First, a program must correctly solve a problem. Second, a program must clearly communicate the solution to the problem. Both of these goals are equally important and you must adhere to them as responsible problem solvers. It is never acceptable to *get the code to work* without documenting the solution to the problem. Think about this carefully. If you were working on a team programming project, would you trust code that you do not understand?

10 Numbers

Recall that a number is either an integer, a real, or a fraction. Number is a primitive type (of data) in BSL. Chapter 1 presented examples of expressions using integers and how to write unit tests using `check-expect`. Now, consider writing a program to compute the circumference of a circle with a radius of 7. Recall that the circumference of a circle is given by $2\pi r$. Type the following program to solve the problem:

```
;; The circumference of a circle with radius r is 2 * pi * r

;; The circumference of a circle with radius 7
(define CIRCUM-7 (* 2 pi 7))

(check-expect CIRCUM-7 43.98)
```

In BSL, pi stores the value of π. Figure 15 displays the failed test message after clicking RUN. The message is informing us that a real number (called `inexact` number in BSL) cannot be checked using `check-expect`. The reason is that numbers in computer are not exactly the same as numbers in Mathematics. In a computer, a real number is limited to a finite number, n, of decimal places. Any decimals after the nth one is discarded. This means that computations using real numbers in BSL may contain errors. This is why they are called inexact. Examining the value on CIRCUM-7 at the prompt reveals that it is #i43.982297150257104.

DrRacket is nice enough to print the value prefixed with #i to warn that it is inexact and, therefore, may contain an error. This problem with real number computations is common among programming languages. Indicating that a value is inexact, however, is not common among other programming languages. When the magnitude of a real number is very small or very large, DrRacket prints it using scientific notation. For example, #i4.3290784900439874e-010 corresponds to the inexact number #i4.3290784900439874 x 10^{-10}.

In order to test computations involving real numbers, the grammar production rules for test must be expanded as follows:

$$\text{test} ::= (\text{check-within expr expr expr})$$

As with check-expect, the first two expressions are, respectively, for the value being tested and the expected value. The third expression defines the error tolerance. For the test to pass, the actual value must be at most the tolerance away from the expected value.

The program to compute the circumference of a circle with a radius of 7 is updated to

```
;; The circumference of a circle with radius r is 2 * pi * r

;; The circumference of a circle with radius 7
(define CIRCUM-7 (* 2 pi 7))

(check-within CIRCUM-7 43.98 0.01)
```

The unit test states that the value of CIRCUM-7 may be at most 0.01 away from 43.98 (the expected value). After clicking RUN, the only test passes.

In summary, use check-expect to test integers and fractions and use check-within to test reals. The example above also demonstrates that bugs do not only appear in expressions. Bugs may also occur in tests.

---

* **Ex. 10** — In Fig. 14, the expression (* 2 2) appears several times. Rewrite the program to eliminate its repetition.

** **Ex. 11** — A horse riding academy has a rectangular field of 25 meters by 5 meters. They wish to convert it to a horse riding outdoor classroom. In the middle of the field, they will fence off a 6 meters by 5 meters rectangle for students to sit and listen to lectures. Write a program to compute the area of the field left for horse riding. Make sure to write unit tests and document your solution.

* **Ex. 12** — Run the following program:
  ```
  (define NUM1 #i0.51467e-99)
  (define NUM2 #i999999999.42477796076938)
  (define NUM3 #i0.8724e-84)


  (check-within (* NUM1 NUM2 NUM3) (* NUM3 NUM2 NUM1) 0)
  ```
  We know from Mathematics courses that multiplication is commutative. Why does the test fail?

11 Strings and Characters

In Chap. 1, a string is described as anything that is inside double quotes. The word "anything" suggests that there may be more than one piece of data in a string. In fact, a string is our first example of a compound data type. Compound data is constructed using several pieces of data. For example, the string `"cat"` may be constructed using the strings: `"c"`, `"a"`, and `"t"`. We build a string by using double quotes. Putting `cat` inside double quotes glues together `"c"`, `"a"`, and `"t"` as a single piece of data. This is exactly the same as typing (`string-append "c" "a" "t"`). In other words, the use of double quotes is simply shorthand for using `string-append`. Functions that build compound data, like `string-append`, are called `constructors`.

When data is compound, it is possible to access some or all of its components. Functions that extract a component from an instance of compound data are called *selectors*. For strings, we can use the following BSL function to extract substrings:

```
;; string N [N] → string
;; Purpose: Extract from s the substring starting in
;;          position i and ending in position j-1
(substring s i j)
```

The signature is stating that the function `substring` requires at least two inputs. The first is a string and the second is a natural number less than or equal to the length of s.[11] The [] indicates that the third argument is optional. The optional third argument is a natural number, j, such that `0<=j<=length` of s. Think of i and j as defining the interval `[i..j)` and `substring` as extracting the substring from position i to position j. Not providing the third argument is shorthand for j being the length of the s. For example, (`substring "Wow!" 2`) is shorthand for (`substring "Wow!" 2 4`). Finally, it is important to note that strings' positions start at 0 (not 1).

The following program illustrates that strings are compound data:

---

[11] A natural number is an integer greater than or equal to 0.

```
(define CAT "cat")
(check-expect CAT (string-append "c" "a" "t"))
(check-expect (substring CAT 0 1) "c")
(check-expect (substring CAT 1 2) "a")
(check-expect (substring CAT 2 3) "t")
(check-expect (substring CAT 3 3) "")
(check-expect (substring CAT 0) CAT)
(check-expect (substring CAT 1) (substring CAT 1 3))
```

The first test illustrates that "cat" is shorthand for (string-append "c" "a" "t"). The second, third, and fourth tests, respectively, demonstrate that substrings of length 1 at the 0th, 1st, and 2nd positions of CAT are "c", "a", and "t". The fifth test demonstrates that the substring starting at 3 and not including 3 is the empty string. The sixth test demonstrates that CAT is the same as the substring starting at 0. Finally, the seventh test demonstrates that the substring starting at 1, "at", is the same as the substring in positions [1..3).

In fact, strings are not really made up of substrings. Every element of a string is a character (abbreviated as char). Therefore, substring in reality is a function that converts the selected characters into a string for the programmer. This function was created to make programming easier.

Expressions may evaluate to characters. Therefore, we need new syntax for characters:

$$\text{expr} ::= \backslash\#<\text{character constant}>$$

To denote characters, they are typed by prefixing them with \# followed by a character constant. For our purposes, a character constant is any single character you can type using a keyboard. As numbers, characters are primitive data and cannot be subdivided into components. To actually access the characters of a string, we may use the following function:

```
;; string N → char
;; Purpose: Extract the i^{th} char from s
(string-ref s i)
```

The index i must satisfy 0<=i<=length of s. The following program illustrates the use of string-ref:

```
(define DOG "dog")

(check-expect (string-ref DOG 0) \#d)
(check-expect (string-ref DOG 1) \#o)
(check-expect (string-ref DOG 2) \#g)
```

---

* **Ex. 13** — There are many useful BSL functions to manipulate strings. Become familiar with, for example, string-ith and string-length by looking them up in DrRacket's Help Desk. Write a program that appends these 3

string: "Program", "By", and "Design". Include tests to illustrate the follow-ing:

1.The appended strings result in "Program By Design".
2.The length of the appended strings is 17.
3."P" is the substring in positions [0..1].
4.\#P is the first character of the appended strings.
5."By" is the substring in positions [8..10].
6.The last character of the appended strings is \#n

* **Ex. 14** — What happens if we add the following tests to the CAT program above? Why does each test pass or fail?

```
(check-expect (substring CAT 3) "")
(check-expect (substring CAT 4) "")
(check-expect (substring CAT 0 3) CAT)
(check-expect (substring CAT 0 4) CAT)
(check-expect (substring CAT -1 1) CAT)
(check-expect (substring CAT 3 1) CAT)
```

* **Ex. 15** — Consider the following program fragment:

```
(define MARCO "Marco")

(define OCRAM (string-append (substring MARCO ...)
                             (substring MARCO ...)
                             (substring MARCO ...)
                             (substring MARCO ...)
                             (substring MARCO ...)))

(check-expect OCRAM "ocraM")
```

Complete the program by filling in each ... with an expression. Make sure the test passes.

* **Ex. 16** — Consider the following program:

```
(define GREETING1 "hello") ;; lowercase greeting
(define GREETING2 "HELLO") ;; uppercase greeting

(check-expect GREETING1 GREETING2)
```

The test fails after running the program. Rewrite the test by applying a function to either GREETING1 or GREETING2. Find a function to change the case of a string.

* **Ex. 17** — Write a program that adds the lengths of "Sena" and "Isa".

12 Symbols

Symbols are like strings that are not decomposable. That is, symbol is a primitive type like number. Symbols are used when we are not interested in manipulating or accessing the characters as can be done with strings. Symbols require extending the BSL grammar explored. The following is a new expr production rule for symbols:

$$expr ::= '<\text{character}>^+$$

An expression may be a symbol, which is written as a ' followed by one or more characters with no spaces.

DrRacket denotes most symbols as a ' followed by the name of the symbol. For example, entering (string->symbol "Apple") at the prompt returns a symbol that is printed as 'Apple to the screen. Entering (string->symbol "1024") returns a symbol, but it is printed differently. Numeric symbols are printed as ', followed by |, followed by the number, and ending with |. Therefore, the symbol for "1024" is printed as '|1024|.

Not surprisingly, a symbol is convertible to a string and vice versa. The following program exemplifies this observation:

```
;; NAME PROGRAM

(define NAME 'Joshua)
(define NAME2 'Sachin)

(define STR-NAME (symbol->string NAME))
(define STR-NAME2 (symbol->string NAME2))

(check-expect STR-NAME "Joshua")
(check-expect STR-NAME2 "Sachin")

(define JOSH (string->symbol STR-NAME))
(define SACH (string->symbol STR-NAME2))

(check-expect JOSH NAME)
(check-expect SACH NAME2)
```

In this program two symbols are converted to strings using symbol->string and then converted back to symbols using string->symbol. Read about these functions in DrRacket's Help Desk.

The functions symbol->string and string->symbol are interesting because they are *inverses* of each other. Informally, this means that they reverse each other. In the program above, for example, symbol->string converts 'Josh into "Josh" and string->symbol converts "Josh" back to 'Josh. More formally, you may recall from high school Mathematics that two functions are inverses if when composed the original input is returned. You may recall it from your Mathematics textbook as

$$(f \circ g)(x_1) = x_1 = (g \circ f)(x_1)$$

Do not panic if you do not remember or recognize function composition and inverses right now. These will be discussed in more detail later in this book. We mention them here, because they are important in programming. For example, you may compress and uncompress your files, encrypt and decrypt your sensitive data, or marshal–unmarshal your data for computer communication. All of these are achieved by a pair of functions that are inverses of each other.

** Ex. 18 — Write a program that defines a symbol for your first name and that computes a symbol that is your first name reversed without the last letter. *Hint*: Make a plan for the values that need to be computed to solve this problem. For example, the program first converts the symbol to a string, then computes a new string for your reversed name without the last letter, and finally computes a symbol from that new string.

* Ex. 19 — Explain what happens and why when the following tests are added to the name program above:
```
(check-expect NAME STR-NAME)
(check-expect SACH STR-NAME2)
```

* Ex. 20 — The functions `string->number` and `number->string` are inverses of each other. Write a program that illustrates this fact.

---

13 Booleans

Boolean is a primitive type of data. There are only two kinds of Boolean values: `#true` and `#false`. This type of data is important because it allows to perform computations that depend on whether conditions hold or fail to hold. For example, in Mathematics you have studied the absolute value function:

$$absValx = \begin{cases} x & \text{if } x \geq 0 \\ -x & \text{otherwise} \end{cases}$$

How do you compute `absVal(-100)`? You plug in -100 for x, evaluate the condition, $-100 \geq 0$, and determine that it is false. Since this condition is false, the value of the function is given by $-(-100)$. Evaluating this expression tells you that the value of `absVal(-100)` is 100.

Two new expr production rules for Booleans are needed:

```
expr ::= #true
     ::= #false
```

These rules state that a # followed by either `true` or `false` represents a Boolean value in BSL. Nothing else is a Boolean.

x	y	x ∧ y	x ∨ y	¬x
false	false	false	false	true
false	true	false	true	true
true	false	false	true	false
true	true	true	true	false

Table 2: Truth table for the basic Boolean functions

Just like numbers have basic functions (i.e., +, -, *, and /) to create new numbers, Booleans have the following basic functions: and (also denoted by ∧), or (also denoted by ∨), and not (also denoted by ¬). A truth table, as the one in Table 2, is used to illustrate the four basic Boolean functions. From the table, we can infer that

1. and is true when all inputs are true and is false otherwise;
2. or is true when any input is true and is false otherwise;
3. not is true when the input is false and is false otherwise.

The above is a complete description on the basic Boolean functions. It is noteworthy that it is not always necessary to evaluate all the arguments to and or to or. Consider the following two expressions:

```
(and #false (≤ x 20))      (or #true (> i 100))
```

After evaluating the first argument to and, the other arguments may be ignored, because the result is known to be false. Similarly, after evaluating the first argument to or, the other arguments may be ignored, because the result is known to be true.

13.1 Basic Boolean Operators in BSL

BSL takes advantage of the fact that not all arguments to and and or may have to be evaluated to make them faster. Instead of evaluating all the arguments to and or or, BSL stops evaluating arguments to and after the first that evaluates to #false. Similarly, BSL stops evaluating arguments to or after the first that evaluates to #true. To achieve this, and and or are not functions in BSL. Instead, they are new types of expressions. The BSL grammar includes the following two production rules for expr:

$$expr ::= (\text{and } expr \ expr \ expr^*)$$
$$::= (\text{or } \ expr \ expr \ expr^*)$$

These production rules tell us that and and or expect at least two values as input. In BSL, not is a one-input function.

Fig. 16 Unevaluated expressions in Boolean table validation program

We can now write a program to validate Table 2 as follows:

```
;; Basic Boolean Functions Validation Program

(define AND-FF (and #false #false))
(define AND-FT (and #false #true))
(define AND-TF (and #true #false))
(define AND-TT (and #true #true))
(define OR-FF  (or #false #false))
(define OR-FT  (or #false #true))
(define OR-TF  (or #true #false))
(define OR-TT  (or #true #true))
(define NOT-F  (not #false))


(define NOT-T  (not #true))

(check-expect AND-FF #false)
(check-expect AND-FT #false)
(check-expect AND-TF #false)
(check-expect AND-TT #true)
(check-expect OR-FF  #false)
(check-expect OR-FT  #true)
(check-expect OR-TF  #true)
(check-expect OR-TT #true)
(check-expect NOT-F #true)
(check-expect NOT-T #false)
```

After running this program, all the tests pass. Observe, as displayed in Fig. 16, that not all the expressions are evaluated. The expressions that remain unevaluated by the tests are highlighted in black. These expressions are unevaluated, because their value is not needed to determine the value of an and or an or expression. In fact, there is no way to test the unevaluated code. As programmers, this means that, at best, thorough testing gives us confidence in the program. Testing, however, never establishes that the program is correct.

** **Ex. 21** — Add the following definitions and tests to the basic Boolean functions validation program:

```
(define AND-FERR (and #false (/ 5 0)))
(define OR-FERR  (and #false (string-append "Is this "
                                            "a Boolean?")))

(check-expect AND-FER #false)
(check-expect OR-FERR #true)
```
What happens with each test? Why?

13.2 Predicates

Functions that return a Boolean are called *predicate* functions. They are useful to determine if the input meets some condition. In BSL, built-in types have a predicate to determine if the input is of that type. These are the predicates for the types presented in this chapter:

Type Predicate
number number?
string string?
character char?
symbol symbol?
boolean boolean?
image image?

For example, (string? "Hi there!") evaluates to #true and (boolean? 103167) evaluates to #false.

You have used predicates in high school Mathematics. For instance, $<$, $>$, $\geq$, $\leq$, and = are all predicates. They are all functions in BSL with the following names: <, >, >=, <=, and =. These functions all require 1 or more inputs. Typing (< 10) at the prompt returns #true. Why does this make sense? It turns out that a numerical predicate returns #true unless one of its input makes it #false. There is nothing in < 10 that makes it #false, and therefore, this expression evaluates to true. What does < 10121831 evaluating to #true mean? This is the BSL expression for $10 < 12 < 18 < 31$. Remember that BSL expressions use prefix, not infix, notation. It evaluates to #true, because $10 < 12 \wedge 12 < 18 \wedge 18 < 31$ is true.

Strings share an important property with numbers: they are *ordinal*. This means that they may be ordered. Strings may be lexicographically ordered (i.e., alphabetically ordered). Therefore, we can ask if one string is less than another or if one string is greater than or equal to another. We cannot, however, use numerical predicates with strings. The corresponding string predicates are `string<?`, `string>?`, `string<=?`, `string>=?`, and `string=?`. Observe that the ? suggests that a question is being asked. For example, (`string<?` "a" "b" "c") is asking if "a" comes before "b" and "b" comes before "c".

Unlike strings, symbols are not an ordinal type. This means that there are no functions to compare symbols like > or `string<?`. There are two predicates to test symbols. The predicate `symbol?` tests if its input is a symbol. The predicate `eq?` may be used to test if two symbols are equal. In fact, `eq?` does not exclusively work with symbols. For example, we can write (`eq?` 1 1) and (`eq?` "Alpha Centauri" "Alpha"). The first evaluates to `#true` and the second evaluates to `#false`. Functions, like `eq?`, that work for many types of inputs are called *generic functions*. We will explore generic functions later in this textbook. For now, we use =, `string=?`, and `eq?`, respectively, to test for numeric, string, and symbol equality.

BSL predicates for Booleans include `boolean?` and `false?`. The first tests if its input is a Boolean. The second tests if its input is `#false`. You may ask yourself, why is `true?` not a predicate in BSL? The answer is that the creators of BSL cannot possibly implement every conceivable function. Therefore, they must choose what functions to provide. One criterion that is used to decide is whether or not a value may be computed using other functions. Can we write expressions to determine if a variable is `#true`? To answer this question, we must carefully think about what it means to be `#true`. First, the value must be a Boolean. Second, the value must not be `#false`. With this insight, we can write an expression to determine if a variable is true using `not`, `and`, and `false?`. This is a sample program to test our observations:

```
(define A-STRING "This is not true.")
(define A-SYMBOL 'not-true)
(define A-NUMBER 87)
(define A-BOOL #true)
(define A-BOOL2 #false)

(define IS-TRUE-A-STRING (and (boolean? A-STRING)
                              (not (false? A-STRING))))
(define IS-TRUE-A-SYMBOL (and (boolean? A-SYMBOL)
                              (not (false? A-SYMBOL))))
(define IS-TRUE-A-NUMBER (and (boolean? A-NUMBER)
                              (not (false? A-NUMBER))))
(define IS-TRUE-A-BOOL   (and (boolean? A-BOOL)
                              (not (false? A-BOOL))))
(define IS-TRUE-A-BOOL2  (and (boolean? A-BOOL2)
                              (not (false? A-BOOL2))))

(check-expect IS-TRUE-A-STRING #false)
(check-expect IS-TRUE-A-SYMBOL #false)
```

```
(check-expect IS-TRUE-A-NUMBER #false)
(check-expect IS-TRUE-A-BOOL #true)
(check-expect IS-TRUE-A-BOOL2 #false)
```

Observe that function composition is used to determine if a variable is #true. That is, the values returned by boolean? and not are inputs to and and the value returned by false? is input to not. We begin to see that function composition is useful to design programs.

---

* **Ex. 22** — BSL provides many useful predicates to us. What are the signature and purpose of the following predicates:

1. odd?
2. even?
3. positive?
4. negative?
5. string-uppercase?
6. string-lowercase?
7. string-numeric?
8. string-alphabetic?
9. string-contains?

* **Ex. 23** — Write a program to determine the number of letters in the symbol 'abracadabra.

** **Ex. 24** — Logical implication (or simply *implies*) is important in program solving. It means that if some condition, ANTECEDENT, is #true, then some other condition, CONSEQUENT, is #true. Traditionally, implies is denoted by ⇒. This is the truth table for implies:

ANTECEDENT	CONSEQUENT	ANTECEDENT ⇒ CONSEQUENT
false	false	true
false	true	true
true	false	false
true	true	true

Write a program to validate the truth table for implies.

*** **Ex. 25** — The nand (not and) boolean function has a property called *functional completeness*. This means that any Boolean expression may be written only using nand expressions. The truth table for nand is

A	B	(nand A B)
false	false	true
false	true	true
true	false	true
true	true	false

The value of nand is given by the expression (not (and A B)). We can compute (not X) using a nand expression as follows: (not (and X X)).

Fig. 17 Examples of outline and solid images

(a) An Outline Rectangle.   (b) A Solid Circle.

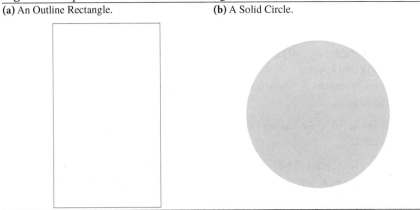

Write a program to demonstrate how to compute and and or using only nand expressions.

* **Ex. 26** — Run the following program:
```
(define NUM1 #i0.51467e-99)

(define NUM2 #i0.8724e-304)

(check-expect (> (* NUM1 NUM2) 0) #true)
```
Why does the test fail?

14 Images

An image is a visual rectangular type of compound data. Every image consists of pixels. A pixel is a picture element representing a colored dot. Every image has a length and a width measured in pixels. In BSL, expressions may evaluate to an image. This means that we need a new production rule for expr:

$$expr ::= <image>$$

Here <image> is a graphic that we either create or copy from elsewhere and paste it into DrRacket. For images we shall not delve into the manipulation of pixels. Instead, we shall focus on image manipulation as one whole value.

BSL provides us with a *teachpack* to create and manipulate images called 2htdp/image. To use the 2htdp/image teachpack, the first line in your program needs to be:

```
(require 2htdp/image)
```

This teachpack contains many functions that are split into three broad categories:

Basic Constructors   These are functions to create basic images like circles, rectangles, ellipses, stars, and text.

Property Selectors   These are functions to extract properties of images such as width and length.

Image Composers   These are functions that combine existing images to create new images.

It is useful to understand two basic definitions before using the 2htdp/image teachpack:

mode   This refers to how basic geometric shapes are drawn: not filled or filled. Use 'outline or "outline" when an outline of a shape is desired. Use 'solid or "solid" when a solid shape is desired.

image color   This is a string or a symbol representing the desired color. Search for image-color? in DrRacket's Help Desk to see the list of predefined colors.

Figure 17 illustrates outline and solid geometric shapes. Figure 17a displays an outline red rectangle created using the rectangle function. Figure 17b displays a solid green circle created using the circle function.

14.1 Basic Image Constructors

To illustrate the use of the basic image constructors, consider the program in Fig. 18 to construct the images in Fig. 17. First, constants for the characteristics of the rectangle and the circle are defined. Next, a constant for each image is defined. The rectangle is created using the basic constructor rectangle. It requires four inputs: a width, a height, a mode, and a color. The circle is created using the basic constructor circle. It requires three inputs: a radius, a mode, and a color. This is followed by tests. We can write the expected value of a test using a function application or an image given that both are valid expressions in BSL. The tests that use images require that the image be created first and then copied and pasted as part of the test.

There are too many basic image constructors to describe them all in this textbook. Therefore, search for 2htdp/image in the Help Desk to learn about and experiment with them. Be creative!

14.2 Property Selectors

There are two property selector functions:

image-width   Returns the width of an image in pixels.
image-height   Returns the height of an image in pixels.

Fig. 18 Basic constructors in BSL

```
(require 2htdp/image)

(define RECT-WIDTH 35)
(define RECT-HEIGHT 55)
(define RECT-MODE 'outline)
(define RECT-COLOR 'red)

(define CIRC-RADIUS 25)
(define CIRC-MODE 'solid)
(define CIRC-COLOR 'green)

(define RED-OUTLINE-RECT    (rectangle RECT-WIDTH RECT-HEIGHT
                                       RECT-MODE   RECT-COLOR))
(define GREEN-SOLID-CIRCLE (circle  CIRC-RADIUS  CIRC-MODE  CIRC-COLOR))

(check-expect RED-OUTLINE-RECT (rectangle 35 55 'outline 'red))
```

```
(check-expect RED-OUTLINE-RECT                )
(check-expect GREEN-SOLID-CIRCLE (circle 25 'solid 'green))
```

```
(check-expect GREEN-SOLID-CIRCLE              )
```

Consider the problem of computing half the width, half the height, and the number of pixels for the following images:

```
(define A-STAR-IMG   (radial-star 10 5 35 'outline 'gold))
(define A-RHOMBUS-IMG (rhombus 60 75 'solid 'red))
```

The first step is to clearly identify what needs to be computed and how it is computed. We need to compute three values as follows:

Half the Width   Divide the image's width by 2.
Half the Height   Divide the image's height by 2.
Number of Pixels   Compute the image's area.

The next question that arises is how are we to test our computations. We know that every image is rectangular, but this does not tell us what is the width or the height of a star image or of a rhombus image. When we do not know what a specific value ought to be or it is too difficult to write a specific value, we can use *property-based testing* to write tests. Instead of testing for the specific value of an expression, we test properties that the value of the expression ought to have. For our problem, we

Fig. 19 Sample program using image selectors and property-based testing

```
(require 2htdp/image)

(define A-STAR-IMG    (radial-star 10 5 35 'outline 'gold))

;; Star computations
(define STAR-W (image-width A-STAR-IMG))
(define STAR-H (image-height A-STAR-IMG))
(define STAR-HALF-W (/ STAR-W 2))
(define STAR-HALF-H (/ STAR-H 2))
(define STAR-PIXELS (* STAR-W STAR-H))

;; Star tests
(check-expect (* 2 STAR-HALF-W) STAR-W)
(check-expect (* 2 STAR-HALF-H) STAR-H)
(check-expect (/ STAR-PIXELS STAR-W) STAR-H)
(check-expect (/ STAR-PIXELS STAR-H) STAR-W)

(define A-RHOMBUS-IMG (rhombus 60 75 'solid 'red))

;; Rhombus computations
(define RHOMBUS-W (image-width A-RHOMBUS-IMG))
(define RHOMBUS-H (image-height A-RHOMBUS-IMG))
(define RHOMBUS-HALF-W (/ RHOMBUS-W 2))
(define RHOMBUS-HALF-H (/ RHOMBUS-H 2))
(define RHOMBUS-PIXELS (* RHOMBUS-W RHOMBUS-H))

;; Rhombus tests
(check-expect (* 2 RHOMBUS-HALF-W) RHOMBUS-W)
(check-expect (* 2 RHOMBUS-HALF-H) RHOMBUS-H)
(check-expect (/ RHOMBUS-PIXELS RHOMBUS-W) RHOMBUS-H)
(check-expect (/ RHOMBUS-PIXELS RHOMBUS-H) RHOMBUS-W)
```

know that an image is always rectangular. This means that twice half the width ought to be the width, twice half the height ought to be the height, the number of pixels divided by the image's height ought to be the image's width, and the number of pixels divided by the image's width ought to be the image's height.

Now that we have a game plan, we can proceed to write our program as displayed in Fig. 19. Observe that related definitions and tests are kept together. First, a data item is defined like A-RHOMBUS-IMG. Second, the result of computations is defined like RHOMBUS-HALF-W. Third, tests are written. Organizing code in such a manner is a good practice because anyone who reads the code (including yourself 6 months from now) will be able to understand the goals.

Fig. 20 An image of nested squares

14.3 Image Composers

Image composers are used to create new images from existing images. The image teachpack provides a myriad of such functions and you ought to experiment with them as you read the documentation in the Help Desk.

Consider the problem of creating the image in Fig. 20. As always, the first step is to determine what needs to be computed. The image consists of 6 nested squares. The largest square is yellow and at the bottom. The smallest square is blue and on the top. This suggests a divide and conquer strategy. First, compute all the needed squares. Second, overlay the squares to create the desired image. We can test the result using property-based testing. A program to implement this strategy is

```
;; Tests
;; NOTE: SQUARE0 is the largest square.
(check-expect (image-width NESTED-SQS)  (image-width SQUARE0))

(check-expect (image-height NESTED-SQS) (image-height SQUARE0))

;; The squares
(define SQUARE0 (square 60 'solid 'yellow)) ;; largest square
(define SQUARE1 (square 50 'solid 'blue))
(define SQUARE2 (square 40 'solid 'yellow))
(define SQUARE3 (square 30 'solid 'blue))
(define SQUARE4 (square 20 'solid 'yellow))
(define SQUARE5 (square 10 'solid 'blue)) ;; smallest square

;; The Nested Squares
(define NESTED-SQS (overlay SQUARE5 SQUARE4 SQUARE3
                            SQUARE2 SQUARE1 SQUARE0))
```

The tests check that the dimensions of the resulting image are correct: the dimensions ought to be the same as the largest square used. The program independently defines the 6 needed squares from largest to smallest. Finally, the needed image is created by using the function `overlay` always placing a smaller image over a larger image.

It is natural to wonder how the placing is done. Recall that an image consists of many pixels. One of these pixels serves as an *anchor point* around which images are placed. Unless otherwise specified, image composing functions use the pixel at the center of the image as the anchor point. This means, for example, that `overlay` places all the center points of the images one on top of another. In our program, the anchor point of SQUARE1 is placed over the anchor point of SQUARE0. Next, the anchor point of SQUARE2 is placed over the anchor point of the SQUARE1 and SQUARE0 composed image, and so on until all the squares are overlayed. You may contrast this behavior with the behavior of the application expression:

```
(overlay/xy img1 i j img2)
```

For `overlay/xy`, the images start aligned with respect to their top-left corner pixel (not the center pixel). The function overlays img1 over img2 but moves img2 i pixels to the right and j pixels down. If i is negative, img2 is moved to the left. If y is negative, img2 is moved up. Experiment with image composers!

Another noteworthy characteristic of our program is that the testing is not very satisfying. Consider what happens if we mistakenly define NESTED-SQS as follows:

```
(define NESTED-SQS (overlay SQUARE0 SQUARE1 SQUARE2
                           SQUARE3 SQUARE4 SQUARE5))
```

No tests fail when running the program despite that NESTED-SQS is the image of a yellow square. Clearly, this is not the desired result and this testing shortcoming ought to be addressed. To remedy such a situation, add unit tests using actual values that are computed. In this case, first experiment with our program. Once the desired image is computed, copy and paste it as the expected result for testing NESTED-SQS. In this manner, any reader of your code can see that both your model and your result are consistent with expectations. You must be very careful when employing such a strategy to write tests. If a computed value is wrong, then its use in a test will make the test pass. Your program, however, still computes the wrong value. It is best to limit the use of this strategy to test computed images that are easy to visually validate.

14.4 Empty Scenes and Placing Images

There are two image composing functions that are used extensively to create animations and video games:

`empty-scene` Creates an empty image of some given width and height. Optionally, the color of the empty image may be provided.

`place-image` Places the first given image at the given x and y coordinates in the second given image.

As characters and elements change in a video game, the displayed image must change. This is done by computing a new image. The empty image is used to create the base

Fig. 21 Computer graphics coordinate system

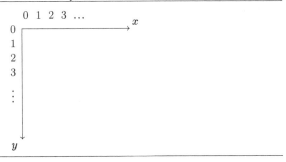

image of the video game or animation. Think of this base image as the empty canvas of an artist. The function `place-image` is used to place elements.

To properly use `place-image`, a brief description of the computer graphics coordinate system is needed. Figure 21 displays the coordinate system used in computer graphics. The possible values of x grow from left to right. To place an image further to the right, the x value is increased. To place an image further to the left the x value is decreased. The possible values of y grow from top to bottom. To place an image further down, the y value is increased. To place an image further up, the y value is decreased. For a given image with dimensions `WIDTH x HEIGHT`, the valid x values are in `[0..WIDTH-1]` and the valid y values are in `[0..HEIGHT-1]`. If any part of a placed image falls outside these coordinate ranges, the image is cropped and parts of the placed image do not appear in the result.

Consider the problem of creating an image with three different alien ships in a black empty scene. To make the task more manageable, use a divide and conquer strategy:

- Define the dimensions of the empty scene.
- Compute three different alien ships.
- Compute an image with one alien ship.
- Compute an image with two alien ships.
- Compute an image with three alien ships.
- Write tests.

There are an infinite number of ways a program can be written following this strategy. Figure 22a displays a proposed partial solution. A black empty scene, 200 x 100, and 3 different alien ships that differ in color are defined. After this, 3 images are defined using `place-image`. Each successive image contains one more ship.

The resulting image with the 3 alien ships is displayed in Fig. 22b. Immediately, you can see there is a bug in the program. The pink alien ship is cropped and only part of it appears in the image. This example highlights the value of testing. The program in Fig. 22a does not contain a test. Although the divide and conquer strategy is a good one, it is always necessary to perform thorough testing to establish a degree of confidence in a problem's solution.

Fig. 22 Program for an image with 3 different alien ships in a black empty image

(a) Program.

```
(require 2htdp/image)

(define WIDTH 200)
(define HEIGHT 100)

(define E-SCENE (empty-scene WIDTH HEIGHT 'black))

(define ALIEN-SHIP0 (overlay (circle 7 'solid 'gray)
                             (rectangle 23 3 'solid 'gray)))

(define ALIEN-SHIP1 (overlay (circle 7 'solid 'pink)
                             (rectangle 23 3 'solid 'pink)))

(define ALIEN-SHIP2 (overlay (circle 7 'solid 'white)
                             (rectangle 23 3 'solid 'white)))

(define SCN0 (place-image ALIEN-SHIP0 15 30 E-SCENE))

(define SCN1 (place-image ALIEN-SHIP1 197 80 SCN0))

(define SCN2 (place-image ALIEN-SHIP2 (/ WIDTH 2) (/ HEIGHT 2) SCN1))
```

(b) Result Image.

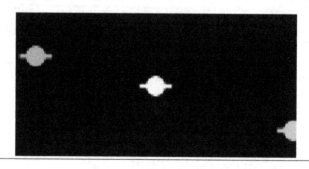

** **Ex. 27** — Debug and complete the design of the program in Fig. 22a. Make sure to test all defined values.

* **Ex. 28** — Write a program that creates an image of a banner with your name on it.

* **Ex. 29** — Write a program that creates an image of a triangle that is over an image of the triangle flipped over the x-axis.

** **Ex. 30** — Write a program that creates the image of a smiley face.

Fig. 23 Sample starry night images

(a) Starry Night I.

(b) Starry Night II

***Ex. 31** — Write a program that creates a starry night image. Your composition must have a representation of at least one moon, three stars, and a stickman. Figure 23a[a] and 23b[b] display sample starry night images created by students. Be creative and have fun!

---

[a] Courtesy of Lindsey M Reams.
[b] Courtesy of Shamil Dzhatdoyev.

15 What Have We Learned in This Chapter?

The important lessons of Chap. 2 are summarized as follows:

Fig. 24 Chapter 2 BSL grammar

```
    program ::= {expr | test | def}*
        def ::= (define <variable name> expr)
       test ::= (check-expect expr expr)
            ::= (check-within expr expr expr)
       expr ::= number | string | <variable name>
            ::= \#<character constant>
            ::= '<character+>
            ::= #true
            ::= #false
            ::= <image>
            ::= (<function> expr+)
            ::= (and expr expr expr*)
            ::= (or expr expr expr*)
     string ::= "<character>*"
     number ::= positive
            ::= negative
   positive ::= mag
   negative ::= -mag
        mag ::= int
            ::= real
            ::= fraction
        int ::= digit+
      digit ::= 0|1|2|3|4|5|6|7|8|9
       real ::= digit*.digit+
   fraction ::= int/nonzero-int
nonzero-int ::= <1|2|3|4|5|6|7|8|9>int
```

- When solving a problem, outline the values that must be computed to guide the development of a solution based on divide and conquer.
- In addition to number and string, BSL includes the character, symbol, Boolean, and image types.
- Primitive type instances, like a Boolean, cannot be decomposed.
- Compound type instances, like a string, can be decomposed.
- The BSL syntax developed so far is displayed in Fig. 24.

  - New expressions for characters, symbols, Booleans, and images.
  - andand orexpressions are syntax for the Boolean functions and and or.
  - not is a Boolean function in BSL.
  - | means or. For example, the first production rule for expr states that it can be a number, a string, or a variable.

- Computations involving numbers and images may contain errors.
- Use check-within to test the computation of a real number.
- Boolean functions are called predicates and allow programmers to determine if the input satisfies a property.
- Model checking tests properties of a computed value.
- The 2htdp/image teachpack provides functions to create, compose, and extract properties of images.

Chapter 3
The Nature of Functions

Every high school student has studied functions. What for? Have you ever wondered where functions come from? Why do they exist? Certainly, many students can state that a function is a mapping from a domain element to a range element. That, however, does not tell anyone where functions come from. Perhaps, looking at an example helps. Consider the following function:

$$f(x) = x^2 + 3x - 10$$

Certainly, many students can state that x is an input element from the domain and that the value of f(10) is 120. Now, we know something about functions. We can use functions to compute values. This is done by "plugging in" 10 for x. That is, all instances of x are substituted with 10 to obtain

$$f(10) = 10^2 + 3 \cdot 10 - 10$$

Now, it is all a matter of evaluating function's body (i.e., the expression to the right of the equal sign). This is screaming to us that functions are likely to play an important role in programming. After all, BSL, as well as other programming languages, is exceptionally good at evaluating expressions. A program in BSL to evaluate f(10) looks like this:

```
;; Evaluating f(x) = x^2 + 3x - 10
(define F-X10 (+ (sqr 10) (* 3 10) -10))
(check-expect F-X10 120)
```

We still, however, do not know where f(x) came from.

This chapter introduces the process of *abstraction over expressions* that leads to functions. It also introduces the BSL syntax needed to define functions (like f(x)). More importantly, it introduces the first *design recipe* to guide problem solvers in function development. A design recipe is a series of steps, each with a specific outcome, that defines a systematic process to implement functions. A design recipe does not tell you the solution to a problem. That you must figure out. It does, however, prove useful to take you from a problem statement and a blank IDE to a program that solves the problem in a manner that is understandable to others.

© The Author(s), under exclusive license to Springer Nature Switzerland AG 2022   47
M. T. Morazán, *Animated Problem Solving*, Texts in Computer Science,
https://doi.org/10.1007/978-3-030-85091-3_3

Fig. 25 Program for f(x) = x² + 3x − 10 at x = 10, 0, 1, 20, 100

```
;; Evaluating f(x) f(x) = x^2 + 3x - 10

(define F-X10  (+ (sqr 10)  (* 3 10)  -10))
(define F-X0   (+ (sqr 0)   (* 3 0)   -10))
(define F-X1   (+ (sqr 1)   (* 3 1)   -10))
(define F-X20  (+ (sqr 20)  (* 3 20)  -10))
(define F-X100 (+ (sqr 100) (* 3 100) -10))

(check-expect F-X10  120)
(check-expect F-X0   -10)
(check-expect F-X1   -6)
(check-expect F-X20  450)
(check-expect F-X100 10290)
```

16 The Rise of Functions

Writing a program to compute the value of f(10) has proven rather easy. Now you are asked to also have your program compute f(0), f(1), f(20), and f(100). After some thought and a bit of typing, your program looks as displayed in Fig. 25. A different constant is defined for each value of f(x) obtained from a different value of x. The tests validate that each value of f(x) has been correctly computed.

Now, you are asked to have your program compute all the values of f(x) for the integers in [11..19]. This is another 9 different values of x and, frankly speaking, many are unlikely to want to do a lot of the same typing over and over again. To avoid this, some may decide to copy, paste, and edit code to account for the changes. This is dangerous, because it is error-prone. It also means that for a new batch of x values you will be doing a lot of copying and pasting again. There must be a better way to get the job done.

Why would anyone decide to cut and paste to write more code? It turns out there is something interesting about the expressions used to compute the different values of f(x). Observe that they are almost identical (see Fig. 26). There is only one difference from one expression to the next: the number plugged in. The elements that vary among similar expressions are called *variables*. That is, we can abstract away the differences among similar expressions by associating each difference with a variable. For the expressions above, let us call the single difference x (as done in the mathematical function f(x)). This reduces all the expressions above to a single expression:

```
(+ (sqr x) (* 3 x) -10))
```

In order to exploit such an expression, a mechanism is needed to provide x with a value.

Let us go back and see how mathematicians provided this mechanism. They chose the syntax f(x) = e, where e is a mathematical expression. We say that f(x) is the function header. A function header contains two parts: the name of the function and the name of the input variables. The input variables are called the function's *parameters*. For f(x), f is the function name and x is the only parameter. We say that

Fig. 26 Expressions for f(x)

```
(+ (sqr 10)  (* 3 10)  -10)
(+ (sqr 0)   (* 3 0)   -10)
(+ (sqr 1)   (* 3 1)   -10)
(+ (sqr 20)  (* 3 20)  -10)
(+ (sqr 100) (* 3 100) -10)
```

e is the function body. Mathematicians use a mathematical application expression to *bind* parameters to values. For example, f(10) binds x to 10. To obtain an expression that can be evaluated, every parameter is substituted with its binding in the body of the function. The process of substituting every variable with its binding is called *β-reduction*. For f(10), *β*-reduction substitutes every x with 10 in $x^2 + 3x - 10$ to obtain $10^2 + 3·10 - 10$. Observe that the *β*-reduction transformation yields an expression that has no variables and may be evaluated.

BSL allows programmers to write their own functions much like mathematicians do. To allow programmers to do so, there is a new def production rule:

def ::= (define (<name> <name>$^+$) expr)

This production rule states that a function definition is written starting with an opening parenthesis, the keyword[12] define, and inside parenthesis the function name and the name of 1 or more parameters.[13] This is called the BSL function header. The function header is followed by a BSL expression and a closing parenthesis (to match the opening parenthesis before define). The expression after the function header is the body of the BSL function.

Developing a function is not quite enough. It is not reasonable to assume that anyone will know how to correctly use a function just by looking at it. Any reader or user of a function needs to know the types of the parameters, the type of the value returned, and the purpose of the function. In other words, functions need to be documented with a signature and a purpose statement (just like it is done in DrRacket's Help Desk). For our current problem, x's type is number and the type returned by the function is number. Therefore, the signature is number $\to$ number. The purpose of the BSL function is to compute the value of f(x).

The program in Fig. 25 can now be updated to compute all the values of f(x) for the integers in [11..19]. Instead of defining 9 constants for the new function values, a single BSL function for f(x) is defined and it is used 9 times to compute the new values. The result of this process is displayed in Fig. 27. Observe that the new tests use f instead of using a constant for the tested value. Now, the value being tested is the value returned by f. Further observe that f's signature and purpose are written before f's definition. This helps anyone reading the program to understand the defined function.

Carefully think about what has been achieved. Ask yourself these questions:

- For the tests, do you prefer to use f or always use defined constants?
- Can this program compute any value of f(x)?

---

[12] A keyword is a word that has a special meaning in a programming language.

[13] A name is a symbol written without the '.

Fig. 27 Program for computing values of f(x) using a BSL function

```
;; Evaluating f(x)  f(x) = x^2 + 3x - 10

(define F-X10  (+ (sqr 10)  (* 3 10)  -10))
(define F-X0   (+ (sqr 0)   (* 3 0)   -10))
(define F-X1   (+ (sqr 1)   (* 3 1)   -10))
(define F-X20  (+ (sqr 20)  (* 3 20)  -10))
(define F-X100 (+ (sqr 100) (* 3 100) -10))

(check-expect F-X10  120)
(check-expect F-X0   -10)
(check-expect F-X1   -6)
(check-expect F-X20  450)
(check-expect F-X100 10290)
(check-expect (f 11) 144)
(check-expect (f 12) 170)
(check-expect (f 13) 198)
(check-expect (f 14) 228)
(check-expect (f 15) 260)
(check-expect (f 16) 294)
(check-expect (f 17) 330)
(check-expect (f 18) 368)
(check-expect (f 19) 408)

;; number → number
;; Purpose: To compute f(x)
(define (f x)
   (+ (sqr x) (* 3 x) -10))
```

- Instead of asking you to modify the program for every value of f(x) needed, can others use the program to compute these values?

To answer the first question, consider a single test. Most individuals find more readable and prefer to type

```
(check-expect (f 11) 144)
```

over

```
(check-expect F-X11 144)
(define F-X11 (+ (sqr 11) (* 3 1) -10))
```

The answer to the second question is yes given enough memory. As a program is evaluated, memory is allocated to store values. Since memory is finite, it is possible that a program may be asked to compute a value that requires more memory than is available. This is something to keep in mind. In practice, however, people around the world execute programs every day without running out of memory. The answer to the third question is an unequivocal yes. Anyone running the program only needs to type the correct application expression at the prompt in the interactions area.

Why were the tests using constants not rewritten to eliminate the need to define the constants? The answer is that many times it is useful to see how a value is

Fig. 28 The general design recipe for functions

1. Outline the representation of values and the computation.
2. Define constants for the value of sample expressions.
3. Identify and name the differences among the sample expressions.
4. Write the function's signature and purpose.
5. Write the function's header.
6. Write tests.
7. Write the function's body.
8. Run the tests and, if necessary, redesign.

computed to understand a program. Therefore, you should write both types of tests: tests that use concrete values (like the last 9 tests) and tests that use defined constants for expressions that show how a value is computed (like the first 4 tests).

17 General Design Recipe for Functions

Abstraction over expressions led to functions. The question now is how do we systematically develop functions to solve problems. There are general steps that ought to be followed to develop every function. Figure 28 presents the steps in the form of a design recipe. Each step has a specific outcome that guides you to a problem's solution.

The first two steps are called problem analysis. Step 1 asks for how values in the real or an imaginary (like in a video game) world are represented in the program. This means that we must represent values in the real or imaginary world in a manner that our programming language can manipulate. Furthermore, this representation must be invertible. That is, a result must be translatable to the world element it represents. It is important for the representation to capture the characteristics needed to carry out the computation. For example, consider the problem of computing the area of a rectangular field. A field in the real world cannot be processed by a computer. Therefore, we need a representation of its characteristics that are needed to compute the area. We can represent the width, length, and area of the field as nonnegative real numbers. Step 1 also asks for the computation of values to be outlined. Returning to the area of a rectangular field, we can state that the area is the product of the length and the width. Step 2 requires the development of sample expressions that illustrate how the needed value is computed.

Step 3 is the abstraction step. The differences among the sample expressions must be identified and each is given a unique variable name. These variables are the parameters of the function. Pick names that identify the value they represent. For example, if a variable represents a number, then a-number is a better choice than z. Step 4 requires that the function's signature be written. To do so, the type of each parameter and the function's return type must be written with an arrow between them. In addition, Step 4 requires a short description of the function's purpose. This purpose statement needs to be clear and concise so that others may understand what

Fig. 29 The basic function template

```
#|
;; type → type
;; Purpose:
(define (f-on-args var)
  ...)

;; Sample expression definitions for f-on-args
(define CONSTANT-1 expr)
    ...
(define CONSTANT-N expr)

;; Tests using sample computations for f-on-args
(check-expect (f-on-args expr) CONSTANT-1)
    ...
(check-expect (f-on-args expr) CONSTANT-N)

;; Tests using sample values for f-on-args
(check-expect (f-on-args expr) value-1)
    ...
(check-expect (f-on-args expr) value-m)
|#
```

is computed by the function. The function header is written to satisfy Step 5. Pick a function name that helps identify the purpose of the function. For example, naming a cubing function f is a poor choice. A better choice is naming the function cube. In addition, the parameters from Step 3 must be written in the order that corresponds to the types in the signature. For Step 6, tests are written using an application of the function as the tested value and using both the constants from Step 2 and other values not defined as constants. The body of the function is developed to satisfy Step 7. β-reduction is performed on any one of the sample expressions. That is, the differences are substituted with the correct parameter. Finally, Step 8 requires the running of the tests. If all the tests pass, you may have guarded optimism in having designed a correct function. If there are any errors, then you need to check your answers to each step of the design recipe.

The design recipe suggests a *function template* may be used for function design. A function template is like a skeleton for functions. It captures the main components a problem solution needs. Figure 29 displays the basic function template. Every time a problem is being solved, the template is copied and specialized. When an answer for a step of the design recipe is formulated, the copied template is edited to reflect the answer.

17.1 The Design Recipe in Action

To illustrate the use of the design recipe, consider the problem of creating name banner images for Craig, Julia (Ohio), Steve, Little Nick, Big Nick, and Jeremy. The name image should contain only the name in a green 36 size font.

The answers to each step of the design recipe are outlined as follows:

STEP 1

Represent each name as a string. The banner image is computed by applying the text function to a name, 36, and 'olive.

STEP 2

Three constants for the value of sample expressions are

```
(define CRAIG (text "Craig"         36 'olive))
(define JULIA (text "Julia (Ohio)" 36 'olive))
(define STEVE  (text "Steve"         36 'olive))
```

STEP 3

The only difference among the three sample expressions is the string representing the name. The variable for this difference is name.

STEP 4

There is only one difference which is a string and the value computed is an image. The signature and purpose statement are

```
;; string → image
;; Purpose: Create a banner for the given name
;;          using font 36 and the color olive
```

STEP 5

The function header contains only one parameter, because a single difference was identified in Step 3. The name make-banner is suggestive of the purpose of the function. The function header is

(define (make-banner name)

STEP 6

The tests using the defined constants and sample values are below.

```
;; Tests using sample computations
(check-expect (make-banner "Craig")         CRAIG)
(check-expect (make-banner "Julia (Ohio)")  JULIA)
(check-expect (make-banner "Steve")         STEVE)
```

Fig. 30 Name banners program

```
(require 2htdp/image)

;; string → image
;; Purpose: Create a banner for the give name using
;;          font 36 and the color olive
(define (make-banner name)
  (text name 36 'olive))

; Sample expression definitions for make-banner
(define CRAIG  (text "Craig"        36 'olive))
(define JULIA  (text "Julia (Ohio)" 36 'olive))
(define STEVE  (text "Steve"        36 'olive))

;; Tests using sample computations for make-banner
(check-expect (make-banner "Craig")        CRAIG)
(check-expect (make-banner "Julia (Ohio)") JULIA)
(check-expect (make-banner "Steve")        STEVE)

;; Tests using sample values for make-banner
```

(check-expect (make-banner "Little Nick") Little Nick)

(check-expect (make-banner "Big Nick") Big Nick)

(check-expect (make-banner "Jeremy") Jeremy)

```
;; Tests using sample values
(check-expect (make-banner "Little Nick")
```
Little Nick)
```
(check-expect (make-banner "Big Nick")
```
Big Nick)
```
(check-expect (make-banner "Jeremy")
```
Jeremy)

STEP 7

The body of the function uses name instead of a concrete string:

```
(text name 36 'olive)
```

STEP 8

All tests pass.

Figure 30 displays the full program written in BSL inside DrRacket.

* **Ex. 32** — Follow the steps of the design recipe to write a program to compute the area of an ellipse.

** **Ex. 33** — Follow the steps of the design recipe to write a program to compute the image of a smiley face.

** **Ex. 34** — Logical equivalence, denoted A $\Leftrightarrow$ B, means that A $\Rightarrow$ B and that B $\Rightarrow$ A. That is, it means that A is true if and only if B is true. The truth table for logical equivalence is

A	**B**	**A $\Leftrightarrow$ B**
F	F	T
F	T	F
T	F	F
T	T	F

Follow the steps of the design recipe to write a program to compute the logical equivalence of two Boolean values.

* **Ex. 35** — Follow the steps of the design recipe to write a program to determine if a string is of even length.

18 Auxiliary Functions

Seldomly, programs only need to compute many instances of a single value as the program in Fig. 30. It is far more common to have to compute several different values to solve a problem. A good designer develops a function for each different value. Such a practice makes it easier for the programmer and for others to understand the solution to the problem. It also endows programs with *modularity*. Modularity enables re-usability of expressions and reduces code duplication. In other words, modularity is tightly connected to abstraction.

If problem analysis reveals that different kinds of values need to be computed, consider which values ought to be computed by an *auxiliary function*. If special knowledge is required to compute a value or if different instances of the same value are needed, then designing an auxiliary function is a good choice. On the other hand, if the expression needed to compute a new value is short, simple, and used only once, then designing a new function may add little clarity to the solution.

If a programmer determines that several functions are needed, she can follow two basic strategies: *bottom-up* or *top-down*. Bottom-up is a programming style in which the simplest (usually the smallest) functions are designed first, and then these functions are used to design more complex functions. Top-down is a programming style in which the complex functions are designed first, and then simpler functions are designed. The most commonly used approach is top-down, because a programmer rarely knows in advance all the simpler functions that are required. Following a top-down approach allows the programmer to discover, as the design advances, needed simpler functions.

Fig. 31 Computing the area of a washer requires two radii

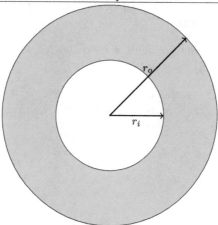

18.1 Bottom-Up Design

To illustrate the bottom-up approach, consider computing the area of a washer as displayed in Fig. 31. The goal is to compute the area of the green section. This area is the area difference of the outer circle with radius r_o and the inner circle with radius r_i. There are two different values to compute: area and difference. This suggests two different functions. Given that computing the difference depends on computing the area, a bottom-up approach starts by designing the area function for circles.

The steps of the design recipe for the area of a circle function may be satisfied as follows:

STEP 1
The area of a circle is given by the product of π and the square of the circle's radius.

STEP 2
Two constants for sample expression values are

```
(define C-AREA5  (* pi 5))
(define C-AREA18 (* pi 18))
```

STEP 3
The only difference among the sample expressions is the radius. The variable for this difference is a-radius.

STEP 4

The signature and purpose statement are

```
;; R>= 0 → R>= 0
;; Purpose: Compute the area of the circle with the given
;;          radius.
```

$\mathbb{R}_{>= 0}$ is any real number greater than or equal to zero.

STEP 5

The function header is
```
(define (area-circle a-radius)
```
Observe that the chosen function name suggests the purpose of the function.

STEP 6

The tests using defined constants and sample values are

```
;; Tests using sample computations
(check-within (area-circle 5)  C-AREA5  0.01)
(check-within (area-circle 18) C-AREA18 0.01)

;; Tests using sample values
(check-within (area-circle 0)  0       0.01)
(check-within (area-circle 10) 314.15 0.01)
```

Observe that the tests include, 0, the lowest possible value for a-radius. It is always good practice to test border values in the domain of a function.

STEP 7

The body of the function is

```
(* pi (sqr a-radius))
```

STEP 8

All tests pass.

With area-circle designed, implemented, and tested, the function for the area of a washer is designed. The steps of the design recipe may be satisfied as follows:

STEP 1

The area of a washer is given by the area difference of its outer and inner circles.

STEP 2

Three constants for the value of sample expressions are

```
;; Sample expression definitions for area-washer
(define W-AREA6-3  (- (area-circle 6)  (area-circle 3)))
```

```
(define W-AREA15-9 (- (area-circle 15) (area-circle 9)))
(define W-AREA4-1  (- (area-circle 4)  (area-circle 1)))
```

Observe that function composition is used to write the tests. The output of area-circle is used as input to -. In addition, observe that the constant names are suggestive of the value they represent.

STEP 3

There are two differences in the sample expressions: the radii of the outer and the inner circles named, respectively, outer-radius and inner-radius.

STEP 4

The signature and purpose statement are

```
;; R>= 0 R>= 0 → R>= 0
;; Purpose: Compute the area of the washer with the given
;;          radii.
;; ASSUMPTION: outer-radius >= inner-radius
```

An assumption statement is added to make clear that outer-radius must be greater than or equal to inner-radius. Such statements help others to correctly use the function.

STEP 5

The function header is

```
(define (area-washer outer-radius inner-radius)
```

The name of the function is suggestive of its purpose. Compare this name choice with a name like g or area.

STEP 6

The tests using defined constants and sample values are

```
;; Tests using sample computations for area-washer
(check-within (area-washer 6 3)  W-AREA6-3  0.01)
(check-within (area-washer 15 9) W-AREA15-9 0.01)
(check-within (area-washer 4 1)  W-AREA4-1  0.01)

;; Tests using sample values for area-washer
(check-within (area-washer 0 0)       0  0.01)
(check-within (area-washer 10 0)  314.15  0.01)
(check-within (area-washer 7 4)   103.67  0.01)
```

Fig. 32 Area of a washer program

```
;; R>= 0 → Real>= 0
;; Purpose: Compute the area of the circle with the given radius.
(define (area-circle a-radius)
  (* pi (sqr a-radius)))

;; Sample expression definitions for area-circle
(define C-AREA5  (* pi (sqr 5)))
(define C-AREA18 (* pi (sqr 18)))

;; Tests using sample computations for area-circle
(check-within (area-circle 5)  C-AREA5  0.01)
(check-within (area-circle 18) C-AREA18 0.01)

;; Tests using sample values for area-circle
(check-within (area-circle 0)  0       0.01)
(check-within (area-circle 10) 314.15 0.01)

;; R>= 0 R>= 0 → Real>= 0
;; Purpose: Compute the area of the washer with the given radii.
;; ASSUMPTION: outer-radius >= inner-radius
(define (area-washer outer-radius inner-radius)
  (- (area-circle outer-radius) (area-circle inner-radius)))

;; Sample expression definitions for area-washer
(define W-AREA6-3 (- (area-circle 6) (area-circle 3)))
(define W-AREA15-9 (- (area-circle 15) (area-circle 9)))
(define W-AREA4-1 (- (area-circle 4) (area-circle 1)))

;; Tests using sample computations for area-washer
(check-within (area-washer 6 3)  W-AREA6-3  0.01)
(check-within (area-washer 15 9) W-AREA15-9 0.01)
(check-within (area-washer 4 1)  W-AREA4-1  0.01)

;; Tests using sample values for area-washer
(check-within (area-washer 0 0)  0       0.01)
(check-within (area-washer 10 0)  314.15  0.01)
(check-within (area-washer 7 4)  103.67  0.01)
```

STEP 7

The body of the function is

```
(- (area-circle outer-radius) (area-circle inner-radius))
```

STEP 8

All tests pass.

The complete program is displayed in Fig. 32. An advantage of bottom-up design is that functions may be tested as soon as they are implemented. For example, the `area-circle` function may be tested as soon as it is written.

It is possible to design a single function to compute the area of a washer. Such a function contains repetitions and may look as follows:

```
;; R>= 0 R>= 0 → R>= 0
;; Purpose: Compute the area of the washer with the given
;;          radii.
;; ASSUMPTION: outer-radius >= inner-radius
(define (area-washer outer-radius inner-radius)
  (- (* pi (sqr outer-radius)) (* pi (sqr inner-radius))))

;; Sample expression definitions for area-washer
(define W-AREA6-3  (- (* pi (sqr 6))   (* pi (sqr 3))))
(define W-AREA15-9 (- (* pi (sqr 15))  (* pi (sqr 9))))
(define W-AREA4-1  (- (* pi (sqr 4))   (* pi (sqr 1))))

;; Tests using sample computations for area-washer
(check-within (area-washer 6 3)  W-AREA6-3  0.01)
(check-within (area-washer 15 9) W-AREA15-9 0.01)
(check-within (area-washer 4 1)  W-AREA4-1  0.01)

;; Tests using sample values for area-washer
(check-within (area-washer 0 0)  0   0.01)
(check-within (area-washer 10 0) 314.15  0.01)
(check-within (area-washer 7 4)  103.67  0.01)
```

This function is obtained by *inlining* `area-circle`. Both versions solve the problem. The question now is which one is clearer? Most people would argue that the version in Fig. 32 is clearer. In the first version, it is easier to see how the area of a washer is computed. Even a person who has forgotten the formula for the area of a circle can discern how the problem is solved. Would that same person as easily discern how the problem is solved in the second version above? Nonetheless, inlining is an important optimization done by compilers[14] and that you will learn more about in a Programming Language or a Compilers course.

---

* Ex. 36 — Use a bottom-up approach following the steps of the design recipe to write a program to determine if `f(a)` equals `f(b)`, where $f(x) = x^2 - 9$.

*** Ex. 37 — Use a bottom-up approach, following the steps of the design recipe, to write a program to implement not, or, and and using only nor (not or). The truth table for nor is displayed in Fig. 33. For example, `(or A B)` = `(nor (nor A B) (nor A B))`.

* Ex. 38 — Use a bottom-up approach following the steps of the design recipe to write a program to determine if two strings of length 3 contain a.

---

[14] A compiler is a program that converts programs written in a language like BSL into machine code that is executable by a computer.

Fig. 33 The truth table for `nor`

A	B	(nor A B)
F	F	T
F	T	F
T	F	F
T	T	F

---

* **Ex. 39** — Use a bottom-up approach following the steps of the design recipe to design and write a program to compute the flag images of Ghana, Honduras, Lithuania, Niger, and Syria.

---

19 Top-Down Design

To illustrate the top-down design process, consider the problem of computing images like those in Fig. 34. Each image has 4 overlayed squares at a $45°$ angle. Instead of first trying to figure out how to compute each square in the image composition, start by writing expressions to compute the image composition. For unknown values, like the length of a square, use a constant. The definitions of these constants are a different problem from the problem of creating the desired image. In other words, use a divide and conquer strategy.

Under this design approach, the steps of the design recipe may be satisfied as follows:

STEP 1
> The image is computed by overlaying squares of alternating colors and differing lengths. Every other overlayed square, starting with the largest square, is rotated by $45°$.

STEP 2
> Observe that it is already known that several squares of different colors and lengths are needed. This immediately suggests that we abstract away the image computation for squares and design (later) a function for this purpose. Furthermore, we know that this function requires two arguments (one for each difference): a length and a color.

Constants for the value of sample expressions may be defined as follows:

```
(define IMG1 (overlay
              (rotate 0  (make-sqr IMG1-LEN4 'brown))
              (rotate 45 (make-sqr IMG1-LEN3 'gold))
              (rotate 0  (make-sqr IMG1-LEN2 'brown))
              (rotate 45 (make-sqr IMG1-LEN1 'gold))))
```

Fig. 34 Nested squares at an angle

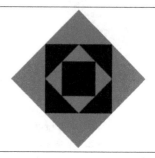

```
(define IMG2 (overlay
               (rotate 0   (make-sqr IMG2-LEN4 'black))
               (rotate 45  (make-sqr IMG2-LEN3 'red))
               (rotate 0   (make-sqr IMG2-LEN2 'black))
               (rotate 45  (make-sqr IMG2-LEN1 'red))))
```

Observe that we do not concern ourselves at this point with how make-sqr is implemented or with how to define the different lengths. We assume that they can all be defined.

STEP 3

There are 6 differences in the sample expressions: 4 lengths and two colors. We name the differences: bot-len, len2, len3, top-len, botclr, and topclr.

STEP 4

The signature and purpose statement are

```
;; R>= 0 R>= 0 R>= 0 R>= 0 color color → image
;; Purpose: Create an image of nested squares at 45
;;          degree angles using the given lengths
;;          and colors.
```

STEP 5

The function header is

```
(define (make-nested-sqs bot-len len2 len3 top-len
                         botclr  topclr)
```

STEP 6

The tests using defined constants and sample values are

```
;; Tests using sample computations
(check-expect (make-nested-sqs IMG1-LEN1 IMG1-LEN2
                               IMG1-LEN3 IMG1-LEN4
                               'gold     'brown)
              IMG1)
(check-expect (make-nested-sqs IMG2-LEN1 IMG2-LEN2
                               IMG2-LEN3 IMG2-LEN4
                               'red      'black)
              IMG2)

;; Tests using sample values
(check-expect (make-nested-sqs 50 35.35 24.99 17.67 'olive 'yellow)
```

```
)
(check-expect (make-nested-sqs 20 14.14  9.99  7.06 'pink  'purple)
```

```
)
```

STEP 7

The body of the function is

```
(overlay (rotate 0  (make-sqr top-len topclr))
         (rotate 45 (make-sqr len3 botclr))
         (rotate 0  (make-sqr len2 topclr))
         (rotate 45 (make-sqr bot-len botclr)))
```

STEP 8

All tests pass.

At this point, we cannot run any tests because make-sqr and the length constants are undefined. The answer written for Step 8 assumes that the tests pass after all required functions and constants are defined. If all tests do not pass, then checking the steps of the design is necessary.

Let us turn our focus now to the design and implementation of make-sqr. We arrive to this function with some clear ideas about the abstraction. There are two differences: side length and color. If we were to discover that more values are needed,

then we have a signal that there is a bug in our abstraction. We proceed assuming
that the function can be designed with the stated differences.

The steps of the design recipe may be satisfied as follows:

STEP 1

The image of a solid square is computed using the square function and the given
side length and color.

STEP 2

Constants for the value of sample expressions may be defined as follows:

```
(define SQ1 (square 500 'solid 'lightbrown))
(define SQ2 (square 70  'solid 'darkblue))
```

STEP 3

There are 2 differences in the sample expressions as expected: a length and a
color. We name the differences: side-len and a-color.

STEP 4

The signature and purpose statement are

```
;; R>= 0 color → image
;; Purpose: Compute the image of a square of the given length and color
             degree angles using the given lengths and colors.
```

STEP 5

The function header is

```
(define (make-nested-sqs botlen len2 len3 toplen
                         botclr topclr)
```

STEP 6

The tests using defined constants and sample values are

```
;; Tests using sample computations
(check-expect (make-sqr 500 'lightbrown) SQ1)
(check-expect (make-sqr 70  'darkblue) SQ2)

;; Tests using sample values
(check-expect (make-sqr 12 'orange)    █    )


(check-expect (make-sqr 35 'skyblue)        )
```

Fig. 35 The length of the next smaller square is the length of a hypotenuse

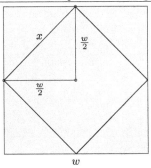

STEP 7

The body of the function is

```
(square side-len 'solid a-color)
```

STEP 8

All tests pass.

The next task is to define the constants for the lengths. For any image of nested squares, the length of the largest square is arbitrary. For example, the length of the largest square can be 100. The length of the next smaller square is not arbitrary as it depends on the length of the outer square. How do we compute the length of the next smaller square? The problem must be carefully analyzed. Figure 35 displays the placement of a smaller square inside a larger square. The length of the outer square is w. Observe that two adjacent midpoints and the center of the outer square form a right triangle. The lengths of the sides forming the 90° are both $\frac{w}{2}$. The length of the inner square is the length of the hypotenuse of the right triangle. We know that the length of the hypotenuse is given by the Pythagorean theorem:

$$x^2 = (\tfrac{w}{2})^2 + (\tfrac{w}{2})^2$$

$$x = \sqrt{(\tfrac{w}{2})^2 + (\tfrac{w}{2})^2}$$

$$= \sqrt{2 * (\tfrac{w}{2})^2}$$

$$= \sqrt{2 * \tfrac{w^2}{4}}$$

$$= \sqrt{\tfrac{w^2}{2}}$$

A function can be defined to compute the length of inner squares. The only difference in computing one inner square length from another is the length of the outer square. Instead of abstracting over similar expressions, we have developed a mathematical expression for the length of an inner circle that is easily translated to BSL. Both approaches to converging on an expression for the body of a function are valid and ought to be part of any problem solver's toolbox.

The steps of the design recipe may be satisfied as follows:

STEP 1

The length of the next smallest square is equal to the length of the line between the two midpoints of two adjacent sides of the enclosing square of length w. The length of the next smaller square is given by $\sqrt{\frac{w^2}{2}}$.

STEP 2

Constants for the value of sample expressions may be defined as follows:

```
(define IMG1-LEN1 100)
(define IMG1-LEN2 (sqrt (/ (sqr IMG1-LEN1) 2)))
(define IMG1-LEN3 (sqrt (/ (sqr IMG1-LEN2) 2)))
(define IMG1-LEN4 (sqrt (/ (sqr IMG1-LEN3) 2)))
```

STEP 3

There is a single difference in the sample expressions as expected: a length. We name the difference side-len.

STEP 4

The signature and purpose statement are

```
;; R>= 0 → R>= 0
;; Purpose: Compute the length of the next smallest square
```

STEP 5

The function header is

```
(define (compute-new-sqr-len side-len)
```

STEP 6

The tests using defined constants and sample values are

```
;; Tests using sample computations
(check-within (compute-new-sqr-len 100)
              IMG1-LEN2
              0.01)
(check-within (compute-new-sqr-len IMG1-LEN2)
              IMG1-LEN3
              0.01)
```

```
(check-within (compute-new-sqr-len IMG1-LEN3)
              IMG1-LEN4
              0.01)
```

Given that constants for the square lengths for a second image are needed, the function being designed may be used to compute these. The tests using sample values based on these constants may be written as follows:

```
;; Tests using sample values
(define IMG2-LEN1 150)
(define IMG2-LEN2 (compute-new-sqr-len IMG2-LEN1))
(define IMG2-LEN3 (compute-new-sqr-len IMG2-LEN2))
(define IMG2-LEN4 (compute-new-sqr-len IMG2-LEN3))

(check-within IMG2-LEN2 106.06 0.01)
(check-within IMG2-LEN3 75 0.01)
(check-within IMG2-LEN4 53.03 0.01)
(check-within (compute-new-sqr-len 0) 0    0.01)
(check-within (compute-new-sqr-len 8) 5.65 0.01)
```

STEP 7

The body of the function is

```
(sqrt (/ (sqr side-len) 2))
```

STEP 8

All tests pass.

An important point to highlight is when a defined function may be applied in BSL. A defined function may be applied any time when it is part of a test. All other times, however, a function must be defined before it is applied to any arguments. That is, the definition of a function must appear in a program before its first use outside tests.

* **Ex. 40** — Implement the nested squares program.

* **Ex. 41** — Use a top-down approach following the steps of the design recipe to write a program to compute the flag images of Armenia, Austria, Bulgaria, Colombia, and Estonia.

* **Ex. 42** — Use a top-down approach following the steps of the design recipe to write a program to compute $f(x) = 4(x^3 - 1)^3 - 6(x^3-1)^2 + 2(x^3-1) + 8$.

* **Ex. 43** — Use a top-down approach following the steps of the design recipe to write a program to append two double copies of a string separated by a space. For example, "abc" results in "abcabc abcabc".

*** **Ex. 44** — Use a top-down approach following the steps of the design recipe to write a program to compute $((a \Rightarrow b) \wedge (b \Rightarrow c)) \Rightarrow (a \Rightarrow c)$. i $\Rightarrow$ j is ¬i $\vee$ j.

20 What Have We Learned in This Chapter?

The important lessons of Chap. 3 are summarized as follows:

- Functions are abstractions over similar expressions.

  - Each difference becomes a function parameter.
  - In the body each difference is replaced with the corresponding parameter.
  - Functions add modularity and help avoid repetition bugs.

- The BSL syntax explored, displayed in Fig. 36, includes a new def production rule to define functions.

  - Recall that | means or.
  - expr ::= #true | #false means an expression may be #true or may be #false.

- The basic function design recipe is a roadmap for developing and implementing functions.
- Auxiliary functions are used when specialized knowledge is needed to compute a needed value or when different instances of the same value are computed.
- There are two general programming development styles.

  - Bottom-up: simplest functions are developed first.
  - Top-down: complex functions are developed first.
  - Regardless of development style, the design recipe guides development.

Fig. 36 Chapter 3 BSL grammar

```
  program ::= {expr | test | def}*
      def ::= (define <variable name> expr)
          ::= (define (<name> <name+>) expr)
     test ::= (check-expect expr expr)
          ::= (check-within expr expr expr)
     expr ::= number | string | <variable name>
          ::= \#<character constant>
          ::= '<character+>
          ::= #true | #false
          ::= <image>
          ::= (<function> expr)
          ::= (and expr expr expr*)
          ::= (or expr expr expr*)
   string ::= "<character>*"
   number ::= positive
          ::= negative
 positive ::= mag
 negative ::= -mag
      mag ::= int
          ::= real
          ::= fraction
      int ::= digit
    digit ::= 0|1|2|3|4|5|6|7|8|9
     real ::= digit*.digit+
 fraction ::= int/nonzero-int
nonzero-int ::= <1|2|3|4|5|6|7|8|9>int
```

Chapter 4
Aliens Attack Version 0

It is time to put your newly acquired skills to work. This chapter develops the first version of a video game that we shall call *Aliens Attack*. This chapter, however, will not develop a full video game. You need to learn more about problem solving and more BSL syntax to write a fully working video game. Therefore, the video game is developed using the process of iterative refinement. That is, as you learn more about problem solving and about BSL syntax, a more complete video game shall be developed. This process culminates with a multiplayer game that you may play with your friends over the internet. That is a promise. If you work hard and absorb all the lessons contained in this textbook, then you will acquire enough skills to develop a multiplayer video game.

Figure 37 displays an image of a single-player version of Aliens Attack. In the scene there is an army of aliens attacking earth and there is a single rocket defending earth. There is no placating the aliens and earth must defend itself. The rocket is at the bottom of the scene over earth and may move left to right without going off the edge of the image. The rocket may also shoot in an attempt to destroy the aliens. The army of aliens starts toward the top of the scene. All the aliens move in the same direction: right, left, or down. The aliens move right one step at a time until an alien reaches the right edge of the scene. At this point all the aliens move down a step. After moving down a step, the aliens move left one step at a time until an alien reaches the left edge of the scene. The aliens then move down a step. This cycle continues until an alien reaches and conquers earth (the player loses the game) or all the aliens are destroyed (the player wins the game). Observe that, like the rocket, the aliens may not go off the scene as they move. When the rocket shoots, a shot starts at the position of the rocket and moves up until it hits an alien or it goes off the top each of the scene.

The first version of Aliens Attack is not truly a video game. That is fine because it will be refined. To start, the focus is on problems that you can solve with the skills you have already developed. The development of Aliens Attack version 0 focuses on the creation and placement of images to render the video game as an image. This is a good starting point because you know the basics of creating and placing images and of writing functions. The first goal is to design the scene where the images of

© The Author(s), under exclusive license to Springer Nature Switzerland AG 2022
M. T. Morazán, *Animated Problem Solving*, Texts in Computer Science,
https://doi.org/10.1007/978-3-030-85091-3_4

Fig. 37 A sample rendering of a single-player Aliens Attack

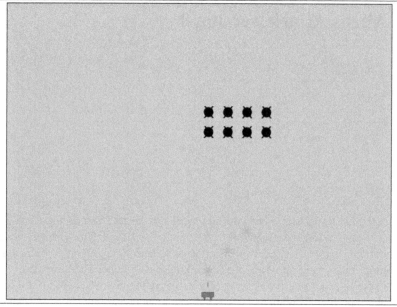

the game are rendered. The second goal is to develop functions to create the images of the rocket, the alien, and the shot. The third goal is to create functions to draw the elements in a scene.

21 The Scene for Aliens Attack

Recall that graphics are created using a coordinate system in which the x coordinate grows from left to right and the y coordinate grows from top to bottom. Also recall that a w_1 x h_1 empty scene into which images are placed may be created as follows:

    (empty-scene w₁ h₁)

Creating an empty scene is only part of what is needed. The question that immediately arises is how do we reason about this empty scene. Figure 38a displays the view of the empty scene as a grid of pixels. Each square in the grid is a pixel and items, like the blue square, are placed in the scene using pixel coordinates. The blue square in Fig. 38a is at pixel coordinate (15, 19). This can work well but seems to mismatch our goal. Our goal is to place images in a scene, not manipulate pixels. If we choose a maximum size for each image in the video game, we can reason about the empty scene as boxes where an image fits. Figure 38b displays this view of the empty scene. A square is placed using image coordinates, not pixel coordinates. For instance, the blue square in Fig. 38a is at image coordinate (3,3).

So, why should we care about the perspective we adopt? It turns out that data representation strongly influences how a problem is reasoned about. Consider, for example, how is an alien hit by a shot is detected. We shall first analyze the problem using the pixel perspective of the game's scene. Assume that the image of an alien has dimensions W x H as illustrated in Fig. 39 and the alien is located at pixel coordinates (x, y). We define a hit as the shot's position being inside the alien's image. That is, if the shot's position is any pixel covered by the alien's image, then the alien is hit. In Fig. 39, for example, the shots at (x_{r_1}, y_{r_1}) and at (x_{r_2}, y_{r_2}) have hit the alien. The shots at (x_{r_3}, y_{r_3}) and (x_{r_4}, y_{r_4}) have not hit the alien. Now, how is a hit detected? After thinking about it, you can see that a hit means that the shot can be at most half the alien's image width (i.e., $W/2$) away on the x-axis and at most half the alien's image height (i.e., $H/2$) away on the y-axis from the alien's coordinates (i.e., (x, y)). This reasoning leads to a function to detect a hit alien that looks as follows:

```
(define HALF-ALIEN-IMG-WIDTH (/ (image-width FUEL-IMG) 2))

(define HALF-ALIEN-IMG-HEIGHT (/ (image-height FUEL-IMG) 2))

(define (alien-hit? x-alien y-alien x-shot y-shot)
  (and (<= (abs (- x-alien x-shot)) HALF-ALIEN-IMG-WIDTH)
       (<= (abs (- y-alien y-shot)) HALF-ALIEN-IMG-HEIGHT)))
```

Now, consider solving the same problem using an image perspective of the game's scene. Under the image perspective, we do not have to worry about every pixel in the scene. Images can only be placed in a box with image coordinates x and y. This means that an alien is hit by a shot if both have the same coordinates. This reasoning leads to a function to detect a hit alien that looks as follows:

```
(define (alien-hit? x-alien y-alien x-shot y-shot)
  (and (= x-alien x-shot) (= y-alien y-shot)))
```

Fig. 38 Empty scene perspectives

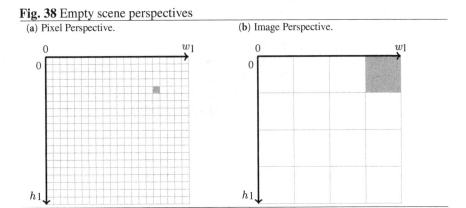

(a) Pixel Perspective. (b) Image Perspective.

Fig. 39 Detecting a hit alien under the pixel perspective

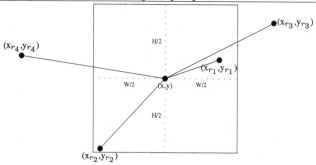

This function is much simpler and easier to understand than the first. The important lesson here is that different representations, like pixel coordinates versus image coordinates, may lead to vastly different solutions/programs. It is worth exploring different representations to determine if any lead to a simpler and easier to understand solution/program.

Given that we have carefully analyzed how to represent coordinates in the game's scene, we may be cautiously confident that using image coordinates leads to simpler problem solutions. We can also surmise that we need to be careful about defining the data representation in the program. For this, we need *data definitions*. A data definition is written to describe a new type of data. For Aliens Attack, the following data definitions and constants are used:

```
;; Character Image Maximum Dimensions
(define IMAGE-WIDTH 30)
(define IMAGE-HEIGHT 30)

;; Video Game Scene Dimensions
(define MAX-CHARS-HORIZONTAL 20)
(define MAX-CHARS-VERTICAL 15)

;; Empty Scene Constants
(define E-SCENE-COLOR 'pink)
(define E-SCENE2-COLOR 'black)
(define E-SCENE-W (* MAX-CHARS-HORIZONTAL IMAGE-WIDTH))
(define E-SCENE-H (* MAX-CHARS-VERTICAL IMAGE-HEIGHT))

#|DATA DEFINITIONS
    A character image (ci) is an image which is at most
    IMAGE-WIDTH x IMAGE-HEIGHT pixels
```

```
    An image-x is an integer in [0..MAX-CHARS-HORIZONTAL-1]

    An image-y is an integer in [0..MAX-CHARS-VERTICAL-1]

    A scene is a E-SCENE-W x E-SCENE-H image

    A pixel-x is an integer in [0..E-SCENE-W-1]

    A pixel-y is an integer in [0..E-SCENE-H-1]            |#

;; Sample image-x
(define AN-IMG-X (/ MAX-CHARS-HORIZONTAL 2))
(define MIN-IMG-X 0)
(define MAX-IMG-X (sub1 MAX-CHARS-HORIZONTAL))

;; Sample image-y
(define AN-IMG-Y (/ MAX-CHARS-VERTICAL 2))
(define MIN-IMG-Y 0)
(define MAX-IMG-Y (sub1 MAX-CHARS-VERTICAL))

;; Sample empty scenes
(define E-SCENE  (empty-scene E-SCENE-W
                              E-SCENE-H
                              E-SCENE-COLOR))
(define E-SCENE2 (empty-scene E-SCENE-W
                              E-SCENE-H
                              E-SCENE2-COLOR))
```

The define constants clearly communicate that for any ci in the game (i.e., rocket, alien, and shot), the maximum width is 30 pixels and the maximum height is 30 pixels. The scene fits 20 ci horizontally and 15 ci vertically. This means image coordinates range from (0,0) to (19, 14). Examples of image-x and image-y values are defined to make writing tests easier. These include the extrema values: the largest and the smallest possible values. Pixel coordinates range from (0,0) to ((sub1 E-SCENE-W), (sub1 E-SCENE-H)). Clearly, we need a mechanism to map image coordinates to pixel coordinates. We shall return to this new problem after tackling the creation of character images.

The data definitions clearly describe what is (and what is not) a ci, an image-x, an image-y, a scene, a pixel-x, and a pixel-y. For example, 2 is a valid image-x because 2 is in [0..(sub1 MAX-CHARS-HORIZONTAL)]. On the other hand, 1000 is not a valid image-x because 1000 is not in [0..(sub1 MAX-CHARS-HORIZONTAL)]. These data definitions guide the development of functions for the video game. Furthermore, the newly defined data types may be used in signatures. That is, the new data types may be used to describe the inputs to and the output of functions.

22 Creating Aliens Attack Images

Creating the images needed for Aliens Attack provides the opportunity to practice
the steps of the design recipe. In addition, it provides us with the opportunity to write
an *application programming interface* (API). An API defines the data formats, the
conventions, and the functions that may be used to create and access data. For Aliens
Attack images, the API is rather simple: the dimensions of any character image must
be 30 x 30 pixels or less and must be created using functions in the image teachpack.
One of the benefits of using or creating an API is *information hiding*. This means,
for example, that the implementation details of a function are hidden from any
programmer who uses the function. A programmer uses the function independent of
how the function is implemented. To be successful, the signature and the purpose of
the function must be clear. Otherwise, programmers will not know how to properly
use a function.

Observe that according to the data definitions, every ci is an image. Every image,
however, is not a ci. A natural question that arises is determining if an image is a
ci. Testing image values is useless, because everybody's idea of a shot, an alien, or
a rocket is different. Furthermore, the data definition ci only specifies ci properties
(not values). This is a clear situation where property-based testing is needed. For
this, a predicate to determine if a given image is a ci is needed. Following the steps
of the design recipe, the predicate may be designed as follows:

STEP 1

Determine that both the image width is less than or equal to IMAGE-WIDTH and
that the image height is less than or equal to IMAGE-HEIGHT.

STEP 2

Definitions for the value of sample expressions are

```
(define IS-CI
        (and (<= (image-width (circle 10 'solid 'red))
                 IMAGE-WIDTH)
             (<= (image-height (circle 10 'solid 'red))
                 IMAGE-HEIGHT)))

(define NOT-CI
        (and (<= (image-width  (square 40 'solid 'blue))
                 IMAGE-WIDTH)
             (<= (image-height (square 40 'solid 'blue))
                 IMAGE-HEIGHT)))

(define NOT-CI2
        (and (<= (image-width
                  (rectangle 2 50 'solid 'blue))
                 IMAGE-WIDTH)
```

```
(<= (image-height
        (rectangle 2 50 'solid 'blue))
    IMAGE-HEIGHT)))
```

Observe that sample expressions are developed for both images that are and that are not ci.

STEP 3

The only difference among the sample expressions is the image tested. The variable for this difference is an-img.

STEP 4

The signature and purpose statement are

```
;; image → Boolean
;; Purpose: To determine if the given image is a ci
```

STEP 5

The function header is
```
(define (ci? an-img)
```

STEP 6

Testing may be satisfied as follows:

```
;; Tests using sample computations for ci?
(check-expect (ci? (circle 10 'solid 'red))  IS-CI)
(check-expect (ci? (square 40 'solid 'blue)) NOT-CI)
(check-expect (ci? (rectangle 20 40 'solid 'blue)) NOT-CI2)

;; Tests using sample values for ci?
(check-expect (ci? (ellipse 10 22 'outline 'green))  #true)
(check-expect (ci? (rectangle 5 33 'solid 'yellow)) #false)
```

Observe that both images that are and are not ci are tested.

STEP 7

The body of the function is

```
(and (<= (image-width an-img)  IMAGE-WIDTH)
     (<= (image-height an-img) IMAGE-HEIGHT))
```

STEP 8

All tests pass.

Recall that this step is only satisfied when the tests are executed and pass.

* **Ex. 45** — Design and implement a predicate to determine if an image is a scene.

* **Ex. 46** — Design and implement a predicate to determine if a number is an `image-x`.

* **Ex. 47** — Design and implement a predicate to determine if a number is an `image-y`.

* **Ex. 48** — Design and implement a predicate to determine if a number is a `pixel-x`.

* **Ex. 49** — Design and implement a predicate to determine if a number is a `pixel-y`.

** **Ex. 50** — A blank pink or black `scene` is rather dull. Personalize your empty scene to provide a more interesting and more pleasant background.

Now that `ci` and non-`ci` images are distinguishable, attention turns to the construction of `cis`. There are three image constructors that are needed: one for a shot, one for an alien, and one for a rocket. The development presented here is only illustrative. This is your video game and you are encouraged to be creative and personalize the game to your liking. Understand the principles for developing the images and then design functions for your own images. Remember that, unlike homework problems in high school Mathematics, there may be many solutions to a problem.

23 Shot Image

The image of the shot is the simplest one in Fig. 37. The shot's image is a radial star and the color is orange. These, of course, may be different depending on your preferences. The goal is to design a constructor for shot images. The steps of the design recipe may be satisfied as follows:

STEP 1
    A shot image is a `ci` of a radial star created using the function `radial-star`.
    Observe that the data definition of a shot image is described in terms of the type
    for character images previously developed.
STEP 2
    Definitions for the value of sample expressions are

```
(define SHOT-COLOR 'orange)

(define SHOT-COLOR2 'skyblue)
```

```
(define SHOT-IMG (radial-star 8
                              (/ IMAGE-WIDTH 8)
                              (/ IMAGE-WIDTH 2)
                              'solid
                              SHOT-COLOR))

(define SHOT-IMG2 (radial-star 8
                               (/ IMAGE-WIDTH 8)
                               (/ IMAGE-WIDTH 2)
                               'solid
                               SHOT-COLOR2))
```

The constants are defined to facilitate changing the color of sample shots. Observe that the outer diameter of the radial star is IMAGE-WIDTH/2 = 15. Therefore, the image of a shot is a ci.

STEP 3

The only difference among the sample expressions is the color of the shot. The variable for this difference is a-color.

STEP 4

The signature and purpose statement are

```
;; color → image
;; Purpose: Create a shot image of the given color
```

STEP 5

The function header is

```
(define (mk-shot-ci a-color)
```

STEP 6

The tests are below.

```
;; Tests using sample computations for mk-shot-ci
(check-expect (mk-shot-ci SHOT-COLOR) SHOT-IMG)
(check-expect (mk-shot-ci SHOT-COLOR2) SHOT-IMG2)
(check-expect (ci? SHOT-IMG) #true)
(check-expect (ci? SHOT-IMG2) #true)

;; Tests using sample values for mk-shot-ci
```

```
(check-expect (mk-shot-ci 'red)           )
```

```
(check-expect (mk-shot-ci 'brown)         )
(check-expect (ci? (mk-shot-img 'red))    #true)
(check-expect (ci? (mk-shot-img 'brown)) #true)
```

Observe that the last two sample computations and sample values tests are property-based testing. They illustrate that the image returned by mk-shot-img is a ci.

STEP 7

The body of the function is

```
(radial-star 8 (/ IMAGE-WIDTH 8) (/ IMAGE-WIDTH 2) 'solid  a-color))
```

STEP 8

All tests pass.

24 Alien Image

The alien image in Fig. 37 is the composition of two images of the same color: an X and a circle. Specifically, the circle is overlayed over the X. A function to achieve this uses function composition. The steps of the design recipe may be satisfied as follows:

STEP 1

The alien image is computed using function composition. The outputs of text and circle are inputs to overlay. The circle image is overlayed over the X image. The alien image must be a ci.

STEP 2

Definitions for the value of sample expressions are

```
(define ALIEN-COLOR 'black)

(define ALIEN-COLOR2 'orange)

(define ALIEN-IMG (overlay (text "X" 25 ALIEN-COLOR)
                           (circle (/ IMAGE-WIDTH 4)
                           'solid
                           ALIEN-COLOR)))

(define ALIEN-IMG2 (overlay (text "X" 25 ALIEN-COLOR2)
                            (circle (/ IMAGE-WIDTH 4)
                            'solid
                            ALIEN-COLOR2)))
```

Getting the alien images to be at most 30×30 pixels requires experimentation. It is not clear from the code above that the resulting images have this property. Property-based testing may be used to demonstrate this.

STEP 3

The only difference among the sample expressions is the color of the alien. The variable for this difference is a-color.

STEP 4

The signature and purpose statement are

```
;; color → image
;; Purpose: Create an alien image of the given color
```

STEP 5

The function header is

```
(define (mk-alien-ci a-color)
```

STEP 6

The tests are below.

```
;; Tests using sample computations for mk-alien-ci
(check-expect (mk-alien-ci ALIEN-COLOR)  ALIEN-IMG)
(check-expect (mk-alien-ci ALIEN-COLOR2) ALIEN-IMG2)
(check-expect (ci? ALIEN-IMG)    #true)
(check-expect (ci? ALIEN-IMG2)   #true)

;; Tests using sample values for mk-alien-ci

(check-expect (mk-alien-ci 'purple)       )

(check-expect (mk-alien-ci 'lightbrown)  )
(check-expect (ci? (mk-alien-img 'purple))     #true)
(check-expect (ci? (mk-alien-img 'lightbrown)) #true)
```

STEP 7

The body of the function is

```
(overlay (text "X" 25 a-color)
         (circle (/ IMAGE-WIDTH 4) 'solid a-color))
```

STEP 8

All tests pass.

Fig. 40 Components of the rocket image

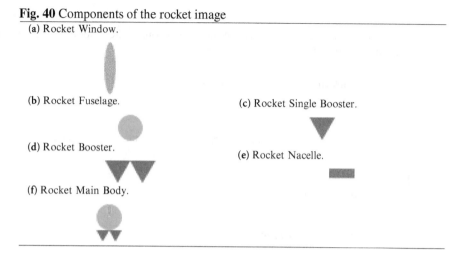

(a) Rocket Window.

(b) Rocket Fuselage.

(c) Rocket Single Booster.

(d) Rocket Booster.

(e) Rocket Nacelle.

(f) Rocket Main Body.

25 Rocket Image

The rocket image is the most complex of the images in Fig. 37. It is composed of the images displayed in Fig. 40. To design a function to create a rocket image, a divide and conquer bottom-up strategy is followed. That is, the simplest components are independently designed first. Then simple components are combined to create more complex figures.

It is important to keep in mind that creating images for the components of a larger image requires experimentation. Rarely, if ever, are the dimensions of a component right after the first attempt. This is another reason why it is important to write sample expressions. Sample expressions may be repeatedly refined until the desired visual effect is achieved. The steps of the design recipe presented for each component below are the final result after several refinements improving the dimensions of each component. Do not be afraid to experiment. Experimenting with sample expressions may lead to insights on how to solve a problem.

25.1 Rocket Window Image Constructor

Creating a rocket window image is a simple exercise with which to practice the steps the design recipe.

STEP 1
    A rocket window is a solid vertical oval.
STEP 2
    Definitions for the value of sample expressions are

```
(define WINDOW-COLOR    'darkgray)

(define WINDOW2-COLOR    'white)

(define WINDOW  (ellipse 3 10 'solid WINDOW-COLOR))

(define WINDOW2  (ellipse 3 10 'solid WINDOW2-COLOR))
```

STEP 3

The only difference among the sample expressions is the color of the oval. The variable for this difference is a-color.

STEP 4

The signature and purpose statement are

```
;; color → image
;; Purpose: Create rocket window image
```

STEP 5

The function header is

```
(define (mk-window-img a-color)
```

STEP 6

Testing may be satisfied as follows:

```
;; Tests using sample computations for mk-window-img
(check-expect (mk-window-img WINDOW-COLOR) WINDOW)
(check-expect (mk-window-img WINDOW2-COLOR) WINDOW2)

;; Tests using sample values for mk-window-img
(check-expect (mk-window-img 'darkblue) ▌ )
(check-expect (mk-window-img 'gray) ▌)
```

STEP 7

The body of the function is

```
(ellipse 3 10 'solid a-color)
```

STEP 8

All tests pass.

In DrRacket, the code ought to be organized as follows:

```
;; color → image
;; Purpose: Create rocket window image
(define (mk-window-img a-color)
  (ellipse 3 10 'solid a-color))

;; Sample expressions for mk-window-img
(define WINDOW  (ellipse 3 10 'solid WINDOW-COLOR))
(define WINDOW2  (ellipse 3 10 'solid WINDOW2-COLOR))

;; Tests using sample computations for mk-window-img
(check-expect (mk-window-img WINDOW-COLOR) WINDOW)
(check-expect (mk-window-img WINDOW2-COLOR) WINDOW2)

;; Tests using sample values for mk-window-img
(check-expect (mk-window-img 'darkblue) ▌ )
(check-expect (mk-window-img 'gray) ▌ )
```

Observe that the steps of the design recipe are written in an organized fashion keeping the function, the sample expressions, and the tests together. The constants WINDOW-COLOR and WINDOW-COLOR2 ought to be defined in a section dedicated to constants toward the top of the program.

25.2 Rocket Fuselage Image Constructor

STEP 1
  The fuselage is a solid circle.
STEP 2
  Definitions for the value of sample expressions are

```
(define FUSELAGE (circle (* 1/3 IMAGE-HEIGHT)
                         'solid
                         FUSELAGE-COLOR))

(define FUSELAGE2 (circle (* 1/3 IMAGE-HEIGHT)
                          'solid
                          FUSELAGE2-COLOR))
```

STEP 3
  The only difference among the sample expressions is the color. The variable for this difference is a-color.

STEP 4

The signature and purpose statement are

```
;; color → image
;; Purpose: Create the fuselage image
```

STEP 5

The function header is
```
(define (mk-fuselage-img a-color)
```
STEP 6

Testing may be satisfied as follows:

```
;; Test using sample computations for mk-fuselage-img
(check-expect (mk-fuselage-img FUSELAGE-COLOR) FUSELAGE)
(check-expect (mk-fuselage-img FUSELAGE2-COLOR) FUSELAGE2)

;; Test using sample values for mk-fuselage-img

(check-expect (mk-fuselage-img 'olive)          )

(check-expect (mk-fuselage-img 'lightgray)         )
```

STEP 7

The body of the function is

```
(circle (* 1/3 IMAGE-HEIGHT) 'solid a-color))
```

STEP 8

All tests pass.

25.3 Rocket Single Booster Image Constructor

The single booster image is an equilateral triangle pointing down. Computing this image requires function composition. The output of triangle is input to rotate.

STEP 1

A rocket single booster is an equilateral triangle image rotated 180°.
STEP 2

Definitions for the value of sample expressions are

```
(define SINGLE-BOOSTER   (rotate 180
                                  (triangle (/ FUSELAGE-W 2)
                                            'solid
                                            NACELLE-COLOR)))
(define SINGLE-BOOSTER2 (rotate 180
                                  (triangle (/ FUSELAGE-W 2)
                                            'solid
                                            NACELLE2-COLOR)))
```

Observe that in Fig. 40, the single booster image is the same color as the nacelle
image. Therefore, constants NACELLE-COLOR and NACELLE2-COLOR are defined
and used to write sample single booster (and nacelle) expressions.

STEP 3

The only difference among the sample expressions is the color. The variable for
this difference is a-color.

STEP 4

The signature and purpose statement are

```
;; color → image
;; Purpose: Create single booster image
```

STEP 5

The function header is

```
(define (mk-single-booster-img a-color)
```

STEP 6

Testing may be satisfied as follows:

```
;; Tests using sample computations for mk-single-booster-img
(check-expect (mk-single-booster-img NACELLE-COLOR) SINGLE-BOOSTER)
(check-expect (mk-single-booster-img NACELLE2-COLOR) SINGLE-BOOSTER2)

;; Tests using sample values for mk-single-booster-img
(check-expect (mk-single-booster-img 'darkred) ▼ )
(check-expect (mk-single-booster-img 'gold) ▼ )
```

STEP 7

The body of the function is

```
(rotate 180 (triangle (/ FUSELAGE-W 2) 'solid a-color)))
```

STEP 8

All tests pass.

25.4 Rocket Booster Image Constructor

Observe that the booster image in Fig. 40d is two copies of a single booster image side by side. This suggests that a constructor for a booster image needs a single booster image as input.

STEP 1
A booster image is two copies of a single booster image side by side.
STEP 2
Definitions for the value of sample expressions are

```
(define BOOSTER (beside SINGLE-BOOSTER SINGLE-BOOSTER))

(define BOOSTER2 (beside SINGLE-BOOSTER2 SINGLE-BOOSTER2))
```

STEP 3
The only difference among the sample expressions is the single booster image. The variable for this difference is a-sb-img.
STEP 4
The signature and purpose statement are

```
;; image → image
;; Purpose: Create booster image
```

STEP 5
The function header is
```
(define (mk-booster-img a-sb-img)
```
STEP 6
Testing may be satisfied as follows:

```
;; Tests using sample computations for mk-booster-img
(check-expect (mk-booster-img SINGLE-BOOSTER) BOOSTER)
(check-expect (mk-booster-img SINGLE-BOOSTER2) BOOSTER2)

;; Tests using sample values for mk-booster-img
(check-expect (mk-booster-img (mk-single-booster-img 'darkred)) ▼▼)
(check-expect (mk-booster-img (mk-single-booster-img 'gold))  ▼▼ )
```

STEP 7
The body of the function is

```
(beside a-sb-img a-sb-img))
```

STEP 8
All tests pass.

25.5 Rocket Main Body Image Constructor

Constructing an image for the rocket's main body, as displayed in Fig. 40f, requires three images: a window image, a fuselage image, and a booster image. It also requires the use of function composition given that the fuselage goes above the booster and the window goes on the fuselage.

STEP 1
The rocket's main body is created by placing the fuselage above the booster and then placing the window one quarter of the way down the height and half away across the width of the fuselage.

STEP 2
Definitions for the value of sample expressions are

```
(define ROCKET-MAIN  (place-image
                      WINDOW
                      (/ (image-width FUSELAGE) 2)
                      (/ (image-height FUSELAGE) 4)
                      (above FUSELAGE BOOSTER)))

(define ROCKET-MAIN2 (place-image
                      WINDOW2
                      (/ (image-width FUSELAGE2) 2)
                      (/ (image-height FUSELAGE2) 4)
                      (above FUSELAGE2 BOOSTER2)))
```

Observe that previously defined sample images are used to write the sample expressions.

STEP 3
There are 3 differences among the sample expressions: the window, the fuselage, and the booster images. The variables for these differences are, respectively, a-window, a-fuselage, and a-booster.

STEP 4
The signature and purpose statement are

```
;; image image image → image
;; Purpose: Create the main rocket image
```

STEP 5

The function header is

```
(define (mk-rocket-main-img a-window a-fuselage a-booster)
```

STEP 6

Testing may be satisfied as follows:

```
;; Tests using sample computations for mk-rocket-main-img
(check-expect (mk-rocket-main-img WINDOW FUSELAGE BOOSTER)
              ROCKET-MAIN)
(check-expect (mk-rocket-main-img
                 WINDOW2 FUSELAGE2 BOOSTER2)
              ROCKET-MAIN2)

;; Tests using sample computations for mk-rocket-main-img
(check-expect (mk-rocket-main-img
                (mk-window-img 'black)
                (mk-fuselage-img 'yellow)
                (mk-booster-img
                  (mk-single-booster-img 'yellow)))


              )

(check-expect (mk-rocket-main-img
                (mk-window-img 'green)
                (mk-fuselage-img 'skyblue)
                (mk-booster-img
                  (mk-single-booster-img 'lightred)))



              )
```

STEP 7

The body of the function is

```
(place-image a-window
             (/ (image-width a-fuselage) 2)
             (/ (image-height a-fuselage) 4)
             (above a-fuselage a-booster))
```

STEP 8

All tests pass.

Fig. 41 Rocket image

25.6 Rocket Nacelle Image Constructor

The image of the rocket's nacelle in Fig. 40e is deceptively simple. At first glance,
it looks like an ordinary rectangle. A closer examination of the rocket image, as
displayed in Fig. 41, reveals that the nacelle and the booster are the same color. In
addition, the nacelle must be the same width as the rocket's main body and about a
quarter of the height of the main body. With these observations, the design of the
constructor for nacelle images follows.

STEP 1

The image of a nacelle is a rectangle that is the same width as the rocket's main
body and a quarter of the height of the rocket's main body height. The color of
the nacelle is the same color as the booster in the rocket's main body.

STEP 2

Definitions for the value of sample expressions are

```
(define NACELLE (rectangle (image-width ROCKET-MAIN)
                           (/ (image-height ROCKET-MAIN)
                              4)
                           'solid
                           NACELLE-COLOR))

(define NACELLE2 (rectangle (image-width ROCKET-MAIN2)
                            (/ (image-height ROCKET-MAIN2)
                               4)
                            'solid
                            NACELLE2-COLOR))
```

Observe that the same constants used to construct single booster images are used
to construct the corresponding nacelle images.

STEP 3

There are two differences among the sample expressions: the main rocket image
and the color of the nacelle. The variables for these differences are, respectively,
a-rocket-main-img and a-color.

STEP 4

The signature and purpose statement are

```
;; image color → image
;; Purpose: Create a rocket nacelle image
```

STEP 5

The function header is

```
(define (mk-nacelle-img a-rocket-main-img a-color)
```

STEP 6

Testing may be satisfied as follows:

```
;; Tests using sample computations for mk-nacelle-img
(check-expect (mk-nacelle-img ROCKET-MAIN NACELLE-COLOR)
              NACELLE)
(check-expect (mk-nacelle-img ROCKET-MAIN2 NACELLE2-COLOR)
              NACELLE2)

;; Tests using sample values for mk-nacelle-img
(check-expect (mk-nacelle-img
                  (mk-rocket-main-img
                    (mk-window-img 'blue)
                    (mk-fuselage-img 'green)
                    (mk-booster-img
                      (mk-single-booster-img 'yellow)))
                  'yellow)
              )
(check-expect (mk-nacelle-img
                  (mk-rocket-main-img
                    (mk-window-img 'blue)
                    (mk-fuselage-img 'green)
                    (mk-booster-img
                      (mk-single-booster-img 'lightorange)))
                  'lightorange)
              )
```

STEP 7

The body of the function is

```
(rectangle (image-width a-rocket-main-img)
           (/ (image-height a-rocket-main-img) 4)
           'solid
           a-color))
```

STEP 8

All tests pass.

25.7 Rocket `ci` Constructor

The final image constructor needed is the rocket image constructor. This constructor
must place the nacelle over the rocket's main body.

STEP 1

The rocket image is constructed by placing the nacelle image half the way across
the rocket's main body and 30% from the bottom of the rocket's main body.

STEP 2

Definitions for the value of sample expressions are

```
(define ROCKET-IMG  (place-image
                     NACELLE
                     (/ (image-width  ROCKET-MAIN) 2)
                     (* 0.7 (image-height ROCKET-MAIN))
                     ROCKET-MAIN))

(define ROCKET-IMG2 (place-image
                     NACELLE2
                     (/ (image-width  ROCKET-MAIN2) 2)
                     (* 0.7 (image-height ROCKET-MAIN2))
                     ROCKET-MAIN2))
```

Notice that 30% from the bottom is the same as 70% from the top of the rocket's
main body image. Since y values grow downward in the graphic plane, 70% of
the rocket's main body image is computed.

STEP 3

There are two differences among the sample expressions: the rocket's main body
image and the rocket's nacelle image. The variables for these differences are
`a-rocket-main-img` and `a-nacelle-img`.

STEP 4

The signature and purpose statement are

```
;; image image → ci
;; Purpose: Create a rocket ci
```

Observe that the signature states that this function returns a `ci`. This is needed
because the returned image is intended for use in Aliens Attack.

STEP 5

The function header is

```
(define (mk-rocket-ci a-rocket-main-img a-nacelle-img)
```

STEP 6

Testing may be satisfied as follows:

```
;; Tests using sample computations for mk-rocket-img
(check-expect (mk-rocket-ci ROCKET-MAIN NACELLE)
              ROCKET-IMG)
(check-expect (mk-rocket-ci ROCKET-MAIN2 NACELLE2)
              ROCKET-IMG2)
(check-expect (ci? ROCKET-IMG)  #true)
(check-expect (ci? ROCKET-IMG2) #true)


;; Tests using sample values for mk-rocket-img
(check-expect (mk-rocket-ci
                (mk-rocket-main-img
                  (mk-window-img
                    'blue)
                  (mk-fuselage-img
                    'green)
                  (mk-booster-img
                    (mk-single-booster-img 'yellow)))
                (mk-nacelle-img
                  (mk-rocket-main-img
                    (mk-window-img
                      'blue)
                    (mk-fuselage-img 'green)
                    (mk-booster-img
                      (mk-single-booster-img 'yellow)))
                  'yellow))

              )
```

Observe that the output of this function must be a character image and, therefore, ci? is used to test its properties. Furthermore, observe that there is a single sample value test and that this test contains a significant amount of repetition. Both of these are considered poor style. Testing ought to be more thorough. The repetitions make it difficult to read and understand the test.

STEP 7

The body of the function is

```
(place-image a-nacelle-img
             (/ (image-width  a-rocket-main-img) 2)
             (* 0.7 (image-height a-rocket-main-img))
             a-rocket-main-img)
```

STEP 8
   All tests pass.

** **Ex. 51** — Refine the tests using sample values for `mk-rocket-ci`. Make
sure to eliminate repeated expressions and include more than one test.

*** **Ex. 52** — Personalize your game with `ci`s for the shot, the alien, and the
rocket of your own creation.

---

26 Drawing Functions

In contrast to the development of `mk-rocket-img`, we shall use a top-down approach
to design the function to draw a `ci` in a `scene`. This computation requires a `ci`, an
`image-x`, an `image-y`, and a `scene`. Note that `place-image` cannot simply be used
to place a `ci` at the coordinate formed by the given `image-x` and `image-y`. Recall
Fig. 38 and the data definitions for image and pixel coordinates. There are many
more pixel coordinates than image coordinates given that one image point, $(x_i,
y_i)$, covers many pixel points. We must now solve the problem of mapping image
coordinates to pixel coordinates. The design starts with the topmost function, which
draws a `ci` in a `scene`.

STEP 1
   The given `ci` is placed in the given `scene` by translating the given image coordi-
   nates to pixel coordinates.
STEP 2
   Definitions for the value of sample expressions are

```
(define ROCKET-Y (sub1 MAX-CHARS-VERTICAL))

(define ROCKET-SCN (place-image
                    ROCKET-IMG
                    (image-x->pix-x
                     (/ MAX-CHARS-HORIZONTAL 2))
                    (image-y->pix-y ROCKET-Y)
                    E-SCENE))

(define ALIEN-SCN (place-image ALIEN-IMG
                               (image-x->pix-x 4)
                               (image-y->pix-y 7)
                               E-SCENE2))
```

```
(define SHOT-SCN (place-image
                 SHOT-IMG
                 (image-x->pix-x 17)
                 (image-y->pix-y 13)
                 E-SCENE2))
```

Observe that the three sample expressions evaluate to a scene because a ci is placed in a scene. Further notice that two auxiliary functions are needed to translate the image coordinates. The constant ROCKET-Y stems from thinking ahead and observing that the rocket's image-y coordinate is a constant in Aliens Attack.

STEP 3

There are four differences among the sample expressions: the ci, the image-x and -y coordinates, and the scene. The variables for these differences are char-img, an-img-x, an-img-y, and scn.

STEP 4

The signature and purpose statement are

```
;; ci image-x image-y scene → scene
;; Purpose: Place the given ci in the given scene at the
;;          given image coordinates
```

STEP 5

The function header is

```
(define (draw-ci char-img an-img-x an-img-y scn)
```

STEP 6

Testing may be satisfied as follows:

```
;; Tests using sample computations for draw-ci
(check-expect (draw-ci ROCKET-IMG
                       (/ MAX-CHARS-HORIZONTAL 2)
                       ROCKET-Y
                       E-SCENE)
              ROCKET-SCN)
(check-expect (draw-ci ALIEN-IMG 4 7 E-SCENE) ALIEN-SCN)
(check-expect (draw-ci SHOT-IMG 17 13 E-SCENE) SHOT-SCN)

;; Tests using sample values for draw-ci
(check-expect (draw-ci
                   (square 10 'solid 'green) 8 8 E-SCENE)
```

Fig. 42 Top-left box of the scene image perspective

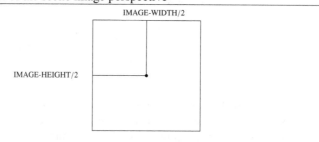

```
(check-expect (draw-ci (ellipse 20 30 'outline 'black)
                11 12 E-SCENE)
```

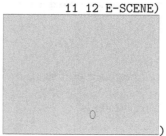

STEP 7

The body of the function is

```
(place-image char-img
             (image-x->pix-x an-img-x)
             (image-y->pix-y an-img-y)
             scn)
```

STEP 8

All tests pass.

The design now focuses on the two auxiliary functions to map image coordinates to pixel coordinates. Let us first consider mapping the image coordinate pair $(0, 0)$ to a pixel coordinate pair. This coordinate pair is the top-left box in Fig. 38b. The center of the image ought to be placed at the center of the box. The dimensions of the box are IMAGE-WIDTH × IMAGE-HEIGHT. As illustrated in Fig. 42, this means that the center of this box is at pixel coordinates (IMAGE-WIDTH/2, IMAGE-HEIGHT/2). What is the pixel coordinate of image coordinate (3, 2)? This pixel coordinate (IMAGE-WIDTH/2, IMAGE-HEIGHT/2) must be translated 3 boxes to the right and 2 boxes down. Therefore, the pixel coordinate for the box at the image coordinate (3, 2) is:

```
(3 *  IMAGE-WIDTH + IMAGE-WIDTH/2,
 2 * IMAGE-HEIGHT + IMAGE-HEIGHT/2)
```

In general, the image coordinate (x, y) maps to the pixel coordinate:

```
(x *  IMAGE-WIDTH + IMAGE-WIDTH/2,
 y * IMAGE-HEIGHT + IMAGE-HEIGHT/2)
```

Observe that the mapping works for image coordinate pair (0, 0).

The above insight guides the design of the image-coordinate to pixel-coordinate functions. The steps of the design recipe to transform an image-x may be satisfied as follows:

STEP 1

For image-x, ix, the corresponding pixel-x is ix * IMAGE-WIDTH + IMAGE-WIDTH/2

STEP 2

Definitions for the value of sample expressions are

```
(define PIX-X5 (+ (* 5 IMAGE-WIDTH) (/ IMAGE-WIDTH 2)))

(define PIX-X12 (+ (* 12 IMAGE-WIDTH) (/ IMAGE-WIDTH 2)))
```

STEP 3

The only difference among the sample expressions is the image-x value. The variable for this difference is ix.

STEP 4

The signature and purpose statement are

```
;; image-x → pixel-x
;; Purpose: To translate the given image-x to a pixel-x
```

STEP 5

The function header is
```
(define (image-x->pix-x ix)
```

STEP 6

```
;; Tests using sample computations for x->pix-x
(check-expect (image-x->pix-x 5) PIX-X5)
(check-expect (image-x->pix-x 12) PIX-X12)

;; Tests using sample values for x->pix-x
(check-expect (image-x->pix-x 0) (/ IMAGE-WIDTH 2))
(check-expect (image-x->pix-x (sub1 MAX-CHARS-HORIZONTAL))
              585)
```

Observe that the tests using sample values are written for extrema values. That is, the minimum and maximum possible values of an image-x are used.

STEP 7

The body of the function is

```
(+ (* ix IMAGE-WIDTH) (/ IMAGE-WIDTH 2)))
```

STEP 8

All tests pass.

The design of image-x->pix-x does not reveal the need for any new auxiliary functions. The only task left is to design a function to translate an image-y to a pixel-y. The steps of the design recipe may be satisfied as follows:

STEP 1

For image-y, iy, the corresponding pixel-y is iy * IMAGE-HEIGHT + IMAGE-HEIGHT/2

STEP 2

Definitions for the value of sample expressions are

```
(define PIX-Y1 (+ (* 1 IMAGE-HEIGHT) (/ IMAGE-HEIGHT 2)))

(define PIX-Y6 (+ (* 6 IMAGE-HEIGHT) (/ IMAGE-HEIGHT 2)))
```

STEP 3

The only difference among the sample expressions is the image-y value. The variable for this difference is iy.

STEP 4

The signature and purpose statement are

```
;; image-y → pixel-y
;; Purpose: To translate the given image-y to a pixel-y
```

STEP 5

> The function header is
>
>> `(define (image-y->pix-y iy)`

STEP 6

> ```
> ;; Tests using sample computations for y->pix-y
> (check-expect (image-y->pix-y 1) PIX-Y1)
> (check-expect (image-y->pix-y 6) PIX-Y6)
>
> ;; Tests using sample values for y->pix-y
> (check-expect (image-y->pix-y 0) (/ IMAGE-HEIGHT 2))
> (check-expect (image-y->pix-y (sub1 MAX-CHARS-VERTICAL))
>                435)
> ```

Once again, observe that the tests using sample values are written for extrema values.

STEP 7

The body of the function is

> `(+ (* iy IMAGE-HEIGHT) (/ IMAGE-HEIGHT 2)))`

STEP 8

All tests pass.

The design of `image-y->pix-y` does not reveal the need for any new auxiliary functions. This means that all the functions needed to draw a `ci` have been designed and implemented.

** **Ex. 53** — What happens if `draw-ci` does not translate image coordinates to pixel coordinates?

* **Ex. 54** — Use `draw-ci` and function composition to create a possible `scene` for Aliens Attack with a rocket, multiple aliens, and multiple shots. Figure 37 is an example of such a scene.

---

27 What Have We Learned in This Chapter?

The important lessons of Chap. 6 are summarized as follows:

- The data representation chosen strongly influences how we think about and solve problems.
- Exploring different data representations may lead to simpler programs.
- Data definitions are written to describe new data types.
- New data types may be used in function signatures.
- An API defines data formats, conventions, constructors, and selectors.
- Signatures and purpose statements make an API's information hiding useful.
- Property-based testing may be useful in illustrating that the conventions of an API are met.

Chapter 5
Making Decisions

Making decisions is part of life. For example, while driving on a highway, the driver monitors the car's speed. If the speed is too fast, then the driver decreases the speed. If the speed is too slow, then the driver increases the speed. Otherwise, the driver does not change the speed. It should not come as a surprise that making decisions is also part of problem solving. Modern cars are equipped with a cruise control system. The driver sets the cruise control at a certain speed. If the speed is too fast, then the cruise control program decreases the speed. If the speed is too slow, then the cruise control program increases the speed. Otherwise, the cruise control program does not change the speed.

Regardless of whether it is a driver or a cruise control program, the decision on how to adjust the speed depends on the car's current speed. This decision is may be represented by one of three possible expressions, say, `'increase`, `'decrease`, or `'steady`. Think carefully about what this means. Multiple expressions for the value of a function means that determining how to adjust the speed is a compound function. We can, in fact, write a mathematical function:

$$\text{speed-change(a-speed)} = \begin{cases} \text{'decrease} & \text{if too-fast?(a-speed)} \\ \text{'increase} & \text{if too-slow?(a-speed)} \\ \text{'steady} & \text{otherwise} \end{cases}$$

Two predicates, `too-fast?` and `too-slow?`, are used to evaluate the given speed. In essence, the above function is stating that there is *data variety* in the domain of the function. The input may be in one of three speed intervals indicating that the car is either traveling too fast, too slow, or neither. In order to determine the speed change a decision must be made as to which of the 3 expressions needs to be evaluated. This decision is based on the speed range a-speed belongs to.

It turns out that speed ranges may be used to solve many problems. For example, a police officer may use the following function to determine a course of action after

© The Author(s), under exclusive license to Springer Nature Switzerland AG 2022
M. T. Morazán, *Animated Problem Solving*, Texts in Computer Science,
https://doi.org/10.1007/978-3-030-85091-3_5

measuring the speed of a car:

$$
\text{police-action(speed)} = \begin{cases} \texttt{"Issue Ticket"} & \texttt{if too-fast?(speed)} \\ \texttt{"Issue Warning"} & \texttt{if too-slow?(speed)} \\ \texttt{"Take No Action"} & \texttt{otherwise} \end{cases}
$$

Observe that this function must also decide which expression to use to provide an answer for a given speed. Furthermore, observe that the two functions have the same basic structure. This structural similarity stems from the fact that they process the same type of data and suggests that a *function template* may be developed to process a speed. A function template is like a skeleton for functions. It captures the expected similarities among function that process the same type of data. For each data type a problem solver defines a function template is developed.

For example, speed may be defined as follows:

```
A speed is a number such that either:
  1. too-fast?(a-speed) is true
  2. too-slow?(a-speed) is true
  3. Neither too-fast?(a-speed) nor too-slow?(a-speed) is true
```

the template for functions that process speed is:

$$
\text{f-on-speed(a-speed)} = \begin{cases} \texttt{...} & \texttt{if too-fast?(a-speed)} \\ \texttt{...} & \texttt{if too-slow?(a-speed)} \\ \texttt{...} & \texttt{otherwise} \end{cases}
$$

This template may be used to design any function that processes a speed. By providing the missing expressions and a function name both functions above are obtained.

We can surmise from the examples above that compound functions arise from data having variety. These functions need to decide which expression to evaluate based on the variety the input belongs to. All functions that process the same data type with variety have the same structure. This chapter introduces how to design functions that make decisions. It introduces new BSL syntax to write *conditional* expressions which are used to make decisions. A design recipe for compound functions is presented that includes the development of data definitions for data with variety and of function templates to capture structural similarities among functions. Several different types of data with variety are explored.

28 Conditional Expressions in BSL

In BSL, there is syntax for expressions to make decisions. These new expressions are called *conditional* expressions. The new expr production rule is:

```
expr ::= (cond [expr expr]⁺
              [else  expr])
```

This rule states that a conditional expression starts with an opening parenthesis and the keyword cond. Afterwards, there is 1 or more *stanzas* delimited by square brackets. Each stanza contains two expressions. The first expression is a condition and must evaluate to a Boolean. Think of this expression as a question whose answer is either true or false. The second expression is called the consequence and is only evaluated if the corresponding condition evaluates to #true. Think of this expression as the value of the conditional expression when the answer to the corresponding question is true. The last stanza in a conditional is called the default stanza and contains in square brackets the keyword else and a single expression. This expression represents the default value of the conditional. The default expression is only evaluated if the conditions in all the other stanzas evaluate to #false.

The mathematical function speed-change(a-speed) is translated into BSL syntax as follows:

```
(define (speed-change-bsl a-speed)
  (cond [(too-fast? a-speed) 'decrease]
        [(too-slow? a-speed) 'increase]
        [else 'steady]))
```

The stanzas of a conditional are evaluated from top to bottom. For each stanza the condition is evaluated first. If the condition evaluates to #true then the value of the consequence is the value of the conditional. If the condition evaluates to #false then evaluation continues with the next stanza. If the default stanza is reached, then the default expression is evaluated to obtain the value of the conditional expression. For example, for speed-change-bsl, if too-fast? evaluates to #true then the value of the conditional is 'decrease. If it evaluates to #false then evaluation continues with the next stanza. If too-slow? evaluates to #true then the value of the conditional is 'decrease. If it evaluates to #false then evaluation continues with the next stanza. The next stanza is the else stanza and, therefore, the default expression is evaluated making the value of the conditional 'steady.

BSL provides shorthand when there are only two varieties of data. That is, shorthand may be used when only the default stanza and one other stanza is needed. The shorthand syntax is called an if-expression:

```
expr ::= (if expr expr expr)
```

This rule states that an if-expression is formed by an open parenthesis, three expressions, and a closing parenthesis. The first expression is called the condition and must evaluate to a Boolean. If the condition is #true then the second expression is evaluated to obtain the value of the if-expression. Otherwise, the third expression is evaluated to obtain the value of the if-expression.

Consider, for example, translating the absolute value mathematical function into BSL. In mathematical syntax the function is defined as follows:

$$\text{abs-value(a-num)} = \begin{cases} \text{a-num} & \text{if a-num} >= 0 \\ \text{-a-num} & \text{otherwise} \end{cases}$$

Observe that there are only two varieties of numbers for this function: nonnegative and negative. Only two varieties means that an `if`-expression may be used to translate it to BSL syntax:

```
(define (abs-value-bsl a-num)
  (if (>= a-num 0)
      a-num
      (* -1 a-num)))
```

If the condition, `(>= a-num 0)`, evaluates to `#true` then the value of the `if`-expression is `a-num`. If the condition evaluates to `#false` then the value of the `if`-expression is `(* -1 a-num)`.

** **Ex. 55** — Write a program to decide the speed change for a car if the maximum speed is 120 kilometers per hour and the minimum speed is 50 kilometers per hour.

** **Ex. 56** — Implement the following mathematical function in BSL:

$$f(a\text{-}num) = \begin{cases} a\text{-}num^2 & \text{if } a\text{-}num < 0 \\ a\text{-}num + 5 & \text{if } anum < 5 \\ e^{a\text{-}num} & \text{otherwise} \end{cases}$$

---

29 Designing Functions to Process Data with Variety

When problem analysis reveals that data with variety needs to be processed then a *data definition* must be created. Given that there is variety in the data, any function that processes this type of data requires a conditional expression in its body. A conditional expression is needed to determine which of the data varieties is being processed. For each variety an expression for the value of the function needs to be developed. A problem solver must also develop a function template to capture the structural similarities among all functions that process the defined data type. Finally, the number of tests must be greater than or equal to the number of varieties in the data. In addition to at least one test per variety, it is also good practice to test border cases that delimit varieties.

Let us examine poem verses as an example. First, we must choose how to represent a verse. We may, for example, represent a verse as a string. Some poets feel that it is good practice to limit the length of each verse to 35 characters. A verse with more than 35 characters is considered too long. A verse with 15 to 35 characters is considered fine. A verse with less than 15 characters is considered too short. Based on this description, a data definition for a verse is formulated as

Fig. 43 Template for functions on a verse

```
;; verse ... → ...
;; Purpose: ...
(define (f-on-verse a-verse ...)
  (cond [(> (string-length a-verse) 35) ...]
        [(<= 15 (string-length a-verse) 35)  ...]
        [else ...])

;; Expressions for sample computations
(define VARIETY1-CONSTANT ...)
(define VARIETY2-CONSTANT ...)
(define VARIETY3-CONSTANT ...)

;; Tests using sample computations
(check-expect (f-on-verse ...) VARIETY1-CONSTANT)
(check-expect (f-on-verse ...) VARIETY2-CONSTANT)
(check-expect (f-on-verse ...) VARIETY3-CONSTANT)
        ⋮

;; Test using sample values
(check-expect (f-on-verse ...) ...) ;; test for verse of length 35
(check-expect (f-on-verse ...) ...) ;; test for verse of length 15
        ⋮
```

follows:

```
;; A verse is either:
;;   1. A string of length greater than 35
;;   2. A string of length 15 to 35
;;   3. A string of length less than 15
```

The data definition for a verse informs problem solvers that any function that processes a verse must have a conditional in its body that determines the variety of the input verse. In addition, it informs problem solvers that at least 3 tests are needed: one for each variety. Remember, we say *at least* because it is always good practice to test boundary values. In this case, 5 tests are reasonable: one for each variety, one for length 35, and one for length 15. It is important to note that verse varieties are *mutually exclusive*. This means that no verse can be part of more than one variety.

Based on the above data definition, observe that all functions that process a verse share these features unique to verses:

1. A signature that has at least a verse as an input type.
2. A conditional in the body that determines if the given verse's length is greater than 35, between 15 and 34, or less than 15.
3. Sample expressions, if any, for each variety that is used to compute a value.
4. One test for each sample expression
5. Sample value tests including tests for borderline cases of length 35 and 15.

This leads to the function template in Fig. 43. Observe that the signature includes a `verse` as input and that each stanza in the skeleton's body has a Boolean expression to determine the variety of the verse. The default stanza, of course, does not explicitly state that its Boolean expression is (< (string-length a-verse) 15). This is unnecessary because verse varieties are mutually exclusive. Mutual exclusion guarantees that if the first two Boolean expressions are false then the verse's length is less than 15. Stated differently:

```
¬(> (string-length a-verse) 35) ∧
¬(<= 15 (string-length a-verse) 35)
⇒
(< (string-length a-verse) 15)
```

This logical expression is stating that if the length of a verse is not greater than 35 and it is not between 15 and 35 then it is less than 15. Finally, observe that the template suggests 3 sample expressions and sample computation tests (one for each variety) and 2 sample computation tests (one for each boundary value). The important point to remember that there must be at least one test for each variety. More tests, of course, may be added in the interest of clarity.

This function template can be specialized to express the solution to any problem that requires processing a verse. Consider the problem of computing a string to describe the length of a verse. To solve the problem, the function must decide which constant string describing its variety to return: "Too Long", "Fine", or "Too Short". Given that a verse is not processed to create any of these constant strings, there are no sample expressions to describe how a verse is used to compute these strings. If there are no sample expressions, there are also no tests using sample computations.

The function's signature, purpose, and header are:

```
;; verse → string
;; Purpose: Determine if the given verse is too long, fine,
;;           or too short
(define (verse-type a-verse)
```

Observe that the signature uses the type, `verse`, defined by the data definition above. Once a type is defined by a data definition it may be used in signatures. Signatures, therefore, may contain types defined by BSL or by a data definition the programmer creates. Further observe that the signature only has one input and, therefore, the function only has one parameter. Finally, observe that the name of the function is suggestive of its purpose and the name of the parameter is suggestive of the value it represents.

Given that there are no sample expressions to test (as noted above), the tests using sample values must be specialized to include a test for each variety of verse and for each borderline length. Sample tests are:

```
;; Tests using sample values
(check-expect
  (verse-type "Here is a sigh to those who love me,")
  "Too Long")
```

Fig. 44 Program to determine verse type

```
;; A verse is either: 1. A string of length greater than 35
;;                    2. A string of length 15 to 35
;;                    3. A string of length less than 15
#| Funtion template for verse
;; verse ... --> ...
;; Purpose: ...
(define (f-on-verse a-verse ...)
  (cond [(> (string-length a-verse) 35) ...]
        [(<= 15 (string-length a-verse) 35)  ...]
        [else ...]))
;; Expressions for sample computations
(define VARIETY1-CONSTANT ...) (define VARIETY2-CONSTANT ...)
(define VARIETY3-CONSTANT ...)
;; Tests using sample computations
(check-expect (f-on-verse ...) VARIETY1-CONSTANT)
(check-expect (f-on-verse ...) VARIETY2-CONSTANT)
(check-expect (f-on-verse ...) VARIETY3-CONSTANT)
;; Test using sample values
(check-expect (f-on-verse ...) ...) ;; test for verse of length 35
(check-expect (f-on-verse ...) ...) ;; test for verse of length 15    |#

;; verse --> string
;; Purpose: Determine if the given verse is too long, fine, or too short
(define (verse-type a-verse)
  (cond [(> (string-length a-verse) 35) "Too Long"]
        [(<= 15 (string-length a-verse) 35)  "Fine"]
        [else "Too Short"]))
;; Tests using sample values
(check-expect (verse-type "Here is a sigh to those who love me,")
              "Too Long")
(check-expect (verse-type "And a smile to those who hate") "Fine")
(check-expect (verse-type "Sorry for fate") "Too Short")
(check-expect (verse-type "The Battle of Culloden started now,") "Fine")
(check-expect (verse-type "Flaming heavens")  "Fine")
```

```
(check-expect
  (verse-type "And a smile to those who hate")
  "Fine")
(check-expect (verse-type "Sorry for fate") "Too Short")
(check-expect
  (verse-type "The Battle of Culloden started now,")
  "Fine") ;; verse length 35
(check-expect
  (verse-type? "Flaming heavens")
  "Fine") ;; verse length 15
```

Fig. 45 The design recipe for decision-making functions

1. Create data definitions with at least one having mutually exclusive varieties.
2. Develop a function template for each data definition.
3. Outline the computation.
4. Define constants for the value of sample expressions for each variety and name the differences.
5. Write the function's signature and purpose.
6. Write the function's header.
7. Write tests for each variety.
8. Write the function's body.
9. Run the tests and, if necessary, redesign.

The next step is to specialize the body of the function in the template. For each verse variety the proper string needs to be returned. The specialized body is:

```
(cond [(> (string-length a-verse) 35) "Too Long"]
      [(<= 15 (string-length a-verse) 35) "Fine"]
      [else "Too Short"]))
```

The complete program is displayed in Fig. 44. To make Fig. 44 easier to read the comments including the data definition and the function template are displayed using an italic font.

The development of verse-type suggests a series of steps that guide the development of a decision-making function. Figure 45 displays the design recipe for decision-making functions. This design recipe is a refinement of the general design recipe for functions in Fig. 28. Therefore, the steps ought to feel familiar. Step 1 requires the development of data definitions. Of these, at least one must have varieties that are mutually exclusive. Step 2 requires the development of a function template. The function's body must be a conditional that has a stanza for each variety. The Boolean expressions to determine the variety of the input are part of the function's body in the template. In addition, there must be at least one test outlined for each data variety. Commonly (but not always), sample expression tests are used to test each variety and sample value tests are used to test boundary values. These first two steps are part of what is called data analysis and do not have to be repeated for every problem being solved using the data type defined. That is, these steps are performed once and the template may be used multiple times.

The rest of the steps are taken to solve a specific problem. These are the steps that need to be repeated for each problem solved. These steps specialize the function template. Step 3 requires an outline of how the function's value is computed. Step 4 requires the specialization of constant definitions for the values of sample expressions. The sample expression illustrates how an answer is computed by processing a given variety. The differences are named and serve as parameters to a function definition. If a variety is not processed to formulate an answer, then no sample expression is written. Steps 5 and 6 specialize the signature, the purpose statement, and the function header. Step 7 requires the specialization of tests. There must be at least one test for each data variety. Tests ought to also be thorough and,

Fig. 46 Function templates for data with variety

```
;; A vdata is either:
;;  1. Variety 1
;;          ⋮
;;
;;  N. Variety N
;; vdata ... → ...
;; Purpose: ...
(define (f-on-vdata a-vdata ...)
  (cond [<Variety 1 Test> ...]
            ⋮
        [<Variety N-1 Test> ...]
        [else ...]))
;; Sample expressions
(define VARIETY1-CONST ...)
        ⋮
(define VARIETYN-CONST ...)
;; Tests using sample computations
(check-expect
  (f-on-vdata <variety 1>  ...)
  VARIETY1-CONST)
        ⋮
(check-expect
  (f-on-vdata <variety N>  ...)
  VARIETYN-CONST)
;; Tests using sample values
(check-expect
  (f-on-vdata <variety i> ...) ...)
    ...
```

(a) Function Template Using cond

```
;; A vdata is either:
;;  1. Variety 1
;;  2. Variety 2
;; vdata ... → ...
;; Purpose: ...
(define (f-on-vdata a-vdata ...)
  (if <Variety 1 Test>
      ...
      ...))
;; Sample expressions
(define VARIETY1-CONST ...)
(define VARIETY2-CONST ...)
;; Tests using sample computations
(check-expect
  (f-on-vdata <variety 1> ...)
  VARIETY1-CONST)
(check-expect
  (f-on-vdata <variety 2>  ...)
  VARIETY2-CONST)
;; Tests using sample values
(check-expect
  (f-on-vdata <variety i> ...) ...)
    ...
```

(b) Function Template Using if

therefore, test boundary values between varieties. Write tests that use the constants defined for sample computations and tests that use sample values. Step 8 requires the specialization of the function's body. Fill in the expressions for the answer of each variety one at a time. Step 9, as before, requires running the tests and redesigning if necessary.

The design recipe for decision-making functions informs us that data variety plays a central role in problem solving. For example, the number of sample expressions, of stanzas in a conditional, and of tests is proportional to the number of varieties in the data. That is, the shape of the data influences the shape of a solution/program. This suggests the function templates displayed in Fig. 46. Figure 46a displays the function template for data with more than two varieties. Figure 46b displays the function template for data with two varieties. In both, the number of constants for sample expressions, of tests, and of needed expressions in the body of the function are equal to the number of varieties. It is, of course, reasonable to increase the number of constants and tests for more thorough testing or to add clarity to the program.

To illustrate the steps of the design recipe we will explore several different types of data that have variety. It is impossible to outline all imaginable types of data with variety. The goal here is to illustrate how to solve problems with several common data type patterns that have variety.

* **Ex. 57** — Write a program to compute a verse whose length is in [15..35] from a given verse. If the given verse is too long, create a new verse by dropping the letters in excess of 35 at the end of the given verse. If the verse is too short, create a new verse by padding it with blanks at the end to make its length 15. Otherwise, return the given verse.

* **Ex. 58** — Implement a program to determine if a verse is printable. A verse is printable if it is not too long. Carefully consider if a conditional is needed. Do you need a conditional to compute a Boolean function?

30 Enumeration Types

A data definition that lists all possible values is called an *enumeration type*. To a programmer this means that the conditional in a function that processes this type of data only needs to distinguish the cases listed in the data definition. This is done by checking for equality with the values listed in the data definition. Although this data type represents the simplest form of variety, it may be cumbersome to use as the number of varieties grows.

To illustrate the design process using an enumerated type consider creating an animation for of a traffic light. We design our program for a simplified traffic light that only changes colors from green to yellow to red to green and so on. That is, the possibilities of a flashing red or a flashing yellow are not included the design. Based on this there are only three possible traffic light images, which may be defined as constants. Each image is created by overlaying the three lights over a background. For example, the three images may be defined as follows:

```
(define BACKGROUND (rectangle 60 180 'solid 'black))

(define R-ON (overlay (above (circle 25 'solid 'red)
                             (square 10 'solid 'transparent)
                             (circle 25 'outline 'yellow)
                             (square 10 'solid 'transparent)
                             (circle 25 'outline 'green))
                      BACKGROUND))
```

```
(define Y-ON (overlay (above (circle 25 'outline 'red)
                             (square 10 'solid 'transparent)
                             (circle 25 'solid 'yellow)
                             (square 10 'solid 'transparent)
                             (circle 25 'outline 'green))
                      BACKGROUND))

(define G-ON (overlay (above (circle 25 'outline 'red)
                             (square 10 'solid 'transparent)
                             (circle 25 'outline 'yellow)
                             (square 10 'solid 'transparent)
                             (circle 25 'solid 'green))
                      BACKGROUND))
```

Each constant for a traffic light has a single light on denoted by a solid circle and two lights off denoted by outline circles. There is a small space between the lights obtained by drawing a transparent square.

To create an animation, the `animate` syntax defined in the `universe` teachpack is used. When an animate expression is evaluated a clock is started that ticks 28 times per second. The programmer must write a function that takes as input a tick: the value of the clock (the number of ticks since the simulation started) and that returns the image to display. To stop a simulation, click `Stop` in DrRacket or close the simulation window. The value of an animate expression is the value of the clock when the animation is stopped.

Let us use a top-down design strategy given that the needed functions are not known. What is known, however, is that clock ticks and a traffic light (which is yet to be defined) must be processed. This is the starting point for the top-down design strategy. To solve this problem, a programmer may decide that a given clock tick is first transformed to a number that represents a traffic light. Observe that a traffic light is not defined as an image. The number representing a traffic light is then used to select the traffic light image. It is necessary to carefully think about how a clock tick may be transformed to a traffic light. Given that there are only three images, we may use three numbers. We need a mechanism to map a tick to one of the three traffic light numbers. If we use 0, 1, and 2 to represent a traffic light, then *modular arithmetic* may be used to map a tick to a traffic light. Observe that the remainder of any tick by 3 is always 0, 1, or 2. Now, all that is left is developing data definitions that attach meaning to each of these numbers chosen to represent a traffic light.

The data analysis steps of the design recipe may be satisfied as follows:

STEP 1

We may define a tick and traffic light as follows:

```
A tick is an integer greater than or equal to 0.

;; A traffic light (tl) is either
;;   1. 0 --means the green light is on
```

```
;;   2. 1 --means the yellow light is on
;;   3. 2 --means the red light is on
```

Observe that if the traffic light is increased by 1 (remainder 3) the next light
is the correct one. For example, increasing from 0 to 1 (remainder 3) means
that the traffic light changes from green to yellow. Similarly, incrementing
2 (remainder 3) results in 0 meaning that the traffic changes from red to
green.

STEP 2

The function template for tick is:

```
;; tick ... → ...
;; Purpose: ...
(define (f-on-tick a-tick) ...)

;; Sample expressions for f-on-tick
(define TICK-V0 ...)
        ⋮
(define TICK-VN ...)

;; Tests using sample computations for f-on-tick
(check-expect (f-on-tick ...) TICK-V0)
        ⋮
(check-expect (f-on-tick ...) TICK-V0)

;; Tests using sample values for f-on-tick
(check-expect (f-on-tick ...) ...)
```

The function template for tl is:

```
;; tl ... --> ...
;; Purpose: ...
(define (f-on-tl a-tl)
  (cond [(= a-tl 0) ...]
        [(= a-tl 1) ...]
        [else ...]))

;; Sample expressions for f-on-tl
(define TL-0 ...)
(define TL-1 ...)
(define TL-2 ...)

;; Tests using sample computations for f-on-tl
(check-expect (f-on-tl ...) TL-0)
```

```
(check-expect (f-on-tl ...) TL-1)
(check-expect (f-on-tl ...) TL-2)

;; Tests using sample values for f-on-tl
(check-expect (f-on-tl ...) ...)
```

There is no variety in the data definition for tick. Therefore, f-on-tick does not have a conditional. No decision needs to be made. The number of tests is also arbitrary as there are no specific values that must be tested.

On the other hand, the data definition for tl has variety. Observe that there is a conditional in the body of f-on-tl. There is a stanza for each variety of tl. The tests for each variety are defined here. The template also suggests writing a sample expression and a corresponding test for each variety of tl.

Now that the steps for data analysis have been completed, we can start solving the problem of creating functions for the traffic light animation. We know that a function to process ticks is needed. This function must return an image of a traffic light. Starting with Step 3, the following the design recipe yields:

STEP 3

Given a tick, two values need to be computed. From a tick a tl value must be computed. From a tl value an image must be computed. The computation of these values is deferred to yet unwritten functions. The function tick->tl converts a tick to a tl. The function image-of-tl converts a tl into a traffic light image.

STEP 4

To specialize the sample expressions, pick three different tick values such that each maps to a different traffic light image. Specializing tests in this manner guarantees to illustrate how a clock tick is mapped to each of the possible images. Here are some sample expressions:

```
;; Sample expressions for draw-tick
(define TICK12-IMG (image-of-tl (tick->tl 12)))
(define TICK25-IMG (image-of-tl (tick->tl 25)))
(define TICK32-IMG (image-of-tl (tick->tl 32)))
```

The only difference among the three sample expressions is the value for tick. The name for this difference is a-tick.

STEP 5

The signature and purpose statement are specialized as:

```
;; tick → image
;; Purpose: Compute the traffic light image for the
;;          given tick
```

STEP 6

The function header is specialized to:

```
(define (draw-tick a-tick)
```

STEP 7

The tests are specialized as follows:

```
;; Tests using sample expressions for ticks to images
(check-expect (draw-tick 12) TICK12-IMG)
(check-expect (draw-tick 25) TICK25-IMG)
(check-expect (draw-tick 32) TICK32-IMG)

;; Tests using sample values for ticks to images
(check-expect (draw-tick 77)  R-ON)
(check-expect (draw-tick 99)  G-ON)
(check-expect (draw-tick 241) Y-ON)
```

The sample value tests illustrate that the function works for more than three predefined computations.

STEP 8

The body of the function is specialized as follows:

```
(image-of-tl (tick->tl a-tick))
```

STEP 9

All tests pass.

The result of Step 9 is expected for now. For the design to be complete all tests must pass after the auxiliary functions are designed and implemented.

Top-down design has revealed that two auxiliary functions, tick->tl and image-of-tl, are needed. Each is designed independently of the other. It does not matter which is designed first. Let us start with tick->tl. Here is an example of how to satisfy the steps of the design recipe:

STEP 3

Given a tick, the corresponding tl is given by the remainder of the tick and 3.

STEP 4

These are specialized sample expressions to illustrate how each variety of tl is computed from a tick value:

```
;; Sample expressions for tick->tl
(define TL-0 (remainder 33 3))
(define TL-1 (remainder 77 3))
(define TL-2 (remainder 152 3))
```

The only difference among the three sample expressions is the value for tick. The variable for this difference is a-tick.

STEP 5

The specialized signature and purpose statement are:

```
;; tick → tl
;; Purpose: Convert the given tick to a tl
```

STEP 6

The specialized function header is:

```
(define (tick->tl a-tick)
```

STEP 7

The specialized tests are:

```
;; Tests for tick->tl using sample expressions
(check-expect (tick->tl 33) TL-0)
(check-expect (tick->tl 77) TL-1)
(check-expect (tick->tl 152) TL-2)

;; Tests for tick->tl using sample values
(check-expect (tick->tl 0) 0)
(check-expect (tick->tl 451) 1)
(check-expect (tick->tl 182) 2)
```

STEP 8

The body of the function is:

```
(remainder a-tick 3)
```

STEP 9

All tests pass.

The design of tick->tl did not reveal the need for any new auxiliary functions. Therefore, the only remaining task is the design of image-of-tl. For this function, the presentation of the design is changed. Instead of outlining the result each step of the design recipe one at a time, the changes made to the template for functions on tl is directly presented.

This function converts a given tl to an image. We also observe that a tl is only used to decide which image to return. Since a tl is not used to compute a value there are no sample expressions or tests using sample expressions to write. Based on these observations, the initial template specialization looks as follows:

```
;; tl → image
;; Purpose: Return the traffic light image for the given tl
(define (image-of-tl a-tl ...)
  (cond [(= a-tl 0) ...]
        [(= a-tl 1) ...]
        [else ...]))
```

```
;; Tests for image-of-tl using sample values
(check-expect (image-of-tl 0) ...)
(check-expect (image-of-tl 1) ...)
(check-expect (image-of-tl 2) ...)
```

Observe that despite not having tests using sample computations, there is still at least one test for every variety of tl.

This rest of the specialization is fairly straight-forward. Our design has already specified what image corresponds to each instance of tl. The final specialization yields:

```
;; tl → image
;; Purpose: Return the traffic light image for the given tl
(define (image-of-tl a-tl)
  (cond [(= a-tl 0)  G-ON]
        [(= a-tl 1)  Y-ON]
        [else  R-ON]))
```

```
;; Tests using sample values
(check-expect (image-of-tl 0) G-ON)
(check-expect (image-of-tl 1) Y-ON)
(check-expect (image-of-tl 3) R-ON)
```

The final step to complete the traffic light simulation program is to require the universe teachpack and to write the animate expression. Figure 47 displays the structure of the program. Elements in angle brackets have been omitted from the figure due to space limitations. It should be clear, however, what needs to be filled in from all the design steps illustrated above. The second line in the program requires the universe teachpack. The last line in the program is telling DrRacket to animate the program using the draw-tick function. Congratulations! You have written your first animation. Run the program. What do you think?

---

* **Ex. 59** — A domesticated mammal is either a dog, a cat, or a horse. Design and implement a program to compute the number of mammary glands of a domesticated mammal.

* **Ex. 60** — Design and implement a program that squares even digits and that doubles odd digits.

Fig. 47 Traffic light animation program

```
(require 2htdp/image)
(require 2htdp/universe)

<Traffic Light Image Constant Definitions>
<Data Definition and function template for tick>
<Data Definition and function template for tl>

;; tick → tl
;; Purpose: Convert the given tick to a tl
(define (tick->tl a-tick)  (remainder a-tick 3))

<Sample expressions for ticks->tl>
<Tests for tick->tl>

;; tl → image
;; Purpose: To return the traffic light image for the given tl
(define (image-of-tl a-tl)
  (cond [(= a-tl 0) G-ON]
        [(= a-tl 1) Y-ON]
        [else R-ON]))

<Sample expressions for image-of-tl>
<Tests for image-of-tl>

;; tick → image
;; Purpose: Compute the traffic light image for the given tick
(define (draw-tick a-tick)
  (image-of-tl (tick->tl a-tick)))

<Sample expressions for draw-tick>
<Tests for draw-tick>

(animate draw-tick)
```

---

* **Ex. 61** — A sequential circuit known as a *flip-flop* can be on (set) or off (reset). When the flip-flop is on the next state is off. When the flip-flop is off the next state is on. Design and implement a program to compute the next state of a flip-flop.

** **Ex. 62** — Design and implement an animation for a pedestrian traffic light. A pedestrian traffic light displays one of two messages: Walk or Don't Walk.

31 Interval Types

Running the traffic light simulation reveals that the light changes too fast–28 times per second. The program is well-designed and works from a certain perspective but needs to be refined. That is, it needs to be improved. This is our first dive into the process of iterative refinement. It is fairly clear that we need the light to change at a slower pace so that the human eye can appreciate the changes. Instead of changing the image 28 times per second, the animation may change the traffic light image, for example, twice per second. This means that, instead of changing every clock tick, the image needs to change every 14 clock ticks.

This refinement means that the data definition of tl must be updated. Instead of defining tl as 0, 1, or 2, tl could define as follows:

```
;; A traffic light (tl) is either
;;   1.    0 --means the green light is on
;;   2.    1 --means the green light is on
      :
;;   13. 13 --means the green light is on
;;   14. 14 --means the yellow light is on
      :
;;   27. 27 --means the yellow light is on
;;   28. 41 --means the red light is on
      :
;;   41. 41 --means the red light is on
```

This data definition leads to a function definition whose conditional has 42 stanzas. That is quite large and error-prone during development. Sometimes such data definitions are unavoidable. Observe, however, that there is something special about this (long) data definition. There is a lot of repetition. This suggests that there is an abstraction that needs to be defined.

Many consecutive numbers have the same meaning. For example, the values from 0 through 13 all mean that the green light is on. We can borrow an idea from high school mathematics called an interval. We can say, for example, that when tl is a member of [0..13] it means that the green light is on. Equivalently, we can say that tl is a member of [0..14), (-1..13], or (-1..14). Remember that a square bracket means included and a parenthesis means not included. This leads to the following data definition:

```
;; A traffic light (tl) is a member of either
;;   1. [0..13]  --means the green light is on
;;   2. [14..27] --means the yellow light is on
;;   3. [28..41] --means the red light is on
```

This is called an *interval type*. An interval type defines orderable data by a set of categories. For example, tl is defined using three intervals. The intervals must be

Fig. 48 Refined `tick->tl` for the traffic light animation

```
#|
;; STEP 3
;; A tl is the remainder of a tick by 42.

   STEP 5:
;; tick --> tl
;; Purpose: Convert the given tick to a tl      |#

;; STEPS 6 and 8
(define (tick->tl a-tick)
  (remainder a-tick 42))

;; STEP 4: Sample expressions for tick->tl
(define TL-0 (remainder 11  42))
(define TL-1 (remainder 60  42))
(define TL-2 (remainder 123 42))

;; STEP 7: TESTS
;;Tests using sample expressions
(check-expect (tick->tl 11) TL-0)
(check-expect (tick->tl 60) TL-1)
(check-expect (tick->tl 123) TL-2)

;; STEP 7: Tests using sample values
(check-expect (tick->tl 0) 0)
(check-expect (tick->tl 325) 31)
(check-expect (tick->tl 650) 20)
```

mutually exclusive. That is, an instance of the data type must be a member of only one interval.

Refining a data definition means that the program must also be refined. Any function that manipulates or creates an instance of the refined data type and its tests must be updated. To determine which functions to update, a programmer must look for expressions that manipulate or create an instance of the updated data type. Functions that are good candidates to be updated are those with signatures that refer to the refined data type. Examining the signatures in the traffic light simulation program reveals:

`tick->tl`: tick → tl   Needs to be updated, because it creates an instance of tl.

`image-of-tl`: tl → image   Needs to be updated, because it makes a decision based on an instance of tl.

`draw-tick`: tick → image   Doest not need to be updated. This function does not manipulate nor creates an instance of tl.

The refinements necessary involve updating expressions and tests. The `tick->tl` function must convert a tick into a tl. Finding the remainder of the given tick by 3 is no longer correct because a tick must be converted to an integer in `[0..41]`. Modular arithmetic, however, can still be used. Now, the remainder of a tick by 42 must be computed. Figure 48 displays the updated `tick->tl` function. The sample

Fig. 49 Refined `image-of-tl` for the traffic light animation

```
#|
STEP 3:
  Determine the interval and return the corresponding image

STEP 5:
;; tl --> image
;; Purpose: To return the traffic light image for the given tl
|#

;; STEPS 6 and 8
(define (image-of-tl a-tl)
  (cond [(<= 0 a-tl 13)  G-ON]
        [(<= 14 a-tl 27) Y-ON]
        [else R-ON]))

;; STEP 4: There are no sample expressions as a tl is not used to
;;         compute a new value. It is only used to make a decision.

;; STEP 7: Tests using sample values
(check-expect (image-of-tl 10) G-ON)
(check-expect (image-of-tl 22) Y-ON)
(check-expect (image-of-tl 37) R-ON)
```

expressions and the body of the function now use 42 instead of 3. The tests have been updated in order to have at least one test for each variety of tl using the new data definition.

Figure 49 displays the refined version of `image-of-tl`. The `image-of-tl` function processes an instance of tl. This means that the conditional expression must be refined to correspond to the new data definition of tl. Observe that the tests inside the conditional now determine what interval contains a-tl. The unit tests for `image-of-tl` are also refined to include at least one test for each interval of tl.

An important lesson to absorb is that data in the real or an imaginary world may be represented in different ways (like tl). Part of the design process is to select a representation. The representation chosen influences how a problem solver thinks about a program. Exploring different representation may provide insight into the problem. It is also important to keep in mind that how data is represented may have a profound impact on performance.

---

* Ex. 63 — Design and implement a program to compute the interest rate of a savings account. The interest rate of a savings account depends on its balance. For a balance larger than $1,000,000 the interest rate is 1.11%. For a balance larger than $100,000 the interest rate is 1.05%. For a balance larger than $50,000 the interest rate is 1%. For a balance less than $50,000 the interest rate is 0.5%.

* **Ex. 64** — Design and implement a program to compute a letter grade on an exam. Less than 60 points is an F. 60-69 points is a D. 70-79 points is a C. 80-89 points is a B. 90-100 points is an A.

* **Ex. 65** — For the traffic light simulation three images are defined: G-ON, Y-ON, and R-ON. Rewrite the traffic light simulation using the following data definition:

```
;; A traffic light (tl) is either
;;   1. G-ON  --means the green light is on
;;   2. Y-ON  --means the yellow light is on
;;   3. R-ON  --means the red light is on
```

** **Ex. 66** — A sequential circuit known as a *flip-flop* can be on (set) or off (reset). When the flip-flop is on the next state is off. When the flip-flop is off the next state is on. Design and implement an animation of a flip-flop that changes state every second.

*** **Ex. 67** — Design and implement an animation for a pedestrian traffic light. A pedestrian traffic light displays one of two messages: Walk or Don't Walk. The Walk message should be displayed for 4 s before it changes. The Don't Walk message should be displayed for 2 s before it changes.

32 Itemization Types

Enumeration types capture variety by exhaustively listing all possible values. Interval types capture variety using a set of intervals to classify orderable data. What is done if both a listing of values and intervals are needed? As it turns out this is sometimes needed. To define such data an *itemization type* is used. An instance of an itemization type may be a specific value or a member of an interval type. Observe that an itemization type is a generalization of enumeration and interval type. When all varieties are specific values an itemization type is called an enumeration type. When all varieties are intervals an itemization type is called an interval type.

To illustrate how to design a program using an itemization type consider the problem of doubling or rotating an image using single alphanumeric or arrow keystrokes. The image is rotated 90, 180, or 270° using, respectively, the right, down, and left arrow keys. The image is doubled using the up arrow key. Nothing is done with the image on an alphanumeric keystroke.

Before proceeding with the design of the solution it is necessary to know how keys are represented and compared. In the universe teachpack, all keys are represented with a string. For example, the z key is represented by "z". The right, down, left, and up keys are represented, respectively, with the strings "right", "down, "left", and "up". The key=? function is a predicate used to compare keys for equality. Do not

Fig. 50 Data definitions for change image and alphanumeric keystrokes

```
STEP 1: DATA DEFINITIONS
;; An alphanumeric keystroke (aks) is a member of either:
;;   1. ["a".."z"] --means a letter keystroke
;;   2. ["0".."9"] --means a numeric keystroke

;; A change image keystroke (ciks) is either:
;;   1. "right" --means rotate image 90 degrees clockwise
;;   2. "down"  --means rotate image 180 degrees clockwise
;;   3. "left"  --means rotate image 270 degrees clockwise
;;   4. "up"    --means double image size
;;   5. aks     --means do nothing to image
```

mistake key=? as being the same as string=?. The former only compares strings that represent keys while the latter compares any two strings.

To facilitate the design, assume that there is a constant ROCKET-IMG whose value is a rocket image created using the functions in the image teachpack. Figure 50 displays Step 1 of the design recipe. An alphanumeric keystroke is an interval type. There are two intervals: one for letters and one for numbers. Nothing else is an alphanumeric keystroke. A change image keystroke is an itemization type. It has four literal values: one for each arrow. It also has one interval type: an alphanumeric keystroke. Observe that a data definition may refer to another data definition. The meaning of each variety is also clearly stated for each variety within each data definition.

Figures 51 and 52 display Step 2 of the design recipe. In Fig. 51, the template for ciks has a function skeleton with a conditional that distinguishes the variety of the value received as input. The template also suggests defining a constant and a test for the value of a sample expression for each variety of ciks. In addition, it suggests the definition of a sample value test for each variety of ciks. In Fig. 52, the template for aks has a function skeleton with a conditional that distinguishes between the varieties of aks. Two sample expressions along with corresponding test are suggested: one for a letter keystroke and one for a digit keystroke. In the same manner, two sample value tests are suggested by the template.

Figure 53 displays Steps 3 through 8 of the design recipe for the function that processes a ciks. Step 3 explains that the rotate and scale functions are used to compute new images. Step 4 illustrates how these two functions are used to compute a new image using the ROCKET-IMG constant. Step 5 results in the specialized signature and purpose statement. The signature states the function takes two inputs: an image and a ciks. The purpose statement indicates that the given image is rotated, doubled, or left untouched. The result of step 6 reflects the requirements stated by the signature. The two parameters are named in a manner that suggest the type of their value. The name of the function is suggestive of its purpose. Step 7 results in tests using sample computations and using sample values. The tests with sample computations illustrate that the function computes the same value as the sample expressions. The tests with sample values use images created

Fig. 51 Function template for `ciks`

```
;; ciks ... --> ...
;; Purpose: ...
(define (f-on-ciks a-ciks ...)
  (cond [(key=? a-ciks "right") ...]
        [(key=? a-ciks "down")  ...]
        [(key=? a-ciks "left")  ...]
        [(key=? a-ciks "up")    ...]
        [else ...]))

;; Sample expressions for f-on-ciks
(define CIKS-RIGHT ...)
(define CIKS-DOWN  ...)
(define CIKS-LEFT  ...)
(define CIKS-UP ...))
(define CIKS-ALPHANUM ...))

;; Tests using sample computations for f-on-ciks
(check-expect (f-on-ciks "right" ...) CIKS-RIGHT)
(check-expect (f-on-ciks "down" ...)  CIKS-DOWN)
(check-expect (f-on-ciks "left" ...)  CIKS-LEFT)
(check-expect (f-on-ciks "up" ...)    CIKS-UP)
(check-expect (f-on-ciks <aks> ...)   CIKS-ALPHANUM)

;; Tests using sample values for f-on-ciks
(check-expect (f-on-ciks "left" ...)  ...)
(check-expect (f-on-ciks "right" ...) ...)
(check-expect (f-on-ciks "down" ...)  ...)
(check-expect (f-on-ciks "up" ...)    ...)
(check-expect (f-on-ciks <aks> ...)   ...)
```

Fig. 52 Function template for aks

```
;; aks ... --> ...
;; Purpose: ...
(define (f-on-aks an-aks ...)
  (cond [(string<=? "a" an-aks "b") ...]
        [(string<=? "0" an-aks "9") ...]))

;; Sample expressions for f-on-aks
(define AKS-LETTER ...)
(define AKS-NUM  ...)

;; Tests using sample computations for f-on-aks
(check-expect (f-on-aks <aks1> ...) AKS-LETTER)
(check-expect (f-on-aks <aks2> ...) AKS-NUM)

;; Tests using sample values for f-on-aks
(check-expect (f-on-aks <aks3> ...) ...)
(check-expect (f-on-aks <aks4> ...) ...)
```

using functions from the image teachpack. The third test uses `flip-vertical`. This test passes because vertically flipping an equilateral triangle results in the

Fig. 53 The change image program

```
;; STEP 3: Use the functions rotate and scale to compute a new image
;; STEP 5: image ciks → image
;;         Purpose: Rotate 90/180/270 degrees, double or untouch image
;; STEP 6 and 8
(define (change-img an-img a-ciks)
  (cond [(key=? a-ciks "right") (rotate 90 an-img)]
        [(key=? a-ciks "down")  (rotate 180 an-img)]
        [(key=? a-ciks "left")  (rotate 270 an-img)]
        [(key=? a-ciks "up")    (scale 2 an-img)]
        [else an-img]))
;; STEP 4: Sample expressions for change-img
(define RRIGHT-RCKT (rotate 90 ROCKET-IMG))
(define RDOWN-RCKT  (rotate 180 ROCKET-IMG))
(define RLEFT-RCKT  (rotate 270 ROCKET-IMG))
(define DOUBLE-RCKT (scale 2 ROCKET-IMG))
;; STEP 7: TESTS
;; Tests using sample computations for change-img
(check-expect (change-img ROCKET-IMG "right") RRIGHT-RCKT)
(check-expect (change-img ROCKET-IMG "down")  RDOWN-RCKT)
(check-expect (change-img ROCKET-IMG "left")  RLEFT-RCKT)
(check-expect (change-img ROCKET-IMG "up")    DOUBLE-RCKT)
(check-expect (change-img ROCKET-IMG "m")     ROCKET-IMG)
;; Tests using sample values for change-img
(check-expect (change-img (rectangle 10 30 'solid 'red) "left")
              (rectangle 30 10 'solid 'red))
(check-expect (change-img (ellipse 75 35 'outline 'pink) "right")
              (ellipse 35 75 'outline 'pink))
(check-expect (change-img (triangle 25 'solid 'gold) "down")
              (flip-vertical (triangle 25 'solid 'gold)))
(check-expect (change-img (square 15 'outline 'green) "up")
              (square 30 'outline 'green))
(check-expect (change-img (star 10 'solid 'yellow) "y")
              (star 10 'solid 'yellow))
```

same image as rotating the triangle 180°. In general, however, this is not true. For example, vertically flipping a right triangle does not result in the same image as rotating the triangle 180°. Finally, Step 8 specializes the body of the function. The expressions for the consequence in each stanza of the conditional are based on the sample expressions and on the last test using a sample value. For the former, the literal ROCKET-IMG is substituted with, an-img, the image parameter of the function. For the latter, observe that the input image is the same as the output image. This means that in the default stanza the value of the parameter must be returned.

The final noteworthy observation is that the design of change-img did not reveal the need for auxiliary functions. This means that the template for aks was never used to design a function. That is fine. Not every problem requires every template to be specialized. Other problems involving ciks may very well require the specialization of the aks function template. Think of the templates developed as different tools in a toolbox. Sometimes you only need a hammer. Other times you only need a wrench. Yet other times you need both.

** **Ex. 68** — Refine the change image program to flip the given image vertically for a letter keystroke and to flip the given image horizontally for a number keystroke. *Hint*: There is no need to change any data definitions for this problem.

** **Ex. 69** — Write a program to provide feedback to a student on their quiz performance. If their average is 100%, then the feedback is `"Excellent Performance"`. If their average is greater than or equal to 90%, then the feedback is `"Very Good Performance"`. If their average is greater than or equal to 80%, then the feedback is `"Good Performance"`. If their average is greater than or equal to 71%, then the feedback is `"Just OK Performance"`. If their average is 70%, then the feedback is `"Borderline Performance"`. If their average is greater than or equal to 60%, then the feedback is `"Poor Performance"`. If their average is less than or equal to 59%, then the feedback is `"Failing Performance"`.

---

33 What Have We Learned in This Chapter?

The important lessons of Chap. 5 are summarized as follows:

- Compound functions arise from data having variety and having to decide which expression to evaluate depending on the variety of the input.
- Compound functions in BSL are written with a conditional expression in the body.
- The BSL provides two types of conditional expressions: `cond-` and `if`-expressions.
- The BSL syntax explored is displayed in Fig. 54.

  – Syntax for data types defined by BSL is omitted.

- Data definitions are needed to describe data that has variety.
- The design recipe for functions that make decisions requires:

  – A data definition to describe data that has variety
  – A function template for every data definition
  – At least one test for every variety of data

- Signatures may use types described by a data definition.
- Function templates are specialized to write functions.

Fig. 54 Chapter 5 BSL grammar

```
program ::= {expr | test | def}*
    def ::= (define <variable name> expr)
        ::= (define (<name> <name>⁺) expr)
   test ::= (check-expect expr  expr)
        ::= (check-within expr  expr  expr)
   expr ::= number
        ::= string
        ::= \#<character constant>
        ::= '<character⁺>
        ::= #true
        ::= #false
        ::= <image>
        ::= (<function> expr⁺)
        ::= (and expr expr expr*)
        ::= (or expr expr expr*)
        ::= (cond [expr expr]⁺
                  [else expr])
        ::= (if expr expr expr)
```

- There are 3 type categories to describe variety:

    - Enumeration types
    - Interval types
    - Itemization types

Chapter 6
Aliens Attack Version 1

We all know that video games are fun to play. Designing them can also be fun despite being complex programs. To manage this complexity, video games are developed using the process of iterative refinement. Adding features to a video game in a piecemeal manner allows the problem solver to conquer the complexity in small steps. For example, for Aliens Attack we have already solved the problem of creating cis (remember, ci is defined as a character image in 4).

Before proceeding, it is a good idea to get a handle on exactly what a video game is. In many ways, a video game is similar to an animation. For instance, scenes are flickered fast enough to create the illusion of movement. Video games, however, allow players to interact with the animation. This interaction may change the evolution of the game. The evolution of the game changes when a *computer event* occurs. A computer event includes any action like pressing a key, the clock ticking, or clicking the mouse. Players change the evolution of the game through, for example, key pressing or mouse actions. For instance, in Aliens Attack a player may use the left arrow and the right arrow keys to move the rocket. Like a simulation, the evolution of a video game may also change by events not controlled by the player like a clock tick. In Aliens Attack, for example, the aliens move every time the clock ticks. It is now clear that functions called *event handlers* (or simply *handlers*) are needed to process computer events.

The ability to design programs that make decisions allows us to implement video games. Handlers need to make decisions. For example, the handler to process a keystroke must distinguish what key has been pressed. If the right arrow key is pressed, then the handler moves the rocket right. If the left arrow key is pressed, then the handler moves the rocket left. Clearly, data definitions are needed to describe the keystroke events that change the evolution of the game.

In addition to providing programmers with the ability to write animations, the universe teachpack provides programmers with the ability to write video games in BSL. This teachpack is an API. It provides the necessary syntax to associate handlers with computer events and it defines the signature that these handlers must have. Using the universe teachpack is an exercise in programming with (the abilities

© The Author(s), under exclusive license to Springer Nature Switzerland AG 2022
M. T. Morazán, *Animated Problem Solving*, Texts in Computer Science,
https://doi.org/10.1007/978-3-030-85091-3_6

provided by and the restrictions imposed by) an API. Programming with an API is a good skill to develop because programming with APIs is standard practice.

34 The Universe Teachpack

The universe teachpack requires the development of a data definition for a *world*. A world is all the values that may change during the evolution of the game. Some of the values may be de displayed when a game image is computed. Other values may only be needed to advance the evolution of the game. In a fully implemented Aliens Attack game, for example, the aliens and the direction the aliens travel in are part of the world. The aliens are displayed in a game image as in Fig. 37. The direction the aliens travel in, on the other hand, is not displayed in the image.

There is a special expression to run a video game called a big-bang expression (bb-expr). This expression allows the programmer to provide the initial value of the world and the handlers needed to advance the evolution of the game. The big-bang expression syntax is:

```
bb-expr ::= (big-bang expr bb-clause⁺)
bb-clause ::= [to-draw function]
              [on-key function]
              [on-tick function]
              [stop-when function]
              [name expr]
                    ⋮
```

A bb-expr has in parenthesis the keyword big-bang followed by an expression that must evaluate to a world value followed by one or more bb-clauses (big-bang clauses). A bb-clause associates an event with a handler function to process the event. Each bb-clause has in square brackets an event describer (e.g., to-draw, on-tick, and stop-when) and a handler for the event. For example, [to-draw draw-world] states to use draw-world to render the image of the world, [on-key process-key] states to use process-key to process a key stroke, [on-tick process-tick] states to use process-tick to process a clock tick, and [stop-when game-over?] states to use game-over? to detect the end of the game (or interactive simulation). The only required bb-clause is the to-draw clause. The only clause that does not follow this scheme is the name clause. This clause associates a name with the world. The expr in this clause must evaluate to a string or symbol. The name appears in title of the scene. The vertical dots mean that there are other varieties of bb-clauses. The big-bang documentation describes all the possible bb-clauses. An important thing to remember is that a bb-clause may not be repeated. For example, a bb-expr may only have one to-draw bb-clause.

The universe API also specifies the signature and purpose of the handlers. Each handler serves a specific purpose like creating a scene, computing the next world after a clock tick or keystroke, or detecting the end of the game/simulation. For

Fig. 55 Fish image

example, the following table displays the signature and purpose for four handlers:

on-draw: world → scene

    Purpose: To create the world's scene

on-key: world key → world

    Purpose: To return the world after the given keystroke

on-tick: world → world

    Purpose: To return the world after a clock tick

stop-when: world → Boolean

    Purpose: To determine if the game/animation has ended

This means that we must write handlers that satisfy the above signatures. To a programmer this suggest using a top-down design strategy to write a video game. Start with the functions needed by the big-bang expression. Design auxiliary functions as their need is revealed.

To illustrate the use of the universe teachpack consider developing an interactive animation to rotate the image of the fish displayed in Fig. 55. The user may rotate the image of the fish to point up, down, left, or right using the arrow keys. In Fig. 55 the fish is pointing up. If the user presses the up arrow key, then the image remains unchanged. If the user presses the right arrow, then the image is rotated to make the fish point right. A similar action takes place pressing the other arrow keys. If the user presses any other key, then the fish image remains unchanged regardless of the direction the fish is pointing in. For example, if the fish is pointing left and the m key is pressed, then the fish image remains unchanged.

To start, first define the constants that are needed. A scene is needed. A scene is defined as follows:

A scene is a WIDTH x HEIGHT image

Here WIDTH and HEIGHT are positive integer constants. Presumably, a scene is large enough to contain the fish image. Otherwise, the fish image is truncated.

The fish image is also a constant. The following code defines all the scene and fish image constants:

```
(define WIDTH 200)
(define HEIGHT 200)
(define E-SCENE-COLOR 'black)
(define E-SCENE (empty-scene WIDTH HEIGHT E-SCENE-COLOR))
```

```
(define FISH-W 46)
(define FISH-H 76)
(define FISH-BODY-IMG
        (place-image
         (ellipse 30 60 'solid 'green)
         (/ FISH-W 2)
         (/ FISH-H 2)
         (rectangle FISH-W FISH-H 'solid E-SCENE-COLOR)))

(define FISH-EYE-IMG (overlay (circle 2 'solid 'lightred)
                              (circle 4 'solid 'white)))

(define FISH-TAIL-IMG (overlay/xy
                       (circle 20 'solid 'black)
                       0
                       -10
                       (circle 20 'solid 'green)))

(define FISH-IMG (place-image FISH-EYE-IMG
                              (- (/ FISH-W 2) 3)
                              (/ FISH-H 4)
                              (place-image
                               FISH-TAIL-IMG
                               (/ FISH-W 2)
                               (+ (/ FISH-H 4/3) 15)
                               FISH-BODY-IMG)))
```

Observe that the fish image is created using a divide and conquer strategy. First, the body, eye, and tail images are defined. Second, these three images are combined to create the fish image.

After defining the first set of constants (others may be needed as the solution progresses), the design process starts with writing a run function that has a bb-expr as its body. By convention in this textbook, the run function is used to start a game or interactive animation and its bb-expr has a name clause. The central question to start is what computer events need to be processed. For this interactive animation only keystrokes need to be processed. Therefore, the run function may be written as follows:

```
;; string → world
;; Purpose: To run the interactive fish simulation
(define (run a-name)
  (big-bang
    INIT-WORLD
    [on-draw draw-world]   ;; world → scene
    [on-key process-key]   ;; world key → world
    [name a-name]))
```

The body of run gives us a starting point for the design process. The initial world, INIT-WORLD, needs to be defined. For this, a world data definition is needed. The function handlers draw-world and process-key and any needed auxiliary functions need to be designed. Recall that the signatures of the handlers are defined by the universe API (noted as comments in run). For the key-processing handler, a data definition is needed for the keys that affect the evolution of the animation.

We start with the data definition for the keys that affect the evolution of the animation. Remember that every data definition means the development of a corresponding function template. A fish keystroke is defined as follows:

```
A fish keystroke (fks) is either:
   1. "up"    --means fish in up direction
   2. "right" --means fish in right direction
   3. "down"  --means fish in down direction
   4. "left"  --means fish in left direction

;; fks ... → ...
;; Purpose: ...
(define (f-on-fks a-fks ...)
  (cond [(string=? a-key "up") ...]
        [(string=? a-key "right") ...]
        [(string=? a-key "down") ...]
        [else ...]))

;; Sample Expressions for f-on-fks
(define UP-FKS-VAL ...)
(define RIGHT-FKS-VAL ...)
(define DOWN-FKS-VAL ...)
(define LEFT-FKS-VAL ...)

;; Tests using sample computations for f-on-fks
(check-expect (f-on-fks "up" ...)    UP-FKS-VAL)
(check-expect (f-on-fks "right" ...) RIGHT-FKS-VAL)
(check-expect (f-on-fks "down" ...)  DOWN-FKS-VAL)
(check-expect (f-on-fks "left" ...)  LEFT-FKS-VAL)

;; Tests using sample values for f-on-fks
(check-expect (f-on-fish-ks ...) ...)
    ...
```

Observe that an fks is an enumeration type. Further observe that four sample expressions and four tests using sample computations are needed as required when designing with data that has variety: one for each variety.

The above data definition now allows for a refinement of the key data definition. Now, keys may be distinguished between keys that are an fks and those that are not. The refined data definition is:

```
A key is either:
  1. fks
  2. not an fks

;; key ... → ...
;; Purpose: ...
(define (f-on-key a-key ...)
  (if (fks? a-key)
      ...
      ...))

;; Sample Expressions for f-on-key
(define FKS-VAL ...)
(define NON-FKS-VAL ...)

;; Tests using sample computations for f-on-key
(check-expect (f-on-key ...)     FKS-VAL)
(check-expect (f-on-key ...) NON-FKS-VAL)
    ...

;; Tests using sample values for f-on-key
(check-expect (f-on-key ...) ...)
    ...
```

Observe that key is an itemization type. There is something different, however, in the formulation of this data definition. The second variety not an fks does not look like an enumeration nor does it look like an interval. It is, however, an enumeration type. Specifically, it is the complement of fks. That is, any key that is not an fks is of the second variety. The use of *not* is simply shorthand for the large number of non-fks keys. Given that keys are itemized in two varieties, the body of f-on-key is an if-expression. This if-expression tests if a given key is an fks using an auxiliary function that needs to be designed. Finally, observe that the number of sample expressions and of tests using sample computations matches the number of varieties.

The final data definition we need is for the world. There are many ways to define the world for this animation. Perhaps, the simplest way to define the world is to make it an fks as follows:

```
A world is an fks

;; world ... → ...
;; Purpose: ...
(define (f-on-world a-world)
  ...(f-on-fks a-world)...)

;; Sample Expressions for f-on-world
(define WORLD-VAL ...))
```

```
;; Tests using sample computations for f-on-world
(check-expect (f-on-world ...) WORLD-VAL)
   ...

;; Tests using sample values for f-on-world
(check-expect (f-on-world ...) ...)
   ...
```

Observe that there is no variety in the world data definition. Therefore, the body of f-on-world is not a conditional expression. This brings to the forefront an important observation. The world and fks are different. They are different data definitions. Therefore, at least two functions are needed to process a world: one to process a world and one to process an fks. This is why there is a call to f-on-fks in the body of f-on-world. You may ask yourself why two are needed when a world is the same as fks. Indeed, this is true for this version of the simulation. However, always design thinking that in the future you or someone else may need to refine the program. For example, the data definition of the world may be refined. If your solution already includes separate world-processing and fks-processing functions, then the process of refinement is easier. A change in the world data definition does not affect the functions that process an fks and only functions that process a world need to be refined. On the other hand, if a single data definition is used, then a change in the world data definition requires refinements to all functions that process a world and functions for an fks need to be designed.

With the data definitions and function templates completed, the design of the elements needed by the big-bang expression is next. The first is INIT-WORLD. Ask yourself what value the initial world needs to be or you want it to be. In this interactive animation, the initial direction the fish is pointing in is arbitrary. Therefore, the initial world value may be defined as follows:

```
(define INIT-WORLD "up")
```

Next, focus turns to designing draw-world. This function processes a world. Therefore, we specialize the template for functions on the world. Ask yourself what this function needs to do. According the universe API, this function needs to compute a scene. This means that the fish image must be placed in E-SCENE. This is enough information to start specializing the template as follows:

```
;; world → scene
;; Purpose: To draw the world in the E-SCENE
(define (draw-world a-world)
  ...(f-on-fks a-world)...)

;; Sample Expressions for draw-world
(define WORLD-VAL1 (place-image <an up fish image>
                                (/ WIDTH 2)
                                (/ HEIGHT 2)
                                E-SCENE))
```

```
(define WORLD-VAL2 (place-image <a left fish image>
                                (/ WIDTH 2)
                                (/ HEIGHT 2)
                                E-SCENE))


;; Tests using sample computations for draw-world
(check-expect (draw-world ...) WORLD-VAL)
(check-expect (draw-world ...) WORLD-VAL2)
    ...


;; Tests using sample values for draw-world
(check-expect (draw-world ...) ...)
    ...
```

The template is first specialized by substituting f-on-world with draw-world and
by creating sample expression to place a fish image in E-SCENE. Placing the fish
image in the middle of the empty scene is a reasonable choice. The fish image to
display depends on the fks value the world represents. This is a different type of
value and an auxiliary function is used to compute it. The template can now be
specialized to:

```
;; world → scene
;; Purpose: To draw the world in the E-SCENE
(define (draw-world a-world)
  (place-image (compute-fish-img a-world)
               (/ WIDTH 2)
               (/ HEIGHT 2)
               E-SCENE))


;; Sample Expressions for draw-world
(define WORLD-VAL1 (place-image
                     (compute-fish-img INIT-WORLD)
                     (/ WIDTH 2)
                     (/ HEIGHT 2)
                     E-SCENE))


(define WORLD-VAL2 (place-image
                     (compute-fish-img "left")
                     (/ WIDTH 2)
                     (/ HEIGHT 2)
                     E-SCENE))


;; Tests using sample computations for draw-world
(check-expect (draw-world "up") WORLD-VAL1)
(check-expect (draw-world "left") WORLD-VAL2)
```

```
;; Tests using sample values for draw-world
```

```
(check-expect (draw-world "down")                      )
```

```
(check-expect (draw-world "right")                     )
```

Observe that the only difference among the sample expressions is the value of the world. This tells us that draw-world does not need any additional parameters. This allows the sample expressions and the sample tests using sample computations to be written. The final specialization step is for the tests using sample values. It is reasonable to use the untested world values: "up" and "down". Now, all the steps of the design recipe are satisfied except running the tests.

Focus now turns to the design of compute-fish-img. This function processes an fks and, therefore, the template to process an fks value is specialized:

```
;; fks ... → image
;; Purpose:  Compute the fish image for the given fks
(define (compute-fish-img a-fks ...)
  (cond [(string=? a-key "up") ...]
        [(string=? a-key "right") ...]
        [(string=? a-key "down") ...]
        [else ...]))

;; Sample Expressions for compute-fish-img
(define UP-FKS-VAL    FISH-IMG)
(define RIGHT-FKS-VAL (rotate 270 FISH-IMG))
(define DOWN-FKS-VAL  (rotate 180 FISH-IMG))
(define LEFT-FKS-VAL (flip-vertical (rotate 90 FISH-IMG)))

;; Tests using sample computations for compute-fish-img
(check-expect (compute-fish-img "up" ...)    UP-FKS-VAL)
(check-expect (compute-fish-img "right" ...) RIGHT-FKS-VAL)
(check-expect (compute-fish-img "down" ...)  DOWN-FKS-VAL)
(check-expect (compute-fish-img "left" ...)  LEFT-FKS-VAL)

;; Tests using sample values for compute-fish-img
(check-expect (compute-fish-img ...) ...)
  ...
```

This function returns an image and this is reflected in the signature and the purpose statement. The sample expressions compute a value for each variety. Observe that each computes a value for a fish image using only constant values and that the conditional only needs the value of the given fks. Thus, compute-fish-img does not require more parameters. Finally, observe that all fks values have a sample expression and that all possible returned fish images are produced by these. Therefore, there is no need for tests using sample values. Based on these observations, the final specialization step yields:

```
;; fks → image
;; Purpose:  Compute the fish image for the given fks
(define (compute-fish-img a-fks)
  (cond [(string=? a-key "up")    FISH-IMG]
        [(string=? a-key "right") (rotate 270 FISH-IMG)]
        [(string=? a-key "down")  (rotate 180 FISH-IMG)]
        [else (flip-vertical (rotate 90 FISH-IMG))]))

;; Sample Expressions for f-on-fks
(define UP-FKS-VAL    FISH-IMG)
(define RIGHT-FKS-VAL (rotate 270 FISH-IMG))
(define DOWN-FKS-VAL  (rotate 180 FISH-IMG))
(define LEFT-FKS-VAL  (flip-vertical (rotate 90 FISH-IMG)))

;; Tests using sample computations for compute-fish-img
(check-expect (compute-fish-img "up")    UP-FKS-VAL)
(check-expect (compute-fish-img "right") RIGHT-FKS-VAL)
(check-expect (compute-fish-img "down")  DOWN-FKS-VAL)
(check-expect (compute-fish-img "left")  LEFT-FKS-VAL)
```

Once again, observe that template specialization completes all the steps of the design recipe except running the tests.

The function process-key, as its name suggests, processes a key. This means the template for functions on a key must be specialized. This function always takes as input a world and a key and returns a world according to the universe API. If the given key is an fks, then the next world is the given key. Otherwise, the world is unchanged. The initial specialization yields:

```
;; world key → world
;; Purpose: To return the next world based on the
;;          given key
(define (process-key a-world a-key ...)
  (if (fks? a-key)
      ...
      ...))

;; Sample Expressions for process-key
(define KEY-VAL     "down")
(define KEY-VAL2    "left")
(define NON-KEY-VAL "up")

;; Tests using sample computations for process-key
(check-expect (process-key  ...) KEY-VAL)
(check-expect (process-key  ...) KEY-VAL2)
(check-expect (process-key  ...) NON-KEY-VAL)

  ...
```

```
;; Tests using sample values for process-key
(check-expect (process-key  ...) ...)
    ...
```

The sample expressions by themselves have an obscured meaning in this case. The expression for KEY-VAL is for inputs "right" and "down" to process-key. The expression for KEY-VAL2 is for inputs "up" and "left" to process-key. The expression for NON-KEY-VAL is for inputs "up" and "j" to process-key. From these sample expressions we can surmise that if the given key is an fks, then the new world is the given key. Otherwise, the next world is the value of the given world. The final specialization is:

```
;; world key → world
;; Purpose: To return the next world based on the
;;          given key
(define (process-key world a-key)
    (if (fks? a-key)
        a-key
        a-world))

;; Sample Expressions for process-key
(define KEY-VAL     "down")
(define KEY-VAL2    "left")
(define NON-KEY-VAL "up")

;; Tests using sample computations for process-key
(check-expect (process-key  "right" "down") KEY-VAL)
(check-expect (process-key  "up"    "left") KEY-VAL2)
(check-expect (process-key  "up"    "j")    NON-KEY-VAL)

;; Tests using sample values for process-key
(check-expect (process-key "left" "up") "up")
(check-expect (process-key "left" "right") "right")
(check-expect (process-key "left" "left") "left")
(check-expect (process-key "left" "v") "left")
(check-expect (process-key "right" "x") "right")
```

The tests using sample values aim to be thorough. The first two test the fks values not present in the tests using sample computations. The third test shows that if the given fks is the same as the given world, then the world is unchanged. The last two tests use two different non-fks values.

The final task is to design fks? Ask yourself how to determine if a key is an fks. If the key is any fks value, then the answer is true. Otherwise, the answer is false. Following the steps of the design recipe yields:

```
;; key → Boolean
;; Purpose: Determine if the given key is an fks
(define (fks? a-key)
  (if (or (key=? a-key "right")
          (key=? a-key "down")
          (key=? a-key "left")
          (key=? a-key "up"))
      #true
      #false))


;; Sample Expressions for fks?
(define FKS-RVAL    #true)
(define NON-FKS-VAL #false)


;; Tests using sample computations for fks?
(check-expect (fks? "right") FKS-RVAL)
(check-expect (fks? "m")     NON-FKS-VAL)


;; Tests using sample values for fks?
(check-expect (fks? "up")   #true)
(check-expect (fks? "down") #true)
(check-expect (fks? "left") #true)
(check-expect (fks? "q")    #false)
(check-expect (fks? "t")    #false)
```

The predicate has the structure suggested by the template. It has an if-expression in its body. The tests using sample values add thoroughness by making sure all fks values are tested and more non-fks values are tested. However, fks? is interesting. It always returns the value of the test. This means that the if-expression is not needed and fks? may be simplified to:

```
;; key → Boolean
;; Purpose: Determine if the given key is an fks
(define (fks? a-key)
  (or (key=? a-key "right")
      (key=? a-key "down")
      (key=? a-key "left")
      (key=? a-key "up")))
```

Certainly, this version of fks? is easier to understand and, therefore, a preferable solution. The important lesson here is that when designing a predicate for data with variety consider using a Boolean expression instead of a conditional. Remember, the template is suggestive of the structure of functions. Sometimes the result of specializing the template can be simplified.

The only step of the design recipe left is to run the tests. Make sure all the tests pass.

* **Ex. 70** — Why is `flip-vertical` used in `compute-fish-img`?

** **Ex. 71** — Redesign the fish interactive simulation using the following data definition for the world:

A world is an image, either:

1.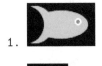

2.

3.

4.

* **Ex. 72** — Consider the following data definition:

A signed integer is either in:
  1. $(-\infty..-1]$
  2. $[1..\infty)$

Write a predicate to determine if an integer is a signed integer. Simplify the predicate as much as possible.

*** **Ex. 73** — Write an interactive animation that echoes up to 80 lowercase letter, space, or period keystrokes in a box. The simulation should stop with an Enter keystroke.

35 A Video Game Design Recipe

This development suggests the design recipe for video game and interactive animations displayed in Fig. 56. Steps 1–3 are problem and data analysis that are performed once. Step 1 requires a data definition for the elements that vary in a game. Step 2

Fig. 56 The design recipe for video game development

1. Create data definitions for the elements that vary.
2. Develop a function template and examples for each data definition.
3. Define the run function with no tests.

   For a needed function:
4. Outline the computation.
5. Define constants for the value of sample expressions for each variety and name the differences.
6. Write the function's signature and purpose.
7. Write the function's header.
8. Write tests.
9. Write the function's body.
10. Run the tests and, if necessary, redesign.

requires the development of a function template and of examples for each data definition. If the defined data has variety, then at least one example for each variety is needed. Step 3 requires the development of the run function. The body must be a bb-expr. This function serves as a map to guide the top-down development of the game. Ask yourself what events may affect the evolution of the game. There must be a clause in the bb-expr for every event that may change the evolution of the game or interactive simulation. This function is written without tests because it is only used to initiate the game or simulation. It is not the solution to a problem. In fact, the run function's template may be defined as follows:

```
; string → world
; Purpose: To run the game
(define (run a-name)
  (big-bang INIT-WORLD
            [on-draw ...]
            [name a-name]
            bb-clause*))
```

The final clauses, of course, may not contain a repetition of any clause.

Steps 4–10 are performed for each function that is needed. This is done by specializing the function template for the data being processed. These steps are the same as those found in previous design recipes.

36 Adding the Rocket to Aliens Attack

The first refinement to Aliens Attack is to add the rocket. Figure 57 displays a scene of the proposed new version of the video game. Before starting save your Aliens Attack version 0 to a new file, say Aliens-Attack-v1. It is this new file that is to be edited with refinements. The version 0 is kept as a safe back-up of work that has been completed.

Fig. 57 Aliens attack scene with a rocket

Recall that the rocket may move left to right without going off the edges of the scene. Given that a rocket may exhibit changes as the game evolves, it needs to be part of the world and, therefore, a data definition for a rocket is needed. Ask yourself what changes about the rocket as the game advances. The characteristics that change must be captured in the rocket's data definition. At this point, it is important to realize that a rocket is not the same as the image of the rocket. The image of the rocket does not change as the rocket moves. When the rocket moves left or right the rocket's image-x changes. For example, if the image coordinates of the rocket are (5, ROCKET-Y) and the rocket moves right, then the new image coordinates of the rocket are (6, ROCKET-Y). That is, the rocket moves to the next image box to the right in the scene. Observe, as noted in Chap. 6, that the rocket's image-y is constant. Now that the rocket's changing characteristics are identified, the rocket's data definition, the template for functions on a rocket, and sample instances (rocket examples) may be stated as follows:

```
#|  A rocket is an image-x

    ;; Sample instances of rocket
    (define ROCKET1 ...)
        ...
```

```
;; rocket ... → ...
;; Purpose: ...
(define (f-on-rocket a-rocket ...)
  ...(f-on-image-x a-rocket ...) ...)


;; Sample expressions for f-on-rocket
(define ROCKET1-VAL (f-on-rocket ROCKET1 ...))
  ...


;; Tests using sample computations for f-on-rocket
(check-expect (f-on-rocket ROCKET1 ...) ROCKET-VAL)
  ...


;; Tests using sample values for f-on-rocket
(check-expect (f-on-rocket ...) ...)
  ...                                                      |#

;; Sample instances of rocket
(define ROCKET1 7)
(define INIT-ROCKET (/ MAX-CHARS-HORIZONTAL 2))
```

Observe that to process a rocket the template suggests calling a function to process an image-x. This design exhibits *separation of concerns*. Separation of concerns reflects that solving a problem for one data type is different from solving a problem for another data type. In this example, processing a rocket may require processing an image-x. The processing of an image-x is done by a function to process an image-x, not a function to process a rocket. Observe that the tests using sample computations refer to the sample instances of a rocket and the values of sample expressions. The tests using sample values do not refer to defined sample instances or defined values for sample expressions. These tests are used to illustrate that a function works for values not previously computed. Finally, when a data definition is developed it is good practice to include at least one sample instance. In this example, two sample instances of a rocket, ROCKET1 and INIT-ROCKET, are defined.

A similar piece of reasoning must be done to define the game's world. Ask yourself what may change as the game evolves. In this version of Aliens Attack, the only characteristic that may change is the rocket. Therefore, the data definition of the world, its function template, and sample instances may be stated as follows:

```
#|  A world is a rocket

    ;; Sample instances of world
    (define WORLD1 ...)

    ;; world ... --> ...
    ;; Purpose: ...
    (define (f-on-world a-world ...)
      ...(f-on-rocket a-world ...) ...)
```

```
;; Sample expressions for f-on-world
(define WORLD1-VAL ...)


;; Tests using sample computations for f-on-world
(check-expect (f-on-world WORLD1 ...) WORLD1-VAL)
     ...


;; Tests using sample values for f-on-world
(check-expect (f-on-world ...) ...)
     ...                                                          |#


;; Sample instances of world
(define WORLD1      ROCKET1)
(define INIT-WORLD  INIT-ROCKET)
```

Observe that despite the world and the rocket being the same in this version of the game, we use two different data definitions. A good designer always has a different data definition for every data type. This makes it easier to make future refinements to the game. We know that the data definition of the world will be expanded to include, for example, the army of aliens. This expansion will be done without having to revisit any code developed to manipulate a rocket. If we use a single definition, then such an expansion would require writing new code for the world, the army of aliens, and the rocket. Further observe that the template suggests that to process a world the processing a rocket may be needed. Again, we see separation of concerns in this design. Observe that, once again, the tests using sample computations refer to previously defined constants. In contrast, once again, the tests using sample values do not refer to previously defined constants. The sample worlds are defined using the sample rockets.

Given that the player moves the rocket using keyboard it is necessary to define what a key is. In this version of Aliens Attack the rocket is moved using the left and right arrow keys. This suggests that a key may be defined as an itemization type. This data definition highlights the keys that change the evolution of the game. The data definition, function template, and sample instances for keys are defined as follows:

```
|#   A key is either:
       1. "right"
       2. "left"
       3. not "right" or "left"

     ;; Sample instances of key
     (define KEY1 ...)
     (define KEY2 ...)
     (define KEY3 ...)
```

```
;; key ... --> ...
;; Purpose: ...
(define (f-on-key a-key ...)
  (cond [(key=? a-key "right") ...]
        [(key=? a-key "left") ...]
        [else ...]))


;; Sample expressions for f-on-key
(define KEY1-VAL ...KEY1...)
(define KEY2-VAL ...KEY2...)
(define KEY3-VAL ...KEY3...)


;; Tests using sample computations for f-on-key
(check-expect (f-on-key KEY1 ...) KEY1-VAL)
(check-expect (f-on-key KEY2 ...) KEY2-VAL)
(check-expect (f-on-key KEY3 ...) KEY3-VAL)
    ...


;; Tests using sample values for f-on-key
(check-expect (f-on-key ...) ...)
    ...                                          |#


;; Sample instances of key
(define KEY1 "right")
(define KEY2 "left")
(define KEY3 "m")
```

Shorthand notation for the third key variety is used. The template suggests three sample instances because there are three key varieties. In the body of f-on-key there is a cond-expression to distinguish among the key varieties. As expected, the tests using sample computations use the key sample instances and the values of the sample expressions. The tests using sample values, on the other hand, do not used defined values as expected.

---

* **Ex. 74 —** Develop function templates for ci, image-x, image-y, pixel-x, pixel-y, and scene.

After completing steps 1 and 2 of the design recipe, we focus on the run template specialization to complete step 3. The player moves the rocket using the left and right arrows keys. This means that an on-key clause is also needed to process key events. The specialization is as follows:

```
; string → world
; Purpose: To run the game
(define (run a-name)
  (big-bang INIT-WORLD
            [on-draw draw-world]
            [name a-name]
            [on-key process-key]))
```

This states that the handler to render the game's scene is draw-world and that the
handler to process key events is process-key.

Let us start by designing draw-world. To draw the world a rocket needs to be
drawn in the empty scene. The steps of the design recipe result in the following
specialization of the template for functions on a world:

```
;; world → scene
;; Purpose: To draw the world in E-SCENE
(define (draw-world a-world)
  (draw-rocket a-world E-SCENE))

;; Sample expressions for draw-world
(define WORLD-SCN1 (draw-rocket INIT-WORLD   E-SCENE))
(define WORLD-SCN2 (draw-rocket INIT-WORDLD2 E-SCENE))

;; Tests using sample computations for draw-world
(check-expect (draw-world INIT-WORLD)  WORLD-SCN1)
(check-expect (draw-world INIT-WORLD2) WORLD-SCN2)

;; Tests using sample computations for draw-world
```

```
(check-expect (draw-world 0)                           )
(check-expect (draw-world (sub1 MAX-CHARS-HORIZONTAL))
```

```
                                                       )
```

The sample expressions maintain the separation of concerns by calling a rocket-processing function to create the world's scene. The only difference in the sample expressions is the value of a world. Therefore, draw-world indeed only needs one parameter. The requirement imposed by the universe API is met. The body of draw-world uses the variable for the single difference instead of using a literal value like the sample expressions. Observe that the tests using sample computations use extrema values for the rocket data type. The design of draw-world awaits the running of the tests.

The design of the auxiliary function draw-rocket is done by specializing the template for functions on a rocket. This function draws the rocket's ci in the given scene using the given rocket as the image-x. Recall that we have already developed the function draw-ci (see Chap. 6). The specialization of the template for functions on a rocket yields:

```
;; rocket scene → scene
;; Purpose: To draw the rocket in the given scene
(define (draw-rocket a-rocket a-scene)
  (draw-ci ROCKET-IMG a-rocket ROCKET-Y a-scene))

;; Sample expressions for draw-rocket

(define RSCN3  (draw-ci ROCKET-IMG 3 ROCKET-Y E-SCENE))
(define RSCN12 (draw-ci ROCKET-IMG 12 ROCKET-Y E-SCENE2))

;; Tests using sample computations for draw-rocket
(check-expect (draw-rocket 3  E-SCENE) RSCN3)
(check-expect (draw-rocket 12 E-SCENE2) RSCN12)

;; Tests using sample values for draw-rocket
(check-expect (draw-rocket 0 E-SCENE)
```

```
)
(check-expect (draw-rocket (sub1 MAX-CHARS-HORIZONTAL)
                           E-SCENE)
```

```
)
```

The sample expressions use `draw-ci` to place the rocket's ci at image coordinates
(3, ROCKET-Y) and (12, ROCKET-Y) in, respectively, E-SCENE and E-SCENE2.
The two differences among the sample expressions are abstracted and become the
parameters to `draw-rocket`. The tests using sample values, once again, test rocket
extrema values. There are no new auxiliary functions to design. Therefore, this
concludes the design of `draw-world` and its auxiliary functions.

The design of `process-key` is done by specializing the `f-on-key` template. The
`universe` API requires that the inputs be a world and a key. If the given key is
`"right"` or `"left"`, then the next world is created by moving the rocket. Otherwise,
the next world is the given world. The specialization of the template yields:

```
;; world key → world
;; Purpose: Process a key event to return next world
(define (process-key a-world a-key)
  (cond [(key=? a-key "right") (move-rckt-right a-world)]
        [(key=? a-key "left")  (move-rckt-left a-world)]
        [else a-world]))

;; Sample expressions for process-key
(define KEY-RVAL (move-rckt-right INIT-WORLD))
(define KEY-LVAL (move-rckt-left INIT-WORLD))
(define KEY-OVAL INIT-WORLD2)

;; Tests using sample computations for process-key
(check-expect (process-key INIT-WORLD  "right") KEY-RVAL)
(check-expect (process-key INIT-WORLD  "left")  KEY-LVAL)
(check-expect (process-key INIT-WORLD2 "m")     KEY-OVAL)

;; Tests using sample values for process-key
(check-expect (process-key (sub1 MAX-CHARS-HORIZONTAL) "right")
              (sub1 MAX-CHARS-HORIZONTAL))
(check-expect (process-key 0 "left")  0)
(check-expect (process-key 0 "o") 0)
(check-expect (process-key 11 ";") 11)
```

Observe that the need for two auxiliary functions is revealed: one to move the rocket
right and one to move the rocket left. Moving a rocket is done in a separate function
because it is a different data type. The sample expressions use the appropriate rocket-
moving function to compute the next world. The third sample expression captures
the idea that a rocket function is not called when the given key is not `"right"` or
`"left"` (like `"m"` in the third test using a sample computation). The first two tests
using sample values are written with extrema values to illustrate that the rocket does
not go off the scene. The last to tests are added for thoroughness.

The design of `move-rckt-right` requires clearly defining how to move a rocket
right. At a first glance, it may appear that adding 1 to the rocket suffices. Ask yourself,
however, can the rocket always be moved to the right. After designing `process-key`,

it is not difficult to see that when the rocket is MAX-CHARS-HORIZONTAL − 1 it cannot move to the right. Adding 1 to MAX-CHARS-HORIZONTAL − 1 results in an integer that is not a rocket. This means that a decision must be made to add or not to add 1 to the given rocket. With this insight, the f-on-rocket template is specialized as follows:

```
;; rocket → rocket
;; Purpose: Move the given rocket right
(define (move-rckt-right a-rocket)
  (if (< a-rocket (sub1 MAX-CHARS-HORIZONTAL))
      (add1 a-rocket)
      a-rocket]))

;; Sample expressions for move-rckt-right
(define ROCKET-VAL3 (add1 3))
(define ROCKET-VALMAX (sub1 MAX-CHARS-HORIZONTAL))

;; Tests using sample computations for move-rckt-right
(check-expect (move-rckt-right 3) ROCKET-VAL3)
(check-expect (move-rckt-right (sub1 MAX-CHARS-HORIZONTAL))
              ROCKET-VALMAX)

;; Tests using sample values for move-rckt-right
(check-expect (move-rckt-right 0) 1)
(check-expect (move-rckt-right 15) 16)
```

The sample expressions illustrate how rockets that may and may not move to the right are computed. In the body of move-rckt-right a new rocket is created by adding 1 only when the given rocket is not at the right edge of the scene. The tests using sample values include an untested extrema value, 0, for the rocket type and add an extra test for thoroughness.

A similar problem analysis leads to concluding that a conditional is needed to decide when a rocket may be moved to the left. In this case, only when the rocket is greater than or equal to 0. The template specialization results in:

```
;; rocket → rocket
;; Purpose: Move the given rocket left
(define (move-rckt-left a-rocket)
  (if (> a-rocket 0)
      (sub1 a-rocket)
      a-rocket))

;; Sample expressions for move-rckt-left
(define ROCKET-VAL7 (sub1 7))
(define ROCKET-VAL0 0)
```

```
;; Tests using sample computations for move-rckt-left
(check-expect (move-rckt-left 7) ROCKET-VAL7)
(check-expect (move-rckt-left 0) 0)

;; Tests using sample values for move-rckt-left
(check-expect (move-rckt-left (sub1 MAX-CHARS-HORIZONTAL))
              (- MAX-CHARS-HORIZONTAL 2))
(check-expect (move-rckt-left 14) 13)
```

Once again, observe that the tests using sample values include an untested extrema value, (sub1 MAX-CHARS-HORIZONTAL), for the rocket type and add an extra test for thoroughness.

The final step of the design recipe is to run all the tests. Make sure that you do not have any syntax errors and that all tests pass. Run the game and try moving the rocket left and right.

** **Ex. 75** — Redesign Aliens Attack version I using the following data definition for a rocket:

> A rocket is an image-x such that it is either:
> 1. 0
> 2. (sub1 MAX-CHARS-HORIZONTAL)
> 3. (0..(sub1 MAX-CHARS-HORIZONTAL))

** **Ex. 76** — Write an interactive simulation of a rocket flying down a scene that stops when it reaches the bottom of the scene. If the user presses "u" the rocket's image points up. If the user presses "d" the rocket's image points down.

*** **Ex. 77** — Design an interactive traffic light simulation such that if the player presses:

1."r" the traffic light goes to flashing red.
2."y" the traffic light goes to flashing yellow.
3."n" the traffic light goes to normal operation.

---

37 What Have We Learned in This Chapter?

The important lessons of Chap. 6 are summarized as follows:

- Video game and interactive animation programs require functions to process computer events.
- The universe teachpack provides an API to program video games and interactive animations.
- Programming with APIs is standard practice in Computer Science.

- The universe's big-bang expression is used to run a video game and allows a programmer to provide the world's initial value and the handlers needed to advance the game's or animation's evolution.
- Predicates for data types with varieties sometimes may be simplified by using a Boolean expression instead of a conditional expression.
- The video game design recipe includes steps to:

  - Develop data definitions and sample instances for every element that varies as the game evolves.
  - Develop a function template for every data definition.
  - Develop a run function.

- Separation of concerns leads to functions that solve a problem for a single data type and simplifies the process of iterative refinement.
- Developing video games is intellectually stimulating and exciting.

Part II
Compound Data of Finite Size

Chapter 7
Structures

As we have seen, one of the important steps in problem solving is choosing a representation for the data that exists in the real or in an imaginary world. In Chap. 6, for example, a rocket is represented as an image-x value. This is an example of what is called *data of finite size*. A single value is used to represent the single characteristic that may change about the rocket as the game evolves.

Now consider the Cartesian plane and the integer-based points displayed in Fig. 58. An integer-based point on the Cartesian plain has two characteristics: an integer x coordinate and an integer y coordinate. This is an example of *compound data* of finite size. Compound data of finite size has a constant number of characteristics that may vary from one instance of the data to another. For example, (0,2) and (-3,-1) vary in both the x and y coordinates. The data is finite because a point is always represented with 2 integer values (as opposed to an arbitrary number of values).

A natural question to ask is how are functions that process compound data of finite size designed? Let us consider the problem of determining if an integer-based point is in the first quadrant following the steps of the design recipe. The first step of the design recipe requires that a representation be chosen for a point. You may very well be thinking that you need two integers. Let us follow this instinct, but there is already something that feels off. Why are we talking about two integers when the problem is about integer-based points? We need to process a point but have no data definition for a point. Instead, this design suggests thinking about x and y coordinates as two separate values instead of a single value. Nonetheless, let us proceed. To determine if a point is in the first quadrant, both the x and y coordinates must be greater than 0. Based on this problem analysis, we can specialize the basic function template (from Fig. 29) as follows:

```
;; integer integer → Boolean
;; Purpose: To determine if the given coordinates for a
;;          point is in Q1
(define (in-Q1? x y)
  (and (> x 0) (> y 0)))
```

M. T. Morazán, *Animated Problem Solving*, Texts in Computer Science,
https://doi.org/10.1007/978-3-030-85091-3_7

Fig. 58 The Cartesian plane with several points

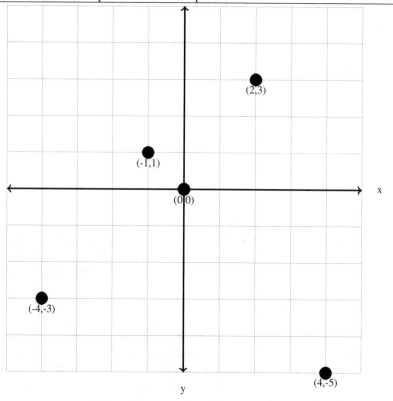

```
;; Sample expression definitions for in-Q1?
(define CONSTANT-1 (and (> 3 0) (> 11 0)))
(define CONSTANT-2 (and (> -5 0) (> 23 0)))

;; Tests using sample computations for in-Q1?
(check-expect (in-Q1? 3 11)  CONSTANT-1)
(check-expect (in-Q1? -5 23) CONSTANT-2)

;; Tests using sample values for in-Q1?
(check-expect (in-Q1? -3 -7) #false)
(check-expect (in-Q1? 83 -4) #false)
```

All the tests pass and this gives you guarded confidence that the program works. However, think carefully about the above solution. There are certain incongruities. The purpose statement for in-Q1? mentions a point, but in the signature there is no point in the input. Instead, there are two integers. The sample expressions have two integers, instead of a point, as differences. The body of in-Q1? processes two integers and not a single point. You may say that it is understood that the two integers represent a point. Perhaps, that is clear to you now. Will it be clear to other people who may read your code? How about to yourself 6 months from now? The truth is that for a two-dimensional point these incongruities may be relatively easy to overcome. What if you were solving a problem using Einstein's Mathematics in which every point has 4 dimensions or in string theory where a point has 10 dimensions? Should every string theory point-processing function have 10 inputs? That certainly begins to sound problematic.

The problem with the above solution is that it does not exhibit separation of concerns. We need a function that takes as input a two-dimensional integer point. We also need a function to process an integer x coordinate and another function to process an integer y coordinate. Our immediate need, therefore, is a mechanism to create a point value out of two coordinates. With such a mechanism, we may rewrite in-Q1? as something similar to

```
;; 2D-ipoint → Boolean
;; Purpose: To determine if the given 2D-ipoint is in Q1
(define (in-Q1? a-2dipoint)
  (and (x-in-Q1? (x-of a-2dipoint))
       (y-in-Q1? (y-of a-2dipoint))))
```

Most will argue that the above function, if it were possible to write, is easier to understand than the previous version. It is likely to be as clear 6 months from now as it is today. To write such nifty functions, it is necessary to learn more about BSL.

38 The posn Structure

In BSL, compound data of finite size may be represented as a single piece of data using a *structure*. A structure combines a fixed number of values into a single piece of data. In addition, for every structure there is a *constructor* and there is a *selector* for each characteristic. A constructor is a function to build instances of the compound data. A selector retrieves the value of a characteristic.

For instance, BSL provides the posn structure. A posn is intended to represent a position in a Cartesian plane. In other words, it is intended to represent what is called a 2D-point (not to be confused with a 2D-ipoint). A posn has two characteristics (or fields) called x and y. The constructor for a posn is make-posn. It requires two inputs: one for x and one for y. There are two selector functions: posn-x to retrieve the value of x and posn-y to retrieve the value of y. Run the following example in DrRacket:

```
(define A-POSN  (make-posn  3.2 9))
(define A-POSN2 (make-posn -8 9))

(check-expect (posn-x A-POSN)   3.2)
(check-expect (posn-x A-POSN2) -8)
```

```
(check-expect (posn-y A-POSN)     9)
(check-expect (posn-y A-POSN2)    9)
(check-expect (= (posn-x A-POSN) (posn-x A-POSN2)) #false)
(check-expect (= (posn-y A-POSN) (posn-y A-POSN2)) #true)
```

This code defines two posn constants that represent, respectively, the points (3.2, 9) and (-8, 9). The first two tests illustrate that posn-x correctly retrieves a posn's x value. Tests 3 and 4 illustrate that posn-y correctly retrieves a posn's y value. The last two tests illustrate that the x values of the two posns are different and that the y values of the two posns are the same. After this example, it becomes easy to understand that two (mathematical) laws govern posns:

```
(posn-x (make-posn  x y)) = x
(posn-y (make-posn  x y)) = y
```

Understanding the above laws, however, is not enough to properly use posns to represent data from the real or an imaginary world. Consider, for example, the following program:

```
(define A-POSN  (make-posn  "Animating" "Programs"))

(check-expect (posn-x A-POSN)    "Animating")
(check-expect (posn-y A-POSN)    "Programs")
(check-expect (string=? (string-append  (posn-x A-POSN)
                                         (posn-y A-POSN))
                    "Animating Programs")
        #true)
```

The tests pass after running the program. What happened? A-POSN certainly does not represent a 2D-point. The explanation is that the constructor make-posn creates a structure that is able to store two values: one called x and another called y. The constructor, however, does not enforce any type rules for x and y. That is, the rules above state that there is an x value and a y value. It does not state anything about the data types of x and y. Therefore, there is nothing from preventing a programmer to use make-posn as done in the above program. The next pressing question, of course, is how do we make clear what a posn represents?

The answer is that to process compound data of fixed size, a data definition is needed. In turn, this means that we need to develop a function template and sample instances of the data defined. An interesting consequence is that a structure suggests how the data ought to be processed. Let us reconsider the representation of a 2D-point. The data definitions and function templates are displayed in Fig. 59. An xcoord and a ycoord are defined as real numbers. Each needs a function template. The most interesting part is the data definition for a 2D-point. A 2D-point is defined as a posn structure whose x is an xcoord and whose y is a ycoord. This suggest that solving a problem about a 2D-point is likely to require solving a problem about an xcoord, a ycoord, or both. Observe that the body of f-on-2D-point captures this observation and exhibits separation of concerns by having references

Fig. 59 The data definitions and function templates for the 2D-point program

```
#|;; An x-coordinate (xcoord) is a real number
 ;; A y-coordinate (ycoord) is a real number
 ;; A 2D-point is a structure (make-posn xcoord ycoord)

(define XCOORD1   ...) ...
(define YCOORD1   ...) ...
(define 2D-POINT1 ...) ...

;; xcoord ... → ...      Purpose: ...
(define (f-on-xcoord an-xcoord ...) ... an-xcoord...)
;; Sample expressions for f-on-xcoord
(define XCOORD1-VAL ...) ...
;; Tests using sample computations for f-on-xcoord
(check-expect (f-on-xcoord XCOORD1 ...) XCOORD1-VAL) ...
;; Tests using sample values for f-on-xcoord
(check-expect (f-on-xcoord ...) ...) ...

;; ycoord ... → ...      Purpose: ...
(define (f-on-ycoord a-ycoord ...) ... a-ycoord...)
;; Sample expressions for f-on-ycoord
(define YCOORD1-VAL ...) ...
;; Tests using sample computations for f-on-ycoord
(check-expect  (f-on-ycoord YCORD1 ...) YCOORD1-VAL) ...
;; Tests using sample values for f-on-ycoord
(check-expect (f-on-ycoord ...) ...) ...

;; 2D-point ... → ...      Purpose: ...
(define (f-on-2D-point a-2Dpoint ...)
 (f-on-xcoord (posn-x a-2Dpoint))...(f-on-ycoord (posn-y a-2Dpoint))...)
;; Sample expressions for f-on-2D-point
(define 2D-POINT1-VAL ...)    ...
;; Tests using sample computations for f-on-2D-point
(check-expect (f-on-2D-point 2D-POINT1 ...) 2D-POINT1-VAL) ...
;; Tests using sample values for f-on-2D-2D-point
(check-expect (f-on-2D-point ...) ...)    ...                |#
```

to functions that process an xcoord and a ycoord. Based on this data analysis, the
2D-point program above may be refined to

```
;; Sample instances of xcoord
(define X1 3.2)
(define X2 -8)

;; Sample instances of ycoord
(define Y1 9)
(define Y2 9)

;; Sample instances of 2D-point
(define A-POSN  (make-posn X1 Y1))
(define A-POSN2 (make-posn X2 Y2))
```

```
(check-expect (posn-x A-POSN)  X1)
(check-expect (posn-x A-POSN2) X2)
(check-expect (posn-y A-POSN)  Y1)
(check-expect (posn-y A-POSN2) Y2)
(check-expect (= (posn-x A-POSN) (posn-x A-POSN2)) #false)
(check-expect (= (posn-y A-POSN) (posn-y A-POSN2)) #true)
```

The results of data analysis may be reused multiple times. For example, design a program to determine if a 2D-point is on the graph of $f(x) = x^3$. Problem analysis tells us that (x, y) is on the graph of $f(x) = x^3$ if $y = x^3$. Observe that determining the answer requires processing x, but there is no need to process y. This means that a function to process a ycoord is not needed. The initial template specialization is

```
(define X1 3)
(define X2 -2.5)

(define Y1 27)
(define Y2 39)

(define 2D-POINT1 (make-posn X1 Y1))
(define 2D-POINT2 (make-posn X2 Y2))

;; 2D-point ... → Boolean
;; Purpose: Determine if the given 2D-point is on the
;;          graph of f(x) = x³
(define (on-x^3? a-2Dpoint)
   ...(f-on-xcoord (posn-x a-2Dpoint))...)

;; Sample expressions for on-x^3?
(define 2D-POINT1-VAL (= (cube (posn-x 2D-POINT1))
                         (posn-y 2D-POINT1)))
(define 2D-POINT2-VAL (= (cube (posn-x 2D-POINT2))
                         (posn-y 2D-POINT2)))

;; Tests using sample computations for on-x^3?
(check-expect (on-x^3? 2D-POINT1) 2D-POINT-VAL1)
(check-expect (on-x^3? 2D-POINT2) 2D-POINT-VAL2)

;; Tests using sample values for on-x^3?
(check-expect (on-x^3? ...) ...)
```

The code first includes sample instances of all the defined data types. The sample instances chosen are a 2D-point that is on the graph of $f(x) = x^3$ and a 2D-point that is not on the graph of $f(x) = x^3$. Observe that the only difference among the sample expressions is the 2D-point processed. Therefore, on-x^3 only needs one parameter.

Tests using sample values are added for testing thoroughly. The complete template specialization is

```
(define X1 3)
(define X2 -2.5)

(define Y1 27)
(define Y2 39)

(define 2D-POINT1 (make-posn X1 Y1))
(define 2D-POINT2 (make-posn X2 Y2))

;; 2D-point → Boolean
;; Purpose: Determine if the given 2D-point is on the
;;            graph of f(x) = x^3 3
(define (on-x^3? a-2Dpoint)
  (= (cube (posn-x a2D-point)) (posn-y a-2Dpoint)))

;; Sample expressions for on-x^3?
(define 2D-POINT1-VAL (= (cube (posn-x 2D-POINT1))
                         (posn-y 2D-POINT1)))
(define 2D-POINT2-VAL (= (cube (posn-x 2D-POINT2))
                         (posn-y 2D-POINT1)))

;; Tests using sample computations for on-x^3?
(check-expect (on-x^3? 2D-POINT1) 2D-POINT1-VAL)
(check-expect (on-x^3? 2D-POINT2) 2D-POINT2-VAL)

;; Tests using sample values for on-x^3?
(check-expect (on-x^3? (make-posn 0 0)) #true)
(check-expect (on-x^3? (make-posn -3.3 -35.937)) #true)
(check-expect (on-x^3? (make-posn 5 25)) #false)
```

The function cube is not part of BSL and must be designed. This is done by specializing the f-on-xcoord template. The answer is computed by raising the given xcoord to the third power. The result of specializing the template is

```
;; xcoord → xcoord
;; Purpose: To cube the given xcoord
(define (cube an-xcoord) (expt an-xcoord 3))

;; Sample expressions for f-on-xcoord
(define XCOORD-VAL1 (expt -2 3))
(define XCOORD-VAL2 (expt 8 3))
(define XCOORD-VAL3 (expt 3 3))
```

Fig. 60 The refined general design recipe for functions

Data Design:

1. Outline data representation and create data definitions.
2. Create sample instances for each data definition.
3. Create a function template for each data definition.

For a needed function:
4. Outline the computation.
5. Define constants for the value of sample expressions.
6. Identify and name the differences among the sample expressions.
7. Write the function's signature and purpose.
8. Write the function's header.
9. Write tests.
10. Write the function's body.
11. Run the tests and, if necessary, redesign.

```
;; Tests using sample computations for f-on-xcoord
(check-expect (cube -2)   XCOORD-VAL1)
(check-expect (cube  8)   XCOORD-VAL2)
(check-expect (cube  X1) XCOORD-VAL3)


;; Tests using sample values for f-on-xcoord
(check-expect (cube 0) 0)
(check-within (cube X2) -15.62 0.01)
```

Observe that there is no need to define new instances of xcoords. Sample instances have already been defined and may be freely used. Running the program reveals that all the tests pass. This completes the design of on-x^3?.

The steps taken suggest that the general design recipe for functions needs to be refined. There are two parts: data design and function design. This division of labor captures the important role that data representation plays in problem solving and in programming. Figure 60 displays the refined general design recipe for functions. The first three steps are part of data design and are performed once. These steps include picking a data representation and creating data definitions, creating sample instances of the data, and creating function templates. Steps 4–11 are the steps followed for each function that needs to be written. These steps are fulfilled by specializing a function template.

39 Going Beyond the Design Recipe

Before proceeding with another example, it is worth to take a pause to analyze the result obtained for on-x^3. It is natural to ask if the solution may be simplified. This step is not necessary but may be performed to aid code readability and/or to reduce the amount of code.

The design steps for on-x³ revealed the need for and the subsequent design of cube. The function cube, however, is rather simple and easy to understand. In fact, defining cube may add little clarity to the program—this, of course, is a matter of opinion. If you feel that function does not add clarity to a program, you may want to consider inlining it. In this case, inlining is straightforward and results in the following refined version of the program:

```
(define X1 3)
(define X2 -2.5)

(define Y1 27)
(define Y2 39)

(define 2D-POINT1 (make-posn X1 Y1))
(define 2D-POINT2 (make-posn X2 Y2))

;; 2D-point → Boolean
;; Purpose: Determine if the given point is on the graph
;;            of f(x) = x^3
(define (on-x^3? a-2Dpoint)
  (= (expt (posn-x a-2Dpoint) 3) (posn-y a-2Dpoint)))

;; Sample expressions for on-x^3?
(define 2D-POINT1-VAL (= (expt (posn-x 2D-POINT1) 3)
                         (posn-y 2D-POINT1)))
(define 2D-POINT2-VAL (= (expt (posn-x 2D-POINT2) 3)
                         (posn-y 2D-POINT1)))

;; Tests using sample computations for on-x^3?
(check-expect (on-x^3? 2D-POINT1) 2D-POINT1-VAL)
(check-expect (on-x^3? 2D-POINT2) 2D-POINT2-VAL)

;; Tests using sample values for on-x^3?
(check-expect (on-x^3? (make-posn 0 0)) #true)
(check-expect (on-x^3? (make-posn -3.3 -35.937)) #true)
(check-expect (on-x^3? (make-posn 5 25)) #false)
```

Observe that all calls to cube in on-x³? and its tests are eliminated, and therefore, the need for defining cube is also eliminated. The program is certainly shorter. Is this refined code clearer? It is certainly not significantly more difficult to understand suggesting that it was fine to perform inlining. You should not, however, expect that inlining code always results in shorter code and in just as clear code. On the contrary, more often than not inlining results in *code explosion*. Code explosion means that the length of the code becomes significantly larger. Instead of using cube once, imagine it was used 100 times. Inlining in this scenario means that similar code is repeated 100 times in the program. Remember that in Chap. 3, this is precisely the situation we wished to avoid. It is better to abstract over similar expressions to create a function than to repeatedly have similar expressions throughout the code. Beyond eliminating repetitions, abstraction over similar expressions also makes revisions easier. Imagine that a better way to compute x^3 is discovered. If cube is inlined 100 times, then the revision to use the better way to compute x^3 requires 100 edits. On the other hand, if cube is not inlined, then only one edit is required. A good problem solver foresees such possibilities and does not forsake separation of concerns in favor of having to design fewer functions.

When should inlining be considered? If a function is only used once and its design does not require any type of specialized knowledge, then you may consider inlining. Keep in mind, however, that inlining is usually left to a compiler. As problem solvers, the rule of thumb is to avoid inlining.

40 Revisiting in-Q1?

Developing the predicate to determine if an integer-based point is in the first quadrant presents an excellent opportunity to put the revised design recipe in action. The first three steps of the design recipe may be satisfied as displayed in Fig. 61. In this program, both an ix and an iy are integers. Do not confuse these data definitions with those developed for the program to determine if a 2D-point is on the graph of f(x) = x^3. A 2D-ipoint is a posn that contains an ix and an iy. The function templates to process an ix and an iy outline the expected structure for the function definition and the tests. This structure is minimal because integers are not decomposable into different pieces. The function template for 2D-ipoint, on the other hand, provides more structure for problem solving because a 2D-ipoint is decomposable into different pieces. To solve a problem about a 2D-ipoint, we can process an ix, an iy, or both. Finally, Step 3 suggests the development of one or more sample instances for each data definition. The minimum for each is one because none of the data definitions has variety. In this case, two sample instances are defined for each data type to exemplify a 2D-ipoint that is in the first quadrant and a 2D-ipoint that is not in the first quadrant.

Function development starts with the specialization of the f-on-2D-ipoint template for in-Q1?. For a given 2D-ipoint to be in the first quadrant, both its ix and iy must be in the first quadrant interval for each dimension. Sample expressions and tests using sample computations may be defined using the two sample instances of 2D-ipoint (one in the first quadrant and one in the second quadrant). The tests using sample values may test 2D-ipoints in quadrants three and four and an additional point in quadrant one. These observations allow for the following template specialization:

```
;; 2D-ipoint → Boolean
;; Purpose: To determine if the given 2D-ipoint is in the first
;;          quadrant
```

Fig. 61 The first three steps of the design recipe defining 2D-ipoint

```
#| ;; An x-coordinate (ix) and a y-coordinate (iy) are integers
   ;; A 2D-ipoint is a structure (make-posn ix iy).
;; Sample instances of ix: (define IX1 ...) ...
;; Sample instances of iy: (define IY1 ...)
;; Sample instances of 2D-ipoint: (define 2D-IPOINT1 (make-posn ... ...))...
;; ix ... → ...       Purpose: ...
(define (f-on-ix an-ix ...) ... an-ix...)
;; Sample expressions for f-on-ix
(define IX-VAL ...)
;; Tests using sample computations for f-on-ix
(check-expect (f-on-ix ...) IX-VAL)   ...
;; Tests using sample values for f-on-ix
(check-expect (f-on-ix ...) ...)     ...
;; iy ... → ...       Purpose: ...
(define (f-on-iy a-iy ...) ... a-iy...)
;; Sample expressions for f-on-iy
(define IY-VAL ...)    ...
;; Tests using sample computations for f-on-iy
(check-expect (f-on-iy ...) IY-VAL)   ...
;; Tests using sample values for f-on-iy
(check-expect (f-on-iy ...) ...)     ...
;; 2D-ipoint ... → ...       Purpose: ...
(define (f-on-2D-ipoint a-2Dipoint ...)
  ...(f-on-ix (posn-x a-2Dipoint))...(f-on-iy (posn-y a-2Dipoint))...)
;; Sample expressions for f-on-2D-ipoint
(define 2D-IPOINT-VAL ...)   ...
;; Tests using sample computations for f-on-2D-ipoint
(check-expect (f-on-2D-ipoint ...) 2D-IPOINT-VAL)   ...
;; Tests using sample values for f-on-2D-ipoint
(check-expect (f-on-2D-ipoint ...) ...) ...                    |#
;; Sample instances of ix
(define IX1 3)      (define IX2 -5)
;; Sample instances of iy
(define IY1 11)      (define IY2 23)
;; Sample instances of 2D-ipoint
(define 2D-IPOINT1 (make-posn IX1 IY1))
(define 2D-IPOINT2 (make-posn IX2 IY2))
```

```
(define (in-Q1? a-2Dipoint)
  (and (ix-in-Q1? (posn-x a-2Dipoint))
       (iy-in-Q1? (posn-y a-2Dipoint))))


;; Sample expressions for in-Q1?
(define 2D-IPOINT1-VAL (and (ix-in-Q1? (posn-x 2D-IPOINT1))
                            (iy-in-Q1? (posn-y 2D-IPOINT1))))


(define 2D-IPOINT2-VAL (and (ix-in-Q1? (posn-x 2D-IPOINT2))
                            (iy-in-Q1? (posn-y 2D-IPOINT2))))
```

```
;; Tests using sample computations for in-Q1?
(check-expect (in-Q1? 2D-IPOINT1) 2D-IPOINT1-VAL)
(check-expect (in-Q1? 2D-IPOINT2) 2D-IPOINT2-VAL)


;; Tests using sample values for in-Q1?
(check-expect (in-Q1? (make-posn -3 -7))   #false)
(check-expect (in-Q1? (make-posn 83 -4))   #false)
(check-expect (in-Q1? (make-posn 100 864)) #true)
```

Observe that the steps of the design recipe, in essence, yield the function at the end of the introduction to this chapter. Any reader of this function, including yourself 6 months from now, will be able to understand the solution to the problem.

The specialization of the template for functions on an ix and on an iy follows the same pattern seen in the previous chapters. To be in the first quadrant interval, an ix must be greater than 0. The same is true for an iy. The specialization process yields

```
;; ix → Boolean
;; Purpose: To determine if the given ix is in the Q1 range
(define (ix-in-Q1? an-ix)
  (> an-ix 0))


;; Sample expressions for ix-in-Q1?
(define IX1-VAL (> IX1 0))
(define IX2-VAL (> IX2 0))


;; Tests using sample computations for ix-in-Q1?
(check-expect (ix-in-Q1? IX1) IX1-VAL)
(check-expect (ix-in-Q1? IX2) IX2-VAL)


;; Tests using sample values for ix-in-Q1?
(check-expect (ix-in-Q1? 0) #false)
(check-expect (ix-in-Q1? 19380) #true)


;; iy → Boolean
;; Purpose: To determine if the given iy is in the Q1 range
(define (iy-in-Q1? an-iy)
  (> an-iy 0))


;; Sample expressions for iy-in-Q1?
(define IY1-VAL (> IY1 0))
(define IY2-VAL (> IY2 0))


;; Tests using sample computations for iy-in-Q1?
(check-expect (iy-in-Q1? IY1) IY1-VAL)
(check-expect (iy-in-Q1? IY2) IY2-VAL)
```

```
;; Tests using sample values for iy-in-Q1?
(check-expect (iy-in-Q1? 0) #false)
(check-expect (iy-in-Q1? 19380) #true)
```

The only new element here is that we exploit the definition of sample instances to write sample expressions and tests using sample computations.

After running the program, all the tests pass. Observe, however, that (iy-in-Q1? (posn-y A-2D-IPOINT2)) in the definition of 2D-IPOINT-VAL2 is highlighted in black. Such highlighting usually means that more tests are needed to reach the untested code. In this case, it is impossible for the program to evaluate the highlighted code. Remember how and works in BSL. The expressions after the first expression that evaluates to #false are not evaluated. The x of A-2D-IPOINT2 is -5. Thus, the value of its y is never tested.

---

* **Ex. 78** — Design and implement predicates to

1. Determine if a 2D-ipoint is in the second quadrant.
2. Determine if a 2D-ipoint is in the third quadrant.
3. Determine if a 2D-ipoint is in the fourth quadrant.

* **Ex. 79** — Design and implement predicates to

1. Determine if a 2D-ipoint is on the x-axis.
2. Determine if a 2D-ipoint is on the y-axis.

* **Ex. 80** — Design and implement a function to determine if a 2D-point is on the graph of f(x) = $2x^3$ - $4x^2$ + 8x - 1.

** **Ex. 81** — Using 2D-points,

- Design and implement a function to compute the distance between two points.
- Design and implement a function to compute the distance between a 2D-point and the origin.

** **Ex. 82** — Design and implement a function to translate a 2D-point. The translation is performed by creating a new 2D-point that moves a given 2D-point by some given amount on the x-axis and by some given amount on the y-axis. For example, (make-posn -2 10) is the result of translating (make-posn 5 -2) by moving it by -7 on the x-axis and by 12 on the y-axis.

** **Ex. 83** — Design and implement a function to compute the length of a person's full name. A full name consists of a first name and a last name.

---

41 What Have We Learned in This Chapter?

The important lessons of Chap. 7 are summarized as follows:

- Compound data of finite size has a constant number of characteristics that may vary from one instance of the data to another.
- Compound data of finite size is represented using structures.
- A structure combines a fixed number of values into a single piece of data.
- Every structure has a constructor and a selector for each characteristic.
- BSL provides the posn structure that has two fields: x and y.
- Processing structures requires a data definition that specifies the types of each characteristic.
- Every data definition requires the development of a function template and sample instances.
- The same structure may be used to represent different types of data.
- The results of the design recipe's data design steps may be used to implement more than one function.
- Inlining may result in code explosion caused by repetitions in the code.
- A good problem solver does not forsake separation of concerns in favor of having to design fewer functions.

Chapter 8
Defining Structures

It turns out that rarely is the input to a function, for example, a single string or number. It is far more common for there to be several pieces of related data that need to be processed. A 2D-point, for instance, may be represented using a `posn` structure. A `posn` structure works well, because a 2D-point only has two varying characteristics. What needs to be done if data has more than two (but finite) varying characteristics? Clearly, a structure with two fields, like a `posn`, cannot be used to represent such data.

Consider representing a student that has a first name, a middle name, a last name, and a grade point average. How can a student be represented? What is needed is a structure that has four fields: one for each varying characteristic. You may imagine that BSL provides a structure with four fields, but it does not. There is actually a good reason for this. As you can imagine, the variety of compound data of fixed size is infinite. Everybody can imagine data with 2, 3, 4, 5, 6, or more varying characteristics. There is no way BSL can provide structures of all possible sizes. Therefore, BSL gives programmers the ability to define their own structures. In this manner, a programmer can define finite compound data of any size and provide custom names to the structure and its fields. The first step is to learn the necessary BSL syntax to define structures.

42 Defining Structures

To define structures the BSL grammar is expanded as follows:
    program ::= {expr | test | def | defs}*
        defs ::= (define-struct <structure name> (<field name>*))
A program may contain zero or more expressions, tests, definitions, and structure definitions. A structure definition starts with an opening parenthesis, followed by the keyword `define-struct`, followed by the structure's name, followed in parentheses by the name of each field. The number of fields a structure has may be zero or more, but must be a finite number.

© The Author(s), under exclusive license to Springer Nature Switzerland AG 2022   167
M. T. Morazán, *Animated Problem Solving*, Texts in Computer Science,
https://doi.org/10.1007/978-3-030-85091-3_8

A structure definition creates much more than just a structure that can store multiple values. It also creates the constructor and selector functions for the structure. The naming conventions for these functions is straightforward. The constructor is always named:

```
make-<structure name>
```

The number of arguments required by a constructor is equal to the number of fields the structure has. The selectors are always named:

```
<structure name>-<field name>
```

The input to a selector must be an instance of `<structure name>`.

We can now define a structure for a 2D-point as follows:

```
(define-struct 2Dpoint (xval yval))
```

This structure definition creates the following functions to manipulate 2D-points:

```
;; X Y → 2Dpoint
;; Purpose: To create a 2Dpoint with the given values
(define (make-2Dpoint an-X an-Y) ...)

;; 2Dpoint → X
;; Purpose: Return the xval of the given 2Dpoint
(define (2Dpoint-xval a-2Dpoint) ...)

;; 2Dpoint → Y
;; Purpose: Return the yval of the given 2Dpoint
(define (2Dpoint-yval a-2Dpoint) ...)

;; Any → Boolean
;; Purpose: To determine if the given value is a 2Dpoint
(define (2Dpoint? any-value) ...)
```

Do not worry about how these functions are implemented in BSL. There is no need to know these details. It is important, however, to understand the structure API provided by BSL. The first function is called a *constructor*. A constructor is a function that is used to create data type instances. The rest of the functions are *observers*. An observer is a function that tells us something about an instance of a data type. The last function, 2Dpoint?, is a predicate observer that distinguishes between data that is a 2Dpoint and data that is not a 2Dpoint.

Take note that the contracts for the constructor and the selectors refer to indeterminate types called X and Y. X and Y are *type variables* and represent a defined type that exists in BSL or that has been defined by a programmer. The type variables indicate that a structure is *generic*. This means that it works equally well for many different data types. BSL assumes nothing about the type of data that the structure stores. Genericity provides programmers with a great deal of flexibility, but must be used with care. For example, a programmer may think that the following are valid 2D-points:

```
(define A (make-2Dpoint 34 90))

(define B (make-2Dpoint "Hello" "World!"))

(define C (make-2Dpoint #true 'CS))
```

How does a programmer know that any of the above are correct uses of the constructor? Without a data definition it is impossible to know, because X and Y may represent any type. A data definition provides the context that defines what X and Y are expected to be. For example, we can define a 2D-point as follows:

```
A 2Dpoint is a structure (make-2Dpoint ℝ ℝ)
```

This data definition states that X is a real number and that Y is a real number. In turn, this tells us that only the definition for A above makes correct use of the 2Dpoint constructor. In essence, the data definition tells you and others that the proper use of a generic structure. In this example, a 2D-point is used properly only when it stores two real numbers.

As you well know, the second step of data analysis in the design recipe tells us that we ought to develop of function template for 2D-point. The template for 2D-point is:

```
;; Sample Instances of 2Dpoint
(define P1 (make-2Dpoint ...))

;; 2Dpoint ... → ...
;; Purpose: ...
(define (f-on-2Dpoint a-2dpoint ...)
  ...(2Dpoint-xval a-2dpoint)...(2Dpoint-yval a-2dpoint)...)

;; Sample expressions for f-on-2Dpoint
(define 2DP-VAL1 ...(2Dpoint-xval P1)...(2Dpoint-xval P1)...)
     ...

;; Tests using sample computations for f-on-2Dpoint
(check-within (f-on-2Dpoint P1 ...) 2DP-VAL1)
     ...

;; Tests using sample values for f-on-2Dpoint
(check-within (f-on-2Dpoint ...) ...)
     ...
```

Now, we can start solving problems with this representation of a 2D-point. For example, write a function to compute the distance of a 2D-point from the origin. The distance to the origin of a 2D-point may be computed using the distance formula. Given that one of the points, the origin, is always $(0, 0)$ the distance formula may be simplified as follows:

$$\text{distance}((x_1, y_1), (x_2, y_2)) = \sqrt{(x_2 - x_1)^2 + (y_2 - y_1)^2}$$

$$\text{distance}((0, 0), (x_2, y_2)) = \sqrt{(x_2 - 0)^2 + (y_2 - 0)^2}$$

$$= \sqrt{x_2^2 + y_2^2}$$

The template specialization may be started as follows:

```
;; A 2Dpoint is a structure (make-2Dpoint R R)
(define-struct 2Dpoint (xval yval))

;; Sample instances of 2Dpoint
(define P1 (make-2Dpoint 5 10))
(define P2 (make-2Dpoint 25 11))

;; 2Dpoint → R
;; Purpose: To compute the distance to the origin for the
;;          given 2Dpoint
(define (distance-to-origin a-2dpoint)
  ...(2Dpoint-xval a-2dpoint)...(2Dpoint-yval a-2dpoint)...)

;; Sample expressions for distance-to-origin
(define 2DP-VAL1 (sqrt (+ (sqr (2Dpoint-xval P1))
                          (sqr (2Dpoint-xval P1)))))
(define 2DP-VAL2 (sqrt (+ (sqr (2Dpoint-xval P2))
                          (sqr (2Dpoint-xval P2)))))

;; Tests using sample computations for distance-to-origin
(check-within (distance-to-origin P1) 2DP-VAL1 0.01)
(check-within (distance-to-origin P2) 2DP-VAL2 0.01)

;; Tests using sample values for distance-to-origin
(check-within (distance-to-origin ...) ...)
```

Observe that the sample expressions are written using the sample instances. There is a single difference among the sample expressions: the 2Dpoint. This tells us that distance-to-origin only needs a 2Dpoint as input. The tests using sample computations use the constants defined for the sample instances and the value of the sample expressions. The final refinement completes the body of distance-to-origin and the tests using sample values as follows:

```
;; A 2Dpoint is a structure (make-2Dpoint R R)
(define-struct 2Dpoint (xval yval))
```

```
;; Sample instances of 2Dpoint
(define P1 (make-2Dpoint 5 10))
(define P2 (make-2Dpoint 25 11))


;; 2Dpoint → real-number
;; Purpose: To compute the distance to the origin for the
;;          given 2Dpoint
(define (distance-to-origin a-2dpoint)
  (sqrt (+ (sqr (2Dpoint-xval a-2dpoint))
           (sqr (2Dpoint-yval a-2dpoint)))))


;; Sample expressions for distance-to-origin
(define 2DP-VAL1 (sqrt (+ (sqr (2Dpoint-xval P1))
                          (sqr (2Dpoint-xval P1)))))
(define 2DP-VAL2 (sqrt (+ (sqr (2Dpoint-xval P2))
                          (sqr (2Dpoint-xval P2)))))


;; Tests using sample computations for distance-to-origin
(check-within (distance-to-origin P1) 2DP-VAL1 0.01)
(check-within (distance-to-origin P2) 2DP-VAL2 0.01)


;; Tests using sample values for distance-to-origin
(check-within (distance-to-origin (make-2Dpoint 0 0))
              0
              0.01)
(check-within (distance-to-origin (make-2Dpoint -3 -4))
              5
              0.01)
```

The final refinement develops the body of distance-to-origin to be similar to the sample expressions. Instead of using a concrete value, it is written using the parameter that represents the difference. The tests using sample values test an extrema value (i.e., the origin) and a 2Dpoint that is different from the sample instances.

43 Computing Structures

Just like numbers, Booleans, strings, and posns, the structures a programmer defines are *first class* is BSL. First class means that they may be passed as input to functions and may be returned as a function value. In other words, functions may compute instances of a structure.

To illustrate the computation of structures consider the problem of updating a student's grade point average. A student, as suggested by the description at the

beginning of this chapter, has a first name, a middle name, a last name, and a grade
point average. This leads to the following data definitions, structure definition, and
function templates:

```
#| DATA DEFINITIONS
   A GPA is a real number in [0..4].

   ;; Sample instances for GPA
   (define GPA1 ...)
         ...


   A student is a structure
      (make-student string string string ℝ)
   that contains a first name, a middle name, a last name,
   and a grade point average.

   ;; Sample instances for student
   (define STUD1 (make-student ... ... ... ...))
         ...
|#


   (define-struct student (fn mn ln gpa))

#| FUNCTION TEMPLATES
   ;; GPA ... → ...
   ;; Purpose: ...
   (define (f-on-GPA a-gpa ...) ...)

   ;; Sample expressions for f-on-GPA
   (define GPA1-VAL ...)
         ...


   ;; Tests using sample computations for f-on-GPA
   (check-expect (f-on-GPA GPA1 ...) GPA1-VAL)
         ...

   ;; Tests using sample values for f-on-GPA
   (check-expect (f-on-student ...) ...)
         ...

   ;; student ... → ...
   ;; Purpose: ...
   (define (f-on-student a-student ...)
     ...(f-on-string (student-fn  a-student))...
     ...(f-on-string (student-mn  a-student))...
     ...(f-on-string (student-ln  a-student))...
```

```
    ...(f-on-GPA(student-gpa a-student))...)

;; Sample expressions for f-on-student
(define STUD1-VAL ...)
      ...


;; Tests using sample computations for f-on-student
(check-expect (f-on-student STUD1 ...) STUD1-VAL)
      ...

;; Tests using sample values for f-on-student
(check-expect (f-on-student (make-student ... ... ... ...))...)
      ...
|#
```

The GPA data definition and its function template are similar to those seen in previous chapters. The template contains a skeleton for sample instances, for sample expressions, for a function definition, and for tests. The student data definition is more interesting. It specifies that a student structure has four fields: 3 strings and a GPA representing, respectively, first, middle, and last names and a grade point average. The structure definition names the structure student and the four fields fn for the first name, mn for the middle name, ln for the last name, and gpa for the grade point average. The template's function definition states that there is at least one student input named a-student. The body of the template's definition contains the four expressions that may be useful in solving problems involving a student: one for each student field. Observe that the template suggests using a string function to process a string and a GPA function to process a GPA. As with all templates, the function template includes the basic skeleton for sample instances, sample expressions to abstract over to obtain a function's body, tests using sample computations and the value of sample expressions, and tests using sample values that use different instances of student.

To start, we can define several instances of GPA and of student. Given that the program is intended to change an old GPA for a new GPA, it is likely a good idea to define several old and new GPAs. In addition, it is a good idea to define a student for each old-new GPA pair. The following are sample instances of GPA and student:

```
(define OLDGPA1 3.8)
(define OLDGPA2 3.7)
(define OLDGPA3 3.58)
(define NEWGPA1 3.93)
(define NEWGPA1 3.9)
(define NEWGPA1 3.8)

(define STUD1 (make-student "Barbara" "" "Mucha" OLDGPA1))
(define STUD2 (make-student "Joan"    "Elizabeth"
                            "Feeney" OLDGPA2))
```

```
(define STUD3 (make-student "Christopher" "Michael"
                            "Dutra"       OLDGPA3))
```

Observe that the student values are defined using the old-GPA constants. These are the GPAs that are to be changed for testing purposes.

To change a student's grade point average, a student and the student's new gpa are needed. The change is done by creating a new student structure with the same names and the new grade point average. This problem analysis leads to the following initial specialization of the student function template:

```
;; student real ... → student
;; Purpose: Update the given student's gpa
(define (update-student-gpa a-student a-gpa ...)
  ...(student-fn  a-student)...
  ...(student-mn  a-student)...
  ...(student-ln  a-student)...
  ...(student-gpa a-student)...)

;; Sample expressions for update-student-gpa
(define STUD1-VAL (make-student (student-fn STUD1)
                                (student-mn STUD1)
                                (student-ln STUD1)
                                NEWGPA1))

(define STUD2-VAL (make-student (student-fn STUD2)
                                (student-mn STUD2)
                                (student-ln STUD2)
                                NEWGPA2))

(define STUD3-VAL (make-student (student-fn STUD3)
                                (student-mn STUD3)
                                (student-ln STUD3)
                                NEWGPA3))

;; Tests using sample computations for update-student-gpa
(check-expect (update-student-gpa STUD1 NEWGPA1 ...)
              STUD1-VAL)
(check-expect (update-student-gpa STUD2 NEWGPA2 ...)
              STUD2-VAL)
(check-expect (update-student-gpa STUD3 NEWGPA3 ...)
              STUD3-VAL)

;; Tests using sample values for update-student-gpa
(check-expect
  (update-student-gpa (make-student ... ... ... ...))
  ...)
```

Observe that the sample expressions create new instances of students that retain the names of an existing student structure and that use one of the new GPA sample instances. There are two differences among the sample expressions: a student and a GPA. This informs us that update-student-gpa only needs two parameters. Further observe, that neither a string nor a GPA is processed. Therefore, there is no need to call string or GPA processing functions. The tests using sample computations utilize the sample students, the sample (new) GPAs, and the values of the evaluated sample expressions. This leads to the following final specializations for update-student-gpa and the tests:

```
;; student real → student
;; Purpose: Update the given student's gpa
(define (update-student-gpa a-student a-gpa)
  (make-student (student-fn a-student)
                (student-mn a-student)
                (student-ln a-student)
                a-gpa))
```

```
;; Tests using sample computations for update-student-gpa
(check-expect (update-student-gpa STUD1 NEWGPA1)
              STUD1-VAL)
(check-expect (update-student-gpa STUD2 NEWGPA2)
              STUD2-VAL)
(check-expect (update-student-gpa STUD3 NEWGPA3)
              STUD3-VAL)
```

```
;; Tests using sample values for update-student-gpa
(check-expect (update-student-gpa
                (make-student "Sandy" "" "Marinakys" 3.1)
                3.4)
              (make-student "Sandy" "" "Marinakys" 3.4))
(check-expect (update-student-gpa
                (make-student "Lidia" "Carolina" "Vazquez" 3.5)
                3.5)
              (make-student "Lidia" "Carolina" "Vazquez" 3.5))
(check-expect (update-student-gpa
                (make-student "Luis" "Manuel" "Diaz" 3.7)
                3.6)
              (make-student "Luis" "Manuel" "Diaz" 3.6))
```

As expected, no auxiliary functions to process a string or a gpa are needed. The new tests demonstrate that update-student-gpa works for students other than those defined. The second test illustrates that a new grade point average may be the same as an existing grade point average resulting in an unchanged student structure. The third test illustrates that update-student-gpa works when a grade point average goes down.

44 Structures for the Masses

Although BSL is exceptionally well-equipped and efficient in creating and manipulating structures, it is not hard to imagine that most people are not as well-equipped. Does the president of your university know what a structure is? Does your grandmother know what a structure is? Yes, it is possible that some university presidents and some grandmothers know about structures. However, it is unlikely that the average university president or average grandmother actually knows about structures in programming. Both, of course, may benefit from structures just like people in a remote Amazon village benefit from vaccines without knowing anything about antibodies. In other words, non-programmers may benefit from the work of programmers without knowing anything about Computer Science.

This poses a challenge for problem solvers because the representation of data in a program may not be easily understood by human beings. The chosen representation commonly has to be transformed into something understood outside of the program. Consider, for example, the values of STUD1 and STUD2 from the program above. Entering these at the prompt displays:

```
(make-student "Barbara" "" "Mucha" 3.8)
```

and

```
(make-student "Joan" "Elizabeth" "Feeney" 3.7)
```

What would your university president or grandmother say if they saw that printed on their computer screen? It is certain that even if they understand structures they will be unable to understand what is being represented. The reason is simple: they are not aware of the data definition of a student.

A common technique to make computer data understandable to people in the real world is to convert it to a string. For example, we can design a function, student2string, to transform a student structure to a string. At the prompt, your university president and your grandmother may have the following interaction:

```
> (student2string STUD1)
"Barbara Mucha has a 3.8 grade point average."
> (student2string STUD2)
"Joan E. Feeney has a 3.7 grade point average."
```

We start by analyzing how the desired string is built. Observe that the returned strings have the following components:

1. The student's first name
2. The student's middle name abbreviation if any
3. The string "has a"
4. The student's grade point average
5. The string "grade point average."

The string for the student's middle name abbreviation and the string for the student's grade point average need to be computed. Once computed, all the strings may be appended to create the returned string. This analysis allows us to start specializing the template for functions on a student. We start with developing sample expressions:

```
;; Sample expressions for student2string
(define STUD1-STR (string-append
                   (student-fn  STUD1)
                   (middle-name-abbrev (student-mn  STUD1))
                   (student-ln  STUD1)
                   " has a "
                   (gpa->string (student-gpa STUD1))
                   " grade point average."))

(define STUD2-STR (string-append
                   (student-fn  STUD2)
                   (middle-name-abbrev (student-mn  STUD2))
                   (student-ln  STUD2)
                   " has a "
                   (gpa->string (student-gpa STUD2))
                   " grade point average."))
```

Observe that computing the middle name abbreviation and grade point average strings are relegated to auxiliary functions and are not the focus of a function to process a student. The only difference among the sample expressions is the student processed. Therefore, student2string only requires one parameter. This leads to the following specialization for the function definition and the tests:

```
;; student → string
;; Purpose: Transform the given student to a string
(define (student2string a-student)
  (string-append
    (student-fn  a-student)
    (middle-name-abbrev (student-mn  a-student))
    (student-ln  a-student)
    " has a "
    (gpa->string (student-gpa a-student))
    " grade point average."))

;; Tests using sample computations for student2string
(check-expect (student2string STUD1) STUD1-STR)
(check-expect (student2string STUD2) STUD2-STR)

;; Tests using sample values for student2string
(check-expect
  (student2string (make-student "Mercedes" "G." "Merayo" 3.97))
  "Mercedes G. Merayo has a 3.97 grade point average.")
```

```
(check-expect
  (student2string (make-student "Manuel" "" "Núñez" 3.89))
  "Manuel Núñez has a 3.89 grade point average.")
```

Let us continue with the task of designing the auxiliary function `middle-name`
`-abbrev`. We can observe that not every student has a last name. In this case, the
middle name string ought to be " " to provide a space in between the first and the last
names. If a student has a middle name, then the string ought to be " " followed by the
first letter of the middle name followed by ". ". Note that this scheme provides for
spaces before and after the middle name abbreviation. Our analysis clearly suggests
that there is variety in the data called middle name and, therefore, a data definition
is required:

```
A middle name (mn) is either:
  1. ""
  2. not ""
```

The corresponding function template is:

```
;; Sample instances for mn
(define MN1 "")
(define MN2 ...)
    ...

;; mn ... --> ...
;; Purpose: ...
(define (f-on-nm an-nm ...)
  (if (string=? an-nm "")
      ...
      ...))

;; Sample expressions for f-on-mn
(define MN1-VAL ...)
(define MN2-VAL ...)
    ...

;; Tests using sample computations for f-on-mn
(check-expect (f-on-mn MN1 ...) MN1-VAL)
(check-expect (f-on-mn MN2 ...) MN2-VAL)
    ...

;; Tests using sample values for f-on-mn
(check-expect (f-on-mn ...) ...)
    ...
```

Observe that the template suggests writing at least one sample instance for each
variety of mn. Of these, one must be " ".

Before proceeding with the design of `middle-name-abbrev`, it is important to note that the above development means that the `student` data definition and function template must be refined. The refinement must reflect that we now realize that a middle name is not just any string. It is an `nm`. The refinements are:

A student is a structure, (make-student string mn string GPA), that contains a first name, a middle name, a last name, and a grade point average.

```
;; student ... → ...
;; Purpose: ...
(define (f-on-student a-student ...)
  ...(f-on-string (student-fn  a-student))...
  ...(f-on-mn (student-mn  a-student))...
  ...(f-on-string (student-ln  a-student))...
  ...(f-on-GPA (student-gpa a-student))...)
```

These refinements make it clear to anyone reading your code what a `student` is and how a `student` might to be processed. Observe that the middle name is now an `nm` and that the middle name may be processed by calling a function that processes an `nm`.

We can now proceed with the design of `middle-name-abbrev`. If the middle name is `""`, then the middle name abbreviation is clearly `" "` according to our design. Otherwise, the middle name abbreviation is a space followed by the first letter of the given `mn` followed by a period and ending with a space. Sample instances of `mn` and sample expressions for `f-on-mn` are:

```
;; Sample instances of mn
(define MN1 " ")
(define MN2 "Jose")
(define MN3 "Francisco")


;; Sample expressions for middle-name-abbrev
(define MN1-VAL " ")
(define MN2-VAL (string-append " " (substring MN2 0 1) ". "))
(define MN3-VAL (string-append " " (substring MN3 0 1) ". "))
```

First observe that computing the middle name abbreviation for `""` does not process the this `nm`. All that is required is returning the constant `" "`. Observe that the sample expressions that process an `mn` only have one difference. This means that `middle-name-abbrev` only needs one parameter. This leads to the following specializations of the template:

```
;; mn → string
;; Purpose: To abbreviated the given middle name
(define (middle-name-abbrev a-mn)
  (if (string=? a-mn "")
      " "
      (string-append " " (substring a-mn 0 1) ". ")))
```

```
;; Tests using sample computations for middle-name-abbrev
(check-expect (middle-name-abbrev MN1) MN1-VAL)
(check-expect (middle-name-abbrev MN2) MN2-VAL)
(check-expect (middle-name-abbrev MN3) MN3-VAL)

;; Tests using sample values for middle-name-abbrev
(check-expect (middle-name-abbrev "Kaliman") " K. ")
```

The next task is to design gpa->string. To compute a string from a number number->string may be used. This leads to the following specialization of the function template for GPA:

```
;; GPA → string
;; Purpose: Transform the given GPA to a string
(define (gpa->string a-gpa)
  (number->string a-gpa))

;; Sample expressions for gpa->string
(define GPA1-VAL "3.8")
(define GPA2-VAL "3.7")

;; Tests using sample computations for gpa->string
(check-expect (gpa->string OLDGPA1) GPA1-VAL)
(check-expect (gpa->string OLDGPA2) GPA2-VAL)

;; Tests using sample values for gpa->string
(check-expect (gpa->string 4.0) "4.0")
(check-expect (gpa->string 2.3) "2.3")
```

To complete the design run the tests. Alas! Six tests fail:

```
Actual value "19/5" differs from "3.8", the expected value.

Actual value "37/10" differs from "3.7", the expected value.

Actual value "4" differs from "4.0", the expected value.

Actual value "23/10" differs from "2.3", the expected value.

Actual value
 "Mercedes G. Merayo has a 397/100 grade point average."
differs from
 "Mercedes G. Merayo has a 3.97 grade point average.",
the expected value.
```

```
Actual value
  "Manuel Núñez has a 389/100 grade point average."
differs from
  "Manuel Núñez has a 3.89 grade point average.",
the expected value.
```

The first four failures are from tests involving gpa->string and the last two failures are from tests using sample values for student2string. What happened? Where did those fractions in the actual values come from? Where do we start refining our solution? To answer the first two questions we must recall the discussion of numbers in Chap. 2 and better understand how BSL stores numbers. Whenever possible, BSL stores a numerical value as exact (instead of inexact) number. This is done in an effort to avoid errors involving computations with inexact numbers. Therefore, a real number that may be exactly represented is stored as an integer or a fraction. For example, 4.0 is stored as the integer 4 and 3.8 is stored as the fraction $\frac{19}{5}$. This explains the test failures for gpa->string.

Observe that the same error is detected by the tests using sample values for student2string. Why is the error not detected by tests using sample computations for student2string? The answer lies in realizing that these tests check if a function computes the same values as the sample expressions. Thus, these tests are unable to detect errors in the sample expressions. Simply stated, the sample expressions using concrete values evaluate to the same erroneous result as using student2string. When abstracting over sample expressions, a logical error in the development of the expressions is test-wise consistent with the use of a function created by the abstraction. On the other hand, the tests using sample values break away from testing that functions and expressions evaluate to the same value. Instead, they test that functions evaluate to the right value. This explains why only the tests using sample values detect the error. This exercise highlights the importance of always writing tests using sample values.

To answer the third question, a good rule of thumb is to always start debugging refinements with the auxiliary functions. An auxiliary function bug that manifests itself in the tests for the function usually also manifests itself in the tests for functions that use said auxiliary function. Therefore, fixing the auxiliary function may fix the bugs in the functions that call the auxiliary function.

Using this principle, we start the debugging process with gpa->string. The problem is that this function needs to return a string representing an inexact number, not an exact number. Therefore, a function to transform an exact number to an inexact number is needed. Exploring the BSL page in the Help Desk reveals the following function:

```
number → number
Purpose: Converts an exact number to an inexact one.
(define (exact->inexact x) ...)
```

This function looks like what is needed. The refined gpa->string is:

```
;; GPA → string
;; Purpose: Transform the given GPA to a string
(define (gpa->string a-gpa)
  (number->string (exact->inexact a-gpa)))
```

Running the program reveals that all the tests pass. This completes the design of student2string.

** **Ex. 84 —** Design a program to compute the distance between two points in a 3D Cartesian coordinate system. A 3D Cartesian coordinate system has three axes: x, y, and z. A point is an ordered triple, (x, y, z), with a coordinate on each axis.

* **Ex. 85 —** [17] An alternate solution to fix gpa->string is to multiply the given GPA and, #i1.0, inexact 1. The product is an inexact number. Redesign gpa->string to use this approach.

** **Ex. 86 —** A DNA sequence consists of four nucleotide bases: adenine, cytosine, guanine, thymine. These bases are denoted, respectively, A, C, G, and T. For example, AATC is a DNA sequence of length 4. The complement of a DNA sequence, S, is S reversed with As and Ts switched and Cs and Gs switched. For example, the complement DNA for AATC is GATT. A DNA sequence of length n is represented by n bases and a symbol for the species the DNA belongs to. Design a program to compute the reverse of a DNA sequence of length 4.

*** **Ex. 87 —** All cars have five characteristics: a brand, a model, a color, a manufacturing year, and a maximum speed in miles per hour. Design and write a program to convert a car to a descriptive string. For example, a car with the following characteristics:

```
Brand: Alpha Romeo
Model: Giulia
Color: Rosso competizione
 Year: 2020
Speed: 160
```
is converted to:
```
The rosso competizione 2020 Alpha Romeo Giulia has a max speed
of 160 mph.
```

* **Ex. 88 —** The cost of running a business is described by fixed costs and by variable costs. The total cost of running a business is given by the sum of fixed and variable costs. Design a function that takes a single input for costs and that returns the total cost.

---

[17] This exercise is due to a discussion with Robby Findler.

Fig. 62 Chapter 8 BSL grammar

```
program ::= {expr | test | def | defs}*
    def ::= (define <variable name> expr)
        ::= (define (<name> <name>+) expr)
   test ::= (check-expect expr expr)
        ::= (check-within expr expr expr)
   defs ::= (define-struct <struct name> (<field name>*))
   expr ::= number
        ::= string
        ::= \#<character constant>
        ::= '<character>+
        ::= #true
        ::= #false
        ::= <image>
        ::= (<function> expr+)
        ::= (and expr expr expr*)
        ::= (or expr expr expr*)
        ::= (cond [expr expr]+
                  [else expr])
        ::= (if expr expr expr)
```

45 What Have We Learned in This Chapter?

The important lessons of Chap. 8 are summarized as follows:

- Programmers may define structures.
- The explored BSL syntax is displayed in Fig. 62 and includes the required syntax to define structures.
- Every structure definition provides a programmer with a constructor and a selector for each field.
- Structures in BSL are generic and require a data definition to understand its correct use and its correct processing.
- Structures in BSL are first class values.
- Internal representation of data inside a programming language (like BSL) sometimes needs to be transformed to make it understandable to people in the real world.
- A common technique to make the internal representation of data understandable to people in the real world is transforming it to a string.
- As a design advances it may become necessary to refine previously created data definitions.
- Abstracting over sample expressions, may embed logical errors in the function defined and these errors may not be detected by tests using sample computations.
- Writing tests using sample values is an effective way to detect logical errors not caught by tests using sample computations.

Chapter 9
Aliens Attack Version 2

The ability to define and solve problems using structures endows us with the power
to refine Aliens Attack version 1 (from Chap. 6). This refinement adds an alien to
the game. The following is a sample scene for Aliens Attack version 2:

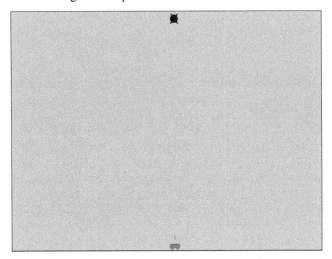

As in Aliens Attack version 1, there is a rocket. In addition, there is an alien. Two
things become immediately obvious. First, the world in this version of the game is
different. It contains, at least, a rocket and an alien. This means a refined world data
definition is needed. Second, a data definition for an alien is needed. These data
definitions are necessary to design a new program for Aliens Attack.

Before proceeding with our design efforts, it is important to note that a refinement
does not mean that we start writing code from scratch. On the contrary, well-designed
code with separation of concerns helps us avoid reinventing the wheel. That is, an
important reason to develop well-designed code is being able to reuse existing code
in a refinement. Inevitably, some functions will change and some new functions will

© The Author(s), under exclusive license to Springer Nature Switzerland AG 2022   185
M. T. Morazán, *Animated Problem Solving*, Texts in Computer Science,
https://doi.org/10.1007/978-3-030-85091-3_9

need to be written. Some functions do not need to be refined and are used unchanged in this new version of the game.

The plan is to follow the steps of the design recipe for video games in Fig. 56. For every handler, a top-down design approach is followed. As the design advances, functions that process instances of a refined data definition are updated. New auxiliary functions are developed as their need arises.

46 Data Definitions

Sometimes it is easier to start defining the simplest data first. In this case, this means starting with the data definition of an alien. To define an alien think about what may change from one instance on an alien to another. An alien moves as follows:

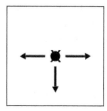

Think carefully about what changes when the alien is moved right, left, or down. Clearly, the image of the alien does not change. As we know, the image of the alien is a constant. Therefore, an alien is not and does not contain an image. What changes when the alien moves right? If you think about it for a while, it becomes clear that the x coordinate of the alien changes. Given that this is an x coordinate in an Aliens Attack scene, it has to be an image-x (defined in Fig. 4). What changes when the alien moves left? Clearly, it is an image-x again. What changes when the alien moves down? The alien's image-x does not change. Instead, its image-y changes. There is nothing more that changes about the alien. Therefore, we now know that an alien has two characteristics that change: its image-x and its image-y. Now, think about how an alien may be represented. Using a posn to represent an alien seems to be a natural fit. Therefore, we may define an alien as follows:

    #| An alien is a posn: (make-posn image-x image-y). |#

Next think about what changes in the world as the game evolves. Just as before, the rocket may change. It is also fairly straightforward to see that the alien changes. Does anything else change? Think about this carefully for a moment. Although not rendered in a game scene, the direction the alien travels in changes. Sometimes the alien is moving right. Sometimes it is moving left. Sometimes it is moving down. Given that nothing else changes in the world, we have that the world has three characteristics that may vary as the game evolves: the rocket, the alien, and the direction that the alien travels in. It now becomes clear that a data definition for a direction and a new data definition for a world are needed.

Again, start by defining the simplest data. Given that a direction can only be one of three values, we may define it as an enumerated type:

```
#|      A direction (dir) is either:
          1. 'right
          2. 'left
          3. 'down                        |#
```

This data definition is clearly stating that a dir may only be one of three symbols at any point during the game's evolution. Making a direction anything else is an improper use of a direction.

We now turn our attention to defining a world. As noted above, a world has three characteristics that may vary. Three is a finite number greater than one. This immediately suggests using a structure with three fields. This means that the world is no longer a rocket. Instead, the world is defined as follows:

```
#| A world is a structure: (make-world rocket alien dir). |#
```

This data definition clearly states that a world is composed of three fields such that the first fields is a rocket, the second field is an alien, and the third field is a dir. If any of these fields is made something different, then it is an improper use of a world structure. Given that we have a data definition for a new type of structure, the program must contain a structure definition for it. The world structure is defined as follows:

```
(define-struct world (rocket alien dir))
```

Observe that the name of the structure and the name of each field is suggestive of the data type they represent.

47 Function Templates and Sample Instances

There are two new data definitions and one refined data definition. This means we need two new function templates and need to refine one function template. The template for functions on an alien and instances of alien are:

```
#|      ;; alien ... → ...
        ;; Purpose: ...
        (define (f-on-alien an-alien ...)
          ...(f-on-image-x (posn-x an-alien)...)
          ...(f-on-image-y (posn-y an-alien)...))

        ;; Sample instances
        (define ALIEN1 (make-posn ... ...))

        ;; Sample expressions for f-on-alien
        (define ALIEN-VAL1 ...)

           ...
```

```
;; Tests using sample computations for f-on-alien
(check-expect (f-on-alien ...) ALIEN-VAL1)
    ...


;; Tests using sample values for f-on-alien
(check-expect (f-on-alien ...) ...)
    ...                                                    |#


;; Sample instances of alien
(define INIT-ALIEN  (make-posn AN-IMG-X 0))
(define INIT-ALIEN2 (make-posn 3 MAX-IMG-Y))
```

Given that an alien is a posn containing an image-x and an image-y, f-on-alien
has function calls to process this type of data. Once again, take note that these
function calls make explicit the separation of concerns. Note that there is no variety
in alien and, therefore, the template suggests only one sample instance, one sample
expression, one test using sample computations, and one test using sample values.
The comments above each of these, however, remain plural to suggest thoroughness
and develop more than one for each. The first alien sample instance defines the
initial alien to be at the top of the scene with 0 as its y coordinate and in the
middle with AN-IMG-X as its x coordinate (recall that AN-IMG-X is defined as
(/ MAX-CHARS-HORIZONTAL 2)). The second alien sample instance defines an
alien at the bottom of the scene with MAX-IMG-Y as its y coordinate and toward the
left half with 3 and its x coordinate. Observe that both x values and both y values,
respectively, are valid instances of image-x and image-y. Therefore, both sample
alien instances are valid.

The template for functions on a dir and sample instances of dir are:

```
#|    ;; dir ... → ...
      ;; Purpose: ...
      (define (f-on-dir a-dir ...)
        (cond [(eq? a-dir 'right) ...]
              [(eq? a-dir 'left) ...]
              [else ...]))


      ;; Sample instances of dir
      (define DIR1 ...)
      (define DIR2 ...)
      (define DIR3 ...)


      ;; Sample expressions for f-on-dir
      (define DIR-VAL1 ...)
      (define DIR-VAL2 ...)
      (define DIR-VAL3 ...)
          ...
```

```
;; Tests using sample computations for f-on-dir
(check-expect (f-on-dir ...) DIR-VAL1)
(check-expect (f-on-dir ...) DIR-VAL2)
(check-expect (f-on-dir ...) DIR-VAL3)
     ...


;; Tests using sample values for f-on-dir
(check-expect (f-on-dir ...) ...)
     ...                                                       |#


;; Sample instances of dir
(define INIT-DIR  'right)
(define INIT-DIR2 'left)
(define INIT-DIR3 'down)
```

Observe that f-on-dir has a conditional expression in its body. This conditional
distinguishes among the 3 varieties of dir. Given that there are 3 varieties of dir
the template suggests defining 3 sample instances. The same is true for the number
of sample expressions and tests using sample computations: at least one for each
variety. It is straightforward to define sample instances for dir given that there are
only 3 varieties: one instance for each.

The refined template for functions on a world and sample instances of world
are:

```
;; world ... → ...
;; Purpose: ...
(define (f-on-world a-world ...)
   ...(f-on-rocket (world-rocket a-world) ...)
   ...(f-on-alien  (world-alien  a-world) ...)
   ...(f-on-dir    (world-dir a-world)    ...)))


;; Sample expressions for f-on-world
(define WORLD-VAL ...)


;; Tests using sample computations for f-on-world
(check-expect (f-on-world ...) WORLD-VAL)
        ...


;; Tests using sample values for f-on-world
(check-expect (f-on-world ...) ...)


;; Sample instances of world
(define INIT-WORLD  (make-world INIT-ROCKET
                                INIT-ALIEN
                                INIT-DIR))
```

```
(define INIT-WORLD2 (make-world INIT-ROCKET2
                                INIT-ALIEN2
                                INIT-DIR2))
```

Observe the separation of concerns suggested by f-on-world a-world. It suggests
that solving a problem about a world may involve solving a problem about a rocket,
an alien, or a dir. This separation of concerns also leads to a divide and conquer
approach to problem solving with worlds. Problems for a rocket, an alien, and a dir
may be solved independently and their solutions combined to, for example, create a
new world. As there is not variety in world, the template suggests a minimum of one
sample expression, one test using sample computations, and one tests using sample
values. Observe that the sample world instances use the samples rocket, alien,
and dir instances previously defined. The number of world instances have been
expanded from those in Chap. 6 to easily write tests.

48 The run Function

We start code refinement with the run function because it informs us of the world-
processing handlers needed. This means we are following a top-down approach to
problem solving. It is necessary to determine what functions are needed in this new
version of Aliens Attack with its new world data definition. In Chap. 6, the run is
defined as follows:

```
; string → world
; Purpose: To run the game
(define (run a-name)
  (big-bang INIT-WORLD
            [on-draw draw-world]
            [name a-name]
            [on-key process-key]))
```

Ask yourself if draw-world and process-key are still needed. Ask yourself is
any other handlers are needed. Given that the world must still be rendered to the
screen and that the player must still be able to move the rocket, it is clear that both
draw-world and process-key are still needed. These functions, however, need to
be refined because they process a world whose data definition has been refined.

To determine if other handlers are needed it is necessary to think about how the
game ought to work. The world's new element is the alien. what is the expected
behavior of the alien in the game? After some thought, it becomes clear that the
player does not control the movements of the alien. Instead, the alien must move
every time the clock ticks. This means that a clock tick handler is needed. Further
thought reveals that it is possible for this version of the game to end. It ends when the
alien reaches earth. This means that a handler to detect the end of the game is also
needed. We must associate these two new handlers with the game in the big-bang
expression. This leads to this refined version of the run function:

```
(define TICK-RATE 1/4)

; string → world
; Purpose: To run the game
(define (run a-name)
  (big-bang INIT-WORLD
            [on-draw draw-world]
            [name a-name]
            [on-key process-key]
            [on-tick process-tick TICK-RATE]
            [stop-when game-over?]))
```

The handler to process clock ticks is process-tick and the handler to detect the
end of the game is game-over?. Observe that an optional argument is given to
on-tick. By limiting the number of clock ticks per second the speed at which the
alien moves is controlled. In this example, the clock ticks 4 times per second or,
equivalently, every $\frac{1}{4}$ seconds. You may, of course, adjust the value of TICK-RATE
to your liking to make the alien move faster or slower.

   The problems that we must solve are now clear. We must refine draw-world and
process-key and we must design process-tick and game-over?. In addition, it
may also be necessary to write new auxiliary functions.

49 Drawing the World

To start, we tackle the problem of drawing the world. It is almost certain that you have
already realized that a function to draw an alien is needed. This is good insight.
You should not, however, immediately jump to write such a function. Instead, be
disciplined about designing your solution to drawing the world. Follow a top-down
design strategy and start with the handler to draw the world. Allow the design process
to reveal all the auxiliary functions that are needed and design them when the need
arises.

49.1 The draw-world Refinement

To update draw-world think about which characteristics of the new definition of
world need to be rendered in the game's scene. Like before, the rocket must be
rendered. In addition, the alien must be rendered. The direction, on the other hand,
is not rendered. Think about how to render the alien with what already exists in the
game's code (from Chap. 6). A scene with the rocket is rendered by the current code.
The draw-world refinement needs to render the alien in the scene that contains the
rocket. This suggests updating the sample expressions for draw-world as follows:

```
;; Sample expressions for draw-world
(define WORLD-SCN1  (draw-alien
                       (world-alien INIT-WORLD)
                       (draw-rocket (world-rocket INIT-WORLD)
                                    E-SCENE)))

(define WORLD-SCN2  (draw-alien
                       (world-alien INIT-WORLD2)
                       (draw-rocket (world-rocket INIT-WORLD2)
                                    E-SCENE)))
```

Based on these sample expressions the definition of `draw-world` is refined to be:

```
;; world → scene
;; Purpose: To draw the world in E-SCENE
(define (draw-world a-world)
  (draw-alien (world-alien a-world)
              (draw-rocket (world-rocket a-world) E-SCENE)))
```

Observe that function composition is used to draw the alien in the scene that contains the rocket. Further observe that a divide and conquer solution has been developed. The problem of drawing a world has been broken into two smaller problems: drawing an alien and drawing a rocket.

Let us carefully analyze the expressions in this function.

```
(draw-rocket (world-rocket a-world) E-SCENE)
```

evaluates to a scene. Specifically, the scene that renders the rocket in the empty scene. This scene is input to (a new) auxiliary function to draw the alien. This expression:

```
(draw-alien (world-alien a-world)
            (draw-rocket (world-rocket a-world) E-SCENE))
```

renders the alien in the scene that contains the rocket.

The tests using sample computations for `draw-world` remain unchanged because they only refer to constants. Referring to constants is not affected by the changes made to `world`. Thus, these tests remain as follows:

```
;; Tests using sample computations for draw-world
(check-expect (draw-world INIT-WORLD)   WORLD-SCN1)
(check-expect (draw-world INIT-WORLD2) WORLD-SCN2)
```

The tests using sample values must now explicitly construct `world` values containing a `rocket`, an `alien`, and a `dir`. Different `world` sample values may be constructed, for example, by using different combinations of the defined sample instances for a `rocket`, an `alien`, and a `dir`. For instance, these refined tests may be:

```
(check-expect
  (draw-world (make-world INIT-ROCKET2 INIT-ALIEN INIT-DIR3))
```

```
                                            )
(check-expect
  (draw-world (make-world INIT-ROCKET INIT-ALIEN2 INIT-DIR2))
```

```
                                            )
```

49.2 Drawing Aliens

The design steps reveal the need for `draw-alien`. This function processes an `alien`.
Thus, we can specialize the template for functions on an alien to implement it. Think
about how to draw the alien. You have two inputs: an `alien` and a scene. To draw the
image of the alien character we may use `draw-ci` (just as is done to draw the rocket's
character image). The image coordinates are obtained from the alien to draw. This
suggests the following initial template specialization:

```
;; alien scene → scene
;; Purpose: Draw the given alien in the given scene
(define (draw-alien an-alien scn)
  ...(f-on-image-x (posn-x an-alien)...)
  ...(f-on-image-y (posn-y an-alien)...))

;; Sample expressions for draw-alien
(define ALIEN-VAL1 (draw-ci ALIEN-IMG
                            (posn-x INIT-ALIEN)
                            (posn-y INIT-ALIEN)
                            E-SCENE))
```

```
(define ALIEN-VAL2 (draw-ci ALIEN-IMG
                           (posn-x INIT-ALIEN2)
                           (posn-y INIT-ALIEN2)
                           E-SCENE2))


;; Tests using sample computations for draw-alien
(check-expect (draw-alien ... ...) ALIEN-VAL1)
(check-expect (draw-alien ... ...) ALIEN-VAL2)


;; Tests using sample values for draw-alien
(check-expect (draw-alien ... ...) ... )
```

The sample expressions do not process the alien's image-x and image-y coordinates. Therefore, there are no calls to functions that process these data types. The only differences in the sample expressions are the alien and the scene. Therefore, draw-alien does not need more parameters. For the body of draw-alien the differences are substituted with the proper parameter. To write the tests using sample computations the differences for each expression are used. Finally, a test using a sample value is written to guard against bugs in our sample expressions. This leads to the following code to draw an alien:

```
;; alien scene → scene
;; Purpose: Draw the given alien in the given scene
(define (draw-alien an-alien scn)
  (draw-ci ALIEN-IMG
          (posn-x an-alien)
          (posn-y an-alien)
          scn))


;; Sample expressions for draw-alien
(define ALIEN-VAL1 (draw-ci ALIEN-IMG
                           (posn-x INIT-ALIEN)
                           (posn-y INIT-ALIEN)
                           E-SCENE))


(define ALIEN-VAL2 (draw-ci ALIEN-IMG
                           (posn-x INIT-ALIEN2)
                           (posn-y INIT-ALIEN2)
                           E-SCENE2))


;; Tests using sample computations for draw-alien
(check-expect (draw-alien INIT-ALIEN  E-SCENE)  ALIEN-VAL1)
(check-expect (draw-alien INIT-ALIEN2 E-SCENE2) ALIEN-VAL2)


;; Tests using sample values for draw-alien
(check-expect (draw-alien INIT-ALIEN2 E-SCENE)
```

)

There are no new auxiliary functions needed. Therefore, the required updates for draw-world are done.

50 The process-key Refinement

The player does not control or affect the aliens nor the direction the aliens travel in. Therefore, as before, key events only affect the rocket. This means that process-key does not have to process an alien nor a dir. The refinement of process-key only requires refining the worlds created in the sample expressions, in the function definitions, and in the tests. Start with the sample expressions. These must now evaluate to a world structure. Use the defined sample world instances to refine them as follows:

```
;; Sample expressions for process-key
(define KEY-RVAL (make-world
                   (move-rckt-right (world-rocket INIT-WORLD))
                   (world-alien INIT-WORLD)
                   (world-dir INIT-WORLD)))
(define KEY-LVAL (make-world
                   (move-rckt-left (world-rocket INIT-WORLD))
                   (world-alien INIT-WORLD)
                   (world-dir INIT-WORLD)))
(define KEY-OVAL INIT-WORLD2)
```

Observe that in the sample expressions the alien and the dir are left unchanged in the new world created. As expected, only the rocket may be changed. The rocket, however, is not always changed and this is illustrated by the third test. The rocket is not moved when, for example, m is pressed by the player. Therefore, a new world is not created and an unchanged existing world is used to define the third constant.

Based on these new sample expressions, it is straightforward to refine the function definition. The process-key body now creates worlds as follows:

```
;; world key → world
;; Purpose: Process a key event to return next world
(define (process-key a-world a-key)
  (cond [(key=? a-key "right")
```

```
          (make-world
            (move-rckt-right (world-rocket a-world))
            (world-alien a-world)
                      (world-dir a-world))]
      [(key=? a-key "left")
       (make-world
         (move-rckt-left (world-rocket a-world))
         (world-alien a-world)
         (world-dir a-world))]
      [else a-world]))
```

The tests using sample computations, as before, remain unchanged given that they only reference constants:

```
;; Tests using sample computations for process-key
(check-expect (process-key INIT-WORLD  "right") KEY-RVAL)
(check-expect (process-key INIT-WORLD  "left")  KEY-LVAL)
(check-expect (process-key INIT-WORLD2 "m")     KEY-OVAL)
```

The tests using sample values are updated to use world structures. These tests illustrate that the rocket may not move off the scene (the first two tests) and that keys other than "left" and "right" beyond "m" leave the input world unchanged (the last two tests). The updated tests are:

```
;; Tests using sample values for process-key
(check-expect (process-key
                 (make-world (sub1 MAX-CHARS-HORIZONTAL)
                             INIT-ALIEN
                             'right)
                "right")
               (make-world (sub1 MAX-CHARS-HORIZONTAL)
                           INIT-ALIEN
                           'right))
(check-expect (process-key (make-world 0
                                       INIT-ALIEN
                                       'left)
                  "left")
               (make-world 0
                           INIT-ALIEN
                           'left))
(check-expect (process-key (make-world 0
                                       INIT-ALIEN
                                       'left)
                  "o")
               (make-world 0
                           INIT-ALIEN
                           'left))
(check-expect (process-key INIT-WORLD2 ";") INIT-WORLD2)
```

The refinement process does not reveal the need for new auxiliary functions. Therefore, the refinements for `process-key` are complete.

51 Processing Ticks

To design the `process-tick` handler think carefully about how the game must evolve every time the clock ticks. What changes? What does not change? The rocket is not affected by clock ticks given that the rocket only moves on keystrokes made by the player. The alien, on the other hand, must move every clock tick. This means that we need to design a function to move an alien.

A bit more subtle is the fact that when the alien moves the direction the new alien must move in may be different. This means that a function to compute the direction for the new alien is needed. This function must distinguish when not to change the direction and between the cases to change the direction. Careful analysis reveals that the direction only changes when the alien is at either the left or right edge of the scene. We can specify how the direction changes as follows:

- New alien at right edge created by moving right means the new direction is down
- New alien at left edge created by moving left means the new direction is down
- New alien at right edge created by moving down means the new direction is left
- New alien at left edge created by moving down means the new direction is right
- Otherwise, the direction does not change.

This analysis suggests that to compute the direction of a new alien two pieces of data are required: the new alien and the direction used to create the new alien.

51.1 The `process-tick` Handler

Based on the above problem analysis, the specialization of the template for a function on a world to design `process-click` is started. The first step is to specialize based on the analysis so far:

```
;; world → world
;; Purpose: Create a new world after a clock tick
(define (process-tick a-world)
   ...(f-on-rocket (world-rocket a-world) ...)
   ...(f-on-alien  (world-alien  a-world)  ...)
   ...(f-on-dir    (world-dir a-world)        ...))

;; Sample expressions for process-tick
(define AFTER-TICK-WORLD1
        (make-world (world-rocket INIT-WORLD)
                    (move-alien (world-alien INIT-WORLD)
                                (world-dir INIT-WORLD))
```

```
                      (new-dir-after-tick
                        (move-alien (world-alien INIT-WORLD)
                                    (world-dir INIT-WORLD))
                        (world-dir INIT-WORLD))))

(define AFTER-TICK-WORLD2
        (make-world (world-rocket INIT-WORLD2)
                    (move-alien (world-alien INIT-WORLD2)
                                (world-dir INIT-WORLD2))
                    (new-dir-after-tick
                      (move-alien (world-alien INIT-WORLD2)
                                  (world-dir INIT-WORLD2))
                      (world-dir INIT-WORLD2))))

;; Tests using sample computations for process-tick
(check-expect (process-tick INIT-WORLD)  AFTER-TICK-WORLD1)
(check-expect (process-tick INIT-WORLD2) AFTER-TICK-WORLD2)

;; Tests using sample values for process-tick
(check-expect (process-tick (make-world INIT-ROCKET
                                        (make-posn 1 5)
                                        'left))
              (make-world INIT-ROCKET
                          (make-posn MIN-IMG-X 5)
                          'down))

(check-expect (process-tick
                (make-world
                  INIT-ROCKET2
                  (make-posn (- MAX-CHARS-HORIZONTAL 2) 10)
                  'right))
              (make-world INIT-ROCKET2
                          (make-posn MAX-IMG-X 10)
                          'down))

(check-expect (process-tick (make-world INIT-ROCKET2
                                        (make-posn MAX-IMG-X 2)
                                        'down))
              (make-world INIT-ROCKET2
                          (make-posn MAX-IMG-X 3)
                          'left))

(check-expect (process-tick (make-world INIT-ROCKET2
                                        (make-posn MIN-IMG-X 2)
                                        'down))
```

```
(make-world INIT-ROCKET2
            (make-posn MIN-IMG-X 3)
            'right))
```

The sample expressions are written using (to be designed) functions to move an alien and to compute a new direction. The arguments to move an alien are fairly straightforward to determine: the alien to move and the direction to move. If more arguments are needed the design of move-alien will reveal them. The arguments for new-dir-after-tick are based on the problem analysis above. The design of new-dir-after-tick will reveal if more arguments are needed. The tests using sample computations are written, as expected, using previously defined constants. In this case, these tests illustrate when the alien does not change direction. The tests using sample values are written building world instances. These tests illustrate that the changes in direction occur as expected when an alien is at either edge of the scene.

The next task is to specialize the body for process-tick. As done before, this is achieved by abstracting over the sample expressions. This yields the following function:

```
;; world → world
;; Purpose: Create a new world after a clock tick
(define (process-tick a-world)
  (make-world
    (world-rocket a-world)
    (move-alien (world-alien a-world) (world-dir a-world))
    (new-dir-after-tick (move-alien (world-alien a-world)
                                    (world-dir a-world))
                        (world-dir a-world))))
```

51.2 The Design of new-dir-after-tick

The design of new-dir-after-tick is interesting because it takes as input two different types of data. Should this function be designed by specializing the template for a function on an alien or a function on a direction? Problem analysis may shed some light on this question.

Every time the clock ticks the direction of the alien may change. When does it change? When does it not change? We can identify the following three conditions:

1. If the direction is right, then the new direction may be left or down.
2. If the direction is left, then the new direction may be down or left.
3. If the direction is down, then the new direction may be right or left.

This analysis suggests that the function ought to be designed around the given direction. Therefore, the template for a function on a direction is specialized.

Given that testing aliens on the left and right edges is needed, the following instances of aliens are defined to facilitate the writing of sample expressions and tests:

```
(define LEFT-EDGE-ALIEN  (make-posn MIN-IMG-X 10))
(define RIGHT-EDGE-ALIEN (make-posn MAX-IMG-X 6))
```

Observe that there are two separate concerns. The first is to determine the given direction instance. Second, is to compute the new direction. The computation of the new direction ought to be split among different auxiliary functions depending on the given direction:

1. `new-dir-after-down` is used when the given direction is down.
2. `new-dir-after-left` is used when the given direction is left.
3. `new-dir-after-right` is used when the given direction is right.

Based on this design idea we can specialize the template for a function on a direction. Sample expressions may be written as follows:

```
;; Sample expressions for new-dir-after-tick
(define NEW-DIR-LEDGE-ALIEN-DOWN
         (new-dir-after-down LEFT-EDGE-ALIEN))
(define NEW-DIR-REDGE-ALIEN-DOWN
         (new-dir-after-down RIGHT-EDGE-ALIEN))
(define NEW-DIR-INIT-ALIEN-LEFT
         (new-dir-after-left INIT-ALIEN))
(define NEW-DIR-LEDGE-ALIEN-LEFT
         (new-dir-after-left LEFT-EDGE-ALIEN))
(define NEW-DIR-INIT-ALIEN-RIGHT
         (new-dir-after-right INIT-ALIEN))
(define NEW-DIR-REDGE-ALIEN-RIGHT
         (new-dir-after-right RIGHT-EDGE-ALIEN))
```

Observe that there are two sample expressions for each auxiliary function. This is due to the fact that for each possible direction the new direction may be one of two values. For example, if the given direction is down, then the new direction may be right if the given alien is at the left edge and may be left if the given alien is at the right edge. Similarly, if the given direction is left, then the new direction is down if the given alien is at the left edge and remains left otherwise. Finally, if the given direction is right, then the new direction is down if the given alien is at the right edge and remains right otherwise. In summary, there is a sample expression for each possible outcome for a given direction.

Based on the conditions and the sample expressions from above the definition template and tests are specialized as follows:

```
;; alien dir → dir
;; Purpose: Return new alien direction
(define (new-dir-after-tick an-alien old-dir)
  (cond [(eq? old-dir 'right)
         (new-dir-after-right an-alien)]
```

```
                    [(eq? old-dir 'left)
                     (new-dir-after-left an-alien)]
                    [else (new-dir-after-down an-alien)]])

    ;; Tests using sample computations for new-dir-after-tick
    (check-expect (new-dir-after-tick LEFT-EDGE-ALIEN 'down)
                  NEW-DIR-LEDGE-ALIEN-DOWN)
    (check-expect (new-dir-after-tick RIGHT-EDGE-ALIEN 'down)
                  NEW-DIR-REDGE-ALIEN-DOWN)
    (check-expect (new-dir-after-tick INIT-ALIEN 'left)
                  NEW-DIR-INIT-ALIEN-LEFT)
    (check-expect (new-dir-after-tick LEFT-EDGE-ALIEN 'left)
                  NEW-DIR-LEDGE-ALIEN-LEFT)
    (check-expect (new-dir-after-tick INIT-ALIEN 'right)
                  NEW-DIR-INIT-ALIEN-RIGHT)
    (check-expect (new-dir-after-tick RIGHT-EDGE-ALIEN 'right)
                  NEW-DIR-REDGE-ALIEN-RIGHT)

    ;; Tests using sample values for new-dir-after-tick
    (check-expect (new-dir-after-tick (make-posn MIN-IMG-X 10)
                                      'down)
                  'right)
    (check-expect (new-dir-after-tick (make-posn MAX-IMG-X 12)
                                      'down)
                  'left)
    (check-expect (new-dir-after-tick (make-posn 10 10)
                                      'left)
                  'left)
    (check-expect (new-dir-after-tick (make-posn MIN-IMG-X 15)
                                      'left)
                  'down)
    (check-expect (new-dir-after-tick (make-posn 10 14)
                                      'right)
                  'right)
    (check-expect (new-dir-after-tick (make-posn MAX-IMG-X 3)
                                      'right)
                  'down)
```

The specialization of the definition template uses the three conditions identified above to call the appropriate auxiliary function. The tests using sample computations illustrate that new-dir-after-tick computes the values of the sample expressions. The tests using sample values further illustrate the possible outcomes for each possible direction instance.

51.3 The Design of Auxiliary Functions for `new-dir-after-tick`

The design of `new-dir-after-tick` revealed the need for three auxiliary functions. Our next task is to design these functions and any further auxiliary functions that are needed. Let us start by designing `new-dir-after-down`, `new-dir-after-left`, and `new-dir-after-right`. For each of these functions the returned direction depends on whether or not the given alien is at one of the edges.

51.3.1 Design of `new-dir-after-down`

Carefully consider what the next direction ought to be if the previous direction is down. When the previous direction is down we know that the given alien must be at one of the edges. If the given alien is at the left edge, then the new direction is right. If the given alien is at the right edge, then the new direction is left. Observe that this function must determine which edge the alien is at. This is a different problem from computing the new direction. In the spirit of separation of concerns, detecting if an alien is at the left or the right edge is delegated to an auxiliary function. Further observe that this means that `new-dir-after-down` does not process the given alien and, therefore, the design of this function does not specialize the template for a function on an alien. Instead, it is designed around the decision that must be made based on the edge the alien is located at.

We are free to choose if the function detects the alien at the left edge or at the right edge because if the detection for an edge fails, then the alien must be at the other edge. We arbitrarily choose to detect if the alien is at the left edge. The function using this strategy looks as follows:

```
;; alien → direction
;; Purpose: Compute the direction of the given alien
;;          when previous direction is down
(define (new-dir-after-down an-alien)
  (if (alien-at-left-edge? an-alien)
      'right
      'left))

;; Sample expressions for new-dir-after-down
(define AT-LEDGE-DOWN 'right)
(define AT-REDGE-DOWN 'left)

;; Tests using sample computations for new-dir-after-down
(check-expect (new-dir-after-down LEFT-EDGE-ALIEN)
              AT-LEDGE-DOWN)
(check-expect (new-dir-after-down RIGHT-EDGE-ALIEN)
              AT-REDGE-DOWN)
```

```
;; Tests using sample values for new-dir-after-down
(check-expect (new-dir-after-down (make-posn MIN-IMG-X 4))
              'right)
(check-expect (new-dir-after-down (make-posn MAX-IMG-X 9))
              'left)
```

The sample expressions are very simple given that once the alien's edge is known all that is needed is to return a direction. The function uses a conditional to decide which direction to return. If the alien is at the left edge the returned direction is right. If the alien is at the right edge, then the returned direction is left. The tests using sample computations illustrate that the function computes the expected new direction. The tests using sample values illustrate that the function works for additional arbitrary aliens at one of the edges.

51.3.2 Design of `new-dir-after-left`

The design of `new-dir-after-left` is similar to that of `new-dir-after-down`. It is designed around making a decision based on whether or not the given alien is at the left edge. If the alien is at the left edge, then the new direction is down. Otherwise, the direction is unchanged because the alien ought to continue moving left. The function may be implemented as follows:

```
;; alien → direction
;; Purpose: Compute the direction of the given alien
;;          when previous direction is left
(define (new-dir-after-left an-alien)
  (if (alien-at-left-edge? an-alien)
      'down
      'left))

;; Sample expressions for new-dir-after-left
(define AT-LEDGE     'down)
(define NOT-AT-LEDGE 'left)

;; Tests using sample computations for new-dir-after-left
(check-expect (new-dir-after-left LEFT-EDGE-ALIEN)  'down)
(check-expect (new-dir-after-left INIT-ALIEN)       'left)

;; Tests using sample values for new-dir-after-left
(check-expect (new-dir-after-left RIGHT-EDGE-ALIEN) 'left)
```

There are two sample expressions: one for each possible outcome. The tests using sample computations use an alien at the left edge and an alien that is not at the left edge to illustrate that the function properly computes the value of the sample expressions. The test using a sample value illustrates that the function works for an extrema value: an alien at the right edge.

51.3.3 Design of `new-dir-after-right`

The design of `new-dir-after-right` is similar to that of `new-dir-after-left`. It is arbitrarily designed around making a decision based on whether or not the given alien is at the right edge. If the alien is at the right edge, then the new direction is down. Otherwise, the direction is unchanged because the alien ought to continue moving right. The function may be implemented as follows:

```
;; alien → direction
;; Purpose: Compute the direction of the given alien
;;          when previous direction is right
(define (new-dir-after-right an-alien)
  (if (alien-at-right-edge? an-alien)
      'down
      'right))

;; Sample expressions for new-dir-after-right
(define AT-REDGE     'down)
(define NOT-AT-REDGE 'right)

;; Tests using sample computations for new-dir-after-right
(check-expect (new-dir-after-right RIGHT-EDGE-ALIEN)
              AT-REDGE)
(check-expect (new-dir-after-right INIT-ALIEN)
              NOT-AT-REDGE)

;; Tests using sample values for new-dir-after-right
(check-expect (new-dir-after-right LEFT-EDGE-ALIEN)
              'right)
```

Once again, we see that there are two sample expressions: one for each possible outcome. The tests using sample computations use an alien at the right edge and an alien that is not at the right edge to illustrate that the function properly computes the value of the sample expressions. The test using a sample value illustrates that the function works for an extrema value: an alien at the left edge.

51.3.4 Design of `alien-at-left-edge?`

The design of the three previous functions reveals the need for two more auxiliary functions. Let us start with the design of `alien-at-left-edge?`. How do we know if an alien is at the left edge? A given alien is at the left edge if its `image-x` coordinate is MIN-IMG-X. This means that the given alien must be processed and, therefore, this function is designed by specializing the template for a function on an alien. This specialization yields:

```
;; alien → Boolean
;; Purpose: Determine if he given alien is at the left edge
(define (alien-at-left-edge? an-alien)
  (= (posn-x an-alien) MIN-IMG-X))

;; Sample expressions for alien-at-left-edge?
(define LEDGE-VAL1 (= (posn-x INIT-ALIEN)       MIN-IMG-X))
(define LEDGE-VAL2 (= (posn-x LEFT-EDGE-ALIEN) MIN-IMG-X))

;; Tests using sample computations for alien-at-left-edge?
(check-expect (alien-at-left-edge? INIT-ALIEN) LEDGE-VAL1)
(check-expect (alien-at-left-edge? LEFT-EDGE-ALIEN) LEDGE-VAL2)

;; Tests using sample values for alien-at-left-edge?
(check-expect (alien-at-left-edge? (make-posn 3 2)) #false)
(check-expect (alien-at-left-edge? (make-posn MIN-IMG-X 8))
              #true)
```

The sample expressions illustrate that the desired Boolean is computed by testing an alien's image-x coordinate with MIN-IMG-X. The definition template specialization uses a posn's x coordinate selector to access the alien's image-x coordinate. The tests using sample values illustrate that the function works for aliens other than those used in the tests using sample computations.

51.3.5 Design of alien-at-right-edge?

How do we know if an alien is at the right edge? A given alien is at the right edge if its image-x coordinate is MAX-IMG-X. This means that the given alien must be processed Once again, this is a function that is designed by specializing the template for a function on an alien. This specialization yields:

```
;; alien → Boolean
;; Purpose: Determine if the given alien is at the
;;          right edge
(define (alien-at-right-edge? an-alien)
  (= (posn-x an-alien) MAX-IMG-X))

;; Sample expressions for alien-at-right-edge?
(define REDGE-VAL1 (= (posn-x INIT-ALIEN) MAX-IMG-X))
(define REDGE-VAL2 (= (posn-x (make-posn MAX-IMG-X 8))
                      MAX-IMG-X))
```

```
;; Tests using sample computations for alien-at-right-edge?
(check-expect (alien-at-right-edge? INIT-ALIEN)
              REDGE-VAL1)
(check-expect (alien-at-right-edge? RIGHT-EDGE-ALIEN)
              REDGE-VAL2)


;; Tests using sample values for alien-at-right-edge?
(check-expect (alien-at-right-edge? (make-posn 1 1)) #false)
(check-expect (alien-at-right-edge? RIGHT-EDGE-ALIEN) #true)
```

The sample expressions illustrate that the desired Boolean is computed by testing an alien's image-x coordinate with MAX-IMG-X. The definition template specialization uses a posn's x coordinate selector to access the alien's image-x coordinate. The tests using sample values illustrate that the function works for aliens other than those used in the tests using sample computations.

Given that the last two functions do not reveal the need for more auxiliary functions the design of new-dir-after-tick is complete. You may have noticed that each of the auxiliary functions is small and easily understandable. This is a direct consequence of respecting the separation of concerns during the design process.

---

* Ex. 89 — Redesign new-dir-after-down to test if the given alien is at the right edge.

* Ex. 90 — Redesign new-dir-after-left to test if the given alien is at the right edge.

* Ex. 91 — Redesign new-dir-after-right to test if the given alien is at the left edge.

** Ex. 92 — Inline   both   alien-at-left-edge?   and alien-at-left-edge? to eliminate them as defined functions. Is this a good idea?

51.4 The Design of move-alien

The next problem to solve is moving an alien. This is another interesting function because we must decide how to design it. It takes two different types of data as input: an alien and a dir. Should it be designed by specializing the template for functions on an alien or the template for functions on a dir? To make this decision requires further problem analysis.

Specializing the template for functions on a dir means that a new alien is created by computing either a new image-x value or a new image-y value depending on the given dir. A conditional is needed to determine which is computed. If the direction is 'right or 'left, then the new alien is constructed with a new image-x coordinate. If the direction is 'down, then the new alien is constructed with a new image-y coordinate. In summary, for each possible direction either a new image-x or a new image-y value must be computed.

Specializing the template for functions on a alien means that a new alien is constructed by computing an image-x value using the given alien's image-x coordinate and the given direction and by computing an image-y value using the given alien's image-y coordinate and the given direction. A consequence of this design path is that the functions to compute the new image-x and image-y coordinates must have a conditional. The image-x value remains unchanged if the direction is 'down. The image-y value remains unchanged if the direction is either 'right or 'left.

As it turns out move-alien may be designed by specializing either template. In such a case, you get to choose which design path to follow. Which design feels more natural? Which design seems easier? Perhaps, specializing the template for functions of a dir is easier. It only requires one conditional as opposed to two required by the other design choice.

Let us choose to specialize the template for functions of a dir. This means deciding how to compute a new alien for each variety of dir. We start by specializing the template as follows:

```
;; alien dir → alien
;; Purpose: Move given alien in given direction
(define (move-alien an-alien a-dir)
  (cond [(eq? a-dir 'right) ...]
        [(eq? a-dir 'left) ...]
            [else ...]))


;; Sample expressions for move-alien
(define MALIEN-VAL1-1
        (make-posn (move-right-image-x (posn-x INIT-ALIEN))
                        (posn-y INIT-ALIEN)))
(define MALIEN-VAL1-2
        (make-posn (move-right-image-x (posn-x INIT-ALIEN2))
                   (posn-y INIT-ALIEN2)))
(define MALIEN-VAL2-1
        (make-posn (move-left-image-x (posn-x INIT-ALIEN))
                        (posn-y INIT-ALIEN)))
(define MALIEN-VAL2-2
        (make-posn (move-left-image-x (posn-x INIT-ALIEN2))
                   (posn-y INIT-ALIEN2)))
(define MALIEN-VAL3-1
        (make-posn (posn-x INIT-ALIEN)
                        (move-down-image-y (posn-y INIT-ALIEN))))
(define MALIEN-VAL3-2
        (make-posn (posn-x INIT-ALIEN2)
                        (move-down-image-y (posn-y INIT-ALIEN2))))
```

```
;; Tests using sample computations for move-alien
(check-expect (move-alien INIT-ALIEN  'right) MALIEN-VAL1-1)
(check-expect (move-alien INIT-ALIEN2 'right) MALIEN-VAL1-2)
(check-expect (move-alien INIT-ALIEN  'left)  MALIEN-VAL2-1)
(check-expect (move-alien INIT-ALIEN2 'left)  MALIEN-VAL2-2)
(check-expect (move-alien INIT-ALIEN  'down)  MALIEN-VAL3-1)
(check-expect (move-alien INIT-ALIEN2 'down)  MALIEN-VAL3-2)


;; Tests using sample values for move-alien
(check-expect (move-alien (make-posn MAX-IMG-X 3) 'down)
              (make-posn MAX-IMG-X 4))
(check-expect (move-alien (make-posn MAX-IMG-X 3) 'left)
              (make-posn (sub1 MAX-IMG-X) 3))
(check-expect (move-alien (make-posn 0 5) 'right)
              (make-posn 1 5))
```

There are two sample expressions for each variety of dir. For each variety the only difference is the alien value. This confirms that move-alien only needs an alien and a dir as input. Observe that among the sample expressions for each dir the new alien is constructed differently. Either the x coordinate is moved right, the x coordinate is moved left, or the y coordinate is moved down. There is, as expected, a test using sample computations for each evaluated sample expression. The tests using sample values explicitly illustrate that a new alien is correctly computed.

The next task is to specialize the body of move-alien. Abstracting over the sample expressions for each dir variety leads to:

```
;; alien dir → alien
;; Purpose: Move given alien in given direction
(define (move-alien an-alien a-dir)
  (cond [(eq? a-dir 'right)
         (make-posn (move-right-image-x (posn-x an-alien))
                    (posn-y an-alien))]
        [(eq? a-dir 'left)
         (make-posn (move-left-image-x (posn-x an-alien))
                    (posn-y an-alien))]
        [else (make-posn
                (posn-x an-alien)
                (move-down-image-y (posn-y an-alien)))]))
```

52 Subtyping

The development of the auxiliary functions needed by move-alien is paused to address a bug in our design. Have you picked up on it? Remember that problem solvers must always be careful about logical mistakes. Consider carefully the following test:

```
(check-expect (move-alien INIT-ALIEN2 'down) MALIEN-VAL3-2)
```

Does this test make sense? Recall that INIT-ALIEN2's image-y coordinate is MAX-IMG-Y. That is the maximum image-y value. Can this alien be moved down? Clearly, moving INIT-ALIEN2 down is impossible because the y coordinate of the new alien would be larger than MAX-IMG-Y. We are facing a situation where the test is suggesting that a function given a valid input value returns an invalid output value.

The problem is that the auxiliary functions should not process an image-x value or an image-y value. Instead, they need to process a subset of the values defined by these data types. This means that we need to define image-x and image-y *subtypes*. A subtype defines a proper subset of the values of an existing type. If you have a type A and B is a subtype of A, then any instance of B is also an instance of A. The opposite is not true. Not every instance of A is also an instance of B. This means that a function that processes data type A can also process data type B and that a function that processes data type B cannot process data type A.

Consider, for example, the following data definition for nonnegative integers:

```
#| A nonnegative integer, nni, is an integer greater than
   or equal to 0. #|

;; nni ... → ...
(define (f-on-nni an-nni) ... an-nni ...)

;; Sample instances of nni
(define NNI1 ...)

;; Sample expression definitions for nni
(define NNI1-VAL ... NNI1 ...)

;; Tests using sample computations for f-on-nni
(check-expect (f-on-nni NNI1 ...) NNI1-VAL)

;; Tests using sample values for f-on-nni
(check-expect (f-on-nni ...) ...)
```

Now consider writing a function to return the ratio of, x and y, two nnis. It is not difficult to see that the ratio, $\frac{x}{y}$, is not always defined. As you know, y cannot be 0. This means that this ratio-computing function cannot process two nnis. Instead, it ought to process an nni (x) and a positive integer (y). That is, we need to define an nni subtype. This may be done as follows:

```
#| A positive integer, posint, is an nni greater than 0. |#
;; posint ... → ...
(define (f-on-posint a-posint) ... a-posint ...)

;; Sample instances of posint
(define POSINT1 ...)

;; Sample expression definitions for posint
(define POSINT1-VAL ... POSINT1 ...)

;; Tests using sample computations for f-on-posint
(check-expect (f-on-posint POSINT1 ...) POSINT1-VAL)

;; Tests using sample values for f-on-posint
(check-expect (f-on-nni ...) ...)
```

Observe that every posint is an nni, but not every nni, specifically 0, is a posint. The definition of this subtype allows us to write the ratio-computing function using the template for functions on a posint as follows:

```
;; nni posint → number
;; Purpose: Return x/y
(define (ratio-x-y x y) (/ x y))

;; Sample instances of posint
(define POSINT1 1)
(define POSINT2 20)
(define POSINT3 3)
(define POSINT4 77)

;; Sample expression definitions for ratio-x-y
(define POSINT1-VAL (/ POSINT1 POSINT2))
(define POSINT2-VAL (/ POSINT3 POSINT4))

;; Tests using sample computations for ratio-x-y
(check-expect (ratio-x-y POSINT1 POSINT2) POSINT1-VAL)
(check-expect (ratio-x-y POSINT3 POSINT4) POSINT2-VAL)

;; Tests using sample values for ratio-x-y
(check-expect (ratio-x-y 2 3)  2/3)
(check-expect (ratio-x-y 3 4)  3/4)
```

Observe that a new data definition, posint, is used in the contract. This communicates to any programmer that to properly use this function y may not be 0. Using this subtype definition (/ x y) is always defined. Any programmer using this function must guarantee that the argument for y always satisfies the signature. Further observe that instances of posint, POSINT1, and POSINT3 are used as nni arguments for x. This can only be done because posint is a subtype of nni.

Subtypes may also be used for the image-x moving functions needed by move-alien. For instance, the image-x values greater than MIN-IMG-X may be defined as:

```
#|
An image-x>min is an image-x in [(add1 MIN-IMG-X)..MAX-IMG-X]

;; image-x>min ... → ...
;; Purpose: ...
(define (f-on-image-x an-img-x>min ...)
  ... an-img-x...)

;; Sample instances of image-x>min
(define IMG-X>MIN1 ...)
      ...

;; Sample expressions for f-on-image-x>min
(define IMGX>MIN-VAL1 ...)
      ...

;; Sample tests using sample computations for f-on-image-x>min
(check-expect (f-on-image-x>min ...) IMGX>MIN-VAL1)
      ...

;; Sample tests using sample computations for f-on-image-x>min
(check-expect (f-on-image-x>min ...) ...)                      |#
```

Armed with this data definition and function template, for example, move-left-image-x may be refined as follows:

```
   ;; image-x>min → image-x
   ;; Purpose: Move the given image-x>min left
   (define (move-left-image-x an-img-x>min)
     (sub1 an-img-x>min))

   ;; Sample expressions for move-left-image-x
   (define IMGX>MIN-VALL1 (sub1 AN-IMG-X))
   (define IMGX>MIN-VALL2 (sub1 MAX-IMG-X))

   ;; Tests using sample computations for move-left-image-x
   (check-expect (move-left-image-x AN-IMG-X)  IMGX>MIN-VALL1)
   (check-expect (move-left-image-x MAX-IMG-X) IMGX>MIN-VALL2)

   ;; Tests using sample values for move-left-image-x
   (check-expect (move-left-image-x 9) 8)
```

It is important to note that move-left-image-x always returns an image-x. That is, the value returned may be MIN-IMG-X and may never be less than MIN-IMG-X. Using the subtype, image-x>min, guarantees this.

The same design strategy results in the following data definitions and function templates for image-x<max and image-y<max:

```
#|
An image-x<max, is an image-x in [MIN-IMG-X..(sub1 MAX-IMG-X)]

;; image-x<max ... → ...
;; Purpose: ...
(define (f-on-image-x<max an-img-x<max ...)
  ... an-img-x...)

;; Sample instances of image-x<max
(define IMG-X<MAX1 ...)
     ...

;; Sample expressions for f-on-image-x<max
(define IMGX<MAX-VAL1 ...)
  ...

;; Tests using sample computations for f-on-image-x<max
(check-expect (f-on-image-x<max ...) IMGX<MAX-VAL1)
     ...

;; Tests using sample computations for f-on-image-x<max
(check-expect (f-on-image-x<max ...) ...)


An image-y<max is an image-y in [MIN-IMG-Y..(sub1 MAX-IMG-Y)]

;; image-y<max ... → ...
;; Purpose: ...
(define (f-on-image-y<max an-img-y<max ...)
  ...˜an-img-y<max...)

;; Sample instances of image-y
(define IMG-Y<MAX1 ...)
     ...

;; Sample expressions for f-on-image-y<max
(define IMGY<MAX-VAL1 ...)
     ...
```

```
;; Tests using sample computations for f-on-image-y<max
(check-expect (f-on-image-y<max ...) IMGY<MAX-VAL1)

       ...


;; Tests using sample values for f-on-image-y<max
(check-expect (f-on-image-y<max ...) ...)                   |#
```

Using these subtypes and function templates the move-right-image-x and
move-down-image-y code is:

```
;; image-x<max → image-x
;; Purpose: Move the given image-x<max right
(define (move-right-image-x an-img-x<max)
  (add1 an-img-x<max))

;; Sample expressions for move-right-image-x<max
(define IMGX<MAX-VALR1 (add1 MIN-IMG-X))
(define IMGX<MAX-VALR2 (add1 11))

;; Tests using sample computations for move-right-image-x
(check-expect (move-right-image-x MIN-IMG-X) IMGX<MAX-VALR1)
(check-expect (move-right-image-x 11)        IMGX<MAX-VALR2)

;; Tests using sample computations for move-right-image-x
(check-expect (move-right-image-x 12) 13)



;; image-y<max → image-y
;; Purpose: To move the given image-y<max down
(define (move-down-image-y an-img-y<max) (add1 an-img-y<max))

;; Sample expressions for move-down-image-y
(define IMG-Y<MAX1 (add1 MIN-IMG-Y))
(define IMG-Y<MAX2 (add1 AN-IMG-Y))

;; Tests using sample computations for move-down-image-y
(check-expect (move-down-image-y MIN-IMG-Y) IMG-Y<MAX1)
(check-expect (move-down-image-y AN-IMG-Y)  IMG-Y<MAX2)

;; Tests using sample values for move-down-image-y
(check-expect (move-down-image-y 2)  3)
```

There is no doubt that creating refined data definitions for subtypes feels like a
lot of extra work now. It is, however, time well spent. It makes solutions to problems
easier to understand. This is important, because it makes it easier to refine and for
others to work with your code. Think about this carefully. If you had to maintain
or refine another person's code, would you not prefer to have code that is easier to

understand? This is a matter of ethics. We need to always strive to develop the easiest code to understand and refine. Otherwise, ourselves and those that maintain our code may have a harder job in the future.

** **Ex. 93** — Design `move-alien` by specializing the template for functions on an `alien`. Is this a better design? Why or why not?

** **Ex. 94** — The `move-alien` design separates the moving on the x-axis in two: moving right and moving left. Redesign `move-alien` to only use two auxiliary functions: `move-image-x` and `move-image-y`. Is this a better design? Why or why not?

52.1 Checking Errors

Most modern programming languages allow a programmer to define subtypes and functions to process subtypes. There are some programming languages, however, that do not provide programmers with these abilities. There are also cases where the programmer is unable to guarantee correct input (e.g., when the input to a function depends on the user of a program). What do you do in such cases? One option is to write *guarded* functions. A guarded function uses a conditional expression to first check if the input is valid. If so, it computes the result. Otherwise, it throws an error and provides an error message.

BSL provides the necessary syntax to generate and check errors. An error always returns a string that ought to help understand error. The syntax for generating an error is:

```
(error expr)
```

Use `error` whenever an error must be thrown. The `expr` must evaluate to a string and is returned as the error message. The syntax to test for an error is similar to `check-expect`:

```
(check-error expr expr)
```

This test states that the first given `expr` throws an error that returns the second given `expr`. The second given expression must evaluate to a string.

As an example, consider again the ratio-computing function. If the subtype `posint` is not defined, the guarded function may look as follows:

```
;; nni nni → number throws error
;; Purpose: Return x/y
(define (x-out-of-y x y)
  (if (> y 0)
      (/ x y)
      (error "x-out-of-y: y cannot be zero.")))
```

```
(check-expect (x-out-of-y 2 3)   2/3)
(check-expect (x-out-of-y 3 4)   3/4)
(check-error (x-out-of-y 10 0) "x-out-of-y: y cannot be zero.")
```

Observe that the purpose of this function is to return a number. However, this is not always possible because division by zero is undefined. The signature reflects this by indicating that the function can throw an error. The function's body has a conditional to test the value of y. Whenever y is zero an error is thrown. The third test checks that the correct error message is returned.

The error message generated contains the name of the function. This is included to help the programmer debug the code. It is important for error messages to be informative without being prescriptive. That is, the error message should not suggest how to fix the bug. Suggesting how to fix a bug is a poor approach because we have no way of knowing what design decisions made the programmer led to the bug.

In addition to the function name, an error message may contain values that led to the error. If values are included in an error message a mechanism to include such information in a string is required. BSL provides the format function to generate strings with customized information. The syntax is:

```
(format string expr*)
```

The given string may contain zero or more times the special character, ~s, that is substituted with the value of one of the expressions provided after the string. The ith ~s is substituted with the value of the ith expression.

Consider the following move-right-image-x implementation designed without defining the posint subtype:

```
;; image-x → image-x throws error
;; Purpose: Move the given image-x right
(define (move-right-image-x an-img-x)
 (if (< an-img-x MAX-IMG-X)
     (add1 an-img-x)
     (error (format "move-right-image-x: The character
                     at x=~s cannot move right."
                    MAX-IMG-X))))

;; Sample expressions for move-right-image-x
(define IMGX-VALR1 (add1 MIN-IMG-X))
(define IMGX-VALR2 (add1 11))
(define IMGX-VALRE (format "move-right-image-x: The character
                           at x=~s cannot move right."
                          MAX-IMG-X))

;; Tests using sample computations for move-right-image-x
(check-expect (move-right-image-x MIN-IMG-X) IMGX-VALR1)
(check-expect (move-right-image-x 11)        IMGX-VALR2)
(check-error  (move-right-image-x MAX-IMG-X) IMGX-VALRE)
```

```
;; Tests using sample values for move-right-image-x
(check-expect (move-right-image-x 12) 13)
```

First observe that move-right-image-x is now a guarded function that may throw as error. The body first checks, in essence, if the given image-x is a posint. Second, observe that error message generated includes the function name and the image-x value that causes the error. Both are likely to be useful to a programmer while debugging their code. Third, observe that the error message generated does not suggest to the programmer how to fix the error. Fourth, observe that a sample expression is added to illustrate the computation of an error message. Fifth, observe that the tests include one error-checking test. There is a single test because there is a single image-x value that generates an error. If there were multiple possible values that generate an error, then there would be more than one error-checking test.

A natural question to ask is how does not defining the posint subtype affect the design of move-alien. Even though the function move-alien itself does not include code to raise an error it may still happen. It happens when one of its auxiliary functions raises an error. This must be reflected in the signature for move-alien. Otherwise, it is impossible to discern that it may throw an error. The error returned by an auxiliary function is returned by move-alien. This means sample expressions and tests must be more carefully designed. Sample expressions may not use values, like INIT-ALIEN2, that generate an error. Tests must check expected error messages from auxiliary functions using values that force throwing an error (like INIT-ALIEN2). The function move-alien may be written as follows:

```
;; alien dir → alien throws error
;; Purpose: Move given alien in given direction
(define (move-alien an-alien a-dir)
  (cond [(eq? a-dir 'right)
         (make-posn (move-right-image-x (posn-x an-alien))
                    (posn-y an-alien))]
        [(eq? a-dir 'left)
         (make-posn (move-left-image-x (posn-x an-alien))
                    (posn-y an-alien))]
        [else
          (make-posn (posn-x an-alien)
                     (move-down-image-y (posn-y an-alien)))]))

;; Sample expressions for move-alien
(define MALIEN-VAL1-1
        (make-posn (move-right-image-x (posn-x INIT-ALIEN))
                   (posn-y INIT-ALIEN)))
(define MALIEN-VAL1-2
        (make-posn (move-right-image-x (posn-x INIT-ALIEN2))
                   (posn-y INIT-ALIEN2)))
```

```
(define MALIEN-VAL2-1
        (make-posn (move-left-image-x (posn-x INIT-ALIEN))
                   (posn-y INIT-ALIEN)))
(define MALIEN-VAL2-2
        (make-posn (move-left-image-x (posn-x INIT-ALIEN2))
                   (posn-y INIT-ALIEN2)))
(define MALIEN-VAL3-1
        (make-posn (posn-x INIT-ALIEN)
                   (move-down-image-y (posn-y INIT-ALIEN))))
(define MALIEN-VAL3-2
        (make-posn (posn-x (make-posn 1 8))
                   (move-down-image-y
                     (posn-y (make-posn 1 8)))))

;; Tests using sample computations for move-alien
(check-expect (move-alien INIT-ALIEN  'right) MALIEN-VAL1-1)
(check-expect (move-alien INIT-ALIEN2 'right) MALIEN-VAL1-2)
(check-expect (move-alien INIT-ALIEN  'left)  MALIEN-VAL2-1)
(check-expect (move-alien INIT-ALIEN2 'left)  MALIEN-VAL2-2)
(check-expect (move-alien INIT-ALIEN  'down)  MALIEN-VAL3-1)
(check-expect (move-alien (make-posn 1 8) 'down)
              MALIEN-VAL3-2)

;; Tests using sample values for move-alien
(check-expect (move-alien (make-posn MAX-IMG-X 3) 'down)
              (make-posn MAX-IMG-X 4))
(check-expect (move-alien (make-posn MAX-IMG-X 3) 'left)
              (make-posn (sub1 MAX-IMG-X) 3))
(check-expect (move-alien (make-posn 0 5) 'right)
              (make-posn 1 5))
(check-error
 (move-alien INIT-ALIEN2 'down)
 (format "move-down-image-y: The character at y=~s cannot
          move down."
         MAX-IMG-Y))
(check-error
 (move-alien (make-posn 0 5) 'left)
 (format "move-left-image-x: The character at x=~s cannot
          move left."
         MIN-IMG-X))
(check-error
 (move-alien (make-posn MAX-IMG-X 15) 'right)
 (format "move-right-image-x: The character at x=~s cannot
          move right."
         MAX-IMG-X))
```

```
(check-error
 (move-alien (make-posn 7 MAX-IMG-Y) 'down)
 (format "move-down-image-y: The character at y=~s cannot
         move down. "
         MAX-IMG-Y))
```

The refinements needed by not defining the subtype `posint` are in italics to make them easier to appreciate. They will not be in italics when typed into `DrRacket`. The contract now clearly indicate that this function may throw an error. Observe that there is a new sample expression to move an alien down that replaces the previous test that used `INIT-ALIEN2`. The tests using sample computations are also refined in the same manner. The most interesting refinements are to the tests using sample values. Error tests have been added. The first error-test is written to make sure an error is thrown and the correct error message is returned when an attempt is made to move `INIT-ALIEN2` down. Error-checks for inappropriately trying to move an alien left or right are also added. An alien cannot be moved left if its `image-x` is 0 nor can an alien be moved right if its `alien-x` is `MAX-IMG-X`.

Overall, it now becomes clear that defining subtypes simplifies the design and the code that is developed. Functions designed using subtypes are shorter, because they do not have a guard. Tests are simpler because throwing errors does not need to be checked. Signatures are simpler because errors are not thrown. All this means that a function is easier to understand, to refine, and to explain to others. Whenever possible design using subtypes. In this textbook the version of `move-alien` developed using the subtype `posint` is adopted.

---

* Ex. 95 — Throughout the semester the *Program Correctness* course has 5 quizzes: Q0-Q4. A lower numbered quiz is always given and graded before a higher numbered quiz. A quiz grade may be an integer in [0..100] or, if the quiz has not been given, 'NA. At the beginning of the semester all the quiz grades are 'NA. Write a function to compute the quiz average to date, which may throw an error.

** Ex. 96 — The lengths of the sides of a triangle, a, b, and c, define a right triangle if $a^2 + b^2 = c^2$. Write a function that given the three lengths of a right triangle returns the image of the right triangle. This function may throw an error with one of two messages communicating that either the hypothenuse is too short or the lengths do not define a right triangle.

---

53 The game-over? Handler

To design the `game-over?` handler it is necessary to think about when this version of the game comes to an end. The only way the game comes to an end is when the alien reaches earth. In other words, the problem of detecting the end of the world is reduced to solving a problem about an alien. Think carefully about how can an alien reaching earth be determined. Visually, the alien has reached earth when it is at the bottom of scene. Now, think it terms of the `alien` data definition. How can it be determined that an alien has reached the bottom of the scene? The alien can only be at the bottom of the scene if its y coordinate is `MAX-IMG-Y`.

The above problem analysis allows specializing the template for functions on a world as follows:

```
;; world → Boolean
;; Purpose: Detect if the game is over
(define (game-over? a-world)
  (alien-reached-earth? (world-alien a-world)))

;; Sample expressions for game-over?
(define GAME-OVER     (alien-reached-earth?
                              (world-alien INIT-WORLD2)))
(define GAME-NOT-OVER (alien-reached-earth?
                              (world-alien INIT-WORLD)))

;; Tests using sample computations for game-over?
(check-expect (game-over? INIT-WORLD2) GAME-OVER)
(check-expect (game-over? INIT-WORLD)  GAME-NOT-OVER)

;; Tests using sample values for game-over?
(check-expect (game-over? (make-world 8
                                      (make-posn 0 3)
                                      'right))
              #false)
(check-expect (game-over? (make-world 8
                                      (make-posn 0 MAX-IMG-Y)
                                      'right))
              #true)
```

An auxiliary function, `alien-reached-earth?`, is used to process the world's alien. Two sample expressions are defined to illustrate each of the possible Boolean outcomes. Observe that `INIT-WORLD2` is used to illustrate when the game is over because its alien has a y coordinate equal to `MAX-IMG-Y`. The tests using sample values illustrate each of the possible Boolean outcomes using explicitly constructed worlds for these tests.

The design of `alien-reached-earth?` is based on specializing the template for functions on an `alien`. The y value of the alien must be tested for equality with `MAX-IMG-Y`. The template specialization yields:

```
;; alien → Boolean
;; Purpose: Determine if the given alien reached earth
(define (alien-reached-earth? an-alien)
  (= (posn-y an-alien) MAX-IMG-Y))
```

Fig. 63 Alternatives for the final scene

(a) Alien Above the Bottom in Last Scene.   **(b)** Alien at Bottom in Last Scene.

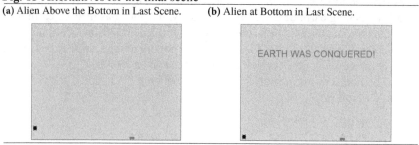

```
;; Sample expressions for alien-reached-earth?
(define ALIEN-EARTH1 (= (posn-y INIT-ALIEN)  MAX-IMG-Y))
(define ALIEN-EARTH2 (= (posn-y INIT-ALIEN2) MAX-IMG-Y))


;; Tests using sample computations for alien-reached-earth?
(check-expect (alien-reached-earth? INIT-ALIEN)  ALIEN-EARTH1)
(check-expect (alien-reached-earth? INIT-ALIEN2) ALIEN-EARTH2)

;; Tests using sample values for alien-reached-earth?
(check-expect (alien-reached-earth? (make-posn 14 0)) #false)
(check-expect (alien-reached-earth? (make-posn 9 MAX-IMG-Y))
              #true)
```

In the sample expressions INIT-ALIEN and INIT-ALIEN2 are used to illustrate, respectively, an alien that has not reached earth and an alien that has reached earth. The tests using sample values illustrate the same using explicitly constructed aliens.

54 Computing the Last Scene

Running the code reveals that all the tests pass. Hooray! Allowing the game to run until the alien reaches earth, however, reveals a small unexpected problem. The final scene is displayed in Fig. 63a. The alien is not at the bottom of the scene. Frankly, it does not look like it quite reached earth. It would be nicer if the final scene displayed were the one in Fig. 63b.

This problem occurs because the universe teachpack stops drawing the world when game-over? evaluates to #true. In the world displayed in Fig. 63a the alien is about to move down and the direction is about to change to right. When this move occurs, however, the universe teachpack detects the end of the game and never draws that final world. To remedy this situation the universe API allows the programmer to specify a function to draw the last world. This function is specified in the stop-when stanza of the big-bang expression as follows:

```
; string → world
; Purpose: To run the game
(define (run a-name)
  (big-bang INIT-WORLD
            [on-draw draw-world]
            [name a-name]
            [on-key process-key]
            [on-tick process-tick TICK-RATE]
            [stop-when game-over? draw-last-world]))
```

The function `draw-last-world` must take as input a world and must return a scene.

To implement `draw-last-world` the template for functions on a world is specialized. The goal is to draw the given final `world` with a message stating that earth was conquered. This message may be placed, for example, half away across and a quarter of the way down in the scene using a font size of 36 and red letters. This analysis yields the following specialization of the template for functions on a `world`:[18]

```
;; world → scene throws error
;; Purpose: To draw the game's final scene
(define (draw-last-world a-world)
 (if (= (posn-y (world-alien a-world)) MAX-IMG-Y)
     (place-image (text "EARTH WAS CONQUERED!" 36 'red)
                  (/ E-SCENE-W 2)
                  (/ E-SCENE-H 4)
                  (draw-world a-world))
     (error
      (format "draw-last-world: Invalid world with ~s as the
               alien's y coordinate. The alien's y coordinate
               must be in [~s..~s]."
              (posn-y (world-alien a-world))
              MIN-IMG-Y
              MAX-IMG-Y))))

;; Sample Instance of (final) world
(define FWORLD1 (make-world 13 (make-posn  0 14) 'right))
(define FWORLD2 (make-world  7 (make-posn 19 14) 'left))

;; Sample expressions for f-on-world
(define FWORLD1-VAL (place-image
                     (text "EARTH WAS CONQUERED!" 36 'red)
                     (/ E-SCENE-W 2)
                     (/ E-SCENE-H 4)
                     (draw-world FWORLD1)))
```

---

[18] The string inputs to `format` should be typed in one line in DrRacket.

Fig. 64 Chapter 9 BSL grammar

```
program ::= {expr | test | def | defs}*
    def ::= (define <variable name> expr)
        ::= (define (<name> <name>+) expr)
   test ::= (check-expect expr expr) | (check-error expr expr)
        ::= (check-within expr expr expr)
   defs ::= (define-struct <struct name> (<field name>*))
   expr ::= number
        ::= string
        ::= \#<character constant>
        ::= '<character+>
        ::= #true
        ::= #false
        ::= <image>
        ::= (<function> expr+)
        ::= (and expr expr expr*)
        ::= (or expr expr expr*)
        ::= (cond [expr expr]+
                  [else expr])
        ::= (if expr expr expr)
```

```
(define FWORLD2-VAL (place-image
                    (text "EARTH WAS CONQUERED!" 36 'red)
                    (/ E-SCENE-W 2)
                    (/ E-SCENE-H 4)
                    (draw-world FWORLD2)))

;; Tests using sample computations for f-on-world
(check-expect (draw-last-world FWORLD1) FWORLD1-VAL)
(check-expect (draw-last-world FWORLD2) FWORLD2-VAL)

;; Tests using sample values for f-on-world
(check-error
 (draw-last-world (make-world 10 (make-posn 7 20) 'right))
 "draw-last-world: Invalid world with 20 as the alien's y
  coordinate. The alien's y coordinate must be in [0..14].")
```

Observe that draw-world is used to draw the given world. When draw-last-world is used by the universe teachpack the given world is the world that stops the game. To make test development easier two sample instances of a (final) world are defined and used both in the sample expressions and in the sample computation tests. The tests using a sample value illustrates that this function throws an error and returns the right error message for a world in which the y coordinate of the alien is not equal to MAX-IMG-Y.

*** **Ex. 97** — Carefully explain why the alien never goes off the scene.

** **Ex. 98** — An alternative ending for the game is the player saving earth if the alien crashes into the rocket. Redesign `game-over?` and `draw-last-world` to implement this alternative ending.

** **Ex. 99** — Redesign the game such that `move-rocket` uses `move-right-image-x` and `move-right-image-y`.

* **Ex. 100** — The `draw-last-world` design did not develop a `world` subtype. As a consequence, `draw-last-world` is a guarded function that may throw an error. Redesign `draw-last-world` by developing a `world` subtype for worlds that end the game.

55 What Have We Learned in This Chapter?

The important lessons of Chap. 9 are summarized as follows:

- The explored BSL syntax is displayed in Fig. 64 and includes the required syntax to test error messages.
- Refining a data definition means that sample instances and functions (sample expressions, defined functions, and tests) must be refined.
- Well-designed code allows for the reuse existing code when a refinement is required.
- Subtypes are defined when a proper subset of a given type needs to be processed.
- If T2 is a subtype of T1, then functions on T1 may process T2 instances. Functions on T2 may not process T1 instances.
- A function may throw an error.
- Error throwing is indicated by having `throws error` in the signature.
- The function `error` is used to throw an error.
- A guarded function returns a value if the input is valid. Otherwise, it throws an error.
- The function `format` is used to create strings customized with values.
- A function to draw a final scene may be specified in the `stop-when` stanza of a `big-bang` expression.

Chapter 10
Structures and Variety

Chapter 9 revealed that functions may consume instances of different data types. This is the case of functions like move-alien and hit?. It turns out that it is common for functions to consume different data types. Functions like move-alien and hit? have a separate parameter for each data type. Now consider designing a function that processes motorized vehicles like cars, motorcycles, and personal transporters or a function that processes geometric shapes like squares, rectangles, triangles, and ellipses. This is a situation that is quite different from designing move-alien and hit?. Now, there is a single input: a motor vehicle. This input, however, may be an instance of several different data types.

This chapter further explores how to design functions that consume data that may vary. Given that there is variety in the data conditional expressions play a central role. Remember that a conditional is needed to distinguish the different varieties. The design may follow a bottom-up or a top-down approach. So far, a top-down approach has been emphasized. In this chapter, a bottom-up approach is taken. Why would you ever take a bottom-up approach? Sometimes it is easier to formulate the simplest forms of data and then use them to define more complex data.

We shall explore the design of a function to process motor vehicles. The characteristics of the different motor vehicles are:

Car   Has a tank capacity in gallons, a miles per gallon, a maximum speed, and a mode. The mode indicates if the car is running in economic mode. When the car is running in economic mode, it may travel 20% further than in normal mode, but the accelerator is less responsive.

Motorcycle   Has a tank capacity in gallons, a miles per gallon, and a maximum speed.

Personal Transporter   Has a maximum miles per hour and maximum hours per charge.

© The Author(s), under exclusive license to Springer Nature Switzerland AG 2022
M. T. Morazán, *Animated Problem Solving*, Texts in Computer Science,
https://doi.org/10.1007/978-3-030-85091-3_10

56 A Bottom-Up Design

A bottom-up design starts with defining the different motor vehicles first. A car has four characteristics and this suggests using a structure. A car and sample instances of a car may be defined as follows:

```
#|
A car is a structure
(make-carr integer>=0 integer>=0 integer>=0 integer>=0 Boolean)
containing tank capacity in gallons, miles per gallon, maximum
speed, and economy mode flag.

;; Sample instances of carr
(define CARR1 ...)

;; carr ... → ...
;; Purpose: ...
(define (f-on-carr a-carr ...)
  ...(carr-gallons a-carr)...(carr-mpg a-carr)
  ...(carr-maxspeed a-carr)...(carr-mode a-carr))

;; Sample expressions for f-on-carr
(define CARR1-VAL ... CARR1 ...)
   ...

;; Tests using sample computations for f-on-carr
(check-expect (f-on-carr CARR1 ...) CARR1-VAL)
   ...

;; Tests using sample values for f-on-carr
(check-expect (f-on-carr ...) ...)
   ...                                                        |#

;; Structure Definition
(define-struct carr (gallons mpg maxspeed mode))

;; Sample Instances of carr
(define CARR1 (make-carr 20 35 140 #true))
(define CARR2 (make-carr 22 15 160 #false))
```

You may think that there is a spelling mistake because carr, not car, is defined. This is not a spelling mistake. There is a function named car in BSL. Therefore, the structure name carr is chosen. Nonetheless, carr represents a car. Given that there is no variety the template suggests at least one sample instance. In this case, two sample instances have been defined: a carr in economic mode and a carr not in economic mode. The definition template lists the four expressions, using carr's selector functions, that may be useful to process a carr. Also given that there is no variety in carr the template suggests at least one test using sample computations and one test using sample values.

We now turn our attention to data analysis for motorcycles. An mc and sample instances of an mc may be defined as follows:

```
#|    A motorcycle, mc, is a structure
         (make-mc integer>=0 integer>=0 integer>=0)
      with a tank capacity in gallons, miles per gallon, and a
      maximum speed.

      ;; Sample instances of mc
      (define MC1 ...)

      ;; mc ... → ...
      ;; Purpose: ...
      (define (f-on-mc an-mc ...)
        ...(mc-gallons an-mc)...(mc-mpg an-mc)
        ...(mc-maxspeed an-mc)...)

      ;; Sample expressions for f-on-mc
      (define MC1-VAL ... MC1 ...)
          ...

      ;; Tests using sample computations for f-on-mc
      (check-expect (f-on-mc MC1 ...) MC1-VAL)
          ...

      ;; Tests using sample values for f-on-mc
      (check-expect (f-on-mc ...) ...)
          ...                                                          |#

      ;; Structure Definition
      (define-struct mc (gallons mpg maxspeed))

      ;; Sample instances of mc
      (define MC1   (make-mc   8  22 135))
      (define MC2   (make-mc  10 20 145))
```

Observe that the defining an mc is similar to defining a carr. Useful expressions to extract data from the given mc instance are found in the function definition template. Given that there is no variety the function template suggests defining at least one sample instance, one sample expression, one test using sample computations, and one test using sample values. Two sample instances are defined for thorough testing and to parallel the work done for carr.

The last motor vehicle to define is the personal transporter. An pt and sample instances of an pt may be defined as follows:

```
#|   A personal transporter, pt, is a structure
        (make-pt integer>=0 integer>=0)
        with a maximum miles per hour and a maximum hours per
        charge.

        ;; Sample instances of pt
        (define PT1 ...)

        ;; pt ... → ...
        ;; Purpose: ...
        (define (f-on-pt a-pt ...)
          ...(pt-mph a-pt)...(pt-hpc a-pt))

        ;; Sample expressions for f-on-pt
        (define PT1-VAL ... PT1 ...)
          ...

        ;; Tests using sample computations for f-on-pt
        (check-expect (f-on-pt PT1 ...) PT1-VAL)
          ...

        ;; Tests using sample values for f-on-pt
        (check-expect (f-on-pt ...) ...)
          ...                                                                |#

        ;; Structure Definition
        (define-struct pt (mph hpc))

        ;; Sample instances of pt
        (define PT1    (make-pt   7  7))
        (define PT2    (make-pt   6 10))
```

Observe that the data design steps are essentially the same as those taken for mc and carr.

It is important to take stock of what has been achieved so far by following a bottom-up approach. There are three data definitions with a function template and sample instances for each. These data definitions correspond to the motor vehicle subtypes. A bottom-up approach, therefore, first defines subtypes.

Once subtypes are defined, the next step is to define a *union type*. A union type enumerates the type varieties that may be used to build instances. If A, B, and C are types, then D may be defined as the union of A, B, and C. A, B, and C are subtypes of D. We say that D is A's, B's, and C's *supertype*. Functions written for a supertype must be able to process instances of each of its subtypes. That is, a function on a supertype must be *polymorphic*. Polymorphic means that a function can process different types of data.

In our example, a supertype for motor vehicles is needed. The supertype mv and instances of mv may be defined as a union type:

```
#|   A motor vehicle, mv, is either:
         1. carr
         2. mc
         3. pt

     ;; Sample instances of mv
     (define MVCARR1 ...)
     (define MVMC1   ...)
     (define MVPT1   ...)


     ;; mv ... → ...
     ;; Purpose: ...
     (define (f-on-mv an-mv ...)
        (cond [(car? an-mv) (f-on-car an-mv ...)]
              [(car? an-mv) (f-on-mc  an-mv ...)]
              [else (f-on-mv an-mv ...)])))

     ;; Sample expressions for f-on-mv
     (define MVCARR1-VAL ... MVCARR1 ...)
     (define MVMC1-VAL   ... MVMC1 ...)
     (define MVPT1-VAL   ... MVPT1 ...)
         ...


     ;; Tests using sample computations for f-on-mv
     (check-expect (f-on-mv MVCARR1 ...) MVCARR1-VAL)
     (check-expect (f-on-mv MVMC1 ...)   MVMC1-VAL)
     (check-expect (f-on-mv MVPT1 ...)   MVPT1-VAL)
         ...


     ;; Tests using sample values for f-on-mv
     (check-expect (f-on-mv ...) ...)
         ...                                                        |#


     ;; Sample instances of mv
     (define MVCARR1 CARR1)
     (define MVCARR2 CARR2)
     (define MVMC1    MC1)
     (define MVMC2    MC2)
     (define MVPT1    PT1)
     (define MVPT2    PT2)
```

Fig. 65 Maximum distance for `mc` and `pt`

```
;; mc → integer>=0
;; Purpose: Return max distance the
;;    given mc may travel on full
(define (mc-maxdist an-mc)
  (* (mc-gallons an-mc)
     (mc-mpg an-mc)))


;; Sample expressions for
;; mc-maxdist
(define MC1-VAL (* (mc-gallons   MC1)
           (mc-mpg   MC1)))
(define MC2-VAL (* (mc-gallons   MC2)
           (mc-mpg   MC2)))


;; Tests using sample computations
;; for mc-maxdist
(check-expect (mc-maxdist MC1)
          MC1-VAL)
(check-expect (mc-maxdist MC1)
          MC1-VAL)


;; Tests using sample values for
;; mc-maxdist
(check-expect (mc-maxdist
          (make-mc 10 10 120))
          100)
(check-expect (mc-maxdist
          (make-mc 8   15 105))
          120)
```

(a) Maximum Distance for mc.

```
;; pt → integer>=0
;; Purpose: Return max distance
;; the given pt may travel on full
(define (pt-maxdist a-pt)
  (* (pt-mph a-pt) (pt-hpc a-pt)))


;; Sample expressions for f-on-pt
(define PT1-VAL (* (pt-mph PT1)
           (pt-hpc PT1)))
(define PT2-VAL (* (pt-mph PT2)
           (pt-hpc PT2)))


;; Tests using sample computations
;; for pt-maxdist
(check-expect (pt-maxdist PT1)
          PT1-VAL)
(check-expect (pt-maxdist PT2)
          PT2-VAL)


;; Tests using sample values
;; for pt-maxdist
(check-expect
  (pt-maxdist (make-pt 4 5))
  20)
```

(b) Maximum Distance for pt.

Observe that a union type is nothing more than a data type that has variety. You have already learned about union types in previous chapters (e.g., speed in Chap. 5 and mn in Chap. 8) although they were not called union types. Therefore, it follows that the definition template has a conditional to distinguish among the subtypes. As expected, the function template also suggests defining at least one sample expression and one test using sample computations for each subtype. Observe that the sample instances are defined using the sample instances of mv's subtypes. This can only be done because an instance of a subtype is also an instance of the supertype. That is, instances of carr, mc, and pt are instances of mv.

With data analysis, finished problems involving motor vehicles may be solved. Consider writing a function to compute the maximum distance a motor vehicle may travel. Following a bottom-up approach means that functions to compute the maximum distance for each subtype (i.e., carr, mc, and pt) are written first. The result of specializing the function templates for mc, pt, and carr is displayed, respectively, in Figs. 65a and 66a. The specialization of the three templates varies in one significant way. In Fig. 65a,b the functions return an integer greater than or equal

Fig. 66 Maximum distance for `carr` and `mv`

```
;; carr → number>=0
;; Purpose: Return max distance the
;;     given carr may travel on full
(define (carr-maxdist a-carr)
  (if (carr-mode a-carr)
      (* 1.2
         (carr-gallons a-carr)
         (carr-mpg a-carr))
      (* (carr-gallons a-carr)
         (carr-mpg a-carr))))
;; Sample expressions for f-on-carr
(define CARR1-VAL
        (* 1.2
           (carr-gallons CARR1)
           (carr-mpg    CARR1)))
(define CARR2-VAL
        (* (carr-gallons  CARR2)
           (carr-mpg  CARR2)))


;; Tests using sample computations
;; for carr-maxdist
(check-expect (carr-maxdist CARR1)
              CARR1-VAL)
(check-expect (carr-maxdist CARR2)
              CARR2-VAL)
;; Tests using sample values
;; for carr-maxdist
(check-expect
  (carr-maxdist
    (make-carr 9 21 10 #true))
  226.8)
(check-expect
  (carr-maxdist
    (make-carr 9 21 10 #false))
  189)


(a) Maximum Distance for carr.
```

```
;; mv → number>=0
;; Purpose: Return max distance
;; the given mv may travel on full
(define (mv-maxdist amv)
  (cond
    [(carr? amv) (carr-maxdist amv)]
    [(mc? amv)   (mc-maxdist  amv)]
    [else (pt-maxdist amv)]))
;; Sample expressions for mv-maxdist
(define MVCARR1-VAL
        (carr-maxdist MVCARR1))
(define MVCARR2-VAL
        (carr-maxdist MVCARR2))
(define MVMC1-VAL
        (mc-maxdist   MVMC1))
(define MVPT1-VAL
        (pt-maxdist   MVPT1))
;; Tests using sample computations
(check-expect (mv-maxdist MVCARR1)
              MVCARR1-VAL)
(check-expect (mv-maxdist MVCARR2)
              MVCARR2-VAL)
(check-expect (mv-maxdist MVMC1)
              MVMC1-VAL)
(check-expect (mv-maxdist MVPT1)
              MVPT1-VAL)
;; Tests using sample values
(check-expect
  (mv-maxdist
    (make-carr 25 40 140 #true))
  1200)
(check-expect
  (mv-maxdist
    (make-carr 25 40 140 #false))
  1000)


(b) Maximum Distance for mv.
```

to zero. In Fig. 66a the function returns a number greater than or equal to zero. This difference in the signatures arises from the observation that `carr-maxdist` may not always return an integer. For example, `(* 1.2 25 40)` evaluates to `1131.6`. All three functions, however, are tested using `check-expect`. Using `check-within` for `carr-maxdist` is not necessary, because `(* 1.2 integer>=0 integer>=0)` is always an exact integer. A careful reader of the code may wonder about not using `check-within`. To mitigate this type of concern an assumption statement may accompany the function definition as follows:

```
;; carr → number>=0
;; Purpose: Return max distance the given carr may travel
;;           on full
```

```
;; Assumption: (* 1.2 integer>=0 integer>=0) is an exact
;;              number>=0
(define (carr-maxdist a-carr)
  (if (carr-mode a-carr)
      (* 1.2 (carr-gallons a-carr) (carr-mpg a-carr))
      (* (carr-gallons a-carr) (carr-mpg a-carr))))
```

After defining the functions for the mv subtypes, the bottom-up design process continues with the design of the function for the supertype: mv-maxdist. The template for functions on an mv suggests using the three auxiliary functions in Figs. 65a and 66a. What is mv-maxdist's return type? Processing an mc or a pt returns an integer>=0. Processing a carr returns a number>=0. These are two different types. An obvious solution is to create a new union type data definition:

```
A distance (dist) is either:
1. integer>=0
2. number>=0
```

Before writing the function template and the sample instances, it is worthwhile to carefully think about this data definition. Observe that integer>=0 is a subtype of number>=0. This means that the value returned by mv-maxdist is always a number>=0. Given that in this problem there is no need to distinguish between the varieties, the data definition for dist is not needed. We can safely claim that mv-maxdist returns a number>=0. With this analysis, the steps of the design recipe may be completed by specializing the template for functions on an mv. The specialization is displayed in Fig. 66b.

*** **Ex. 101** — Change the data definition of a motor vehicle to include a boat:
```
A boat is either:
```
  1. Cruise Boat that has two gas tanks in gallons, a
     miles per gallon, and a mode. The mode indicates
     if the boat is empty. When empty, a cruise boat
     may travel 50 more miles per gallon than when not
     empty.
  2. Speed Boat that has a gas tank per gallon, a
     miles per gallon, and a number of passengers: 1
     or 2. When the boat has 2 passengers it travels
     10 fewer miles per gallon than when it only has 1
     passenger.

Refine mv-maxdist for the new motor vehicle definition.

*** **Ex. 102** — Consider the following data definition:
```
A geometric shape is either:
```
  1.   square: Has a length
  2. rectangle: Has a length and a width
  3.   circle: Has a radius
  4.   ellipse: Has a major axis length and a minor axis length

Design and implement a function to compute the area of a geometric shape.

*** **Ex. 103** — Design and implement a function to compute the perimeter of a geometric shape as defined in the previous problem.

* **Ex. 104** — A flag is a Boolean value used to indicate if a property is present or not. Consider the following data definition:

```
A university student is either:
  1.   freshman: Has a name, last name, enrollment year, and gpa
  2. sophomore: Has a name, last name, enrollment year, gpa,
                and Dean's List flag
  3.     junior: Has a name, last name, enrollment year, gpa,
                and Dean's List flag
  4.     senior: Has a name, last name, enrollment year, gpa,
                and Dean's List flag
```
Write a function that converts a university student to a string.

57 Code Refactoring

Although we have a well-designed and working program, it is possible to do better. Take a close look at the expressions used in the auxiliary functions:

```
(* 1.2 (carr-gallons a-carr) (carr-mpg a-carr)) ;;in mv-maxdist
(*     (carr-gallons a-carr) (carr-mpg a-carr)) ;;in mv-maxdist
(*     (mc-gallons an-mc)    (mc-mpg an-mc))    ;;in mc-maxdist
(*     (pt-hpc a-pt)         (pt-mph a-pt))     ;;in pt-maxdist
```

These expressions all look very similar. The last three expressions are structurally the same. They compute the product of energy units and miles per energy unit. This suggests that abstraction over expressions ought to be used to create a single function to compute these values.

We cannot, however, directly use abstraction over expressions to include the first expression. Although similar, it is structurally different from the other expressions. The first expression multiplies three, not two, quantities. In such a case, consider using a technique called *code refactoring*. Code refactoring restructures existing expressions (or functions) without changing their external behavior. Expressions may be restructured to look the same and, therefore, allow for abstraction over similar expressions. These changes, however, must be done without changing the purpose of the expressions. The first expression above has, 1.2, a constant of proportionality not present in the other three expressions. We can refactor the last three expressions to contain a constant of proportionality as follows:

```
(* 1.2 (carr-gallons a-carr) (carr-mpg a-carr))
(* 1   (carr-gallons a-carr) (carr-mpg a-carr))
```

Fig. 67 The `mv-maxdist` helper function after code refactoring

```
;; number>=0 integer>=0 integer>=0 --> number>=0
;; Purpose: Compute the maximum distance
(define (refactored-helper k energy-units miles/energy-unit)
  (* k energy-units miles/energy-unit))


;; Sample expressions for refactored-helper
(define DIST1 (* 1.2 (carr-gallons CARR1) (carr-mpg CARR1)))
(define DIST2 (* 1   (carr-gallons CARR2) (carr-mpg CARR2)))
(define DIST3 (* 1   (mc-gallons MC1)     (mc-mpg MC1)))
(define DIST4 (* 1   (pt-hpc PT1)         (pt-mph PT1)))


;; Tests using sample computations for refactored-helper
(check-expect
 (refactored-helper 1.2 (carr-gallons CARR1) (carr-mpg CARR1))
 DIST1)
(check-expect
 (refactored-helper 1   (carr-gallons CARR2) (carr-mpg CARR2))
 DIST2)
(check-expect
 (refactored-helper 1   (mc-gallons MC1)     (mc-mpg MC1))
 DIST3)
(check-expect
 (refactored-helper 1   (pt-hpc PT1)         (pt-mph PT1))
 DIST4)


;; Tests using sample values for refactored-helper
(check-expect (refactored-helper 1.2 11 30) 396)
```

```
  (* 1   (mc-gallons an-mc)     (mc-mpg an-mc))
  (* 1   (pt-hpc a-pt)          (pt-mph a-pt))
```

With this new insight, the function in Fig. 67 is designed and written. Observe that for each of the three differences in the sample expressions, there is a parameter in `refactored-helper`. This one function is able to do the work of the three functions in Figs. 65a and 66a. Therefore, we can substitute all the code in Figs. 65a and 66a with the code in Fig. 67.

Eliminating the code to compute the maximum distance for each subtype of motor vehicle means that `mv-maxdist` needs to be refined to use a single helper function. Only the sample expressions and the function definition need to be updated. The tests remain unchanged because `mv-maxdist`'s external behavior remains unchanged. For an `mc` and a `pt` the constant of proportionality is always 1. The energy and energy units and the miles per energy unit are extracted from the given structure. The constant of proportionality may vary from one `carr` to another. Therefore, it is necessary to determine which constant of proportionality to use. This is achieved using a conditional to distinguish if the given `carr` is running in economic mode. The refined code is displayed in Fig. 68. Observe that in the conditional's `carr` stanza there is an `if`-expression to determine the constant of proportionality to use. Further observe that the tests are the same as the tests in Fig. 66b.

Fig. 68 Refined `mv-maxdist` using refactored helper function

```
;; mv → number>=0
;; Purpose: Return max distance the given mv may travel on full
(define (mv-maxdistance an-mv)
 (cond
  [(carr? an-mv)
   (if (carr-mode an-mv)
       (refactored-helper 1.2 (carr-gallons an-mv) (carr-mpg an-mv))
       (refactored-helper 1   (carr-gallons an-mv) (carr-mpg an-mv)))]
  [(mc? an-mv)
   (refactored-helper 1 (mc-gallons an-mv) (mc-mpg an-mv))]
  [else (refactored-helper 1 (pt-hpc an-mv) (pt-mph an-mv))]))

;; Sample expressions for mv-maxdistance
(define MVCARR1-VAL
        (refactored-helper 1.2 (carr-gallons MVCARR1) (carr-mpg MVCARR1)))
(define MVCARR2-VAL
        (refactored-helper 1   (carr-gallons MVCARR2) (carr-mpg MVCARR2)))
(define MVMC2-VAL
        (refactored-helper 1   (mc-gallons MVMC2) (mc-mpg MVMC2)))
(define MVPT1-VAL
        (refactored-helper 1   (pt-hpc MVPT1) (pt-mph MVPT1)))

;; Tests using sample computations for mv-maxdistance
(check-expect (mv-maxdist MVCARR1) MVCARR1-VAL)
(check-expect (mv-maxdist MVCARR2) MVCARR2-VAL)
(check-expect (mv-maxdist MVMC2)   MVMC2-VAL)
(check-expect (mv-maxdist MVPT1)   MVPT1-VAL)

;; Tests using sample values for mv-maxdistance
(check-expect (mv-maxdist (make-carr 25 40 140 #true))  1200 )
(check-expect (mv-maxdist (make-carr 25 40 140 #false)) 1000 )
(check-expect (mv-maxdist (make-mc 12 25 140)) 300 )
(check-expect (mv-maxdist (make-pt 8 5)) 40 )
```

Code refactoring has significantly reduced the size of the code. The original code's four functions are reduced to two. Code refactoring plays a central role in software development. It is used to improve design, structure, and efficiency without changing software functionality.

** **Ex. 105** — The expressions used to compute the maximum distance may instead be refactored as follows:

```
(* (* 1.2 (carr-gallons a-carr)) (carr-mpg a-carr))
(* (carr-gallons a-carr)         (carr-mpg a-carr))
(* (mc-gallons an-mc)            (mc-mpg an-mc))
(* (pt-hpc a-pt)                 (pt-mph a-pt))
```

The computation of the maximum distances is always the product of two numbers. Use this code refactoring idea to refine the implementation of mv-maxdist in Fig. 66b.

** **Ex. 106** — *Horner's Method*. Implement functions for:
$$f(x) = 4x^3 + 10x^2 + 5x + 8$$
$$g(x) = 3x^4 + x^3 + 17x^2 + 7x + 2$$
Now that you have implemented the two functions, observe that many of the same values are repeatedly computed. For example, in f the value of x^2 is computed for $10x^2$ and $4x^3$ and in g the value of x^2 is computed for $17x^2$, x^3, and $3x^4$. Repeatedly computing the same value is inefficient.

In 1819, William George Horner observed that a function's expression may be refactored to avoid repeating computations. For example, consider the following h:
$$h(x) = 87x^4 + 31x^2 + 17x + 99$$
Computing the value of h(x) naively requires 9 multiplications and 3 additions. Horner observed that h(x) may be refactored to:
$$h(x) = 99 + x(17 + x(31 + x(0 + x(87))))$$
Observe that computing the value of h(x) only requires 4 multiplications and 4 additions now. Refactor your code for f(x) and g(x) to take advantage of Horner's method. Make sure you only refine the sample expressions and the definition bodies.

58 What Have We Learned in This Chapter?

The important lessons of Chap. 10 are summarized as follows:

- Use a bottom-up design approach when it is easier to define the simplest forms of data first.
- A supertype is a collection of one or more subtypes that define a data type.
- A union type is an enumeration of subtypes that may be used to define a supertype.
- A bottom-up design of a function that processes a supertype instance starts with the auxiliary functions, one for each subtype, and then designs the function for the supertype.
- If a supertype has variety, has a subtype, A, that contains all the other subtypes, and had no need to distinguish among the varieties of the supertype, then A may be used instead of defining subtypes.
- Code refactoring restructures existing expressions or functions without changing their external behavior.
- Abstracting over refactored expressions may be an effective means to simplify the function design.

- When the subtype code is refactored, supertype sample expressions and functions may have to be refined.
- Code refactoring is used to improve design, structure, and efficiency without changing software functionality.

Chapter 11
Aliens Attack Version 3

Writing union types that contain structure-based subtypes endows us with the power
to refine Aliens Attack version 2 (from Chap. 9). This chapter discusses adding a
shot to the game. As in Aliens Attack version 2, the world in version 3 has a rocket,
an alien, and a direction. The world data definition is now refined to contain a shot.
We emphasize the singular here. There can be at most one shot in the game at any
time. A player may shoot only when there is no shot in the game. At the beginning
of the game, for example, the player may shoot. A player may not shoot again until
the last shot created goes off the top of the scene.

Now that a shot is part of the world it becomes possible for the player to win the
game. When does this happen? It is fairly straightforward to see that the player ought
to win when the alien is hit by the shot. It is less straightforward to precisely define
when an alien has been hit. Clearly, the alien has been hit when the coordinates of
the alien and the shot are the same. For example, if the alien and the shot are both (4
2) then the alien has been hit and the player wins the game. Now consider an alien
at (0 7), a shot at (0 6), and the direction being 'down. This puts the alien and
the shot at the left edge of the scene. The alien moves to coordinate (0 6) and the
shot moves to coordinates (0 7). Has the alien been hit? On the one hand, the alien
and the shot are never the same. On the other hand, the alien and the shot cross each
other. This is a situation that forces game designer to choose feature. If it is not a hit,
it makes the game a bit more challenging for the player to win. If it is a hit, it makes
the game a bit easier to win. The presented design chooses the former feature. An
alien moving down "sees" the shot coming and skittles beneath it to avoid the hit.

Adding a shot to the world means that world's function template and world
sample instances must also be refined. In addition, any functions and tests that build
a world must be updated. This is the same process followed to develop Aliens Attack
2. The refinement presented follows a top-down design. The first step is to refine
the world data definition. The second step is to define a shot. The third step is
the refinement of the program and the design of new functions. Observe that data
analysis is performed first. Remember that if you do not have a clear understanding
of the data being processed, then it is impossible to design a solution to a problem.

Fig. 69 A sample rendering of Aliens attack with a shot

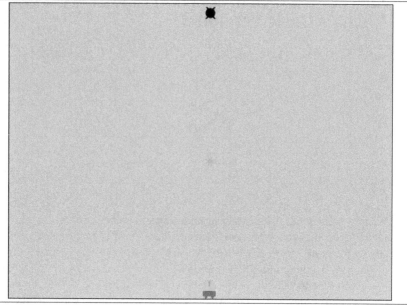

59 Data Definitions

Figure 69 displays a rendering of the game that now includes a shot. The only new component is the shot. Therefore, the world data definition is refined as follows:

```
#| A world is a structure: (make-world rocket alien dir shot).

   ;; world ... → ...
   ;; Purpose: ...
   (define (f-on-world a-world ...)
      ...(f-on-rocket (world-rocket a-world) ...)
      ...(f-on-alien  (world-alien  a-world) ...)
      ...(f-on-dir    (world-dir a-world)    ...)
      ...(f-on-shot   (world-shot a-world)   ...))

   ;; Sample instances for world
   (define WORLD1 (make-world ...))

   ;; Sample expressions for f-on-world
   (define WORLD-VAL1 ...)

   ;; Tests using sample computations for f-on-world
   (check-expect (f-on-world WORLD1 ...) WORLD-VAL1)

      ...
```

```
;; Tests using sample values for f-on-world
(check-expect (f-on-world ...) ...)                              #|
```

The data definition includes a new field of type shot. This new type is not yet defined. Therefore, the world data definition is written assuming that the shot data definition will be developed. Observe that the sample instances of the world are not yet refined for this reason. Their refinement requires instances of shot and, therefore, must be postponed until shot is defined. Nonetheless, the definition template contains an expression, (f-on-shot (world-shot a-world) ...), to process a shot. Once again, we see a disciplined separation of concerns. A function on a world does not process a shot. Instead, a function on a shot is used to process the given world's shot.

Now, let us think about what a shot is. Remember that a shot is not an image of a shot. A player uses a key, say the space bar key (or simply the space key), to shoot. Think about what may change from one instance on a shot to another. A shot moves as follows:

A shot always moves up. What changes when a shot moves up? Clearly, an image-y coordinate is needed to represent a shot that moves up. Is an image-x coordinate needed? As the shot moves up the image-x coordinate never changes. However, the image-x coordinate may vary among shots. This coordinate is determined by the position of the rocket when the shot is created. If the rocket is 4 when the player shoots, then the new shot's image-x coordinate is 4. If the rocket is 10 when the player shoots, then the new shot's image-x coordinate is 10. This means that an image-x coordinate is needed. Using a posn to represent a shot is a good option.

What posn should be used for the shot at the beginning of the game? This is an interesting question because the player has not created a shot. If a shot has not been created, how can it have image-x and image-y coordinates? This situation is suggesting that there is variety in shots: non-existing and existing shots. We have already determined to represent an existing shot using a posn. The representation choice for a non-existing shot is arbitrary. We shall define, NO-SHOT, a symbol constant to represent such a shot. Based on this data analysis the data definition for a shot and the template for a function on a shot are:

```
(define NO-SHOT 'no-shot)
```

```
#|   A shot is either:
       1. NO-SHOT
       2. A structure (make-posn image-x image-y)
```

```
;; Sample instances of shot
(define SHOT1 ...)
(define SHOT2 ...)

;; shot ... → ...
;; Purpose: ...
(define (f-on-shot a-shot ...)
  (if (eq? a-shot NO-SHOT)
      ...
      ...(f-on-image-x (posn-x a-shot))
      ...(f-on-image-y (posn-y a-shot))...)))

;; Sample expressions for f-on-shot
(define SHOT1-VAL ...)
(define SHOT2-VAL ...)
  ...

;; Tests using sample computations for f-on-shot
(check-expect (f-on-shot SHOT1 ...) SHOT1-VAL)
(check-expect (f-on-shot SHOT2 ...) SHOT2-VAL)
  ...

;; Tests using sample values for f-on-shot
(check-expect (f-on-shot ...) ...)
  ...                                                                    |#
```

Observe that a posn is used to represent both an `alien` and a `shot`. Although the same representation is used, the expected behavior is quite different. A posn representing a shot may only be moved up. On the other hand, a shot representing an `alien` may be may be moved right, left, and down. This further highlights why data definitions are important. They clearly outline that not all data represented using a posn is the same.

Now that a shot is defined it is possible to define sample instances of a shot and refined the sample instances of a world. These are:

```
;; Sample instances of shot
(define INIT-SHOT NO-SHOT)
(define SHOT2 (make-posn (/ MAX-CHARS-HORIZONTAL 2)
                         (/ (sub1 MAX-CHARS-VERTICAL) 2)))
(define SHOT3 (make-posn 4 MAX-IMG-Y))
(define SHOT4 (make-posn 14 MIN-IMG-Y))

;; Sample instances of world
(define INIT-WORLD  (make-world INIT-ROCKET INIT-ALIEN
                                INIT-DIR    INIT-SHOT))
(define INIT-WORLD2 (make-world INIT-ROCKET2 INIT-ALIEN2
                                DIR2         SHOT2))
```

```
(define WORLD3 (make-world 7        (make-posn 3 3)
                           'right (make-posn 3 3)))
```

As suggested by the template for a function on a shot, there is at least one shot instance for each variety. In addition, shots are defined for extrema image-y values. The world instances now contain a shot. The first instance is a world that does not contain a shot. The second instance is a world that contains a shot. The third world instance illustrates that the same posn instance may be an alien or a shot.

60 The draw-world Refinement

In addition to rendering the rocket and the alien, the shot must be rendered. The only decision that needs to be made is whether the alien or the shot is rendered on top when a hit occurs. This is mostly a matter of personal preferences. In order to clearly see that a hit has occurred, the chosen design renders the shot on top of the alien. This means that the shot must be rendered in a scene that contains the alien. Given that we have already developed code to render a scene that has the alien and the rocket, all we need is function composition to draw the shot in such a scene. First, let us refine the sample expressions for draw-world:

```
;; Sample expressions for draw-world
(define WORLD-SCN1
        (draw-shot (world-shot INIT-WORLD)
                   (draw-alien (world-alien INIT-WORLD)
                               (draw-rocket
                                   (world-rocket INIT-WORLD)
                                               E-SCENE))))

(define WORLD-SCN2
        (draw-shot (world-shot INIT-WORLD2)
                   (draw-alien (world-alien INIT-WORLD2)
                               (draw-rocket
                                   (world-rocket INIT-WORLD2)
                                               E-SCENE))))
```

Observe that the shot is rendered in a scene that contains the alien (and the rocket) using function composition. In addition to such a scene, the new function to draw the shot takes as input the world's shot.

The above sample expressions lead to the following refinement of the function definition for draw-world:

```
;; world → scene
;; Purpose: To draw the world in E-SCENE
```

```
(define (draw-world a-world)
  (draw-shot (world-shot a-world)
             (draw-alien (world-alien a-world)
                         (draw-rocket (world-rocket a-world)
                                      E-SCENE))))
```

The final step for draw-world is to refine the tests. The tests using sample computations do not need to be refined because they do not build a world. The tests using sample values, on the other hand, need to be refined given that they build worlds. These are refined to construct a world in which the player has not created a shot and a world in which the player has not created a shot:

```
(check-expect
  (draw-world (make-world INIT-ROCKET2 INIT-ALIEN
                          INIT-DIR3    NO-SHOT))
```

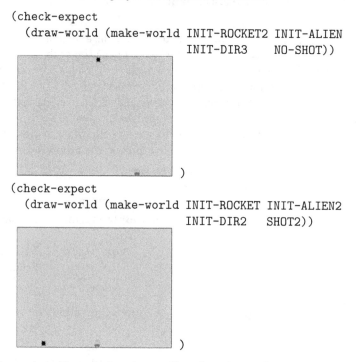

```
                                                     )
(check-expect
  (draw-world (make-world INIT-ROCKET INIT-ALIEN2
                          INIT-DIR2    SHOT2))
```

```
                                                     )
```

The next step is to design the auxiliary function to draw a shot. To do so, the template for a function on a shot is specialized. Think carefully about how to draw a shot. There are two varieties of shot. Think about each variety independently. If the given shot is 'NO-SHOT, then there is nothing to draw in the given scene. If the given shot is a posn, then the shot must be drawn at the image coordinates contained in the shot. This problem analysis leads to the following template specialization:

```
;; shot scene → scene
;; Purpose: To draw the shot in the given scene
(define (draw-shot a-shot scn)
  (if (eq? a-shot NO-SHOT)
      scn
      (draw-ci SHOT-IMG (posn-x a-shot) (posn-y a-shot) scn)))
```

```
;; Sample expressions for draw-shot
(define INIT-SHOT-VAL E-SCENE)
(define SHOT2-VAL (draw-ci SHOT-IMG       (posn-x SHOT2)
                           (posn-y SHOT2) E-SCENE))
(define SHOT3-VAL (draw-ci SHOT-IMG       (posn-x SHOT3)
                           (posn-y SHOT3) E-SCENE2))


;; Tests using sample computations for draw-shot
(check-expect (draw-shot INIT-SHOT E-SCENE)  INIT-SHOT-VAL)
(check-expect (draw-shot SHOT2     E-SCENE)  SHOT2-VAL)
(check-expect (draw-shot SHOT3     E-SCENE2) SHOT3-VAL)


;; Tests using sample values for draw-shot
(check-expect (draw-shot INIT-SHOT E-SCENE2) E-SCENE2)
(check-expect (draw-shot SHOT2 E-SCENE2)
```

```
)
```

The signature identifies a shot and a scene as input values and a scene as the output
value. The purpose statement concisely describes what the function does. The sample
expressions illustrate the computations that are performed for the different shot
varieties. The first sample expression illustrates that nothing needs to be computed for
INIT-SHOT (which is 'NO-SHOT). The second and third sample expressions illustrate
how to compute a scene that contains a shot using draw-ci (the same function used
to draw an alien a rocket). The conditional expression in the body of the function
definition first determines if the given shot is 'NO-SHOT. If so, the given scene
is returned without any further computation as done in the first sample expression.
Otherwise, the shot ci is rendered in the given scene at the image coordinates
contained in the given shot as done in the other sample expressions. The tests using
sample computations employ the differences among the sample expressions and the
defined constants, as before, to illustrate that the defined function returns the same
values as those obtained from the sample expressions. Finally, the tests using sample
values further illustrate that the function works for each variety of shot using a
combination of input values not used in the sample expressions.

61 The `process-key` Refinement

The key event handler must be updated to construct `world`s that contain a `shot`. In addition, this function must also process the key event associated with shooting. The key choice is arbitrary, but as indicated before a popular choice is to use the space key to allow a player to shoot.[19] This means that the key data definition and the template for a function on a key must be refined. This is done as follows:

```
A key is either:
  1. "right"
  2. "left"
  3. " "
  4. not "right", "left", or " "

;; Sample instances of key
(define KEY1 ...)
(define KEY2 ...)
(define KEY3 ...)
(define KEY4 ...)

;; key ... → ...
;; Purpose: ...
(define (f-on-key a-key ...)
  (cond [(key=? a-key "right") ...]
        [(key=? a-key "left") ...]
        [(key=? a-key " ") ...]
        [else ...]))

;; Sample expressions for f-on-key
(define KEY1-VAL ... KEY1 ...)
(define KEY2-VAL ... KEY2 ...)
(define KEY3-VAL ... KEY3 ...)
(define KEY4-VAL ... KEY4 ...)

;; Tests using sample computations for f-on-key
(check-expect (f-on-key KEY1 ...) KEY1-VAL)
(check-expect (f-on-key KEY2 ...) KEY2-VAL)
(check-expect (f-on-key KEY3 ...) KEY3-VAL)
(check-expect (f-on-key KEY4 ...) KEY4-VAL)
    ...

;; Tests using sample values for f-on-key
(check-expect (f-on-key ...) ...)
    ...
```

---

[19] Another popular choice is to use the up-arrow key.

The data definition now contains four key varieties. Therefore, there are now four sample instances, four sample expressions, four stanzas in the definition-template's conditional, and four tests using sample computations. The refined template clearly informs us that there must be at least 4, not 3, of each of these items in the definition of process-key.

Next, analyze the problem of processing the space key. When should a shot be created? There can only be at most one shot in a world. This means a new shot cannot be created every time the player tries to shoot. A decision must be made as to whether to construct a new shot or not. The details of how this is done are left to an auxiliary function, but there are two cases. If there is no shot in the game, then a new shot is created and added to the world. Otherwise, a new shot is not created and the shot in the world is left unchanged.

Start by refining the sample instances. It is logical to start with this refinement because these constants may be used to simplify sample expression refinement and development. The four needed sample instances may be defined as follows:

```
;; Sample instances of key
(define KEY1 "right")
(define KEY2 "left")
(define KEY3 "m")
(define KEY4 " ")
```

Next, refine the sample expressions for process-key. Recall that the new world data definition tells us that worlds must be constructed with a shot and that the template for a function on a key tells us there must be at least four sample expressions. The sample expressions may be refined as follows:

```
;; Sample expressions for process-key
(define KEY-RVAL  (make-world (move-rckt-right
                                 (world-rocket INIT-WORLD))
                              (world-alien INIT-WORLD)
                              (world-dir INIT-WORLD)
                              (world-shot INIT-WORLD)))
(define KEY-LVAL  (make-world (move-rckt-left
                                 (world-rocket INIT-WORLD))
                              (world-alien INIT-WORLD)
                              (world-dir INIT-WORLD)
                              (world-shot INIT-WORLD)))
(define KEY-SVAL  (make-world (world-rocket INIT-WORLD)
                              (world-alien INIT-WORLD)
                              (world-dir INIT-WORLD)
                              (process-shooting
                                (world-shot INIT-WORLD)
                                (world-rocket INIT-WORLD)))))
(define KEY-SVAL2 (make-world (world-rocket INIT-WORLD2)
                              (world-alien INIT-WORLD2)
                              (world-dir INIT-WORLD2)
```

```
                              (process-shooting
                               (world-shot INIT-WORLD2)
                               (world-rocket INIT-WORLD2))))
(define KEY-OVAL INIT-WORLD2)
```

The sample expressions for "right" and "left", KEY-RVAL and KEY-LVAL, are refined to build a world with an unchanged shot. The sample expression for the fourth key variety, KEY-OVAL, remains unchanged because a world is not constructed. The remaining sample expressions, KEY-SVAL and KEY-SVAL2, illustrate how a new world is computed, respectively, when a world does not contain a shot and when it contains a shot. In either case, as per the problem analysis above, the processing of the shooting key is left to an auxiliary function. This function requires at least two inputs: the world's shot and the world's rocket. The shot is needed to determine if a new shot may be created. The rocket is needed to provide the image-x coordinate if a new shot is created. If any further inputs are needed by this function its design ought to reveal them.

Abstracting over the sample expressions confirms that process-key must be refined to have a conditional with four stanzas. The refined function is:

```
;; world key → world
;; Purpose: Process a key event to return next world
(define (process-key a-world a-key)
  (cond [(key=? a-key "right")
         (make-world (move-rckt-right (world-rocket a-world))
                     (world-alien a-world)
                     (world-dir a-world)
                     (world-shot a-world))]
        [(key=? a-key "left")
         (make-world (move-rckt-left (world-rocket a-world))
                     (world-alien a-world)
                     (world-dir a-world)
                     (world-shot a-world))]
        [(key=? a-key " ")
         (make-world (world-rocket a-world)
                     (world-alien a-world)
                     (world-dir a-world)
                     (process-shooting
                       (world-shot a-world)
                       (world-rocket a-world)))]
        [else a-world]))
```

Observe that there is now a stanza for the new key variety (i.e., " ") and that world construction always includes a shot.

Tests using sample computations are refined by adding tests using KEY-SVAL and KEY-SVAL2:

```
(check-expect (process-key INIT-WORLD  " ") KEY-SVAL)
(check-expect (process-key INIT-WORLD2 " ") KEY-SVAL2)
```

The other tests using sample computations remain unchanged. Tests using sample values are updated to correctly construct worlds and to further illustrate how the space key is processed. For example, the following are refined tests using sample values:

```
;; Tests using sample values for process-key
(check-expect (process-key (make-world
                               (sub1 MAX-CHARS-HORIZONTAL)
                               INIT-ALIEN
                               'right
                               INIT-SHOT)
                            "right")
              (make-world (sub1 MAX-CHARS-HORIZONTAL)
                          INIT-ALIEN
                          'right
                          INIT-SHOT))

(check-expect (process-key (make-world 0
                                       INIT-ALIEN
                                       'left
                                       INIT-SHOT)
                           " ")
              (make-world 0
                          INIT-ALIEN
                          'left
                          (make-posn 0 MAX-IMG-Y)))
```

---

* Ex. 107 — Refine all the process-key tests using sample values that are in Aliens Attack 2.

* Ex. 108 — Add tests using sample values to further illustrate how the space key is processed.

* Ex. 109 — There are repetitions in the process-key tests using sample values. For example, the first test above creates the same world twice. Rewrite the tests without repetitions. Make sure not to change what is being tested.

With the refinement of process-key completed focus turns to the design of the auxiliary function to process the space key. This function takes as input two different types of data: a shot and a rocket. Which template ought to be used to design this function? To answer this question it is necessary to do careful problem analysis. This function must create a new shot only when the game does not already have a posn shot. When ought a new shot be created? A new shot is created only when the game's shot is 'NO-SHOT. This immediately suggests designing this function by specializing the template for a function on a shot because its body distinguishes among shot varieties.

Can this function be designed by specializing the template for a function on a rocket? If you think carefully about this the answer is no. The given rocket does not have enough information to decide whether or not a shot ought to be created. This is a situation in which one input dominates another input. When facing such a problem design around the dominating input.

Given that the dominating input is the given shot, the function template for a function on a shot is specialized as follows:

```
;; shot rocket → shot
;; Purpose: To process a shooting attempt
(define (process-shooting a-shot a-rocket)
  (if (eq? a-shot NO-SHOT)
      (make-posn a-rocket MAX-IMG-Y)
      a-shot))


;; Sample expressions for process-shooting
(define PS-SHOT-VAL1 (make-posn INIT-ROCKET MAX-IMG-Y))
(define PS-SHOT2-VAL SHOT2)
(define PS-SHOT3-VAL SHOT3)


;; Tests using sample computations for process-shooting
(check-expect (process-shooting INIT-SHOT INIT-ROCKET)
              PS-SHOT-VAL1)
(check-expect (process-shooting SHOT2 INIT-ROCKET)
              PS-SHOT2-VAL)
(check-expect (process-shooting SHOT3 INIT-ROCKET2)
              PS-SHOT3-VAL)


;; Tests using sample values for process-shooting
(check-expect (process-shooting NO-SHOT 8)
              (make-posn 8 MAX-IMG-Y))
(check-expect (process-shooting (make-posn 17 9) 8)
              (make-posn 17 9))
```

The sample expressions illustrate the returned value for each shot variety. When it is 'NO-SHOT a new posn shot is created using the rocket as the shot's image-x coordinate. Otherwise, a new shot is not created. The body of the definition returns a new posn shot when the game does not have a shot. Otherwise, it returns the given shot. The tests using sample computations illustrate that process-shooting computes the same values as the sample expressions. The tests using sample values further illustrate that process-shooting works for both shot varieties. This completes the design of process-key.

62 The `process-tick` **Refinement**

To refine `process-tick`, like any other problem, first perform problem analysis. Outline what needs to happen when the clock ticks. In Aliens Attack 2 tick processing created a new world by moving the alien and computing a direction. These tasks must still be performed in this new Aliens Attack version. To construct a new `world`, however, a `shot` instance is needed. Does a shot change after a clock tick? Once again, reason about each `shot` variety. If the `shot` is `'NO-SHOT`, then it does not change. If the shot is a `posn`, then it either must move up or disappear because it has reached the top of the `scene`. The details of how the new `shot` is computed is left to an auxiliary function that processes a `shot`.

62.1 The Refinement

The sample expressions must now illustrate that the alien is moved, a new direction is computed, and the shot is moved (if possible). The sample expressions are refined as follows:

```
;; Sample expressions for process-tick
(define AFTER-TICK-WORLD1
        (make-world
          (world-rocket INIT-WORLD)
          (move-alien (world-alien INIT-WORLD)
                      (world-dir INIT-WORLD))
          (new-dir-after-tick (move-alien
                                (world-alien INIT-WORLD)
                                (world-dir INIT-WORLD))
                              (world-dir INIT-WORLD))
          (move-shot (world-shot INIT-WORLD))))

(define AFTER-TICK-WORLD2
        (make-world
          (world-rocket INIT-WORLD2)
          (move-alien (world-alien INIT-WORLD2)
                      (world-dir INIT-WORLD2))
          (new-dir-after-tick (move-alien
                                (world-alien INIT-WORLD2)
                                (world-dir INIT-WORLD2))
                              (world-dir INIT-WORLD2))
          (move-shot (world-shot INIT-WORLD2))))
```

Observe that, just as in Aliens Attack 2, the rocket is unchanged, the alien is moved, and a new direction is computed. Moving the shot is left to an auxiliary function, `move-shot`, that is to be designed after completing the `process-tick` refinement.

The refinement of process-tick's definition is accomplished by adding the call to move-shot:

```
;; world → world
;; Purpose: Create a new world after a clock tick
(define (process-tick a-world)
  (make-world (world-rocket a-world)
              (move-alien (world-alien a-world)
                          (world-dir a-world))
              (new-dir-after-tick (move-alien
                                    (world-alien a-world)
                                    (world-dir a-world))
                                  (world-dir a-world))
              (move-shot (world-shot a-world))))
```

Observe that the specialization is similar to code refactoring. The function body is restructured without changing the behavior of the function. When a function is refined or refactored without changing its external behavior, the function's signature remains unchanged.

Given that the external behavior of the function is unchanged, the tests using sample computations remain unchanged. The tests using sample values, on the other hand, must be refined because worlds are built. The worlds built for the call to process-tick must now contain a shot. Think carefully about the expressions needed for the expected values. If there is no shot or the shot is at the top of the scene in the given world, then the expected world must be built using 'NO-SHOT. Otherwise, the shot is moved up. The refined tests are:

```
;; Tests using sample values for process-tick
(check-expect (process-tick (make-world INIT-ROCKET
                                        (make-posn 1 5)
                                        'left
                                        INIT-SHOT))
              (make-world INIT-ROCKET
                          (make-posn MIN-IMG-X 5)
                          'down
                          INIT-SHOT))

(check-expect (process-tick
                (make-world
                  INIT-ROCKET2
                  (make-posn (- MAX-CHARS-HORIZONTAL 2) 10)
                  'right
                  SHOT2))
              (make-world INIT-ROCKET2
                          (make-posn MAX-IMG-X 10)
                          'down
                          (move-shot SHOT2)))
```

```
(check-expect (process-tick (make-world INIT-ROCKET2
                                        (make-posn MAX-IMG-X 2)
                                        'down
                                        (make-posn 15 6)))
              (make-world INIT-ROCKET2
                          (make-posn MAX-IMG-X 3)
                          'left
                          (make-posn 15 5)))

(check-expect (process-tick (make-world
                             INIT-ROCKET2
                             (make-posn MIN-IMG-X 2)
                             'down
                             (make-posn 2 MIN-IMG-Y)))
              (make-world INIT-ROCKET2
                          (make-posn MIN-IMG-X 3)
                          'right
                          NO-SHOT))
```

Remember that `image-y` coordinates grow from top to bottom. Thus, moving the shot is accomplished by decreasing its `image-y` coordinate.

62.2 The `move-shot` Design

Writing tests for `process-tick` has provided an insight into how to move a shot: a `posn` shot is moved by decreasing its `image-y` coordinate. It is still necessary to perform problem analysis. There are two `shot` varieties. How is a `'NO-SHOT` shot moved? If there is no `shot` in the game, then there is nothing to move. Therefore, the `shot` remains unchanged. Now, carefully think about how a `posn` shot is moved. Does a `shot` always move up? If it did, then the player would only be able to shoot once during the game. This, however, is not what is needed. We wish to allow the player to shoot again when a `shot` goes off the top of the scene. How does this affect how a `shot` is moved? In order to allow the player to shoot again a `posn` shot must become a `'NO-SHOT` shot when it moves off the top of the scene. This analysis suggests that there are three conditions that must be tested:

```
            (eq? a-shot NO-SHOT) → shot remains unchanged
      (= (posn-y a-shot) MIN-IMG-Y) → shot changes to 'NO-SHOT
(not (= (posn-y a-shot) MIN-IMG-Y)) → shot's image-y is decreased
```

Armed with the insights provided by problem analysis, the template for functions on a shot is specialized. We start with sample expressions. Given that there are three conditions at least 3 sample expressions need to be defined:

```
;; Sample expressions for move-shot
(define MSHOT1-VAL INIT-SHOT)
(define MSHOT2-VAL (make-posn
                        (posn-x SHOT2)
                        (move-up-image-y (posn-y SHOT2)))))
(define MSHOT4-VAL NO-SHOT)
```

The first sample expression is for a 'NO-SHOT shot. The second sample expression is for a posn shot that may move up. The third sample expression is for a posn shot that may not be moved up. Observe that separation of concerns is maintained by requiring a new auxiliary function to move an image-y instance up. The design of this new function is delayed until the design of move-shot is completed.

The tests for move-shot are as follows:

```
;; Tests using sample computations for move-shot
(check-expect (move-shot INIT-SHOT) MSHOT1-VAL)
(check-expect (move-shot SHOT2) MSHOT2-VAL)
(check-expect (move-shot SHOT4) MSHOT4-VAL)

;; Tests using sample values for move-shot
(check-expect (move-shot (make-posn 5 5)) (make-posn 5 4))
(check-expect (move-shot (make-posn 5 MIN-IMG-Y)) NO-SHOT)
```

The tests using sample computations use, as expected, the values of the sample expressions. The tests using sample values further illustrate how posn shots are moved. They clearly show when the image-y coordinate is decreased and when a posn shot becomes a 'NO-SHOT shot.

The definition template may now be specialized. The conditional must have three stanzas (not two as suggested by the template):

```
;; shot → shot
;; Purpose: To move the given shot
(define (move-shot a-shot)
  (cond [(eq? a-shot NO-SHOT) a-shot]
        [(= (posn-y a-shot) MIN-IMG-Y) NO-SHOT]
        [else (make-posn (posn-x a-shot)
                          (move-up-image-y (posn-y a-shot)))]))
```

Observe that the first and second stanzas always return the same value: 'NO-SHOT. This means that the function may be refactored in an attempt to simplify it. The first two stanzas may be combined into one stanza. The resulting function is:

```
;; shot → shot
;; Purpose: To move the given shot
(define (move-shot a-shot)
  (cond [(or (eq? a-shot NO-SHOT)
             (= (posn-y a-shot) MIN-IMG-Y))
         NO-SHOT]
```

```
[else (make-posn (posn-x a-shot)
                 (move-up-image-y (posn-y a-shot)))]))
```

This simplification step is not necessary. Such simplification steps ought to be performed only if you feel it makes the program easier to understand.

We move onto solving the problem of moving an image-y value up. Moving up simply means decreasing the value of the given image-y. Specializing the template for a function on an image-y is fairly straightforward. The result of the specialization is:

```
;; image-y>min → image-y
;; Purpose: To move the given image-y>min up
(define (move-up-image-y an-img-y>min)
  (sub1 an-img-y>min))


;; Sample expressions for move-up-image-y
(define IMGY>MIN-VAL1 (sub1 IMG-Y>MIN1))
(define IMGY>MIN-VAL2 (sub1 IMG-Y>MIN2))


;; Tests using sample computations for move-up-image-y
(check-expect (move-up-image-y AN-IMG-Y)  IMGY>MIN-VAL1)
(check-expect (move-up-image-y MAX-IMG-Y) IMGY>MIN-VAL2)


;; Tests using sample values for f-on-image-y>min
(check-expect (move-up-image-y 6)  5)
(check-expect (move-up-image-y 11) 10)
```

At this point, you have hopefully developed enough expertise with template specialization that a detailed explanation for the design of move-up-image-y is no longer necessary. Nonetheless, make sure you understand how each step of the design recipe is satisfied. It is important to note, however, that the signature of the function is carefully crafted. Observe that the input is not an image-y value. Instead, it is a subtype of image-y: the image-y instances greater than MIN-IMG-Y. This is necessary to guarantee that the returned value is always an image-y instance.

---

* **Ex. 110** — The design of move-shot may more strictly adhere to the template for a function on a shot by not changing the number of conditions from 2 to 3. The following is an alternative design using the conditional to strictly discriminate among the shot varieties:

```
;; shot → shot
;; Purpose: To move the given shot
(define (move-shot a-shot)
  (cond [(eq? a-shot NO-SHOT) a-shot]
        [else
          (cond [(= (posn-y a-shot) MIN-IMG-Y) NO-SHOT]
                [else (make-posn
```

```
                                (posn-x a-shot)
                                (move-up-image-y (posn-y a-shot))))])))
```

This design clearly communicates how each shot variety is processed. The processing of a posn shot requires a conditional expression. Is this design easier to understand? Do you prefer this design or the design that does not have a nested conditional expression?

63 The game-over? Refinement

By now, it is likely clear that the game may end in two ways. The first, as before, occurs when the alien reaches earth and the player loses. The second occurs when the alien is hit by a shot and the player wins.

The above problem analysis suggests that at least three sample expressions are needed. One is needed to illustrate when the game is not over. Two are needed to illustrate when the game ends. One for when the player loses and one for when the player wins. For example, the following are sample expressions that satisfy these constraints:

```
;; Sample expressions for game-over?
(define GAME-OVER1 (or (alien-reached-earth?
                          (world-alien INIT-WORLD2))
                        (hit? (world-shot INIT-WORLD2)
                              (world-alien INIT-WORLD2))))

(define GAME-OVER2 (or (alien-reached-earth?
                          (world-alien WORLD3))
                        (hit? (world-shot WORLD3)
                              (world-alien WORLD3))))

(define GAME-NOT-OVER (or (alien-reached-earth?
                             (world-alien INIT-WORLD))
                           (hit? (world-shot INIT-WORLD)
                                 (world-alien INIT-WORLD))
```

The first sample expression is written using a world in which the alien has reached earth. The second sample expression is written using a world in which the alien has been hit by a shot. The third sample expression is written using a world for which the game is not over.

The tests are written as follows:

```
;; Tests using sample computations for game-over?
(check-expect (game-over? INIT-WORLD2) GAME-OVER1)
(check-expect (game-over? WORLD3)      GAME-OVER2)
(check-expect (game-over? INIT-WORLD)  GAME-NOT-OVER)
```

```
;; Tests using sample values for game-over?
(check-expect (game-over? (make-world 8
                                      (make-posn 0 3)
                                      'right
                                      NO-SHOT))
              #false)
(check-expect (game-over? (make-world
                           8
                           (make-posn 0 MAX-IMG-Y)
                           'right
                           (make-posn 12 11)))
              #true)
(check-expect (game-over? (make-world 8
                                      (make-posn 0 5)
                                      'right
                                      (make-posn 0 5)))
              #true)
```

As expected, there is a test using each value computed from the sample expressions. The tests using sample values further illustrate when a world has ended and when it has not ended. The first builds a world that has not ended. The second builds a world that has ended because the alien has reached earth. The third builds a world that has ended because the alien has been hit by the shot.

The function definition is refined using or, as in the sample expressions, to detect each of the possible ways the game is over. The refined function is:

```
;; world → Boolean
;; Purpose: Detect if the game is over
(define (game-over? a-world)
   (or (alien-reached-earth? (world-alien a-world))
       (hit? (world-shot a-world) (world-alien a-world))))
```

Observe that the problems of determining either way the world may end are delegated to auxiliary functions. As before, alien-reached-earth? is used to detect when the player has lost the game. On the other hand, hit? needs to be designed and written to detect when the player has won the game. It is straightforward to observe that determining a hit requires at least an alien and a shot.

63.1 The hit? Design

We must now analyze how to determine if a given alien is hit by a given shot. A 'NO-SHOT shot can never hit an alien. This means that the given shot must be a posn shot to have a hit. If the given shot is a posn shot, then its image-x and image-y coordinates must be the same as those of the given alien. Observe that nothing in this problem analysis suggests that a decision must be made. Thus, a conditional is not needed. Given this observation, we proceed by specializing the template for a function on an `alien` (and not the template for a function on a `shot` that contains a conditional).

We start by writing sample expressions for `hit?`. The idea is to write at least two sample expressions: one that returns `#false` and one that returns `#true`. The following are two such sample expressions:

```
(define ALIEN3 (make-posn 4 MAX-IMG-Y))


;; Sample expressions for hit?
(define NHIT-VAL (and (posn? INIT-SHOT)
                      (= (posn-x INIT-SHOT)
                         (posn-x INIT-ALIEN))
                      (= (posn-y INIT-SHOT)
                         (posn-y INIT-ALIEN))))
(define HIT-VAL  (and (posn? SHOT3)
                      (= (posn-x SHOT3)
                         (posn-x ALIEN3))
                      (= (posn-y SHOT3)
                         (posn-y ALIEN3))))
```

The first sample expression illustrates an `alien` and a `shot` that have not hit. For the sample expression that illustrates a hit an `alien` and a `shot` with same coordinates are needed. None of the sample `aliens` and `shots` has this characteristic. Therefore, a new sample `alien` is defined with the same coordinates as SHOT3. Observe that for NHIT-VAL no error is thrown by trying to extract coordinates from INIT-SHOT. This occurs because INIT-SHOT is not a posn. Given that `(posn? INIT-SHOT)` is `#false` the other inputs to `and` are never evaluated as explained in Chap. 2. Thus, no error is thrown.

The following are the tests for `hit?`:

```
;; Tests using sample computations for hit?
(check-expect (hit? INIT-SHOT INIT-ALIEN) NHIT-VAL)
(check-expect (hit? SHOT3 ALIEN3) HIT-VAL)


;; Tests using sample values for hit?
(check-expect (hit? (make-posn 0 0)  (make-posn 0 0)) #true)
(check-expect (hit? (make-posn 15 6) (make-posn 1 2)) #false)
```

Both sets of tests illustrate when there is and there is not a hit. The tests using sample values make it clear to any reader of the code that the coordinates must be equal to have a hit.

The function definition is developed by abstracting over the sample expressions. This abstraction yields:

```
;; shot → Boolean
;; Purpose: To determine if the given shot has hit the
;;          given alien
```

```
(define (hit? a-shot an-alien)
  (and (posn? a-shot)
       (= (posn-x a-shot) (posn-x an-alien))
       (= (posn-y a-shot) (posn-y an-alien)))))
```

63.2 The `draw-last-world` Refinement

The computation of the last scene must also be refined. Now, the player may win and, if so, a winning message ought to be displayed. To start, it is best to define a sample final world representing a player win such as:

```
(define FWORLD3 (make-world  7     (make-posn 19 3)
                                'left (make-posn 19 3)))
```

Now, think carefully. How do we decide to display a winning or a losing message? How do we know that FWORLD1 and FWORLD2 represent a loss for the player and FWORLD3 represents a win for the player? As before, it is a loss if the image-y of the alien is MAX-IMG-Y. It is a win if the alien is hit.

The sample expression using FWORLD3 is:

```
(define FWORLD3-VAL (place-image
                     (text "EARTH WAS SAVED!" 36 'green)
                     (/ E-SCENE-W 2)
                     (/ E-SCENE-H 4)
                     (draw-world FWORLD3)))
```

Observe that the message is different from the other two sample expressions in Aliens Attack 2. The development of a third sample expression means that a test using this new sample value must be added:

```
(check-expect (draw-last-world FWORLD3) FWORLD3-VAL)
```

The other tests using sample values remain unchanged. The test using a sample value is changed to build a world that contains a shot. It is still used to test the error thrown. The refined test is:

```
;; Tests using sample values for draw-last-world
(check-error
 (draw-last-world (make-world 10
                              (make-posn 7 20)
                              'right
                              (make-posn 2 3)))
 "draw-last-world: Invalid world with #(struct:posn 7 20)
as the alien value and #(struct:posn 2 3) as the shot value.")
```

Observe that the world constructed does not represent a game-ending world and, thus, is expected to force draw-last-world to throw an error.

The function definition refinement adds a stanza to the conditional to determine if the player has won. Clearly, this is when the alien is hit. If so, an *EARTH WAS SAVED!* message is displayed. The refined function is:

```
;; world → scene throws error
;; Purpose: To draw the game's final scene
(define (draw-last-world a-world)
 (cond [(= (posn-y (world-alien a-world)) MAX-IMG-Y)
        (place-image (text "EARTH WAS CONQUERED!" 36 'red)
                     (/ E-SCENE-W 2)
                     (/ E-SCENE-H 4)
                     (draw-world a-world))]
       [(hit? (world-shot a-world) (world-alien a-world))
        (place-image (text "EARTH WAS SAVED!" 36 'green)
                     (/ E-SCENE-W 2)
                     (/ E-SCENE-H 4)
                     (draw-world a-world))]
       [else (error
              (format
               "draw-last-world: Invalid world with ~s as the
               alien value and ~s as the shot value."
               (world-alien a-world)
               (world-shot a-world)))]))
```

This completes the refinement for Aliens Attack 3. Good job! Run and enjoy the game!

---

* **Ex. 111** — Change the data definition of a key to:
```
A key is either:
1. "right"
2. "left"
3. "up"
4. not "right", "left", or "up"
```
Refine the code to use this new data definition.

**** **Ex. 112** — Change the data definition of an alien to be:
```
An alien is a structure: (make-alien posn integer>=0).
```
The nonnegative integer represents the health of the alien. That is, the number of times the alien must be hit before it is destroyed. Carefully analyze how the handlers must be refined before editing the code.

64 What Have We Learned in This Chapter?

The important lessons of Chap. 11 are summarized as follows:

- When a representation choice is arbitrary you may choose any (simple) representation. For example, a non-existing shot is represented by a symbol (i.e., 'NO-SHOT).
- Two different types may have the same representation like a posn is used to represent both an alien and a shot.
- The operations valid on an instance of a type do not depend on the representation. For example, an alien may move left, right, and down while a shot may only move up.
- The implementation of an operation may vary for each variety. For example, a 'NO-SHOT shot is not drawn, but a posn shot is drawn.
- If a function has an input of type A that dominates the other inputs, design the function by specializing the template for a function on A.
- Sometimes a function to process a type with variety may need to distinguish more conditions beyond the number of varieties. For instance, move-shot has three, not two, conditions.
- Refactoring may simplify well-designed code.
- Sometimes defining new instances of a type makes writing tests easier.

Part III
Compound Data of Arbitrary Size

Chapter 12
Lists

Congratulations! You are no longer a beginning student. Change your language in DrRacket to Intermediate Student with lambda. We shall refer to this language as ISL+. All your programs written in BSL will still work in ISL+. In fact, BSL is a subset of ISL+.

In this chapter, we begin to study data of arbitrary size. By data of arbitrary size, we mean data whose size is not constant. In a practical sense, this means that we shall begin to learn how to solve problems involving compound data that may have a varying number of elements. This does not mean that data may be of infinite size. Every instance of our data will be of finite size. Unlike structures, however, not every instance shall be of the same size.

Data of arbitrary size is a natural part of human life. For example, it is typical for persons to make a grocery list before going to the supermarket. My grocery list, of course, may very well be different than your grocery list. This is no surprise given that we may have different tastes. For example, a vegetarian's grocery list will not contain animal proteins while a non-vegetarian will contain animal proteins. Beside content, there is another important difference between these lists. They may contain a different number of items. For example, one grocery list may contain milk, walnuts, and bread while another grocery list may contain sliced turkey, milk, bread, onions, and salmon. Yet, someone else's grocery list may be empty. Regardless of the size, we all agree that they are valid grocery lists. That is a grocery list is data of arbitrary size.

Lists may be used to represent much more than just the groceries that we need to buy. For example, in Aliens Attack we would like to have more than one alien and we would like to allow the player to shoot more than one shot at a time. Consider carefully what it means to have multiple aliens and multiple shots in Aliens Attack. Is the number of aliens constant? Is the number of shots constant? Clearly, the answer to both questions is no. As the game advances the number of aliens decreases as they are hit. That is, the number of aliens is not constant. Similarly, the number of shots varies. At the beginning of the game, the number of shots is 0. Every time the player shoots the number of shots increases. Every time a shot hits an alien or goes off the scene, the number of shots decreases. This tells us that aliens and shots are data of

© The Author(s), under exclusive license to Springer Nature Switzerland AG 2022
M. T. Morazán, *Animated Problem Solving*, Texts in Computer Science,
https://doi.org/10.1007/978-3-030-85091-3_12

arbitrary size just as a grocery list. Thus, we may consider using a list to represent the aliens and the shots.

65 Creating and Accessing Lists in ISL+

Given that many different types of data are naturally represented as lists, ISL+ provides support for lists. The smallest possible list is the empty list. In ISL+, the empty list is represented as '(). We can use the empty list to define many different types of list. For example, an empty grocery list, an empty list of aliens, and an empty list of shots may be defined as follows:

```
(define E-GLIST '())
(define E-LOA   '())
(define E-LOS   '())


(check-expect (empty? E-GLIST) #true)
(check-expect (empty? E-LOA) #true)
(check-expect (empty? E-LOS) #true)
```

In essence, '() is an ISL+ constant that represents any type of empty list. It is the basis of all lists. The ISL+ predicate empty? returns true if its input is '() and #false otherwise.

Non-empty lists, may be constructed by adding an element to the front of an existing list. Just like constructors are needed to create structures, a constructor is needed to build a new list. In ISL+ this function is cons (for **cons**truct). The signature and purpose statement for cons are the following:

```
any list → list
Purpose: To construct a new list by adding the given value
         to the front of the given list
```

The contract is stating that the first argument may be of any type, that the second argument must be a list (of any type), and that it returns a list (of any type). This means that cons is a generic function that may be used to construct any type of list. We can now use cons to build a grocery list, a list of aliens, and a list of shots of any (finite) size. For example, a grocery list with 2 elements, a list of 5 aliens, and list of 3 shots may be defined as follows:

```
(define A-GLIST (cons "milk"
                  (cons "apples"
                        E-GLIST)))
(define A-LOA   (cons (make-posn 10 2)
                  (cons (make-posn 5 12)
                        (cons (make-posn 4 8)
                              (cons (make-posn 15 7)
                                    (cons (make-posn 6 6)
                                          E-LOA))))))
```

```
(define A-LOS    (cons (make-posn 4 2)
                     (cons NO-SHOT
                           (cons (make-posn 17 3)
                                 E-LOS))))

(check-expect (cons? E-GLIST) #false)
(check-expect (cons? E-LOA) #false)
(check-expect (cons? E-LOS) #false)
(check-expect (cons? A-GLIST) #true)
(check-expect (cons? A-LOA) #true)
(check-expect (cons? A-LOS) #true)
```

The arguments to cons are lined up for you to easily confirm that its second argument is always a list. That is, the second argument is always a list constructed using cons or is the empty list (i.e., E-GLIST, E-LOA, or E-LOS). The first argument varies depending on the type of list constructed. For the grocery list, the first argument is always a string. For a list of aliens, the first argument is always an alien. For the list of shots, the first argument is always a shot. Now, it should be even clearer that lists, just as structures, are generic. The tests use the ISL+ predicate cons? that returns true when its input is a non-empty list. Otherwise, it returns false.

As with structures, selectors are needed to extract the elements used to construct a list. Given that a non-empty list is always constructed using cons, two selectors are needed to extract the components of a list. The selector to extract the first element of a given list is first. The selector to extract the list containing the rest of the elements (not including the first element) of a given list is rest. Care must be taken when using these selector functions because the empty list does not have a first element nor does it have a value for the rest of the elements. If either list-selector function is applied to the empty list, an error is thrown. The following tests illustrate how the list-selector functions work:

```
(check-error (first E-GLIST))
(check-error (first E-LOA))
(check-error (first E-LOS))

(check-expect (first A-GLIST) "milk")
(check-expect (first A-LOA)    (make-posn 10 2))
(check-expect (first A-LOS)    (make-posn 4 2))

(check-error (rest E-GLIST))
(check-error (rest E-LOA))
(check-error (rest E-LOS))

(check-expect (rest A-GLIST) (cons "apples" E-GLIST))
```

```
(check-expect (rest A-LOA)
              (cons (make-posn 5 12)
                    (cons (make-posn 4 8)
                          (cons (make-posn 15 7)
                                (cons (make-posn 6 6)
                                      E-LOA)))))
(check-expect (rest A-LOS)
              (cons NO-SHOT (cons (make-posn 17 3) E-LOS)))
```

Here a special form of check-error is used that only checks if an error is thrown. It does not require an error message to check. This form of check-error is particularly useful when testing functions whose error messages we did not design.

How is the second element of a list extracted? The third element? To achieve extractions beyond the first list element you need to compose calls to first and rest. For example, the second element of A-LOS, NO-SHOT, is given by (first (rest A-LOS)). Let us examine how this works:

```
(first (rest A-LOA)) = (first
                          (rest (cons (make-posn 4 2)
                                      (cons NO-SHOT
                                            (cons
                                              (make-posn 17 3)
                                              E-LOS)))
                     = (first (cons NO-SHOT
                                    (cons (make-posn 17 3)
                                          E-LOS)))

                     = NO-SHOT
```

The first step substitutes A-LOA for its value. In the second step, the inner most function application (using rest) is evaluated and is replaced with its value. The third step applies the outermost function application to obtain NO-SHOT.

---

* Ex. 113 — Design and implement a function, third-of-list, to extract the third element of a list. Use compositions of first and rest.

* Ex. 114 — Design and implement a function, fourth-of-list, to extract the fourth element of a list. Use compositions of first and rest.

* Ex. 115 — Design and implement a function, fifth-of-list, to extract the fifth element of a list. Use compositions of first and rest.

** Ex. 116 — Design and implement a function, tenth-of-list, to extract the tenth element of a list. Use compositions of first and rest.

Extracting the second, third, fourth, and so on up to the eighth element of a list is common enough that ISL+ provides functions to do so directly. Not surprisingly, these functions are called second, third, fourth, and so on up to eighth. Be mindful when using these functions because if given a list that is too short they throw an error. These function provide a useful shorthand notation to access list elements up to the eighth. From the ninth on you must write your own function.

66 Shorthand for Building Lists

Consider constructing a list of first 7 digits. Your code may look something like this:

```
(define SEVEN-DIGITS
        (cons
          0
          (cons 1
                (cons 2
                      (cons 3
                            (cons 4
                                  (cons 5
                                        (cons 6 empty))))))))
(check-expect (first SEVEN-DIGITS)   0)
(check-expect (second SEVEN-DIGITS)  1)
(check-expect (third SEVEN-DIGITS)   2)
(check-expect (fourth SEVEN-DIGITS)  3)
(check-expect (fifth SEVEN-DIGITS)   4)
(check-expect (sixth SEVEN-DIGITS)   5)
(check-expect (seventh SEVEN-DIGITS) 6)
```

Observe that there is a lot of repetition in the code to construct the list. Specifically, there is an application of cons for every element of the list. This may not be too cumbersome for a list with seven elements, but what if you are now asked to define a list with the integers in [0..19]? You would need to write cons twenty times. To avoid all this repetition ISL+ provides three shorthand constructors for lists.

The first is used when the elements of the list are known in advance. A *quoted list* has the elements listed inside parenthesis preceded by a '. For example, we may refactor the SEVEN-DIGITS definition as follows:

```
(define SEVEN-DIGITS '(0 1 2 3 4 5 6))

(check-expect (first   SEVEN-DIGITS)  0)
(check-expect (second  SEVEN-DIGITS)  1)
(check-expect (third   SEVEN-DIGITS)  2)
(check-expect (fourth  SEVEN-DIGITS)  3)
(check-expect (fifth   SEVEN-DIGITS)  4)
(check-expect (sixth   SEVEN-DIGITS)  5)
(check-expect (seventh SEVEN-DIGITS)  6)
```

Using a quoted list eliminates the need to repeatedly write cons to construct the list. It is important to note that nothing after the quote (inside the parenthesis) is evaluated. That means all the listed elements are literal values in the list. This is important because there can be no expressions that need to be evaluated inside the parenthesis. For example, consider the following code:

```
(define SOME-SQRS1 (cons (sqr 0)
                         (cons (sqr 1)
                               (cons (sqr 2)
                                     empty))))


(define SOME-SQRS2 '((sqr 0) (sqr 1) (sqr 2)))

(check-expect SOME-SQRS1 '(0 1 4))
(check-expect (not (equal? SOME-SQRS1 SOME-SQRS2)) #true)
```

Both tests pass. For SOME-SQRS1 the expressions using sqr are evaluated. For SOME-SQRS2 they are not evaluated because they are inside a quoted list. Instead of being evaluated, they are considered literal sublists. Thus, the value of SOME-SQRS2 is:

```
(cons (cons 'sqr (cons 0 empty))
      (cons (cons 'sqr (cons 1 empty))
            (cons (cons 'sqr (cons 2 empty))
                  empty)))
```

Naturally, you must be asking yourself if there is shorthand notation to create a list from evaluated expressions. After all, it would be nice not to repeatedly write cons to define SOME-SQRS1. The shorthand provided by ISL+ is list. This is a list-constructor function that evaluates all of its arguments and creates a list of the results. The number of arguments is arbitrary. If no arguments are provided list returns '(). We can refactor the SOME-SQRS2 definition and update the tests as follows:

```
(define SOME-SQRS1 (cons (sqr 0)
                         (cons (sqr 1)
                               (cons (sqr 2)
                                     empty))))


(define SOME-SQRS2 (list (sqr 0) (sqr 1) (sqr 2)))

(check-expect SOME-SQRS1 '(0 1 4))
(check-expect (equal? SOME-SQRS1 SOME-SQRS2) #true)
```

Use list when you want all the expressions to be evaluated to construct a list.

The third shorthand is a *quasiquoted list*. A quasiquoted list is a combination of ' and list. Instead of preceding the opening parentheses with a ', it is preceded with `. The ` indicates that some subexpression inside the parenthesis may have to be evaluated. To indicate that an expression needs to be evaluated, it must be preceded by a ,. If there are no expressions preceded by a comma inside the parenthesis, then ` and ' yield the same value when evaluated. To illustrate the use of quasiquote consider the following code:

```
(define X 2)
(define Y 3)
(define Z 4)
```

```
(define A-LIST  '((add1 X)  J  (* Z Y)))
(define A-LIST2 `(,(add1 X) J ,(* Z Y)))

(check-expect (first A-LIST)  '(add1 X))
(check-expect (first A-LIST2) 3)

(check-expect (second A-LIST)  'J)
(check-expect (second A-LIST2) 'J)

(check-expect (third A-LIST)  '(* Z Y))
(check-expect (third A-LIST2) 12)
```

The expressions (add1 X) and (* Z Y) are evaluated to construct A-LIST2 because they are preceded by a comma in a quasiquoted list. The same expressions are
treated as literal values for A-LIST because they are inside a quoted list.

67 Recursive Data Definitions

We have explored how to create and access lists. As part of our exploration, we have
discovered that lists may be used to store different types of data. We have not yet
explored how to process a list. To do so we first need to be able to develop a data
definition and a function template for a given type of list. Consider defining a list of
numbers. Let us look at some examples based on our knowledge of lists so far:

```
'()
(cons 87 '())
(cons 24 (cons 87 '()))
(cons 16 (cons 24 (cons 87 '())))
(cons 31 (cons 16 (cons 24 (cons 87 '()))))
```

If you think about it carefully, you can see a distinct pattern. There are two list-of-
numbers varieties. The first is the empty list of numbers. The second is a non-empty
list of numbers constructed using cons. This immediately suggests that to define a
list of numbers, we need a data definition with two varieties:

```
;; A list of numbers (lon) is either
;;   1. '()
;;   2. (cons ??? ???)
```

Now, we must be precise about the types of the arguments to cons. Given that we
are defining a list of numbers, it is clear that the first argument must be a number.
This takes us a step closer to the needed data definition:

```
;; A list of numbers (lon) is either
;;   1. '()
;;   2. (cons number ???)
```

What is the type of the second argument to cons? To answer this question, let us analyze one of our examples: '(cons 31 (cons 16 (cons 24 (cons 87 '()))))). In this example, 31 is the first number of the list. Clearly, it fulfills what is required by the data definition we have so far. What is '(cons 16 (cons 24 (cons 87 '()))))? If you think about it carefully, the inescapable conclusion is that it is a lon. Is this really the case? Does this make sense? Let us look at another example: '(cons 87 '()). Here the argument types to cons are number (the 87) and, once again, a lon ('()). You can verify that all other examples satisfy this pattern. This analysis is telling us that the type of the second argument to cons is lon. Thus, the lon data definition is:

```
;; A list of number (lon) is either
;;   1. '()
;;   2. (cons number lon)
```

A list of numbers is defined in terms of itself. That is, it is a circular data definition. A type defined in terms of itself is a *recursive* data type.

Does this make any sense? Can this data definition be used to build any list of numbers? It turns out that you can build any list of numbers using this data definition. To build the empty list of numbers, we simply use the first rule and write: '(). How about a list that is not empty? Here is how you build '(cons 24 (cons 87 '())):

```
lon → (cons 24 lon)              using rule 2 to substitute lon
    → (cons 24
            (cons 87 lon))       using rule 2 to substitute lon
    → (cons 24
            (cons 87 empty))     using rule 1 to substitute lon
```

This is an example of a derivation. A derivation is the series of steps used to show how to build an instance of a data type using the varieties of a data definition. It is not difficult to see that any valid list of numbers can be derived using the above data definition. Can anything that is not a list of numbers be derived? Let us try to derive '(cons 42 (cons -6 (cons "Hi" (cons 87 '())))):

```
lon → (cons 42 lon)   using rule 2 to substitute lon
    → (cons 42
            (cons -6 lon))   using rule 2 to substitute lon
```

The derivation fails because there is no lon variety whose first element is a string. Therefore, '(cons 31 (cons 16 (cons "Hi" (cons 87 '()))))) is not a lon. It is also not difficult to see that according to our data definition all the elements of a lon must be numbers. If any element of a given list is not a number, then it is not a lon.

It is very likely that you have been taught to steer away from recursive data definitions. This is unfortunate because as we have seen recursive data definitions are useful to define data of arbitrary size like lists. In fact, any data of arbitrary size requires a recursive data definition. So, why are students steered away from recursive data definitions? This is likely rooted in the fact that recursive data definitions may be nonsense. For example, someone may attempt to define a list of numbers as follows:

```
; A list of numbers (lon2) is a (cons number lon2)
```

Is this a useful data definition? Let us try to derive `'(cons 24 (cons 87 '()))`:

```
lon2 → (cons 24 lon2)              substitute lon2 using rule 2
     → (cons 24
            (cons 87 lon2))        substitute lon2 using rule 2
```

The derivation fails because we are unable to instantiate the `lon2` in `(cons 87 lon2)`. You may say that clearly it should be `'()`. In fact, this would be wrong. Nowhere in this data definition does it say that `'()` is a `lon2`. It is important to be precise with our data definitions. Otherwise, we will be unable to solve problems.

This leads to asking ourselves what constitutes a useful recursive data definition. In order to be useful, a recursive data definition must have the following characteristics:

1. At least two subtypes (varieties)
2. At least one subtype that does not contain a selfreference
3. At least one subtype that contains a selfreference

The subtypes that do not contain a selfreference are known as `base subtypes`. These are concrete values that are known to be instances of the data type defined. These concrete values break the circularity in a derivation. The subtypes that do contain a selfreference are known as `recursive subtypes`. These are the varieties that introduce circularity which endows us with the power to define data of arbitrary size. In the recursive data definition for `lon`, we have `'()` as a base subtype and `(cons number lon)` as a recursive subtype. The recursive data definition for `lon2` is not useful because it does not have a base subtype.

With our newly acquired knowledge, we can now define a representation for multiple aliens and multiple shots in Aliens Attack. Given that both are data of arbitrary size, we need a recursive data definition for each. At this point, the only recursive data type we know is list. Thus, let us try to use a list to define an arbitrary number of aliens. Remember that it must have the three characteristic above required for a useful recursive data definition. A list of aliens may be defined as follows:

```
;; A list of alien (loa) is either:
;;   1. '()
;;   2. (cons alien loa)

;; Sample instances of loa
(define E-LOA '())
(define INIT-LOA
        (list
          (make-posn 8 0)  (make-posn 9 0)  (make-posn 10 0)
          (make-posn 11 0) (make-posn 12 0) (make-posn 13 0)
```

```
(make-posn 8 1)   (make-posn 9 1)   (make-posn 10 1)
(make-posn 11 1)  (make-posn 12 1)  (make-posn 13 1)
(make-posn 8 2)   (make-posn 9 2)   (make-posn 10 2)
(make-posn 11 2)  (make-posn 12 2)  (make-posn 13 2)))
```

Observe that the `loa` data definition has two subtypes: one base subtype and one recursive subtype. In addition, following the steps of the design recipe, an instance of each variety of `loa` is defined. The initial list of aliens, `INIT-LOA`, contains 18 aliens. This ought to make the game more interesting. You are encouraged to make the initial list of aliens shorter or longer to personalize the game to your liking.

A list of shots is defined as follows:

```
;; A list of shot (los) is either:
;;  1. '()
;;  2. (cons shot los)

;; Sample instances of los
(define INIT-LOS '())
(define LOS2 (list (make-posn 8 0) (make-posn 10 5)))
```

Observe that the requirements for a useful data definition are satisfied and that sample instances are also defined.

---

* **Ex. 117** — Define sample instances for `lon`.

* **Ex. 118** — Create a data definition and sample instances for a grocery list.

* **Ex. 119** — In Chap. 7 a data definition for a 2D-point is developed. Why or why not is this a useful recursive data definition?

*** **Ex. 120** — Create a data definition for a composed image. A composed image may contain one or more rectangles and circles that are above, next, or overlaid in relation to each other.

---

68 Generic Data Definitions

The next natural step is to develop a function template for `lon`, `loa`, and `los`. However, notice that the three data definitions are almost identical. In other words, there is a lot of repetition among them. When we have repetition among expressions, an abstraction step introduces a variable to obtain a function. Can we apply an abstraction step to avoid repetitions among data definitions?

The situation we face is a bit different from abstraction over expressions. When you abstract over expressions, a difference is always a value and a variable is used to represent the value. This felt quite natural because you are familiar with variables from your Mathematics courses. The difference among the data definitions for `lon`, `loa`, and `los` is a type. For `lon` the type used is `number`. For `loa` the type used is `alien`. For `los` the type used is `shot`. When abstracting over data definitions the variables used to capture the differences are `type variables`. Type variables represent types not instances of types (i.e., values). A type variable is needed for each difference.

Let `X` be the single difference among `lon`, `loa`, and `los`. Instead of using a concrete type (like `number`, `alien`, or `shot`), we write a data definition using `X`:

```
;; A list of X ((listof X)) is either:
;;   1. '()
;;   2. (cons X (listof X))
```

The data definition is recursive just like the data definitions for `lon`, `loa`, and `los`. Observe that if we plug in `number` for `X` we obtain the data definition for `lon`. Similarly, plugging in `alien` and `shot` for `X` yields, respectively, the data definitions for `loa` and `los`. The notation `(listof X)` is used to emphasize that a type must be plugged in to obtain a concrete data definition. Clearly, this data definition works for many different types. A data definition that works for many different types is called a `generic` (or `parameterized`) data definition.

As we shall see, a generic data definition may be used in two ways in our signatures. We may substitute `X` with a concrete type to specify a concrete data definition or we may use `(listof X)` directly. We shall start with examples of the former. The use of the latter will follow after we learn how to abstract over functions.

69 Function Templates for Lists

We can write a function template for a `(listof X)` and use it to define the templates for `lon`, `loa`, and `los`. Before that, however, we must learn to write a function template for a recursive data definition. Using the knowledge you have accumulated so far, we can begin to develop the function template for `(listof X)`:

```
;; Sample instances of (listof X)
(define LOX1 ...)
(define LOX2 ...)

;; (listof X) ... → ...
;; Purpose: ...
(define (f-on-loX a-loX ...)
  (if (empty? a-loX)
      ...
      ...))

;; Sample expressions for f-on-loX
(define LOX1-VAL ...)
(define LOX2-VAL ...)

   ...
```

```
;; Tests using sample computations for f-on-loX
(check-expect (f-on-loX LOX1 ...) LOX1-VAL)
(check-expect (f-on-loX LOX2 ...) LOX2-VAL)
    ...

;; Tests using sample values for f-on-los
(check-expect (f-on-loX ...) ...)
    ...
```

A function template for a generic type contains all the same elements as a concrete function template: sample instances templates, a function definition template, sample expression templates, and test templates. The definition template has a conditional expression because there is variety in the data. So far, there is nothing really new here except not knowing what X is at this time. That is fine because when a type is plugged in for X, the yield is a concrete function template. The question we must answer is how do we deal with selfreferences in the data definition. Specifically, how is ... substituted in the definition template's else clause. This clause tells us how to process a list constructed using cons. Let us examine carefully what needs to be processed:

```
(cons X (listof X))
```

There are two different types that need to be processed: X and (listof X). Processing an X is done by calling a function on an X. How do we process a (listof X)? The natural answer is to call a function that processes a (listof X). In other words, the function must call itself. Let us finalize the template using this new insight:

```
;; Sample instances of (listof X)
(define LOX1 ...)
(define LOX2 ...)
...

;; (listof X) ... → ...
;; Purpose: ...
(define (f-on-loX a-loX ...)
  (if (empty? a-loX)
      ...
      ...(f-on-X (first a-loX))...
      ...(f-on-loX (rest a-loX) ...)...))

;; Sample expressions for f-on-loX
(define LOX1-VAL ...)
(define LOX2-VAL ...)
    ...
```

```
;; Tests using sample computations for f-on-loX
(check-expect (f-on-loX LOX1 ...) LOX1-VAL)
(check-expect (f-on-loX LOX2 ...) LOX2-VAL)
   ...


;; Tests using sample values for f-on-loX
(check-expect (f-on-loX ...) ...)
   ...
```

A new principle now becomes clear. Every selfreference in a data definition becomes
a selfreference in the definition template and, eventually, a selfreference in a function definition. That is, *data of arbitrary size is processed by a recursive function.*
Recursion that is based on the structure of your data is called *structural recursion*
(or natural recursion). As before with structures, the structure of your data suggests
the structure of your functions. Observe that a divide and conquer strategy naturally
arises from the structure of a (listof X). To solve a problem for a (listof X) to
subproblem for an X and a subproblem for a (smaller) (listof X) must be solved.
The fascinating part is that the subproblem for the smaller (listof X) is solved the
same way as the larger (listof X). When using structural recursion, it is always the
case that the subproblem is smaller and, therefore, closer to a base case. This means
that when structural recursion is correctly used, your code is guaranteed to eventually
stop. It becomes impossible for a function to implement an infinite recursion.

70 Designing List-Processing Functions

We can use the generic data definition for a (listof X) to define a list of numbers:

> A lon is a (listof number)

Let us take a close look at what this means. Plugging in number for X in the generic
data definition for (listof X) yields:

```
;; A list of number (lon) is either
;;  1. '()
;;  2. (cons number lon)
```

This is exactly the data definition derived above. Plugging in number for X in the
function template for a function on a (listof X) yields a concrete function template
for a lon:

```
;; Sample instances of lon
(define LON1 ...)
(define LON2 ...)
   ...
```

```
;; lon ... → ...
;; Purpose: ...
(define (f-on-lon a-lon ...)
  (if (empty? a-lon)
      ...
      ...(f-on-number (first a-lon))...
      ...(f-on-lon (rest a-lon) ...)...))

;; Sample expressions for f-on-lon
(define LON1-VAL ...)
(define LON2-VAL ...)
  ...


;; Tests using sample computations for f-on-lon
(check-expect (f-on-lon LON1 ...) LON1-VAL)
(check-expect (f-on-lon LON2 ...) LON2-VAL)
  ...


;; Tests using sample values for f-on-lon
(check-expect (f-on-lon ...) ...)
  ...
```

We can now use the template to write functions to process a list of numbers. For example, write a function that squares a list of numbers. The design idea is to traverse the given list and construct a new list with the square of each number in the list. Specializing the template yields:

```
;; Sample instances of lon
(define LON1 '())
(define LON2 '(1 2 3 4))

;; lon → lon
;; Purpose: Return a list of the squares of the given lon
(define (square-lon a-lon)
  (if (empty? a-lon)
      '()
      (cons (sqr (first a-lon))
            (square-lon (rest a-lon)))))

;; Sample expressions for square-lon
(define LON1-VAL '())
(define LON2-VAL (cons (sqr (first '(1 2 3 4)))
                       (square-lon (rest '(1 2 3 4)))))

;; Tests using sample computations for square-lon
(check-expect (square-lon LON1) LON1-VAL)
(check-expect (square-lon LON2) LON2-VAL)
```

```
;; Tests using sample values for square-lon
(check-expect (square-lon '(10 8 4)) '(100 64 16))
```

It is worth carefully analyzing the expressions used in the function definition:

`(sqr (first a-lon))`	square of the first number in `a-lon`
`(square-lon (rest a-lon))`	list of squares obtained from the rest of `a-lon`

In the function definition `cons` is used to construct the new list. A new square is added to the front of the list of squares obtained from the rest of the given list. There is a sample expression and corresponding test for each `lon` variety. Finally, as always, there is one or more tests using sample values.

To close this chapter, it is worth noting that there is a popular legend among students and professionals that recursion is hard. If you understand the design of `square-lon`, then you know better. Recursion is not hard nor should it be feared. Understanding how to design solutions to problems based on data definitions makes recursion quite natural. In the next chapter, you will gain more experience designing recursive functions. Enjoy the journey!

---

* **Ex. 121** — Design a function to cube a given `lon`.

*** **Ex. 122** — Design a function that returns a list of the lengths of all the strings in a list of strings. Make sure you have a data definition for all the list data types needed.

**** **Ex. 123** — A student's backpack may be modeled using a (`listof` `symbol`). For example, a backpack containing a notebook, a laptop, and a pen is represented as '(notebook laptop pen). Design a function to determine if a given item is contained in a given backpack.

*** **Ex. 124** — For the previous exercise, do you need a conditional to define the predicate as suggested by the data definition for (`listof X`)? If you used a conditional for the previous exercise refactor your solution to not use a conditional.

---

71 What Have We Learned in This Chapter?

The important lessons of Chap. 12 are summarized as follows:

- Data of arbitrary size occurs naturally in real life and in virtual worlds.
- A list is data of arbitrary size with two varieties:
  - '()
  - A list built using cons

- The constructor for a non-empty list, cons, builds a new list by adding an element to the front of an existing list.
- The selectors for lists are first and rest.
- When using an error-throwing function, we did not write use check-error to test that an error is thrown.
- A quoted list may be used when all the list values are known and can be enumerated.
- The function list may be used when the expressions for each list value are known and can be enumerated.
- A quasiquoted list may be used when for the list elements either a value or an expression for the value is known. Expressions that need to be evaluated must be preceded by a comma.
- A recursive data definition is needed to define data of arbitrary size like lists.
- A recursive data definition always has a variety of subtypes of which at least one is a base subtype and at least one is a recursive subtype.
- A recursive subtype contains a selfreference to its supertype.
- A generic data definition is an abstraction over types and may be used to define many different concrete data types.
- For (listof X) there are two varieties: '() is the base subtype and (cons X (listof X)) is the recursive subtype.
- A generic data definition leads to a generic function template.
- In a function template for data of arbitrary size, the definition template has a recursive call for every selfreference in the data it is designed to process.
- Data of arbitrary size is processed using a recursive function.
- Recursion based on the structure of the data is called structural recursion.
- Structural recursion implements a divide and conquer design.
- Proper use of structural recursion guarantees that functions are not infinite recursions.
- A concrete type and a concrete function template is obtained from a generic type and its generic template by plugging in a type for each type variable.
- A concrete type and its concrete template are used to design functions. For example, (listof number) and its function template are used to design any function that processes a list of numbers.

Chapter 13
List Processing

In this chapter, we explore common list operations. These include summarizing, searching, mapping, filtering, and sorting. A summarizing operation is one that computes an aggregate value from the list elements. For example, you may need to compute the length of a list or the sum of a list of numbers. A search operation is used when list membership needs to be determined. You may want to know if a list contains a value or if any list element satisfies a property. Mapping is used when you want to apply a function to every list element and return a new list with the results. Filtering is used when you need to extract all the list elements that satisfy a property. Finally, list sorting is used when the list elements need to be put in order. In order to sort a list, the list elements must be numerical or ordinal data. That is, it must be possible to naturally put list elements in order. For example, a list of numbers may be ordered in non-decreasing or non-increasing order. On the other hand, a list of colors cannot be ordered. This is because colors are nominal data. There is no natural way to order colors. Does brown come before green or does green come before brown?

Given that lists must be processed, the functions we design will be recursive. We shall bring all our accumulated program design knowledge to bear on the functions developed. Chief among these is careful problem analysis and separation of concerns. Remember that for every value that needs to be computed, a separate function needs to be designed.

72 List Summarizing

As a student, you are likely to keep track of your quiz grades in a class throughout the semester. Why would you want to do this? Perhaps, your quiz average is 15% of your final grade. Therefore, you would like to compute your quiz average every time you earn a new quiz grade. How can you represent your quiz grades? Ask yourself if you know the number of quizzes in advance. The most likely answer is that you do not. After all, professors are likely to have pop quizzes or not announce the number of quizzes in advance. Therefore, they may be, for example, 0, 19, or 7 quizzes.

© The Author(s), under exclusive license to Springer Nature Switzerland AG 2022   281
M. T. Morazán, *Animated Problem Solving*, Texts in Computer Science,
https://doi.org/10.1007/978-3-030-85091-3_13

The point is that the number of quizzes is arbitrary and must be represented using compound data of arbitrary size. Thus, a structure is a poor choice to represent the quiz grades, and a list of numbers is a much better representation.

A first attempt to define a list of quiz grades may be:

```
A list of quiz grades (loq) is a (listof number).
```

Is this a reasonable representation of quiz grades? Unfortunately, it is not. Given this data definition, the following is a valid list of quiz grades:

```
'(87 65 92 -45 88 -7 98)
```

Clearly, this is a list of numbers. Is it a list of quiz grades? Clearly, it is not because a quiz grade cannot be negative. We need to refine our data definition to be more specific about what a quiz grade is. Assuming a quiz grade is based on a 100-point scale, we may say:

```
;; A quiz grade (qg) is a number in [0..100]

;; A list of quiz grades (loq) is a (listof qg)

;; Sample values of loq
(define LOQ1 '())
(define LOQ2 '(87 65 92 88 98))
```

Now we have a data definition that is specific for quiz grades. A loq is a subtype of a list of numbers. This means that a function on a list of numbers can process a loq, but a function on a loq may not be able to process a list of numbers.

As we learned in Chap. 12, we can use qg to derive a concrete function template for a loq:

```
;; Sample instances of loq
(define LOX1 ...)
(define LOX2 ...)

;; loq ... → ...
;; Purpose: ...
(define (f-on-loq a-loq ...)
  (if (empty? loq)
      '()
      ...(f-on-qg (first a-loq))...
      ...(f-on-loq (rest a-loq) ...)...))))

;; Sample expressions for f-on-loq
(define LOQ1-VAL ...)
(define LOQ2-VAL ...)

    ...
```

```
;; Tests using sample computations for f-on-loq
(check-expect (f-on-loq LOQ1 ...) LOQ1-VAL)
(check-expect (f-on-loq LOQ2 ...) LOQ2-VAL)
   ...

;; Tests using sample values for f-on-loq
(check-expect (f-on-loq ...) ...)
   ...
```

Consider writing a function to compute the average of a `loq`. With data analysis done, the next step of the design recipe is problem analysis to outline the computation. Ask yourself how a quiz average is computed. You need to know the sum of all the quiz grades. You need to know the number of quiz grades. You need to divide the sum of quiz grades by the number of quiz grades. We can now specify what needs to be computed:

1. Compute the length of the given `loq`
2. Compute the sum of the given `loq`
3. Divide the sum by the length

Given that three different values are needed, how many different functions are needed? The most natural answer is three: one for each needed value. This is underlined by the principle of separation of concerns.

Let us start with the function that computes the average of a `loq`. This function needs to summarize a property of the given `loq` by dividing its sum by its length. Take note of two facts. First, this function does not process the given `loq`. Instead, it manipulates two list-summarizing values. This means that using the template for a function on a `loq` is incorrect. This template is needed only when a function needs to traverse a list. Second, the given `loq` may not be empty. It is impossible to compute the average of an empty `loq` because division by 0 is undefined. Therefore, this function throws an error if the given `loq` is empty. The design of this function assumes that functions to compute the sum and the length exist. Following the steps of the design recipe results in:

```
;; loq → number throws error
;; Purpose: To compute the given loq's average
(define (avg-loq a-loq)
  (if (empty? a-loq)
      (error (avg-loq expects an non-empty loq))
      (/ (sum-loq a-loq) (loq-len a-loq)))))

;; Sample expressions for avg-loq
(define LOQ2-VAL (avg-loq LOQ2))

;; Tests using sample computations for avg-loq
(check-expect (avg-loq LOQ2) LOQ2-VAL)
```

```
;; Tests using sample values for avg-loq
(check-error (avg-loq LOQ1) "avg-loq expects an non-empty.")
```

Observe that both subtypes of loq are tested, albeit, not as tests using sample expressions.

---

* Ex. 125 — Define more sample instances of loq and more tests using sample expressions for avg-log.

*** Ex. 126 — Develop a data definition for a non-empty (listof X). Re-design avg-loq around processing a non-empty (listof qg).

We now proceed to design the auxiliary functions for the sum and the length of a loq. The sum of an empty loq is 0. The sum of a non-empty loq is the sum of the rest of the given loq and the first element of the given loq. Observe that we statically reason about the loq. That is, we reason about what to do with the needed value obtained from the first quiz grade and the needed value obtained from the rest of the list. We do not dynamically reason about the loq. That is, we do not say that we add the first element of the list, the second element of the list, the third element of the list, and so on. We do not because it is not always clear what "and so on" means. Furthermore, static reasoning is easily translated to a solution expressed as a program. That is, it is clear that two things are needed to be done: process the first element and process the rest of the given list. This problem analysis leads to the following specialization of the template for a function on a loq:

```
;; Sample values of loq
(define LOQ3 '(50 90 80 60 70))

;; loq → number
;; Purpose: To compute the sum of the given loq
(define (sum-loq a-loq)
  (if (empty? a-loq)
      0
      (+ (first a-loq) (sum-loq (rest a-loq)))))

;; Sample expressions for sum-loq
(define SUM-LOQ1-VAL 0)
(define SUM-LOQ2-VAL (+ (first LOQ2) (sum-loq (rest LOQ2))))
(define SUM-LOQ3-VAL (+ (first LOQ3) (sum-loq (rest LOQ3))))

;; Tests using sample computations for sum-loq
(check-expect (sum-loq LOQ1) SUM-LOQ1-VAL)
(check-expect (sum-loq LOQ2) SUM-LOQ2-VAL)

;; Tests using sample values for sum-loq
(check-expect (sum-loq '(96 97 99 100)) 392)
```

An extra sample `loq` instance is defined to improve the illustration of the abstraction
that leads to the function definition. Observe that it is easy to see that the code
implements the strategy suggested by static reasoning.

The final task is to design a function to compute the length of a `loq`. The length
is 0 if the given `loq` is empty. What is the answer if the `loq` is not empty? Use static
reasoning to determine the solution. According to the template for a function on a
`loq`, you need a value obtained from the first qg, a value obtained from the rest of the
qgs, and a function to combine these two values. Ask yourself, what does the first qg
contribute to the length? It contributes 1 to the length of the given `loq`. What does
the rest of the quiz grades contribute to the length? It contributes its length. How do
we combine these two numbers to obtain the length of the given `loq`? The length
of the given `loq` is obtained by adding these two numbers. This problem analysis
yields the following template specialization:

```
;; loq → number
;; Purpose: To compute the length of the given loq
(define (length-loq a-loq)
  (if (empty? a-loq)
      0
      (+ 1 (length-loq (rest a-loq)))))

;; Sample expressions for length-loq
(define LEN-LOQ1-VAL 0)
(define LEN-LOQ2-VAL (+ 1 (length-loq (rest LOQ2))))
(define LEN-LOQ3-VAL (+ 1 (length-loq (rest LOQ3))))

;; Tests using sample computations for length-loq
(check-expect (length-loq LOQ1) LEN-LOQ1-VAL)
(check-expect (length-loq LOQ2) LEN-LOQ2-VAL)
(check-expect (length-loq LOQ3) LEN-LOQ3-VAL)

;; Tests using sample values for length-loq
(check-expect (length-loq '(96 97 99 100 89 94)) 6)
```

Once again observe that the code implements the strategy suggested by static reasoning. Developing static reasoning skills is important because, as we will discover,
it makes proving the correctness of a program easier.

---

* Ex. 127 — Design and implement a function to compute the average of a list
of numbers.

** Ex. 128 — Design and implement a function to compute the product of a
list of numbers.

* Ex. 129 — Design and implement a function to count the number of aliens in a (listof alien).

** Ex. 130 — Design and implement a function to append the strings in a list of strings.

73 List Searching

Another common operation is searching a given list for a value. For example, given a list of numbers, a-lon, and a number, x, you need the sublist of a-lon that starts with the first occurrence of x. We start with problem analysis. If a-lon is empty the answer is '() because a-lon does not contain x. What if the list is not empty? Think about where x may be in terms of the structure of a-lon. We observe that x may be the first element of the list. In this case, the answer is a-lon given that (first a-lon) is the first occurrence of x. It is also possible that (first a-lon) is not equal to x. In this case, (rest a-lon) must be searched. This, of course, is done recursively as suggested by the template for a function on an lon. Will this design idea work if x is not in a-lon? If you think carefully about it you realize that it does. When x is in (rest a-lon), the recursive search stops when x equals (first a-lon). When x is not in (rest a-lon), the recursive search stops when a-lon equals '() and returns '()—the correct answer. Finally, observe that there are three conditions that need to be detected (not two as suggested by the template for a function on a lon).

We now need to develop sample expressions using sample lon instances to illustrate how the result is computed for each of the three conditions. We define the following sample lon instances:

```
;; Sample instances of lon
(define LON1 '())
(define LON2 '(1 2 3 4))
```

Using these sample instances, we define the following sample expressions:

```
;; Sample expressions for xsublist-lon
(define XSUBLIST-LON1-VAL '())
(define XSUBLIST-LON2-VAL1 LON2)
(define XSUBLIST-LON2-VAL2 (xsublist-lon 3 (rest LON2)))
(define XSUBLIST-LON2-VAL3 (xsublist-lon 0 (rest LON2)))
```

The first sample expression illustrates the answer when searching for, say, 7 in the empty lon. The second sample expression illustrates the answer when searching for 1 in an lon that has 1 as its first number. The third and fourth sample expressions illustrate how to compute the answer when the given number (3 and 0, respectively) is not the first number in the given lon. Observe that the third sample expression illustrates searching for a number that is in the rest of the given list while the fourth sample expression searches for a value not contained in the rest of the list. These last two sample expressions illustrate the expression needed to make a recursive call to search the rest of the given lon–just as suggested by the function template for a function on a lon.

We can now finalize the specialization of the function template as follows:

```
;; number lon → lon
;; Purpose: To return the sublist of the given lon that
;;          starts with the first instance of the given
;;          number.
(define (xsublist-lon x a-lon)
  (cond [(empty? a-lon) '()]
        [(equal? x (first a-lon)) a-lon]
        [else (xsublist-lon x (rest a-lon))]))


;; Tests using sample computations for xsublist-lon
(check-expect (xsublist-lon 7 LON1)  XSUBLIST-LON1-VAL)
(check-expect (xsublist-lon 1 LON2)  XSUBLIST-LON2-VAL1)
(check-expect (xsublist-lon 3 LON2)  XSUBLIST-LON2-VAL2)
(check-expect (xsublist-lon 0 LON2)  XSUBLIST-LON2-VAL3)


;; Tests using sample values for xsublist-lon
(check-expect (xsublist-lon 99 '(96 97 99 100)) '(99 100))
(check-expect (xsublist-lon 87 '(86 47 10)) '())
```

Observe that the conditional in the function's body has three stanzas: one for each condition that must be detected. The first is used when the given lon is empty. The second is used when the given lon has x as its first element. The third is used when the rest of the list must be searched. The tests using sample values further illustrate that the function works for searches that are successful and that are unsuccessful.

---

* Ex. 131 — Design and implement a function that returns the sublist of a given (listof string) that starts with the first instance of a string that has a length less than 5.

*** Ex. 132 — Design and implement a function that returns the first instance of an even number in a given (listof number). If there are no even numbers in the given (listof number), the function returns #false. For this problem, you need a data definition for the function's result type.

**** Ex. 133 — A list of alphabet symbols is a list that only contains the symbols either in ['a..'z] or in ['A..'Z]. Design and implement a function that returns the first instance of a symbol in ['a..'z] in a given list of alphabet symbols. Make sure to follow all the steps of the design recipe. You need to develop two data definitions to solve this problem.

74 List ORing

A variant of list searching is list ORing. ORing determines if there exists a list value in a given list, L, that satisfies some property P. That is, we seek to determine if any element in L satisfies P. Think about the varieties of L. What is the answer if L is empty? The answer may not be clear to you. That is fine. Let us delay the answer for now and think about a list of length 1 whose only element, p, does not satisfy P. The list looks as follows:

```
L = (cons p '())
```

Is there an element in L that satisfies P? Clearly the answer is no. Now, think about how L is processed. You need to apply P to p to obtain #false. This result must be ored with the result obtained from the rest of L. The rest of L is always recursively processed. This means that '() must be recursively processed. The only way processing (cons p '()) returns #false is if processing '() returns #false. This means that the answer is #false when L is empty. If L is not empty, then you must apply or to the result of applying P to p and of recursively processing the rest of L.

For example, in Aliens Attack with multiple aliens all the aliens move in the same direction. The direction only changes when there exists an alien that is either at the left or the right edge of the scene. This means that we need predicates to determine if there exists an alien located at either the right or left edge in a list of aliens.

74.1 Determining If an Alien Is at the Left Edge

Carefully think about what it means for there to exist an alien that is at the left edge of the scene. One condition is that the given list of aliens cannot be empty. This is a *necessary* condition for such an alien to exist, but it is not *sufficient*. A necessary condition is one that must be true for a predicate to be true, but is not enough to conclude that the predicate is true. A sufficient condition is one that allows us to conclude that the predicate is true. A list of aliens must not be empty for there to be an alien at the left edge of the scene. A list of aliens that is not empty is not sufficient, because it may not have an alien at the left edge. This means we need more conditions to hold in order to conclude that there exists an alien at the left edge. What other condition(s) must hold? Once again, think in terms of the structure of the list you need to process. Either the first alien is at the left edge or an alien in the rest of the list of aliens is at the left edge. Observe that no decision must be made to compute this value. That is, a conditional as suggested by the template for a function on a list of aliens is not needed. Instead, we can use and to detect if both conditions hold. We can use or to detect if the first alien is at the left edge or if any alien in the rest of the list is at the left edge.

Based on the above problem analysis, we can specialize the template for a function on a loa as follows:

```
(define ALIEN-8-0 (make-posn 8 0))


;; Sample instances of loa
(define EDGE-LOA  (list ALIEN-8-0
                        (make-posn MIN-IMG-X 11)
                        (make-posn 5 5)))
(define EDGE-LOA2 (list (make-posn 1 11)
                        (make-posn MAX-IMG-X 5)))


;; loa → Boolean
;; Purpose: To determine if any alien is at scene's left edge
(define (any-alien-at-left-edge? a-loa)
  (and (not (empty? a-loa))
       (or (alien-at-left-edge? (first a-loa))
           (any-alien-at-left-edge? (rest a-loa)))))


;; Sample expressions for any-alien-at-left-edge?
(define LEDGE-E-LOA-VAL
        (and (not (empty? E-LOA))
             (or (alien-at-left-edge?    (first E-LOA))
                 (any-alien-at-left-edge? (rest E-LOA)))))


(define LEDGE-INIT-LOA-VAL
        (and (not (empty? INIT-LOA))
             (or (alien-at-left-edge?    (first INIT-LOA))
                 (any-alien-at-left-edge? (rest INIT-LOA)))))


(define LEDGE-LOA-VAL
        (and (not (empty? EDGE-LOA))
             (or (alien-at-left-edge?    (first EDGE-LOA))
                 (any-alien-at-left-edge? (rest EDGE-LOA)))))


(define LEDGE-LOA2-VAL
        (and (not (empty? EDGE-LOA2))
             (or (alien-at-left-edge?    (first EDGE-LOA2))
                 (any-alien-at-left-edge? (rest EDGE-LOA2)))))


;; Tests using sample computations any-alien-at-left-edge?
(check-expect (any-alien-at-left-edge? E-LOA)
              LEDGE-E-LOA-VAL)
(check-expect (any-alien-at-left-edge? INIT-LOA)
              LEDGE-INIT-LOA-VAL)
```

```
(check-expect (any-alien-at-left-edge? EDGE-LOA)
              LEDGE-LOA-VAL)
(check-expect (any-alien-at-left-edge? EDGE-LOA2)
              LEDGE-LOA2-VAL)


;; Tests using sample values for any-alien-at-left-edge?
(check-expect (any-alien-at-left-edge?
                (list (make-posn MIN-IMG-X 8)
                      (make-posn 6 3)
                      (make-posn MAX-IMG-X 10)))
              #true)
(check-expect (any-alien-at-left-edge?
                (list (make-posn 3  8)
                      (make-posn MIN-IMG-X 3)
                      (make-posn 5 2)))
              #true)
(check-expect (any-alien-at-left-edge?
                (list (make-posn MAX-IMG-Y 8)))
              #false)
(check-expect (any-alien-at-left-edge?
                (list (make-posn 3 8)
                      (make-posn 5 2)))
              #false)
```

The constant ALIEN-8-0 is defined to help write loa instances and future tests. Two new sample loa instances are defined to facilitate the development of tests. The first new sample instance has an alien at the left edge. The second new sample instance has an alien at the right edge. The sample expressions use and to determine that the list is not empty and that at least one of the aliens is at the left edge. To determine if there is at least one alien at the left side or is used. The job of determining if a single alien is at the left edge is delegated to an auxiliary function because an alien is not the same type as the one that the function processes (i.e., alien ≠ loa). Observe that the only difference among the sample expressions is the list of aliens used. Thus, any-alien-at-left-edge? has only one parameter. As expected, any-alien-at-left-edge? uses its parameter, instead of a concrete value, in its body. The tests using sample computations illustrate the function works for four interesting loas: empty, does not contain an alien at either edge, contains an alien at the left edge, and contains an alien at the right edge. The tests using sample values further illustrate how the function works when the given loa is not empty.

The auxiliary function needed, alien-at-left-edge?, was already for Aliens Attack version 2 (in Chap. 9). Therefore, any-alien-at-left-edge?'s design and implementation is complete.

74.2 Determining If an Alien Is at the Right Edge

Naturally, the next task is to design a function to determine if any alien is at the right edge. Its design is similar to `any-alien-at-left-edge?`'s design. The sufficient condition tests if an alien is at the right edge instead of the left edge. That is, a given `loa` has an alien at the right edge if the `loa` is not empty and either the first alien is at the left edge or an alien in the rest of the `loa` is at the left edge. The specialization of the template for functions on a `loa` yields:

```
;; loa → Boolean
;; Purpose: To determine if any alien is at scene's right edge
(define (any-alien-at-right-edge? a-loa)
  (and (not (empty? a-loa))
       (or (alien-at-right-edge? (first a-loa))
           (any-alien-at-right-edge? (rest a-loa)))))

;; Sample expressions for any-alien-at-right-edge?
(define EDGE-E-LOA-VAL
        (and (not (empty? E-LOA))
             (or (alien-at-right-edge?    (first E-LOA))
                 (any-alien-at-right-edge? (rest E-LOA)))))

(define EDGE-INIT-LOA-VAL
        (and (not (empty? INIT-LOA))
             (or (alien-at-right-edge?    (first INIT-LOA))
                 (any-alien-at-right-edge? (rest INIT-LOA)))))

(define EDGE-LOA-VAL
        (and (not (empty? EDGE-LOA))
             (or (alien-at-right-edge?    (first EDGE-LOA))
                 (any-alien-at-right-edge? (rest EDGE-LOA)))))

(define EDGE-LOA2-VAL
        (and (not (empty? EDGE-LOA2))
             (or (alien-at-right-edge?    (first EDGE-LOA2))
                 (any-alien-at-right-edge? (rest EDGE-LOA2)))))

;; Tests using sample computations any-alien-at-right-edge?
(check-expect (any-alien-at-right-edge? E-LOA)
              EDGE-E-LOA-VAL)
(check-expect (any-alien-at-right-edge? INIT-LOA)
              EDGE-INIT-LOA-VAL)
(check-expect (any-alien-at-right-edge? EDGE-LOA)
              EDGE-LOA-VAL)
```

```
(check-expect (any-alien-at-right-edge? EDGE-LOA2)
              EDGE-LOA2-VAL)

;; Tests using sample values for any-alien-at-right-edge?
(check-expect (any-alien-at-right-edge?
                (list (make-posn MIN-IMG-X 8)
                      (make-posn 6 3)
                      (make-posn MAX-IMG-X 10)))
              #true)
(check-expect (any-alien-at-right-edge?
                (list (make-posn 3  8)
                      (make-posn MAX-IMG-X  3)
                      (make-posn 5 2)))
              #true)
(check-expect (any-alien-at-right-edge?
                (list (make-posn MIN-IMG-Y  8)))
              #false)
(check-expect (any-alien-at-right-edge?
                (list (make-posn 3  8)
                      (make-posn 5 2)))
              #false)
```

Test coverage is similar to that of `any-alien-at-left-edge?`. The auxiliary function needed, `alien-at-right-edge?`, has already been written for Aliens Attack version 2 (in Chap. 9). Therefore, `any-alien-at-right-edge?`'s design and implementation is complete.

74.3 Determining If an Alien Has Reached Earth

As a final example consider determining if any alien in a given `loa` has reached earth. This is another problem that requires oring a list. Such an alien exists in a given `loa` if it is not empty and either the first alien has reached earth or one of the rest of the aliens has reached earth. Once again we specialize the template for a function on a `loa` and obtain:

```
(define EARTH-REACHED-LOA
        (list (make-posn 1 11)
              (make-posn MAX-IMG-X MAX-IMG-Y)))


;; loa → Boolean
;; Purpose: Determine if any alien has reached earth
(define (any-alien-reached-earth? a-loa)
  (and (not (empty? a-loa))
       (or (alien-reached-earth? (first a-loa))
           (any-alien-reached-earth? (rest a-loa)))))
```

```
;; Sample expressions for any-alien-reached-earth?
(define ANY-REACHED-VAL1
        (and (not (empty? E-LOA))
             (or (alien-reached-earth? (first E-LOA))
                 (any-alien-reached-earth? (rest E-LOA)))))
(define ANY-REACHED-VAL2
        (and (not (empty? INIT-LOA))
             (or (alien-reached-earth? (first INIT-LOA))
                 (any-alien-reached-earth? (rest INIT-LOA)))))
(define ANY-REACHED-VAL3
        (and (not (empty? EARTH-REACHED-LOA))
             (or (alien-reached-earth?
                   (first EARTH-REACHED-LOA))
                 (any-alien-reached-earth?
                   (rest EARTH-REACHED-LOA)))))


;; Tests using sample computations for any-alien-reached-earth?
(check-expect (any-alien-reached-earth? E-LOA)
              ANY-REACHED-VAL1)
(check-expect (any-alien-reached-earth? INIT-LOA)
              ANY-REACHED-VAL2)
(check-expect (any-alien-reached-earth? EARTH-REACHED-LOA)
              ANY-REACHED-VAL3)


;; Tests using sample values for any-alien-reached-earth?
(check-expect (any-alien-reached-earth?
                (list (make-posn 3 MAX-IMG-Y)
                      (make-posn 7 5)
                      (make-posn 8 2)))
              #true)
(check-expect (any-alien-reached-earth? (list (make-posn 3 12)
                                              (make-posn 7 5)
                                              (make-posn 8 2)))
              #false)
```

To make the development of tests easier a new loa instance with an alien that has reached earth is defined. The auxiliary function, alien-reached-earth?, was developed in Chap. 9. The tests cover both loa varieties and lists that contain and do not contain an alien that reached earth.

Observe that any-alien-at-left-edge?, any-alien-at-right-edge?, and any-alien-reached-earth? are all very similar. What does this suggest to you? How do we avoid so much repetition? If you are thinking that an abstraction step is needed, then you are on the right track. We shall soon learn how to avoid repetitions among functions.

* **Ex. 134** — Design and write a function to determine if a given list of numbers contains an even number.

* **Ex. 135** — Design and write a function to determine if a given list of numbers contains a multiple of 10.

* **Ex. 136** — Design and write a function to determine if a given list of strings contains `"Ekaterina Ermilkina"`.

** **Ex. 137** — A car is defined by a brand, a model, and a price. Design and write a function to determine if a given list of cars contains a car that costs less than $20,000.

* **Ex. 138** — Design and write a function to determine if a given list of images contains an image with a width greater than 100 pixels.

75 List ANDing

Another variant of list searching determines if all elements of some list, L, satisfy some property. That is, we seek to determine if all of L's elements satisfy a predicate P. How is this determined? Think about the list varieties. What is the answer if L is empty? The answer may not be obvious to you. That is fine. Let us once again consider a list of length 1 whose only element, p, satisfies P. In this case, do all the list elements satisfy *P*? Clearly, the answer is yes. Now, think about how this is computed. The list looks as follows:

```
L = (cons p '())
```

Let us name the function that processes L: `all-satisfy-P?`. To process p you apply P to p to obtain `#true`. The rest of the list is processed recursively by calling `all-satisfy-P?`. All the list elements, if any, in the rest of L must also satisfy P. This means that the following expression must evaluate to `#true`:

```
(and (P p) (all-satisfy-P? (rest L)))
```

Given that the rest of L is `'()`, `(all-satisfy-P? (rest L))` must evaluate to `#true` in order for `(all-satisfy-P? L)` to evaluate to `#true`. Thus, we have that the answer must be `#true` when L is empty. When the list is not empty you and the result of applying P to the first element of the list and the result obtained from recursively processing the rest of the list.

75.1 All Even in a `lon`

Consider determining if all the numbers in a list of numbers are even. If the given `lon` is empty then, as suggested above, the answer is true. It is certainly true that all the numbers (i.e., none) in the empty list are even. If the given `lon` is not empty, then the first number must be even and the rest of the numbers must be even. Observe that no decision must be made to solve this problem. Therefore, the use of a condition expression as suggested by the template for a function on a `lon` is not needed. Instead, the result for the different varieties of `lon` is ored.

To start specializing the template for a function on a `lon` as suggested by our problem analysis let us start by defining useful sample `lon` instances and sample expressions for our function `all-even?`:

```
;; Sample instances of lon
(define E-LON   '())
(define AE-LON  '(88 98 22 78 506))
(define NAE-LON '(8 561 683 788))


  ;; Sample expressions for all-even-lon?
(define E-LON-VAL    (or (empty? E-LON)
                         (and (even? (first E-LON))
                              (all-even-lon? (rest E-LON)))))
(define AE-LON-VAL   (or (empty? AE-LON)
                         (and (even? (first AE-LON))
                              (all-even-lon? (rest AE-LON)))))
(define NAE-LON-VAL  (or (empty? NAE-LON)
                         (and (even? (first NAE-LON))
                              (all-even-lon? (rest NAE-LON)))))
```

At least one example of each `lon` variety and sample `lon`s that are and are not all even are defined. The sample expressions state that the elements of a given `lon` are all even if the list is empty or if all the elements satisfy Racket's `even?` predicate.

The process of abstracting over the sample expressions identifies that there is only one difference: the `lon` being processed. This step leads to the following specialization of the definition template:

```
;; lon → Boolean
;; Purpose: To determine if the given lon only has even numbers
(define (all-even-lon? a-lon)
  (or (empty? a-lon)
      (and (even? (first a-lon))
           (all-even-lon? (rest a-lon)))))
```

The steps of the design recipe are completed by specializing and running the tests. The result of specializing the tests are:

```
;; Tests using sample computations for all-even-lon?
(check-expect (all-even-lon? E-LON)   E-LON-VAL)
(check-expect (all-even-lon? AE-LON)  AE-LON-VAL)
(check-expect (all-even-lon? NAE-LON) NAE-LON-VAL)

;; Tests using sample values for all-even-lon?
(check-expect (all-even-lon? '(9 1 7)) #false)
(check-expect (all-even-lon? '(4 6 8)) #true)
```

The tests using sample values employ the sample lon instances and the constants
defined for the values of the sample expressions. The tests using sample values
further illustrate how the function works using lists that have either all even or all
odd numbers.

75.2 Determining if a lon Is Sorted

Consider the problem of determining of a list of numbers is sorted in non-decreasing
order. For example, '(73 87 87 99 104) is in non-decreasing order and '(73 87
87 17 205) is not in non-decreasing order. How do you know if a lon is or is not
in non-decreasing order? As you traverse the list from left to right the first number
must be less than or equal to the second number. What if the lon does not have two
numbers? In this case, the lon must be either '() or (cons number '()). In both
cases the lon is sorted in non-decreasing order.

The data analysis above suggests that for this problem we need a different data
definition for a list of numbers. Observe that there are two base cases: '() and
(cons number '()). If the length of the list is greater than 1, then there must be
at least two numbers in the list. This means that we need to define a list of numbers
as follows:

```
;; A lon2 is either:
;; 1. '()
;; 2. (list number)
;; 3. (list number number lon2)
```

A list of length greater than one is defined recursively. Notice that this is a valid data
definition. There are at least two varieties. Two varieties are nonrecursive and one
variety is recursive.

The corresponding template for a function on a lon2 is:

```
;; Sample instances of lon2
;; (define E-LON2 ...)
;; (define A-LON2 ...)
;; (define B-LON2 ...)
;;      ...
```

```
;; lon2 ... --> ...
;; Purpose: ...
;; (define (f-on-lon2 a-lon2 ...)
;;    (cond [(empty? a-lon2) ...)
;;          [(= (length a-lon2) 1) ...]
;;          [else ...(f-on-number (first a-lon2))
;;                ...(f-on-number (second a-lon2))
;;                ...(f-on-lon2 (rest a-lon2))
;;                ...(f-on-lon2 (rest (rest a-lon2)))]))

;; Sample expressions for sorted-lon2
;; (define E-LON2-VAL ...)
;; (define A-LON2-VAL ...)
;; (define B-LON2-VAL ...)
;;      ...

;; Tests using sample computations for sorted-LON2
;; (check-expect (sorted-lon2? E-LON2 ...) E-LON2-VAL)
;; (check-expect (sorted-lon2? A-LON2 ...) A-LON2-VAL)
;; (check-expect (sorted-lon2? B-LON2 ...) B-LON2-VAL)
;;      ...

;; Tests using sample values for sorted-lon2
;; (check-expect (sorted-lon2? ...) ...)
;;      ...
```

The template suggests at least three sample instances need to be defined given that there are three varieties of lon2. The definition template suggests using a conditional with three clauses to capture each lon2 variety. Of these, the else clause is the most interesting. It states that the first and second numbers may be processed by calling a function on a number. Furthermore, the rest of the numbers may be processed in one of two ways. The first eliminates the number in the first position of the list for the recursive call. The second eliminates the first two numbers for the recursive call. Why is there two ways to process the rest of the numbers? Observe that both (rest a-lon2) and (rest (rest a-lon2)) are a lon2. The first of these may be used when the first number no longer needs to be processed. The second is used when the first two numbers no longer need to be processed. In the template there are also at least three sample expressions to illustrate how a computation is performed for each lon2 variety. The suggested number of tests correspond to the number of sample instances and sample expressions for a lon2. Finally, the tests using sample values will be used to illustrate that the function works for concrete values other than those defined as sample instances.

Armed with a data definition and a function template, we can proceed with problem solving. If the given lon2 is empty, then the numbers are sorted in non-decreasing order. The same is true if the given lon2 only has one number. This suggests that the first two varieties may be combined in our function definition because they yield the same answer. If the given lon2 has two or more elements, then the first two elements must be in non-decreasing order. How is the recursive call made? It must not eliminate the second number in the given lon2 because it is needed to make sure it is in non-decreasing order relative to the third number if it exists. That is, the recursive call is made with the rest of the given lon2. Observe that a decision must not be made to compute the needed answer. We can or the result of determining if the list is of at most length 1 and the result of anding the result of comparing the first two numbers and the result of recursively processing the rest of the given lon2. This analysis leads to the following specialization of the function template:

```
;; Sample instances of lon2
(define E-LON2          '())
(define A-LON2          '(88))
(define SORTED-LON2     '(8 56 68 788))
(define UNSORTED-LON2 '(5 7 8 4 9))


;; lon2 → Boolean
;; Purpose: To determine if the given lon2 is sorted in
;;          nondecreasing order
(define (sorted-lon2? a-lon2)
  (or (<= 0 (length a-lon2) 1)
      (and (<= (first a-lon2) (second a-lon2))
           (sorted-lon2? (rest a-lon2)))))

;; Sample expressions for sorted-lon2
(define E-LON2-VAL
        (or (< (length E-LON2) 2)
            (and (<= (first E-LON2) (second E-LON2))
                 (sorted-lon2? (rest E-LON2)))))
(define A-LON2-VAL
        (or (< (length A-LON2) 2)
            (and (<= (first A-LON2) (second A-LON2))
                 (sorted-lon2? (rest A-LON2)))))
(define SORTED-LON2-VAL
        (or (< (length SORTED-LON2) 2)
            (and (<= (first SORTED-LON2) (second SORTED-LON2))
                 (sorted-lon2? (rest SORTED-LON2)))))
(define UNSORTED-LON2-VAL
        (or (< (length UNSORTED-LON2) 2)
            (and (<= (first UNSORTED-LON2)
                     (second UNSORTED-LON2))
                 (sorted-lon2? (rest UNSORTED-LON2)))))

;; Tests using sample computations for sorted-LON2
(check-expect (sorted-lon2? E-LON2)        E-LON2-VAL)
```

```
(check-expect (sorted-lon2? A-LON2)        A-LON2-VAL)
(check-expect (sorted-lon2? SORTED-LON2)   SORTED-LON2-VAL)
(check-expect (sorted-lon2? UNSORTED-LON2) UNSORTED-LON2-VAL)

;; Tests using sample values for sorted-lon2
(check-expect (sorted-lon2? '(8 7 6 5)) #false)
(check-expect (sorted-lon2? '(5 6 7 8)) #true)
```

The sample instances have an instance of each lon2 variety. In addition, there are two instances of the third lon2 variety: one that is sorted in non-decreasing order and one that is not. These instances make illustrating how the function works through tests easier. The sample expressions illustrate that a lon2 sorted in non-decreasing order is either of length less than 2 or has the first two numbers in non-decreasing order and the rest of the numbers (not including the first one) in non-decreasing order. Abstracting over the sample expressions yields a function definition. Finally, the tests illustrate that the function works for the sample lon2 instances and for other concrete lon2 instances.

** **Ex. 139** — Design and write a function to determine if a list of posns only contains aliens as defined for Aliens Attack.

** **Ex. 140** — Design and write a function to determine if a list of images only contains images that have an area less than 200 squared pixels.

* **Ex. 141** — Design and write a function to determine if a list of Booleans only contains #trues.

** **Ex. 142** — Design and write a function to determine if a list of Booleans only contains #falses.

* **Ex. 143** — Design and write a function to determine if a list of numbers is in non-decreasing order using the conditional suggested by the template for a function on a lon2.

* **Ex. 144** — Design and write a function to determine if a list of numbers is in non-increasing order.

** **Ex. 145** — Design and write a function to determine if a list of strings is in alphabetical order. You may use Racket's string<=? predicate.

*** **Ex. 146** — Design and write a function to determine if in a list of numbers, L, for every even i in [0..(sub (length L))] the i + 1 number, if it exists, has a different parity than the ith number.

---

76 List Mapping

List mapping refers to the process of applying a function to every element of a list and returning a list of the results. This type of operation is very common when solving problems involving lists. For example, in Aliens Attack multiple aliens and multiple shots may be represented using, respectively, a list of aliens and a list of shots. Every time the clock ticks all the aliens and all the shots must be moved. How is this accomplished?

76.1 Moving a List of Aliens

First consider how to move every alien. Imagine the world in Aliens Attack contains a list of aliens and a direction. All the aliens must move in the same direction every time the clock ticks. This means that the function move-alien must be mapped over the given loa to create the list of the moved aliens. This list of moved aliens becomes the world's list of aliens after the clock tick. The list of aliens must be processed, thus, suggesting specializing the template for a function on a list of aliens. Think about how to process the list of aliens based on its structure. If the list of aliens is empty, then there are no aliens to move and the list of moved aliens is empty. Otherwise, the first alien is moved using the function move-alien and the rest of the aliens are moved. The list of moved aliens is created by consing these two values. Based on this problem analysis, the template for a function on a list of aliens may be specialized starting with the sample expressions as follows:

```
;; Sample expressions for move-loa
(define MELOA-VAL  E-LOA)
(define MILOA-VAL  (cons (move-alien (first INIT-LOA) 'left)
                         (move-loa (rest INIT-LOA) 'left)))
(define MILOA-VAL2 (cons (move-alien (first INIT-LOA) 'right)
                         (move-loa (rest INIT-LOA) 'right)))
(define MILOA-VAL3 (cons (move-alien (first INIT-LOA) 'down)
                         (move-loa (rest INIT-LOA) 'down)))
```

The first sample expression states that when the empty list of aliens is moved the resulting list of moved aliens is the empty list of aliens. The other three sample expressions state that a non-empty list of aliens is moved by creating a list containing the first alien moved in a given direction and the rest of the aliens moved in the same given direction. There is such a sample expression for each possible instance of dir. Abstracting over the sample expressions yields the specialization of the definition template:

```
;; loa dir → loa
;; Purpose: To move the given loa in the given dir
(define (move-loa a-loa dir)
```

```
(if (empty? a-loa)
    E-LOA
    (cons (move-alien (first a-loa) dir)
          (move-loa (rest a-loa) dir))))
```

To complete the steps of the design recipe the tests must be specialized for move-loa. The tests using sample computations used the defined instances of loa and the defined constants for the value of sample expressions. The tests using sample computations utilize concrete lists of aliens and each of the possible dir instances. We may specialize the testing suite as follows:

```
;; Tests using sample computations for move-loa
(check-expect (move-loa E-LOA 'right)    MELOA-VAL)
(check-expect (move-loa INIT-LOA 'left)  MILOA-VAL)
(check-expect (move-loa INIT-LOA 'right) MILOA-VAL2)
(check-expect (move-loa INIT-LOA 'down)  MILOA-VAL3)

;; Tests using sample values for move-loa
(check-expect (move-loa (cons (make-posn 1 1)
                              (cons (make-posn 1 2) '()))
                        'right)
              (cons (make-posn 2 1)
                    (cons (make-posn 2 2) '())))

(check-expect (move-loa (cons (make-posn 1 1)
                              (cons (make-posn 1 2) '()))
                        'left)
              (cons (make-posn 0 1)
                    (cons (make-posn 0 2) '())))
(check-expect (move-loa (cons (make-posn 1 1)
                              (cons (make-posn 1 2) '()))
                        'down)
              (cons (make-posn 1 2)
                    (cons (make-posn 1 3) '())))
```

76.2 Moving a List of Shots

Designing a function to move a list of shots is also a mapping operation. The function move-shot must be mapped over a given list of shots. Given that a list of shots must be processed, the template for a function on a list of shots must be specialized. The result of this specialization is:

```
;; los → los
;; Purpose: To move the given list of shots
(define (move-los a-los)
```

```
(if (empty? a-los)
    E-LOS
    (cons (move-shot (first a-los))
          (move-los  (rest a-los)))))
```

```
;; Sample expressions for move-los
(define MOVED-E-LOS-VAL E-LOS)
(define MOVED-A-LOS-VAL (cons (move-shot (first A-LOS))
                             (move-los  (rest A-LOS))))
```

```
;; Tests using sample computations for move-los
(check-expect (move-los E-LOS) MOVED-E-LOS-VAL)
(check-expect (move-los A-LOS) MOVED-A-LOS-VAL)
```

```
;; Tests using sample values for move-los
(check-expect (move-los (cons (make-posn 12 7)
                             (cons NO-SHOT E-LOS)))
             (cons (make-posn 12 6)
                   (cons NO-SHOT E-LOS)))
```

Observe the remarkable similarity between move-loa and move-los. This is not terribly surprising because both map a function over a list. It does, however, cement our idea that there must be an abstraction step to eliminate repetitions among functions.

76.3 Returning a Different List Type

Both move-loa and move-los return the same type of list that they get as input. This occurs for move-loa because the mapped function move-alien returns an alien. Similarly, this occurs for move-los because the mapped function move-shot returns a shot. This is not a property of mapping a function over a list. Instead, it is a property of the function mapped. A mapping function may take as input a (listof X) and return a (listof Y) if the signature of the mapped function is: X → Y.

Consider, for example, computing the lengths of each string in a (listof string). The length of a string is always a number. More specifically, it is always a, natnum, natural number (i.e., a nonnegative integer). Therefore, the result type for a function that solves this problem is: (listof string) → (listof natnum). The function must process the given (listof string) and compute the length of each string.

We start the process of specializing the template for a function on a (listof string) by creating sample instances of (listof string):[20]

---

[20] Verses courtesy of Lord Byron.

```
;; Sample instances of a (listof string)
(define E-LOSTR   '())
(define NE-LOSTR '("Here's" "a" "sigh" "to" "those" "who"
                              "love"   "me."))
(define NE-LOSTR2 '("And" "a" "smile" "for" "to" "those"
                    "who" "hate")
```

These sample (listof string) are used to define variables for the values of
sample expressions to illustrate how the answer is computed:

```
;; Sample expressions for lengths-lostr
(define E-LOSTR-VAL '())
(define NE-LOSTR-VAL  (cons (string-length (first NE-LOSTR))
                            (lengths-lostr (rest NE-LOSTR))))
(define NE-LOSTR2-VAL (cons (string-length (first NE-LOSTR))
                            (lengths-lostr (rest NE-LOSTR))))
```

The sample expressions state that when the given (listof string) is empty,
then the answer is the empty (listof natnum). When the (listof string) is
not empty, then the answer is obtained by consing the length of the first string
in the given (listof string) and the lengths of the rest of the strings in the
given (listof string). Observe that the rest of the given (listof string)
is processed recursively by the function that computes the lengths of a (listof
string).

To specialize the definition template, the empty string is returned if the given
(listof string) is empty. The expression for when the given (listof string)
is not empty is obtained by abstracting over the second and third sample expressions.
This yields the following function definition:

```
;; (listof string) → lon
;; Purpose: Return a list of the string lengths in the
;;          given (listof string)
(define (lengths-lostr a-lostr)
  (if (empty? a-lostr)
      '()
      (cons (string-length (first a-lostr))
            (lengths-lostr (rest a-lostr)))))
```

The tests using sample computations illustrate that the function properly computes
the value of the sample expressions. The tests using sample values illustrate the
function works for different sample values. The tests are:

```
;; Tests using sample computations for lengths-lostr
(check-expect (lengths-lostr E-LOSTR)  E-LOSTR-VAL)
(check-expect (lengths-lostr NE-LOSTR) NE-LOSTR-VAL)
```

```
;; Tests using sample values for lengths-lostr
(check-expect (lengths-lostr
               (list "And" "whatever" "sky's" "above" "me"))
              (list 3 8 5 5 2))
(check-expect (lengths-lostr
               (list "Here's" "a" "heart" "for" "every"
                     "fate"))
              (list 6 1 5 3 5 4))
```

---

* **Ex. 147** — Design and write a function to cube the numbers in a list of numbers.

** **Ex. 148** — Design and write a function to return a list of x values from a list of posns.

* **Ex. 149** — Display the template for a function on a list of strings.

** **Ex. 150** — Display the data definition and the template for a function on a list of images. Design and write a function to compute the perimeters of a list of images.

*** **Ex. 151** — Design and write a function to double the even numbers and to triple the odd numbers in a list of numbers.

**** **Ex. 152** — A numstr is either a number or a string representing a number. Design and write a function to change the numbers into strings (representing the numbers) and change the strings into numbers. For example, the following test ought to pass:

```
(check-expect (transform-lonumstr (list 10 "10" "-5" -8))
              (list "10" 10 -5 "-8"))
```

Search the documentation for functions that transform a number into a string and vice versa.

---

77 List Filtering

List filtering refers to the process of removing/filtering elements from a given list that do not satisfy a condition. Alternatively, you may think of list filtering as returning/extracting a list of the elements that satisfy a given condition. This is achieved by testing every element of the list as it is traversed.

Three examples are presented. The first extracts the even numbers out of a given list of numbers. The second filters out the aliens hit by a shot for a given list of aliens and a given list of shots. The third extracts shots that have not hit an alien from a given list of shots and a given list of aliens.

77.1 Extracting Even numbers

Consider the problem of returning the even numbers found in a list of numbers. The list must be traversed. This means that the list must be processed and you ought to think in terms of the structure of a list of numbers. If the given list is empty, then it contains no even numbers and the empty list is the list of all even numbers in the given list. If the given list is not empty, then we think in terms of the first number and the rest of the numbers. The first number is included in the resulting list if it is even and it is not included if it is odd. The rest of the list is processed recursively as suggested by the template for a function on a lon. This analysis suggests that there are three conditions that need to be determined: the list is empty, the first element of the list is even, and the first element of the list is not even.

Given our problem analysis, we can proceed to specialize the template for a function on a lon. First we define sample instances of a lon to use in our tests:

```
;; Sample instances of lon
(define LON1 '())
(define LON2 '(0 1 2 -3 4 5 -6 7 8 9))
(define LON3 '(11 75 -31 49))
```

Observe that each list satisfies one of the conditions. LON1 is empty. LON2 has an even number as its first element. LON3 has an odd number as its first element.

We can now write sample expressions to illustrate how each of the different lists is processed:

```
;; Sample expressions for extract-evens
(define LON1-VAL '())
(define LON2-VAL (cons (first LON2)
                       (extract-evens (rest LON2))))
(define LON3-VAL (extract-evens (rest LON3)))
```

When the input list is empty, the answer is the empty list. When the first number is even this number is consed to the result of extracting the even numbers from the rest of the list. When the first number is not even, then it is not consed to the result of extracting the even numbers from the rest of the list.

Abstracting over the sample expressions helps us specialize the definition template:

```
;; lon → lon
;; Purpose: To return list of the even numbers in the
;;          given list
(define (extract-evens a-lon)
  (cond [(empty? a-lon) '()]
        [(even? (first a-lon))
         (cons (first a-lon) (extract-evens (rest a-lon)))]
        [else (extract-evens (rest a-lon))]))
```

Instead of two stanzas, the conditional has three stanzas as per our problem analysis. When the given lon is not empty, even? is used to determine if the first number is even and if so it is added to the resulting list. If it is not even, then number must be odd and is not added to the resulting list.

The tests using sample computations, as always, are specialized using the sample lon instances and the defined constants for the values of the sample expressions:

```
;; Tests using sample computations for extract-evens
(check-expect (extract-evens LON1) LON1-VAL)
(check-expect (extract-evens LON2) LON2-VAL)
(check-expect (extract-evens LON3) LON3-VAL)
```

The tests using sample computations are specialized using extrema lon instances. In this case, we use a list that only contains even numbers and a list that only contains odd numbers:

```
;; Tests using sample values for extract-evens
(check-expect (extract-evens '(2 4 6 8)) '(2 4 6 8))
(check-expect (extract-evens '(-71 -9 -909 -55)) '())
```

77.2 Removing Hit Aliens

In Aliens Attack, we wish to have multiple shots and multiple aliens. Among other things, this means that aliens hit by a shot must be removed from the world's list of aliens. This is accomplished by traversing the loa and testing each alien. If the first alien has been hit by any shot, then it is not added to the resulting loa. Otherwise the first alien is added to the resulting loa. Consider carefully how to design such a function. There are two inputs: a list of aliens and a list of shots. We must decide which template to specialize to write the function. Our problem analysis suggests that for each alien we must traverse the list of shots to determine if it has been hit by any of the shots. This means that the function ought to be designed to traverse the aliens using the template for a function on a loa.

Observe that our problem analysis reveals that there are three conditions and, therefore, a conditional expression with three stanzas is needed to specialize the template. This means we need at least three sample expressions to illustrate how each condition is processed. The following are sample expressions for this purpose:

```
;; Sample expressions for remove-hit-aliens
(define EMP-LOA-VAL '())
(define INIT-LOA-VAL (cons (first INIT-LOA)
                           (remove-hit-aliens (rest INIT-LOA)
                                              INIT-LOS)))
(define INIT-LOA-VAL2 (remove-hit-aliens (rest INIT-LOA) LOS2))
```

These sample expressions use previously defined loa and los instances. The first expression states that when the given loa is empty the answer is empty. There are no aliens that have been hit in the empty loa. The second expression corresponds to the case when the first alien in the given loa is not hit by any shot. In this case, the first alien is added to the result list. The third sample expression corresponds to the case when the first alien is hit. In this case, the first alien is not added to the result list.

Using a variable instead is concrete values for the loa and the los allows us to specialize the template definition:

```
;; loa los → loa
;; Purpose: To remove the aliens from the given loa hit by any
;;          shot in the given los
(define (remove-hit-aliens a-loa a-los)
  (cond [(empty? a-loa) '()]
        [(hit-by-any-shot? (first a-loa) a-los)
         (remove-hit-aliens (rest a-loa) a-los)]
        [else (cons (first a-loa)
                    (remove-hit-aliens (rest a-loa) a-los))]))
```

Observe that there is a stanza for each of the conditions identified. The function hit-by-any-shot? is an auxiliary predicate to determine if any shot has hit the first alien. It needs to be designed and written. For now, we assume that the function exists to fulfill the separation of concerns principle.

The tests using sample computations use the previously defined loa and los instances and the defined constants for the value of the sample expressions:

```
;; Tests using sample computations for remove-hit-aliens
(check-expect (remove-hit-aliens E-LOA LOS2) EMP-LOA-VAL)
(check-expect (remove-hit-aliens INIT-LOA INIT-LOS)
              INIT-LOA-VAL)
(check-expect (remove-hit-aliens INIT-LOA LOS2) INIT-LOA-VAL2)
```

The first test using sample values illustrates that the function works when more than one alien must be removed. Observe that the los includes both shot varieties. The second test illustrates that the function works when none of the aliens need to be removed given a non-empty loa and a non-empty los. The tests are the following:

```
(check-expect (remove-hit-aliens
               (cons (make-posn 1 1)
                 (cons (make-posn 2 2)
                   (cons (make-posn 3 3)
                     (cons (make-posn 4 4) '()))))
               (cons (make-posn 3 3)
                 (cons NO-SHOT
                   (cons (make-posn 1 1) '()))))
              (cons (make-posn 2 2)
                (cons (make-posn 4 4) '())))
```

```
(check-expect
  (remove-hit-aliens (cons (make-posn 1 1)
                           (cons (make-posn 2 2)
                     (cons (make-posn 3 3) '())))
                           (cons (make-posn 7 4)
                                 (cons NO-SHOT
                                       (cons (make-posn 3 5)
                                             '())))))
  (cons (make-posn 1 1)
        (cons (make-posn 2 2)
              (cons (make-posn 3 3) '()))))
```

Now, we must design the auxiliary function hit-by-any-shot?. Given an alien, how do we determine if the alien has been hit by any shot in a given los? The los must be traversed to determine if hit?[21] holds for any of the shots. Determining if a predicate holds for any member of a list is a list oring function. Based on our previous experience in this chapter, a conditional is not required for such a function. Instead, an and-expression is used to determine that the given list of shots is not empty and an or-expression is used to determine if the first shot has hit the alien or some other shot has hit the alien.

Based on our problem analysis, we may write the following sample expressions:

```
;; Sample expressions for hit-by-any-shot?
(define HIT-LOS1-VAL (and (not (empty? LOS2))
                          (or (hit? (first LOS2) ALIEN-8-0)
                              (hit-by-any-shot? ALIEN-8-0
                                                (rest LOS2)))))
(define HIT-LOS2-VAL (and (not (empty? INIT-LOS))
                          (or (hit? (first INIT-LOS) ALIEN-8-0)
                              (hit-by-any-shot?
                               ALIEN-8-0
                               (rest INIT-LOS)))))
```

Each sample expression tests if the a los is not empty. If the list of shots is not empty, then both expressions test if the first shot has hit the alien and test if any other shot has hit the alien. The first expression uses a non-empty los that contains a shot that has hit the given alien. The second uses an empty los that, of course, does not contain any shot that has hit the given alien.

Abstraction over the concrete expressions informs us how to specialize the definition template for a function on a los as follows:

```
;; alien los → Boolean
;; Purpose: To determine if the given alien is hit by any shot
;;          in the given los
(define (hit-by-any-shot? an-alien a-los)
  (and (not (empty? a-los))
       (or (hit? (first a-los) an-alien)
           (hit-by-any-shot? an-alien (rest a-los)))))
```

---

[21] The predicate hit? was designed in Sect. 63.1.

Finally, we can write tests as follows:

```
;; Tests using sample computations for hit-by-any-shot?
(check-expect (hit-by-any-shot? ALIEN-8-0 LOS2)
              HIT-LOS1-VAL)
(check-expect (hit-by-any-shot? ALIEN-8-0 INIT-LOS)
              HIT-LOS2-VAL)

;; Tests using sample values for hit-by-any-shot?
(check-expect (hit-by-any-shot?
                (make-posn 8 3)
                (list (make-posn 1 1) (make-posn 10 7)))
              #false)
(check-expect (hit-by-any-shot?
                (make-posn 10 7)
                (list (make-posn 1 1) (make-posn 10 7)))
              #true)
```

The tests using sample values illustrate that the function returns the correct answer when the given alien is and is not hit. Given that no more auxiliary functions are needed, this completes the design of remove-hit-aliens.

---

* **Ex. 153** — Design and write a function to return the odd numbers in a given list of numbers.

* **Ex. 154** — Design and write a function to extract the strings of length greater than 5 from a given list of strings.

*** **Ex. 155** — Consider the following data definition:
```
;; A TV character (character) is a structure,
;; (make-character string image), with a name
;; and an image of the character.
(define-struct character (name img))
```

Design and write a function to extract the images that have an area less than 10,000 pixels^2 from a given list of characters.

** **Ex. 156** — Design and write a function that extracts the multiples of 3 and 7 from a given list of numbers.

* **Ex. 157** — Design and write a function to remove the strings that start with "M" from a given list of strings.

77.3 Removing Shots

In Aliens Attack, we need to filter the list of aliens. We must now decide if we must also filter the list of shots. Should a single shot be able to hit multiple aliens or should it only be able to hit one alien? We adopt the second posture. This means that the list of shots must be filtered to eliminate shots that have hit an alien. As we now know, filtering requires traversing a given list to create a new list with elements that satisfy a property. In this case, we need to extract the shots that have not hit an alien. Think carefully about what it means to have a shot that has not hit an alien. Which shots are these? Clearly, a posn shot that does not have the same image-x and image-y coordinates as any alien is a shot that must be preserved. What shots need to be filtered out? A posn shot that has the same coordinates as any alien must be filtered out. In addition, all NO-SHOT will also be filtered out because such a shot no longer can affect the evolution of the game. To filter the shots we need as input the list of shots and the list of aliens. As the list of shots is traversed any shot that is NO-SHOT or a posn shot that has hit an alien is not added to the resulting list of shots. Otherwise, the shot is added to the resulting list of shots.

The sample expressions in the template for a function on a list of shots may be specialized as follows:

```
;; Sample loa instances
(define LOA3 (list (make-posn 1 9) (make-posn 8 0)))
(define LOA4 (list (make-posn 1 9) (make-posn 8 5)))

;; Sample expressions for remove-shots
(define RM-INIT-LOS-VAL INIT-LOS)
(define RM-LOS2-VAL     (remove-shots (rest LOS2) LOA3))
(define RM-LOS2-VAL2    (cons (make-posn 8 0)
                             (remove-shots (rest LOS2)
                                           LOA4)))
```

Two new loa sample instances are defined to easily define variables for the values of the sample expressions. There is a sample expression for each possible condition. Either the given los is empty, the first shot is removed, or the first shot is not removed.

Based on the sample expressions, the definition template is specialized as follows:

```
;; los loa → los
;; Purpose: To remove hit and NO-SHOTs from the given loa
(define (remove-shots a-los a-loa)
  (cond [(empty? a-los) a-los]
        [(or (eq? (first a-los) NO-SHOT)
             (hit-any-alien? (first a-los) a-loa))
         (remove-shots (rest a-los) a-loa)]
        [else (cons (first a-los)
                    (remove-shots (rest a-los) a-loa))]))
```

Observe that a shot is filtered out if it is either NO-SHOT or it has hit an alien. That is, the shot is not consed into the resulting list of shots. Determining if the first shot has hit an alien requires the given loa to be traversed. This means processing a different kind of data and, therefore, this task is relegated to an auxiliary function that needs as input a shot and an loa. Once again, we see the importance of separation of concerns in program design.

The tests are specialized as follows:

```
;; Tests using sample computations for remove-shots
(check-expect (remove-shots INIT-LOS INIT-LOA)
              RM-INIT-LOS-VAL)
(check-expect (remove-shots LOS2 (list (make-posn 1 9)
                                       (make-posn 8 0)))
              RM-LOS2-VAL)
(check-expect (remove-shots LOS2 (list (make-posn 1 9)
                                       (make-posn 8 5)))
              RM-LOS2-VAL2)


;; Tests using sample values for remove-shots
(check-expect (remove-shots (list (make-posn 2 9)
                                  (make-posn 10 10))
                            INIT-LOA)
              (list (make-posn 2 9) (make-posn 10 10)))
(check-expect (remove-shots (list (make-posn 8 2)
                                  (make-posn 13 1))
                            INIT-LOA)
              '())
```

The tests using sample computations, as always, illustrate that the function correctly computes the values of the sample expressions. The tests using sample values illustrate that the function works when none of the shots must be filtered out and when all of the shots must be filtered out.

Now our focus turns to the design of the needed auxiliary function. To determine if a shot has hit an alien for a given loa, the given loa must be traversed. We may use a conditional expression as suggested by the template for a function on an loa, but careful problem analysis reveals that it is not needed. A given shot has hit any alien if the given loa is not empty and either the shot has hit the first alien or the shot has hit any other alien. This is a list ORing operation.

Based on this problem analysis, sample expressions may be written as follows:

```
;; Sample instance of a shot
(define SHOT5 (make-posn 11 1))


;; Sample expressions for hit-any-alien?
(define HIT-ANY-ALIEN0
```

```
            (and (not (empty? E-LOA))
                 (or (hit? NO-SHOT (first E-LOA))
                     (hit-any-alien? NO-SHOT (rest E-LOA)))))
(define HIT-ANY-ALIEN1
            (and (not (empty? E-LOA))
                 (or (hit? SHOT3 (first INIT-LOA))
                     (hit-any-alien? NO-SHOT (rest INIT-LOA)))))
(define HIT-ANY-ALIEN2
            (and (not (empty? INIT-LOA))
                 (or (hit? NO-SHOT (first INIT-LOA))
                     (hit-any-alien? NO-SHOT (rest INIT-LOA)))))

(define HIT-ANY-ALIEN3
            (and (not (empty? INIT-LOA))
                 (or (hit? SHOT5 (first INIT-LOA))
                     (hit-any-alien? SHOT5 (rest INIT-LOA)))))
```

A new shot instance is defined to facilitate the writing of the sample expressions. There are four sample expressions in order to have expressions for both varieties of aliens and shots. There are four possible combinations as input. The computation for an empty loa and a NO-SHOT is illustrated by the first sample expression. The computation for an empty loa and a posn shot is illustrated by the second sample expression. The computation for a non-empty loa and a NO-SHOT is illustrated by the third sample expression. The computation for a non-empty loa and a posn shot is illustrated by the fourth sample expression. The previously defined hit? (in Chap. 11) is used to detect if a shot has hit an alien. This is consistent with the goal to recycle as much code as possible during a refinement step.

Abstracting over the sample expressions leads to the following function definition:

```
;; shot loa → Boolean
;; Purpose: Determine if the given shot has hit any alien
;;          in the given loa
(define (hit-any-alien? a-shot a-loa)
  (and (not (empty? a-loa))
       (or (hit? a-shot (first a-loa))
           (hit-any-alien? a-shot (rest a-loa)))))
```

Observe that this is, indeed, very similar to other list ORing functions developed in this chapter.

The function is tested as follows:

```
;; Tests using sample computations for hit-any-alien?
(check-expect (hit-any-alien? NO-SHOT E-LOA)
              HIT-ANY-ALIEN0)
(check-expect (hit-any-alien? SHOT3   E-LOA)
              HIT-ANY-ALIEN1)
```

```
(check-expect (hit-any-alien? NO-SHOT INIT-LOA)
              HIT-ANY-ALIEN2)
(check-expect (hit-any-alien? SHOT5   INIT-LOA)
              HIT-ANY-ALIEN3)


;; Tests using sample values for hit-any-alien?
(check-expect (hit-any-alien? (make-posn 9 3)
                              (list (make-posn 6 2)
                                    (make-posn 9 3)
                                    (make-posn 9 11)))
              #true)
(check-expect (hit-any-alien? (make-posn 11 3)
                              (list (make-posn 6 2)
                                    (make-posn 9 3)
                                    (make-posn 9 11)))
              #false)
(check-expect (hit-any-alien? NO-SHOT
                              (list (make-posn 6 2)
                                    (make-posn 9 3)
                                    (make-posn 9 11)))
              #false)
```

The tests using sample computations test every possible combination of the varieties of the input. The first test using sample values illustrates that the function works when a posn shot has hit an alien other than the first. The second test using sample values illustrates that the function works when a posn shot has not hit an alien. The third test using sample values illustrates that the function works when a NO-SHOT is given as input using a new loa.

---

* **Ex. 158** — Design and write a function to extract the odd numbers from a given list of numbers.

** **Ex. 159** — Design and write a function to filter out numbers that are not a multiple of 9 from a given list of numbers.

** **Ex. 160** — Design and write a function to filter out the NO-SHOTs from a given list of shots.

*** **Ex. 161** — Design and write a function to filter out from a list of numbers any number that appears in another given list of numbers.

*** **Ex. 162** — Consider the following data definition:

```
#|  A store item (item) is a structure,
    (make-item string number number),
    that has the item's name, price, and quantity in stock.
|#
(define-struct item (name price quantity))
```

Design and write a function to extract from a list of items those that are below
a given price.

78 List Sorting

The solution to many problems requires sorting a list. In order for a list to be sortable,
it must contain numerical or ordinal data. That is, any two elements are comparable
to determine which goes first and which goes second. For example, a list of numbers
and a list of strings may be sorted. A list that contains nominal data is not sortable.
For example, a list of symbols or a list of religions is not sortable.[22] For sortable data,
we need a predicate that determines which of two elements goes first. For example,
$\leq$ and $\geq$ are two such predicates for numbers depending on whether the list must be
sorted in non-decreasing order or in non-increasing order.

Let us take as an example sorting a list of numbers in non-decreasing order. For
example, '(87 65 90 21) after sorted in non-decreasing order is '(21 65 87
90). How is this accomplished? Clearly, the given list must be traversed and a new
list must be constructed. Therefore, think about the varieties of a list of numbers.
If the given lon is empty, then the sorted lon is also empty. If the given list is not
empty, think about its structure. The template for a function on an lon tells us to
process the rest of the list recursively. Assuming the function is named sort-lon
and the given list is a-lon, think about what this expression evaluates to:

```
(sort-lon (rest a-lon))
```

This expression ought to evaluate to a sorted list containing all the elements of
a-lon except a-lon's first element. This means that we must combine a-lon's first
element with a sorted list. How is this done? The sorted list must be traversed to
find the right place to insert a-lon's first element. If this is done, then we have a
sorted list that contains all the elements of the given list. Take note that inserting
a number into a sorted list of numbers is a different problem from sorting a list of
numbers. A different problem means we need an auxiliary function to perform this
computation. Keeping consistent with the principle of separation of concerns, we
assume this inserting function exists and works.

---

[22] The words (i.e., strings) that represent the names of different religions are sortable, but this is a
property of strings and not a property of religions.

Based on our problem analysis, template specialization begins with a-lon instances and sample expressions as follows:

```
;; Sample instances of a lon
(define E-LON        '())
(define SORTED-LON   '(17 18 29 37 41 52))
(define UNSORTED-LON '(89 21 1 77 23))


;; Sample expressions for sort-lon
(define E-LON-VAL '())
(define SORTED-LON-VAL
         (insert (first SORTED-LON)
                 (sort-lon (rest SORTED-LON))))
(define UNSORTED-LON-VAL
         (insert (first UNSORTED-LON)
                 (sort-lon (rest UNSORTED-LON))))
```

Two instances of a non-empty lon are defined to illustrate that the function works for a sorted and unsorted list. The first sample expression illustrates the answer when the given lon is empty. The second and third sample expressions illustrate that for a given non-empty lon, the sorted list is obtained by inserting the first number of the given list in the list obtained by sorting the rest of the list.

Abstracting over the sample expressions helps use specialize the template definition:

```
;; sort-lon: lon '() lon
;; Purpose: To sort the given lon in non-decreasing order
(define (sort-lon a-lon)
  (cond [(empty? a-lon) '()]
        [else (insert (first a-lon) (sort-lon (rest a-lon)))]))
```

Observe that insert still needs to be designed and implemented.

The tests are may be written as follows:

```
;; Tests using sample computations for sort-lon
(check-expect (sort-lon E-LON)        E-LON-VAL)
(check-expect (sort-lon SORTED-LON)   SORTED-LON-VAL)
(check-expect (sort-lon UNSORTED-LON) UNSORTED-LON-VAL)


;; Tests using sample values for sort-lon
(check-expect (sort-lon (list 5 4 3 2 1))
              (list 1 2 3 4 5))
(check-expect (sort-lon (list 63 12 76 99 0))
              (list 0 12 63 76 99))
```

The tests using sample values illustrate that the function works for a list that is in non-increasing order and a different unsorted list.

With the design and implementation of sort-lon completed, we turn to the design and implementation of the insert function. We have a number and a lon

sorted in non-decreasing order. We need a `lon` sorted in non-decreasing order that
contains the given number and all the numbers in the given sorted `lon`. Let us analyze
the problem based in the `lon` varieties. If the given sorted list is empty, then the
resulting list must only contain the given number. What if the given sorted list is not
empty? Then we must determine if the given number is less than or equal to the first
number in the given sorted list. If so, we obtain the needed sorted list by `cons`ing
the two. For example, given

> 9 and '(10 43 88 100)

the complete sorted list is obtained by the following expression:

> (cons 9 '(10 43 88 100))

What if the given number is greater than the first number in the given sorted list? In
this case, the first number of the resulting sorted list is the first number of the given
sorted list. The given number must be inserted in the rest of the given sorted list.
Processing the rest of the list, as we know, is done recursively. For example, given

> 53 and '(10 43 88 100)

the complete sorted list is obtained by the following expression:

> (cons 10 (insert 53 '(43 88 100)))

Here the result of the call to `insert` is:

> '(43 53 88 100)

Adding the 10 to the front of this list is the sorted list that is needed. Based on this
analysis we may conclude that the function must determine which one of 3 possible
is faced: the list is empty, the given number is less than or equal to the first number
of the list, and the given number is greater than the first number of the list.

To develop sample expressions, a sorted `lon` and two numbers to insert are
defined:

```
(define SORTED-LON2 '(31 87 95 102))
(define INSERT-NUM1 20)
(define INSERT-NUM2 90)
```

We display a sample expression for each possible condition:

```
;; Sample expressions for insert
(define ELON-VAL        (list INSERT-NUM1))
(define SORTEDLON-VAL   (cons INSERT-NUM1 SORTED-LON2))
(define UNSORTEDLON-VAL (cons (first SORTED-LON2)
                             (insert INSERT-NUM2
                                     (rest SORTED-LON2))))
```

The first sample expression illustrates how a number is inserted into the empty list
of numbers. The second illustrates how a number is inserted when it is less than or
equal than the first number in the sorted list. The third expression illustrates how a
number is inserted when it is greater than the first number in the sorted list.

Building on the sample expressions, the definition template is specialized as follows:

```
;; insert: number lon → lon
;; Purpose: To insert the given number in the given lon to
;;          create an lon in non-decreasing order
;; ASSUMPTION: Given lon is sorted in nondecreasing order
(define (insert a-num a-lon)
  (cond [(empty? a-lon) (list a-num)]
        [(<= a-num (first a-lon)) (cons a-num a-lon)]
        [else (cons (first a-lon)
                    (insert a-num (rest a-lon)))]))
```

Observe, the assumption that the given `lon` is sorted in non-decreasing is made explicit. This communicates clearly to the readers and users of our code how the solution was designed.

The tests for `insert` are the following:

```
;; Tests using sample computations for insert
(check-expect (insert INSERT-NUM1 E-LON) ELON-VAL)
(check-expect (insert INSERT-NUM1 SORTED-LON2)
              SORTEDLON-VAL)
(check-expect (cons (first SORTED-LON2)
                    (insert INSERT-NUM2 (rest SORTED-LON2)))
              UNSORTEDLON-VAL)

;; Tests using sample values for insert
(check-expect (insert 3 '(1 2 4 5))
              '(1 2 3 4 5))
(check-expect (insert 101 '(-7 -5 0 2 232))
              '(-7 -5 0 2 101 232))
```

The tests using sample values explicitly illustrate with concrete values how a number is inserted into a sorted list in non-decreasing order.

---

* **Ex. 163** — Design and write a function that sorts a list of numbers in non-increasing order.

*** **Ex. 164** — Consider the following data definition:
```
#| A store item (item) is a structure,
(make-item string number number),
that has the item's name, price, and quantity in stock. |#
(define-struct item (name price quantity))
```

Design and write a function that sorts a list of items in non-decreasing order by price.

*** **Ex. 165** — Stores usually need space for new inventory and put on sale the items they have the most of in stock. Using the item data definition from the previous problem, design and write a function that sorts a list of items in non-increasing order by quantity.

79 What Have We Learned in This Chapter?

The important lessons of Chap. 13 are summarized as follows:

- List summarizing computes an aggregate value from the values in a given list.
- List searching determines if a given value is contained in a list. Two common variants of list searching are:

  - List ORing determines if there is any value in a given list that satisfies a property.
  - List ANDing determines if all the values in a given list satisfy a property.

- List mapping applies a function to every element of the list and returns a list with the results.
- List filtering extracts the elements of a list that satisfy a given predicate.
- List sorting orders lists of ordinal values based on a predicate that can be used to compare any two list values.
- Think statically about the structure of a list during problem analysis to design a list-processing function.
- A necessary condition is one that must be true for a predicate to be true, but is not enough to conclude that the predicate is true.
- A sufficient condition is one that allows us to conclude that the predicate is true.
- Careful problem analysis reveals which functions that take a list as input processes the list. These are the functions that are developed using a template for a function on a list.
- List processing may require a conditional expression with more than two conditions.
- Functions may take as input a (listof X) and may return a (listof Y).
- There is a rumor among beginner programmers that recursion is hard. Now you know better!

Chapter 14
Natural Numbers

In this chapter we explore a different data type of arbitrary size. This is a data type
that is a subtype of the number type. It is likely that you have seen this data type in
your Mathematics textbooks. In a Mathematics textbook you may see the following
definition for the natural numbers:

    The natural numbers are 0, 1, 2, ...

You probably interpret the ... as meaning all the way to infinity. Thus, you are
confident that you understand what the natural numbers are. A natural question that
you may be asked is: What is a natural number? You may answer that a natural
number is an element of the set of the natural numbers. This may be true, but is
it useful in problem solving? That is, can you solve a problem if the given data is
a natural number? How do you process a natural number? You may say that you
process a natural number the same way you process a number. Yes, of course, this is
possible for some problems because the natural numbers are a subset of the numbers.
Is it always the case? If n is a natural number how you compute n!? In a Mathematics
textbook you may find the following:

    n! = 1 * 2 * * 3 * ... * n-1 * n

Do you understand how to compute n!? You can probable compute 3! and 5!.
Can you compute 1000!? If the answer is no then you need to write a function
to perform the computation. Can you do this? There are several problems with the
approach taken in some Mathematics textbooks for our purposes. A value needs to
be computed from a natural number, but we do not have a data definition for a natural
number. In addition, we do not know how to program . . . .

Consider more carefully developing a data definition for the set of natural numbers.
A natural number may be small like 0. It may be large like 10000. It may be of medium
size like 1587. It may be super large like 100000000. What is all this telling us?
It is telling us that a natural number is data of arbitrary size. What do we need to
design functions that process a natural number? You have probably already realized
the answer. We need a recursive data definition and a function template.

© The Author(s), under exclusive license to Springer Nature Switzerland AG 2022
M. T. Morazán, *Animated Problem Solving*, Texts in Computer Science,
https://doi.org/10.1007/978-3-030-85091-3_14

80 Data Definition for a Natural Number

Recall that for a recursive data definition we need at least two varieties. At least
one variety must not have a selfreference and at least one variety must have a
selfreference. Let us start with the variety that does not have a selfreference. When
we studied lists, the nonrecursive variety was the smallest list possible: '(). What
is the smallest natural number? Clearly, it is 0. Therefore, for our data definition we
can say that a natural number is 0. Now, ask yourself how can other natural numbers
be created? To make a larger list we use cons. What can we use to make a bigger
natural number? Let us start with 0, which we know is a natural number. Can we
create the next natural number, 1, using 0? Sure, we increment 0 by 1. Can we build,
2, the next natural number? Well we can increment the natural number 1 by 1. We
can build 3 by incrementing 2 by 1. There is a pattern here. If n is a natural number,
the next natural is obtained by incrementing it by 1. We can now write the needed
data definition:

```
A natural number (natnum) is either:
  1. 0
  2. (add1 natnum)
```

Observe that there are two natnum varieties of which one does not have a selfreference and other does.

We can use add1 to create a new natnum. What is the selector function to extract
the natnum used to build a given nonzero natnum? What natnum is used to build 5?
It is 4. What natnum is used to build 10? It is 9. Again we see a pattern. The selector
function is sub1.

Observe that there is one selfreference in the data definition. This means that
processing a nonzero natnum requires one recursive call. Based on this observation
the template for a function on a natnum is the following:

```
#|  ;; Sample instances of natnum
    (define ZERO 0)
    (define NATNUMA ...)
       ...


    ;; natnum ... → ...
    ;; Purpose: ...
    (define (f-on-natnum a-natnum ...)
      (if (= a-natnum 0)
          ...
          (...a-natnum...(f-on-natnum (sub1 a-natnum) ...)))))


    ;; Sample expressions for f-on-natnum
    (define ZERO-VAL ...)
    (define NATNUMA-VAL ...)
       ...
```

```
                ;; Tests using sample computations for f-on-natnum
                (check-expect (f-on-natnum ZERO ...)    ZERO-VAL)
                (check-expect (f-on-natnum NATNUMA ...) NATNUMA-VAL)
                    ...

                ;; Tests using sample values for f-on-natnum
                (check-expect (f-on-natnum ...) ...)
                (check-expect (f-on-natnum ...) ...)
                    ...
        |#
```

The template has all the expected components: sample instances, a function definition template, sample expressions, tests using sample computations, and tests using
sample values. Observe that one of the sample instances is 0. This is because it is the
only instance of the first variety. You may also observe that in the definition template
the expression for the recursive call contains sub1 applied to the input natnum.

81 Computing Factorial

Armed with the data definition and the template for a function on a natnum we are
ready to tackle problem solving. We start with designing a function to compute the
factorial of a natural number. First we define a few sample natnums as follows:

```
        ;; Sample instances of natnum
        (define ZERO  0)
        (define TEN   10)
        (define FIFTY 50)
```

Two nonzero natnums are defined to facilitate the abstraction process over the sample
expressions. The values chosen are ones for which anyone is unlikely to compute its
factorial by hand. Thus, a function is really needed.

Next, we must analyze how to solve the problem. For this we reason statically
about the structure of a natnum (just as we reason statically about the structure of a
list). Start with the nonrecursive variety. What is the factorial of 0? The mathematical
definition for factorial above does not specify this. It is not clear what the value of
0! is. Let us proceed with the second variety and come back to the first variety later.
If the given natnum, n, is not 0, the template suggests combining the given number
and the factorial of n − 1. For example, for the factorial of 4 the template suggests
combining 4 and 3!. We know from the mathematical definition above that:

```
        3! = 1 * 2 * 3
```

Given that value of 3! and the value 4, how do we get the value of 4!? Let us use
the mathematical definition again to examine what 4! is

```
        4! = 1 * 2 * 3 * 4
```

It now becomes clear that 4 and the value of 3! must be multiplied. This informs us that when the given natnum, n, is not 0, then n and (n - 1)! must be multiplied to obtain n!. We can now turn back to think about what the value of 0! must be. A value must be returned when n is 0. Let us look at how 4! is computed:

```
4! = 4 * 3 * 2 * 1 * ??
```

This sample computation captures the design idea of multiplying 4 by 3!. At each step n is decremented by 1. Eventually, n becomes 0. The ?? represents the value of 0!. Observe that the product of 4 through 1 is 4!. It now becomes clear that 0! is 1. Any other value for 0! would make the product not equal to 4!. Finally, observe that the product of natural numbers is a natural number. For example, 4! is 24, which is a natnum. This means that any function that computes the factorial of a natnum must return a natnum.

With a clear idea of how to compute the factorial of a natnum, we write sample expressions:

```
;; Sample expressions for factorial
(define ZERO-VAL  1)
(define TEN-VAL   (* 10 (factorial (sub1 10))))
(define FIFTY-VAL (* 50 (factorial (sub1 50))))
```

The first sample expression illustrates the computation when the given natnum is 0. The other two sample expressions illustrate the computation when the given natnum is not 0. As per our problem analysis the given natnum is multiplied by the factorial of said number decremented by 1.

Abstraction over the sample expressions yields the specialization of the definition template

```
;; natnum → natnum
;; Purpose: Compute the factorial of the given natnum
(define (factorial a-natnum)
  (if (= a-natnum 0)
      1
      (* a-natnum (factorial (sub1 a-natnum)))))
```

Observe that the return type is natnum as suggested by our problem analysis. In the body of the function 1 is returned if the given natnum is 0. Otherwise, the product of the given natnum, a-natnum, and the factorial of a-natnum - 1 is returned. In other words, the values returned are consistent with our problem analysis.

The final template specialization step is to develop the tests. The tests using sample computations are

```
;; Tests using sample computations for factorial
(check-expect (factorial ZERO)  ZERO-VAL)
(check-expect (factorial TEN)    TEN-VAL)
(check-expect (factorial FIFTY) FIFTY-VAL)
```

These tests, as before, illustrate that the function correctly computes the values of the sample expressions. They validate the abstraction over the sample expressions. The tests using sample values are

```
;; Tests using sample values for f-on-natnum
(check-expect (factorial 3) 6)
(check-expect (factorial 5) 120)
```

The sample values chosen are small enough that any reader of the code can easily verify that the expected values are correct. To finalize the steps of the design recipe run the program to make sure all the tests pass.

---

* Ex. 166 — Design and implement a function to compute the sum of the first n squares, where n is a natural number. For example, for n = 3 the sum of the first 3 nonzero squares is: $3^2 + 2^2 + 1^2$.

*** Ex. 167 — Design and implement a function to compute n^2, where n is a natural number, using only addition. Hint: $n^2 =$ the sum of the first n odd natural numbers. For example, $4^2 = 7 + 5 + 3 + 1$.

** Ex. 168 — Design and implement a function to compute the product of two natural numbers only using addition. For example, 3 * 4 = 3 + 3 + 3 + 3.

---

82 Computing Tetrahedral Numbers

A tetrahedral is a triangular pyramid. At each layer of a tetrahedral we find a set of objects, all the same, that form an equilateral triangle. Figure 70 displays three tetrahedra of different heights made of disks. In Fig. 70a the tetrahedral is of height one and is built using a single disk. In Fig. 70b the tetrahedral is of height two and is built using 4 disks: 3 for the bottom level and one for the top level. In Fig. 70c the tetrahedral is of height three and is built using 10 disks: 6 for the bottommost layer, 3 for the middle layer, and 1 for the top layer. In Fig. 70c it is easy to see the triangles that form each layer of the tetrahedral. The numbers 1, 4, and 10 are the first three numbers in a sequence of numbers called the tetrahedral numbers. The tetrahedral number in position n of the sequence is the number of objects needed to build a tetrahedral of height n.

Imagine that you wish to build a tetrahedral of disks (all the same) of height 20. How many disks do you need? In other words, what is the 20th tetrahedral number? Given that the answer is not immediately obvious, we need to write a function to compute tetrahedral numbers. Observe that the position, n, of the desired tetrahedral number is always a natnum: the first, the fifth, the twentieth, etc. This gives us insight into how we may design a function to compute tetrahedral numbers. We need to process a natnum. Thus, we ought to specialize the template for a function on a natnum.

Fig. 70 Three tetrahedra

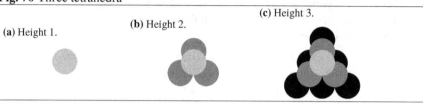

(a) Height 1.

(b) Height 2.

(c) Height 3.

Fig. 71 Division of tetrahedral of height 3

(a) Top Layers.

(b) Bottom Layer.

Consider the structure of a natural number. How many disks are needed to build a tetrahedral of height 0? If the height is 0, it means that it contains no disks. Therefore, the 0th tetrahedral number is 0. How many disks are needed if the height is not 0? Once again, consider the tetrahedral in Fig. 70c. We can use a divide and conquer strategy to determine how to compute its tetrahedral number. Divide the tetrahedral into two parts: the bottommost layer and all the other layers. This division is displayed in Fig. 71. Figure 71a is a tetrahedral of height 2. The template suggests that this value be computed recursively. How do we compute the number of disks in the bottom layer? Recall that each layer is a triangle. Observe that the bottommost layer is a triangle of height 3 (i.e., three layers). This means that we need to compute the number of coins needed for a triangle of height 3. The number of disks needed to build a triangle is a triangular number. In general, when the height, h, is not zero, we need to compute h^{th} triangular number and the $(h - 1)^{th}$ tetrahedral. How are these two numbers combined to obtain the hth tetrahedral number? Once again looking at Fig. 71, it becomes clear that these two numbers must be added.

Based on the problem analysis we define `natnum` instances and sample expressions as follows:

```
;; Sample instances of natnum
(define ZERO 0)
(define NINE 9)
(define SIXTY 60)


;; Sample expressions for nth-tetra
(define ZERO-VAL 0)
(define NINE-VAL  (+ (nth-tri NINE) (nth-tetra (sub1 NINE))))
(define SIXTY-VAL (+ (nth-tri SIXTY) (nth-tetra (sub1 SIXTY))))
```

The chosen names for the functions, `nth-tetra` and `nth-tri`, reflect their purpose. The first sample expression illustrates that for height 0 the number of needed disks

Fig. 72 Three triangles of disks

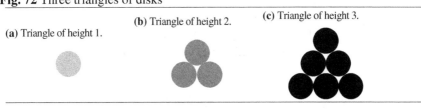

(a) Triangle of height 1.

(b) Triangle of height 2.

(c) Triangle of height 3.

is simply 0 as per our problem analysis. The second and third sample expressions illustrate that for a given nonzero `natnum` you add the triangular number for the given `natnum` and recursively compute the tetrahedral number for the input's previous `natnum`.

To specialize the template abstraction over the sample expressions is performed to obtain:

```
;; natnum → natnum
;; Purpose: Compute the nth tetrahedral number
(define (nth-tetra a-natnum)
  (if (= a-natnum 0)
      0
      (+ (nth-tri a-natnum) (nth-tetra (sub1 a-natnum))))))
```

Once again, our design assumes that the auxiliary function exists and works correctly. The tests are the following:

```
;; Tests using sample computations for nth-tetra
(check-expect (nth-tetra ZERO) ZERO-VAL)
(check-expect (nth-tetra NINE) NINE-VAL)

;; Tests using sample values for nth-tetra
(check-expect (nth-tetra 3) 10)
(check-expect (nth-tetra 2) 4)
```

Once again, observe that small values have been chosen to make it easy for the reader of our code to verify that the expected value is correct.

We now proceed to design and implement the auxiliary function `nth-tri`. For every natural number there is a different disk of triangles. Each of these triangles has a different height. For example, Fig. 72 displays three triangles of disks of different heights. Our goal is to compute the number of disks for a given height. Given that the height is a `natnum`, reason about the structure of a `natnum`. How many disks are used for a triangle of height 0? Height zero means that 0 disks are used. How many disks are used for a triangle whose height is not 0? The disks at each level of the triangle must be added. Let us use the triangles in Fig. 72 to reason about this. For height 1, 1 disk is needed for the bottommost (only) level and the disks needed for the rest of the levels (0 levels) ought to be computed recursively. This means we have 1 and 0. These numbers are combined by addition to obtain the total number of disks needed (i.e., $1 + 0 = 1$). For height 2, we need two disks for the bottommost

level and recursively compute the disks needed for a triangle of height 1. Observe
that 2 + 1 = 3, the number of disks needed for a triangle of height 2. For height 3
the number of disks is 3 + the number of disks needed for height 2 = 6. The pattern
holds. The given height is added to the triangular number obtained from height −1.
For example, for height 3:

```
triangular number for 3
  =    3  + 2 + 1
  =    3  + 3
  =    3  + triangular number for 2
  = height + triangular number for (height - 1)
```

Based on our problem analysis, we can write sample expressions for nth-tri:

```
;; Sample expressions for nth-tri
(define ZERO-VAL-TRI  0)
(define NINE-VAL-TRI  (+ NINE (nth-tri (sub1 NINE))))
(define SIXTY-VAL-TRI (+ SIXTY (nth-tri (sub1 SIXTY))))
```

The same natnum instances defined for nth-tetra are used. The first expression
illustrates that for 0 the answer is simply 0 as per our problem analysis. The second
and third sample expressions illustrate that for a nonzero natnum the given natnum
is added to the triangular number obtained from the decremented given natnum.

Abstraction over the sample expressions is used to specialize the function definition template:

```
;; natnum → natnum
;; Purpose: Compute the triangular number for the given natnum
(define (nth-tri a-natnum)
  (if (= a-natnum 0)
      0
      (+ a-natnum (nth-tri (sub1 a-natnum))))))
```

Observe that the return value is a natnum because 0 is a natnum and adding two
natnums results in a natnum. The body of the function implements the design
obtained from our problem analysis.

The tests may be written as follows:

```
;; Tests using sample computations for nth-tri
(check-expect (nth-tri ZERO)  ZERO-VAL-TRI)
(check-expect (nth-tri NINE)  NINE-VAL-TRI)
(check-expect (nth-tri SIXTY) SIXTY-VAL-TRI)

;; Tests using sample values for f-on-natnum
(check-expect (nth-tri 4) 10)
(check-expect (nth-tri 8) 36)
```

Once again, observe that small natnums are used in the tests using sample values.
To complete the implementation run the program and make sure all the tests pass.

> * **Ex. 169** — The number of disks used for a triangle is equal to the sum of
> the natural numbers from the given height, h, down to 0. This sum is equal to
> $\frac{h(h+1)}{2}$. Refactor `nth-tri` to take advantage of this formula.

83 Making Copies

Consider making photocopies of a one-page document. You go to a copy machine,
punch in the number of copies needed, and hit the copy button. There is a program
that controls the copy machine that stops when the desired number of copies have
been made. How does that program work?

Instead of making photocopies of a one-page document, we will focus on making
copies of a given BSL+ value. It is straightforward to see that two input values are
needed: the number of copies to make and the value to copy. A user of this function
may need 20 copies. Another user may need 100. Yet another user may need 0. The
first thing to notice is that the number of copies needed is always a natural number.
This gives us insight into how to solve the problem. The function that makes the
copies must process a natural number. What type of value does this function need to
return? How can you represent 20 copies of a value? 100 copies? 0 copies? Observe
that the size of the output must be proportional to the number of copies needed. This
means that the value returned must also be of arbitrary size. That is, it must be a
recursive data type. Given that multiple values must be stored (all the same) using
a (`listof X`) is natural. Now we know the signature, purpose, and header of the
function:

```
;; natnum X → (listof bsl-value)
;; Purpose: To make the given number of copies of the
;;          given value
(define (make-n-copies n val)
```

To determine how to build the result list reason about the structure of the natural
number being processed. If the given natural number is 0, then the resulting list is
empty. The empty list contains 0 copies of the given value. What if the given natural
number is not 0? If it is not 0, then at least once copy must be added to the result
list and the rest of the copies are added recursively. The rest of the copies, of course,
may be 0 or more.

The specialization of the template for a function on a `natnum` starts with the
following value constants and sample `natnum`s:

```
(define ORIGIN  (make-posn 0 0))
(define CSPROF  "Marco T. Morazán")

;; Sample instances of natnum
(define ZERO   0)
```

```
(define TWENTY 20)
(define FIFTY  50)
```

The sample expressions are based on the problem analysis above:

```
;; Sample expressions for make-n-copies
(define ZERO-VAL   '())
(define TWENTY-VAL
          (cons ORIGIN (make-n-copies (sub1 TWENTY)
                                        ORIGIN)))
(define FIFTY-VAL
          (cons CSPROF (make-n-copies (sub1 FIFTY)
                                        CSPROF)))
```

The first sample expression illustrates how to make 0 copies of, say #true, a value. The second and third sample expressions illustrate how to make 1 or more copies of a value. For example, FIFTY copies of CSPROF are needed. Observe that

```
(make-n-copies (sub1 FIFTY) CSPROF)
```

is a list containing 49 copies of CSPROF. The 50 needed copies are made by adding one copy to the front of this list using cons.

Abstraction over the sample expressions leads to the following definition of template specialization:

```
;; natnum X → (listof X)
;; Purpose: To make the given number of copies of the
;;          given value
(define (make-n-copies n val)
  (if (= n 0)
      '()
      (cons val (make-n-copies (sub1 n) val))))
```

The tests are the following:

```
;; Tests using sample computations for make-n-copies
(check-expect (make-n-copies ZERO    #true)
              ZERO-VAL)
(check-expect (make-n-copies TWENTY (make-posn 0 0))
              TWENTY-VAL)
(check-expect (make-n-copies FIFTY   CSPROF)
              FIFTY-VAL)

;; Tests using sample values for make-n-copies
(check-expect (make-n-copies 3 100) '(100 100 100))
(check-expect (make-n-copies 5 'x)  '(x x x x x))
```

* **Ex. 170 —** Design and implement a function that returns the first n squares, where n is a natural number.

** **Ex. 171 —** Let f be
$$f(x) = 5x^5 - 10x^3 + 5x + 87$$

Design and implement a function that takes a natural number, n, as input and that returns a list of the values of f(x), for natural number x in [n..0].

**** **Ex. 172 —** The natural numbers greater than 100, natnum>100, are a subtype of the natural numbers. Provide a data definition for natnum>100. Design and write a function that takes as input a natnum>100, k, and that returns the sum of the natural numbers greater than 100 and less than or equal to k.

84 What Have We Learned in This Chapter?

The important lessons of Chap. 14 are summarized as follows:

- Natural numbers are of arbitrary size and are a subtype of the number type.
- Natural numbers are processed recursively.
- The constructor for natural numbers is add1.
- The selector for natural numbers is sub1.
- Reasoning statically about the structure of a natnum is a powerful technique to solve problems involving natnums.
- Functions that process natural numbers may return any type of data.
- Structural recursion is a form of divide-and-conquer problem solving.

Chapter 15
Interval Processing

Chapter 5 introduced interval types to describe a value and used to design functions
that make decisions. This chapter returns to intervals, but not as a mechanism solely
used to describe a value. Instead, intervals are considered compound data that may
be processed. Chapter 14 hinted at the concept of an interval as data that may be
processed. If you think about it carefully, processing a `natnum`, n, means that all the
natural numbers in `[0..n]` must be processed. The first call to the function does
something for n, the second call does something for n - 1, and so forth until the last
call does something for 0. Processing natural numbers fixes the lower end of the
interval to 0, while the higher end of the interval is of arbitrary size.

This chapter generalizes the concept of an interval such that both ends may
vary. For example, in your Mathematics textbooks you may have seen an interval of
integers described as

        `[i..j]`, where i < j

This is intended to represent all the integers between i and j. The square brackets
indicate that i and j are included in the interval. In other words, `[i..j]` represents
all the integers greater than or equal to i and less than or equal to j. If a parenthesis
is used, it means that the value is not included. For example, the following means
that i is not included in the interval:

        `(i..j]`, where i < j

From this you can surmise the intended meaning of `[i..j)` and `(i..j)`.

The question now is how do you process an interval of integers. The description
found in many Mathematics textbooks hides the structure of an interval making it hard
to reason about how an interval is processed. Clearly, an interval is data of arbitrary
size and, therefore, we need a recursive data definition. Can you discern from the
mathematical description above what the base case or cases are? For example, can
an interval be empty?

Understanding to how to process intervals is important. In future courses you will
study compound data called a `vector` (or `array`). Usually, the part of the vector
that needs to be processed is defined by an interval of natural numbers (a subtype

© The Author(s), under exclusive license to Springer Nature Switzerland AG 2022   331
M. T. Morazán, *Animated Problem Solving*, Texts in Computer Science,
https://doi.org/10.1007/978-3-030-85091-3_15

of the integers). Before studying vector intervals, however, this chapter focuses on integer intervals.

85 Interval Data Definition

Without loss of generality, we shall focus on intervals that include their end points, that is, on intervals such as [i..j]. It is straightforward for you to extend the work presented to an interval that does not include one or both end points.

Consider what the interval [-2..4] represents

    [-2 -1 0 1 2 3 4]

It represents 7 consecutive integers. This fact, however, tells us nothing about the structure of an interval that we need to determine in order to process an interval. A natural question to ask what is the smallest interval possible. For example, is [23..23] the smallest an interval can be? It only contains 1 number: 23. Can an interval contain 0 numbers? Thinking carefully about this ought to lead you to the conclusion that an interval can contain 0 numbers. In other words, an interval may be empty—a fact well-hidden in the mathematical description above. For example, [0..-1] is an empty interval. There are no integers greater than or equal to 0 and less than or equal to -1. Given an interval [low..high], how do we know that the interval is empty? If low is greater than high, then the interval is empty.

How do we define a non-empty interval? Once again consider [-2..4]:

    [-2 -1 0 1 2 3 4]

Here low = -2 and high = 4. Is there any natural way to decompose this interval into two or more parts? Given that the interval is not empty it must have at least one number. Let us take that number to be, 4, the high-end of the interval. We have left:

    [-2 -1 0 1 2 3]

This is an interval. Specifically, it is [-2..3]. We can rewrite [-2..4] as follows:

    [[-2..3] 4]

This means that a non-empty interval has a structure: the high number and the subinterval with the rest of the numbers. Observe that the high number of the subinterval is 3. That is, the high end of the given interval is decremented by 1 (i.e., (sub1 4) = 3). We can now write a data definition for an interval as follows:

    An interval ([low..high]) is two integers such that it is
    either the:
    1. empty interval   (interpretation: low > high)
    2. non-empty interval (interpretation: low ≤ high)
       [[low..(sub1 high)] high]

Fig. 73 Template for a function on an interval

```
|#    ;; Sample instances of interval
      (define LOW1  ...) (define HIGH1 ...)
      (define LOW2  ...) (define HIGH2 ...)
          ...

      ;; [int..int] ... → ...
      ;; Purpose: ...
      (define (f-on-interval low high ...)
        (if (> low high)
              ...
            (...high...(f-on-interval low (sub1 high)...
             ...low....(f-on-interval (add1 low) high)...)))

      ;; Sample expressions for f-on-interval
      (define LOW1-HIGH1-VAL ...)
      (define LOW2-HIGH2-VAL ...)
          ...
      ;; Tests using sample computations for f-on-interval
      (check-expect (f-on-interval LOW1 HIGH1 ...) LOW1-HIGH1-VAL)
      (check-expect (f-on-interval LOW2 HIGH2 ...) LOW2-HIGH2-VAL)
          ...
      ;; Tests using sample values for f-on-interval
      (check-expect (f-on-interval ...) ...)
      (check-expect (f-on-interval ...) ...)
          ...
#|
```

Observe that an interval is compound data. It is always represented using two integers. At first, this might suggest it is data of finite size. However, remember that an interval represents an arbitrary number of consecutive integers. Further observe that the data definition contains information about how to interpret each variety of interval. This is important because it explains how the two varieties are distinguished. For an empty interval `low` is greater than `high`. For a non-empty interval, we have `high` and the subinterval `[low..(sub1 high)]`. This definition suggests that an interval is processed from `high` down to `low` until the lower subinterval is empty.

The choice of dividing an interval into `high` and `[low..(sub1 high)]` seems rather arbitrary. Just as easily we can define a non-empty interval as

```
[low [(add1 low)..high]
```

The subinterval may be on the high end. This definition suggests that an interval is processed from `low` to `high` until the higher subinterval is empty. Which is correct? They are both correct. Observe that in both cases the subinterval is smaller, which tells us that the circularity in the data definition is not infinite. Eventually, the subinterval is empty and the circularity stops. This means we can refine the interval data definition to be:

An interval (`[low..high]`) is two integers such that it is either:

1. empty interval   (interpretation: low > high)
2. non-empty interval (interpretation: low ≤ high)
   [[low..(sub1 high)] high] or [low [(add1 low)..high]

This data definition is different from any other we have seen before. It states that we can choose how to decompose a non-empty interval. In terms of computing this means that an interval may be processed from high down to low or from low to high. In fact, a computation may combine both ways of decomposing an interval. It is important to emphasize that there are only two varieties of intervals, not three. Different manners of decomposing a variety do not add varieties to a data definition.

Figure 73 displays the template for a function on an interval. The template suggests defining at least two intervals (one for each variety). Observe that each interval instance requires defining two integer constants: a low and a high value. The signature for the definition template uses our interval notation to indicate that the two integers represent an interval. The fact that an interval is represented by two integers is captured in the function header that has least two parameters: low and high. The body of the definition template distinguishes between the interval varieties by testing (> low high) as per our interpretation of an empty interval. The template also clearly suggests that a non-empty interval may be processed in two different ways: process the low or the high element and recursively process the rest of the elements. The rest of the template is what ought to be expected. There is a sample expression for each defined interval instance. The values of these expressions, the sample instances, and the function are used to define the tests using sample computations. Finally, as before, tests using sample values are also required to validate that the function works beyond correctly computing the value of sample expressions.

86 Revisiting Factorial

In Chap. 14, factorial was designed around processing a natural number. We now consider a different design around processing an interval. We know that n! is the product of all the natural numbers in [1..n]. This means that we may design factorial around processing this interval. The refactored code is displayed in Fig. 74. Observe that in the sample expressions the auxiliary function interval-product is called to compute the product of the integers in the interval from 1 to a given natural number. Given that the natural numbers are a subset of the integers, the intervals are valid. Abstraction over the sample expressions yields the refactored function definition. The tests remain unchanged as expected because refactoring does not change the purpose of the function. Further observe that factorial is no longer recursive because it does not process the given natural number. Instead, it calls the auxiliary interval-processing function on [1..a-natnum].

Now we must design the auxiliary function to compute the product of a given interval. We know from high school algebra that multiplication is commutative. This means that it does not matter if the given interval is processed from high down to low or from low to high. Arbitrarily, we choose to process the interval from high down

Fig. 74 Factorial refactored using interval processing

```
;; Sample intances of natnum
(define ZERO 0)   (define TEN  10)   (define FIFTY 50)

;; natnum → natnum
;; Purpose: Compute the factorial of the given natnum
(define (factorial a-natnum) (interval-product 1 a-natnum))

;; Sample expressions for factorial
(define ZERO-VAL  (interval-product 1 ZERO))
(define TEN-VAL   (interval-product 1 TEN))
(define FIFTY-VAL (interval-product 1 FIFTY))

;; Tests using sample computations for factorial
(check-expect (factorial ZERO)  ZERO-VAL)
(check-expect (factorial TEN)   TEN-VAL)
(check-expect (factorial FIFTY) FIFTY-VAL)

;; Tests using sample values for f-on-natnum
(check-expect (factorial 3) 6)
(check-expect (factorial 5) 120)
```

to low. Now, think about the structure of an interval. If the given interval is empty, a number that does not change a product must be returned. The only such value is 1. Recall that any number, x, times 1 is x. If the interval is not empty, the function template suggests creating the final product using `high` and the product obtained from `[low..high-1]`. All that is needed is to multiply these two values.

Based on this problem analysis, we may write interval instances and sample expressions as follows:

```
;; Sample instances of interval
(define LOW1   1)
(define HIGH1  0)
(define LOW2  -3)
(define HIGH2  5)
(define LOW3   4)
(define HIGH3  7)

;; Sample expressions for interval-product
(define LOW1-HIGH1-VAL 1)
(define LOW2-HIGH2-VAL
        (* HIGH2 (interval-product LOW2 (sub1 HIGH2))))
(define LOW3-HIGH3-VAL
        (* HIGH3 (interval-product LOW3 (sub1 HIGH3))))
```

The first interval is empty. Therefore, the sample expression to compute its product is simply 1 as suggested by our problem analysis. The second and third intervals are not empty. The sample expressions to compute their product, as suggested by our problem analysis, multiply the high-end value with the product of the rest of the interval.

Abstracting over the sample expressions yields the following specialization of the definition template:

```
;; [int..int] → int
;; Purpose: Compute the product of the integers in the
;;          given interval
(define (interval-product low high)
  (if (> low high)
      1
      (* high (interval-product low (sub1 high))))))
```

Observe that the function implements our design idea by distinguishing between an empty and a non-empty interval.

Finally, tests may be written as follows:

```
;; Tests using sample computations for interval-product
(check-expect (interval-product LOW1 HIGH1) LOW1-HIGH1-VAL)
(check-expect (interval-product LOW2 HIGH2) LOW2-HIGH2-VAL)
(check-expect (interval-product LOW3 HIGH3) LOW3-HIGH3-VAL)

;; Tests using sample values for interval-product
(check-expect (interval-product 3 5) 60)
(check-expect (interval-product 6 9) 3024)
```

Each test provides a valid interval to the function as input. The tests using sample values make use of intervals for which any reader of the code may easily verify that the expected value is correct. Run the program and make sure all the tests pass.

We now have two different function implementations to compute the factorial of a natural number. Which one is preferable? They both compute the correct value. Therefore, in that regard there is no difference. Is there a difference in the number of multiplications performed? They both perform the same number of multiplications and, therefore, no difference there. Is one design more versatile? Here there is a difference. The factorial design in Chap. 14 is limited to only computing a factorial value. In contrast, the design in this chapter can be used to do more than just compute a factorial value. The tests for interval-product illustrate computations that cannot be performed by the factorial function from Chap. 14. More versatile designs allow programmers to solve different problems with the same function.

87 Creating an Army of Aliens

For the next Aliens Attack version an initial army of aliens must be created. This army of aliens is represented as a list of aliens. Consider the problem of creating this list. Figure 75 displays Aliens Attack with an initial list of aliens. The list of aliens

Fig. 75 Aliens attack with an army of aliens

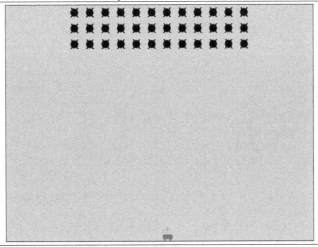

contains aliens in three different lines. Each line has the same number of aliens lined up to form columns. Therefore, a decision must be made on the number of alien lines and the number of aliens per line. For the army of aliens displayed in Fig. 75 the following constants are defined:

```
(define ALIEN-LINES 3)
(define ALIENS-PER-LINE 12)
```

The aliens start at the top row. That is, each alien in the top row of the scene has an image-y of 0. The alien line is placed toward the scene's horizontal middle and the aliens span the same range of image-x values in every line.

These observations give us insight into how to create the initial list of aliens. The number of alien lines that need to be computed, num-lines, is a natural number. We can process this natural number to create the needed list of aliens. At each step, a new alien line is added to the list of aliens using the number of lines that still need to be computed to determine the image-y value for the aliens in the new line. Each line of aliens may be of arbitrary size and, therefore, is represented as a list of aliens.

Now, think about the structure of a natural number. If num-lines is 0, then no more alien lines need to be added and the empty list of aliens is returned. Otherwise, a line of aliens is created for the target range of image-x values and this new line is added to the list of aliens obtained by recursively processing num-lines's predecessor. Observe that the range of image-x values are consecutive values. That is, it may be represented using an interval.

This design idea is still incomplete, but it allows us to start specializing the sample instances and the sample expressions required by the template for a function on a natural number as follows:

Fig. 76 Number of alien lines left and `image-y` values for alien line

num-lines	image-y Value
3	2
2	1
1	0

num-lines	image-y Value
5	4
4	3
3	2
2	1
1	0

```
;; Sample instances of natnum
(define ZERO  0)
(define THREE 3)
(define FIVE  5)


;; Sample expressions for create-alien-army
(define ZERO-VAL  '())
(define THREE-VAL (... (make-alien-line image-y low high)
                       (create-alien-army (sub1 THREE))))
(define FIVE-VAL  (... (make-alien-line image-y low high)
                       (create-alien-army (sub1 FIVE))))
```

When the number of lines is 0, as per our design idea, the empty list is returned. When the number of lines is not 0, the previous natural number is recursively processed to obtain a list of aliens that is only missing the first line. An auxiliary function is used to compute a single alien line. This auxiliary function needs the `image-y` value for the aliens in the line and the interval for `image-x` values.

What should the `image-y` value be? To answer this question consider the tables in Fig. 76. The tables present the values for, `num-lines`, the number of lines still not computed and the corresponding `image-y` value for the next alien line. Do you see the pattern? The `image-y` value is always one less than `num-lines`. This means that for each call to `make-alien-line` the needed `image-y` value is (`sub1 num-lines`).

What is the needed interval for `image-x` values? Given that the aliens ought to be relatively centered on the x-axis the aliens can be placed around the midpoint of possible `image-x` values: (`/ MAX-CHARS-HORIZONTAL 2`). Half the aliens ought to be placed before the midpoint and half after the midpoint. This leads to the following interval definition for image-x values:

```
(define ALIEN-LINE-XLOW  (- (/ MAX-CHARS-HORIZONTAL 2)
                            (/ ALIENS-PER-LINE 2)))
(define ALIEN-LINE-XHIGH (sub1 (+ (/ MAX-CHARS-HORIZONTAL 2)
                                  (/ ALIENS-PER-LINE 2))))
```

Half the number of aliens per line is added and subtracted from the midpoint. This makes the interval one number too big. Therefore, 1 is subtracted from the high end of the interval. The choice of subtracting 1 from the high end of the interval is arbitrary. Instead, 1 could be subtracted from the low end of the interval.

Finally, we need to decide how to combine an alien line (i.e., a (`listof alien`)) and a (`listof alien`). Consider this example using `cons`:

```
(cons (list (make-posn 9 0) (make-posn 10 0) (make-posn 11 0))
      (list (make-posn 9 1) (make-posn 10 1) (make-posn 11 1)
            (make-posn 9 2) (make-posn 10 2) (make-posn 11 2)))
```

The resulting list is

```
(list
  (list (make-posn 9 0) (make-posn 10 0) (make-posn 11 0))
  (make-posn 9 1)
  (make-posn 10 1)
  (make-posn 11 1)
  (make-posn 9 2)
  (make-posn 10 2)
  (make-posn 11 2))
```

Observe that this is not a list of aliens. The first element of the list is not an alien. Instead, it is a list of aliens. Remember that cons adds its first argument to the front of its second (list) argument. This is the wrong thing to do in this case. We need a function that combines two lists into one list. Such a function exists in BSL+: append. The append function takes as input zero or more lists and creates a new list that contains all the elements in the given lists starting with the first given list. For example, consider:

```
(append
  (list (make-posn 9 0) (make-posn 10 0) (make-posn 11 0))
  (list (make-posn 9 1) (make-posn 10 1) (make-posn 11 1)
        (make-posn 9 2) (make-posn 10 2) (make-posn 11 2)))
```

The resulting list is:

```
(list
  (make-posn 9  0) (make-posn 10 0) (make-posn 11 0)
  (make-posn 9  1) (make-posn 10 1) (make-posn 11 1)
  (make-posn 9  2) (make-posn 10 2) (make-posn 11 2))
```

Observe that the result is a list of aliens. That is, every list element is an alien.

We can now finish the specialization of the create-alien-army sample expressions as follows:

```
;; Sample expressions for create-alien-army
(define ZERO-VAL '())
(define THREE-VAL (append (make-alien-line (sub1 THREE)
                                           ALIEN-LINE-XLOW
                                           ALIEN-LINE-XHIGH)
                          (create-alien-army (sub1 THREE))))
(define FIVE-VAL  (append (make-alien-line (sub1 FIVE)
                                           ALIEN-LINE-XLOW
                                           ALIEN-LINE-XHIGH)
                          (create-alien-army (sub1 FIVE))))
```

To specialize the definition template we use abstraction over the sample expressions to obtain

```
;; natnum → loa
;; Purpose: Create initial alien army with the given number
;;          of lines
(define (create-alien-army num-lines)
  (if (= num-lines 0)
      '()
      (append (make-alien-line (sub1 num-lines)
                               ALIEN-LINE-XLOW
                               ALIEN-LINE-XHIGH)
              (create-alien-army (sub1 num-lines)))))
```

The tests are written as follows:

```
;; Tests using sample computations for create-alien-army
(check-expect (create-alien-army ZERO)  ZERO-VAL)
(check-expect (create-alien-army THREE) THREE-VAL)
(check-expect (create-alien-army FIVE)  FIVE-VAL)

;; Tests using sample values for create-alien-army
(check-expect
  (create-alien-army 1)
  (list (make-posn 4  0) (make-posn 5 0)  (make-posn 6  0)
        (make-posn 7  0) (make-posn 8 0)  (make-posn 9  0)
        (make-posn 10 0) (make-posn 11 0) (make-posn 12 0)
        (make-posn 13 0) (make-posn 14 0) (make-posn 15 0)))
```

A small natural number, 1, is used in the test using a sample value to make it easy for any code reviewer to verify that the expected value is correct.

We may now proceed to design and implement make-alien-line. This function must traverse the given interval and create a list of aliens. Think in terms of the structure of an interval. If the interval is empty, there are no aliens to create and the empty list of aliens is returned. Otherwise, a new alien is created using low-end value of the given interval and the given image-y value. This new alien is added to the front of the list of aliens obtained from processing the rest of the interval.

The function is implemented by specializing the template for a function on an interval. The following sample interval instances and sample expressions are defined:

```
;; Sample instances of interval
(define LOW1  THREE)
(define HIGH1 ZERO)
(define LOW2  ZERO)
(define HIGH2 THREE)
(define LOW3  THREE)
(define HIGH3 FIVE)
```

```
;; Sample expressions for make-alien-line
(define LOW1-HIGH1-VAL '())
(define LOW2-HIGH2-VAL (cons (make-posn LOW2 3)
                            (make-alien-line 3
                                             (add1 LOW2)
                                             HIGH2)))
(define LOW3-HIGH3-VAL (cons (make-posn LOW3 2)
                            (make-alien-line 2
                                             (add1 LOW3)
                                             HIGH3)))
```

The first interval is empty and the remaining two are not empty. As per our problem analysis, when the interval is empty, the line of aliens returned is empty. Otherwise, a new alien is added to the front of the list containing the rest of the aliens in the line. Observe that the new alien is constructed using the low-end value of an interval and a given image-y value (i.e., 3 and 2 in the tests).

Specializing the definition template is done by abstracting over the sample expressions:

```
;; image-y [image-x..image-x] → loa
;; Purpose: Create an loa with an alien for each value in
;;          the given interval using the given image-y
(define (make-alien-line an-image-y low high)
  (if (> low high)
      '()
      (cons (make-posn low an-image-y)
            (make-alien-line an-image-y (add1 low) high))))
```

As per our problem analysis, each alien constructed contains the low value of the given interval and the given image-y value.

The tests may be written as follows:

```
;; Tests using sample computations for make-alien-line
(check-expect (make-alien-line 3 LOW2 HIGH2) LOW2-HIGH2-VAL)
(check-expect (make-alien-line 2 LOW3 HIGH3) LOW3-HIGH3-VAL)

;; Tests using sample values for make-alien-line
(check-expect (make-alien-line 1 17 19)
              (list (make-posn 17 1)
                    (make-posn 18 1)
                    (make-posn 19 1)))
```

Once again, observe that the interval used in the sample value test is small enough that any code reviewer may verify that the expected value is correct. Run the program and make sure all the tests pass.

88 Largest Prime in an Interval

You may recall from high school Mathematics that a prime number is a natural number greater than 1 that is not the product of smaller natural numbers. For example, 7 is a prime number because it is not divisible by any natural number in [2..6]. On the other hand, 51 is not a prime number because it is divisible by 3 and 17. To determine if a given natural number, n, greater than 1 is prime, we must establish that it is not divisible by any natural number in [2..n]. It is not necessary to check all the natural numbers in this interval. Observe that it suffices to check if any natural in [2..(quotient n 2)] divides n because none of the natural numbers in [(quotient n 2)..n-1] divide n.

Consider the problem of finding the largest prime number in a given interval. As you know, you have two options: you can process the interval from low to high or from high down to low. Does it matter which one you choose? Consider finding the largest prime in [9..22]. If this interval is processed from low to high, you discover that 9 and 10 are not prime. This means that may think of the interval as divided into two pieces:

[9..10] : interval has no primes
[11..22] : interval not explored and may have a largest prime

In the next step you determine that 11 is prime. Now, you may think of the interval in three pieces:

[9..10] : interval has no primes
[11..11] : 11 is the smallest prime
[12..22] : interval not explored and may have a larger prime

How do you determine if 11 is the largest prime? You need to find, if it exists, the largest prime in [12..22]. If it exists, then that number is the largest prime. If it does not exist, then 11 is the largest prime. In this example, it is clear that 11 is not the largest prime but you do not know that until the entire unexplored interval is processed. This uncertainty requires the function to somehow remember 11 as the previous largest prime in case the unexplored interval does not have a prime.

Now consider processing the interval from high down to low. This means that you first discover that 22, 21, and 20 are not primes. You may think of the interval divided as follows:

[20..22] : interval has no primes
[9..19] : interval not explored and may have a largest prime

In the next step you determine that 19 is a prime and you may think of the interval divided as follows:

[20..22] : interval has no primes
[19..19] : 19 is the largest prime
[9..18] : interval not explored and may have a largest prime

You immediately know that the first prime found is the largest one. There is no need to process the unexplored interval. Clearly, for this problem it is easier to process the interval from `high` down to `low`. If the given interval is empty, the function returns -1 to indicate that the interval does not contain a prime number. If the interval is not empty, the largest number, `high`, in the interval is tested to see if it is not divisible by any natural number in `[2..(quotient high 2]`. If so, `high` is returned as it is the largest prime. Otherwise, the rest of the interval is recursively processed. Observe that there are three, not two, conditions that need to be distinguished.

Based on the problem analysis, the following three interval instances and three sample expressions are developed:

```
;; Sample instances of interval
(define LOW1  2)
(define HIGH1 1)
(define LOW2  2)
(define HIGH2 23)
(define LOW3  13)
(define HIGH3 16)


;; Sample expressions for largest-prime
(define LOW1-HIGH1-VAL -1)
(define LOW2-HIGH2-VAL HIGH2)
(define LOW3-HIGH3-VAL (largest-prime LOW3 (sub1 HIGH3)))
```

The first interval is empty. The second interval has a high-end number that is prime. The third interval does not have a high-end number that is prime. The sample expressions illustrate how the answer is computed for each different type of interval. For the empty interval, as per our design idea, the answer is -1. If the interval is not empty and the high-end number is prime, then the high-end number is returned. Finally, if the high-end number is not prime, then the rest of the interval is processed.

We can now proceed with the specialization of the definition template. A conditional with three stanzas is required as follows:

```
;; [int..int] → int
;; Purpose: Return largest prime in given interval.
;;          If none, return -1
;; ASSUMPTION: low > 1
(define (largest-prime low high)
  (cond [(> low high) -1]
        [(not (is-divisible? high 2 (quotient high 2))) high]
        [else (largest-prime low (sub1 high))]))
```

The first thing to observe is that the function returns an `int` and not a prime natural number. This is because the function may return -1. The second observation is the explicit assumption that `low` is greater than 1. This is because a prime number must be greater than 1. The body of the function implements the design idea. The auxiliary function `is-divisible?` is used to determine if `high` is divisible by any natural number in $[2..(\texttt{quotient high 2})]$. If it is not, `high` is the largest prime as outlined in our problem analysis. Otherwise, the rest of the interval is recursively searched for a prime.

We may specialize the tests as follows:

```
;; Tests using sample computations for largest-prime
(check-expect (largest-prime LOW1 HIGH1) LOW1-HIGH1-VAL)
(check-expect (largest-prime LOW2 HIGH2) LOW2-HIGH2-VAL)
(check-expect (largest-prime LOW3 HIGH3) LOW3-HIGH3-VAL)

;; Tests using sample values for largest-prime
(check-expect (largest-prime 2 2)    2)
(check-expect (largest-prime 24 28) -1)
(check-expect (largest-prime 29 35) 31)
```

The tests using sample values illustrate that the function correctly works for non-empty intervals when there is and there is not a prime number in the given interval.

An important lesson to derive from this problem so far is that it is worth exploring different designs. In this case, one design led to a simpler solution to the problem. A good problem solver explores different designs, whenever possible, before committing to one.

We turn our attention to the design of `is-divisible?`. This function must also process an interval. Once again, we must decide in what direction to process the given interval. If the given natural number is not divisible by any number in the given interval, then the entire interval must be processed to determine this. The direction of the processing uses makes no difference. If the given number is divisible, the search for a factor may stop when any factor is found. It also does not matter what direction the search is done in. We arbitrarily choose from `low` to `high`. Observe that this is an ORing operation on an interval (not a list). We need to determine if any natural number in the given interval is a factor of the given natural number. The given natural number is divisible if the given interval is not empty and the interval's low-end number divides the given natural number or a number in the rest of the interval divides the given natural number. Observe that, just as with lists, an ORing operation does not require a conditional expression as suggested by the template for a function on an interval.

Based on our problem analysis we can write sample intervals and sample expressions as follows:

```
;; Sample instances of interval
(define LOW4  21)
(define HIGH4 20)
(define LOW5  2)
(define HIGH5 13)
(define LOW6  2)
(define HIGH6 8)
```

```
;; Sample expressions for is-divisible?
(define LOW4-HIGH4-VAL
         (and (not (> LOW4 HIGH4))
                  (or (= (remainder 11 LOW4) 0)
                      (is-divisible? 11 (add1 LOW4) HIGH4)))))
(define LOW5-HIGH5-VAL
         (and (not (> LOW5 HIGH5))
                (or (= (remainder 27 LOW5) 0)
                    (is-divisible? 27 (add1 LOW5) HIGH5)))))
(define LOW6-HIGH6-VAL
         (and (not (> LOW6 HIGH6))
                (or (= (remainder 17 LOW6) 0)
                    (is-divisible? 17 (add1 LOW6) HIGH6)))))
```

The sample expressions illustrate the computation for empty and non-empty intervals using both numbers that are and that are not divisible by the any member of an interval. As expected all the expressions are similar because there is no need for a conditional expression.

Abstraction over the sample expressions yields the specialized definition template:

```
;; natnum [natnum..natnum] → Boolean
;; Purpose: Determine if the given natnum is divisible by
;;          any natnum in the given interval
(define (is-divisible? target low high)
  (and (not (> low high))
       (or (= (remainder target low) 0)
           (is-divisible? target (add1 low) high))))
```

Finally, the test templates are specialized as follows:

```
;; Tests using sample computations for is-divisible?
(check-expect (is-divisible? 11 LOW4 HIGH4) LOW4-HIGH4-VAL)
(check-expect (is-divisible? 27 LOW5 HIGH5) LOW5-HIGH5-VAL)
(check-expect (is-divisible? 17 LOW6 HIGH6) LOW6-HIGH6-VAL)

;; Tests using sample values for largest-prime
(check-expect (is-divisible?  2 2  2) #true)
(check-expect (is-divisible? 51 2 25) #true)
(check-expect (is-divisible? 53 2 26) #false)
```

The tests using sample computations illustrate that the abstraction is correctly done. The first test using a sample value illustrates that the function works when the interval only contains the smallest possible value. The second such test illustrated that the function works when the number is divisible by some number in the interval. Finally, the third such test illustrates that the function works when the number is not divisible by some number in the interval. Run the program and make sure all the tests pass.

Another important lesson from this example is that a problem may require processing several intervals. Frequently, although not always, each interval that needs to be processed requires a different function to be designed. Such is the case for this example. Furthermore, the different intervals do not have to be processed in the same direction.

---

* Ex. 173 — Design and implement a function to sum the integers in a given interval.

** Ex. 174 — Design and implement a function to sum the even positive integers in a given interval.

** Ex. 175 — Design and implement a function to determine if an interval contains a square. For example, [2..5] contains a square because $4 = 2^2$.

*** Ex. 176 — BSL+ includes the function `list-ref` that has the following signature:

```
(listof X) natnum → X throws error
```

This function returns the ith element of the list (counting from 0). If the list is too short, then it does not have an ith element and the function throws an error. Design and implement a function to determine if a given (`listof String`) contains a given string in a given interval. For example, the following tests should pass:

```
(check-expect
  (contains-in? "Basia"
                (list "Walter" "Skyler" "Basia" "Madrid")
                0
                2)
  #true)
(check-expect
  (contains-in? "Bob"
                (list "Walter" "Skyler" "Basia" "Madrid")
                0
                1)
  #false)
```

** Ex. 177 — Design and implement a function to determine if an interval does not contain any prime numbers.

** Ex. 178 — Carefully explain why the following test passes:
```
(check-expect (is-divisible? 2 2  2) #true)
```

89 What Have We Learned in This Chapter?

The important lessons of Chap. 15 are summarized as follows:

- An interval is compound data of arbitrary size consisting of 0 or more consecutive integers.
- Four different interval types may be defined:

    - [low..high] includes low and high.
    - (low..high] does not include low and includes high.
    - [low..high) includes low and does not include high.
    - (low..high) does not include both low and high.

- An interval may be processed from the low-end value to the high-end value or it may be processed from the high-end value down to the low-end value.
- We may reason about the structure of an interval to solve problems.
- Different manners of decomposing a variety of data do not add varieties to the data definition.
- Functions that can be used to solve more than one problem provide powerful versatility to programmers that make problem solving easier.
- Problem solving using intervals may require more than one interval to be processed.
- Different intervals processed by a program can be processed in different directions.
- Exploring different designs may lead to a simpler solution to a problem.

Chapter 16
Aliens Attack Version 4

This chapter presents the next refinement for Aliens Attack that adds multiple aliens and shots. In the past few chapters some of the needed auxiliary functions have been designed. This chapter brings together the design of the refinement with the already designed auxiliary functions. The first step is to refine the data definition for a world and, consequently, the template for functions on a world. This will lead us to the refinements needed to update the game.

This refinement is the largest one so far. This is why auxiliary functions were defined throughout the previous chapters (Chaps. 13–15). In this manner, the refinement is not overwhelming. Such an approach is common in software engineering. With a data representation idea in place, auxiliary functions may be designed first. In other words, a bottom-up approach may be used. A primary lesson is that in the software development process both top-down and bottom-up designs may coexist.

90 New `world` Data Definition and Function Template

The `world` refinement changes the game from having a single alien and a single shot to having multiple aliens and multiple shots. The data definitions for a list of aliens (`loa`) and a list of shots (`los`) were defined in Sect. 67. We integrate these to the world data definition as follows:

```
;; A world is a structure: (make-world rocket loa dir los)
(define-struct world (rocket aliens dir shots))
```

Observe that the names of the selectors change from `world-alien` and `world-shot` to, respectively, `world-aliens` and `world-shots`. We do so to make sure the structure's field names convey to any reader of our code what they represent. This refinement also means that the template for a function on a `world` must also be refined. Specifically, a function on a `world` should no longer call a function on an `alien` or a function on a `shot`. Instead, it must call functions on a `loa` and on a `los`.

Based on these observations the template for a function on a `world` is refined to
be

```
;; world ... → ...
;; Purpose: ...
(define (f-on-world a-world ...)
   ...(f-on-rocket (world-rocket a-world) ...)
   ...(f-on-loa   (world-aliens  a-world) ...)
   ...(f-on-dir   (world-dir a-world)     ...)
   ...(f-on-los   (world-shots a-world)   ...))

;; Sample instances for world
(define WORLD1 (make-world ...))

;; Sample expressions for f-on-world
(define WORLD-VAL1 ...)

;; Tests using sample computations for f-on-world
(check-expect (f-on-world WORLD1 ...) WORLD-VAL1)
   ...

;; Tests using sample values for f-on-world
(check-expect (f-on-world ...) ...)
```

The changes are all in the definition template. The changes clearly inform us that
solving a `world` problem now may involve solving `loa` and `los` problems. A world-
processing function should not call functions that solve an `alien` or a shot problem.
This is important to realize because it helps organize your thoughts as a problem
solver.

The sample `world`s may now be updated as follows:

```
(define INIT-LOA   (create-alien-army ALIEN-LINES))

(define INIT-WORLD (make-world  INIT-ROCKET
                                INIT-LOA
                                INIT-DIR
                                E-LOS))

(define INIT-WORLD2 (make-world INIT-ROCKET2
                                (list INIT-ALIEN2)
                                DIR2
                                (list SHOT2)))

(define WORLD3      (make-world 7
                                (list (make-posn 3 3))
                                'right
                                (list (make-posn 3 3))))
```

The initial list of aliens, INIT-LOA, is defined using the create-alien-army developed in Sect. 87. This list of aliens and the initial list of shots (defined in Sect. 67) are used to define, INIT-WORLD, the initial world. The remaining two worlds are updated to contain the single alien and the single shot used in Aliens Attack 3.

Now, our job will follow a top-down approach to the refinement. The run function and its big-bang expression remain unchanged. The refinements needed, as before, start with the world-processing functions in the big-bang expression.

91 The draw-world Refinement

Instead of drawing an alien and a shot, drawing the world now means drawing a loa and a los. The sample expressions for draw-world must be refined. To do so we must realize that two new problems must be solved: drawing a list of aliens and drawing a list of shots. We assume these functions exist and that they need as input the proper list to draw and the scene to draw in. The refined sample expressions are

```
;; Sample expressions for draw-world
(define WORLD-SCN1
        (draw-los (world-shots INIT-WORLD)
                  (draw-loa  (world-aliens INIT-WORLD)
                             (draw-rocket
                               (world-rocket INIT-WORLD)
                               E-SCENE)))))

(define WORLD-SCN2
        (draw-los (world-shots INIT-WORLD2)
                  (draw-loa (world-aliens INIT-WORLD2)
                            (draw-rocket
                              (world-rocket INIT-WORLD2)
                              E-SCENE)))))
```

Abstracting over the sample expressions yields the refined world drawing function:

```
;; world → scene
;; Purpose: To draw the world in E-SCENE
(define (draw-world a-world)
  (draw-los (world-shots a-world)
            (draw-loa (world-aliens a-world)
                      (draw-rocket (world-rocket a-world)
                                   E-SCENE))))
```

It is important not to forget to refine the tests. The tests using sample computations do not need to be refined because they do not explicitly refer to a world. The tests using sample values, on the other hand, do explicitly refer to world instances. Each test is refined as follows to use a loa and a los:

```
;; Tests using sample computations for draw-world
(check-expect (draw-world (make-world INIT-ROCKET2
                                      (list INIT-ALIEN)
                                      DIR3
                                      empty))
```

```
                                                            )
```

```
(check-expect (draw-world (make-world INIT-ROCKET
                                      (list INIT-ALIEN2)
                                      DIR2
                                      (list SHOT2)))
```

```
                                                            )
```

Next, it is necessary to design the two auxiliary functions. To draw the aliens a list of aliens must be processed. This suggests reasoning about the structure of a loa. If the given list of aliens is empty, there are no aliens to draw and the result is the given scene. If the given list of aliens is not empty, then the rest of the aliens are recursively processed to obtain a scene that contains all the aliens except the first. In this scene the first alien is drawn to obtain a scene that contains all the aliens.

Based on this design idea we can write the following sample expressions:

```
;; Sample expressions for draw-loa
(define ELOA-VAL E-SCENE)
(define ILOA-VAL (draw-alien (first INIT-LOA)
                             (draw-loa (rest INIT-LOA)
                                       E-SCENE)))
```

There is a sample expression for each loa variety. The sample expression for a non-empty loa uses the previously designed draw-alien function from Sect. 49.2. Based on the sample expressions the definition template is specialized as follows:

```
;; loa scene → scene
;; Purpose: To draw the given loa in the given scene
(define (draw-loa a-loa scn)
  (if (empty? a-loa)
      scn
      (draw-alien (first a-loa)
                  (draw-loa (rest a-loa) scn))))
```

The test templates are specialized as follows:

```
;; Tests using sample computations for draw-loa
(check-expect (draw-loa E-LOA E-SCENE)   ELOA-VAL)
(check-expect (draw-loa INIT-LOA E-SCENE) ILOA-VAL)
```

```
;; Tests using sample values for draw-loa
(check-expect (draw-loa (cons (make-posn 3 4)
                              (cons (make-posn 15 8) empty))
              E-SCENE2)
```

```
)
```

Given that there are no new problems to solve for drawing a list of aliens the design of draw-aliens is complete.

To draw the shots a list of shots must be processed. This suggests reasoning about the structure of a los. If the given list of shots is empty, there are no shots to draw and the result is the given scene. If the given los is not empty, then the rest of the shots are recursively processed to obtain a scene that contains all the shots except the first. In this scene the first shot is drawn to obtain a scene that contains all the shots.

This problem analysis leads to the following sample expressions:

```
;; Sample expressions for draw-los
(define ELOS-VAL E-SCENE)
(define ALOS-VAL (draw-shot (first A-LOS)
                            (draw-los (rest A-LOS) E-SCENE)))
```

Observe that the `draw-shot` function, developed in Sect. 60, is used when the given `los` is not empty. As with the sample expressions for `draw-aliens`, abstraction over the sample expressions for `draw-los` leads to the definition template specialization:

```
;; los scene → scene
;; Purpose: To draw the given los in the given scene
(define (draw-los a-los scn)
  (if (empty? a-los)
      scn
      (draw-shot (first a-los)
                 (draw-los (rest a-los) scn)))))
```

Observe that `draw-los` is remarkably similar to `draw-loa`. This is clearly suggesting that an abstraction ought to be possible to avoid all the repetition. We shall explore this soon in the next part of this book.

The tests may be written as follows:

```
;; Tests using sample computations for draw-los
(check-expect (draw-los E-LOS E-SCENE) ELOS-VAL)
(check-expect (draw-los A-LOS E-SCENE) ALOS-VAL)

;; Tests using sample values for draw-los
(check-expect (draw-los (cons (make-posn 14 8)
                              (cons (make-posn 3 2) empty))
                   E-SCENE2)
```

```
                                                     )
```

The tests complete the design of `draw-los`. Given that there are no more problems to solve the refinement of `draw-world` is completed.

92 The `process-key` Refinement

The `process-key` function must be refined, because it builds `world`s. In addition, it must now always add new shots to the list of shots when the player presses the space bar. When the space bar is pressed, a posn shot is always created and added to the world's list of shots. This can be accomplished using cons given that it does not matter where the shot is added.

Based on this problem analysis the refined sample expressions are

```
;; Sample expressions for process-key
(define KEY-RVAL
        (make-world
          (move-rckt-right (world-rocket INIT-WORLD))
          (world-aliens INIT-WORLD)
          (world-dir INIT-WORLD)
          (world-shots INIT-WORLD)))
(define KEY-LVAL
        (make-world
          (move-rckt-left (world-rocket INIT-WORLD))
          (world-aliens INIT-WORLD)
          (world-dir INIT-WORLD)
          (world-shots INIT-WORLD)))
(define KEY-SVAL
        (make-world
          (world-rocket INIT-WORLD)
          (world-aliens INIT-WORLD)
          (world-dir INIT-WORLD)
          (cons (process-shooting (world-rocket INIT-WORLD))
                (world-shots INIT-WORLD))))
(define KEY-SVAL2
        (make-world
          (world-rocket INIT-WORLD2)
          (world-aliens INIT-WORLD2)
          (world-dir INIT-WORLD2)
          (cons (process-shooting (world-rocket INIT-WORLD2))
                (world-shots INIT-WORLD2))))
(define KEY-OVAL INIT-WORLD2)
```

Observe that every world created has a list of aliens and a list of shots. In addition, processing the space bar key adds the result of process-shooting to the front of the given world's list of shots.

Based on the sample expressions, the refined function definition is

```
;; world key → world
;; Purpose: Process a key event to return next world
(define (process-key a-world a-key)
  (cond [(key=? a-key "right")
         (make-world (move-rckt-right (world-rocket a-world))
                     (world-aliens a-world)
                     (world-dir a-world)
                     (world-shots a-world))]
```

```
      [(key=? a-key "left")
       (make-world (move-rckt-left (world-rocket a-world))
                   (world-aliens a-world)
                   (world-dir a-world)
                   (world-shots a-world))]
      [(key=? a-key " ")
       (make-world (world-rocket a-world)
                   (world-aliens a-world)
                   (world-dir a-world)
                   (cons (process-shooting
                           (world-rocket a-world))
                         (world-shots a-world)))]
      [else a-world]))
```

The tests using sample computations do not change because they do not contain
any world references. The tests using sample values, on the other hand, do need to
be refined to have world references updated. These all involve using a loa and los
as follows:

```
;; Tests using sample values for process-key
(check-expect
 (process-key
  (make-world (sub1 MAX-CHARS-HORIZONTAL) INIT-LOA
              'right                        E-LOS)
  "right")
 (make-world (sub1 MAX-CHARS-HORIZONTAL) INIT-LOA
             'right                        E-LOS))

(check-expect (process-key (make-world 0 INIT-LOA 'left E-LOS)
                           "left")
              (make-world 0 INIT-LOA 'left E-LOS))

(check-expect (process-key (make-world 0 INIT-LOA 'left E-LOS)
                           "o")
              (make-world 0 INIT-LOA 'left E-LOS))

(check-expect (process-key INIT-WORLD2 ";") INIT-WORLD2)

(check-expect
  (process-key (make-world 0     INIT-LOA
                           'left  E-LOS)
               " ")
  (make-world 0 INIT-LOA 'left (list (make-posn 0 MAX-IMG-Y))))
```

```
(check-expect
  (process-key (make-world 0 INIT-LOA 'left (list SHOT2))
               "left")
  (make-world 0 INIT-LOA 'left (list SHOT2)))
```

As before, these tests still explicitly illustrate how a key is processed.

Having refined process-key to integrate the world refinements it is fairly easy to mistakenly believe the design and implementation are done. It is important to implement all the changes made to the game. Recall that a shot must be added every time the space bar is pressed by the player. This means that process-shooting must always return a posn shot. In Aliens Attack 3, this function makes a decision to return either 'NO-SHOT or a posn shot. Therefore, it must be refined to always return an alien.

Given that a posn shot must always be returned by process-shooting, the image-x value must be the given rocket value and the image-y value must be MAX-IMG-Y to put the shot at the bottom at the scene. This problem analysis leads to these new sample expressions:

```
;; Sample expressions for process-shooting
(define PS-SHOT-VAL1 (make-posn INIT-ROCKET  MAX-IMG-Y))
(define PS-SHOT2-VAL (make-posn INIT-ROCKET2 MAX-IMG-Y))
```

Abstraction over the sample expression yields the new function definition:

```
;; shot rocket → shot
;; Purpose: To create a new shot
(define (process-shooting a-rocket)
  (make-posn a-rocket MAX-IMG-Y))
```

The new tests may be written as follows:

```
;; Tests using sample computations for process-shooting
(check-expect (process-shooting INIT-ROCKET)  PS-SHOT-VAL1)
(check-expect (process-shooting INIT-ROCKET2) PS-SHOT2-VAL)
```

```
;; Tests using sample values for process-shooting
(check-expect (process-shooting 8)  (make-posn 8  MAX-IMG-Y))
(check-expect (process-shooting 16) (make-posn 16 MAX-IMG-Y))
```

Observe that all the tests clearly illustrate that a posn shot is always returned.

This completes the design and implementation of process-key. The primary lesson from this example is that refinements do not only involve changes in data definition. They also include refinements in functionality.

93 The `process-tick` Refinement

In Aliens Attack 3, `process-tick` moves the alien, computes a new direction, and moves the shot. What does `process-tick` have to do in Aliens Attack 4? This function must perform the same tasks for multiple aliens and shots. That is, `process-tick` must move a list of aliens, compute a new direction, and move a list of shots. The function to move a list of aliens is designed in Sect. 76.1. The function to move a list of shots is designed in Sect. 76.2. Moving aliens and shots, however, is not enough. As aliens and shots move, they may hit each other and must be removed. Therefore, functions to remove hit aliens and hit shots are required. The function to remove hit aliens is designed in Sect. 77.2. The function to remove hit shots is designed in Sect. 77.3.

What is required to compute a new direction? In Aliens Attack 3, computing new direction uses the next (moved) alien and the current direction. If the moved alien is at the left or right edge, then a new direction is returned. With multiple aliens the direction changes if any of the aliens is either at the left or right edge. Does it make sense to follow the same strategy as in Aliens Attack 3? That is, does it make sense to compute the new direction using the (moved) list of aliens for the next world and the current direction? It seems perfectly reasonable because the new direction is for the next list of aliens.

Based on this problem analysis, we begin to specialize the template for a function on a world. We use the defined `world` instances to write the following refined sample expressions:

```
;; Sample expressions for process-tick
(define AFTER-TICK-WORLD1
        (make-world
          (world-rocket INIT-WORLD)
          (remove-hit-aliens
            (move-loa (world-aliens INIT-WORLD)
                      (world-dir INIT-WORLD))
            (move-los (world-shots INIT-WORLD)))
          (new-dir-after-tick
            (remove-hit-aliens
              (move-loa (world-aliens INIT-WORLD)
                        (world-dir INIT-WORLD))
              (move-los (world-shots INIT-WORLD)))
            (world-dir INIT-WORLD))
          (remove-shots (move-los (world-shots INIT-WORLD))
                        (move-loa (world-aliens INIT-WORLD)
                                  (world-dir INIT-WORLD)))))
```

```
(define AFTER-TICK-WORLD2
        (make-world
          (world-rocket INIT-WORLD2)
          (remove-hit-aliens
            (move-loa (world-aliens INIT-WORLD2)
                      (world-dir INIT-WORLD2))
            (move-los (world-shots INIT-WORLD2)))
          (new-dir-after-tick
            (remove-hit-aliens
              (move-loa (world-aliens INIT-WORLD2)
                        (world-dir INIT-WORLD2))
              (move-los (world-shots INIT-WORLD2)))
            (world-dir INIT-WORLD2))
          (remove-shots (move-los (world-shots INIT-WORLD2))
                        (move-loa (world-aliens INIT-WORLD2)
                                  (world-dir INIT-WORLD2)))))
```

Observe that the only function not yet designed is new-dir-after-tick. For now, we assume this function exists and we will design it later. The input to new-dir-after-tick is the given list of aliens for the world being built as input. That is, the moved list of aliens with the hit aliens removed. This is following the design, as mentioned above, of Aliens Attack 3.

Abstracting over the sample expressions yields the specialized definition template:

```
;; world → world
;; Purpose: Create a new world after a clock tick
(define (process-tick a-world)
  (make-world (world-rocket a-world)
              (remove-hit-aliens
                (move-loa (world-aliens a-world)
                          (world-dir a-world))
                (move-los (world-shots a-world)))
              (new-dir-after-tick
                (remove-hit-aliens
                  (move-loa (world-aliens a-world)
                            (world-dir a-world))
                  (move-los (world-shots a-world))))
                (world-dir a-world))
              (remove-shots (move-los (world-shots a-world))
                            (move-loa (world-aliens a-world)
                                      (world-dir a-world)))))
```

The final step is to specialize the tests. The tests using sample computations do not
change as they do not directly refer to a world. We use the same tests using sample
values as in Aliens Attack 3, but these tests are specialized to use the new world
data definition:

```
;; Tests using sample values for process-tick
(check-expect
  (process-tick (make-world INIT-ROCKET
                            (cons (make-posn 1 5) '())
                            'left
                            E-LOS))
                (make-world INIT-ROCKET
                            (cons (make-posn MIN-IMG-X 5) '())
                            'down
                            E-LOS))

(check-expect
  (process-tick (make-world
                  INIT-ROCKET2
                  (list (make-posn (- MAX-CHARS-HORIZONTAL 2)
                                   10))
                  'right
                  (cons SHOT2 '())))
  (make-world INIT-ROCKET2
              (list (make-posn MAX-IMG-X 10))
              'down
              (cons (move-shot SHOT2) '())))

(check-expect (process-tick (make-world INIT-ROCKET2
                            (cons (make-posn MAX-IMG-X 2) '())
                            'down
                            (cons (make-posn 15 6) '())))
              (make-world INIT-ROCKET2
                          (cons (make-posn MAX-IMG-X 3) '())
                          'left
                          (cons (make-posn 15 5) '())))

(check-expect (process-tick (make-world INIT-ROCKET2
                            (list (make-posn MIN-IMG-X 2))
                            'down
                            (list (make-posn 2 MIN-IMG-Y))))
              (make-world INIT-ROCKET2
                          (list (make-posn MIN-IMG-X 3))
                          'right
                          '()))
```

This completes the design and implementation of `process-tick`. Remember that all auxiliary functions except `new-dir-after-tick` are designed in the previous chapters.

93.1 The `new-dir-after-tick` Design

We now turn our focus to the design and implementation of `new-dir-after-tick`. Recall from the design of `new-dir-after-tick` in Sect. 51.2 that the new direction computed depends on the given (current) direction. If the given direction is down, then the new direction may be right or left. If the given direction is right, then the new direction may be right or down. If the given direction is left, then the new direction may be left or down. This design is still valid for Aliens Attack 4 albeit it for a `loa`, instead of an `alien`, now. The implementation proceeds by specializing the template for a function on a direction.

The sample expressions ought to illustrate how the given direction is processed. To this end we write two sample expressions for each direction. Each expression illustrates the computation of one of the two possible next directions. The sample expressions are as follows:

```
;; Sample expressions for new-dir-after-tick
(define NEW-DIR-EDGE-LOA-DOWN   (new-dir-after-down EDGE-LOA))
(define NEW-DIR-EDGE-LOA2-DOWN  (new-dir-after-down EDGE-LOA2))
(define NEW-DIR-INIT-LOA-LEFT   (new-dir-after-left INIT-LOA))
(define NEW-DIR-EDGE-LOA-LEFT   (new-dir-after-left EDGE-LOA))
(define NEW-DIR-INIT-LOA-RIGHT  (new-dir-after-right INIT-LOA))
(define NEW-DIR-EDGE-LOA2-RIGHT
          (new-dir-after-right EDGE-LOA2))
```

Recall from Sect. 74.1 that EDGE-LOA has an alien at the left and EDGE-LOA2 has an alien at the right edge. INIT-LOA does not have an alien at either edge. The first two tests illustrate how to compute the new direction when the given direction is down. The next two tests do the same when the given direction is left. The final two tests do so when the given direction is right.

Abstracting over the sample expressions yields the definition template specialization. The abstraction over each pair of sample expressions for a given direction yields the expression needed in each stanza of the conditional:

```
;; loa dir → dir
;; Purpose: Return new aliens direction
(define (new-dir-after-tick a-loa old-dir)
  (cond [(eq? old-dir 'down)
         (new-dir-after-down a-loa)]
        [(eq? old-dir 'left)
         (new-dir-after-left a-loa)]
        [else (new-dir-after-right a-loa)]))
```

The tests are written as follows:

```
;; Tests using sample computations for new-dir-after-tick
(check-expect (new-dir-after-tick EDGE-LOA  'down)
               NEW-DIR-EDGE-LOA-DOWN)
(check-expect (new-dir-after-tick EDGE-LOA2 'down)
               NEW-DIR-EDGE-LOA2-DOWN)
(check-expect (new-dir-after-tick INIT-LOA  'left)
               NEW-DIR-INIT-LOA-LEFT)
(check-expect (new-dir-after-tick EDGE-LOA  'left)
               NEW-DIR-EDGE-LOA-LEFT)
(check-expect (new-dir-after-tick INIT-LOA  'right)
               NEW-DIR-INIT-LOA-RIGHT)
(check-expect (new-dir-after-tick EDGE-LOA2 'right)
               NEW-DIR-EDGE-LOA2-RIGHT)

;; Tests using sample values for new-dir-after-tick
(check-expect
  (new-dir-after-tick (list (make-posn MIN-IMG-X 10))
                      'down)
  'right)
(check-expect
  (new-dir-after-tick (list (make-posn MAX-IMG-X 12))
                      'down)
  'left)
(check-expect
  (new-dir-after-tick (list (make-posn 10 10))
                      'left)
  'left)
(check-expect
  (new-dir-after-tick (list (make-posn MIN-IMG-X 15))
                      'left)
  'down)
(check-expect
  (new-dir-after-tick (list (make-posn 10 14))
                      'right)
  'right)
(check-expect
  (new-dir-after-tick (list (make-posn MAX-IMG-X 3))
                      'right)
  'down)
```

The tests using sample values also illustrate the computation of the next direction
using explicit values. Recall that MIN-IMG-X and MAX-IMG-X are the minimum and
maximum image-x values. We now proceed with the design of the needed auxiliary
functions.

93.1.1 The `new-dir-after-down` Design

This function must decide for the given list of aliens if the next direction is right or left. The needed conditional must determine if the given loa has an alien at the right edge or at the left edge. The assumption is made that the given loa does not have aliens at both edges. Without loss of generality, we choose to determine if the given loa contains an alien at the left edge. To do so we use `any-alien-at-left-edge?` designed in Sect. 74.1.

The design of the function is straightforward and its implementation is

```
;; loa → direction
;; Purpose: Compute the direction of the given alien
;;          when previous direction is down
;; ASSUMPTION: The given loa does not have aliens at
;;             both edges
(define (new-dir-after-down a-loa)
  (if (any-alien-at-left-edge? a-loa) 'right 'left))

;; Sample expressions for new-dir-after-down
(define AT-LEDGE-DOWN 'right)
(define AT-REDGE-DOWN 'left)

;; Tests using sample computations for new-dir-after-down
(check-expect (new-dir-after-down EDGE-LOA2) AT-REDGE-DOWN)
(check-expect (new-dir-after-down EDGE-LOA) AT-LEDGE-DOWN)

;; Tests using sample values for new-dir-after-down
(check-expect (new-dir-after-down
                (list (make-posn MIN-IMG-X 4)))
              'right)
(check-expect (new-dir-after-down
                (list (make-posn MAX-IMG-X 9)))
              'left)
```

The tests using sample values use an explicit loa and illustrate that the function works correctly for a variety of loas.

93.1.2 The `new-dir-after-left` Design

This function must decide for the given list of aliens if the next direction is down or left. The needed conditional must determine if the given loa has an alien at the left edge. If so, the next direction is down. Otherwise, it is left. To do so we, once again, use `any-alien-at-left-edge?` designed in Sect. 74.1.

The design of the function is straightforward and its implementation is

```
;; alien → direction
;; Purpose: Compute the direction of the given alien
;;          when previous direction is left
(define (new-dir-after-left a-loa)
  (if (any-alien-at-left-edge? a-loa) 'down 'left))


;; Sample expressions for new-dir-after-left
(define AT-LEDGE     'down)
(define NOT-AT-LEDGE 'left)



;; Tests using sample computations for new-dir-after-left
(check-expect (new-dir-after-left EDGE-LOA) AT-LEDGE)
(check-expect (new-dir-after-left INIT-LOA) NOT-AT-LEDGE)

;; Tests using sample values for new-dir-after-left
(check-expect (new-dir-after-left (list RIGHT-EDGE-ALIEN))
              'left)
```

Observe that the test using a sample value illustrates that the function works when the given loa only has an alien on the right edge of the scene. It uses an alien constant defined in Sect. 51.2.

93.1.3 The new-dir-after-right Design

This function must decide for the given list of aliens if the next direction is down or right. The needed conditional must determine if the given loa has an alien at the right edge. If so, the next direction is down. Otherwise, it is right. To do so we use any-alien-at-right-edge? designed in Sect. 74.2.

The design of the function is straightforward and its implementation is

```
;; loa → direction
;; Purpose: Compute the direction of the given loa
;;          when previous direction is right
(define (new-dir-after-right a-loa)
  (if (any-alien-at-right-edge? a-loa)
      'down
      'right))

;; Sample expressions for new-dir-after-right
(define AT-REDGE     'down)
(define NOT-AT-REDGE 'right)
```

```
;; Tests using sample computations for new-dir-after-right
(check-expect (new-dir-after-right EDGE-LOA2)
              AT-REDGE)
(check-expect (new-dir-after-right INIT-LOA)
              NOT-AT-REDGE)

;; Tests using sample values for new-dir-after-right
(check-expect (new-dir-after-right (list LEFT-EDGE-ALIEN))
              'right)
```

Observe that the test using a sample value illustrates that the function works when the given loa only has an alien on the left edge of the scene. It uses an alien constant defined in Sect. 51.2.

94 The game-over? Refinement

Ask yourself when should the game be over in Aliens Attack 4. When does the player lose the game? The player loses when any alien reaches earth. A predicate to detect this condition, any-alien-reached-earth?, is designed in Sect. 74.3. When does the player win the game? The player wins when there are no more aliens left.

Based on our problem analysis we can define a world instance and write sample expressions as follows:

```
(define WORLD4 (make-world 4 '() 'left '()))

;; Sample expressions for game-over?
(define GAME-OVER1
        (or (any-alien-reached-earth?
              (world-aliens INIT-WORLD2))
            (not (any-aliens-alive?
                    (world-aliens INIT-WORLD2)))))

(define GAME-OVER2
        (or (any-alien-reached-earth?
              (world-aliens WORLD4))
            (not (any-aliens-alive?
                    (world-aliens WORLD4)))))

(define GAME-NOT-OVER
        (or (any-alien-reached-earth?
              (world-aliens INIT-WORLD))
            (not (any-aliens-alive?
                    (world-aliens INIT-WORLD)))))
```

The sample world is defined to facilitate writing the sample expressions. The first sample expression computes the answer for a world having an alien that has reached earth. The second sample expression computes the answer for a world that has no aliens. The third sample expression computes the answer using a world for which the game is not over. Determining whether there are aliens left in the world, just like any-alien-reached-earth?, is a loa problem. In the interest of separation of concerns, a loa-processing function is needed.

Abstraction over the sample expressions yields

```
;; world → Boolean
;; Purpose: Detect if the game is over
(define (game-over? a-world)
   (or (any-alien-reached-earth? (world-aliens a-world))
       (not (any-aliens-alive? (world-aliens a-world)))))
```

The tests for the function are

```
;; Tests using sample computations for game-over?
(check-expect (game-over? INIT-WORLD2) GAME-OVER1)
(check-expect (game-over? WORLD4)      GAME-OVER2)
(check-expect (game-over? INIT-WORLD)  GAME-NOT-OVER)

;; Tests using sample values for game-over?
(check-expect (game-over?
                 (make-world
                   8 (list (make-posn 0 3)) 'right NO-SHOT))
              #false)
(check-expect (game-over?
                 (make-world 8
                             (list (make-posn 0 MAX-IMG-Y))
                             'right
                             (list (make-posn 12 11))))
              #true)
(check-expect (game-over?
                 (make-world 8
                             (list (make-posn 0 5))
                             'right
                             (list (make-posn 0 5))))
              #false)
```

The auxiliary function any-aliens-alive? does not have to process the given loa. Instead, it needs to test if the given loa is not empty. This may be achieved using cons?. The function is implemented as follows:

```
;; loa Boolean → Boolean
;; Purpose: Determine if there is a posn alien in the given loa
(define (any-aliens-alive? a-loa) (cons? a-loa))
```

```
;; Sample expressions for any-aliens-alive?
(define NOT-ALIVE-VAL (cons? E-LOA))
(define ALIVE-VAL     (cons? INIT-LOA))


;; Tests using sample computations any-aliens-alive?
(check-expect (any-aliens-alive? E-LOA)    NOT-ALIVE-VAL)
(check-expect (any-aliens-alive? INIT-LOA) ALIVE-VAL)
;; Tests using sample values for any-aliens-alive?
(check-expect (any-aliens-alive? '()) #false)
(check-expect (any-aliens-alive? (list (make-posn 9 2)
                                       (make-posn 6 4)))
              #true)
```

94.1 The draw-last-world Refinement

The final refinement involves the function used to draw the last world. Recall that this function is used only when game-over? returns #true. How do we determine if the player has won or lost? We may use any-alien-reached-earth? and any-aliens-alive? to determine this. Based on this problem analysis we may write sample worlds and sample expressions as follows:

```
;; Sample Instance of (final) world
(define FWORLD1 (make-world 13
                            (list (make-posn  0 MAX-IMG-Y))
                            'right
                            E-LOS))
(define FWORLD2 (make-world 7
                            (list (make-posn 19 MAX-IMG-Y))
                            'left
                            (list (make-posn 2 4))))
(define FWORLD3
        (make-world 7 '() 'left (list (make-posn 19 3))))


;; Sample expressions for draw-last-world
(define FWORLD1-VAL (place-image
                     (text "EARTH WAS CONQUERED!" 36 'red)
                     (/ E-SCENE-W 2)
                     (/ E-SCENE-H 4)
                     (draw-world FWORLD1)))
(define FWORLD2-VAL (place-image
                     (text "EARTH WAS CONQUERED!" 36 'red)
                     (/ E-SCENE-W 2)
                     (/ E-SCENE-H 4)
                     (draw-world FWORLD2)))
```

```
(define FWORLD3-VAL (place-image
                     (text "EARTH WAS SAVED!" 36 'green)
                     (/ E-SCENE-W 2)
                     (/ E-SCENE-H 4)
                     (draw-world FWORLD3)))
```

The first and second sample worlds represent a loss for the player given that they contain an alien with MAX-IMG-Y as their y coordinate. The first world has no shots and the second has a non-empty los. The third sample world represents a win for the player given that it contains no aliens. The first two sample expressions illustrate how to draw a final losing world, while the third illustrates how to draw a final winning world.

The function's signature and purpose are the same as for Aliens Attack 3. The only difference in the function are the predicates used in the conditional expression:

```
;; world → scene throws error
;; Purpose: To draw the game's final scene
(define (draw-last-world a-world)
  (cond [(any-alien-reached-earth? (world-aliens a-world))
         (place-image (text "EARTH WAS CONQUERED!" 36 'red)
                      (/ E-SCENE-W 2)
                      (/ E-SCENE-H 4)
                      (draw-world a-world))]
        [(not (any-aliens-alive? (world-aliens a-world)))
         (place-image (text "EARTH WAS SAVED!" 36 'green)
                      (/ E-SCENE-W 2)
                      (/ E-SCENE-H 4)
                      (draw-world a-world))]
        [else
         (error (format
                 "draw-last-world: Given world has ~s aliens and
                 none have reached earth."
                 (length (world-aliens a-world))))]))
```

Recall that an error is thrown if a non-final world is given as input.

The tests are written as follows:

```
;; Tests using sample computations for draw-last-world
(check-expect (draw-last-world FWORLD1) FWORLD1-VAL)
(check-expect (draw-last-world FWORLD2) FWORLD2-VAL)
(check-expect (draw-last-world FWORLD3) FWORLD3-VAL)
```

```
;; Tests using sample values for draw-last-world
(check-expect (draw-last-world (make-world 10 '() 'left '())))
```

```
)
(check-error
 (draw-last-world
  (make-world 10
              (list (make-posn 3 3) (make-posn 7 8))
              'right
              (list (make-posn 2 3))))
  "draw-last-world: Given world has 2 aliens and none have
  reached earth.")
```

The tests using sample values test a final and a non-final world. For the non-final world, as in Aliens Attack 3, check-error is used to check the error thrown.

To complete the design run the program. Make sure all the tests pass and play the game several games. Does it all work as expected? Make sure that you play the game several times before proceeding.

95 A Bug Despite Hundreds of Tests Passing

After playing the game several times you may or may not have noticed that there is a bug. If you did not notice it, do not be concerned. This is a bug that does not always manifests itself. A special set of conditions must occur to be able to see the bug. To illustrate the bug define the following world:

```
(define BUG-WORLD (make-world
                   10
                   (list
                     (make-posn 4  6)
                     (make-posn 10 6)
                     (make-posn 11 6)
                     (make-posn 12 6)
                     (make-posn 10 7)
                     (make-posn 11 7)
                     (make-posn 13 7)
                     (make-posn 15 8))
                   'left
                   (list (make-posn 0 12))))
```

Observe that there is an alien that is farther left than all the other aliens and that the aliens are moving left. Now, edit the run function to use BUG-WORLD as follows:

```
; string → world
; Purpose: To run the game
(define (run a-name)
  (big-bang BUG-WORLD
            [on-draw draw-world]
            [name a-name]
            [on-key process-key]
            [on-tick process-tick TICK-RATE]
            [stop-when game-over? draw-last-world]))
```

Run the game several times and see if you can notice the bug. What do you notice about how the aliens move?

Let us closely analyze what happens. In particular, we shall focus on the first alien, the only shot, and the direction. The following table captures how these values change as the clock ticks:

TICK	ALIEN	SHOT	DIRECTION
0	(make-posn 4 6)	(make-posn 0 12)	'left
1	(make-posn 3 6)	(make-posn 0 11)	'left
2	(make-posn 2 6)	(make-posn 0 10)	'left
3	(make-posn 1 6)	(make-posn 0 9)	'left
4	(make-posn 0 6)	(make-posn 0 8)	'left
5	(make-posn 0 7)	(make-posn 0 7)	'down

The alien starts at image coordinates (4 6) and the shot starts at image coordinates (0 12). The alien moves left and the shot moves up until tick 4. At tick 4 the alien is at the left edge and the direction changes to down. At tick 5 the alien has moved down and the shot has moved up. Observe that the shot hits the alien. Therefore, process-tick removes both from the world. The new direction is computed by new-dir-after-tick using the list of aliens that does not contain the hit alien and 'down. This function, in turn, calls new-dir-after-down. Pay close attention to what new-dir-after-down does. It tests if any alien is at the left edge. This test returns #false and the function returns 'left. The aliens go back to moving left when they should move right. This means that we were not careful enough in our original problem analysis. It is not perfectly reasonable to compute the new direction using the moved and filtered list of aliens for the next world being built. Take note of the fact that despite hundreds of tests passing there is still a bug in the program. This ought to drive home an important lesson. Tests do not guarantee that a program is correct. They only give us cautious optimism that it is correct. As problem solvers it is our responsibility to make sure a program is correct. In a future course in Discrete Mathematics, Program Correctness, or Formal Verification you will learn how to prove programs correct.

> ** **Ex. 179** — Define a world that manifests the bug when the aliens are moving right.

For now, we must revisit our problem analysis to fix the bug. The problem in our example is that the hit alien is removed before computing the new direction. If the hit alien is not removed, then `new-dir-after-down`'s test returns `#true` and the function returns `'right`. That is, the returned direction is correct. Therefore, we must refine `process-tick` to be

```
;; world → world
;; Purpose: Create a new world after a clock tick
(define (process-tick a-world)
  (make-world (world-rocket a-world)
              (remove-hit-aliens
                (move-loa (world-aliens a-world)
                          (world-dir a-world))
                (move-los (world-shots a-world)))
              (new-dir-after-tick
                (move-loa (world-aliens a-world)
                          (world-dir a-world))
                (world-dir a-world))
              (remove-shots
                (move-los (world-shots a-world))
                (move-loa (world-aliens a-world)
                          (world-dir a-world))))))
```

Observe that the new direction is computed without removing hit aliens. Run the program and make sure all the tests pass. Enjoy the new version of the game!

> ***** **Ex. 180** — **PROJECT**: Change the `world` and `alien` data definitions to:
> ```
> ;;  A world is a structure
> ;;     (make-world rocket loa dir los natnum)
> (define-struct world (rocket aliens dir shots ticks2shoot))
>
> ;; An alien is a structure: (make-alien posn natnum)
> (define-struct alien (pos health))
> ```

The player is limited to shoot every `ticks2shoot` tick. When a player shoots a world with `ticks2shoot` equal to some natural number, a constant is created. After every tick `ticks2shoot` is decreased by 1. The player may shoot again when `ticks2shoot` is 0.

Aliens have a level of health representing how many times they must be hit before destroyed. Every time an alien is hit its health is decreased by 1. When an alien's health is 0, it is removed. Pick an alien color scheme to indicate the health of the alien. For example, if an alien starts with a health of 3, then at 3 it is drawn black, at two it is drawn orange, and at 1 it is drawn red.

96 What Have We Learned in This Chapter?

The important lessons of Chap. 15 are summarized as follows:

- Top-down and bottom-up designs may both be used when developing a large piece of software.
- Refinements reflect changes in both data definitions and in functionality.
- Designs may vary between refinements. A design idea implemented in one refinement may not work in the next.
- Decision-making functions may not need to make a decision in a new refinement.
- All tests passing does not guarantee that there are no bugs in a program.
- Some bugs do not always manifest themselves and as programmers we must be aware of this.
- Careful problem analysis helps protect us from subtle bugs whose existence is difficult to realize.

Chapter 17
Binary Trees

We have explored data of arbitrary size whose definitions only contain one selfreference. For example, (listof X) and `natnum` only have one selfreference:

A list of X is either:
1. '()
2. (cons X (listof X))

A natural number is either:
1. 0
2. (add1 natnum)

There are, however, many data types that contain more than one selfreference. Consider, for example, representing the results of an arbitrary number of coin flips. Each time you flip a coin the result is either heads or tail. How can we represent all the possible outcomes of flipping a coin an arbitrary number of times? Figure 77 displays a graphical representation of all possible outcomes for 3 coin flips. At the top level, 0 heads and 0 tails have been flipped. To the left at the next level, after a head is flipped, we have 1 head and 0 tails. To the right at the next level, after a tail is flipped, we have 0 heads and 1 tail. You may confirm that going left represents that a head is flipped and going right represents that a tail is flipped as you traverse down to the next level.

The data representation in Fig. 77 is called a *binary tree*. A binary tree may be empty. A non-empty binary tree is made up of 1 or more nodes. A node has data, like the number of heads and tails flipped, and at most two children. The parent node is connected to its children by an *edge*. If an edge goes left, it connects the parent with its `left child`. If an edge goes right, it connects the parent with its `right child`. The top node of a binary tree is called the `root`. A node that does not have any children is called a `leaf`. In Fig. 77, the root is the node that contains `H:0 T:0` and all the nodes in the bottommost level are leaves. Binary trees are commonly used to efficiently access data contained in nodes and to represent data with a bifurcating structure—a structure where placement of a node (e.g., left or right) is part of the information being represented.

© The Author(s), under exclusive license to Springer Nature Switzerland AG 2022
M. T. Morazán, *Animated Problem Solving*, Texts in Computer Science,
https://doi.org/10.1007/978-3-030-85091-3_17

Fig. 77 A tree of coin flips

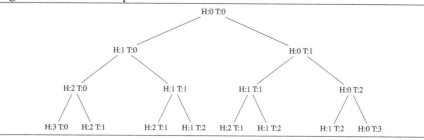

Fig. 78 A tree of natural numbers

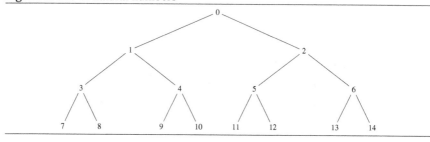

97 Binary Tree Data Definition

Like a list, a binary tree may contain any kind of data. As problem solvers we are free
to define that type of data each node contains. For example, Fig. 77 depicts a binary
tree of `coin-tally`, where a `coin-tally` is a structure with two numbers, and
Fig. 78 depicts a binary tree of `natnum`. You may have already observed that binary
trees are generic. The question now, of course, is how are binary trees defined. Let
us focus closely on Fig. 78. Every node contains a natural number and two edges.
What do the edges represent? Let us closely examine the root. The root is connected
to its left child that contains 1. In addition to 1, the left child also has two children
(containing 3 and 4). The left child is a binary tree. Let us examine the right child of
the root. It contains 2 and two children. It is also a binary tree. How about the node
containing 12? It has 12 and two children (both are empty). We can now define a
binary tree of natural numbers:

```
;; A binary tree of natural numbers, (btof natnum), is either:
;;   1. '()
;;   2. (list natnum (btof natnum) (btof natnum))
```

Observe that we arbitrarily chose to represent the empty (`btof natnum`) as the empty
list and the non-empty `btnatnum` as a non-empty list. This may seem awkward for
the non-empty (`btof natnum`) given that there are always three elements: a `natnum`
and two (`btof natnum`). A structure would seem to be a better fit. We shall revisit
this issue in Chap. 18. Also observe that the circularity in the recursive definition
is useful. There are two varieties. One is not recursive and the other is recursive.

The recursive variety, however, has two selfreferences not one like a list or a natural number. What does this tells us? It tells us that solving a problem involving a (btof natnum) may require recursive calls to solve the same problem for the left subtree and the right subtree.

Let us define a binary tree of coin tallies. In Fig. 77 we see the same structure as in Fig. 78. This tells us that the data definitions will be similar. We define a binary tree for coin tallies as follows:

```
;; A cointally is a structure: (make-cointally natnum natnum)
(define-struct cointally (heads tails))
```

```
;; A binary tree of coin tallies, (btof cointally), is either:
;;    1. '()
;;    2. (list cointally (btof cointally) (btof cointally))
```

The cointally data definition is used to capture the two counts that every node has. Observe that, indeed, the (btof cointally) data definition is very similar to the (btof natnum) data definition. This informs us that an abstraction is needed to obtain a generic data definition. Otherwise, we will need to write a new data definition for every type of binary tree we need to process.

Abstracting over the data definitions above yields the following generic data definition:

```
;; A binary tree of X, (btof X), is either:
;;    1. '()
;;    2. (list X (btof X) (btof X))
```

Recall that X is a type variable. Plugging in natnum for X yields the data definition for (btof natnum). Plugging in cointally for X yields the data definition for (btof cointally). We must also develop a template for a function on a (btof X). There are a couple of things that the definition template needs. The first is a conditional expression because there is a variety in the data. The second is that the conditional's stanza for the non-empty (btof X) needs two recursive expressions: one for each subtree. The function template is

```
;; Sample instances of btX
(define E-BTX '())
(define BTX2  ...)

;; (btof X) ... → ...
;; Purpose: ...
(define (f-on-btx a-btx ...)
  (if (empty? a-btx)
      ...
      ...(f-on-X   (first a-btx))
         (f-on-btx (second a-btx))
         (f-on-btx (thrid a-btx))...)))
```

```
;; Sample expressions for f-on-btx
(define E-BTX-VAL ...)
(define BTX2-VAL  ...)
   ...


;; Tests using sample computations for f-on-btx
(check-expect (f-on-btx E-BTX ...) E-BTX-VAL)
(check-expect (f-on-btx BTX2  ...) BTX2-VAL)
   ...


;; Tests using sample values for f-on-btx
(check-expect (f-on-btx ...) ...)
   ...
```

The template for a function on a (btof X) ought to look familiar. It contains all the elements needed to complete the steps of the design recipe. One of the (btof X) sample instances is directly defined as the empty list given that this is found in the data definition and never varies. Observe that the definition template has expressions to recursively process the left and right subtrees of the given tree.

98 Traversing a Binary Tree

The structure of a list must be traversed from its first element to the last element. Unlike a list, there are different ways a binary tree may be traversed. In this regard, binary trees are similar to intervals. An interval may be traversed from its low-end value to its high-end value and vice versa. Variety in the traversal possibilities offers problem solvers flexibility in problem solving.

If we examine the definition template for a function on a (btof X), we see that there is a call to a function on a X. This call processes the value at the root. There are two recursive calls. These traverse the left and right subtrees to process all their values. The template does not prescribe the order in which these calls are made. That is, we are free to make these calls in any order depending on the problem being solved and the design we choose to follow. Three of the basic strategies are preorder traversal, inorder traversal, and postorder traversal. A preorder traversal first processes the value at the root, then processes the left subtree, and ends by processing the right subtree. An inorder traversal first processes the right subtree, then processes the value at the root, and ends by processing the left subtree. A postorder traversal first processes the left subtree, then processes the right subtree, and ends by processing the value at the root.

Consider extracting all the strings from a (btof string). Given that binary trees are data of arbitrary size, the returned value must also be data of arbitrary size. A natural fit is to return a (listof string). Now reason in terms of the structure of a binary tree. If the tree is empty, it contains no strings and the returned value is the empty list. Otherwise, we must decide how to traverse the tree. The problem statement does not specify the order in which the strings must be returned. Therefore, we arbitrarily choose to return the list of strings following a preorder traversal of the given binary tree. This means that the function adds the root string to the list of strings that first contains the strings in the left subtree and then the strings in the right subtree.

We define sample (btof string) as follows:

```
;; Sample instances of (btof X)
(define E-BTSTRING '())
(define BTSTRING2  (list
                    "Pokemon"
                    (list "Attack on Titan"
                          (list "Dragon Ball" '() '())
                          (list "One Piece" '() '()))
                    (list "Naruto"
                          (list "Death Note" '() '())
                          (list "Detective Conan" '() '())))))
```

The non-empty binary tree of strings represents a set of popular anime. The root of the tree contains "Pokemon". Its left subtree is rooted at "Attack on Titan" and its right tree is rooted at "Naruto". The leaves of the binary tree are the children of the nodes containing "Attack on Titan" and "Naruto". Observe that the leaves all have empty subtrees.

We formulate sample expressions as follows:

```
;; Sample expressions for max-btnatnum
(define EBTSTRING-VAL  '())
(define BTSTRING2-VAL
        (cons (first BTSTRING2)
              (append (btstring-extract (second BTSTRING2))
                      (btstring-extract (third  BTSTRING2)))))
```

As per our problem analysis, processing the empty (btof string) results in an empty list of strings. If the given (btof string) is not empty, like BTSTRING2, the right subtree's list of strings in preorder is recursively computed. The same is done for the left subtree. These two lists are made into one using append. To the front of this list the string at the root is added. Observe that this is precisely a list of all the strings in BTSTRING2 in preorder.

The sample expressions provide us with the structure needed to specialize the definition template as follows:

```
;; (btof string) → (listof string)
;; Purpose: Extract the strings in the given (btof string)
;;          in preorder
(define (btstring-extract a-btstring)
  (if (empty? a-btstring)
      '()
      (cons (first a-btstring)
            (append (btstring-extract (second a-btstring))
                    (btstring-extract (third  a-btstring)))))))
```

The final step is to specialize the tests. As with all data types, we have tests using sample computations and tests using sample values. The tests developed are:

```
;; Tests using sample computations for btstring-extract
(check-expect (btstring-extract E-BTSTRING) EBTSTRING-VAL)
(check-expect (btstring-extract BTSTRING2)  BTSTRING2-VAL)


;; Tests using sample values for btstring-extract
(check-expect (btstring-extract
                (list "Attack on Titan"
                      '()
                      (list "Sailor Moon"
                            (list "Fullmetal Alchemist"
                                  '()
                                  '())
                            '()))))
              (list "Attack on Titan"
                    "Sailor Moon"
                    "Fullmetal Alchemist"))

(check-expect (btstring-extract
                (list "This"
                      (list "BT"
                            (list "is"
                                  (list "like"
                                        (list
                                         "a"
                                         (list "list." '() '())
                                         '())
                                        '())
                                  '())
                            '())
                      '()))
              (list "This" "BT" "is" "like" "a" "list."))
```

The tests using sample values illustrate that the function works for binary trees that are not full. That is, for binary trees containing leaf nodes at different levels or containing nodes that have one subtree. Observe that the second of the tests using sample values illustrates that a binary tree may have a structure similar to a list. This occurs when either all left subtrees are empty or all right subtrees are empty.

99 The Maximum of a (`btof int`)

Consider the problem of finding the maximum in a (`btof int`). For example, the maximum of the (`btof int`) in Fig. 78 is 14. How did you determine this? You probably scanned all the numbers in the tree. That is, you traversed the tree. Think about what is needed to determine the maximum value and how the (`btof int`) may be traversed to find the maximum. What does the root value need to be compared to determine the maximum? It is not difficult to see that the root value needs to be compared to the maximum of the left subtree and the maximum of the right subtree. That means that a postorder traversal is a natural fit to this problem.

Now reason in terms of the structure of a (`btof int`). What is the answer if the (`btof int`) is empty? If the given (`btof int`) is empty, then it contains no maximum number. This informs us that we either need to define a subtype for a non-empty (`btof int`) or the function must throw an error if it is given a empty (`btof int`) as input. On this occasion, we design using the second option and have the function throw an error. If the given (`btof int`) is not empty, then the function needs to determine the maximum among the left subtree maximum, the right subtree maximum, and the root value. Care must be taken because any of the subtrees or both may be empty. A recursive call must not be made with an empty subtree to avoid having the function throw and error. This means that there are 5 conditions that must be tested for. For each, the value returned depends on the non-empty subtrees:

(`btof int`)	Return
Empty	Throw error
Leaf	Root value
Left subtree empty	Max of the root value and the right subtree max
Right subtree empty	Max of the root value and the left subtree max
Neither subtree empty	Max of root value, left subtree max, and right subtree max

Based on this problem analysis, we define 5 sample (btof int) instances as follows:

```
;; Sample instances of (btof int)
(define E-BTINT '()) ;; empty tree
(define BTINT1  (list 200 '() '())) ;; leaf
(define BTINT2  (list 100    ;; neither subtree is empty
                 (list 1
                       (list 3 '() '())
                       (list 4 '() '()))
                 (list 2
                       (list 5 '() '())
                       (list 6 '() '()))))
(define BTINT3  (list -10    ;; left subtree is empty
                 '()
                 (list 78 '() '()))))
(define BTINT4  (list -8     ;; right subtree is empty
                 (list -5
                       (list 47 '() '())
                       (list -1 '() '()))
                 '())))
```

There is a sample instance for each condition above as indicated by the comments. In this manner, we can easily write a sample expression for each condition.

Assuming the function name is max-btint, we may write sample expressions as follows:

```
;; Sample expressions for max-btint
(define BTINT1-VAL  (first BTINT1))
(define BTINT2-VAL  (max (first BTINT2)
                         (max-btint (second BTINT2))
                         (max-btint (third BTINT2))))
(define BTINT3-VAL  (max (first BTINT3)
                         (max-btint (third  BTINT3))))
(define BTINT4-VAL  (max (first BTINT4)
                         (max-btint (second BTINT4))))
```

First, there is no sample expression for the empty (btof int) because a value is not computed. The error message generated is tested as part of the tests using a sample value. Second, observe that for each non-empty (btof int) there are no calls to max-btint with an empty tree.

We can now specialize the definition template as follows:

```
;; (btof int) → int throws error
;; Purpose: Find the maximum in the given (btof int)
(define (max-btint a-btint)
  (cond [(empty? a-ntint)
           (error "An empty (btof int) has no maximum value.")]
        [(and (empty? (second a-btint))
              (empty? (third  a-btint)))
         (first a-btint)]
        [(empty? (second a-btint))
         (max (first a-btint) (max-btint (third a-btint)))]
        [(empty? (third a-btint))
         (max (first a-btint) (max-btint (second a-btint)))]
        [else (max (first a-btint)
                   (max-btint (second a-btint))
                   (max-btint (third a-btint)))]))
```

Observe that the conditional has 5 stanzas. That is, one stanza for each condition identified. As with all conditionals, the first two stanzas are for nonrecursive cases. The last three are recursive cases. Observe that only the fifth stanza (the else stanza) has two recursive calls, two traverse both subtrees. These recursive calls appear in an argument position to max. This means that the subtrees are traversed first before examining the root value. The same is true for the non-empty subtree in stanzas 3 and 4. That is, this function implements a postorder traversal as expected by the problem analysis.

The tests are the following:

```
;; Tests using sample computations for max-btint
(check-expect (max-btint BTINT1) BTINT1-VAL)
(check-expect (max-btint BTINT2) BTINT2-VAL)
(check-expect (max-btint BTINT3) BTINT3-VAL)
(check-expect (max-btint BTINT4) BTINT4-VAL)

;; Tests using sample values for max-btint
(check-error
  (max-btint E-BTINT)
  "An empty (btof natnum) has no maximum value.")
(check-expect (max-btint (list -67
                               (list -50 '() '())
                               (list -8  '() '()))))
              -8)
```

Observe that the error message when an empty binary tree is provided as input is tested. The second test using a sample value illustrates that the function works when all the integers in the binary tree are negative. Run the program and make sure all the tests pass.

*** **Ex. 181** — Provide a data definition for a non-empty (`btof int`). Design and implement `max-btint` using your new data definition.

* **Ex. 182** — Design and implement a function to compute the minimum of a (`btof int`).

** **Ex. 183** — Design and implement a function to return the longest string (`btof string`).

*** **Ex. 184** — Design and implement a function to return the subtree in a (`btof int`) that has the tree's maximum as its root. If the root value is the maximum value in the tree, then the entire tree is the subtree that has the tree's maximum as its root.

100 Binary Search Trees

A database stores organized information in a computer program. Consider representing a database of criminals for a law enforcement agency. We may define a criminal record as follows:

```
;; A criminal record (cr) is a structure
;;     (make-cr natnum string string)
;; with an id number, a nickname, and a name.
(define-struct cr (id nickname name))
```

The following are sample `cr` instances that may be used to populate a database:

```
(define TEFLONDON (make-cr 241
                          "The Teflon Don"
                          "John Gotti Jr."))

(define BABYFACE  (make-cr 77
                          "Babyface Nelson"
                          "Lester Joseph Gillis"))

(define SCARFACE (make-cr 23
                          "Scarface"
                          "Alphonse Gabriel Capone"))

(define DILLINGER (make-cr 675
                          "Gentleman John"
                          "John Herbert Dillinger"))

(define BUGSY     (make-cr 874 "Bugsy" "Benjamin Siegel"))
```

```
(define PAULIE    (make-cr 1
                            "Big Pauli"
                            "Paul Castellano"))

(define VITO      (make-cr 55  "Don Vitone" "Vito Genovese"))
```

The next question we must think about is how will the database be represented. Given that the number of criminals is not known in advance, a database is of arbitrary size. This means we need a recursive data structure to represent it. We shall explore three possible representations: a list of cr, a binary tree of cr, and a binary search tree of cr.

100.1 A (listof cr) Representation

A natural way to represent the criminal database is to use a list. We may define a criminal database and sample instances as follows:

```
;; A criminal database is a (listof cr).

;; Sample instances
(define CR-DB0 '())
(define CR-DB1 (list TEFLONDON BABYFACE SCARFACE
                     DILLINGER BUGSY))
```

Is this a good and efficient representation? Answering such a question is at the heart of many problems. That is, it is not only important to solve a problem. It is equally important to have a fast and efficient solution. Here is where representation plays a significant role. A representation influences how a problem solver thinks about a problem and how efficient a solution is.

Consider the problem of returning a cr in a database given an id number. To solve this problem, as before, we think in terms of the structure of the database. What is the answer if the database is empty? In this case, the wanted cr does not exist. Therefore, we define the following cr to signal that the a cr with the given id number does not exist:

```
(define DNE-CR (make-cr 0 "DNE" "CR DOES NOT EXIST"))
```

When the database is empty, the answer is DNE-CR. What is the answer if the database is not empty? This means that there is at least a cr in the database. The id of the first cr is compared with the given id. If they match, then the first cr is returned. Otherwise, the rest of the database is recursively searched. The function to retrieve a cr from a database represented using a (listof cr) is displayed in Fig. 79. The function is designed using the template for a function on a (listof cr).

Fig. 79 The function to retrieve a cr from a (`listof cr`)

```
;; number (listof cr) → cr
;; Purpose: To return list of the even numbers in the given list
(define (get-record-locr id a-locr)
  (cond [(empty? a-locr) DNE-CR]
        [(= (cr-id (first a-locr)) id) (first a-locr)]
        [else (get-record-locr id (rest a-locr))]))


;; Sample expressions for get-record-locr
(define GR1-VAL DNE-CR)
(define GR2-VAL TEFLONDON)
(define GR3-VAL (get-record-locr 675 (rest CR-DB1)))


;; Tests using sample computations for get-record-locr
(check-expect (get-record-locr 899 CR-DB1) GR1-VAL)
(check-expect (get-record-locr 241 CR-DB1) GR2-VAL)
(check-expect (get-record-locr 675 CR-DB1) GR3-VAL)


;; Tests using sample values for get-record-locr
(check-expect (get-record-locr 55 (list PAULIE VITO)) VITO)
(check-expect (get-record-locr 1  (list PAULIE VITO)) PAULIE)
```

100.2 A (btof cr) Representation

Another representation option for the criminal database is to use a binary tree. The idea here is to have a cr at the root and distribute the remaining crs among the two subtrees. For example, we may define the same database from the previous subsection as

```
(define CR-DB3 (list
                DILLINGER
                (list BABYFACE  '() (list SCARFACE '() '()))
                (list TEFLONDON (list BUGSY '() '()) '())))
```

DILLINGER is at the root of the tree and the rest of the criminal records are evenly distributed among the subtrees.

Once again, consider how to retrieve a criminal record given an id number. Reason in terms of the structure of a binary tree. If the given binary tree is empty, then the answer is DNE-CR. What is the answer if the binary tree is not empty? In this case, the tree must be traversed. It is reasonable to first check the root's cr. Therefore, a preorder traversal is appropriate. There are several cases that must be distinguished. We start by checking if the root's cr's id matches the given id. If they match, then the answer is the root cr and there is no need to traverse the subtrees. If they do not match, then we traverse the left subtree first. The cr being searched for may or may not be in the left subtree. How do we know if it is or it is not? Thinking about this carefully reveals that we may determine the answer by examining the result obtained by traversing the left subtree. If the result is DNE-CR, then the right subtree must be

Fig. 80 The function to retrieve a cr from a (btof cr)

```
;; number (btof cr) → cr
;; Purpose: To return list of the even numbers in the given list
(define (get-record-btocr id a-btocr)
  (cond [(empty? a-btocr) DNE-CR]
        [(= (cr-id (first a-btocr)) id) (first a-btocr)]
        [(equal? (get-record-btocr id (second a-btocr)) DNE-CR)
         (get-record-btocr id (third a-btocr))]
        [else (get-record-btocr id (second a-btocr))]))

;; Sample expressions for get-record-btocr
(define GRBT1-VAL DNE-CR)
(define GRBT2-VAL DILLINGER)
(define GRBT3-VAL (get-record-btocr 874 (third  CR-DB3)))
(define GRBT4-VAL (get-record-btocr 77  (second CR-DB3)))

;; Tests using sample computations for get-record-btocr
(check-expect (get-record-btocr 899 CR-DB0) GRBT1-VAL)
(check-expect (get-record-btocr 675 CR-DB3) GRBT2-VAL)
(check-expect (get-record-btocr 874 CR-DB3) GRBT3-VAL)
(check-expect (get-record-btocr 77  CR-DB3) GRBT4-VAL)

;; Tests using sample values for get-record-locr
(check-expect (get-record-btocr 55 (list PAULIE '() (list VITO '() '())))
              VITO)
(check-expect (get-record-btocr 1  (list PAULIE '() (list VITO '() '())))
              PAULIE)
(check-expect (get-record-btocr 16 (list BABYFACE
                                         (list SCARFACE '() '())
                                         (list BUGSY    '() '()))))
              DNE-CR)
```

traversed for the answer. Otherwise, the answer is the result obtained from traversing the left subtree.

The specialized template is displayed in Fig. 80. Observe that problem analysis reveals 4 conditions that must be distinguished. There is a sample expression for each. The first two sample expressions are for the nonrecursive cases, respectively, the empty binary tree and CR-DB3's root id matching the given id. The third sample expression illustrates how to traverse CR-DB3's right subtree when the left subtree traversal returns DNE-CR. The fourth sample expression illustrates how to compute the answer if CR-DB3's left subtree contains the searched for cr.

Based on the problem analysis and the sample expressions the definition template is specialized to have a conditional expression with 4 stanzas. The nonrecursive cases are straightforward to understand. The recursive cases, on the other hand, need to be scrutinized. As per our problem analysis, the left subtree is traversed first. It is traversed, however, to determine if the result is DNE-CR and not to actually return a result. As per our problem analysis, the right subtree is traversed if the traversal of the left subtree is DNE-CR. If the result of the left subtree is not DNE-CR, then this result is recomputed to return the answer. In other words, the function may traverse the left subtree twice. This does not seem very efficient. Why do the same work twice? For small binary trees this may not matter. However, the repetition of a computation may be costly if the given binary tree contains millions of criminal records.

Finally, observe that the first test using a sample computation searches the empty database. The tests using sample values show that successful and unsuccessful searches return the correct value.

100.3 A (bstof cr) Representation

We have implemented two different ways to search the criminal-record database using two different representations. The first was relatively straightforward. The second is inefficient because it repeats work done. The question now is can searching the database be made faster. A possible optimization is to represent the database using a (listof cr) sorted by id number. In this manner, a search may sometimes be able to determine that a cr does not exist before traversing the entire list. For example, consider CR-DB1 sorted by id number. Searching for a record with an id of 10 ends with the first record (given that SCARFACE's id is 23) and searching for an id record with an id of 300 ends after four comparisons (given that DILLINGER's id is 675). In both cases, the entire (listof cr) does not have to be searched to determine that the record with the given id number does not exist.

Can we improve searching when using a binary tree representation? This is an interesting and nontrivial question. There is potential for significant improvements if we can guarantee certain binary tree properties. For example, we can avoid traversing the whole tree searching for a cr if, for example, all the ids less than the root are in the left subtree and all the ids greater than the root are in the right subtree. In this manner if the given id does not match the root, then only the left or only the right subtree needs to be traversed.

A (btof X) that satisfies these *invariant* properties is called a *binary search tree*. We may define a binary search tree of X as follows:

```
;; A (bstof X) is either
;;   1. '()
;;   2. (list X (bstof X) (btsof X))
;;     SUCH THAT
;;       A. All Xs in the left subtree are less than the root X
;;       B. All Xs in the right subtree are greater than the root X
```

Observe that the data definition lists the invariant properties. In this manner, it is clear to all readers and problem solvers what a (bstof X) is. That is, (bstof X) is a subtype of (btof X). Take note of the fact that the invariants define content properties of a binary tree and do not affect the structure of a binary tree. Therefore, the template of a function on a (btof X) is specialized when a binary search tree problem is solved.

The sample database used in the previous subsections may now be represented as a binary search tree:

```
(define CR-DB4 (list TEFLONDON
                     (list BABYFACE
                           (list SCARFACE '() '())
                           '())
                     (list DILLINGER
                           '()
                           (list BUGSY '() '()))))
```

Observe that all the crs with ids less than the root's id are in the left subtree and all the crs with an id larger than the root's id are in the right subtree. The same is true for the subtrees rooted at BABYFACE, SCARFACE, DILLINGER, and BUGSY. In other words, the invariant properties always hold and, therefore, CR-DB4 is a (bstof cr).

Given an id and a (bstof X), how do we search for the needed cr? We reason about the structure of a (bstof X). That is, we reason about the structure of a (btof X). If the (bstof X) is empty, once again, the answer is DNE-CR. If the given id matches the id at the root, then the answer is the root cr. If the given id is less than the root's id, then the left subtree is recursively searched. Otherwise, the right subtree is recursively searched.

Following the steps of the design recipe, we define a constant for the value of an expression for each of the four conditions:

```
;; Sample expressions for get-record-bstocr
(define GRBST1-VAL DNE-CR)
(define GRBST2-VAL (first CR-DB4))
(define GRBST3-VAL (get-record-bstocr 23  (second CR-DB4)))
(define GRBST4-VAL (get-record-bstocr 675 (third  CR-DB4)))
```

The sample expressions correspond, respectively, to searching a an empty (bstof X), matching the root id number, needing to search the left subtree for an id number less than the root id number, and needing to search the right subtree for an id number greater than the root id number.

Based on the sample expressions we can specialize the definition template to be

```
;; number (btof cr) → cr
;; Purpose: To return the cr with the given id if it
;;          exists in the given (bstof cr)
(define (get-record-bstocr id a-bstocr)
  (cond [(empty? a-bstocr) DNE-CR]
        [(= (cr-id (first a-bstocr)) id) (first a-bstocr)]
        [(< id (cr-id (first a-bstocr)))
         (get-record-bstocr id (second a-bstocr))]
        [else (get-record-bstocr id (third a-bstocr))]))
```

The stanzas for the nonrecursive cases appear first in the conditional. Observe that both subtrees are never traversed. Based on the relation between the given id number and the root's id number only the left or the right subtree is traversed. Furthermore, observe that neither subtree is ever traversed twice. Clearly, searching a (bstof X) is more efficient than searching a (btof X) when the needed cr is in the left subtree.

The tests are written following the same motivating guidelines as the tests using a (btof cr). The tests are

```
;; Tests using sample computations for get-record-bstocr
(check-expect (get-record-bstocr 899 CR-DB0) GRBST1-VAL)
(check-expect (get-record-bstocr 241 CR-DB4) GRBST2-VAL)
(check-expect (get-record-bstocr 23  CR-DB4) GRBST3-VAL)
(check-expect (get-record-bstocr 675 CR-DB4) GRBST4-VAL)

;; Tests using sample values for get-record-bstocr
(check-expect (get-record-bstocr 55
                                 (list PAULIE
                                       '()
                                       (list VITO '() '()))))
              VITO)
(check-expect (get-record-bstocr 1
                                 (list PAULIE
                                       '()
                                       (list VITO '() '()))))
              PAULIE)
(check-expect (get-record-bstocr 14
                                 (list PAULIE
                                       '()
                                       (list VITO '() '()))))
              DNE-CR)
```

As with the tests using a (btof cr), the first test using a sample computation searches the empty database. The tests using sample values show that successful and unsuccessful searches return the correct value.

101 Abstract Running Time

We have three different ways to search a criminal database based on three different representations. Which one should we choose? The answer depends on the criteria that must be met. If the most important criteria is code simplicity, then it is likely that the representation using a (listof cr) is the best. Most of the time, however, it is more important for a program to be efficient in terms of execution time, memory usage, or both.

Fig. 81 The function to build a list of random natural numbers less than 10,000,000

```
;; natnum → (listof natnum<10000000)
;; Purpose: Create a list on n random natnums < 10000000
(define (build-random-list n)
  (if (= n 0)
      '()
      (cons (random 10000000) (build-random-list (sub1 n)))))


;; Sample expressions for build-random-list
(define L1 '())
(define L2 (cons (random 10000000) (build-random-list (sub1 1000))))


;; Tests using sample computations for build-random-list
(check-expect (build-random-list 0) '())
(check-expect (length (build-random-list 1000)) 1000)
(check-expect (all<10000000 (build-random-list 1000)) #t)

;; Tests using sample values for build-random-list
(check-expect (build-random-list 0) '())
(check-expect (length (build-random-list 1000)) 1000)
(check-expect (all<10000000 (build-random-list 1000)) #t)
```

Let us focus on execution time. How can we describe the efficiency of a program? In other words, how can we compare two programs to decide which one is more efficient in terms of execution time? Clearly, we all dislike slow programs and want all our programs to be fast. One way to measure efficiency is by timing the programs, given the same input, that are being compared. In ISL+ we can time programs using the time function. The time function takes as input an expression to evaluate and returns its value. Before returning the value of the expression it prints information about execution time in milliseconds including CPU time. For example consider timing the sorting of a (listof natnum) using insertion sorting (from Sect. 78) and ISL+'s built-in sorting function[23] as follows:

```
(define LST1 (build-random-list 5000))

(define SORTED1 (time (sort-lon LST1)))
(define SORTED2 (time (sort     LST1 <)))
```

The same list is sorted by two different functions. The function build-random-list is displayed in Fig. 81. The expression (random 10000000) evaluates to a random number in [0..10000000). Property-based testing is used given that we do not have a way of knowing which random number is generated. The properties tested are the length of the list and proper membership in the list. The auxiliary predicate, all<10000000, used to write property-based tests is displayed in Fig. 82.

---

[23] The second argument to sort tells the function to use < to compare numbers.

Fig. 82 The predicate to determine if (listof natnum) members are all less than 10,000,000

```
;; (listof natnum) → Boolean
;; Purpose: Determine if all natnums in the given list are in
;;              [0..10000000)
(define (all<10000000 L)
  (or (empty? L)
      (and (<= 0 (first L) 9999999)
           (all<10000000 (rest L)))))

;; Sample expressions for all<10000000
(define B1 (or (empty? '())
               (and (<= 0 (first '()) 9999999)
                    (all<10000000 (rest '())))))
(define B2 (or (empty? '(5000 34 893499))
               (and (<= 0 (first '(5000 34 893499)) 9999999)
                    (all<10000000 (rest '(5000 34 893499))))))

;; Tests using sample computations for all<10000000
(check-expect (all<10000000 '()) B1)
(check-expect (all<10000000 '(5000 34 893499)) B2)

;; Tests using sample values for all<10000000
(check-expect (all<10000000 '(500 -9 38928)) #f)
```

Running the program 5 times yields the following CPU-time measurements:

Run	Insort	Sort
1	26406	15
2	25922	0
3	25719	16
4	25109	16
5	26344	47

At first glance, the collected data suggests that ISL+'s sort function is faster than our sort-lon function. The most salient feature from the above table, however, is that execution timing is an unreliable measure. For neither sorting function do we always get the same result given the same input. Furthermore, the variation between different runs is noticeable. In fact, if you run the same experiments on your computer, you are likely to get different results also. The lesson here is that execution times may vary on a computer and may vary among different computers. There must be a better way to compare the expected execution time of programs.

In fact there is a better way to compare the expected execution time of programs. Instead of counting milliseconds, we can count the number of operations performed in relation to the size of the input. For example, we may count the number of (recursive) function calls or the number of comparisons made. For a given input, these do not vary among different runs nor among different computers. This means that we expect a program that performs fewer of the counted operations to be faster regardless of the computer used. This is what is called `abstract running time` or the `complexity` of a program. It is important to note that we do not count every single operation done by the computer. Instead, we count abstract operations, like recursive calls or comparisons, that may involve many computer operations. How abstract operations are implemented may vary from one computer to another. Some computer systems may use more or may use less computer operations to implement an abstract operation. The number of abstract operations themselves does not vary and that is what makes abstract running time a good basis for comparison when evaluating the efficiency of a program. If a program performs n abstract operations and on a given machine each operation performs k computer operations, then the number of computer operations is k * n. That is, the number of computer operations is proportional to some constant k. This constant of proportionality is different for different computers and is ignored when determining abstract running time.

Typically, we are concerned with the worst-case scenario to establish the abstract running time of a program. The number of abstract operations is described in terms of the size of the input by a mathematical function that we must derive from the code. If the size of the input is n, then we say that the complexity is the highest power of n in this function. Big O `notation` is used to describe the complexity of a program in terms of the input size. If a program performs $5n^2+2n+1$ abstract operations, we say the complexity of the program is $O(n^2)$, where n is the size of the input. Observe that the constant of proportionality, the lower powers of n, and constant factors are ignored. For example, consider the `build-random-list` function in Fig. 81. If the input is 5, then there are five recursive calls performed for: 4, 3, 2, 1, 0. When n is 0, the recursion stops. Similarly, if the input is 3, then there are three recursive calls performed for: 2, 1, 0. In general, the function is recursively called n times. Thus, we say that the complexity of the function is $O(n)$.

102 The Complexity of Searching the Criminal Database

To determine if any of the criminal-record database implementations is superior we compare their abstract running time. To start, consider the database represented as a (`listof cr`) and the searching function from Sect. 100.1. In the best case `get-record-locr` is called only once. This occurs when the function is called with the empty list or when the record searched for is the first one in the list. Therefore, in the best case the function performs $O(1)$, or simply $O(k)$, calls. What is the worst-case scenario? Searching for an id number not in the database means that the function is called once for every criminal record in the database to determine that a criminal record with the given id number does not exist. If the given list has n records, then the complexity is $O(n)$. This is a linear function. If the size of the input is doubled, then the number of operations performed is also doubled.

Is searching the database any better if it is represented as a sorted (`listof cr`)? Clearly, in the best case the function performs $O(k)$ calls for the same reasons above. What is the worst-case scenario? In the worst case the given id number is larger than any id number in the database. This means that the entire database must be searched to determine that a criminal record with the given id number does not exist, thus making the complexity $O(n)$. This tells us that the best and worst cases for both representations (unsorted and sorted (listof cr)) are expected to have the same performance. Neither is superior to the other.

Let us now consider the search complexity for the representation using a (btof cr) from Sect. 100.2. In the best case get-record-btocr is called only once. That is, in the best case the complexity is $O(k)$. The worst-case scenario is searching for an id number that is not in the tree. The left subtree is traversed to determine that the left subtree does not contain the given id number and, subsequently, the right subtree is traversed. This means that the number of calls to get-record-btocr is equal to the number of nodes in the binary tree. Therefore, the search complexity is $O(n)$. This is the same complexity as using a (listof cr) and, therefore, using a binary tree provides no improvement.

We now turn our attention to representing the database using a (bstof cr). In the best case, as with the other representations, get-record-bstocr is only called once and the search complexity is $O(k)$. Analyzing the worst-case scenario is more subtle. It occurs when a search is performed for an id number that is larger (or smaller) than any id number in the binary search tree. A careless glance at the code may suggest that at each step half of the criminal records are eliminated from the search because only the left or the right subtree is traversed. Is it guaranteed that half of the criminal records are eliminated from the search every time the function is called? Consider, for example, the following database represented using a binary search tree:

```
(define BST-LST
  (list
    PAULIE
    '()
    (list SCARFACE
          '()
          (list VITO
                '()
                (list BABYFACE
                      '()
                      (list TEFLONDON
                            '()
                            (list DILLINGER
                                  '()
                                  (list BUGSY '() '()))))))))))
```

Observe that every left subtree is empty. This means that the structure of this binary search tree is similar to the structure of a list. In an arbitrary binary search tree with n nodes and the same type of structure searching for a cr with an id number greater than anything in the database requires n calls to get-record-bstocr. Therefore, in the worst case the complexity of this function is $O(n)$. This means that all three of our database representations have a searching function with the same complexity. None are expected to always be better than any of the others.

103 Balanced (bstof cr)

Our efforts to date, regardless of the database representation, have yielded a linear time searching algorithm. When using binary search trees, the problem is that in the worst case only the record at the root is eliminated from the search, thus forcing the examination of all records in the database. To overcome this problem we can represent the database using a *balanced* binary search tree. A balanced binary tree is one in which the height of the left and right subtrees of any node differs by no more than 1. In other words, the binary tree is not lopsided and the descendants of a node are roughly evenly distributed in its subtrees. We define a balanced binary search tree as follows:

```
;; A (bbstof X) is either
;; 1. '()
;; 2. (list X (bbstof X) (bbtsof X))
;; SUCH THAT
;; A. All Xs in the left subtree are less than the root X
;; B. All Xs in the right subtree are greater than the root X
;; C. (<= (- (height left-subtree) (height right-subtree)) 1)
```

The third invariant guarantees that the nodes are evenly distributed and, therefore, at each step of the search roughly half of the nodes left to explore are eliminated.

103.1 Creating a Balanced Binary Search Tree

However, can a balanced binary search tree be created in the first place? Without loss of generality, we assume that we have a (listof cr) sorted in non-decreasing order by id number. The middle element of the list must be the root of the balanced binary search tree. All the crs before the middle element must be placed in the left (balanced) subtree and all the crs after the middle element must be placed in the right (balanced) subtree. Accessing the middle element of the given list is fairly straightforward. If the input list, a-locr, is not empty, then we know that its first element is indexed by 0 and its last element is indexed by (sub1 (length a-locr)). Therefore, the middle element is indexed by (quotient (length a-locr) 2). How then are the elements before and after the middle element referenced? Observe that the valid indexes into a-locr may be represented by an interval: [0..(sub1 (length a-locr))]. This means that the elements before the middle element are indexed by the interval elements in [0..(sub1 (quotient (length a-locr) 2))] and that the elements after the middle element are indexed by the interval elements

in [(add1 (quotient (length a-locr) 2))..(sub1 (length a-locr))].
This analysis suggests that we can, indeed, create a balanced binary search tree using
a function that processes an interval. If the given (listof cr) is empty, then the
interval to process must be empty given that there are no crs in the list. Otherwise,
the interval to process is defined by the minimum and maximum indexes into the
list. We may write sample expressions as follows:

```
(define SORTED-LOCR (list PAULIE    SCARFACE  VITO BABYFACE
                          TEFLONDON DILLINGER BUGSY))


;; Sample expressions for locr->bstocr
(define LOCR->BBST1 (create-bstofcr CR-DB0     0 -1))
(define LOCR->BBST2 (create-bstofcr SORTED-LOCR 0 6))
```

A sorted (listof cr) is defined to facilitate writing sample expressions and tests.
The first sample expression is for the empty (listof cr) and the second is for the
non-empty SORTED-LOCR.

Based on the sample expressions we can write the function as follows:

```
;; (listof cr) → (bbstof cr)
;; Purpose: Create (bbst cr) from the given sorted (listof cr)
;; ASSUMPTION: The given (listof cr) is sorted in nondecreasing
;;             order by id number
(define (locr->bbstocr a-locr)
  (create-bbstofcr a-locr 0 (sub1 (length a-locr))))
```

Observe that locr->bbstocr only calls a function to process an interval. When the
given list is empty, the interval is [0..-1], and when it is not empty, it is [0..(sub1
(length a-locr))], which are the intervals suggested by our problem analysis.
Finally, the function is tested as follows:

```
    ;; Tests using sample computations for locr->bstocr
    (check-expect (locr->bbstocr CR-DB0)       LOCR->BBST1)
    (check-expect (locr->bbstocr SORTED-LOCR) LOCR->BBST2)


    ;; Tests using sample values for locr->bstocr
    (check-expect (locr->bbstocr (list PAULIE VITO BUGSY))
                  (list VITO
                        (list PAULIE '() '())
                        (list BUGSY  '() '())))
```

Recall that CR-DB0 is defined as '(). The single test using a sample value illustrates
the structure of the generated balanced binary tree.

We now focus on the design of `create-bbstofcr`. This function has as input a (listof cr) and an interval of indexes, [low..high], into the list. We reason about the structure of the interval. If the interval is empty, then the needed tree is '(). If the tree is not empty, then the root of the needed tree is the middle list element in the interval. That element is indexed by `low` plus half the length of the interval:

```
(+ low (quotient (- high low) 2))
```

The elements for the left and right subtrees, respectively, are indexed by the elements in the following intervals:

```
[low..(sub1 (+ low (quotient (- high low) 2)))]
```

```
[(add1 (+ low (quotient (- high low) 2)))..high]
```

Observe that the high-end for the left subtree elements is exactly one less than the middle element index and that low-end for the right subtree elements is exactly one more than the middle element index. To build the desired balanced binary search tree all that is needed is to create a list with the middle element, the tree obtained by processing the first subinterval, and the tree obtained by processing the second subinterval.

Based on our problem analysis above we write the following sample expressions:

```
;; Sample expressions for create-bbstofcr
(define CBST1 '())
(define CBST2
        (list (list-ref SORTED-LOCR (+ 0 (quotient (- 6 0) 2)))
              (create-bbstofcr
               SORTED-LOCR
               0
               (sub1 (+ 0 (quotient (- 6 0) 2))))
              (create-bbstofcr
               SORTED-LOCR
               (add1 (+ 0 (quotient (- 6 0) 2)))
               6)))
```

As per the problem analysis, the empty binary search tree is returned when the given (listof cr) is empty. When the given (listof cr) is not empty, a non-empty binary search tree is built using the middle cr and the trees obtained by processing the subintervals before and after the middle element.

Based on the sample expressions we specialize the template for a function on an interval as follows:

```
;; (listof cr) [natnum..natnum] → (bbstof cr)
;; Purpose: To create a bbst from the sorted list elements in
;;          the given interval
(define (create-bbstofcr a-locr low high)
  (if (< high low)
      '()
```

```
(list (list-ref a-locr (+ low (quotient (- high low) 2)))
      (create-bbstofcr
        a-locr
        low
        (sub1 (+ low (quotient (- high low) 2))))
      (create-bbstofcr
        a-locr
        (add1 (+ low (quotient (- high low) 2)))
        high))))
```

Observe that instead of using concrete values, like 0 and 6, the parameters low and high are used in their place. Finally, the tests are written as follows:

```
;; Tests using sample computations for create-bstofcr
(check-expect (create-bbstofcr CR-DB0      0 -1) CBST1)
(check-expect (create-bbstofcr SORTED-LOCR 0 6)  CBST2)

;; Tests using sample values for create-bstofcr
(check-expect
  (create-bbstofcr
    (list PAULIE SCARFACE VITO DILLINGER BUGSY)
    0
    4)
  (list VITO
        (list PAULIE
              '()
              (list SCARFACE '() '()))
        (list DILLINGER
              '()
              (list BUGSY  '() '()))))
```

Observe that the test using a sample value is another example that illustrates that the resulting binary search tree is balanced.

103.2 Analysis

Does representing a database as a balanced binary search tree improve the complexity of searching? Consider the balanced binary search tree in Fig. 83 (that only depicts id numbers). Consider searching for a cr record with an id of 87. After comparing 87 with 70 (the root id number) all the elements in the left subtree are discarded from the search. That is, roughly half of the remaining elements are discarded. After the comparison with 110 half of the remaining elements are discarded again from the search. This happens again after the comparison with 90 and with 80. Finally, after the comparison with 85 get-record-bbstocr is called with the empty tree and the function halts. Notice that 6 calls are made to get-record-bbstocr. The

Fig. 83 A balanced binary search tree

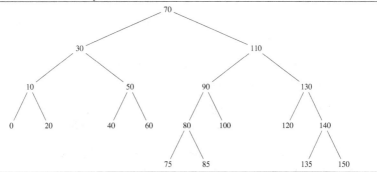

same number of calls occurs if a cr with an id of 200 is searched for. If a cr with an id of 45 is searched for, 5 calls to the function occur. Observe that in the worst case the number of calls is equal to the height of the tree plus 2. That is a call for every node on the longest path plus one call with the empty tree. Such is the case, for example, for this path:

$$70 \rightarrow 110 \rightarrow 130 \rightarrow 140 \rightarrow 135$$

What is the length of the longest path in a balanced binary search tree with n nodes? After each step down the tree about half of the elements are discarded. How many times can we divide n by 2? If n is a power of 2, then the answer is $\lg n$ (i.e., $\log_2 n$). If n is not a power of 2, then the answer is $\lfloor \lg n \rfloor$, the largest integer less than or equal to $\lg n$. This means that in the worst case $\lfloor \lg n \rfloor + 2$ calls are made. For example, the balanced binary search tree in Fig. 83 has 19 nodes and in the worst case the maximum number of calls is

$$\lfloor \lg\ n \rfloor\ +\ 2\ =\ \lfloor \lg\ 19 \rfloor\ +\ 2$$
$$=\ 6$$

This means that the complexity of searching a balanced binary search tree is $O(\lg n)$. This is significantly better than an $O(n)$. For instance, in the worst case, the number of function calls to search a database with 1024 crs represented as a (listof cr) is proportional to 1024. The number of calls is proportional to 10 when the database is represented as a balanced binary search tree.

Equally noteworthy is that create-bstofcr is a recursive function that is not based on structural recursion. That is, the recursive calls are not made with the subinterval used to build the given interval. Instead, new intervals are generated for the recursive calls. This is called *generative recursion*. We shall study generative recursion more in-depth in the next volume of this textbook. For now, you need to be aware that there are other useful forms of recursion that we have not studied yet.

** **Ex. 185** — Design and implement a function that takes as input a (bbstof cr) and that returns the criminal record with the largest id number. Make sure to do careful problem analysis to make the function as simple as possible.

*** **Ex. 186** — Design and implement a function that takes as input a (bbstof cr) and that returns its height.

*** **Ex. 187** — Design and implement a function that takes as input a (bbstof cr) and that returns a list of criminal names in order by id number.

*** **Ex. 188** — Design and implement a function that takes as input a (bbstof number) and that returns the tree's second largest number.

**** **Ex. 189** — Design and implement a predicate that takes as input a number and a (bbstof number) and that determines if the given number is a member of the tree. Also design and implement a predicate that takes as input a number and a (listof number) and that determines if the given number is a member of the list. Which do you expect to be faster? Justify your answer using abstract running time.

**** **Ex. 190** — Design and implement a predicate that takes as input a (bbstof number) and that determines if all tree elements are even. Also design and implement a predicate that takes as input a (btof number) and that determines if all tree elements are even. Which do you expect to be faster? Justify your answer using abstract running time.

** **Ex. 191** — What is the complexity of sum-loq from Sect. 72?

**** **Ex. 192** — What is the complexity of remove-hit-aliens from Sect. 77.2?

104 What Have We Learned in This Chapter?

The important lessons of Chap. 17 are summarized as follows:

- A binary tree, (btof X), is used to represent data of arbitrary size.
- The data definition for binary trees has two selfreferences.
- The definition template for a function on a (btof X) has two expressions for recursive calls: one for each subtree.
- Three common binary tree traversal strategies visit nodes in the following order:

  - Preorder: root, left subtree, right subtree
  - Inorder: left subtree, root, right subtree
  - Postorder: left subtree, right subtree, root

- A binary search tree, (bstof X), is a subtype of (btof X).
- In a (bstof X) anything in the left subtree is less than that the root value and anything in the right subtree is greater than the root value. This is an invariant property for all nodes in the binary search tree.
- Timing programs is an unreliable metric to compare expected execution time.
- Abstract running time counts the number of major operations based on the size of the input.
- Abstract running time is a more reliable measure to compare expected running time.
- Typically programmers are interested in the complexity of the worst-case scenario.
- Big O notation is used to describe the complexity of a program in terms of the input size.
- A balanced binary search tree, (bbstof X), is a binary search tree subtype in which the height of the left and right subtrees of any node differs by no more than 1.
- The use of a (bbstof X) reduces the complexity of a search from $O(n)$ to $O(\lg n)$.
- Unlike structural recursion that uses the structure of an input to make recursive calls, generative recursion creates new instances of the input type to make recursive calls.

Chapter 18
Mutually Recursive Data

So far, we have only considered data types that only refer to themselves. For example, look at the data definitions for a (listof X) and a natnum:

```
A list of X is either:      A natural number (natnum) is either:
  1. '()                      1. 0
  2. (cons X (listof X))      2. (add1 natnum)
```

These recursive data definitions only refer to themselves. Now, take a look at the data definition for a binary tree:

```
;; A binary tree of X, (btof X), is either:
;;   1. '()
;;   2. (list X (btof X) (btof X))
```

This data definition also only refers to itself. However, as discussed in Chap. 17, representing a non-empty binary tree as a list is a bit awkward given that it is not of arbitrary size. A binary tree is of arbitrary size, but a non-empty binary tree always has 3 elements: something of type X and two subtrees of type X. That is, the number of elements needed to represent a non-empty binary tree is finite. This suggests that a non-empty binary tree ought to be represented using a structure with three fields. A first attempt to refine the binary tree data definition may be

```
;; A binary tree of X, (btof X), is either:
;;   1. '()
;;   2. A structure, (make-node X (btof X) (btof X)), with
;;      an X value and two subtrees of X values
```

This data definition ought to feel more natural. An item of finite size is represented using a structure and not a list.

This revised data definition, however, is still a bit awkward. We have a data definition within a data definition. That is, we define a node inside the definition of

M. T. Morazán, *Animated Problem Solving*, Texts in Computer Science,
https://doi.org/10.1007/978-3-030-85091-3_18

Fig. 84 Templates for node and (btof X)

```
#| ;; Sample instances of (nodeof X)
   (define NODE0 (make-node ... ... ...))     ...
   ;; node ... → ...          Purpose:
   (define (f-on-node a-node)
     ...(f-on-X (node-val a-node))
     ...(f-on-btx (node-ltree a-node))
     ...(f-on-btx (node-rtree a-node)))
   ;; Sample expressions for f-on-node
   (define NODE0-VAL ...)

          ...

   ;; Tests using sample computations for f-on-node
   (check-expect (f-on-node NODE0 ...) NODE0-VAL)  ...
   ;; Tests using sample values for f-on-node
   (check-expect (f-on-node (make-node ... ... ...) ...) ...) ...)  ...

   ;; Sample instances of (btof X)
   (define BTX0 '())     (define BTX1 (make-node ...))  ...
   ;; btx ... → ...     Purpose:
   (define (f-on-btx a-btx ...)
     (if (empty? a-node)

          ...

          (f-on-node a-btx ...))))
   ;; Sample expressions for f-on-btx
   (define BTX0-VAL (f-on-btx  BTX0 ...))
   (define BTX1-VAL (f-on-node BTX1 ...))

          ...

   ;; Tests using sample computations for f-on-btx
   (check-expect (f-on-btx BTX0 ...) BTX0-VAL)
   (check-expect (f-on-btx BTX1 ...) BTX1-VAL)

          ...

   ;; Tests using sample values for f-on-btx
   (check-expect (f-on-btx ...) ...)
          ...                                               |#
   (define-struct node (val ltree rtree))
```

a binary tree. It is much more natural to have distinct and separate data definitions,
one for a binary tree and one for a node, as follows:

```
;; A (nodeof X) is a structure, (make-node X (btof X) (btof X)),
;; with an X value and two (btof X) values.

;; A binary tree of X, (btof X), is either:
;;   1. '()
;;   2. node
```

Observe that there is something new about these data definitions. These data
definitions are *mutually recursive*. This means that they define intertwined data. The
data definitions refer to each other. A binary tree cannot be defined without knowing
what a node is and a node cannot be defined without knowing what a binary tree is.

105 Designing with Mutually Recursive Data

What impact does mutually recursive data have on problem solving? In a very real sense we already know what references to a data definition mean for our code. For example, in the data definition for a (list of X) there is a reference to a (listof X). This means that we must call a function to process a (list of X). Given that it is a selfreference it turns into a recursive call in our code.

The same principle applies to mutually recursive data definitions. The reference to a node in the data definition for a (btof X) means that processing a non-empty binary tree requires calling a function on a node. Similarly, the references to a (btof X) in the data definition of a node require calls to a function that processes a (btof X). Observe that the data definition for a (btof X) is still circular. A (btof X) refers to node and a node refers (back) to (btof X). That is, it defines data of arbitrary size. The definition is useful because the circularity ends when a (btof X) is '(). These observations lead to the function templates and structure definition displayed in Fig. 84. Immediately you can observe that the templates embody the principle of separation of concerns. A node is processed by a node-processing function and a (btof X) is processed by a (btof X)-processing function.

105.1 Revisiting the Maximum of a (btof int)

In Sect. 99 we designed a function to find the maximum of a (btof int). Now, we revisit this problem and solve it based on our refined data definition. To start, we define sample instances of node and (btof int). Care must be taken writing these in our program because the definitions are mutually recursive. Remember that we may not use a value before it is defined. In other words, we may not use a node or a (btof int) to build another before defining them. For example, we may not define a binary tree that only contains 177 as follows:

```
(define NODE177 (make-node 177 BTI0 BTI0))
```

```
(define BTI0 '())
```

We cannot define NODE177 in terms of BTI0 before defining BTI0. The proper way to build this tree is

```
(define BTI0 '())
```

```
(define NODE177 (make-node 177 BTI0 BTI0))
```

Observe that anything needed to build NODE177 is defined before its definition. This indicates the general strategy that we must follow to build instances of mutually recursive data. Build nonrecursive instances first and then build instances that only depend on existing instances. For binary trees this means that the empty tree must be defined first. Once the empty tree is defined, all the leaves may by defined. Once

Fig. 85 A binary tree of integers

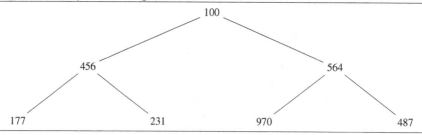

Fig. 86 Mutually recursive sample instances of (btof int) and (nodeof X)

```
(define BTI0 '())

(define NODE177 (make-node 177 BTI0 BTI0))
(define NODE231 (make-node 231 BTI0 BTI0))
(define NODE970 (make-node 970 BTI0 BTI0))
(define NODE487 (make-node 487 BTI0 BTI0))

(define BTI177 NODE177)
(define BTI231 NODE231)
(define BTI970 NODE970)
(define BTI487 NODE487)

(define NODE456 (make-node 456 BTI177 BTI231))
(define NODE564 (make-node 564 BTI970 BTI487))

(define BTI456 NODE456)
(define BTI564 NODE564)

(define NODE100 (make-node 100 BTI456 BTI564))

(define BTI100 NODE100)
```

all the leaves are defined, all nodes that only have leaves as children may be defined. This process continues until the root node is defined. In other words, we build the instances needed from the bottom of the binary tree to the root of the tree level by level. Consider defining the (btof int) displayed in Fig. 85. First, we define the empty tree. Second, we define all the leaf nodes using the defined empty tree. Third, we define binary trees rooted at the leaves. Fourth, we define nodes for the parents of the leaves. Fifth, we define binary trees rooted at the parents of the leaves. Finally, we define the root node and the corresponding binary tree. The definitions for the binary tree in Fig. 85 are displayed in Fig. 86. The tree in Fig. 85 is BTI100.

Based on our sample instances we may write sample expressions for the maximum of a (btof int) as follows:

```
;; Sample expressions for max-btint
(define BTI100-VAL (max-node BTI100))
(define BTI456-VAL (max-node BTI456))
```

Observe that there is no sample expression for the empty (btof int) as this would throw an error. For a non-empty binary tree a function to find the maximum of a node is called. As usual, we assume that auxiliary functions exist and work.

These expressions lead to the following specialization of the definition template:

```
;; (btof int) → int throws error
;; Purpose: Return the maximum of the given (btof int)
(define (max-btint a-btint)
  (if (empty? a-btint)
      (error "An empty (btof int) has no maximum value.")
      (max-node a-btint)))
```

Observe that this function is now much simpler and easier to read than the function developed in Sect. 99. It is clear how the answer is computed. If the given binary tree is empty, then there is no maximum integer. Otherwise, the maximum of the given (btof int) is the maximum of a node.

The tests may be written as follows:

```
;; Tests using sample computations for max-btint
(check-expect (max-btint BTI100) BTI100-VAL)
(check-expect (max-btint BTI456) BTI456-VAL)

; Tests using sample values for f-on-btx
(check-error
  (max-btint BTI0)
  "An empty (btof int) has no maximum value.")
(check-expect (max-btint (make-node -97
                                    (make-node -89 BTI0 BTI0)
                                    (make-node -99 BTI0 BTI0)))
              -89)
```

Observe that once again error checking is part of the tests using sample values. The second of these tests illustrates that the function works when the tree contains negative numbers.

We now turn to the problem of finding the maximum integer in a node. As in Sect. 99, we must take care not to call max-btint with an empty tree. If a node is a leaf, then the node's value is the maximum. Otherwise, the maximum of the node's value and the maximum of any non-empty subtree are computed. This leads to the following new node instances and four sample expressions:

```
(define NODE200 (make-node 200 BTI0 (make-node 311 BTI0 BTI0)))
(define NODE650 (make-node 650 (make-node 912 BTI0 BTI0) BTI0))

;; Sample expressions for max-node
(define NODE487-VAL (node-val NODE487))
(define NODE200-VAL (max (node-val NODE200)
                         (max-node (node-rtree NODE200))))
```

```
(define NODE650-VAL (max (node-val NODE650)
                         (max-node (node-ltree NODE650))))
(define NODE456-VAL (max (node-val NODE456)
                         (max-node (node-ltree NODE456))
                         (max-node (node-rtree NODE456))))
```

The two new node instances are written to make the development of sample expressions easier. The first has an empty left tree and the second has an empty right tree. Observe that there is an expression for each node condition possible: leaf, only left subtree is empty, only right subtree is empty, and no subtrees are empty.

Based on the sample expressions, we may specialize the definition template for a function on a node as follows:

```
;; node → int
;; Purpose: Return the max int in the given node
(define (max-node a-node)
  (cond [(and (empty? (node-ltree a-node))
              (empty? (node-rtree a-node)))
         (node-val a-node)]
        [(empty? (node-ltree a-node))
         (max (node-val a-node)
              (max-btint (node-rtree a-node)))]
        [(empty? (node-rtree a-node))
         (max (node-val a-node)
              (max-btint (node-ltree a-node)))]
        [else (max (node-val a-node)
                   (max-btint (node-ltree a-node))
                   (max-btint (node-rtree a-node)))]))
```

Observe the absence of first, second, and third to access the components of a node. These list functions needed to be used in Sect. 99 because a non-empty tree was represented as a list. Now the interface is cleaner and more elegant. For instance, any reader of our code easily understands that (node-rtree a-node) evaluates to a-node's right subtree. In Sect. 99, (third a-btint) was used to access the right subtree. Does this expression in any way suggest that it ought to evaluate to the right subtree? You are now beginning to understand the importance of writing elegant code by using separation of concerns.

The tests may be written as follows:

```
;; Tests using sample computations for max-node
(check-expect (max-node NODE487) NODE487-VAL)
(check-expect (max-node NODE200) NODE200-VAL)
(check-expect (max-node NODE650) NODE650-VAL)
(check-expect (max-node NODE456) NODE456-VAL)
```

```
;; Tests using sample values for max-node
(check-expect (max-node (make-node
                          789
                          (make-node -1000 BTI0 BTI0)
                          (make-node 3000  BTI0 BTI0)))
               3000)
```

Observe that any reader can determine that the function properly computes the value of the sample expressions. In addition, they can see that max-node works for an arbitrary node that contains both positive and negative integers.

106 Evaluating Arithmetic Expressions

In a seminal 1960 research article, *Recursive Functions of Symbolic Expressions and Their Computation by Machine, Part I*, Prof. John McCarthy from The Massachusetts Institute of Technology defined *symbolic expressions* to represent the expressions that we use today to program in ISL+.[24] McCarthy developed a set of mutually recursive data definitions for symbolic expressions that may be used to represent a computation that, subsequently, may be evaluated by a computer.

In this section, we shall not tackle the problem of evaluating ISL+ programs. Instead, we tackle the problem of evaluating the subset of symbolic expressions representing arithmetic expressions using +, −, and *. To start, let us look at a few sample expressions:

```
45                87
(+ 67 54)         (* (- 56 43) 44 (+ 7 4))
```

Observe that there are two varieties of symbolic expressions. The simplest symbolic expression is a number. The second variety is a list that contains a symbol representing a function followed by a list of symbolic expressions. This list of symbolic expressions represents the arguments to the function.

The above data analysis naturally leads to the following set of mutually recursive data definitions:

```
A symbolic expression (sexpr) is either:
  1. number
  2. slist

A symbolic list (slist) is: (cons function losexpr)

A function is either:        A list of sexpr (losexpr) is either:
  1. '+                        1. '()
  2. '-                        2. (cons sexpr losexpr)
  3. '*
```

---

[24] In fact, many other programming languages represent programs as symbolic expressions such as LISP, Scheme, Racket, and BSL.

Fig. 87 The function templates for `sexpr` and `slist`

```
#|   ;; Samples of sexpr
     (define SEXPR1 ...)      (define SEXPR2 ...)


     ;; sexpr ... --> ...     Purpose:
     (define (f-on-sexpr a-sexpr)
       (if (number? a-sexpr)
           (f-on-number a-sexpr ...)
           (f-on-slist a-sexpr ...)))
     ;; Sample expressions for f-on-sexpr
     (define SEXPR1-VAL ...)        (define SEXPR2-VAL ...)


     ;; Tests using sample computations for f-on-sexpr
     (check-expect (f-on-sexpr SEXPR1) SEXPR1-VAL)
     (check-expect (f-on-sexpr SEXPR2) SEXPR2-VAL)
     ;; Tests using sample values for f-on-sexpr
     (check-expect (f-on-sexpr ... ...) ...)


     ;; Samples of slist
     (define SLIST1 '())       (define SLIST2 ...)


     ;; slist ... --> ...     Purpose:
     (define (f-on-slist an-slist)
       (if (empty? an-slist)
           ...
           (cons (f-on-sexpr (first an-slist) ...)
                 (f-on-slist (rest an-slist) ...))))
     ;; Sample expressions for f-on-slist
     (define SLIST1-VAL ...)        (define SLIST2-VAL ...)


     ;; Tests using sample computations for f-on-slist
     (check-expect (f-on-slist SLIST1 ...) SLIST1-VAL)
     (check-expect (f-on-slist SLIST2 ...) SLIST2-VAL)
     ;; Tests using sample values for f-on-slist
     (check-expect (f-on-slist ... ...) ...)
|#
```

Observe that processing an `sexpr` requires processing either a number or an `slist`. Processing an `slist` requires processing a `function` and a `losexpr`. Processing a `function` requires processing one of the three symbols. Finally, processing a `losexpr` requires either processing the empty list or processing a `sexpr` and a `losexpr`. It is clear that `sexpr`, `slist`, and `losexpr` are mutually recursive. With this understanding the function templates in Figs. 87 and 88 are developed. It is worth noting now that below functions are developed following the steps of the design recipe. Given that the functions are mutually recursive, however, in DrRacket all the functions must appear before the sample expressions and tests. Otherwise, DrRacket will throw an error telling you that a function is used before its definition.

Fig. 88 The template for function

```
#|    ;; function ... --> ...      Purpose:
(define (f-on-function a-function)
  (cond [(eq? a-function '+) ...]
        [(eq? a-function '-) ...]
        [else ...]))

;; Sample expressions for f-on-function
(define PLUS-VAL ...)
(define SUBT-VAL ...)
(define MULT-VAL ...)

;; Tests using sample computations for f-on-function
(check-expect (f-on-function PLUS ...) PLUS-VAL)
(check-expect (f-on-function SUBT ...) SUBT-VAL)
(check-expect (f-on-function MULT ...) SUBT-VAL)

;; Tests using sample values for f-on-function
(check-expect (f-on-function ... ...) ...)
|#
```

We first start by defining the following sample instances for the different data types:

```
;; Sample instances of slist
(define SLIST1 '(* (+ 44 -44) (- 20 10)))
(define SLIST2 '(* 3 (+ 6 4)))

;; Sample instances of sexpr
(define SEXPR1 67)
(define SEXPR2 SLIST2)

;; Sample instances of (listof sexpr)
(define LOSEXPR1 '())
(define LOSEXPR2 '(80 (+ 70 20) (* 4 (- 30 5))))

;; Sample instances of (listof number)
(define LON1 '())
(define LON2 '(1 2 3 4 5))
(define LON3 '(-10 -20 -30))
```

These sample instances are used to develop the steps of the design recipe for the program to evaluate arithmetic expressions. The `function` sample instances are omitted because it is simple enough to directly use the three possible symbols. The `(listof number)` instances are explicitly written to make it easier to develop the function that applies a given function to a list of arguments.

Now that we know what is required to process the different data types, we may proceed with problem analysis for evaluating arithmetic expressions. We start with analyzing how to evaluate a `sexpr`. The evaluation of a number `sexpr` is the number itself. The evaluation of an `slist` `sexpr` requires calling a function to evaluate an `slist`. This analysis leads to the following sample expressions:

```
;; Sample expressions for eval-sexpr
(define SEXPR1-VAL SEXPR1)                    ;; for a number
(define SEXPR2-VAL (eval-slist SEXPR2)) ;; for a slist
```

Observe that the sample expressions illustrate how to implement our problem analysis.

The next step is to specialize the definition template and tests. This is accomplished as follows:

```
;; sexpr → number throws error
;; Purpose: To evaluate the given sexpr
(define (eval-sexpr a-sexpr)
  (if (number? a-sexpr)
      a-sexpr
      (eval-slist a-sexpr)))

;; Tests using sample computations for eval-sexpr
(check-expect (eval-sexpr SEXPR1) SEXPR1-VAL)
(check-expect (eval-sexpr SEXPR2) SEXPR2-VAL)

;; Tests using sample values for eval-sexpr
(check-expect (eval-sexpr 42) 42)
(check-expect (eval-sexpr '(+ -1 (* 6 (+ 8 2)))) 59)
```

At this point, the function and tests ought to feel quite straightforward to you. They are the direct results of our problem analysis and of following the steps of the design recipe. The only detail that remains unclear is why does the signature state that this function can throw an error. Bear with this for now. The answer will become clear as our design progresses.

As expected, our function design has revealed the need for an auxiliary function: `eval-slist`. This function must evaluate an `slist` `sexpr`. Recall that an `slist` represents the application of a function to its arguments. To do so, the arguments to the function must be evaluated; then the function must be applied to them. Observe that these are two different tasks and, therefore, two auxiliary functions are needed: one to evaluate the arguments and one to apply the function. The template for a function of an `slist` is specialized as follows:

```
;; Sample expressions for eval-slist
(define SLIST1-VAL (apply-f (first SLIST1)
                            (eval-args (rest SLIST1))))
(define SLIST2-VAL (apply-f (first SLIST2)
                            (eval-args (rest SLIST2))))
```

```
;; slist → number
;; Purpose: To evaluate the given slist
(define (eval-slist an-slist)
  (apply-f (first an-slist) (eval-args (rest an-slist))))

;; Tests using sample computations for eval-slist
(check-expect (eval-slist SLIST1) SLIST1-VAL)
(check-expect (eval-slist SLIST2) SLIST2-VAL)

;; Tests using sample values for eval-slist
(check-expect (eval-slist
                '(- (* 10 10) (+ 5 (* 2 3) 7))) 82)
```

Observe that the sample expressions clearly illustrate that the arguments are evaluated first and then the function is applied to them. Given that there is only one difference among the sample expressions eval-slist only needs one parameter. The test using a sample value illustrates that the function works for all functions with multiple nested levels.

To evaluate the list of arguments each sexpr in the given list must be evaluated and a list of the results must be returned. This is a mapping operation (as we studied in Sect. 76). Therefore, the template for a function on a (listof sexpr) is specialized. If the given list is empty, the empty list is returned. Otherwise, cons is used to create a new list containing the result of evaluating the first sexpr and recursively evaluating the rest of the sexprs. The template specialization is

```
;; Sample expressions for eval-args
(define LOSEXPR1-VAL '())
(define LOSEXPR2-VAL (cons (eval-sexpr (first LOSEXPR2))
                          (eval-args (rest LOSEXPR2))))

;; (listof sexpr) arrow (listof number) throws error
;; Purpose: To evaluate the sexprs in the given list
(define (eval-args a-losexpr)
  (if (empty? a-losexpr)
      '()
      (cons (eval-sexpr (first a-losexpr))
            (eval-args (rest a-losexpr)))))

;; Tests using sample computations for eval-args
(check-expect (eval-args LOSEXPR1) LOSEXPR1-VAL)
(check-expect (eval-args LOSEXPR2) LOSEXPR2-VAL)

;; Tests using sample values for eval-args
(check-expect (eval-args '((- 1 1) 89)) '(0 89))
```

As before, the reason for the signature stating that the function may throw an error will become clear as our design advances.

We may now proceed to design `apply-f`. This function takes as input a `function` and a (`listof` number). It is necessary to determine the value of the given `function` to properly combine the given numbers. The combination of the given numbers involves one of three different tasks. Each of these tasks is performed by a different auxiliary function. Therefore, the template for a function on a `function` is specialized as follows:

```
;; Sample expressions for apply-f
(define APPLY1-VAL (sum-lon  LON1))
(define APPLY2-VAL (subt-lon LON2))
(define APPLY3-VAL (mult-lon LON3))

;; function (listof number) → number throws error
;; Purpose: Apply the given function to the given numbers
(define (apply-f a-function a-lon)
  (cond [(eq? a-function '+) (sum-lon  a-lon)]
        [(eq? a-function '-) (subt-lon a-lon)]
        [else (mult-lon a-lon)]))

;; Tests using sample computations for apply-f
(check-expect (apply-f '+ LON1) APPLY1-VAL)
(check-expect (apply-f '- LON2) APPLY2-VAL)
(check-expect (apply-f '* LON3) APPLY3-VAL)

;; Tests using sample values for apply-f
(check-expect (apply-f '+ '(10 10 10)) 30)
(check-expect (apply-f '- '(20 0)) 20)
(check-expect (apply-f '* '(9 -2)) -18)
```

The design of `sum-lon` is exactly the same as the design of `sum-loq` in Sect. 72. The design of `mult-lon` is very similar and the results of following the steps of the design recipe are displayed in Fig. 89.

Of the three auxiliary functions the most interesting one is `subt-lon`. We must carefully analyze how the arithmetic minus function is applied to an arbitrary number of arguments. Let us look at a few interactions with DrRacket:

```
> (- 1)
-1
> (- 2 -4)
6
> (- 10 20 -5)
-5
```

How is − applied to its arguments? According the ISL+ documentation this is how subtraction works:

```
Subtracts the second (and following) number(s) from the first;
negates the number if there is only one argument.
```

Fig. 89 The function to multiply the numbers in a list of numbers

```
;; Sample instances of (listof number)
(define LON1 '())
(define LON2 '(1 2 3 4 5))
(define LON3 '(-10 -20 -30))

;; lon → number
;; Purpose: To multiply the numbers in the given lon
(define (mult-lon a-lon)
  (if (empty? a-lon)
      1
      (* (first a-lon) (mult-lon (rest a-lon)))))

;; Sample expressions for mult-lon
(define LON1-MULT 1)
(define LON2-MULT (* (first LON2) (mult-lon (rest LON2))))

;; Tests using sample computations for mult-lon
(check-expect (mult-lon LON1) LON1-MULT)
(check-expect (mult-lon LON2) LON2-MULT)

;; Tests using sample computations for mult-lon
(check-expect (mult-lon '(-10 0 10)) 0)
```

Therefore, we have

```
(- 1)        = -1
(- 2 -4)     = 2 - -4
(- 10 20 -5) = 10 - 20 - -5
```

What happens if - is provided no arguments? Try it in DrRacket. You can see that an error is thrown. This is why eval-sexpr, eval-slist, eval-args, and apply-f may throw an error. The function subt-lon is called by apply-f and, therefore, calling apply-f may generate an error. In turn, apply-f is called by eval-slist, which itself is called by eval-sexpr. Thus, these two functions may also throw an error. Finally, eval-args may throw an error because it calls eval-sexpr. In general, if a function f may lead to a call to function g that throws an error, then f may also throw an error.

Now that we understand how to apply -, we can determine how to implement a function to perform this task. If the given list of numbers is empty, then an error is thrown. Otherwise, we need to subtract the rest of the numbers from the first number. How can this be done? Observe that a - is placed before each number in the rest of the list. By using a little Algebra we can factor out the -. For example, the last two expressions above may be rewritten as follows:

```
(- 2 -4)     = 2 - -4      = 2 - (-4)
(- 10 20 -5) = 10 - 20 - -5 = 10 - (20 + -5)
```

We can subtract from the first number the sum of the rest of the numbers.

We can now specialize the template for a function on a (listof number) as follows:

```
;; lon → number throws error
;; Purpose: To subtract the given lon
(define (subt-lon a-lon)
  (if (empty? a-lon)
      (error "No numbers provided to -.")
      (- (first a-lon) (sum-lon (rest a-lon)))))

;; Sample expressions for subt-lon
(define LON2-SUBT (- (first LON2) (sum-lon (rest LON2))))

;; Tests using sample computations for subt-lon
(check-error  (subt-lon LON1) "No numbers provided to -.")
(check-expect (subt-lon LON2) LON2-SUBT)

;; Tests using sample computations for subt-lon
(check-expect (subt-lon '(-10 10 10)) -30)
```

Observe that we make use of sum-lon in our implementation. In this manner, there is no need for us to write a function that does repeated subtractions for us.

107 Trees

The concept of a binary tree may be generalized. Instead of each node having at most two children, in a *tree* a node may have an arbitrary number of children. Figure 90 displays a tree representing moves on a Tic Tac Toe board.[25] At level 0, the root has 3 children. At level 1, the children of the root each have two children. At level 2, the grandchildren of the root each have 1 child. Finally, at level 3 the nodes do not have any children. As you can observe the number of children a node has is arbitrary. How many children does the node representing the empty board at the beginning of a game has? Clearly, such a node would have 9 children—one for each possible move the first player may make.

Trees are versatile and may be used to represent many real or imaginary objects. One use of trees is to represent a *search space*. A search space defines all possible solutions to a problem and is searched to find a solution. For example, Fig. 90 represents all possible paths in a Tic Tac Toe gaming starting at the root node. Such a tree, for instance, may be taken as input by a function that determines the next move the computer ought to make.

---

[25] Tic Tac Toe is played on a 3×3 board formed by using two vertical and two horizontal lines. There are two players. One is designated 'X and the other 'O. The player's goal is to get three symbols in a row.

Fig. 90 A tree of Tic Tac Toe paths

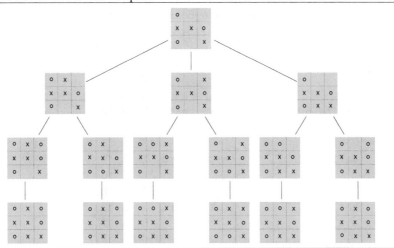

We must now decide how to represent a search tree for Tic Tac Toe. Observe that a search tree is made of nodes. Stop and think carefully what this means to a problem solver. It suggests that two data definitions are needed: one for a node and one for a search tree. Let us think carefully about a node. A node has a board (i.e., the current state of the game) and a list of children. We use of list because the number of children is arbitrary. Observe two more things. The first is the need for a third data definition: a board. The second is that a node is of finite size and always contains two elements. Now, let us think carefully about what a search tree is. What should the search tree be if there is no game? We are free to choose any representation. Without loss of generality, we shall say it is '(). If there is a game, then the search tree must be a node. This data analysis suggests the following data definitions:

```
;; A node is a structure: (make-node board (listof st))
(define-struct node (board children))

;; A solution tree (st) is either:
;;   1. '()
;;   2. node

;; A board value (bval) is either:
;;   1. 'X
;;   2. 'O
;;   3. 'B

;; A board is a structure:
;;   (make-board bval bval bval bval bval bval bval bval bval)
(define-struct board (p0 p1 p2 p3 p4 p5 p6 p7 p8))
```

```
;; Sample board values
(define INIT-BOARD (make-board 'B 'B 'B
                               'B 'B 'B
                               'B 'B 'B))
(define BOARD1     (make-board 'X 'O 'X
                               'O 'X 'O
                               'X 'O 'X))
(define BOARD2     (make-board 'X 'B 'B
                               'O 'B 'B
                               'B 'B 'B))
(define BOARD3     (make-board 'X 'B 'B
                               'X 'O 'B
                               'B 'B 'B))
(define BOARD4     (make-board 'X 'B 'B
                               'B 'B 'B
                               'B 'B 'B))
(define BOARD5     (make-board 'X 'X 'O
                               'B 'X 'X
                               'O 'O 'O))
(define BOARD6     (make-board 'X 'B 'B
                               'B 'X 'X
                               'O 'B 'O))
```

A board is a structure with nine bvals and a bval is one of three symbols. Observe
that node, (listof st), and st are mutually recursive. That is, node refers to
(listof st), (listof st) refers to st, and st refers to node. As problem solvers
this immediately tells us that writing a function to process a node requires writing
functions to process a (listof st) and a function to process an st.

Given out insights we can now write the required function templates as follows:

```
#| TEMPLATES
;; Sample instances of (listof st)
(define LOST1 '())
(define LOST2 ...)

;; (listof st) ... → ...
;; Purpose:
(define (f-on-lost an-lost)
  (if (empty? an-lost)
      ...
      ...(f-on-st (first an-lost))...(f-on-lost (rest an-lost)))))

;; Sample expressions for f-on-st
(define ST1-VAL ...)
(define ST2-VAL ...)
```

```
;; Tests using sample computations f-on-st
(check-expect (f-on-st ST1 ...) ST1-VAL)
(check-expect (f-on-st ST2 ...) ST2-VAL)

;; Tests using sample values f-on-st
(check-expect (f-on-st ... ...) ...)


;; Sample instances of node
(define NODE1 ...)

;; node ... → ...
;; Purpose:
(define (f-on-node a-node)
  ...(f-on-board (node-board a-node))...
  ...(f-on-lost  (node-children a-node))...)

;; Sample expressions for f-on-node
(define NODE1-VAL ...)

;; Tests using sample computations f-on-node
(check-expect (f-on-node NODE1 ...) NODE1-VAL)

;; Tests using sample values f-on-node
(check-expect (f-on-node ... ...) ...)


;; Sample instances of ST
(define ST1 '())
(define ST2 ...)

;; st ... → ...
;; Purpose:
(define (f-on-st an-st)
  (if (empty? an-st)
      ...
      (f-on-node an-st)))

;; Sample expressions for f-on-st
(define ST1-VAL ...)
(define ST2-VAL ...)

;; Tests using sample computations f-on-st
(check-expect (f-on-node ST1 ...) ST1-VAL)
(check-expect (f-on-node ST2 ...) ST2-VAL)
```

```
;; Tests using sample values f-on-st
(check-expect (f-on-st ... ...) ...)
|#
```

As expected, f-on-node has an expression to call f-on-lost, f-on-lost has an
expression to call f-on-st, and f-on-st has an expression to call f-on-node. The
function templates for board and bval are left as exercises.

---

* **Ex. 193** — Develop a template for a function on a board.

* **Ex. 194** — Develop a template for a function on a bval.

107.1 Creating a Search Tree for Tic Tac Toe

A natural question that you may have is how to create a tree representing, for example,
the complete st for Tic Tac Toe starting from the blank board. To create an st we
need to know whose turn it is. Therefore, we create the following data definition and
sample instances:

```
;; A turn is either 'X or 'O

(define INIT-TURN 'X)
(define O-TURN 'O)
```

By convention the first move is made by 'X and this is the convention we shall follow.
Given a board and a turn the blanks in the board must be identified. A child for the
given board must be created for each blank. Observe that this data analysis suggests
that the function to create an st does not process neither the given board nor the
given turn. Instead, a function to find the blanks in the given board and a function
to process the blanks (by creating an st for each possible successive board) are
needed. A node, therefore, is created using the given board and the sts created by
processing the blanks of the given board. Sample expressions may be written as
follows:

```
;; Sample expressions for create-st
(define BOARD1-VAL (make-node BOARD1
                              (process-blanks
                                BOARD1
                                (find-blanks BOARD1)
                                'O)))
(define BOARD2-VAL (make-node BOARD2
                              (process-blanks
                                BOARD2
                                (find-blanks BOARD2)
                                'X)))
```

The function process-blanks returns a (listof st) containing one st for each blank in the given board.

Abstracting over the sample expressions yields the following function:

```
;; board turn → st
;; Purpose: Create the st for the given board
(define (create-st a-board a-turn)
  (make-node a-board
             (process-blanks a-board
                             (find-blanks a-board)
                             a-turn)))
```

This function may be tested as follows:

```
;; Tests using sample computations for create-st
(check-expect (create-st BOARD1 'O) BOARD1-VAL)
(check-expect (create-st BOARD2 'X) BOARD2-VAL)

;; Tests using sample values for create-st
(check-expect (create-st (make-board 'X 'O 'X
                                     'O 'X 'O
                                     'X 'B 'B)
                         'O)
              (make-node
               (make-board 'X 'O 'X
                           'O 'X 'O
                           'X 'B 'B)
               (list
                (make-node
                 (make-board 'X 'O 'X
                             'O 'X 'O
                             'X 'O 'B)
                 (list
                  (make-node
                   (make-board 'X 'O 'X
                               'O 'X 'O
                               'X 'O 'X)
                   '()))
                (make-node
                 (make-board 'X 'O 'X
                             'O 'X 'O
                             'X 'B 'O)
                 (list
                  (make-node
                   (make-board 'X 'O 'X
                               'O 'X 'O
                               'X 'X 'O)
                   '())))))))
```

The test using a sample value is written using a board that only has a couple of moves left to make it feasible to write the expected `st`.

*** **Ex. 195** — Write the function `find-blanks` by specializing the template for a function on a `board`. To do so, you may find the following data definition useful:

```
;; A board position (bpos) is a natnum in [0..8]
```

The board positions may be numbered starting at the top left corner at 0 and ending at the bottom right corner at 8. The function, `find-blanks`, must return a (`listof bpos`).

*** **Ex. 196** — Write model checking tests using boards that have a large number of moves left. What properties can you test about an `st`?

We can now turn our attention to the design of `process-blanks`. We assume that you have implemented a solution to the first exercise above. This function must process the given (`listof bpos`). For each blank position in the given list a new board is created by placing the given `bval` at that position in the given `board`. This board is then used to create an `st` for the (`listof st`) returned. We may write sample expressions as follows:

```
;; Sample expressions for process-blanks
(define PROC-0BLANKS  '())
(define PROC-6BLANKS
       (cons (create-st (place-on-board BOARD3
                                        (first '(1 2 5 6 7 8))
                                        'O)
                        (if (eq? 'O 'X) 'O 'X))
             (process-blanks
               BOARD3 (rest '(1 2 5 6 7 8)) 'O)))
```

If the given (`listof bpos`) is empty, then there are no `st`s to create and the empty (`listof st`) is the answer. Otherwise, a non-empty (`listof st`) is returned. For BOARD3, the first `st` is created using the board obtained by placing an O in position 1 and the next turn (i.e., X). The rest of the `st`s are recursively created by processing '(2 5 6 7 8) along with the same board (i.e., BOARD3) and the same turn (i.e., O).

Based on the insights obtained from our problem analysis and sample expressions we may write the function as follows:

```
;; board (listof bpos) turn → (listof st)
;; Purpose: Build the st for the given board and its given list
;;          of blank positions
(define (process-blanks a-board a-lobpos a-turn)
  (if (empty? a-lobpos)
      '()
      (cons (create-st
             (place-on-board a-board (first a-lobpos) a-turn)
             (if (eq? a-turn 'X) 'O 'X))
            (process-blanks a-board (rest a-lobpos) a-turn)))))
```

Observe that the if-expression is used to swap X to O and O to X for the call to create-st. Finally, tests are written as follows:

```
;; Tests using sample computations for process-blanks
(check-expect (process-blanks BOARD1 '()                    'X)
              PROC-0BLANKS)
(check-expect (process-blanks BOARD3 '(1 2 5 6 7 8) 'O)
              PROC-6BLANKS)

;; Tests using sample values for process-blanks
(check-expect (process-blanks
                  (make-board 'B 'X 'O
                              'O 'X 'X
                              'O 'X 'O)
                  '(O)
                  'X)
                  (list (make-node
                          (make-board 'X 'X 'O
                                      'O 'X 'X
                                      'O 'X 'O)
                          '()))))
```

The test using a sample value is written using a board that only has one move left to make it feasible to write the expected (listof st). Finally, given that the functions are mutually recursive, remember to place the functions first in your file and after them the results of the other steps of the design recipe.

** **Ex. 197** — Write the function place-on-board by specializing the template for a function on a bpos.

*** **Ex. 198** — Write model checking tests for process-blanks. What properties can you test for a returned (listof st)?

*** **Ex. 199** — The design of `create-st` continues to place moves on boards where one of the players has already won. Redesign `create-st` so that it does not create children for such boards.

107.2 Can Win Tic Tac Toe?

We now turn to an example of processing an `st`. Given an `st` consider determining if it is possible for a given player to win by any number of moves. We must clearly define what a move may be. It is not difficult to see that a move is a whole number in [0..8]. This means that the root `board` in the given `st` and all the `boards` under it must be checked for a win by the given `turn`. If the given `st` is empty, then the answer is `#false`. Otherwise, according to the template for a function on an `st`, a function to determine if the given `turn` may win in any number of moves for a given node must be called. Based on this problem analysis, we may right sample instances and expressions as follows:

```
;; Sample st instances
(define INIT-ST (create-st INIT-BOARD 'X))
(define BRD7-ST (create-st BOARD7      'O))

;; Sample expressions for st-can-win?
(define WIN-ST1-VAL #false)
(define WIN-ST2-VAL (node-can-win? INIT-ST 'X))
(define WIN-ST3-VAL (node-can-win? BRD7-ST 'O))
```

The first `st` sample instance is created using the initial board and the second from `BOARD7` that has two moves left. The first sample expression is for the empty `st`. The second sample expression ought to evaluate to `#true` because X can still win the game. The third sample expression ought to evaluate to `#false` because O cannot win the game.

Abstracting over the sample expressions leads to the following function definition:

```
;; st turn → Boolean
;; Purpose: Determine if there is a sequence of moves for
;;          the given turn to win
(define (st-can-win? an-st a-turn)
  (if (empty? an-st)
      #false
      (node-can-win? an-st a-turn)))
```

Observe that separation of concerns renders a function that is straightforward to understand. The answer is false if the given `st` is empty. Otherwise, the answer is given by processing a node.

The tests may be written as follows:

```
;; Tests using sample computations st-can-win?
(check-expect (st-can-win? WIN-ST1 'X) WIN-ST1-VAL)
(check-expect (st-can-win? WIN-ST2 'X) WIN-ST2-VAL)
(check-expect (st-can-win? WIN-ST3 'O) WIN-ST3-VAL)


;; Tests using sample values can-win-st?
(check-expect (st-can-win? (create-st (make-board 'O 'X 'B
                                                  'X 'O 'X
                                                  'O 'X 'O)
                                       'X)
                           'X)
              #false)

(check-expect (st-can-win? (create-st (make-board 'B 'B 'B
                                                  'X 'O 'X
                                                  'B 'B 'B)
                                       'O)
                           'O)
              #true)
```

As always, the tests using sample computations illustrate that the abstraction over the sample expressions computes the expected values. The tests using sample values illustrate using explicit values for which both possible outcomes are properly computed.

With st-can-win? designed and implemented, we can now turn our attention to designing node-can-win?. Recall that a node has a board and a list of children sts. What does it mean that the given turn can win? The given turn can win if it has won in the node's board. This means two things. First, the given turn has three of its values in any row. Second, the given turn's opponent has not won. The given turn can also win if it can win through any of the given node's children. Based on this problem analysis we may write sample instances and expressions as follows:

```
;; Sample instances of node
(define WIN-NODE2 WIN-ST2)
(define WIN-NODE3 WIN-ST3)


;; Sample expressions for node-can-win?
(define WIN-NODE2-VAL
        (or
          (and (not (has-win? (node-board WIN-NODE2)
                              (flip 'X)))
               (has-win? (node-board WIN-NODE2) 'X))
          (lost-can-win?  (node-children WIN-NODE2) 'X)))
```

```
(define WIN-NODE3-VAL
          (or
           (and (not (has-win? (node-board WIN-NODE3)
                               (flip 'O)))
                (has-win? (node-board WIN-NODE3) 'O))
           (lost-can-win?  (node-children WIN-NODE3) 'O)))
```

The sample expressions test if the given node's board is a win for the given turn or
if any of the children lead to a win. The auxiliary function, flip, is used to change
an 'X to an 'O and vice versa. As expected, the children are processed by calling a
function on a lost.

Abstracting over the sample expressions leads to the following function definition:

```
;; node turn → Boolean
;; Purpose: To determine if the given turn can reach a win
(define (node-can-win? a-node a-turn)
  (or (and (not (has-win? (node-board a-node) (flip a-turn)))
           (has-win? (node-board a-node) a-turn))
      (lost-can-win?  (node-children a-node) a-turn)))
```

This function may be tested as follows:

```
;; Tests using sample computations node-can-win?
(check-expect (node-can-win? WIN-NODE2 'X) WIN-NODE2-VAL)
(check-expect (node-can-win? WIN-NODE3 'O) WIN-NODE3-VAL)

;; Tests using sample values node-can-win?
(check-expect (node-can-win?
               (create-st (make-board 'B 'B 'B
                                      'B 'X 'B
                                      'B 'B 'B)
                          'O)
               'O)
              #true)

(check-expect (node-can-win?
               (create-st (make-board 'O 'O 'O
                                      'X 'X 'B
                                      'X 'B 'B)
                          'X)
               'X)
              #false)
```

The tests using sample computations, once again, illustrate that the function computes
the values of the sample expressions. The tests using sample values provide examples
of nodes for which a win is possible and a win is not possible for the given turn.

> * **Ex. 200** — Design and implement the function flip.

The function lost-can-win? must determine if for a given turn any of its sts lead to a win. If the given list is empty, then the answer is #false. Otherwise, a win is possible if the first st leads to a win or any of the rest of the sts leads to a win. Observe that a Boolean value is computed. This means we may opt to use a Boolean function without using a conditional expression as suggested by the template for a function on a lost. We may write sample instances and expressions as follows:

```
;; Sample instances of lost
(define WIN-LOST1 '())
(define WIN-LOST2 (node-children WIN-NODE2))
(define WIN-LOST3 (node-children WIN-NODE3))

;; Sample expressions for lost-can-win?
(define WIN-LOST1-VAL (and (not (empty? WIN-LOST1))
                           (or (st-can-win? (first WIN-LOST1)
                                            'X)
                               (lost-can-win? (rest WIN-LOST1)
                                              'X))))
(define WIN-LOST2-VAL (and (not (empty? WIN-LOST2))
                           (or (st-can-win? (first WIN-LOST2)
                                            'X)
                               (lost-can-win? (rest WIN-LOST2)
                                              'X))))
(define WIN-LOST3-VAL (and (not (empty? WIN-LOST3))
                           (or (st-can-win? (first WIN-LOST3)
                                            'O)
                               (lost-can-win? (rest WIN-LOST3)
                                              'O))))
```

Observe that the sample expressions are communicating the ideas in our problem analysis. A win is possible only if the given lost is not empty and either the first st leads to a win or any of the other sts lead to a win.

Abstracting over the sample expressions allows us to continue specializing the template for a function on a lost as follows:

```
;; (listof st) turn → Boolean
;; Purpose: Determine if the given turn can win through any st
(define (lost-can-win? an-lost a-turn)
  (and (not (empty? an-lost))
       (or (st-can-win? (first an-lost) a-turn)
           (lost-can-win? (rest an-lost) a-turn))))
```

Finally, the function may be tested as follows:

```
;; Tests using sample computations lost-can-win?
(check-expect (lost-can-win? WIN-LOST1 'X) WIN-LOST1-VAL)
(check-expect (lost-can-win? WIN-LOST2 'O) WIN-LOST2-VAL)
(check-expect (lost-can-win? WIN-LOST3 'O) WIN-LOST3-VAL)

;; Tests using sample values lost-can-win?
(check-expect
  (lost-can-win?
    (node-children (create-st (make-board 'X 'B 'O
                                          'O 'X 'O
                                          'B 'X 'X)
                    'O))
    'O)
  #false)

(check-expect (lost-can-win?
                (node-children
                  (create-st (make-board 'B 'B 'O
                                         'O 'X 'O
                                         'B 'X 'X)
                    'X))
                'X)
              #true)
```

The tests using sample values clearly communicate that both possible expected values are properly computed. For the tests using sample values, any reader of our code can easily observe that for the first test O cannot win and for the second test X can win. As with all mutually recursive functions, place all function definitions before the results of the other steps of the design recipe in order to run the program.

108 Project: Tic Tac Toe

The goal of this project is for you to design and implement a Tic Tac Toe game. In this game a player and the computer are opponents. The player is X and plays first. The game initially displays an initial board similar to the one displayed in Fig. 91. Feel free to embellish the game with graphics that you like. The player uses the mouse to click on a board box to make a move. If it is the player's turn and the clicked box is blank, then an X is placed in the clicked box. After this the computer makes a move by placing an O in any of the remaining boxes. The game cycles in this manner until there is a winner or when there is a draw when all the boxes in the board are not blank.

Fig. 91 The initial board image for Tic Tac Toe

To get you started here is the run function for the game:

```
(define (run a-name)
  (big-bang INIT-WORLD
    (on-draw draw-world)
    (on-mouse process-mouse)
    (on-tick process-tick)
    (stop-when game-over? draw-last-world)
    (name A-NAME)))
```

You need to follow a top-down design strategy starting with the event-handling functions in the big-bang expression. The rest of the section will help you with each of these.

108.1 Data Analysis

There are two basic components that must be represented: the world and the image for representing the world. Of these the easiest is the image of the world. This image ought to include the game's current board. For example, at the beginning of the game the image rendered must include the initial board displayed in Fig. 91. If you examine this image, you can see that the scene contains the board that has 9 tiles of the same size and same color. You may find the following constants useful:

```
(define TILE-LEN 100)
(define TILE-CLR 'green)
(define WIDTH    (* 3 TILE-LEN))
(define HEIGHT   (* 3 TILE-LEN))
(define E-SCENE  (empty-scene WIDTH HEIGHT))
```

How can we represent the world? We can take advantage of the work we have done in Sect. 107.1. As the game advances, we are stepping through the st that has the initial board at the root. For a given st, the next board must be one of the children. This child becomes the world's st after each move. In addition, we need to track the current turn to determine if the player is allowed to make a move. This analysis leads the following data definition:

```
;; A world is a structure: (make-world st turn).
(define-struct world (st turn))
```

* **Ex. 201** — Develop the template for a function on a world.

* **Ex. 202** — Define, INIT-WORLD, the initial world.

108.2 Design draw-world

Drawing the world requires drawing a board and any embellishments that you like to personalize the game to your liking (e.g., whose turn it is). What board ought to be rendered? In accordance with our data representation, this board ought to be at the root in the world's st.

* **Ex. 203** — Design and implement a function to draw the world.

108.3 Design process-mouse

In the universe API, a mouse event handler needs four inputs: a world, an x coordinate, a y coordinate, and a mouse event. The given x and y coordinates correspond to the position of the mouse in the scene when a mouse event happens. There are several mouse events defined and you may read about them through the Help Desk. Of interest for us is the "button-down" event. This occurs when the player clicks. When the player clicks on a tile, an X is placed in the clicked tile if:

1. It is X's turn.
2. The clicked box is empty (i.e., blank).
3. The mouse event is "button-down".

To do so, a new world must be created by choosing the appropriate child from the world's st. If any of the conditions above do not hold, then handler returns the given world.

The above problem analysis suggests that at least two auxiliary functions are needed. One is needed to convert the x and y coordinates into a bpos. Another is needed to search an st's children for the child st that is rooted at a given board. In all likelihood you may find it useful to use the place-on-board function left as an exercise above.

---

* Ex. 204 — Create data definitions and function templates for, ttt-x and ttt-y, valid x and y coordinates for the Tic Tac Toe game.

*** Ex. 205 — Design and implement process-mouse, a function to process mouse events.

** Ex. 206 — Design and implement mouse-tile that takes as input ttt-x and ttt-y values and returns the corresponding bpos corresponding to the clicked tile.

*** Ex. 207 — Design and implement get-st that takes as input a board and a lost and that returns the st in the given lost that has the given board at its root.

108.4 Design process-tick

The computer ought to make a move when the clock ticks and it is O's turn. If it is X's turn, then the given world ought to be returned. To make a move the program must decide the move to make and then extract the right child st from the given world.

The natural question that arises is how does the computer make a move. Two popular approaches to have a program make a move in a game are rule-based moves and heuristic-based moves. In the rule-based approach there is a rule that, given a board, decides what the next move ought to be. In the heuristic-based approach there is a function that assigns a score to each possible board after a move and the move with the best score is chosen. We shall pursue a rule-based approach for our version of Tic Tac Toe. In follow-up courses, you shall study the heuristic-based approach that is commonly used in Artificial Intelligence.

Think carefully about how you play Tic Tac Toe. It is fairly clear that if you can win you make the winning move. Otherwise, you determine if you can block and do so if possible. What if you cannot win or block? We need to decide what move the program ought to make. A reasonable strategy may be to play the center box if it is empty. Otherwise, play a blank corner. If all corners are taken, then play a middle space. This analysis means that we have a compound function with 5 conditions:

```
(cond [(can-o-win? a-board)        (make-o-win a-board)]
      [(can-o-block? a-board)      (make-o-block a-board)]
      [(center-empty? a-board)     (make-o-center a-board)]
      [(any-corner-empty? a-aboard) (make-o-corner a-board)]
      [else (make-o-mid a-board)])
```

The moves with the highest priorities must be tested for first (i.e., win then block) to guarantee they take precedence.

*** **Ex. 208** — Design and implement a function to make a computer (i.e., O) move based on the rule outlined above.

*** **Ex. 209** — Design and implement a function to process a clock tick.

***** **Ex. 210** — The rule to make a computer move outlined above does not consider creating or preventing the player from creating a fork. A fork is a board in which there are two winning moves. Redesign your function to make a computer move to take into account forking.

108.5 Design `game-over?`

The game is over if either player has won or if the board is full. A player has won if there are three of the same symbols on any row, column, or diagonal. A board is full if there are no 'Bs left in the board.

The function to draw the last world may simply be `draw-world`. A better design indicates the winning player or a draw.

** **Ex. 211** — Design and implement a function to detect when the game is over.

* **Ex. 212** — Design and implement a function to draw the last world by indicating the winner or a draw.

---

109 What Have We Learned in This Chapter?

The important lessons of Chap. 18 are summarized as follows:

- Data definitions that refer to each other are said to be mutually recursive.
- In a data definition, references to a different type of data, X, mean that in our code there needs to be a call to an X-processing function.
- For mutually recursive data, build nonrecursive instances first and then build instances that only depend on existing instances.
- To write a function for mutually recursive data, write a function for each data type assuming the functions to process the other data types exist.
- In a tree each node has an arbitrary number of children.
- Two popular ways to have a program make a move in a game are the rule-based approach and the heuristic-based approach.

- In the rule-based approach there is a rule that, given a board, decides what the next move ought to be.
- In the heuristic-based approach there is a function that assigns a score to each possible board after a move and the move with the best score is chosen.
- The use of heuristic functions is common in Artificial Intelligence.

Chapter 19
Processing Multiple Inputs of Arbitrary Size

Our focus up to know has mostly been on the design of functions that consume a single instance of data of arbitrary size. This chapter discusses how functions that consume multiple inputs of arbitrary size are designed. To simplify this initial discussion we shall focus on designing functions that consume two inputs of arbitrary size. How do you design such a function?

We outline three basic properties that you may establish once problem analysis is performed. These are:

- One input has the dominant role.
- The two inputs must be processed simultaneously.
- There is no clear relationship between the inputs.

If one of the inputs, say of type X, has a dominant role, then the function may be designed using the template for a function on X. You were exposed to this idea in Sect. 61 albeit to process data of finite size. If the two inputs must be processed at the same time, then pick one of the inputs and design the function using the template for a function on the type of the given input. If there is not a clear relationship between the inputs, then you need to analyze all possible combinations of the inputs' subtypes.

110 One Input Has a Dominant Role

Imagine that ISL+ did not include a function, append, to append two given lists. If the programming language you are using does not include a function, you need then you must design your own. How you design and implement a function to append two lists? How did the creators of ISL+ design the append function? We shall follow the steps of the design recipe to determine the answer.

© The Author(s), under exclusive license to Springer Nature Switzerland AG 2022   433
M. T. Morazán, *Animated Problem Solving*, Texts in Computer Science,
https://doi.org/10.1007/978-3-030-85091-3_19

We always start with problem analysis. We are given, say, L1 and L2. Ask yourself what the result of appending the two lists ought to look like. It is not difficult to see that a new list must be created that has all the elements of L1 followed by all the elements of L2. To add all the elements of L1 to the resulting list L1 must be traversed. Do we need to also traverse L2? As L1 is traversed cons is used to created a list that contains the first element of L1 and the result of appending the rest of L1 and L2. Consider what occurs with the last element of L1. This element must be consed with the result of appending the rest of L1, which is empty, and L2. What ought to be the result of appending empty with L2? Since L1 (i.e., empty) has no elements, nothing ought to appear before the elements of L2. In other words, L2 is the answer. Observe that L2 does not need to be traversed and, therefore, L1 plays a dominant role. This informs us that we ought to design this function around processing L1.

We shall be careful with the next step of the design recipe, data analysis, to make sure the design is sound. The types of the two inputs may be defined as (listof X) and (listof Y). Observe that the two inputs may or may not be of the same type. They are the same type (not value) when X = Y. Otherwise, they are of different types. The natural question to ask, therefore, is what is the type of the returned list? If X ≠ Y, then the result is neither of type (listof X) nor (listof Y). We know, however, that every element of the result list is either of type X or Y. This means there is variety among the elements of the result list. To capture this variety we need the following data definition:

```
An XY is either:
  1. X
  2. Y
```

Armed with this data definition, we can now write the returned type as (listof XY). Note that this means that every element of the returned list is either an X or a Y. It does not specify that all the X elements must appear before the Y elements. Such a specification is done by the purpose statement of the function.

We can now specialize the template for a function on X to write a function to append two lists. Start by writing sample instances for a (listof X) and (listof Y). For example, we may write:

```
;; Sample instances of (listof X), where X = number
(define LON1 '())
(define LON2 '(10 20 30 40))

;; Sample instances of (listof Y), where Y = string
(define LOS1 '())
(define LOS2 '("" "A" "BB"))
```

Following the design recipe, we next develop sample expressions for myappend based on the varieties of (listof X):

```
;; Sample expressions for myappend
(define LON1-LOS1-VAL LOS1)
(define LON1-LON2-VAL LON2)
(define LOS2-LOS1-VAL (cons (first LOS2)
                           (myappend (rest LOS2) LOS1)))
(define LON2-LOS2-VAL (cons (first LON2)
                           (myappend (rest LON2) LOS2)))
```

Observe that we test every possible combination of inputs' subtypes. As per our problem analysis if the first given list is empty then the answer is the second given list. Otherwise, a new list is created by consing the first element of the first given list to the result of appending the rest of the first given list and the second given list.

Abstracting over the sample expressions yields the following function:

```
;; (listof X) (listof Y) → (listof XY)
;; Purpose: Create a new list with members of the first given
;;          list followed by members of the second given list
(define (myappend L1 L2)
  (if (empty? L1)
      L2
      (cons (first L1) (myappend (rest L1) L2))))
```

Observe that the signature states the return type as the one we developed as part of data analysis. Further observe that the purpose statement specifies that a new list is created with the elements of L1 followed by the elements of L2.

Finally, test may be written as follows:

```
;; Tests using sample computations for myappend
(check-expect (myappend LON1 LOS1)  LON1-LOS1-VAL)
(check-expect (myappend LON1 LON2)  LON1-LON2-VAL)
(check-expect (myappend LOS2 LOS1)  LOS2-LOS1-VAL)
(check-expect (myappend LON2 LON2)  LON2-LOS2-VAL)

;; Tests using sample values for myappend
(check-expect (myappend '(#true #false) '(a b c))
              '(#true #false a b c))
(check-expect (myappend '(M) '(T M)) '(M T M))
```

Observe that the tests using sample values illustrate that the function works for lists of different sizes that both have and do not have the same types of elements. As always, the tests using sample computations illustrate that the function correctly computes the values of the sample expressions.

***Ex. 213** — Design and implement a function that takes as input a natural number, n, and a (listof X), L, and that returns a list with n copies of L.

***Ex. 214** — Design and implement a predicate to determine if all the elements of a given list are members of a second given list. You may find the ISL+ function member? useful.

****Ex. 215** — Design and implement a function that takes as input a (btof X), btx, and a (listof X), L, of length 2 and that returns btx with all occurrences of the first element of L substituted with the second element of L.

***Ex. 216** — Design and implement a function that takes as input two natural numbers and that returns the product of the two numbers. Your function may not use * and must use +. Recall, for example, that 4 * 3 = 4 + 4 + 4.

111 Inputs Must Be Processed Simultaneously

Consider the problem of multiplying corresponding numbers in two lists of numbers and returning a list of the products. This operation is useful to solve the following problems:

1. Compute employees' gross pay from a list of hours worked and a list of hourly rates. The ith number of hours worked is paid using the ith hourly rate.
2. Compute the total inventory value of the different items in a store from a list of item quantities and a list of item prices. Each item in the ith quantity has the ith price.

Observe that for both problems the ith elements of each list must be multiplied to compute a list of products. Further observe that both lists must be of the same size.

For this type of problem, we cannot process one of the lists and simply return the other list when the first list is processed. In other words, neither list is dominant. Note that both lists must be processed at the same time. As the lists are traversed, the first element of both lists is multiplied and consed to the result of processing the rest of both lists. That is, the processing of the lists is *synchronized*. When the processing of two instances of data of arbitrary size is synchronized, the function may be designed using the template for functions on the type of either input. There is, however, a significant difference. The recursive call must be made using the selector for the substructure of both inputs. For example, the recursive call for the synchronized processing of two list of numbers, L1 and L2, is made with (rest L1) and (rest L2).

Given that to multiply corresponding numbers the two lists must be of the same size, the lists are either both empty or they are both not empty. What is the answer if the lists are empty? There are no corresponding numbers to multiply. Therefore, the result must be the empty list. If the two lists are not empty, then this is when the product of first element of each list is consed to the result of multiplying the rest of both lists. The function may be designed by specializing the template for a function on a (listof number).

Based on our problem analysis we can write sample instances and sample expressions as follows:

```
;; Sample instances of lon
(define ELON '())
(define HOURS-WORKED '(1 23 39 27))
(define HOURLY-RATES '(13 22 18 34))
(define QUANTITIES   '(10 3 86 27 8))
(define PRICES       '(80 50 5 10 20))


;; Sample expressions for mlist
(define NOTHING '())
(define GROSSPAY
        (cons (* (first HOURS-WORKED) (first HOURLY-RATES))
              (mlist (rest HOURS-WORKED) (rest HOURLY-RATES))))


(define TOTALS
        (cons (* (first QUANTITIES) (first PRICES))
              (mlist (rest QUANTITIES) (rest PRICES))))
```

The first sample expression illustrates that the result is empty when the given lists are empty. The two other sample expressions illustrate that for non-empty lists a new list is constructed using the product of the first element of each list and recursively processing the rest of both lists.

Abstracting over the sample expressions yields the following function:

```
;; (listof num) (listof num) → (listof num)
;; Purpose: Return a list with the products of corresponding
;;          elements in the given lists
;; Assumption: The given lists are of the same length
(define (mlist L1 L2)
  (if (empty? L1)
      '()
      (cons (* (first L1) (first L2))
            (mlist (rest L1) (rest L2)))))
```

Observe that the assumption that the two lists are of the same size is clearly indicated. This informs any reader of the code that the function is specifically designed for two lists of the same size.

The function may be tested as follows:

```
;; Tests using sample computations for mlist
(check-expect (mlist ELON            '())           NOTHING)
(check-expect (mlist HOURS-WORKED HOURLY-RATES) GROSSPAY)
(check-expect (mlist QUANTITIES    PRICES)      TOTALS)

;; Tests using sample values for mlist
(check-expect (mlist '(1 2 3) '(1 2 3)) '(1 4 9))
```

In addition to illustrating that the function computes the expected values, the second and third tests using sample computations illustrate some of the practical purposes of `mlist`: computing gross pay and inventory value. The test using a sample value illustrates how to compute the squares of a list of numbers.

---

* **Ex. 217** — Design and implement a function that takes as input two (`listof number`) and that returns a (`listof number`) containing the sums of corresponding numbers in the given list.

** **Ex. 218** — Redesign and re-implement `mlist` by removing the assumption that both lists are of the same size. The function ought to terminate when either list is empty.

** **Ex. 219** — Design and implement a function that takes as input a list of first names and a list of last names and that returns a list of full names.

**** **Ex. 220** — Design and implement a function that takes as input two (`listof Boolean`) and that returns a (`listof Boolean`) indicating if the corresponding elements in the given lists are the same.

**** **Ex. 221** — Design and implement a function that takes as input two (`listof number`) and that returns an intertwined list of numbers. For example, given '(1 3 5) and '(2 4 6) the function returns '(1 2 3 4 5 6).

---

112 No Clear Relationship Between the Inputs

It is not uncommon to have more than one complex input and not be able to identify a relationship between the inputs. That is, neither input dominates the other and the processing of the inputs is not synchronized. In such cases, it is necessary to analyze each possible combination of the inputs' subtypes. A conditional expression is needed in which the number of conditions is equal to the number of possible input subtype combinations. Each stanza in the conditional expression tests for a specific combination of subtypes. For instance, consider a function that processes a (`listof X`) and a natural number. Each of these types has two subtypes. Thus, there are four possible subtype combinations. The needed conditional expression identifies the combination that the inputs represent. Assuming the list is a-lox and the natural number is a-natnum, the needed conditional expression for the function called f may be outlined as follows:

```
(cond [(and (empty? a-lox) (zero? a-natnum))             ...]
      [(and (empty? a-lox) (not (zero? a-natnum))) ...]
      [(and (cons? a-lox) (zero? a-natnum))             ...]
      [else ...(f a-lox (sub1 n))...
            ...(f (rest a-lox) n)...
            ...(f (rest a-lox) (sub1 n))...])
```

Observe that this is a divide and conquer strategy. The problem of processing (listof X) and a natural number is divided into four smaller subproblems. The solution for each subproblem is developed independently. In the case when a-lox is not empty and a-natnum is not zero the recursive call to f may be done with the substructure of either input or the substructure of both inputs. This is why the else clause of the conditional has three different expressions that may be used for the recursive call. As a designer you must decide which of these expressions to use (for any recursive call in f). It is important to note that this design strategy may always be used when processing more than one input of arbitrary size.

Consider the problem of merging two lists of numbers sorted in non-decreasing order. The goal is to create a sorted list that only contains all the elements of the given lists. For example, given '(15 31 67) and '(22 44 87 100) the resulting list is '(15 22 31 44 67 87 100). Ask yourself if one list dominates the other. Clearly, this is not the case because the next element to add to the result list may come from either of the given lists. That is, the first element of the result list may be the first element of the first given list or the first element of the second given list. Now, we know that both lists must be processed. Ask you yourself if the processing of the lists must be synchronized. Once again, the answer is no because the first element of the result may come from either given list.

We are left to conclude that there is no clear relationship between the inputs. This means processing the inputs by determining the subtype combination of the given inputs. If the function is called merge and the inputs are called sl1 and sl2, then the needed conditional expression is outlined as follows:

```
(cond [(and (empty? sl1) (empty? sl2)) ...]
      [(and (empty? sl1) (cons? sl2))   ...]
      [(and (cons? sl1)  (empty? sl2)) ...]
      [else ...(merge sl1          (rest sl2))...
            ...(merge (rest sl1) sl2)...
            ...(merge (rest sl1) (rest sl2)) ...])])
```

We can now reason about each case in the conditional independently. If both given lists are empty, then there is nothing to add to the result and the answer is '(). If only one of the lists is empty, then only the elements in the other list must be added. Therefore, the answer is the other list. If both lists are not empty, then a decision must be made to either create a new list using sl1's or sl2's first element. The element chosen must be the smaller of the two. The recursive call, therefore, is made with the rest of the list whose first element is added to the result and the other list.

Let us now use the following instances of a (listof number) to develop our design and implementation:

```
;; Sample instances of (listof number)
(define ELON '())
(define SL1  '(1 22 30))
(define SL2  '(13 22 108 346))
(define SL3  '(-89 -50 0 6 90))
(define SL4  '(-240))
```

We start by writing sample expressions for each of the possible subtype combinations. If both given lists are empty, the answer is the empty list. We define a sample expression as follows:

```
;; Sample expressions for merge
(define ELON-ELON-VAL '())
```

If only one of the given lists is empty, then the answer is the other list. We define sample expressions as follows:

```
(define ELON-SL1-VAL SL1)
(define ELON-SL2-VAL SL2)
(define SL3-ELON-VAL SL3)
(define SL4-ELON-VAL SL4)
```

The first two sample expressions illustrate the answer when the first given list is empty. The second two sample expressions illustrate the answer when the second given list is empty. For the final combination (i.e., when both lists are not empty) we need examples that make the first element of the result the first element of the first given list and examples that make the first element of the result the first element of the second given list. We may write the following sample expressions:

```
(define SL1-SL2-VAL (cons (first SL1) (merge (rest SL1) SL2)))
(define SL3-SL2-VAL (cons (first SL3) (merge (rest SL3) SL2)))
(define SL3-SL4-VAL (cons (first SL4) (merge SL3 (rest SL4))))
(define SL1-SL4-VAL (cons (first SL4) (merge SL1 (rest SL4))))
```

The first two sample expressions take the first element of the first given list and the second two sample expressions take the first element of the second given list. Observe that the recursive call is always made with the rest of the list whose first element is added to the result and with the other list untouched. It ought to be clear that the processing of the lists is not synchronized.

To write the function definition we abstract over the sample expressions for each subtype combination. This process yields the following function:

```
;; (listof num) (listof num) → (listof num)
;; Purpose: Return a list sorted in nondecreasing order that
;;          only contains all the elements of the given lists
;; Assumption: Given lists are sorted in nondecreasing order
(define (merge sl1 sl2)
  (cond [(and (empty? sl1) (empty? sl2)) '()]
        [(and (empty? sl1) (cons? sl2))  sl2]
        [(and (cons? sl1)  (empty? sl2)) sl1]
        [else (if (<= (first sl1) (first sl2))
                  (cons (first sl1) (merge (rest sl1) sl2))
                  (cons (first sl2) (merge sl1 (rest sl2))))]))
```

Observe that when both given lists are not empty a conditional expression is used to determine from which list to take the first of the result. Further observe that the recursive call is always done with the rest of the list from which the first element is selected and the other list.

All conditions must be tested including the two in the else stanza of the cond-expression. The tests may be written as follows:

```
;; Tests using sample computations for merge
(check-expect (merge ELON ELON) ELON-ELON-VAL)
(check-expect (merge ELON SL1)  ELON-SL1-VAL)
(check-expect (merge ELON SL2)  ELON-SL2-VAL)
(check-expect (merge SL3 ELON)  SL3-ELON-VAL)
(check-expect (merge SL4 ELON)  SL4-ELON-VAL)
(check-expect (merge SL1 SL2)   SL1-SL2-VAL)
(check-expect (merge SL3 SL2)   SL3-SL2-VAL)
(check-expect (merge SL3 SL4)   SL3-SL4-VAL)
(check-expect (merge SL1 SL4)   SL1-SL4-VAL)

;; Tests using sample values for merge
(check-expect (merge '() '()) '())
(check-expect (merge '() '(8 77)) '(8 77))
(check-expect (merge '(43 67 91) '())  '(43 67 91))
(check-expect (merge '(15 31 67) '(22 44 87 100))
                     '(15 22 31 44 67 87 100))
(check-expect (merge '(66 99) '(1 56 83)) '(1 56 66 83 99))
```

The tests using sample computations are organized in the same manner as the conditional expression in merge. The first test is for when both given lists are empty. The second and third tests are for when only the first given list is empty. The next two tests are for when only the second given list is empty. The final four tests are for when both given lists are not empty. Of these, the first two are for when the first given list's first element is used to construct the result. The last two are for when the second given list's first element is used to construct the result. The tests using sample values are organized in the same order, but there is only a single test for each possible condition.

*** **Ex. 222** — Design and implement a function that extracts the nth element of a list. The elements of the list are numbered 0 to n-1. If there is no n^{th} element, then the function ought to throw an error. You may not use `list-ref` in your solution.

* **Ex. 223** — Design and implement a function that merges two lists of numbers sorted in non-decreasing order.

*** **Ex. 224** — Design and implement a function that consumes two (`listof Boolean`) and intertwines them based on the first element of each list. If the first elements are the same, then put the first element of the first list in the result. Otherwise, put the first element of the second list in the result. If either given input is empty, nothing more is added to the result. For example, given `'(#true #true #true #false #false)` and `'(#true #false #false)` the result is `'(#true #true #true #true #false #false)`.

*** **Ex. 225** — Design and implement a function that takes as input two (`listof number`) and a Boolean and that returns an intertwined list of numbers. For example, given `'(1 3 5)` and `'(2 4 6)` the function returns `'(1 2 3 4 5 6)`. The Boolean input is used to decide from which given list to add its first element to the result. If the Boolean is true, take the first element from the first list. Otherwise, take the first element from the second list. Do you prefer this version of the function over the version that synchronizes the processing of the lists? Why or why not?

113 What Have We Learned in This Chapter?

The important lessons of Chap. 19 are summarized as follows:

- Three common scenarios that may be identified when processing multiple instances of data of arbitrary size are: one input dominates the other, the processing of the inputs must be synchronized, and there is no clear relationship between the inputs.
- If one input of type X dominates the other inputs, then specialize the template for a function on X.
- If processing inputs of type X and Y must be synchronized, specialize either the template for a function on X or the template for a function on Y, but make recursive calls using the substructure of both inputs.
- If there is no clear relationship between the inputs, use a conditional to determine which combination of input subtypes is faced and independently formulate the answer for each possible subtype combination.
- Subtype combination analysis may always be used when processing more than one input of arbitrary size.
- Sometimes a data definition for the type returned by a function must be defined.

Part IV
Abstraction

Chapter 20
Functional Abstraction

Chapter 3 discusses how to abstract over similar expressions to eliminate repetitions, which leads to the development of functions. Section 68 discusses how to eliminate repetitions among data definitions, which leads to the development of generic data definitions. This chapter discusses *functional abstraction*. In other words, it discusses how to eliminate repetitions among functions. This leads to powerful *abstract functions* (or generic functions) that can perform many different jobs for us. It will also conceptually change the meaning of data in your mind. As we shall see functions are data just like a number, a list, and an image are data. Thus, you will soon realize that the conceptual line between data and functions is imaginary.

If you already have code that works, why would you want to perform abstraction to eliminate differences? The answer is twofold. On the one side there are practical programming reasons. By eliminating repetition among functions you make your code easier to understand and maintain, shorter, and more elegant. Collectively this means that it becomes easier to make improvements or necessary changes in the future. On the other side it allows you to think about solutions to problems more abstractly, thus making problem solving and programming easier.

To illustrate the process consider the functions displayed in Fig. 92. These are functions to determine, correspondingly, if `'laptop` and `'pen` are contained in a `(listof symbol)`. Observe that the two functions are nearly identical. They only vary in the use of the symbol `'laptop` or `'pen`. Recall that the body of each function is an expression and a variable is used to abstract away differences among expressions to create functions. This suggest the same ought to happen here. That is, use a variable to represent the symbol that varies and create a new *abstract function* that has a parameter for this varying symbol. The other parameter in the original functions is still needed and all the parameters (including the new one for the varying

M. T. Morazán, *Animated Problem Solving*, Texts in Computer Science,
https://doi.org/10.1007/978-3-030-85091-3_20

Fig. 92 Two very similar functions

```
;; contains-laptop?: (listof symbol) → Boolean
;; Purpose: Determine if the given list contains 'laptop
(define (contains-laptop? a-los)
  (and (not (empty a-los))
       (or (symbol=? (first a-los) 'laptop)
           (contains-laptop? (rest a-los)))))

;; contains-pen?: (listof symbol) → Boolean
;; Purpose: Determine if the given list contains 'pen
(define (contains-pen? a-los)
  (and (not (empty a-los))
       (or (symbol=? (first a-los) 'pen)
           (contains-pen? (rest a-los)))))
```

symbol) are used in the body of the abstract function. This abstraction step yields the following function:

```
;; contains?: symbol (listof symbol) → Boolean
;; Purpose: Determine if the given list contains the
;;            given symbol
(define (contains? a-symbol a-los)
  (and (not (empty a-los))
       (or (symbol=? (first a-los) a-symbol)
           (contains? a-symbol (rest a-los)))))
```

We can now use the abstract function to refactor contains-laptop? and contains-pen? as follows:

```
;; contains-laptop?: (listof symbol) → Boolean
;; Purpose: Determine if the given list contains 'laptop
(define (contains-laptop? a-los) (contains? 'laptop a-los))

;; contains-pen?: (listof symbol) → Boolean
;; Purpose: Determine if the given list contains 'pen
(define (contains-pen? a-los) (contains? 'pen a-los))
```

Observe how much shorter and readable these functions are now. Furthermore, observe that now there is only one recursive function instead of two. The benefit of the abstract function goes even further. It can be used to write functions to determine if a (listof symbol) contains 'book, 'keys, and 'money as follows:

```
;; contains-book?: (listof symbol) → Boolean
;; Purpose: Determine if the given list contains 'book
(define (contains-book? a-los) (contains? 'book a-los))

;; contains-keys?: (listof symbol) → Boolean
;; Purpose: Determine if the given list contains 'keys
(define (contains-keys? a-los) (contains? 'keys a-los))
```

```
;; contains-money?: (listof symbol) → Boolean
;; Purpose: Determine if the given list contains 'money
(define (contains-money? a-los) (contains? 'money a-los))
```

This illustrates the power of abstract functions. They can perform many different tasks that allows us to simplify code design and development. Using abstract functions means that we need to write less code and may have fewer bugs.

** **Ex. 226** — Write tests for `contains?`.

* **Ex. 227** — Write tests for `contains-laptop?`, `contains-pen?`, `contains-book?`, `contains-keys?`, and `contains-money?`.

---

114 A Design Recipe for Abstraction

The goal for functional abstraction is to abstract over similar expressions in the body of different functions with a similar number of parameters. The process followed to abstract over `contains-laptop?` and `contains-pen?` may be generalized into the following design recipe for functional abstraction:

Mark Differences   Compare and mark the differences in the bodies of the functions.

Create the Abstraction   Define an abstract function that has the same number of parameters as the functions abstracted over plus a parameter for every difference identified in the previous step. The body of the abstract function references the parameters for the differences instead of the values found in the functions abstracted over. Make sure the signature takes into account that the new parameters' types may vary making the function generic.

Refactor   Refactor the functions abstracted over to use the abstract function.

The first step asks you to identify the significant differences in the expressions that constitute the bodies of the functions. This means you ought to identify different values. It does not mean differences in function or variable names. The second step asks you to define the abstract function. This requires you to pick a descriptive name for the function. The parameter list must include a parameter for each difference and a set of parameters representing the parameters in the functions abstracted over. The third step asks you to refactor the bodies of the functions abstracted over to use the new abstract function. The tests for these refactored functions unchanged.

115 Functions as Values

To illustrate the design recipe for abstraction in practice consider computing the slope of a secant line. A secant line crosses the graph of a function, $f(x)$, at exactly two points: $(x_1, f(x_1))$ and $(x_2, f(x_2))$. When the distance between x_1 and x_2

Fig. 93 Functions for the slope of the secant line

```
;; number number → number
;; Purpose: Compute slope of secant line for given x-values for f(x) = x^2
(define (x^2-sec-slope x1 x2) (/ (- (sqr x2) (sqr x1)) (- x2 x1)))


;; Sample expressions for x^2-sec-slope
(define MSEC1 (/ (- (sqr 4) (sqr 2)) (- 4 2)))
(define MSEC2 (/ (- (sqr 3.75) (sqr -2.03)) (- 3.75 -2.03)))


;; Tests using sample computations for x^2-sec-slope
(check-within (x^2-sec-slope 2 4)        MSEC1 0.01)
(check-within (x^2-sec-slope -2.03 3.75) MSEC2 0.01)


;; Tests using sample values for x^2-sec-slope
(check-within (x^2-sec-slope 1.5 3.2) 4.7 0.01)


;; number number → number
;; Purpose: Compute slope of the secant line for given x-values
;;          for f(x)= x^3
(define (x^3-sec-slope x1 x2) (/ (- (cube x2) (cube x1)) (- x2 x1)))


;; Sample expressions for x^2-sec-slope
(define MSEC3 (/ (- (cube 5)    (cube 1))    (- 5 1)))
(define MSEC4 (/ (- (cube 10.1) (cube -4.6)) (- 10.1 -4.6)))


;; Tests using sample computations for x^3-sec-slope
(check-within (x^3-sec-slope 1 5)      MSEC3 0.01)
(check-within (x^3-sec-slope -4.6 10.1) MSEC4 0.01)


;; Tests using sample values for x^3-sec-slope
(check-within (x^3-sec-slope 1.5 3.2) 17.29 0.01)
```

is very small, the slope of the secant line may be used as an approximation for the slope of f(x) at the midpoint between the two points. The slope of a (secant) line is fairly easy to compute as you learned in your high school algebra course:

$$m = \frac{fx_2 - fx_1}{x_2 - x_1}$$

This formula informs us that to compute the slope of the secant line we need two x-values. Figure 93 displays two functions, x^2-sec-slope and x^3-sec-slope, to compute the slope of the secant line, respectively, for $f(x) = x^2$ and $f(x) = x^3$.[26]

Observe that x^2-sec-slope and x^3-sec-slope are very similar and, therefore, good candidates for abstraction. Following the steps of the design recipe for abstraction we find that the only significant difference is the function that is applied to an x-value. In x^2-sec-slope sqr is used and in x^3-sec-slope cube is used. There is something new to learn here. The differences are functions. This means that functions must be data just like a natural number and a posn are data.

_____

[26] The design of a function to cube its input is found in Sect. 38.

In programming languages that provide support for functions as data we say that the language has *first-class functions*. Among other things this means that functions may be passed as arguments to a function. ISL+ is one such language and, therefore, we may proceed with the process of functional abstraction.

The next step of the design recipe is to create an abstract function. For our current problem this means that the abstract function needs a parameter for the single difference, say f, and two parameters for the two x-values (as x^2-sec-slope and x^3-sec-slope have). To write this function, however, we need to denote a function in the signature. This is accomplished by writing a signature for the type of function the parameter denotes. In this case both $f(x) = x^2$ and $f(x) = x^3$ have the same signature: number number → number. The result of this step of the design recipe for abstraction is

```
;; (number → number) number number → number
;; Purpose: Approximate the slope of the secant line between
;;          the given x-values for the given function
(define (f-sec-slope f x1 x2) (/ (- (f x2) (f x1)) (- x2 x1)))
```

Observe that parentheses are placed around function values in the signature to aid readability. It makes it clear that f-sec-slope returns a number. The body of the function looks the same as the bodies of x^2-sec-slope and x^3-sec-slope except that references to sqr and cube are now references to the parameter f.

The third step of the design recipe has refactor x^2-sec-slope and x^3-sec-slope to use f-sec-slope. This means, in essence, that each of these functions must call f-sec-slope with the right arguments. In practical terms, this means x^2-sec-slope must make the call with sqr and the x-values it gets as input and x^3-sec-slope must make the call with cube and the x-values it gets as input. The result of this step is

```
;; number number → number
;; Purpose: Approximate the slope of the secant line between
;;          the given x-values for f(x) = x^2
(define (x^2-secant-slope x1 x2) (f-sec-slope sqr x1 x2))
```

```
;; number number → number
;; Purpose: Approximate the slope of the secant line between
;;          the given x-values for f(x) = x^3
(define (x^3-secant-slope x1 x2) (f-sec-slope cube x1 x2))
```

Observe that nothing changes except the bodies of the functions. This includes the tests for both functions. Go ahead and run the tests to make sure they all pass.

By now you may find it strange that this discussion has ignored writing tests for abstract functions. There is a good reason for this. When an abstract function returns a value that is not a function we can write tests for it. However, we do not for two reasons. The first is the refactoring performed on the functions that are abstracted. These refactored functions use the abstract function and have tests. If the testing is thorough, bugs in the abstract function will be caught by the existing tests. More importantly, however, is the fact that first-class functions push programmers against the limits of what is possible. Chapter 22 discusses how a function may be returned as the value of a function just like a string or a number may be returned. To directly test such a function the returned function and another function must be proven equivalent. As you will learn in a Formal Languages and Automata Theory course or a Computability course, testing the equivalence of functions is an *unsolvable problem*. That is, there is no solution to the problem of determining if two functions are equivalent. It is for this reason that abstract functions are tested through the functions that make use of them.

116 Abstraction Over List-Processing Functions

Chapter 13 discusses several common operations over lists. If you think about it for a minute, it is not unreasonable to expect functions that perform the same operation for different types of lists to be almost identical. If this is the case, then they are good candidates for abstraction. Sometimes, however, the expressions in the bodies of these functions may not be the same. In such cases code refactoring may be used to make the functions almost identical before performing functional abstraction.

This section presents the abstraction over functions that perform common list-processing operations. Specifically, this section looks at the operations outlined in Chap. 13: list summarizing, list searching, list ORing, list ANDing, list mapping, list filtering, and list sorting.

116.1 List Summarizing

In Sect. 72 the following functions to sum and to compute the length of a list of quiz grades are developed:

```
;; (listof quizgrade) → number
;; Purpose: To compute the sum of the given
;;          (listof quizgrade)
(define (sum-loq a-loq)
  (if (empty? a-loq)
      0
      (+ (first a-loq) (sum-loq (rest a-loq))))))

;; (listof quizgrade) → number
;; Purpose: To compute the length of the given
;;          (listof quizgrade)
(define (length-loq a-loq)
  (if (empty? a-loq)
      0
      (+ 1 (length-loq (rest a-loq))))))
```

In the same section two different exercises ask you to design and implement a function to compute the product of a list of numbers and a function to append the strings in a list of strings. Your solutions likely look like this:

```
;; (listof number) → number
;; Purpose: Compute the product of the given (listof number)
(define (product-lon a-lon)
  (if (empty? a-lon)
      1
      (* (first a-lon) (product-lon (rest a-lon)))))

;; (listof string) → string
;; Purpose: Append the strings in the given (listof string)
(define (append-los a-lostr)
  (if (empty? a-lostr)
      ""
      (string-append (first a-lostr)
                     (append-los (rest a-lostr)))))
```

We can immediately observe that all four functions are very similar, but not structurally identical. Observe that only length-loq does not explicitly use the first element of the list. Instead of having an application expression involving the first list element it has the constant expression 1.

This is a situation where code refactoring may be useful to create similarities. How can length-loq use its first element? At first glance it may seem that it cannot. If you think about it carefully, however, the first element of the list given to length-loq always contributes 1 to its length. This represents a constant function like f(x) = 1. Therefore, length-loq may be refactored to

```
;; X → 1
;; Purpose: Return 1
(define (constant-f1 an-x) 1)

;; loq → number
;; Purpose: To compute the length of the given loq
(define (length-loq a-loq)
  (if (empty? a-loq)
      0
      (+ (constant-f1 (first a-loq))
         (length-loq (rest a-loq)))))
```

Now, length-loq uses its first element. It is still, however, different from the other 3 functions. It applies a function to its first element and the other 3 functions use the first element directly.

To perform functional abstraction we need all 4 functions abstracted over to apply a function to the first element of the given list. That is, sum-loq, product-lon, and append-los need to apply a function to their first list element. This function must return the value it gets as input. In Mathematics, such a function is known as the identity function: $f(x) = x$. We can implement the identity function and refactor the three functions as follows:

```
;; X → X
;; Purpose: Return the given input
(define (id an-x) an-x)

;; (listof quizgrade) → number
;; Purpose: Compute the sum of the given
;;          (listof quizgrade)
(define (sum-loq a-loq)
  (if (empty? a-loq)
      0
      (+ (id (first a-loq)) (sum-loq (rest a-loq)))))

;; (listof number) → number
;; Purpose: Compute the product of the given
;;          (listof number)
(define (product-lon a-lon)
  (if (empty? a-lon)
      1
      (* (id (first a-lon)) (product-lon (rest a-lon)))))

;; (listof string) → string
;; Purpose: Append the strings in the given
;;          (listof string)
(define (append-los a-lostr)
  (if (empty? a-lostr)
      ""
      (string-append (id (first a-lostr))
                     (append-los (rest a-lostr)))))
```

All four functions now look almost identical. That is, their structure is the same because they use the same types of expressions. This means they are good candidates for abstraction.

The first step is to mark the differences. There are three differences among the four functions: the base value returned when the given list is empty, the function applied to the first element of the list, and the function used to combine the value obtained from the first element of the given list and the value obtained from recursively processing the rest of the given list.

Armed with a clear understanding of the differences we may sketch the abstract function as follows:

```
;; ? (? → ?) (? ? → ?) (listof ?) → ?
;; Purpose: Summarize given list
(define (accum base-val ffirst comb a-lox)
  (if (empty? a-lox)
      base-val
      (comb (ffirst (first a-lox))
            (accum base-val ffirst comb (rest a-lox)))))
```

Observe that the abstract function preserves the structure of the functions abstracted over. That is, it uses the same type of expressions in its body. The question that remains is the signature of the abstract function. The types of lists processed by the functions abstracted over vary. Let us denote the type of list processed by the abstract as (listof X). This yields the following partial signature:

```
? (? → ?) (? ? → ?) (listof X) → ?
```

If the elements of the given list are of type X, then the input to the function applied to the first element of the list must be also of type X. Therefore, the partial signature now is

```
? (X → ?) (? ? → ?) (listof X) → ?
```

Observe that the returned type of the functions abstracted over varies. Let us denoted this type as Z making the partial signature:

```
? (X → ?) (? ? → ?) (listof X) → Z
```

Whenever the abstract returns a value, it must be of type Z. This means that the base value and the value returned by the combining function must also be Z. These observations allow us to make the partial signature:

```
Z (X → ?) (? ? → Z) (listof X) → Z
```

Observe that the result of the recursive call in the abstract function is the second input to the combining function. Thus, the partial signature now is

```
Z (X → ?) (? Z → Z) (listof X) → Z
```

Observe that the type of value returned by the function applied to the first element of the list varies in the functions abstracted over. Furthermore, this value is the first input to the combining function. If we denote its type as Y, the signature for accum is

```
Z (X → Y) (Y Z → Z) (listof X) → Z
```

Finally, note that the signature defines a generic function. That is, the types X, Y, and Z are not known until the function receives its input. Just like functions have parameters signatures also have parameters. For functions the parameters must be declared. We shall adopt the same policy for signatures. To declare type parameters for signatures we shall write the type variables inside angled brackets before the signature. The signature for `accum` is

```
<X Y Z> Z (X → Y) (Y Z → Z) (listof X) → Z
```

This signature informs any reader of our code that the types represented by X, Y, and Z only become known when arguments are provided to `accum`.

The final step is to refactor the functions abstracted over to use the abstract function. The result of this step is

```
;; (listof quizgrade) → number
;; Purpose: To compute the length of the given
;;          (listof quizgrade)
(define (length-loq a-loq) (accum 0 constant-f1 + a-loq))

;; (listof quizgrade) → number
;; Purpose: To compute the sum of the given
;;          (listof quizgrade)
(define (sum-loq a-loq) (accum 0 id + a-loq))

;; (listof number) → number
;; Purpose: To compute the product of the given
;;          (listof number)
(define (product-lon a-lon) (accum 1 id * a-lon))

;; (listof string) → string
;; Purpose: To append the strings in the given
;;          (listof string)
(define (append-los a-lostr)
   (accum "" id string-append a-lostr))
```

Observe that the abstract function is always given as input the values used in the original functions. Is the abstract function properly used? At the very least the arguments provided to `accum` must satisfy `accum`'s signature. Let us consider the call to `accum` in `product-lon`. These are the types of the arguments:

```
base-val: number                   ffirst: (number → number)
   comb: (number number → number)  a-lox: (listof number)
```

If we let X = Y = Z = number, we may rewrite the types of the arguments as follows:

```
base-val: Z            ffirst: (X → Y)
   comb: (Y Z → Z)     a-lox: (listof X)
```

Observe that the types of the arguments satisfy the types expected by `accum`'s signature. In accordance with this new convention, the proper way to write `id` is

```
;; <X> X → X
;; Purpose: Return the given input
(define (id an-x) an-x)
```

Fig. 94 A function to extract the X-values from a (`listof posn`)

```
;; Sample instances of (listof posn)
(define ELOP '())
(define LOP1 (list (make-posn 1 9) (make-posn 2 8)
                   (make-posn 3 7) (make-posn 4 6))))

;; (listof posn) → lon
;; Purpose: To extract the x-values in the given list of posns
(define (get-xs-lop a-lop) (accum '() posn-x cons a-lop))

;; Sample expressions for get-xs-lop
(define ELOP-VAL (accum '() posn-x cons ELOP))
(define LOP1-VAL (accum '() posn-x cons LOP1))

;; Tests using sample computations for get-xs-lop
(check-expect (get-xs-lop ELOP) ELOP-VAL)
(check-expect (get-xs-lop LOP1) LOP1-VAL)

;; Tests using sample values for get-xs-lop
(check-expect (get-xs-lop (list (make-posn -10 2) (make-posn -5 7)))
              '(-10 -5))
```

Take time to appreciate what has been achieved by using abstraction. The most obvious achievement is that instead of having 4 recursive functions there is only one recursive function (i.e., the abstract function). This makes the code shorter and more elegant. Elegance in this case refers to using a common function to accumulate (thus the name `accum`) the summarizing value being computed. It is also noteworthy that tests do not have to be rewritten for the functions abstracted over. Go ahead and run your tests to verify that they all pass. After refactoring, however, the sample expressions no longer reflect the expressions abstracted over to write the bodies of the functions. We are now using a new way (i.e., the abstract function) to compute the same value.

The most important achievement, however, is that we now have a powerful function to perform list-summarizing computations that may be directly used to solve other problems. Figure 94 displays the solution to extracting the x-values from a (`listof posn`). Observe that the sample expressions use `accum`. That is, `get-xs-lop` is directly designed using our abstract function. There is no need to design a recursive function because the needed recursion is done by `accum`.

---

* **Ex. 228** — Design and implement a nonrecursive function to extract the y-values of a (`listof posn`).

*** **Ex. 229** — Design and implement a nonrecursive function to make a copy of a given (`listof X`).

*** **Ex. 230** — Design and implement a nonrecursive function to find the maximum of a non-empty list of natural numbers.

**** **Ex. 231** — Design and implement a nonrecursive function to count the number of strings that have a length less than 5 in a given list of strings.

**** **Ex. 232** — Design and implement a nonrecursive function that only uses accum as an auxiliary function to compute the average of a given non-empty list of numbers.

*** **Ex. 233** — Argue that the calls to accum in length-loq, sum-loq, and append-lostr satisfy accum's signature.

116.2 List Searching

Section 73 discusses the design of the following function:

```
;; number (listof number) → (listof number)
;; Purpose: To return the sublist of the given lon that starts
;;          with the first instance of given number.
(define (xsublist-lon x a-lon)
  (cond [(empty? a-lon)            '()]
        [(equal? x (first a-lon)) a-lon]
        [else (xsublist-lon x (rest a-lon))]))
```

It is not difficult to now design a function that returns the sublist of a given list of symbols that starts with the first instance of a symbol that is not equal to a given symbol. The resulting function definition may be implemented as

```
;; symbol (listof symbol) → (listof symbol)
;; Purpose: To return the sublist of the given list that starts
;;          with the first symbol not equal to given symbol.
(define (nonxsublist-los x a-los)
  (cond [(empty? a-los)                  '()]
        [(not (equal? x (first a-los))) a-los]
        [else (notxsublist-los x (rest a-los))]))
```

Structurally these functions are almost the same. The only structural difference is the function composition in nonxsublist-los's second condition. This means we need to refactor the code, if possible, to make it a two-argument application expression as in xsublist-lon.

Recall from Mathematics that $(g \circ h)(x) = g(h(x))$. This means that any expression for a function composition may be refactored into an expression that applies a new function (namely $(g \circ h)(x)$). For this problem we need to design a function to compute the negation of the equal? function. The result of this design is

Fig. 95 The function for the complement of equals?

```
;; <A B> A B → Boolean
;; Purpose: To determine is the given values are not equal?
(define (not-equal? v1 v2) (not (eq? v1 v2)))

;; Sample expressions for not-equal?
(define VAL1 (not (equal? 5 3)))
(define VAL2 (not (equal? '(1 2) '(1 2))))

;; Tests using sample computations for not-equal?
(check-expect (not-equal? 5 3)            VAL1)
(check-expect (not-equal? '(1 2) '(1 2)) VAL2)

;; Tests using sample values for not-equal?
(check-expect (not-equal? "MATTHIAS" "SHRIRAM") #true)
(check-expect (not-equal? (make-posn (sub1 1) 10) (make-posn 0 (+ 5 5)))
              #false)
```

displayed in Fig. 95. Armed with this function nonxsublist-lon may be refactored to

```
;; symbol (listof symbol) → (listof symbol)
;; Purpose: To return the sublist of the given list that starts
;;          with the first symbol not equal to given symbol.
(define (nonxsublist-los x a-los)
  (cond [(empty? a-los)          '()]
        [(not-equal? x (first a-los)) a-los]
        [else (notxsublist-los x (rest a-los))]))
```

Observe that the structures of xsublist-lon and nonxsublist-los are now the same and, therefore, are good candidates for abstraction. The only difference is the predicate used to compare the first element of the list. The abstraction step results in

```
;; (? → Boolean) ? (listof ?) → (listof ?)
;; Purpose: To return the sublist of the given list that starts
;;          with first element that satisfies given predicate.
(define (pred-sublist pred x a-lox)
  (cond [(empty? a-lox) '()]
        [(pred x (first a-lox)) a-lox]
        [else (pred-sublist pred x (rest a-lox))]))
```

Once again, care must be taken to write the signature of the abstract function. Observe that the list type processed varies among the functions abstracted over. If we denote this type as (listof X), the partial signature is

```
<X> (? ? → Boolean) ? (listof X) → (listof ?)
```

Observe that the second argument to the given predicate is a list element. This means the partial signature becomes

```
<X> (? X → Boolean) ? (listof X) → (listof ?)
```

Now observe that in the second line of the conditional the given list is returned. This suggests that the return type for accum is (listof X) making the partial signature:

```
<X> (? X → Boolean) ? (listof X) → (listof X)
```

Finally, observe that the type of the first argument to the functions abstracted over varies but is always the same as the list elements' type. Furthermore, this argument is also the first input to the given predicate. Thus, we may conclude that the signature of pred-sublist is

```
<X> (X X → Boolean) X (listof X) → (listof X)
```

It is now possible to refactor xsublist-lon and nonxsublist-lon to

```
;; number (listof number) → (listof number)
;; Purpose: To return the sublist of the given lon that starts
;;          with the first instance of the given number.
(define (xsublist-lon x a-lon) (pred-sublist equal? x a-lon))

;; symbol (listof symbol) → (listof symbol)
;; Purpose: To return the sublist of the given los that starts
;;          with first symbol not equal to given symbol.
(define (nonxsublist-los x a-los)
  (pred-sublist not-equal? x a-los))
```

Once again, observe that the difference among the functions is part of the input to the abstract function.

Always ask yourself if the arguments provided to an abstract function satisfy the abstract function's signature. The arguments in xsublist-lon's call have the following types:

```
pred: A B → Boolean      x: number      a-lox: (listof number)
```

This means that in the contract for pred-sublist X = number. Finally, observe that this also means that A = B = X = number, which satisfies equal?'s signature. Based on these observations we may conclude that the arguments provided to the abstract function satisfy the abstract function's signature.

Once again, take time to think about what abstraction has accomplished. We now have a powerful function that can return the sublist that starts with the first element that satisfies any predicate we can write. Figure 96 displays the implementation of a function that returns the sublist of a list of strings that starts with the given string.

Fig. 96 Function to return the sublist that starts with a given string

```
;; string (listof string)→ (listof string)
;; Purpose: To return the sublist of the given (listof string) that starts
;;          with the first instance of the given string.
(define (strsublist-lostr str a-lostr) (pred-sublist string=? str a-lostr))

;; Sample expressions for strsublist-lostr
(define STRSUBLIST-LOS1-VAL (pred-sublist string=? "Janice"   LOS1))
(define STRSUBLIST-LOS2-VAL (pred-sublist string=? "Matthias" LOS2))

;; Tests using sample computations for strsublist-lostr
(check-expect (strsublist-lostr "Janice"   LOS1) STRSUBLIST-LOS1-VAL)
(check-expect (strsublist-lostr "Matthias" LOS2) STRSUBLIST-LOS2-VAL)

;; Tests using sample values for strsublist-lostr
(check-expect (strsublist-los "Eladio" '("Rob" "Eladio" "Juan" "Eladio"))
              '("Eladio" "Juan" "Eladio"))
(check-expect (strsublist-los "zed" '("u" "v" "x" "y" "z" "ZED")) '())
```

*** **Ex. 234 —** Design and implement a nonrecursive function that takes as input a number and a (listof number) sorted in non-decreasing order and that returns the list of numbers greater than the given number.

*** **Ex. 235 —** Design and implement a nonrecursive function that consumes an x-value and a (listof posn) and that returns the sublist starting with the first posn that has an x-value greater than the given x-value.

* **Ex. 236 —** Design and implement a nonrecursive function that takes as input a negative number and a (listof natnum) sorted in nonincreasing order and that returns the (listof natnum) greater than the given negative number.

** **Ex. 237 —** Argue that the call to pred-sublist in nonxsublist-los satisfies pred-sublist's signature.

116.3 List ORing

Section 74.1 discusses the development of the following function to determine if any alien in a (listof alien) is at the left edge:

```
;; (listof alien) → Boolean
;; Purpose: To determine if any alien is at scene's left edge
(define (any-alien-at-left-edge? a-loa)
  (and (not (empty? a-loa))
       (or (alien-at-left-edge? (first a-loa))
           (any-alien-at-left-edge? (rest a-loa)))))
```

As an exercise you were also asked to write a function to determine if a given list of numbers contains an even number. Your solution likely looked as follows:

```
;; (listof number) → Boolean
;; Purpose: To determine if the list of numbers contains an
;;          even number
(define (has-even-lon? a-lon)
  (and (not (empty? a-lon))
       (or (even? (first a-lon))
           (has-even-lon? (rest a-lon)))))
```

Observe that both functions are structurally the same and, therefore, candidates for abstraction.

The only significant difference between the functions is the predicate that is applied to the first element of the list. Performing the abstraction step leads to the following function:

```
;; <X> (X → Boolean) (listof X) → Boolean
;; Purpose: Determine if any list element satisfies the
;;          given predicate
(define (ormap-pred pred? a-lox)
  (and (not (empty? a-lox))
       (or (pred? (first a-lox))
           (ormap-pred pred? (rest a-lox)))))
```

Observe the list input types for any-alien-at-left-edge? and has-even-lon? are different. Therefore, the type of ormap-pred's second parameter is (listof X). Its first parameter must be a predicate that takes as input a list element of type X and returns a Boolean. Thus, the type of ormap-pred's first parameter is (X → Boolean).

Refactoring any-alien-at-left-edge? and has-even-lon? yields

```
;; alien → Boolean
;; Purpose: Determine if he given alien is at the left edge
(define (alien-at-left-edge? an-alien)
  (= (posn-x an-alien) MIN-IMG-X))

;; (listof alien) → Boolean
;; Purpose: To determine if any alien is at scene's left edge
(define (any-alien-at-left-edge? a-loa)
  (ormap-pred alien-at-left-edge? a-loa))

;; (listof number) → Boolean
;; Purpose: Determine if the list of numbers contains an even
;;          number
(define (has-even-lon? a-lon)
  (ormap-pred even? a-lon))
```

Observe that calling `ormap-pred` with `alien-at-left-edge?` and `a-loa` makes its signature:

```
;; (alien → Boolean) (listof alien) → Boolean
```

That is, X = `alien`. The abstract function applies the given `alien`-predicate to all the elements of the given list of `aliens` and returns the `oring` of all the results. This is exactly what `any-alien-at-left-edge?` must do. Similarly, calling `ormap-pred` with `even?` and `a-lon` makes its signature:

```
;; (number → Boolean) (listof number) → Boolean
```

That is, X = number and it applies the given number-predicate to all the elements of the given list of numbers and returns the `oring` of all the results. This is exactly what `has-even-lon?` must do.

Take time again to reflect on what has been achieved. We now have a powerful function to perform list `oring` operations. For example, `any-alien-reached-earth?` from Sect. 74.3 and `any-alien-at-right-edge?` from Sect. 74.2 may be refactored to

```
;; (listof alien) → Boolean
;; Purpose: Determine if any alien has reached earth
(define (any-alien-reached-earth? a-loa)
  (ormap-pred alien-reached-earth? a-loa))
```

```
;; (listof alien) → Boolean
;; Purpose: To determine if any alien is at scene's right edge
(define (any-alien-at-right-edge? a-loa)
  (ormap-pred alien-at-right-edge? a-loa))
```

The abstract function we named `ormap-pred` is so powerful and useful that ISL+ provides it and is called `ormap`. Now that you understand the abstraction use `ormap` in your programs.

---

* Ex. 238 — Design and implement a nonrecursive predicate to determine if a given list of numbers contains an odd number.

*** Ex. 239 — Section 43 defines a `student`. A student makes the Dean's list if their grade point average is 3.5 or above. Design and implement a nonrecursive predicate to determine if there are any students on the Dean's list for a given (`listof student`).

*** Ex. 240 — Design and implement a nonrecursive predicate to determine if there are any images with an area of more than 500 pixels in a given (`listof image`).

**** Ex. 241 — Design and implement a nonrecursive predicate to determine if there are any prime numbers in a given (`listof number`).

*** **Ex. 242** — Argue that the calls to ormap-pred in
any-alien-reached-earth? and any-alien-at-right-edge? satisfy
ormap-pred's signature.

116.4 List ANDing

In Sect. 75.1 the following predicate to determine if all the elements in a list of
numbers are even is designed:

```
;; (listof number) → Boolean
;; Purpose: Determine if the given list of numbers only has
;;          even numbers
(define (all-even-lon? a-lon)
  (or (empty? a-lon)
      (and (even? (first a-lon))
           (all-even-lon? (rest a-lon)))))
```

If you were asked to write a predicate to determine if all strings in a list of strings
had a length less than or equal to 5, your function definitions would look as follows:

```
;; string → Boolean
;; Purpose: Determine if the length of the given string is ≤ 5
(define (string-len<5? a-str) (<= (string-length a-str) 5))


;; (listof string) → Boolean
;; Purpose: Determine if the given (listof string) only has
;;          strings of length ≤ 5
(define (string-all-len<5? a-lostr)
 (or (empty? a-lostr)
     (and (string-len<5? (first a-lostr))
          (string-all-len<5? (rest a-lostr)))))
```

You can immediately observe that all-even-lon? and string-all-len<5? are
good candidates for abstraction. The structure of their bodies is exactly the same and
no refactoring is required.

The only significant difference is the predicate applied to the first element of
the given list. Therefore, the abstract function only needs one extra parameter. The
abstraction step yields

```
;; <X> (X → Boolean) (listof X) → Boolean
;; Purpose: Determine if the elements of the list satisfy
;;          the given predicate
(define (andmap-pred pred a-lox)
  (or (empty? a-lox)
```

```
          (and (pred (first a-lox))
               (andmap-pred pred (rest a-lox)))))
```

Observe that the functions abstracted from process different types of lists. Therefore, the list processed by the abstract function is denoted by (listof X). In the functions abstracted from, the predicate is applied to the first element of the list and returns a Boolean. In the abstract function the elements of the list are of type X. Therefore, the type of the predicate is (X → Boolean).

The functions abstracted from can now be refactored to

```
;; lon → Boolean
;; Purpose: Determine if the given lon only has even numbers
(define (all-even-lon? a-lon) (andmap-pred even? a-lon))
```

```
;; (listof string) → Boolean
;; Purpose: Determine if the given (listof string) only
;;          has strings of length <= 5
(define (string-all-len<5? a-lostr)
  (andmap-pred string-len<5? a-lostr))
```

Once again you can see that the elegance and clarity provided by the abstract function are truly remarkable. Furthermore, we have a powerful abstract function to perform list anding operations on a (listof X). This list operation is so useful that ISL provides it and it is called andmap. Now that you understand the abstraction, use andmap in your programs.

---

* **Ex. 243 —** Design and implement a nonrecursive predicate to determine if a given list of numbers contains only odd numbers.

*** **Ex. 244 —** Design and implement a nonrecursive predicate to determine if all the elements in a (listof posn) are in the first quadrant of the Cartesian plane.

* **Ex. 245 —** Design and implement a nonrecursive predicate to determine if all the elements in a (listof Boolean) are #true.

***** **Ex. 246 —** Section 75.2 discusses the design of a predicate, sorted-lon2?, to determine if the given (listof number) is sorted in non-decreasing order. Design and implement a predicate to determine if the given (listof number) is sorted in nonincreasing order. Perform functional abstraction over the two functions and refactor them to use the abstract function.

*** **Ex. 247 —** Argue that the calls to andmap-pred in all-even-lon? and string-all-len<5? satisfy andmap-pred's signature.

116.5 List Mapping

Section 76 discusses the design of the following functions to apply a function to all
the elements of a list and return the list of obtained results:

```
;; (listof shot) → (listof shot)
;; Purpose: To move the given list of shots
(define (move-los a-los)
  (if (empty? a-los)
      E-LOS
      (cons (move-shot (first a-los))
            (move-los  (rest a-los)))))


;; (listof string) → (listof number)
;; Purpose: Return the string lengths in the given
;;          (listof string)
(define (lengths-lostr a-lostr)
  (if (empty? a-lostr)
      '()
      (cons (string-length (first a-lostr))
            (lengths-lostr (rest a-lostr)))))
```

By now you have probably noticed that these functions process different types of
lists and are good candidates for abstraction. The only significant difference between
them is the function applied to the given list's first element.

Abstracting over the functions leads to the following abstract function:

```
;; <X Y> (X → Y) (listof X) → (listof Y)
;; Purpose: Return the values from applying the given function
;;          to the given list's elements
(define (map-f f a-lox)
  (if (empty? a-lox)
      '()
      (cons (f (first a-lox))
            (map-f f (rest a-lox)))))
```

Given that functions abstracted over process different types of lists, the list type for
map-f's list parameter is (listof X). The given function is applied to the elements
of this list. Thus, the input to the given function must be of type X. The result of
this given function varies among the functions abstracted from. Therefore, the return
type of the given function is Y. This means that the type of the given function is
(X →Y). Note that X may or may not be the same as Y. The results of applying the
given function are placed in a list and this list is the returned value. The result list,
therefore, is of type (listof Y).

Refactoring the functions abstracted over to use the abstract function yields

```
;; los → los
;; Purpose: To move the given list of shots
(define (move-los a-los) (map-f move-shot a-los))

;; (listof string) → lon
;; Purpose: Return the string lengths in the given
;;            (listof string)
(define (lengths-lostr a-lostr)
  (map-f string-length a-lostr))
```

Now that we have a function to perform list mapping operations, observe how short and elegant the above functions have become. Many experienced programmers argue that the use of abstract functions is the poetry of programming. The abstract function we named map-f is named map in ISL+. Now that you understand the abstraction go ahead and use map in your programs.

*** **Ex. 248** — Section 76 discusses the design of move-alien. Can this function be implemented using map? Justify your answer.

* **Ex. 249** — Design and implement a nonrecursive to add 1 to the elements of a list of numbers.

**** **Ex. 250** — Design and implement a nonrecursive function to extract the full names from a list of students. Section 43 defines the type student. Define your function twice: once using map and once using accum. Which version do you prefer? Why?

*** **Ex. 251** — Implement map-f using accum.

**** **Ex. 252** — Design and implement a nonrecursive function to compute the second largest factor of each natural number in a list of natural numbers. Keep in mind that the largest factor of a natural number, n, is n. Any auxiliary functions you need to write may be recursive.

** **Ex. 253** — Design and implement a nonrecursive function to make a copy of a given list.

*** **Ex. 254** — Argue that the calls to map-f in move-los and lengths-lostr satisfy map-f's signature.

116.6 List Filtering

Section 77 discusses the design of a function to extract the even numbers from a list
of numbers and has an exercise to extract the posn shots from a list of shots. Both
functions are

```
;; (listof number) → (listof number)
;; Purpose: Return a list of the even numbers in the given list
(define (extract-evens a-lon)
  (cond [(empty? a-lon) '()]
        [(even? (first a-lon))
         (cons (first a-lon) (extract-evens (rest a-lon)))]
        [else (extract-evens (rest a-lon))]))
```

```
;; (listof shot) → (listof shot)
;; Purpose: To return a list of posn shots in the given list
(define (extract-posn-shots a-los)
  (cond [(empty? a-los) '()]
        [(posn? (first a-los))
         (cons (first a-los) (extract-posn-shots (rest a-los)))]
        [else (extract-posn-shots (rest a-los))]))
```

A visual inspection reveals that both functions have the same type of expression in
their bodies and, therefore, are good candidates for abstraction.

The only significant difference is the predicate applied to the first element of the
list. The abstraction step yields the following function:

```
;; <X> (X → Boolean) (listof X) → (listof X)
;; Purpose: Return the elements in the given list that
;;          satisfy the given predicate
(define (filter-pred pred a-lox)
  (cond [(empty? a-lox) '()]
        [(pred (first a-lox))
         (cons (first a-lox)
               (filter-pred pred (rest a-lox)))]
        [else (filter-pred pred (rest a-lox))]))
```

The functions abstracted over process different types. Therefore, filter-pred's list
argument is of type (listof X). The predicates in functions abstracted over take
as input a list element and return a Boolean. Thus, the filter-pred's predicate
type is (X → Boolean). Finally, the functions abstracted over always return a list
of the same type they get as input. This means that filter-pred's return type must
be (listof X).

The functions abstracted over are refactored to use `filter-pred` as follows:

```
;; lon → lon
;; Purpose: Return list of the even numbers in the given list
(define (extract-evens a-lon) (filter-pred even? a-lon))
```

```
;; los → los
;; Purpose: Return list of posn shots in the given list
(define (extract-posn-shots a-los) (filter-pred posn? a-los))
```

The elegance of the refactored functions is appreciated by those that understand the abstract function. This abstraction is so powerful and useful that ISL+ provides this abstract function and it is named `filter`. Now that you understand the abstraction, go ahead and use `filter` in your programs.

---

* **Ex. 255** — Design and implement a nonrecursive function to extract the odd numbers from a list of numbers.

** **Ex. 256** — Design and implement a nonrecursive function to extract the multiples of 10 from a list of numbers.

*** **Ex. 257** — Design and implement a nonrecursive function to extract the prime numbers from a list of numbers. Your auxiliary function to determine if a given number is prime may be recursive.

*** **Ex. 258** — Section 77 discusses the design of `remove-hit-aliens`. Can this function be refactored to use `filter`? Justify your answer.

*** **Ex. 259** — Design and implement a nonrecursive function to extract the posns from a `(listof posn)` that are either on the x-axis or the y-axis.

*** **Ex. 260** — Argue that the calls to `filter-pred` in `extract-evens` and `extract-posn-shots` satisfy `filter-pred`'s signature.

116.7 List Sorting

Section 78 discusses insertion sorting. The following functions are designed to sort a list in non-decreasing order:

```
;; number (listof number) → (listof number)
;; Purpose: Insert the given number in the given list to
;;          create an list of numbers in non-decreasing order
;; ASSUMPTION: The given lon is sorted in nondecreasing order
(define (insert a-num a-lon)
  (cond [(empty? a-lon) (list a-num)]
```

```
          [(<= a-num (first a-lon)) (cons a-num a-lon)]
          [else (cons (first a-lon)
                      (insert a-num (rest a-lon)))]]))
;; (listof number) → (listof number)
;; Purpose: Sort the given list of numbers in non-decreasing
;;          order
(define (sort-lon a-lon)
  (cond [(empty? a-lon) '()]
        [else
          (insert (first a-lon) (sort-lon (rest a-lon)))]]))
```

If you needed to write code to sort a list of numbers in nonincreasing order, the functions you develop would likely look like this:

```
;; number (listof number) → (listof number)
;; Purpose: Insert the given number in the given list to create
;;          a list of numbers in nonincreasing order
;; ASSUMPTION: The given lon is sorted in nonincreasing order
(define (insert>= a-num a-lon)
  (cond [(empty? a-lon) (list a-num)]
        [(>= a-num (first a-lon)) (cons a-num a-lon)]
        [else (cons (first a-lon)
                    (insert>= a-num (rest a-lon)))]]))
;; (listof number) '() (listof number)
;; Purpose: Sort the given list of numbers in nonincreasing
;;          order
(define (sort-lon>= a-lon)
 (cond [(empty? a-lon) '()]
        [else
          (insert>= (first a-lon) (sort-lon>= (rest a-lon)))]]))
```

Finally, consider the following code to sort a (listof item) in non-decreasing order by price:

```
;; An item (item) is a structure
;;     (make-item string number number)
;; that has the item's name, price, and quantity in stock.
(define-struct item (name price quantity))

;; item item → Boolean
;; Purpose: Determine if the first given item's price is <=
;;          to the second given item's price
(define (leq-item item1 item2)
  (<= (item-price item1) (item-price item2)))
;; item (listof item) → (listof item)
;; Purpose: Insert the given item in the given loi to create an
;;          loi in nondecreasing order by price
```

```
;; ASSUMPTION: The given loi is sorted in nondecreasing order
;;              by price
(define (insert-loi an-item a-loi)
  (cond [(empty? a-loi) (list an-item)]
        [(leq-item an-item (first a-loi)) (cons an-item a-loi)]
        [else (cons (first a-loi)
                    (insert-loi an-item (rest a-loi)))]))
;; loi → loi
;; Purpose: Sort the given loi in nonincreasing order by price
(define (sort-loi a-loi)
  (cond [(empty? a-loi) '()]
        [else (insert-loi (first a-loi)
                          (sort-loi (rest a-loi)))]))
```

Immediately you may notice that these functions are good candidates for abstraction. Observe that the only significant difference between the inserting functions is the predicate used to compare two values. The sorting functions are essentially the same also. They call an inserting function and make a recursive call. Their only significant difference is the inserting function called.

Abstracting over the inserting functions yields the following abstract function:

```
;; <X> (X → Boolean) X (listof X) → (listof X)
;; Purpose: Insert the given number in the given lox to
;;          create sorted lox using the given predicate
;; ASSUMPTION: Given lon is sorted as defined by the given
;;             predicate
(define (insert-pred pred an-x a-lox)
  (cond [(empty? a-lox) (list an-x)]
        [(pred an-x (first a-lox)) (cons an-x a-lox)]
        [else (cons (first a-lox)
                    (insert-pred pred an-x (rest a-lox)))]))
```

The list types processed by the inserting functions vary. Therefore, the list type for insert-pred is (listof X). The value to insert is always of the same type as the values in the given list. This means that for insert-pred the value to insert must be of type X. Finally, the predicate always takes as input a list value and returns a Boolean. Thus, for insert-pred, the predicate type is (X →Boolean).

Refactoring the inserting functions yields

```
;; insert: number (listof number) → (listof number)
;; Purpose: To insert the given number in the given lon to
;;          create a list of numbers in non-decreasing order
;; ASSUMPTION: The given list is sorted in non-decreasing order
(define (insert a-num a-lon) (insert-pred <= a-num a-lon))

;; number (listof number) → (listof number)
;; Purpose: To insert the given number in the given lon to
```

```
;;              create a list of numbers in nonincreasing order
;; ASSUMPTION: The given list is sorted in nonincreasing order
(define (insert>= a-num a-lon) (insert-pred >= a-num a-lon))


;; item (listof item) → (listof item)
;; Purpose: To insert the given item in the given loi to
;;          create a list of numbers in nondecreasing order
;;          by price
;; ASSUMPTION: The given list is sorted in nondecreasing order
;;             by price
(define (insert-loi an-item a-loi)
  (insert-pred leq-item an-item a-loi))
```

The simplification of these three functions is, indeed, very impressive.

The only difference in the functions sort-lon, sort-lon>=, and sort-loi needs to also be abstracted away. Instinctively, we may create an abstract function that takes as input the proper inserting function. Such an approach yields the following abstract sorting function:

```
;; <X> (X (listof X) → (listof X)) (listof X) → (listof X)
;; Purpose: Sort given lox using the given inserting function
(define (sort-lox insert-f a-lox)
  (cond [(empty? a-lox) '()]
        [else (insert-f (first a-lox)
              (sort-lox (rest a-lox)))]))
```

Although technically correct this is the wrong abstraction for anyone using our sorting function. It forces the user of the function to provide an inserting function. The average user may not find this abstraction useful. The average user is likely to only want to sort a list using a predicate. They are not interested in nor inclined to develop the proper inserting function even if they can use insert-pred to do so.

The proper abstraction for sorting only requires the user to specify the predicate they wish to use to sort the given list. In other words, the user provides a predicate and a list to sort. How can we develop an abstract sorting function that provides the right abstraction? In essence, we need to eliminate the inserting function as the difference and make the sorting predicate the difference. This can be achieved by refactoring the sorting functions before performing the abstraction step. More concretely, we can inline the proper use of insert-pred into the bodies of the sorting functions. This yields the following refactored sorting functions:

```
;; (listof number) → (listof number)
;; Purpose: Sort the given list of numbers in nondecreasing
;;          order
(define (sort-lon a-lon)
  (cond [(empty? a-lon) '()]
        [else (insert-pred <=
                           (first a-lon)
                           (sort-lon (rest a-lon)))]))
```

```
;; (listof number) '() (listof number)
;; Purpose: Sort the given list of numbers in nonincreasing
;;          order
(define (sort-lon>= a-lon)
 (cond [(empty? a-lon) '()]
       [else (insert-pred >=
                          (first a-lon)
                          (sort-lon>= (rest a-lon)))]))

;; (listof item) → (listof item)
;; Purpose: To sort the given list of items in nonincreasing
;;          order by price
(define (sort-loi a-loi)
 (cond [(empty? a-loi) '()]
       [else
         (insert-pred leq-item
                      (first a-loi)
                      (sort-loi (rest a-loi)))]))
```

There are two important consequences of inlining the use of `insert-pred`. The first is the only difference among the sorting functions is the predicate used to perform the sorting. The second is that `insert`, `insert>=`, and `insert-loi` are no longer needed and may safely be deleted from our program.

Performing the abstraction step on the sorting functions now yields the following abstract sorting function:

```
;; <X> (X → Boolean) (listof X) → (listof X)
;; Purpose: To sort the given lox using the given predicate
(define (sort-pred pred a-lox)
 (cond [(empty? a-lox) '()]
       [else (insert-pred pred
                          (first a-lox)
                          (sort-pred (rest a-lox)))]))
```

In the functions abstracted from, the list type processed varies. For `sort-pred` this means that the given list's type is `(listof X)`. Observe that the given predicate's input must be the same type as the elements in the given list. Therefore, its type is `(X → Boolean)`.

Refactoring the sorting functions to use `sort-pred` yields

```
    ;; (listof number) → (listof number)
    ;; Purpose: To sort the given list of numbers in
    ;;          non-decreasing order
    (define (sort-lon a-lon) (sort-pred <= a-lon))
```

```
;; (listof number) → (listof number)
;; Purpose: To sort the given list of numbers in
;;          nonincreasing order
(define (sort-lon>= a-lon) (sort-pred >= a-lon))


;; (listof item) → (listof item)
;; Purpose: To sort the given list of items in
;;          nonincreasing order
;;          by price
(define (sort-loi a-loi) (sort-pred leq-item a-loi))
```

What do you think about how simple it is now to write sorting functions? Be aware, however, that the elimination of `insert`, `insert>=`, and `insert-loi` requires that you update the sample expressions for the sorting functions. This powerful abstract function to write sorting functions is called `sort` in ISL+.

The efforts to perform functional abstraction using the sorting functions had left us an important lesson. Not all possible abstractions are useful or make code easier to understand. The first attempt to abstract the sorting functions yielded an abstraction that is unlikely to be useful. It is important to be mindful about the usefulness of the abstractions we create. Experience will teach you that the wrong abstraction makes programs harder to understand or harder to understand.

** **Ex. 261** — Section 43 defines the type `student`. Design and implement a nonrecursive function to sort a list of students in non-decreasing order by grade point average.

** **Ex. 262** — Design and implement a nonrecursive function to sort a list of images in nonincreasing order by area.

*** **Ex. 263** — Design and implement a nonrecursive function to sort a list of aliens in non-decreasing order by how high they are in a scene.

*** **Ex. 264** — Argue that the calls to `sort-pred` in `sort-lon`, `sort-lon>=`, and `sort-loi` satisfy `sort-pred`'s signature.

---

117 Abstraction over Interval-Processing Functions

Consider the following functions to process an interval. The first computes the sum of the squares of the integers in the given interval. The second computes the list of strings representing the integers in the interval.

```
;; [int..int] → int
;; Purpose: Compute the product of the squares of the ints
;;          in the given interval
```

```
(define (interval-product-sqrs low high)
  (if (> low high)
      1
      (* (sqr low) (interval-product-sqrs (add1 low) high))))

;; [int..int] → (listof string)
;; Purpose: Construct the list of strings for the ints in
;;          the given interval
(define (interval->lostr low high)
  (if (> low high)
      '()
      (cons (number->string low)
            (interval->lostr (add1 low) high))))
```

A visual examination reveals that they are good candidates for abstraction. Both functions have the same number of parameters and process the interval from the low value to the high value. They both have the same type of expression in their body: an if-expression that tests if the given interval is empty, a consequent expression that is a concrete value, and alternative expression that applies a two-input function to the values obtained from applying a one-input function to the first element of the list and the result of recursively processing the rest of the list.

There are three significant differences: the base value returned, the function applied to the first element of the interval, and the combining function. This is reminiscent of the differences among list-summarizing functions in Sect. 116.1 suggesting that the above functions are interval-summarizing functions. The result of the abstraction step yields

```
;; <X Y> X (int → Y) (Y X → X) [int..int] → X
;; Purpose: Compute a value by traversing the given interval
;;          from low to high using the given base value,
;;          function to apply to low, and combining function.
(define (interval-accum-12h base-val ffirst comb low high)
  if (> low high)
     base-val
     (comb (ffirst low)
           (interval-accum-12h base-val ffirst
                               comb       (add1 low) high))))
```

The type of the interval ought to be clear. The base value, the second input and the return type of the combining function, and the return type of the abstract function must all be the same and it is denoted by X. The type applied of the function to the low element of the interval must be (int → Y) given that the low element is an integer and it may return any type of data. Finally, the first input to the combining function must be of type Y making the type of the combining function (Y X → X).

The final step refactoring the functions abstracted over yields

```
;; [int..int] → (listof string)
;; Purpose: Construct the list of strings for the ints in
;;          the given interval
(define (interval->lostr low high)
  (interval-accum-12h '() number->string cons low high))


;; [int..int] → int
;; Purpose: Compute the product of the squares of the ints
;;          in the given interval
(define (interval-product-sqrs low high)
  (interval-accum-12h 1 sqr * low high))
```

Once again, observe that the functions abstracted over have been greatly simplified. This abstract function, like the others in this chapter, allows the programmers to spend more time on problem solving and less time on mundane typing of repetitions, which usually means fewer bugs in the software developed.

** **Ex. 265** — Design and implement a nonrecursive function to sum the integers in a given interval.

*** **Ex. 266** — Design and implement a nonrecursive predicate to determine if a given interval contains a multiple of 7.

*** **Ex. 267** — ISL+'s random function takes as input, n, a nonzero natural number and returns a random natural number in [0..n-1]. Design and implement a nonrecursive function that takes as input an interval, [i..j], and that returns a list of random numbers less than 1000, one for each integer in the given interval. For example, (generate-randoms 10 12) may return '(786 31 87).

*** **Ex. 268** — Argue that the calls to interval-accum-12h in interval->lostr and interval-product-sqrs satisfy interval-accum-12h's signature.

***** **Ex. 269** — Design and implement an abstract function to process an interval from right to left (i.e., from the high end to the low end of the interval). Refactor interval-product in Sect. 86 to use the abstract function you develop.

118 What Have We Learned in This Chapter?

The important lessons of Chap. 20 are summarized as follows:

- Functional abstraction allows us to eliminate repetitions in our programs and to write a code that is more elegant, shorter, easier to maintain, and with fewer bugs.
- Abstract (or generic) functions can perform many different tasks.
- Thinking abstractly makes problem solving and programming easier.
- The design recipe for abstraction has three steps: mark the differences, create the abstract function, and refactor the functions abstracted over.
- Functions are a type of value. Programming languages that provide support for functions as values are said to have first-class functions.
- Care must be taken to develop the signature of an abstract function and signatures need to be explicitly parameterized (i.e., type variables in angled brackets before the signature).
- Care must be taken to make sure the arguments provided to an abstract function satisfy the abstract function's signature.
- ISL+ provides the following abstract functions: `ormap`, `andmap`, `map`, `filter`, and `sort`.
- Not all possible abstractions are useful or make code easier to understand.
- Inlining can help to create useful abstractions.
- Two useful abstract functions may be developed to process an interval: one that processes from the low end to the high end and one that processes from the high end to the low end.
- Many experienced programmers consider abstract functions the poetry of programming.

Chapter 21
Encapsulation

As the use of auxiliary functions increases, the size of programs grows. You may
have already noticed in Aliens Attack, for example, that you have related functions
scattered all over your program's file. This makes it difficult to understand a design
and to make refinements. It is therefore desirable to *encapsulate* the definitions in
our programs. Encapsulation means that we package together all related definitions
as a single piece of software. This allows any reader of our code to more easily
understand the design and makes the process of program refinement easier.

New syntax is required to encapsulate definitions. This new syntax is a *local-
expression*. In essence, a local-expression allows us to have definitions inside of
functions. In this manner auxiliary functions are defined inside the functions that
need them instead of being defined elsewhere (possibly far away) in our program.
As this chapter and Chap. 25 illustrate, the power of encapsulation has consequences
for design and for performance.

119 Local-Expressions

A local-expression is used to group together an arbitrary number of related definitions. The local-expression syntax is
```
expr ::= (local [def*] expr)
```
A local-expression has inside parenthesis the keyword local, then inside square
brackets zero or more definitions, and finally an expression. The expression after
the local definitions is called the body of the local-expression. This body may
refer to any of the definitions locally defined. The value of a local-expression is
the value of its body. We say that the local definitions are encapsulated inside the
local-expression.

Consider, for example, the function to move a (listof shot) designed for the Aliens Attack game in Sect. 76.2:

```
;; los → los
;; Purpose: To move the given list of shots
(define (move-los a-los)
  (if (empty? a-los)
      E-LOS
      (cons (move-shot (first a-los))
            (move-los (rest a-los)))))
```

Revisiting this function makes us realize that the same one-input function, move-shot, is applied to every shot in the given list. This suggest that the function may be refactored and simplified using map(similar to the design in Sect. 116.5:

```
;; los → los
;; Purpose: To move the given list of shots
(define (move-los a-los) (map move-shot a-los))
```

Can any reader fully understand and can any programmer easily make refinements to this code? To a certain degree yes, but not fully. Any refinement to move-los, for example, is likely to involve changes to move-shot. Therefore, it is desirable to encapsulate both of these functions into a single package. Using a local-expression allows us to refactor the dispersed code to

```
;; los → los
;; Purpose: To move the given list of shots
(define (move-los a-los)
  (local [;; shot → shot
          ;; Purpose: To move the given shot
          (define (local-move-shot a-shot)
            (cond [(eq? a-shot NO-SHOT) a-shot]
                  [else
                   (cond [(= (posn-y a-shot) MIN-IMG-Y)
                          NO-SHOT]
                         [else
                          (make-posn
                            (posn-x a-shot)
                            (move-up-image-y
                              (posn-y a-shot)))])]))
    (map local-move-shot a-los))
```

The body of move-los is now a local-expression. This expression locally defines the auxiliary function local-move-los. The name of move-los has been prefixed by local to highlight that it is now a locally defined function. Such prefixing is not necessary in practice. The body of the local-expression is the body of the original move-los. Now, move-los is a complete package containing all the functions needed to move a list of shots.

No new computational power is offered by local-expressions. Anything computed using a local-expression may be computed without it. In other words, they are simply syntactic sugar to make program development easier. Any local-expression may be eliminated as follows:

1. Give every local definition a unique name not found elsewhere in the program and change all references using the old name to be references using the new names.
2. Move the renamed definitions out of the local-expression.
3. Replace the local-expression with its body.

In essence, these steps are a *refactoring recipe* to eliminate local-expressions. This refactoring recipe is not presented to develop a practical skill. It is presented to clarify the role of local-expressions. In addition, be aware that this refactoring recipe is incomplete as we shall see later in this chapter. Nonetheless, let us consider the following concrete example:

```
(define DELTA 10)
(+ DELTA (local [(define DELTA 100)
                 (define VAL (+ DELTA DELTA))]
          VAL))
```

What is the value of the sum? 30? 210? 300? Some other value? Let us refactor the program to eliminate the local-expression. After Step 1 we have

```
(define DELTA 10)
(+ DELTA (local [(define DLT 100)
                 (define VAL (+ DLT DLT))]
          VAL))
```

Observe that inside the original local-expression all references to DELTA are to the locally defined variable. Therefore, all of them are changed to DLT. Now that all the defined names do no clash with names defined outside the local-expression Step 2 may be completed to yield

```
(define DELTA 10)
(define DLT 100)
(define VAL (+ DLT DLT))
(+ DELTA (local [] VAL))
```

Given that there are no local definitions Step 3 replaces the local-expression with its body to yield

```
(define DELTA 10)
(define DLT 100)
(define VAL (+ DLT DLT))
(+ DELTA VAL)
```

In this form it becomes clear that the value of the sum is 210.

120 Lexical Scoping

Why is it necessary to rename definitions before lifting them outside a `local`-expression? How do we know which references need to be updated to use the new name? The answer is *lexical scoping* (or *static scoping*). The lexical scope of a definition or a variable (as the parameters of a function) is the part of the program where the definition or variable is valid. Consider the following program fragments that contain a function definition to multiply two natural numbers:

```
  ⋮
;; natnum natnum → natnum
;; Purpose: Multiply the given natural numbers
(define (mult x y)
  (if (= x 0)
      0
      (+ y (mult (sub1 x) y))))
  ⋮
```

There are three names declared in this program fragment: `mult` is the name of a function that takes two inputs, x is the name of the first parameter, and y is the name of the second parameter. These three declarations do not have the same lexical scope. That is, the program defines where these variables are valid. We say that `mult` has *global scope* (or simply is global) because it is not locally defined (inside a `local`-expression) nor is it a parameter. The lexical scope of x and y, on the other hand, is the body of the function. That is, the parameters x and y are only valid in the body of `mult` (emphasized in slanted fonts) and are invalid elsewhere. We say that x and y are bound variables in the body of `mult`. That is, there is a declaration for these variables in `mult` (specifically the parameters in the function header).

Now, consider this larger fragment of the program:

```
  ⋮
(define x 2)

;; natnum → natnum
;; Purpose: Add x to the given number
(define (add-x-y-and-z y) (+ x y z))

;; natnum → natnum
;; Purpose: Compute the factorial of the given number
(define (fact x)
  (if (= x 0)
      1
      (* x (fact (sub1 x)))))
```

```
;; natnum natnum → natnum
;; Purpose: Multiply the given natural numbers
(define (mult x y)
  (if (= x 0)
      0
      (+ y (mult (sub1 x) y))))
    ⋮
```

In this program fragment there are 4 declarations that have global scope: x (the one defined as 2), add-x, fact, and mult. There are four declarations that do not have global scope. The y parameter of add-x-y-and-z is only valid in its body. The x parameter of fact is only valid in its body. The x and y parameters of mult are only valid in its body. Observe that x is declared and referenced multiple times. In (* x (fact (sub1 x))), for example, the references to x are bound to fact's x parameter. Similarly, in (+ x y z, for example, the x referenced is bound to addd-x-y-z's x parameter. Lexical scoping allows programmers to use the same variable names multiple times. The scoping rules make it possible to understand where a variable is bound or if it is *free*. In the body of addd-x-y-z we say that y and z are *free variables*. A free variable is one that is not bound to a declaration. In this case, y and z are free because they are not declared in addd-x-y-z.

Most programming languages use lexical scoping. Lexical scoping determines where a variable is bound based on the syntax of the programming language. Global definitions are valid everywhere unless they are *shadowed* by a local declaration. If the same variable name is reused in a program, the local declaration is the bounding declaration. All other declarations of this variable are shadowed and unaccessible in the scope of the local declaration. In other words, the closest declaration is always the bounding declaration. For example, in the program fragment above the definition that binds x to 2 is shadowed by the declarations of x (as parameters) in fact and mult. In these functions, references to x are always to the parameter of the function and not to the global x. In contrast, the reference to the free variable x in add-x-y-z is bound to the global x. The same is true for the reference to z that must be defined in the part of the program not displayed. A free variable that is not bound to a declaration is said to be unbound and is an error.

The lexical scoping rules are:

1. The definitions not typed inside a local-expression have global lexical scope and are valid everywhere unless shadowed.
2. The lexical scope of parameters is the function that declares them unless shadowed.
3. The lexical scope of a local definition is the declarations and the body of the local-expression unless shadowed.

We can now revisit the example used to illustrate the refactoring recipe to eliminate local-expressions:

```
(define DELTA 10)
(+ DELTA (local [(define DELTA 100)
                 (define VAL (+ DELTA DELTA))]
           VAL))
```

We do not need to refactor this code to understand it. The declaration of DELTA as 10 has global scope. This declaration is shadowed by the local declaration of DELTA inside the local-expression. According to Rule 3 above, inside this expression DELTA is 100. This makes VAL 200. Given that VAL is returned in the body of the local, the value of the local-expression is 200. The local declaration of DELTA is not valid outside of the local-expression. Therefore, the reference to DELTA as the first argument to + must be to a different declaration of DELTA. In this case, the closest declaration of DELTA is the global one making +'s first argument 10. It is now also clear, without refactoring, that the value of the sum is 210.

As a final example, consider the following program:

```
(define X 2)
(define Y 3)

(+ X Y (local [(define X 10)]
         (+ X (local [(define Y 10)]
                (+ X Y)))))
```

What is the value of the sum? The X and Y defined before the summing expression have global scope. Inside first local-expression the X bound to 5 shadows the global X. Inside the innermost local-expression X is a free variable and the Y bound to 10 shadows the global Y. Where does the value of X come from? It comes from the closest declaration in scope: the declaration of X in the containing local-expression. This makes the value of the sum 35. If this is not clear, you can always refactor to remove the local-expressions. Start with the innermost local-expression to get:

```
(define X 2)
(define Y 3)
(define Y-INNERMOST 10)
(+ X Y (local [(define X 10)]
         (+ X (+ X Y-INNERMOST))))
```

The Y declaration in the innermost local-expression has been renamed to Y-INNERMOST and moved to the global level. The innermost local-expression is replaced with its body. Observe that the reference to X in (+ X Y-INNERMOST) is not free. That is, the previously free variable X is now a bound variable. The same steps are taken to remove the only local-expression left. This process yields

```
(define X 2)
(define Y 3)
(define Y-INNERMOST 10)
(define X-MIDDLE 10)
(+ X Y (+ X-MIDDLE (+ X-MIDDLE Y-INNERMOST)))
```

The local X bound to 10 is renamed to X-MIDDLE and the local-expression is substituted with its body. It this form it becomes clear that the value of the sum is 35.

121 Using Local-Expressions

As with any new type of expression it is important to understand when and how to use a `local`-expression. There are four reasons to use a `local`-expression. The first, as we begun to discuss above, is encapsulation. Use to a `local`-expression to organize your code to package together related functions. The second is to make code more readable. The third is to make the use of abstract functions possible. The fourth is to eliminate multiple evaluations of the same expression.

The following subsections discuss each of these reasons in more detail. Keep in mind that sometimes the use of a `local`-expression is subjective. For example, what does it mean for code to be more readable? For some people. the use of a `local`-expression may make understanding the design of a function easier and for others the same function is perfectly understandable without it. If you feel that a `local`-expression makes your code more readable, then do not hesitate to use it.

121.1 Encapsulation

Encapsulation is a good practice to develop because it makes refinements easier. When a refinement is needed, all the code is located in one place (i.e., one package). In addition, it also makes it easier to move code from one file to another given that all the needed code is packaged together. To encapsulate code use these steps:

1. Develop your program using any of the design recipes.
2. Test your functions thoroughly.
3. Identify related definitions to package together.
4. Identify the main function among the functions to be packaged.
5. Place all the functions inside a `local`-expression.
6. Place the `local`-expression inside a new function that has the same signature, purpose, and header as the main function.
7. In the body of the `local`-expression call the main function with the given arguments.
8. Comment out the sample expressions and the tests for all functions except the main function and comment out the sample expressions and the tests using sample computations for the main function.

It is important to remember not to encapsulate functions before thorough testing has been performed and you are relatively sure that the functions are bug free. Otherwise, you risk making untested buggy functions local. This is important because localized functions cannot be tested due to scoping rules. Localized functions do not exist outside the `local`-expression and, therefore, tests cannot be written for them. In essence, test before encapsulation.

Fig. 97 Draft encapsulated `draw-world` function definition

```
;; world → scene    Purpose: To draw the world in E-SCENE
(define (draw-world a-world)
  (local
    [(define E-SCENE-COLOR 'pink)
     (define E-SCENE (empty-scene E-SCENE-W E-SCENE-H E-SCENE-COLOR))
     ;; los scene → scene    Purpose: Draw given los in given scene
     (define (draw-los a-los scn)
       (if (empty? a-los) scn
           (draw-shot (first a-los)
                      (draw-los (rest a-los) scn))))
     ;; loa scene → scene    Purpose: Draw given loa in given scene
     (define (draw-loa a-loa scn)
       (if (empty? a-loa) scn
           (draw-alien (first a-loa) (draw-loa (rest a-loa) scn))))
     ;; rocket scene → scene    Purpose: Draw rocket in given scene
     (define (draw-rocket a-rocket a-scene)
       (draw-ci ROCKET-IMG a-rocket ROCKET-Y a-scene))
     ;; world → scene    Purpose: To draw the world in E-SCENE
     (define (draw-world a-world)
       (draw-los (world-shots a-world)
                 (draw-loa
                  (world-aliens a-world)
                  (draw-rocket (world-rocket a-world) E-SCENE))))]
    (draw-world a-world)))
```

Consider the function `draw-world` from Aliens Attack (its design is discussed in Sect. 91):

```
;; world → scene
;; Purpose: To draw the world in E-SCENE
(define (draw-world a-world)
  (draw-los (world-shots a-world)
            (draw-loa (world-aliens a-world)
                      (draw-rocket (world-rocket a-world)
                                   E-SCENE))))
```

Observe that 3 auxiliary functions and a constant are used. Where are these functions and constant defined? Clearly, they are defined elsewhere in the program that forces any reader of the code to search for them. Further observe that the auxiliary functions and the constant are not needed elsewhere in the program. Given that the functions have been thoroughly tested, they are ideal for encapsulation along with the constant. The definitions to encapsulate are E-SCENE, E-SCENE-COLOR (only used to define E-SCENE in the program), `draw-world`, `draw-loa`, and `draw-rocket`. The main function is `draw-world`.

The draft new code after encapsulation for `draw-world` is displayed in Figs. 97 and 98. Observe that in Fig. 97 all the related definitions identified are localized. The interface with the rest of the program (e.g., using `draw-world` in the big-bang expression inside `run`) is unchanged because the signature, purpose, and function

Fig. 98 Tests for draft encapsulated `draw-world` function

```
;; Tests using sample computations for draw-world
(check-expect (draw-world (make-world INIT-ROCKET2 (list INIT-ALIEN)
                                      DIR3          empty))
```

```
                                                               )
(check-expect (draw-world (make-world INIT-ROCKET (list INIT-ALIEN2)
                                      DIR2        (list SHOT2)))
```

```
                                                               )
```

header of the new (global) draw-world implementation remain unchanged. Take some time to think about the call to `draw-world` inside the `local`-expression. Is this a recursive call? Why or why not? Remember the scoping rules. It is not a recursive call because it is calling the local `draw-world` function. There are no sample expressions or tests using sample computations in Fig. 98 because the local functions are not in scope and, therefore, may not be used to write sample expressions. This highlights the importance of testing before encapsulation.

Observe that `draw-shot` is an auxiliary function that is only needed by `draw-los`. The same observation may be made for `draw-alien` and `draw-loa`. Respectively encapsulating these functions yield these new implementations for `draw-los` and `draw-loa`:

```
;; los scene → scene
;; Purpose: To draw the given los in the given scene
(define (draw-los a-los scn)
  (local [;; shot scene → scene
          ;; Purpose: To draw the shot in the given scene
          (define (draw-shot a-shot scn)
            (if (eq? a-shot NO-SHOT)
                scn
                (draw-ci SHOT-IMG
                         (posn-x a-shot)
                         (posn-y a-shot)
                         scn)))
```

Fig. 99 Encapsulated `draw-world` function, part I

```
;; world → scene      Purpose: To draw the world in E-SCENE
(define (draw-world a-world)
  (local
   [(define E-SCENE-COLOR 'pink)
    (define E-SCENE (empty-scene E-SCENE-W E-SCENE-H E-SCENE-COLOR))
    ;; image image-x image-y image → image
    ;; Purpose: Place first image in second image at given coordinates
    (define (draw-ci char-img an-img-x an-img-y scn)
     (local [;; image-x → pixel-x  Purpose: Translate image-x to pixel-x
             (define (image-x->pix-x ix)
               (+ (* ix IMAGE-WIDTH) (/ IMAGE-WIDTH 2)))
             ;; image-y → pixel-y  Purpose: Translate image-y to pixel-y
             (define (image-y->pix-y iy)
               (+ (* iy IMAGE-HEIGHT) (/ IMAGE-HEIGHT 2)))
             ;; image image-x image-y image → image
             ;; Purpose: Place first image in second image at given
             ;;          coordinates
             (define (draw-ci char-img an-img-x an-img-y scn)
              (place-image char-img
                           (image-x->pix-x an-img-x)
                           (image-y->pix-y an-img-y)
                           scn))]
      (draw-ci char-img an-img-x an-img-y scn)))
    ;; los scene → scene
    ;; Purpose: To draw the given los in the given scene
    (define (draw-los a-los scn)
     (local [;; shot scene → scene      Purpose: Draw shot in given scene
             (define (draw-shot a-shot scn)
               (if (eq? a-shot NO-SHOT) scn
                   (draw-ci SHOT-IMG (posn-x a-shot) (posn-y a-shot) scn)))
             ;; los scene → scene
             ;; Purpose: To draw the given los in the given scene
             (define (draw-los a-los scn)
              (if (empty? a-los) scn
                  (draw-shot (first a-los) (draw-los (rest a-los) scn))))]
      (draw-los a-los scn)))
```

```
    ;; los scene → scene
    ;; Purpose: To draw the given los in the given scene
    (define (draw-los a-los scn)
      (if (empty? a-los)
          scn
          (draw-shot (first a-los)
                     (draw-los (rest a-los) scn))))]
  (draw-los a-los scn)))
```

Fig. 100 Encapsulated draw-world function, part II

```
;; loa scene → scene
;; Purpose: Draw given loa in given scene
(define (draw-loa a-loa scn)
  (local
    [;; alien scene → scene      Purpose: Draw alien in given scene
     (define (draw-alien an-alien scn)
       (draw-ci ALIEN-IMG (posn-x an-alien) (posn-y an-alien) scn))
     ;; loa scene → scene      Purpose: Draw given loa in given scene
     (define (draw-loa a-loa scn)
       (if (empty? a-loa) scn
           (draw-alien (first a-loa) (draw-loa (rest a-loa) scn))))]

     ;; rocket scene → scene  Purpose: Draw given rocket in given scene
     (define (draw-rocket a-rocket a-scene)
       (draw-ci ROCKET-IMG a-rocket ROCKET-Y a-scene))

     ;; world → scene      Purpose: To draw the world in E-SCENE
     (define (draw-world a-world)
       (draw-los (world-shots a-world)
                 (draw-loa (world-aliens a-world)
                           (draw-rocket (world-rocket a-world)
                                        E-SCENE))))]
  (draw-world a-world)))
```

```
;; loa scene → scene
;; Purpose: To draw the given loa in the given scene
(define (draw-loa a-loa scn)
  (local [;; alien scene → scene
          ;; Purpose: Draw the given alien in the given scene
          (define (draw-alien an-alien scn)
            (draw-ci ALIEN-IMG
                     (posn-x an-alien)
                     (posn-y an-alien)
                     scn))
          ;; loa scene → scene
          ;; Purpose: To draw the given loa in the given scene
          (define (draw-loa a-loa scn)
            (if (empty? a-loa)
                scn
                (draw-alien (first a-loa)
                            (draw-loa (rest a-loa) scn))))]
    (draw-loa a-loa scn)))
```

Observe that draw-ci is an auxiliary function used by draw-rocket, draw-shot, and draw-alien. If draw-ci is made local to these functions, there would be repeated code and this ought to be avoided. Instead, what is needed is to place draw-ci in a location where it is in scope of all three of these functions. This means that `draw-ci` cannot be local to, for example, `draw-shot` because it would be out of scope for the remaining two functions. If left at the global level `draw-ci` would be in scope for all three functions. This, however, leaves `draw-ci` outside of the only package that needs it. Therefore, the best solution is to make `draw-ci` local to `draw-world`. Figures 99 and 100 display the completed encapsulated version of `draw-world`. Observe that the auxiliary functions only needed by `draw-ci` are also locally encapsulated.

Take a moment to appreciate what has been accomplished. The code is now organized in a manner that allows any reader (including yourself 6 months from now) to easily find related functions. It also means that when a refinement is necessary we know where the new tested functions must be placed. For example, if a score is added to the world, then after testing you know that the `draw-score` function ought to be local to `draw-world`.

> ***** Ex. 270 —** Section 106 discusses the design of `eval-sexpr`. Encapsulate this function and its auxiliary functions.
>
> ****** Ex. 271 —** Section 88 discusses the design of `largest-prime`. Encapsulate this function and its auxiliary functions.

121.2 Readability

Section 106 discusses the design of the following functions to evaluate arithmetic expressions using +, -, and *:

```
;; (listof sexpr) arrow (listof number) throws error
;; Purpose: To evaluate the sexprs in the given list
(define (eval-args a-losexpr)
  (if (empty? a-losexpr)
      '()
      (cons (eval-sexpr (first a-losexpr))
            (eval-args (rest a-losexpr)))))

;; function (listof number) → number throws error
;; Purpose: To apply the given function to the given numbers
(define (apply-f a-function a-lon)
  (cond [(eq? a-function '+) (sum-lon  a-lon)]
        [(eq? a-function '-) (subt-lon a-lon)]
        [else (mult-lon a-lon)]))

;; slist → number
;; Purpose: To evaluate the given slist
(define (eval-slist an-slist)
  (apply-f (first an-slist) (eval-args (rest an-slist))))
```

```
;; sexpr → number throws error
;; Purpose: To evaluate the given sexpr
(define (eval-sexpr a-sexpr)
  (if (number? a-sexpr)
      a-sexpr
      (eval-slist a-sexpr))))
```

What does (first a-losexpr) represents? Do you remember? Is it reasonable to expect others reading this code for the first time to know or easily figure it out? It is unlikely that you remember what all the expressions in the program represent and it is even more unlikely that someone reading your code will be able to discern the meaning of every expression. To mitigate this problem a local-expression may be used to define intermediate values using descriptive variable names.

To start consider the function eval-slist. In its body there is an application expression to apply apply-f to the first element of the given slist and the result obtained from applying eval-args to the rest of the given slist. Anyone that is familiar with ISL+ can make these observations, but such a verbatim description of the code does not elucidate the reader about why the code does this. Anyone, of course, can go read Sect. 106 to understand what this function does, but this is time consuming. Instead of placing this burden on the readers of the code we can define local variables with names that elicit the meaning of the expressions. The idea is that we do not rely on list selector applications to showcase the meaning of expressions to evaluate arithmetic expressions. Instead, local variables may be used to easily discern that (first an-slist) represents the arithmetic operator and that (eval-args (rest an-slist)) the arguments for the arithmetic operator. This idea leads to the following refactoring:

```
;; slist → number
;; Purpose: To evaluate the given slist
(define (eval-slist an-slist)
  (local [(define operator  (first an-slist))
          (define arg-exprs (rest an-slist))]
    (apply-f operator (eval-args arg-exprs))))
```

Observe that eval-slist is more readable now. Any reader can now immediately understand that the slist's operator is applied to the arguments obtained from evaluating the argument-expressions in the given slist.

A similar refactoring can be done to make it easier to understand what the function eval-args does. Observe that the expressions (first a-losexpr) and (rest a-losexpr) give the reader no indication of what they represent. The former represents the first argument and the latter represents the rest of the arguments. With this in mind, a local-expression may be used to refactor eval-args as follows:

```
;; (listof sexpr) arrow (listof number) throws error
;; Purpose: To evaluate the sexprs in the given list
(define (eval-args a-losexpr)
  (if (empty? a-losexpr)
      '()
      (local [(define first-arg (first a-losexpr))
              (define rest-args (rest a-losexpr))]
        (cons (eval-sexpr first-arg)
              (eval-args  rest-args)))))
```

As you solve a problem remember that the goal of a program is not only to produce a solution. An equally important goal is to clearly communicate how a problem is solved. The use of local-expressions can be very useful to make clear what expressions represent.

***
Ex. 272 — Section 107.1 discusses the design of process-blanks. Refactor this function to make it more readable.

****
Ex. 273 — Section 107.2 discusses the design of node-can-win?. Refactor this function to make it more readable. Make sure not to unnecessarily evaluate any arguments for and and or. Your refactored code should not do more work than the original function.

***
Ex. 274 — Section 98 discusses the design of btstring-extract. Refactor this function to make it more readable.

121.3 Furthering Functional Abstraction

Consider the function to move a (listof alien):

```
;; (listof alien) dir → (listof alien)
;; Purpose: To move the given list of aliens in the
;;          given direction
(define (move-loa a-loa dir)
  (if (empty? a-loa)
      E-LOA
      (cons (move-alien (first a-loa) dir)
            (move-loa (rest a-loa) dir))))
```

The same function, `move-alien`, is applied to every `alien` in the given list and a list of the results is returned. This suggests using `map` to re-implement this function. Recall, however, the signature for `map`:

```
(X → Y) (listof X) → (listof Y)
```

It expects a one-input function as input. Do you see the problem? Look at the signature for `move-alien`:

```
alien direction → alien
```

It is a two-input function and, therefore, cannot be given as input to `map`.

Observe, however, that to move an alien the only thing that varies is the alien to be moved. The direction is the same for all aliens. Given that only one thing varies, this suggests that inside `move-loa` the moving of an alien may be implemented as a one-input function. This function may be defined locally and given to `map` as input:

```
;; (listof alien) dir → (listof alien)
;; Purpose: To move the given list of aliens in the
;;          given direction
(define (move-loa a-loa dir)
  (local [(define (alien-mover an-alien)
            (move-alien an-alien dir))]
    (map alien-mover a-loa)))
```

Why is such refactoring possible? Note that the value of `dir` does not change in the recursive call. Therefore, inside `move-loa` `dir` may be considered a constant value and a simpler function may be defined that does not have `dir` as input. Instead, `dir` becomes a free variable inside the new local function. In general, within a function any variables that do not change from one recursive call to the next may be treated as constants to define a local function in which these variables are free variables. In this case, it makes it possible to refactor a two-input function to move an `alien` into a one-input function in which the direction to move the `alien` in is a free variable.

A note of caution is in order at this time. The `local`-expression in `move-loa` cannot be eliminated using the draft refactoring recipe presented in Sect. 119. The problem is that `alien-mover` has a free variable, `dir`, that only exists inside `move-loa`. Therefore, `alien-mover` cannot simply be moved outside the scope of `dir`. We shall discuss how to solve this problem in Chap. 22.

** Ex. 275 — Refactor `move-posns` to use `map`. Write and run tests to validate your transformation.

```
;; number number (listof posn) → (listof posn)
;; Purpose: Move the posns by the given amounts
(define (move-posns deltax deltay a-loposn)
  (if (empty? a-loposn)
      '()
      (cons (move-posn  deltax deltay (first a-loposn))
            (move-posns deltax deltay (rest a-loposn)))))
```

**** **Ex. 276** — Refactor `get-all-in-interval` to use `filter`. Write and
run tests to validate your transformation.

```
;; [int..int] (listof number) → (listof number)
;; Purpose: Extract the list numbers that are in the
;;          given interval
(define (get-all-in-interval low high a-lon)
  (cond [(empty? a-lon) '()]
        [(<= low (first a-lon) high)
         (cons (first a-lon)
               (get-all-in-interval low high (rest a-lon)))]
        [else  (get-all-in-interval low high (rest a-lon))]))
```

**** **Ex. 277** — Refactor `all-outside-interval?` to use andmap. Write
and run tests to validate your transformation.

```
;; [int..int] (listof number) → Boolean
;; Purpose: Determine if all list numbers are outside
;;          given interval
(define (all-outside-interval? low high a-lon)
  (or (empty? a-lon)
      (and (not (<= low (first a-lon) high))
           (all-outside-interval? low high (rest a-lon)))))
```

121.4 One-Time Expression Evaluation

It may be surprising to you that `local`-expressions may be used to improve program
performance. That is, the use of `local`-expressions may make a program faster.
Programs may be noticeably slowed down by having to compute the value of an
expression more than once. In fact the abstract running time of a program may be
worsened by programs that evaluate the same expression multiple times.

Consider, for example, the program to return the last `item` in a given (`listof`
`item`) that costs less than a given price displayed in Fig. 101. Observe that the
expression (`get-last a-price (rest a-loi)`)) may be evaluated twice for
every call to `get-last`. This expression is evaluated once to test if the result is
empty and then again if the result is not empty. At a glance you can immediately tell
this is inefficient. It is simply silly to evaluate the same expression to get the same
value twice.

Fig. 101 A program to get last item under a given price

```
;; An item is a structure, (make-item string number), with a name & price.
(define-struct item (name price))


;; A result is either: 1. '() or 2. item
;; Sample items
(define IT0 (make-item "ball"  10))   (define IT1 (make-item "doll"  8))
(define IT2 (make-item "bat"   12))   (define IT3 (make-item "glove" 15))
(define IT4 (make-item "cap"    7))   (define IT5 (make-item "bike"  100))


;; Sample (listof item)
(define LOI0 '())
(define LOI1 (list IT0 IT1 IT2 IT3 IT4 IT5))
(define LOI2 (list IT1 IT2 IT3 IT5))
(define LOI3 (list IT1 IT2 IT4 IT5))


;; number (listof item) → result    Purpose: Get last item < given price
(define (get-last a-price a-loi)
  (cond [(empty? a-loi) '()]
        [(< (item-price (first a-loi)) a-price)
         (if (empty? (get-last a-price (rest a-loi))) (first a-loi)
             (get-last a-price (rest a-loi)))]
        [else (get-last a-price (rest a-loi))]))


;; Sample expressions for get-last
(define L0-V '())            (define L1-V (get-last 10 (rest LOI1)))
(define L2-V (first L2))     (define L3-V (get-last 11 (rest LOI3)))


;; Tests using sample computations for get-last
(check-expect (get-last 120 L0) L0-V)
(check-expect (get-last 10  L1) L1-V)
(check-expect (get-last 9   L2) L2-V)
(check-expect (get-last 11 L3)  L3-V)


;; Tests using sample values for get-last
(check-expect (get-last 150
                        (list (make-item "pen" 100)
                              (make-item "ring" 600)
                              (make-item "knife" 125)))
              (make-item "knife" 125))
(check-expect (get-last 120
                        (list (make-item "pen" 100)
                              (make-item "ring" 600)
                              (make-item "knife" 125)))
              (make-item "pen" 100))
```

Instead of evaluating the same expression multiple times to obtain the same value, locally define a variable and only evaluate the expression once. In the remainder of the code reference the local variable instead of evaluating the expression again. Following this principle get-last is refactored to

```
;; number (listof item) → result
;; Purpose: Get last item < given price
(define (get-last a-price a-loi)
  (cond [(empty? a-loi) '()]
        [(< (item-price (first a-loi)) a-price)
         (local [(define rest-result (get-last a-price
                                               (rest a-loi)))]
            (if (empty? rest-result)
                (first a-loi)
                rest-result))]
        [else (get-last a-price (rest a-loi))]))
```

Observe that rest-result captures the value obtained from processing the rest of the list of items. Therefore, this local variable may be used instead of processing the rest of the list of items multiple times.

Is this type of refactoring nitpicking or can it have a significant impact on performance? To answer this question let us identify the input that exhibits the worst possible performance. This occurs when the price given to get-last is larger than the price of all the items in the given list. In such a case there is always an item with a smaller price in the rest of a non-empty list. Let us define a list of with all identical items using interval-accum-12h (from Sect. 117) as follows:

```
;; int → item
;; Purpose: Returns a doll item that costs 30
(define (make-doll-item n) (make-item "doll" 30))

;; Sample expressions for make-doll-item
(define DOLL1 (make-item "doll" 30))
(define DOLL2 (make-item "doll" 30))

;; Tests using sample computations for make-doll-item
(check-expect (make-doll-item 4) DOLL1)
(check-expect (make-doll-item 8) DOLL2)

;; Tests using sample values for make-doll-item
(check-expect (make-doll-item -5) (make-item "doll" 30))
(check-expect (make-doll-item 0)  (make-item "doll" 30))

(define LOIL
        (interval-accum-12h '() make-doll-item cons 0 19))
```

Fig. 102 A tree of natural numbers

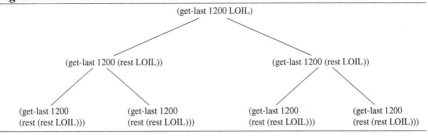

LOIL is a (short) list of 20 identical items. If we rename the second version of the function as get-last2, we can time the two versions as follows:

```
(time (get-last  1200 LOIL))
(time (get-last2 1200 LOIL))
```

The results obtained for CPU time are

Function	CPU Time
get-last	1547
get-last2	0

On your computer the measured numbers might vary, but it is undeniable that there is a significant difference in actual running time in favor of the version that uses a local-expression.

How is this explained? Why is the get-last2 much faster? To answer this let us look at the abstract running time of both functions. To ascertain the abstract running time for get-last let us visualize the beginning of the function calls made. These calls are displayed in Fig. 102. The initial call to get-last generates two calls using the rest of the given list. Each of these two calls generates two calls with the rest of the given list. We can extrapolate that every call to get-last will generate two more recursive calls until the list is empty. How many calls are made for a list of length n? The binary tree of calls in Fig. 102 would have height n (remember that the root of the binary tree is at height 0). Each node in the binary tree represents a function call. The binary tree would be a full binary tree (i.e., all leaves are at level n). Therefore, the number of calls is equal to the number of nodes in a full binary tree. The following table illustrates the number of nodes in a full binary tree of height h:

h	Number of Nodes
0	0
1	3
2	7
3	15
4	31
⋮	⋮

From the table we can extrapolate that a full binary tree of height h has $2^{h+1} - 1$ nodes. This means that the number of function calls for a list of length n is $2^{n+1} - 1$ making get-last $O(2^n)$. That is, the amount of work done by get-last grows exponentially as the length of the input list grows.

What is the abstract running time of get-last2? Observe that for every function call there is at most only one recursive call generated. This means that the total number of function calls for a list of length n is n. This makes get-last2 $O(n)$. In other words, the work done is proportional to the size of the list. This explains why get-last2 is much faster than get-last.

The lesson you should walk away with is that evaluating the same expression multiple times may have a profound impact on abstract and actual running time. It is not the case, however, that eliminating the repetitive evaluation of the same expression always leads to better abstract running time. In fact, it may not even have a noticeable impact on actual running time. Another thing worth noting is that a program that has an exponential abstract running time is not a practical solution to a problem. The amount of work done grows too quickly and makes the computation of a solution unfeasible even for input of moderate size. In future courses in Computer Science you will study techniques to approximate a solution using, for example, heuristics that have a polynomial (not exponential) abstract running time.

*** **Ex. 278 —** The *powerset* of a set, S, is the set of all subsets of S, including the empty set and S itself. A colleague has written the following function to compute the powerset of a set (foolishly not all the steps of the design recipe have been followed):

```
;; A set is a (listof X)

;; set → (listof set)
;; Purpose: Return the power set of the given set
(define (powerSet a-set)
  (if (empty? a-set)
      (list '())
      (local [(define (add2subset a-subset)
                (cons (first a-set) a-subset))]
        (append (powerSet (rest a-set))
                (map add2subset (powerSet (rest a-set)))))))

(check-expect (powerSet '()) (list '()))
(check-expect (powerSet '(1 2))
              (list '() (list 2) (list 1) (list 1 2)))
(check-expect (powerSet '(a b c))
              '(()     (c) (b)
                (b c) (a) (a c)
                (a b) (a b c)))
```

If you run the code the tests pass. However, your colleague believes there is a bug in the code. The following use of the function seems to never return an answer or simply takes too long to be of practical use:

```
(powerSet '(a b c d e f g h i j k l m n o p q r s
                                  t u v w x y z))
```

Help your colleague to make the function faster.

** **Ex. 279** — Design and write a function that takes as input an x-value and a list of posns and that returns the last posn in the given list that has the given x-value. If no such posn exists, then your function ought to return #false.

**** **Ex. 280** — Your friend is studying Computer Science at a university that does not teach students about program design. Your friend wrote the following function that takes as input a (btof number) and then returns the maximum between the sum of the left and right subtrees:

```
(define (bt-sum t)
  (if (empty? t)
      0
      (+ (first t)
         (first (rest t))
         (first (rest (rest t)))))))

(define (leftsum>rightsum? a-numbt)
  (if (> (numbt-sum (second a-numbt))
         (numbt-sum (third a-numbt)))
      (numbt-sum (second a-numbt))
      (numbt-sum (third a-numbt))))
```

You are horrified, of course, by such unreadable code that computes the value of the same expression more than once. Redesign the code to make it more readable and avoid evaluating expressions more than once by following the steps of the design recipe.

122 What Have We Learned in This Chapter?

The important lessons of Chap. 21 are summarized as follows:

- Encapsulation means that we package together all related functions as a single piece of software.
- A local-expression allows us to define new variables and functions inside of functions.
- The local-expression syntax is expr ::= (local [def*] expr)

- No new computational power is provided by `local`-expressions. They are syntactic sugar to help programmers better organize and design programs.
- The lexical scope of a variable is the section of the program where it is valid.
- Within its lexical scope a variable may be shadowed by a declaration of the same variable.
- In lexical scoping a reference is always to the nearest declaration.
- Encapsulate functions only after thoroughly testing them.
- Local definitions can improve communicating how a problem was solved.
- Local definitions can aid in furthering the use of abstract functions by defining functions where only values that change are parameters and that have one or more free variables whose values do not change for a given function call (like in `move-loa`).
- A repeated expression inside a function may be eliminated by defining a local variable for its value and referencing the variable instead of evaluation the expression multiple times.
- Repeated expressions inside a function may make it have an exponential abstract running time and, therefore, be an impractical solution to a problem.

Chapter 22
Lambda Expressions

Section 115 introduces the idea that functions are a type of value just like numbers, strings, and images are types of values. It presents how functions may be passed as arguments to other functions. This ability allows us to develop powerful abstract functions like map, filter, and ormap. This chapter continues the exploration of functions as data. Specifically, it explores how to create a function value and how to return a function as the value of a function application. This ability has profound implications for problem solving and program design. For example, it leads to functions that compute functions and to object-oriented programming (as Chap. 25 discusses).

Why would you want to compute a function in the first place? The short answer is that it is a common operation in human life. Consider, for example, the composition of two functions as you have studied in high school Mathematics. You may recall how function composition is typically written:

        (f ○ g)(x) = f(g(x))

This equation is stating that the composition of f and g provides the output of g as input to f. Although it is more subtle and not very emphasized in a high school Mathematics course, the composition of f and g is a function. If we have two functions f and g, the above equation tells us how to build a new function that we call the composition of f and g. For example, Fig. 103 displays two functions. One adds four to its input and the other doubles its input. If you were asked to compose add4 and double (i.e., write a function that adds 4 to the doubling of its input) and to compose double and add4 (i.e., write a function that doubles the sum of its input and 4), your code may look as displayed in Fig. 104.

Observe that in Fig. 104 add4-o-double and double-o-add4 are good candidates for abstraction. As you expect the differences are the composed functions.

© The Author(s), under exclusive license to Springer Nature Switzerland AG 2022   499
M. T. Morazán, *Animated Problem Solving*, Texts in Computer Science,
https://doi.org/10.1007/978-3-030-85091-3_22

Fig. 103 Functions to add 4 and double a given number

```
;; number → number     Purpose: Add 4 to the given number
(define (add4 x) (+ x 4))


;; Sample expressions for add4
(define ADD4-VAL1 (+ 5 4))              (define ADD4-VAL2 (+ -7 4))


;; Tests using sample computations for add4
(check-expect (add4 5) ADD4-VAL1)    (check-expect (add4 -7) ADD4-VAL2)
;; Tests using sample values for add4
(check-expect (add4 0) 4)               (check-expect (add4 -10) -6)


;; number → number     Purpose: Double the given number
(define (double x) (* 2 x))


;; Sample expressions for double
(define DBL-VAL1 (* 2 10))              (define DBL-VAL2 (* 2 -3))


;; Tests using sample computations for double
(check-expect (double 10) DBL-VAL1)  (check-expect (double -3) DBL-VAL2)
;; Tests using sample values for double
(check-expect (double -7) -14)          (check-expect (double 65) 130)
```

Using the design recipe for functional abstraction yields the following abstract function and refactored functions:

```
;; (number → number) (number → number) number → number
;; Purpose: Return f(g(x))
(define (f-o-g f g x) (f (g x)))


;; number → number
;; Purpose: Add 4 to the double of the given number
(define (add4-o-double x) (f-o-g add4 double x))


;; number → number
;; Purpose: Double the sum of the given number and 4
(define (double-o-add4 x) (f-o-g double add4 x))
```

All tests pass after running them. The abstract function, however, is not quite what we want. Observe that x is a parameter in the abstract function, but not a difference in the original functions. We want f-o-g to return a function and not the value of said function for some value x. This means x should not be a parameter in the abstract function. In other words, we want an abstract function with the following signature and purpose:

```
;; (number → number) (number → number) → (number → number)
;; Purpose: Return the composition of the given functions
(define (f-o-g f g) ...)
```

Fig. 104 Two ways of composing add2 and double

```
;; number → number    Purpose: Add 4 to the double of the given number
(define (add4-o-double x) (add4 (double x)))


;; Sample expressions for add4-o-double
(define ADD4-DBL-VAL1 (add4 (double 0)))
(define ADD4-DBL-VAL2 (add4 (double -1)))


;; Tests using sample computations for add4-o-double
(check-expect (add4-o-double 0)  ADD4-DBL-VAL1)
(check-expect (add4-o-double -1) ADD4-DBL-VAL2)
;; Tests using sample values for add4-o-double
(check-expect (add4-o-double -8) -12)
(check-expect (add4-o-double 50) 104)


;; number → number    Purpose: Double the sum of the given number and 4
(define (double-o-add4 x) (double (add4 x)))


;; Sample expressions for double-o-add4
(define DBL-ADD4-VAL1 (double (add4 10)))
(define DBL-ADD4-VAL2 (double (add4 -2)))


;; Tests using sample computations for double-o-add4
(check-expect (double-o-add4 10) DBL-ADD4-VAL1)
(check-expect (double-o-add4 -2) DBL-ADD4-VAL2)
;; Tests using sample values for double-o-add4
(check-expect (double-o-add4 40) 88)
(check-expect (double-o-add4 -6) -4)
```

123 Anonymous Functions

You probably suspect already that returning a function is easy. You simply need to return the function you want just like you return a number or a string of your choice. This is partially correct. Consider, for example, the following program:

```
;; number → (number → number)
;; Purpose: Return + if the given number is even.
;;          Otherwise, return -.
(define (choose-f x) (if (even? x) + -))

(check-expect ((choose-f 4) 1 5) 6)
(check-expect ((choose-f 3) 1 5) -4)
```

The function choose-f returns a function. Specifically, it returns + if its input is even and it returns − if its input is odd. Therefore, ((choose-f 4) 1 5) is (+ 1 5) and ((choose-f 3) 1 5) is (− 1 5). The application of choose-f to a number returns a function that is then applied to the given arguments.

The above example works because it handles functions that exist and have a name. This is why it is easy to return a function. If a function has a name, it may be returned as the value of a function. In other words, a function name is simply a variable whose value is a function. In contrast, we want f-o-g to return a function that does not exist in the program or in the programming language and, of course, does not have a name. Therefore, we need an expression that returns a function when it is evaluated. Such an expression is a lambda-expression (or λ-expression). The syntax for a λ-expression in ISL+ is

expr ::= (lambda (symbol⁺) expr)

::= (λ (symbol⁺) expr)

These two expressions mean exactly the same thing. To type a "λ" in DrRacket use Ctrl-\ (hold down the control key and press the backslash key). In parenthesis, a λ-expression has the keyword lambda or the symbol λ followed by a list of symbols and an expression. The list of symbols are the parameters of the function and the expression is the body of the function. For example, the following expression returns a function that adds 10 to its input:

(λ (a-number) (+ a-number 10))

We may apply this function to a number just like any other function that takes as input a number. Consider, for example, the following expression:

((λ (a-number) (+ a-number 10)) 25)

When this application expression is evaluated, the λ-expression returns a function that has a parameter called a-number and that has a body that adds 10 to a-number. This function is applied to 25 to obtain 35 (the value of the application expression).

In essence, a λ-expression allows us to create an *anonymous function*. That is a function without a name. If we wish to give such a function a name, then we need to use define. For example, the function above to add 10 to its input may be bound to a name as follows:

(define add10 (λ (a-number) (+ a-number 10)))

It is now possible for you to understand that

(define (<name> <name>$^+$) expr)

is syntactic sugar for

(define <name> (lambda (<name>$^+$) expr))

In other words, define binds a variable to value. The value may be any valid value in ISL+ including functions.

You should consider using a λ-expression on its own (i.e., without binding its value to a variable) when:

- A new function is needed.
- The needed function is not recursive.
- The needed function is only used once.

Keep in mind that a λ-expression evaluates to an anonymous function. Therefore, it cannot recursively call itself. In order for a function to be recursive, it must have a name. Commonly, a λ-expression is used to provide an argument to a function or to return a function as the value of a function call.

** **Ex. 281** — Write a λ-expression to create a function that computes $f(x)$ = $5x^3 + 10x^2 + 2x + 31$. Use it to compute $f(0)$ and $f(10)$.

*** **Ex. 282** — Write a λ-expression to create a function that returns the absolute value of its input. Use it to compute the absolute value of 0, 22, and -40.

**** **Ex. 283** — Write a λ-expression to create a function that returns the second largest value of three given numbers. Apply it to 87, 27, and 100.

*** **Ex. 284** — Write a λ-expression to create a function that moves a shot for Aliens Attack. Apply it to (make-posn 4 5) and to NO-SHOT.

*** **Ex. 285** — Write a λ-expression to create a predicate to determine if a given number is in a given interval. Apply it to 10 and [89..100] and to 67 and [50..85].

*** **Ex. 286** — An item has a name and a price. Write a λ-expression to create a predicate to determine if a given item's price is less than a given price. Write application expressions that illustrate that the function works.

---

124 Revisiting Function Composition

Given add4 and double, we need two functions: (add4 ∘ double)(x) and (double ∘ add4)(x). We can define these functions using a λ-expression as follows:

```
;; number → number
;; Purpose: Add 4 to the double of the given number
(define add4-o-double (λ (x) (add4 (double x))))

;; number → number
;; Purpose: Double the sum of the given number and 4
(define double-o-add4 (λ (x) (double (add4 x))))
```

Observe that using a λ-expression does not change the steps of the design recipe. You can substitute these new definitions for the definitions in Fig. 104 and all the tests will pass. Try it out!

Observe that the two expressions are nearly identical. This strongly suggests abstracting over the expressions. This abstraction step yields the following function:

```
;; (number → number) (number → number) → (number → number)
;; Purpose: Return f(g(x))
(define (f-o-g f g) (λ (x) (f (g x))))
```

We now have the correct abstraction. We have a function that given two functions returns a function for the composition of the two functions. We can now refactor the original definitions to use the abstraction to get

```
;; number → number
;; Purpose: Add 4 to the double of the given number
(define add4-o-double (f-o-g add4 double))
```

```
;; number → number
;; Purpose: Double the sum of the given number and 4
(define double-o-add4 (f-o-g double add4))
```

You can now add f-o-g to and substitute these two functions in Fig. 104. All the test will pass. Try it out!

Take some time to ponder what has been accomplished. We can design functions that compute functions. This means we can now use functions that we did not write. We use functions that were computed for us. This is a powerful tool in your design arsenal. A program can create specialized functions as needed. In fact, the abstraction provided by f-o-g is so useful that it is provided by ISL+ as compose.

** **Ex. 287** — In high school Mathematics you learned that an invertible function, f, maps a value from its domain to a value in its range. The inverse of f, f^{-1}, maps the range value back to the domain value. This suggests that the composition of f and f^{-1} is the identity function (implemented as id in Sect. 116.1). Write a program to test this hypothesis. Your different definitions for the identity function and corresponding tests ought to look like this:

```
;; number → number
;; Purpose: Return the given number
(define id-f1 (make-id f1 f1⁻¹))
```

```
;; number → number
;; Purpose: Return the given number
(define id-f2 (make-id f2 f2⁻¹))
```

```
(check-expect (id-f1 100) 100)
(check-expect (id-f2 4)    4)
```

*** **Ex. 288** — You have a software company that supports manufacturing companies. The total costs of any manufacturing company is given by the sum of its variable costs and its fixed costs. The variable cost is proportional to the number of units produced each month, while fixed costs are the same every month. For example, assume that for company C1 the cost per unit is $5 and the fixed costs are $100 and that for company C2 the cost per unit is $3 and the fixed costs are $75. The respective functions for the total costs of companies C1 and C2 may be written as follows:

```
;; number → number
;; Purpose: Return the total costs of C1
(define (total-costs-C1 units-produced)
  (+ (* units-produced 5) 100))

(check-expect (total-costs-C1 10) 150)

;; number → number
;; Purpose: Return the total costs of C1
(define (total-costs-C2 units-produced)
  (+ (* units-produced 3) 75))

(check-expect (total-costs-C2 20) 135)
```

As the number of companies you develop total costs functions for grows, you discover that typing similar functions over and over is a waste of your time. Abstract over the above functions to develop an abstract function that computes a total cost function. Refactor the above functions to make use of your abstract function.

125 Curried Functions

Creating specialized recursive functions as a program is evaluated may be implemented using both local- and λ-expressions. Consider the following functions from Aliens Attack to draw a list of aliens and a list of shots:

```
;; loa scene → scene
;; Purpose: To draw the given loa in the given scene
(define (draw-loa a-loa scn)
  (if (empty? a-loa)
      scn
      (draw-alien (first a-loa)
                  (draw-loa (rest a-loa) scn))))
```

```
;; los scene → scene
;; Purpose: To draw the given los in the given scene
(define (draw-los a-los scn)
  (if (empty? a-los)
      scn
      (draw-shot (first a-los)
                 (draw-los (rest a-los) scn)))))
```

These functions are clear candidates for abstraction. The only significant difference between them is the function used to draw the first list element. Performing the abstraction step yields the following function:

```
;; (listof X) image → image
;; Purpose: To draw the given list in the given scene
(define (draw-lox draw-x a-lox scn)
  (if (empty? a-lox)
      scn
      (draw-x (first a-lox)
              (draw-lox draw-x (rest a-lox) scn)))))
```

Given an X-drawing function draw-lox draws a given (listof X) in the given scene. Observe that draw-lox has a structure very similar to accum from Sect. 116.1. It can easily be refactored to have the same structure using id (also from Sect. 116.1) as follows:

```
;; (listof X) image → image
;; Purpose: To draw the given list in the given scene
(define (draw-lox draw-x a-lox scn)
  (if (empty? a-lox)
      scn
      (draw-x (id (first a-lox))
              (draw-lox draw-x (rest a-lox) scn)))))
```

This means draw-lox may be refactored using accum as follows:

```
;; (listof X) image → image
;; Purpose: To draw the given list in the given scene
(define (draw-lox draw-x a-lox scn)
  (accum scn id draw-x a-lox))
```

Refactoring the functions abstracted over yields

```
;; (listof alien) scene → scene
;; Purpose: To draw the given loa in the given scene
(define (draw-loa a-loa scn) (draw-lox draw-alien a-loa scn))
```

```
;; (listof shot) scene → scene
;; Purpose: To draw the given los in the given scene
(define (draw-los a-los scn) (draw-lox draw-shot a-los scn))
```

Observe that there is still a lot of repetition among these two functions. The only significant difference is the function used to draw either an `alien` or a `shot`. Abstracting over these functions suggests creating a function that may be outlined as follows:

```
;; (X → image) → ???
;; Purpose: ???
(define (draw-lox-maker draw-x) (...))
```

What should such a function return? This proposed abstract function only takes as input a drawing function. This drawing function by itself is of little use without the list of elements to draw and the scene to draw them into. This means that this list and scene are still needed as input. If they are needed as input, then `draw-lox` must return a function that consumes these inputs. The returned function must capture the similarities in `draw-loa` and `draw-los`. With this understanding the abstraction step yields

```
;; (X image → image) → ((listof X) image → image)
;; Purpose: Return a function to draw a (listof X)
(define (draw-lox-maker draw-x)
   (λ (a-lox scn) (draw-lox draw-x a-lox scn)))
```

The contract states that this function takes as input a function that consumes an X and an `image` and that returns an `image` (i.e., a drawing function). It returns a function that consumes a (`listof` X) and an `image` and that returns an `image` (i.e., a function to draw the given list). The resulting function is obtained by evaluating a λ-expression.[27] Observe that `draw-lox-maker` returns a specialized list-drawing function.

The abstract function `draw-lox-maker` is an example of a curried function. A curried function is one that consumes part of its input and returns a function that consumes the rest of the input. In this example, `draw-lox-maker` consumes a drawing function and returns a function that consumes a list of elements to draw and an image. The returned function is specialized using the value given as input. For example, consider the result of refactoring the functions abstracted over:

```
;; loa scene → scene
;; Purpose: To draw the given loa in the given scene
(define draw-loa (draw-lox-maker draw-alien))

;; los scene → scene
;; Purpose: To draw the given los in the given scene
(define draw-los (draw-lox-maker draw-shot))
```

---

[27] The body of `draw-lox-maker` could also be implemented using a `local`-expression that defines the returned function.

What are `draw-loa` and `draw-los`? Like any other function, we may plug-in the given arguments to `draw-lox-maker` and substitute the result into the above definitions:

```
;; loa scene → scene
;; Purpose: To draw the given loa in the given scene
(define draw-loa (λ (a-lox scn)
                   (draw-lox draw-alien a-lox scn)))

;; los scene → scene
;; Purpose: To draw the given los in the given scene
(define draw-los (λ (a-lox scn)
                   (draw-lox draw-shot a-lox scn)))
```

Observe that if we use the `define` syntactic sugar and change the name of `a-lox`, we obtain exactly the functions that were abstracted over.

Curried functions allow programmers to stage providing the inputs to a function. This allows for the partial evaluation of functions to produce specialized functions (as done by `draw-lox-maker`). Do you feel this is strange? Consider that without knowing it you have been using curried functions. The `big-bang` expression used to create video games and simulations is an example of currying in action. As a programmer you provide the functions, for example, to process keystrokes and to process clock ticks. Later a player and the computer provide the rest of the input (i.e., the keystrokes and the world).

The power of curried functions allows us to revisit `move-loa` from Sect. 121.3:

```
;; (listof alien) dir → (listof alien)
;; Purpose: To move the given list of aliens in the
;;               given direction
(define (move-loa a-loa dir)
  (local [(define (alien-mover an-alien)
            (move-alien an-alien dir))]
    (map alien-mover a-loa)))
```

Recall that we were unable to remove the `local`-expression because `alien-mover` has a free variable (i.e., `dir`). To remove the `local`-expression an `alien-mover` function specialized with the value of `dir` is needed. This can be done using a curried function. When a local function has free variables, a function that takes as input the free variables and that returns a specialized function is needed. In this case, the function needs to consume `dir` and return a specialized function for `alien-mover`. The refactored code without the `local`-expression is

```
;; dir → (alien → alien)
;; Purpose: Return a function to move an alien in the
;;               given direction
(define (alien-mover-maker a-dir)
  (λ (an-alien) (move-alien an-alien a-dir)))
```

```
;; (listof alien) dir → (listof alien)
;; Purpose: To move the given list of aliens in the
;;          given direction
(define (move-loa a-loa dir)
  (map (alien-mover-maker dir) a-loa))
```

Observe that for the first input to map a specialized alien-mover function is computed using the value of dir. The function alien-mover-maker contains no free variables and, therefore, may be moved outside the local-expression allowing for the elimination of said expression.

A cautionary note is warranted at this point. Computing a function's complete set of free variables and lifting it out of its lexical scope is a nontrivial process. Such lifting becomes harder when local functions are mutually recursive. The free variables of a function f are the free variables referenced in its body and the free variables in f's scope that are referenced by any function reachable from f by one or more function calls. The process to lift functions outside of their scope is called λ-*lifting* and you may study it in a future course on the implementation of programming languages or on your own.

*** Ex. 289 — You have a physicist friend who routinely writes functions to scale a list of numbers as the following (pardon the physicist who does not know about the steps of the design recipe):

```
(define (scale-by-2 L) (map (lambda (x) (* 2 x)) L))

(define (scale-by-5 L) (map (lambda (x) (* 5 x)) L))

(define (scale-by-3 L) (map (lambda (x) (* 3 x)) L))
                    ⋮
```

She complains that programming is too tedious because she must write almost the same code over and over again. Help your friend by writing a curried function to scale a list of numbers. Refactor the above functions to show your friend how all the list-scaling functions can be computed for her.

*** Ex. 290 — In Sect. 117 the following functions that accumulate a value by processing an interval from low to high are developed:

```
;; [int..int] → (listof string)
;; Purpose: Construct the list of strings for the ints in
;;          the given interval
(define (interval->lostr low high)
  (interval-accum-12h '() number->string cons low high))

;; [int..int] → int
;; Purpose: Compute the product of the squares of the ints
;;          in the given interval
(define (interval-product-sqrs low high)
  (interval-accum-12h 1 sqr * low high))
```

Observe the similarities between the two functions. Develop a curried function that produces specialized functions to accumulate a value by processing an interval from low to high. The specialized functions produced should only take an interval as input.

*** **Ex. 291** — The following functions combine three images:
```
;; image image image → image
;; Purpose: Create an image by putting the images
;;          above each other
(define (above-3imgs img1 img2 img3)
  (above img1 img2 img3))

(check-expect (above-3imgs (circle 10 'outline 'red)
                           (circle 20 'outline 'red)
                           (circle 40 'outline 'red))
```

)

```
;; image image image → image
;; Purpose: Create an image by putting the images beside
;;          each other
(define (beside-3imgs img1 img2 img3)
  (beside img1 img2 img3))

(check-expect (beside-3imgs (circle 10 'outline 'red)
                            (circle 20 'outline 'red)
                            (circle 40 'outline 'red))
```

)

Develop a curried function that produces specialized functions to combine three images. Refactor the above functions to use your curried function. Use your curried function to define a function that puts the first image above the image containing the other two images besides each other.

126 Designing Using Existing Abstractions

You may have the impression that designing abstract functions is a lot of work. You may feel that it always requires abstracting over similar functions and refactoring the functions abstracted over. Without a doubt this is an effective way to write more elegant and easier to maintain code. An abstract function, however, may be directly designed just like any other function. This section explores two examples that illustrate how this can be done. If an abstraction already exists in another domain, it can be directly designed and implemented. The two examples explored are computing a series and computing an approximation for π.

126.1 Computing the Value of a Series

In Mathematics, a set of ordered terms is called a *sequence*. For example, the sequence of the first 5 odd natural numbers is

    1 3 5 7 9

This sequence is finite. A sequence may also be infinite. For example, you have probably seen the sequence of odd natural numbers written as follows:

    1 3 5 7 9 ...

Each term in a sequence may be computed using its index in the sequence. Indexing starts at 0. This means, for example, that the 0th odd natural number is 1 and the 4th odd natural number is 9. The following function computes the ith element of the sequence of odd natural numbers:

```
;; natunum → natnum    Purpose: Return ith odd number
(define (ith-odd i) (add1 (* 2 i)))

;; Sample expressions for ith-odd
(define 0TH-ODD (add1 (* 2 0)))
(define 9TH-ODD (add1 (* 2 9)))

;; Tests using sample computations for ith-odd
(check-expect (ith-odd 0) 0TH-ODD)
(check-expect (ith-odd 9) 9TH-ODD)

;; Tests using sample values for ith-odd
(check-expect (ith-odd 2) 5)
(check-expect (ith-odd 4) 9)
```

The sum of the elements of a sequence is called a *series*. Summing up the elements of a sequence may provide the means by which to compute a number. For example, the sum of the first n elements of the sequence of natural odd numbers is equal to n^2. We will not prove this here, but we will illustrate it with the following examples:

$$0^2 = 0$$

$$3^2 = 1 + 3 + 5$$

$$5^2 = 1 + 3 + 5 + 7 + 9$$

Mathematicians would never explicitly write out all the elements of the sum for two reasons. The first is that it is too cumbersome. The second is that it is impossible to do so when the sequence is infinite. Instead, they have created syntax to abstractly capture and compactly write the idea of summing the terms of a sequence:

$$0^2 = 0$$

$$3^2 = \Sigma_{i=0}^{2}(\text{ith-odd i})$$

$$5^2 = \Sigma_{i=0}^{4}(\text{ith-odd i})$$

Look closely at what the mathematical notation is communicating. Adding zero terms is 0^2. For all other natural numbers a square is obtained by adding n terms produced using `ith-odd`. It is not difficult to see that a function for the terms for any sequence may be used. In fact, we may write

$$\text{series}_f(\text{n}) = \Sigma_{i=0}^{n-1}(\text{f i})$$

Observe that this defines a curried function. It first takes as input the term function and then to actually compute a value it takes the number of terms to add. We can implement a function to return a series-computing function as follows:

```
;; (natnum → number) → (natnum → number)
;; Purpose: Return a function to compute the series for
;;          the sequence defined by the given function
(define (series term-f)
  (lambda (n)
    (local [;; natnum → number
            ;; Purpose: Compute the series using the given
            ;;          number of terms
            (define (add-terms n)
              (if (= n 0)
                  (term-f 0)
                  (+ (term-f n) (add-terms (sub1 n)))))]
      (if (= n 0)
          (term-f 0)
          (add-terms (sub1 n))))))
```

This function returns a function to compute the value of a series that is specialized for the given term function. The returned function expects as input, n, a natural number (i.e., the number of terms to add). If n is 0, it returns the 0th term. Otherwise, it adds the first n terms using structural recursion. Observe that 1 is subtracted from n to add the terms. This is done because the number of integers in [0..n-1] is n. Given that recursion is needed to process a given natural number greater than 0, the function that does this work must be locally defined.

It now becomes straightforward to define a function to compute n^2. All that is needed is to give `series` the function `ith-odd` as input. The computed function may be defined and tested as follows:

```
;; natnum → natnum
;; Purpose: Compute the square of the given number
(define n-square (series ith-odd))

;; Sample expressions for nth-square
(define ZERO-SQ  (n-square 0))
(define THREE-SQ (n-square 3))

;; Tests using sample computations for nth-square
(check-expect (n-square 0) ZERO-SQ)
(check-expect (n-square 3) THREE-SQ)

;; Tests using sample values for nth-square
(check-expect (n-square 10) 100)
(check-expect (n-square 4)    16)
(check-expect (n-square 325) (sqr 325))
(check-expect (n-square 57)  (sqr 57))
```

Observe that the tests using sample values use ISL+'s sqr function. This clearly communicates that the functions are expected to be equivalent. It would be nice to simply write:

```
(check-expect n-square sqr)
```

Remember, however, that establishing the equivalence of two functions is an unsolvable problem. Therefore, it is impossible to write such a test.

*** **Ex. 292 —** Redesign `series` using the following contract for `add-terms`:
```
;; natnum>=1 → number
```

Admittedly, computing a series is hardly impressive if all we do is compute the square of a number. After all, we can use sqr or * to compute n^2. Let us continue to explore the power of the `series` function.

Your Discrete Mathematics Professor proposes the following hypothesis: the series of the first n cubes is always a square. Do you know if this is true or false? You may or may not know the answer already. Regardless of that you can (very) quickly write a program to test the hypothesis. The idea is to define a function to compute the series for cubes and test if the result is always a square. Here is a sample program to do so:

```
;; natnum → natnum
;; Purpose: Return the sum of the first n cubes
(define sum-cubes (series (lambda (n) (* n n n))))

(check-expect (integer? (sqrt (sum-cubes 0)))   #true)
(check-expect (integer? (sqrt (sum-cubes 5)))   #true)
(check-expect (integer? (sqrt (sum-cubes 209))) #true)
```

Observe that a λ-expression is used to define a function that cubes its input because it is not recursive and is only needed once. After running the tests you discover that they all pass and you begin to suspect that the Professor's hypothesis is true. In your Discrete Mathematics course you will learn how to actually prove that the Professor's hypothesis is true. The lesson to walk away with is that abstractions offer you the opportunity to easily experiment and test a hypothesis.

126.2 Approximating π

An irrational number, like π, cannot be exactly represented by a fraction. How then can the value of π be represented? The answer is that it cannot. All that we can do is approximate the value of π. In the fourteenth century the Indian mathematician Madhava of Sangamagrama discovered an infinite series to approximate the value of π (known today as the Madhava–Leibniz series, also named after the German mathematician Gottfried Wilhelm (von) Leibniz). The infinite series is

$$\pi = \Sigma_{i=0}^{\infty} (4 * \frac{-1^i}{(\text{ith-odd } i)})$$

This formula states that if we add an infinite number of terms the value of π is obtained. It is, of course, impossible to add an infinite number of terms. Therefore, the value of π is approximated by adding the first n terms of the series.

Using the abstract `series` function we can create a function to approximate π as follows:

```
;; natnum → number
;; Purpose: Approximate pi using the given number of terms
(define pi-series (series (lambda (i)
                            (* 4 (/ (expt -1 i) (ith-odd i)))))))
```

Observe that a λ-expression is used to define the term function given as input to `series`. Once again, this is done because the term function is not recursive and is only needed once.

The question now is to determine how to test this function. Given that an approximation is being computed our tests need to illustrate that as the number of terms used to approximate π increases the approximation gets better. This requires experimenting with the function to make sure it *converges*. That is, the approximation error gets smaller as the number of terms grows. The following tests achieve this goal:

```
(check-within (pi-series 500)   3.1415 0.01)   ;; 3.139592
(check-within (pi-series 3000)  3.1415 0.001)  ;; 3.141259
(check-within (pi-series 12000) 3.1415 0.0001) ;; 3.141509
```

The tests clearly illustrate that as the number of terms increases the accuracy of the results gets better. The values returned by `pi-series` are written as comments so that any reader can easily see how the approximation of π is converging.

In closing, developing your design and abstraction skills using λ-expressions and first-class functions is important. They are becoming more prevalent across all programming languages. Virtually all functional programming languages (e.g., `ISL+`, `Racket`, `Haskell`, `Clean`, and `F#`) have λ-expressions and support first-class functions. This support is now also found in object-oriented programming languages (e.g., `Java`, `Kotlin`, and `Scala`). In fact, now you may even use λ-expressions in `Excel`.

**** Ex. 293 — The product of the terms of a sequence from a to b whose elements are produced by f is defined as follows:
$$\Pi_{i=a}^{b} f(i) = \texttt{f(a)} * \texttt{f(a+1)} * \texttt{f(a+2)} * \ldots * \texttt{f(b-1)} * \texttt{f(b)}$$

Design a curried function, `pseries`, to implement $\Pi_{i=a}^{b} f(i)$. Use your curried function to define a function to compute `n!`.

***** Ex. 294 — The number of ways to choose k elements out of a finite set with n elements is
$$\binom{n}{k} = \Pi_{i=1}^{k} \frac{n+1-i}{i}$$

$\binom{n}{k}$ is read as n chooses k. Use your `pseries` function from the previous exercise to define a function to compute the value of $\binom{n}{k}$. <u>HINT</u>: n is a free variable in your term function.

*** Ex. 295 — Your Discrete Mathematics Professor postulates that
$$\Sigma_{i=1}^{b} k^4 = \frac{1}{30} n(n+1)(2n+1)(3n^2+3n-1)$$

Write a program to test this hypothesis. Do you suspect the Professor is right or wrong?

*** Ex. 296 — The Mathematics Professor claims that the constant e, an irrational number, may be approximated using the first n values of the following infinite series:
$$e = \Sigma_{i=0}^{\infty} \frac{1}{i!}$$

Write a program to illustrate that the series converges as n grows.

127 What Have We Learned in This Chapter?

The important lessons of Chap. 22 are summarized as follows:

- Functions are a type of value.
- Computing functions are common in human life.
- A function name is simply a variable whose value is a function.
- A λ-expression evaluates to an anonymous function.
- The syntax for a λ-expression in ISL+ is

  expr ::= (lambda (symbol$^+$) expr)

        ::= (λ (symbol$^+$) expr)

- Use a λ-expression on its own when a nonrecursive function that is only used once is needed.
- Functions can compute functions.
- A curried function is one that consumes part of its input and returns a function that consumes the rest of the input.
- Curried functions allow programmers to partially evaluate a function to produce a specialized function.
- Abstractions offer you the opportunity to easily experiment and test a hypothesis.
- Tests for functions that approximate a value must illustrate that the approximation error gets smaller as the number of terms grows.

Chapter 23
Aliens Attack Version 5

This chapter illustrates the use of encapsulation, abstract functions, and λ-expressions in the context of a larger piece of software. In essence, this chapter refactors Aliens Attack from Chap. 16. The goal is to group together related functions and to streamline the implementation of functions. The refactored code for the video game will have a set of constants needed by multiple functions or for testing, 6 global functions, and tests for the global functions. The global functions needed are run and the functions used in the big-bang expression in run's body.

Technically, the functions used in the big-bang expression can be encapsulated inside of run. This may be a perfectly reasonable choice for thoroughly tested code. We abstain from doing so for two reasons. First, run becomes too large and obfuscated. Second, as discussed in Part V, different components in a multiplayer game may need a different subset of the global functions. Therefore, it is best not to encapsulate them for now.

An outline of the desired refactored code for Aliens Attack is displayed in Fig. 105. The code is organized in 9 sections: data definitions, constants that are needed by more than a single function or test, structure definitions and sample instances, and 6 functions. No new data definitions nor changes to existing data definitions are required for this new version of the video game. Therefore, these remain unchanged and are not furthered discussed in this chapter. The constants that are only needed by a single handler are encapsulated. The constants at the global level include those that are needed by more than one handler or that are used in any handler's test. After the constants, the structure definitions and sample instances are written. In our game we only have one structure definition: world. This is followed by the code for each handler. The code for each handler includes the function definition, sample expressions, and its tests. The results from the steps of the design recipe must still be displayed for all global functions. The sample expressions and tests for auxiliary functions are not included given that they are encapsulated. Finally, the program ends with the refactored run function.

© The Author(s), under exclusive license to Springer Nature Switzerland AG 2022   517
M. T. Morazán, *Animated Problem Solving*, Texts in Computer Science,
https://doi.org/10.1007/978-3-030-85091-3_23

Fig. 105 Structure of Aliens Attack version 5

```
(require 2htdp/image)
(require 2htdp/universe)
;; Data Definitions
        ⋮

;; Constants
        ⋮

(define-struct world (rocket aliens dir shots))
;; Sample world instances
        ⋮

<draw-world code>
        ⋮

<process-key code>
        ⋮

<process-tick code>
        ⋮

<game-over? code>
        ⋮

<draw-last-world code>
        ⋮

<run code>
```

Each code section is discussed in the remaining sections of this chapter. The presented refactoring is based on the code presented in previous chapters. Quite a bit of editing is required, but mostly the editing is straightforward: encapsulating functions and simplifying definitions. There are a small number of testing updates or removal (due to encapsulation). The test updates involve making sure that every line of code is covered by the tests.

128 Constants

Two varieties of constants must be identified: those needed globally and those needed locally. Global constants are defined to be those that are needed by more than one global function or by the tests of a global function. All other constants ought to be encapsulated. We organize the global constants in three broad categories: general constants needed to define elements of the video game, constants to define images, and constants to define an initial world.

The general constants needed to define elements of the video game include those needed to define a scene, to define coordinates inside a scene, and NO-SHOT. Examining the game's code reveals the following general constants:

```
;; General Constants
(define MAX-CHARS-HORIZONTAL 20)
(define MAX-CHARS-VERTICAL 15)
(define IMAGE-WIDTH 30)
(define IMAGE-HEIGHT 30)
(define MIN-IMG-X 0)
(define MAX-IMG-X (sub1 MAX-CHARS-HORIZONTAL))
(define MIN-IMG-Y 0)
(define MAX-IMG-Y (sub1 MAX-CHARS-VERTICAL))
(define E-SCENE-W (* MAX-CHARS-HORIZONTAL IMAGE-WIDTH))
(define E-SCENE-H (* MAX-CHARS-VERTICAL IMAGE-HEIGHT))
(define NO-SHOT 'no-shot)
```

Observe that no changes are made to any of these constants. Each of these constants is either needed by more than one function or test or is needed by another constant definition.

The constants needed to define images that must remain global are those used only to test the draw-world function. Image constants used while the game is running are encapsulated in draw-world. The global image constants used in testing are

```
;; Drawing Testing Constants
(define SHOT-COLOR2    'skyblue)
(define ALIEN-COLOR2    'orange)
(define WINDOW2-COLOR    'white)
(define FUSELAGE2-COLOR 'orange)
(define NACELLE2-COLOR 'brown)
(define ALIEN-IMG2   ...)
(define SHOT-IMG2    ...)
(define FUSELAGE2    ...)
(define WINDOW2 (ellipse 3 10 'solid WINDOW2-COLOR))
(define SINGLE-BOOSTER2 ...)
(define BOOSTER2 (beside SINGLE-BOOSTER2 SINGLE-BOOSTER2))
(define ROCKET-MAIN2 ...)
(define NACELLE2    ...)
(define ROCKET-IMG2 ...)
```

The values of all these constants remain unchanged from how they are defined in Chap. 4. In the interest of clarity and brevity some of the code above is omitted as indicated by the ellipsis.

The constants to define initial worlds are those needed to construct the initial world used in the run function or in the testing of the handlers. These constants are

```
;; Constants for INIT-WORLD
(define AN-IMG-X (/ MAX-CHARS-HORIZONTAL 2))
(define INIT-ROCKET  AN-IMG-X)
(define INIT-DIR  'right)
(define INIT-SHOT NO-SHOT)
(define INIT-LOA ...)
(define INIT-LOS '())


;; Constants for INIT-WORLD2
(define INIT-ROCKET2 15)
(define INIT-ALIEN2 (make-posn 3 MAX-IMG-Y))
(define DIR2 'left)
(define SHOT2 (make-posn AN-IMG-X
                         (/ (sub1 MAX-CHARS-VERTICAL) 2)))
```

These constants remain mostly unchanged. To build SHOT2 AN-IMG-X is used to eliminate having to evaluate (/ MAX-CHARS-HORIZONTAL 2) twice. We shall now focus on the definition of INIT-LOA. Section 87 discusses the design of create-alien-army using interval processing to define INIT-LOA. We take the opportunity to discuss a new approach using ISL+'s build-list abstract function. The signature for this function is

```
<X> natnum (natnum → X) → (listof X)
```

Let us call the given natural number k. This abstract function builds a list of size k with the results of applying the given function to every integer, n, in the interval [0..k-1] from low to high.

Four constants may be defined to build an initial army of aliens using build-list:

```
(define NUM-ALIENS 18)
(define NUM-ALIEN-LINES 3)
(define ALIENS-PER-LINE (/ NUM-ALIENS NUM-ALIEN-LINES))
(define STARTING-X-LINE (add1 (/ (- MAX-CHARS-HORIZONTAL
                                    ALIENS-PER-LINE)
                                 2)))
```

The first constant is the number of aliens in the initial army. The second is the number of rows in the alien army. To make the design easy to understand we make the first constant divisible by the second constant and their quotient is the number of aliens per line (the third constant). Finally, the alien army ought to start in the middle of the horizontal axis and at the top of the scene. This means that the number of empty image-x coordinates before and after a row of aliens is given by dividing by 2 the difference of the maximum number of characters on the horizontal axis and the aliens per row. Adding 1 to this integer gives us the initial image-x coordinate for each row (the fourth constant).

Modular arithmetic (first discussed in Sect. 30) may be used to compute the image-x and image-y coordinates of each alien as follows:

```
x = (+ STARTING-X-LINE (remainder n ALIENS-PER-LINE))
y = (quotient n ALIENS-PER-LINE)
```

Here n is the number of the aliens to be created (e.g., the 12th or the 3rd). Using these formulas we define INIT-LOA as follows:

```
(define INIT-LOA
        (build-list NUM-ALIENS
                    (λ (n)
                       (make-posn (+ STARTING-X-LINE
                                     (remainder n
                                                ALIENS-PER-LINE))
                                  (quotient n
                                            ALIENS-PER-LINE)))))
```

The function given to build-list creates a new alien instance using the alien number it gets as input. Take time to compare the above approach to create an initial army of aliens with the approach first presented in Sect. 87. You ought to be able to appreciate how much more concise and elegant the code is now.

---

* **Ex. 297** — Modify the constants to increase the number of aliens and the number of rows in the initial alien army. Make sure a row of aliens fits and able to move within confines of the scene.

*** **Ex. 298** — Modify the constants to have the alien army in the initial world displayed in the following formation:

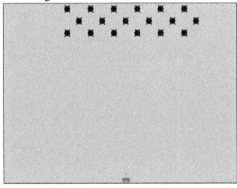

129 Structure Definitions

Given that new characteristics are not being added to Aliens Attack there are no
changes made to the world structure nor to the sample worlds used in testing. They
remain as

```
;; A world is a structure: (make-world rocket loa dir los)
(define-struct world (rocket aliens dir shots))

(define INIT-WORLD  (make-world INIT-ROCKET  INIT-LOA
                                INIT-DIR     INIT-LOS))

(define INIT-WORLD2 (make-world INIT-ROCKET2 (list INIT-ALIEN2)
                                DIR2         (list SHOT2)))

(define WORLD3 (make-world 7           (list (make-posn 3 3))
                           'right      (list (make-posn 3 3))))
```

If INIT-WORLD were not used in testing, it could be encapsulated inside of run.
Since it is used in testing, it is left at the global level for it to be in scope for all
the tests. In contrast, the structure definition cannot be encapsulated unless all the
handlers are encapsulated with it (given that the need the world selector functions).
In general, if a structure definition is to be encapsulated, then all functions that use
the structure's selectors, constructor, or predicate must be encapsulated with it.

130 Encapsulating and Refactoring Handlers

Each handler is a function. Therefore, a handler may encapsulate any constants and
auxiliary functions only it uses. In addition, the handler and any of its auxiliary
functions may be refactored to use abstract functions. You will be well-served,
however, if you refactor and test before encapsulating. Always keep in mind that
the process of refactoring may (accidentally) introduce a bug. It is better to catch
bugs before a refactored function is encapsulated. Once encapsulated the refactored
function cannot be directly tested.

130.1 The draw-world Handler

One of the goals is to encapsulate within the drawing handler anything that only
it uses. Inspecting the video game code immediately reveals that color constants,
the empty scene, the image-y coordinate of the rocket, and all the image-creating
functions (designed in Chap. 4) along with constants defined using them may be
encapsulated. We note that the image-creating functions do not require refactoring

because they are simple and do not exhibit repetition among them. The definitions to encapsulate are

```
(define SHOT-COLOR     'orange)
(define ALIEN-COLOR    'black)
(define WINDOW-COLOR   'darkgray)
(define FUSELAGE-COLOR 'green)
(define NACELLE-COLOR  'red)
(define E-SCENE-COLOR  'pink)
(define E-SCENE
        (empty-scene E-SCENE-W E-SCENE-H E-SCENE-COLOR))
(define ROCKET-Y (sub1 MAX-CHARS-VERTICAL))


;; color → image  Purpose: Create an alien image of the
;;                          given color
(define (mk-alien-img a-color) ...)
(define ALIEN-IMG (mk-alien-img ALIEN-COLOR))


;; color → image  Purpose: Create shot image of the
;;                          given color
(define (mk-shot-img a-color) ...)
(define SHOT-IMG (mk-shot-img SHOT-COLOR))


;; color → image  Purpose: Create the fuselage image
;;                          of the given color
(define (mk-fuselage-img a-color) ...)
(define FUSELAGE (mk-fuselage-img FUSELAGE-COLOR))
(define FUSELAGE-W (image-width FUSELAGE))
(define FUSELAGE-H (image-width FUSELAGE))


;; color → image  Purpose: Create rocket window image
(define (mk-window-img a-color) ...)
(define WINDOW  (mk-window-img WINDOW-COLOR))


;; color → image  Purpose: Create single booster image
(define (mk-single-booster-img a-color) ...)
(define SINGLE-BOOSTER
        (mk-single-booster-img NACELLE-COLOR))


;; image → image  Purpose: Create booster image
(define (mk-booster-img a-sb-img) ...)
(define BOOSTER (mk-booster-img SINGLE-BOOSTER))


;; image image image → image  Purpose: Create the main
;;                                      rocket image
(define (mk-rocket-main-img a-window a-fuselage a-booster)
        ...)
```

```
(define ROCKET-MAIN
         (mk-rocket-main-img WINDOW FUSELAGE BOOSTER))
;; image color → image  Purpose: Create a rocket nacelle
;;                                      image
(define (mk-nacelle-img a-rocket-main-img a-color) ...)
(define NACELLE (mk-nacelle-img ROCKET-MAIN NACELLE-COLOR))


;; image image → ci    Purpose: Create a rocket ci
(define (mk-rocket-ci a-rocket-main-img a-nacelle-img) ...)
(define ROCKET-IMG (mk-rocket-ci ROCKET-MAIN NACELLE))
```

In the interest of brevity and clarity the bodies of the functions are not included above.

In Sect. 125 the functions to draw a list of aliens and a list of shots were refactored to

```
;; loa scene → scene
;; Purpose: To draw the given loa in the given scene
(define draw-loa (λ (a-lox scn)
                    (draw-lox draw-alien a-lox scn)))


;; los scene → scene
;; Purpose: To draw the given los in the given scene
(define draw-los (λ (a-lox scn)
                    (draw-lox draw-shot a-lox scn)))
```

Recall that the auxiliary function each uses (i.e., draw-alien and draw-shot) is not recursive and is only referenced once (i.e., in the above functions). This suggests using a λ-expression instead of defining the two auxiliary functions. The above functions are refactored to

```
;; loa scene → scene
;; Purpose: To draw the given loa in the given scene
(define draw-loa (draw-lox-maker (λ (an-alien scn)
                                    (draw-ci ALIEN-IMG
                                             (posn-x an-alien)
                                             (posn-y an-alien)
                                             scn))))


;; los scene → scene
;; Purpose: To draw the given los in the given scene
(define draw-los (draw-lox-maker (λ (a-shot scn)
                                    (if (eq? a-shot NO-SHOT)
                                        scn
                                        (draw-ci SHOT-IMG
                                                 (posn-x a-shot)
                                                 (posn-y a-shot)
                                                 scn)))))
```

Implemented in this manner there is no longer a need for `draw-alien` and for `draw-shot` to be defined. They may be deleted from the game's program. Encapsulating the above functions means that `draw-ci` (refactored using encapsulation in Fig. 99), `draw-lox-maker`, and `draw-lox` may also be encapsulated inside `draw-world` given that they are not referenced elsewhere.

To complete the refactoring of `draw-world` add `draw-rocket` and `draw-world` (from Chap. 16) as local functions. The body of the local ought to call the locally defined `draw-world`. The tests for (the new global) `draw-world` remain unchanged.

130.2 The `process-key` Handler

This handler is the only one that uses `process-shooting`, `move-rckt-left`, and `move-rckt-right` as auxiliary functions. Therefore, these functions ought to be encapsulated inside `process-key`. Observe, however, that `move-rckt-left` and `move-rckt-right` are very similar:

```
;; rocket → rocket
;; Purpose: Move the given rocket right
(define (move-rckt-right a-rocket)
  (if (< a-rocket (sub1 MAX-CHARS-HORIZONTAL))
      (add1 a-rocket)
      a-rocket))

;; rocket → rocket
;; Purpose: Move the given rocket left
(define (move-rckt-left a-rocket)
  (if (> a-rocket 0)
      (sub1 a-rocket)
      a-rocket))
```

This suggests using a curried function to eliminate the repetitions and to create the rocket-moving functions. There are three significant differences: the comparing predicate, the second value given to this predicate, and the function used to create a new rocket. Abstracting over the functions yields

```
(define (make-rocket-mover cmp val f)
  (λ (rckt) (if (cmp rckt val) (f rckt) rckt)))
```

The rocket-moving functions are refactored to

```
;; rocket → rocket
;; Purpose: Move the given rocket left
(define move-rckt-left (make-rocket-mover > 0 sub1))

;; rocket → rocket
;; Purpose: Move the given rocket right
(define move-rckt-right
        (mk-rckt-mvr < (sub1 MAX-CHARS-HORIZONTAL) add1))
```

The above three functions, `process-shooting`, and `process-key` from Aliens Attack version 4 are encapsulated using a `local`-expression in the body of `process-key` for Aliens Attack version 5. The body of the `local`-expression calls the local `process-key`. The tests for this handler remain unchanged.

130.3 The `process-tick` Handler

This is the handler with the most auxiliary functions. We shall comment on all the functions that ought to be encapsulated. We start with the refactored function to move a list of aliens from Sect. 125:

```
;; dir → (alien → alien)
;; Purpose: Return a function to move an alien in the
;;          given direction
(define (alien-mover-maker a-dir)
  (λ (an-alien) (move-alien an-alien a-dir)))

;; (listof alien) dir → (listof alien)
;; Purpose: To move the given list of aliens in the
;;          given direction
(define (move-loa a-loa dir)
  (map (alien-mover-maker dir) a-loa))
```

It is unlikely that `move-loa` can be further simplified. The `alien-mover-maker` function, on the other hand, refers to a function, `move-alien`, that is only referenced once. This suggests encapsulating it inside `alien-mover-maker`. Before doing so, however, observe that `move-alien` is the only function that refers to `move-down-image-y`, `move-left-image-x`, and `move-right-image-x`. Therefore, these functions ought to be encapsulated inside `move-alien`. The resulting function is

```
;; dir → (alien → alien)
;; Purpose: Return a function to move an alien in the
;;          given direction
(define (move-alien-maker a-dir)
 (local
  [;; alien → alien
   ;; Purpose: Move the given alien in a-dir
   (define (move-alien an-alien)
     (local [;; image-y<max → image-y
             ;; Purpose: To move the given image-y<max down
             (define (move-down-image-y an-img-y<max)
               (add1 an-img-y<max))
```

```
;; image-x>min → image-x
;; Purpose: Move the given image-x>min left
(define (move-left-image-x an-img-x>min)
  (sub1 an-img-x>min))


;; image-x<max → image-x
;; Purpose: Move the given image-x<max right
(define (move-right-image-x an-img-x<max)
  (add1 an-img-x<max))]
(cond [(eq? a-dir 'right)
       (make-posn (move-right-image-x (posn-x an-alien))
                  (posn-y an-alien))]
      [(eq? a-dir 'left)
       (make-posn (move-left-image-x (posn-x an-alien))
                  (posn-y an-alien))]
      [else (make-posn
             (posn-x an-alien)
             (move-down-image-y (posn-y an-alien)))]))))]
move-alien))
```

Observe that move-alien is locally defined, but it is only referenced once and it is not recursive. This suggests using a λ-expression to represent it instead of locally defining it. The auxiliary functions to move image coordinates become local to the new λ-expression as follows:

```
;; dir → (alien → alien)
;; Purpose: Return a function to move an alien in the
;;          given direction
(define (move-alien-maker a-dir)
 (lambda (an-alien)
  (local [;; image-y<max → image-y
          ;; Purpose: To move the given image-y<max down
          (define (move-down-image-y an-img-y<max)
            (add1 an-img-y<max))


          ;; image-x>min → image-x
          ;; Purpose: Move the given image-x>min left
          (define (move-left-image-x an-img-x>min)
            (sub1 an-img-x>min))


          ;; image-x<max → image-x
          ;; Purpose: Move the given image-x<max right
          (define (move-right-image-x an-img-x<max)
            (add1 an-img-x<max))]
     (cond [(eq? a-dir 'right)
            (make-posn (move-right-image-x (posn-x an-alien))
                       (posn-y an-alien))]
```

```
[(eq? a-dir 'left)
 (make-posn (move-left-image-x (posn-x an-alien))
            (posn-y an-alien))]
[else (make-posn
       (posn-x an-alien)
       (move-down-image-y (posn-y an-alien)))]))))
```

In this form it is easier to see that `alien-mover-maker` is a curried function to create specialized versions of an `alien`-moving function. This is the function to encapsulate inside `process-tick`.

** Ex. 299 — The conditional in the above function contains some repetition. Use abstraction to eliminate repetitions. Is the resulting function easier to understand?

In Sect. 119 the function to move a list of shots is refactored to

```
;; los → los
;; Purpose: To move the given list of shots
(define (move-los a-los)
 (local [;; shot → shot
         ;; Purpose: To move the given shot
         (define (local-move-shot a-shot)
          (cond [(eq? a-shot NO-SHOT) a-shot]
                [else
                 (cond [(= (posn-y a-shot) MIN-IMG-Y)
                        NO-SHOT]
                       [else
                        (make-posn
                         (posn-x a-shot)
                         (move-up-image-y (posn-y a-shot)))])]))
   (map local-move-shot a-los))
```

Once again, we see a local function defined that is not recursive and is only referenced once. This suggests using a λ-expression. This yields the following refactored `move-los`:

```
;; los → los
;; Purpose: To move the given list of shots
(define (move-los a-los)
  (map (lambda (a-shot)
         (cond [(eq? a-shot NO-SHOT) a-shot]
               [(= (posn-y a-shot) MIN-IMG-Y) NO-SHOT]
               [else (make-posn
                      (posn-x a-shot)
                      (sub1 (posn-y a-shot)))]))
       a-los))
```

In this example the nonrecursive function only referenced once, `move-up-image`, is inlined instead of making it local to the λ-expression. In this case, inlining seems not to affect the function's readability. Be warned, however, that inlining may be taken too far and render a function incomprehensible. In fact, the same is true for abstraction. You have done too much abstraction when the code is too far removed from its concrete goals. There must always be a balance between code readability and refactoring techniques like abstraction and inlining.

Another auxiliary function used by `process-tick` is

```
;; loa dir → dir
;; Purpose: Return new aliens direction
(define (new-dir-after-tick a-loa old-dir)
  (cond [(eq? old-dir 'down)
         (new-dir-after-down a-loa)]
        [(eq? old-dir 'left)
         (new-dir-after-left a-loa)]
        [else (new-dir-after-right a-loa)]))
```

This function is designed in Sect. 93.1. It references three auxiliary functions that are simple and may be inlined without sacrificing readability as follows:

```
;; loa dir → dir
;; Purpose: Return new aliens direction
(define (new-dir-after-tick a-loa old-dir)
  (cond [(eq? old-dir 'down)
         (if (any-alien-at-left-edge? a-loa) 'right 'left)]
        [(eq? old-dir 'left)
         (if (any-alien-at-left-edge? a-loa) 'down 'left)]
        [else (if (any-alien-at-right-edge? a-loa)
                  'down
                  'right)]))
```

Examining the code reveals that now this function is the only function that references `any-alien-at-left-edge?` and `any-alien-at-right-edge?`. These functions, therefore, ought to be encapsulated. Before doing so, however, we refactor them to use `ormap` as suggested in Sect. 116.3. The new refactored function is

```
;; loa dir → dir
;; Purpose: Return new aliens direction
(define (new-dir-after-tick a-loa old-dir)
  (local [;; loa → Boolean
          ;; Purpose: Determine if any alien is at scene's
          ;;          right edge
          (define (any-alien-at-right-edge? a-loa)
            (ormap (lambda (an-alien)
                     (= (posn-x an-alien) MAX-IMG-X))
                   a-loa))
```

```
;; loa → Boolean
;; Purpose: Determine if any alien is at scene's
;;           left edge
(define (any-alien-at-left-edge? a-loa)
  (ormap (lambda (an-alien)
           (= (posn-x an-alien) MIN-IMG-X))
         a-loa))]
  (cond [(eq? old-dir 'down)
         (if (any-alien-at-left-edge? a-loa) 'right 'left)]
        [(eq? old-dir 'left)
         (if (any-alien-at-left-edge? a-loa) 'down 'left)]
        [else (if (any-alien-at-right-edge? a-loa)
                  'down
                  'right)]])))
```

You may be thinking that we can streamline the function by inlining the two local functions in the body of the cond-expression. Although there is no technical difficulty in doing so, this is likely to reduce the readability of the code. Therefore, in the interest of making sure our code clearly communicates how the problem is solved we refrain from further inlining. You may, of course, disagree and perform the inlining of the local functions.

** **Ex. 300** — Inline any-alien-at-left-edge? and
any-alien-at-right-edge? in the function above. Why is the result more
or less readable?

Section 77.2 discusses the design of remove-hit-aliens and Sect. 77.3 discusses the design of remove-shots. Both of these auxiliary functions are only used by process-tick:

```
;; loa los → loa
;; Purpose: Remove aliens hit by any shot
(define (remove-hit-aliens a-loa a-los)
  (cond [(empty? a-loa) '()]
        [(hit-by-any-shot? (first a-loa) a-los)
         (remove-hit-aliens (rest a-loa) a-los)]
        [else (cons (first a-loa)
                    (remove-hit-aliens (rest a-loa) a-los))]))


;; los loa → los
;; Purpose: Remove NO-SHOTs and hit shots
(define (remove-shots a-los a-loa)
  (cond [(empty? a-los) a-los]
        [(or (eq? (first a-los) NO-SHOT)
             (hit-any-alien? (first a-los) a-loa))
         (remove-shots (rest a-los) a-loa)]
        [else (cons (first a-los)
                    (remove-shots (rest a-los) a-loa))]))
```

Immediately, encapsulation comes to mind. Take a minute, however, to think about the functions themselves. Can they be simplified? Both of these functions are removing elements from the list they get as input. In other words, these functions are good candidates to be simplified using `filter`. For `remove-hit-aliens` `filter` needs a predicate that negates the result of testing if an alien is hit by any shot. For `remove-shots` `filter` needs a predicate that negates the result of testing if a shot is `NO-SHOT` or has been hit by any alien. Both of these needed predicates may be implemented using a λ-expression and `ormap` as follows:

```
;; loa los → loa
;; Purpose: Remove aliens hit by any shot
(define (remove-hit-aliens a-loa a-los)
  (filter (lambda (an-alien)
            (not (ormap (lambda (a-shot) (hit? a-shot an-alien))
                        a-los)))
          a-loa))
```

```
;; los loa → los
;; Purpose: Remove NO-SHOTs and hit shots
(define (remove-shots a-los a-loa)
  (filter (lambda (a-shot)
            (not (or (eq? a-shot NO-SHOT)
                     (ormap (lambda (an-alien)
                              (hit? a-shot an-alien))
                            a-loa))))
          a-los))
```

These functions may now be encapsulated in `process-tick`. Observe that `hit?` is now referenced only by these two functions in the entire program. This means that `hit?` may not be encapsulated in either. It also means that `hit?` may be encapsulated in `process-tick` because it will be in scope for the functions that need them.

The last function that needs to be encapsulated is `process-tick` from Aliens Attack version 4. The body of the `local`-expression in `process-tick` for Aliens Attack version 5 calls the local `process-tick`.

Observe that running the existing tests after encapsulation fails to test all the code. Specifically, not all the code in `hit?` and in `move-los` is covered by the existing tests. None of the tests for `process-tick` has an alien hit nor test moving a `NO-SHOT`. To remedy this we add the following test:

```
(check-expect (process-tick
               (make-world INIT-ROCKET
                           (list (make-posn 2 5))
                           'left
                           (list (make-posn 1 6) NO-SHOT)))
              (make-world INIT-ROCKET
                          '()
                          'left
                          '()))
```

Observe that in this test the alien is hit by the first shot and the second shot is
NO-SHOT. This means that all the code is now fully tested. The important lesson to
remember is that encapsulation may remove tests that cover code not covered by the
tests for the function encapsulated into and, thus, requires new tests to be developed.

130.4 The game-over? Handler

The only references to any-alien-reached-earth? and any-aliens-alive?
are in this handler and draw-last-world. This suggests that these two functions
should not be encapsulated. For the sake of argument, however, let us proceed as if
only game-over? references these two auxiliary functions. That is, let us not decide
a priori that these functions should not be encapsulated and engage in speculative
encapsulation. After encapsulation the refactored function is[28]

```
;; world → Boolean
;; Purpose: Detect if the game is over
(define (game-over? a-world)
  (local [;; (listof alien) → Boolean
          ;; Purpose: Determine if any alien has reached earth
          (define (any-alien-reached-earth? a-loa)
            (local [(define (alien-reached-earth? an-alien)
                      (= (posn-y an-alien) MAX-IMG-Y))]
              (ormap alien-reached-earth? a-loa)))
          ;; loa Boolean → Boolean
          ;; Purpose: Determine if there is an alien in the
          ;;          given loa
          (define (any-aliens-alive? a-loa) (cons? a-loa))]
    (or (any-alien-reached-earth? (world-aliens a-world))
        (not (any-aliens-alive? (world-aliens a-world))))))
```

Observe that negating the value returned by any-aliens-alive? is the same
as testing if the given list of aliens is empty. Further observe that the body of
any-alien-reached-earth? is easily inlined into the local-expression's body.
Finally, observe that alien-reached-earth? may be represented using a λ-
expression given that it is not recursive and is only needed once. These observations mean that the local-expression may be removed resulting in the following
refactored handler:

```
;; world → Boolean
;; Purpose: Detect if the game is over
(define (game-over? a-world)
  (or (ormap (λ (an-alien) (= (posn-y an-alien) MAX-IMG-Y))
             (world-aliens a-world))
      (empty? (world-aliens a-world))))
```

---

[28] The use of ormap-pred is substituted with ISL+'s ormap.

The tests for this handler are unchanged. This refactoring exercise illustrates two important lessons. The first is that logic is a useful tool to simplify functions. In this example, it led to the elimination of `any-aliens-alive?` and the use of `not`. The second is that speculative encapsulation may make us aware of possible simplifications.

** **Ex. 301** — A fellow student proposes that the following `game-over?` implementation communicates better how the problem is solved:

```
;; world → Boolean
;; Purpose: Detect if the game is over
(define (game-over? a-world)
  (local [(define ANY-REACHED-EARTH
                  (ormap (lambda (an-alien)
                           (= (posn-y an-alien) MAX-IMG-Y))
                         (world-aliens a-world)))
          (define ALL-ALIENS-DEFEATED
                  (empty? (world-aliens a-world)))]
    (or ANY-REACHED-EARTH ALL-ALIENS-DEFEATED)))
```

Is she right? What is better and worse about this implementation? Remember to consider how an `or`-expression is evaluated (discussed in Sect. 13.1).

130.5 The `draw-last-world` Handler

Recall that this handler must determine why `game-over?` returns #true. Given that in Aliens Attack 4 it references the same auxiliary functions as `game-over?` we can employ the same observations that led to `game-over?`'s refactoring: logic and inlining. The refactored function is

```
;; world → scene throws error
;; Purpose: To draw the game's final scene
(define (draw-last-world a-world)
  (cond [(ormap (lambda (an-alien)
                  (= (posn-y an-alien) MAX-IMG-Y))
                (world-aliens a-world))
         (place-image (text "EARTH WAS CONQUERED!" 36 'red)
                      (/ E-SCENE-W 2)
                      (/ E-SCENE-H 4)
                      (draw-world a-world))]
```

```
[(empty? (world-aliens a-world))
 (place-image (text "EARTH WAS SAVED!" 36 'green)
              (/ E-SCENE-W 2)
              (/ E-SCENE-H 4)
              (draw-world a-world))]
[else
 (error (format "draw-last-world: Given world has ~s
                 aliens and none have reached earth."
                (length (world-aliens a-world))))])]))
```

Remember that the same refactoring strategies may work for different functions that refer to the same auxiliary functions.

131 Refactoring run

The run function is the only function that references TICK-RATE. Therefore, TICK-RATE's definition ought to be encapsulated. This straightforward refactoring yields

```
;; string → world
;; Purpose: To run the game
(define (run a-name)
  (local [(define TICK-RATE 1/4)]
    (big-bang INIT-WORLD
              [on-draw draw-world]
              [name a-name]
              [on-key process-key]
              [on-tick process-tick TICK-RATE]
              [stop-when game-over? draw-last-world])))
```

Recall that INIT-WORLD cannot be encapsulated because it is used to test the handlers.

The only task remaining is to decide where to place accum and id. These functions are only referenced by draw-lox, which is encapsulated in draw-world. Therefore, these functions may also be encapsulated inside draw-world.

This ends the development of Aliens Attack version 5. Take time to appreciate how much better organized and clearer the game's code is now. Do you feel that the code for Aliens Attack version 5 better communicates how the game works than the code for Aliens Attack version 4? Have you developed a bigger appreciation for encapsulation, anonymous functions, and abstract functions?

132 What Have We Learned in This Chapter?

The important lessons of Chap. 23 are summarized as follows:

- Use `build-list` to create a list of a given size k with the results obtained from applying a given function to the integers in [0..k-1] from low to high.
- If a structure definition is to be encapsulated, then all functions that use the structure's selectors, constructor, or predicate must be encapsulated with it.
- Refactor and test before encapsulating.
- Constants and auxiliary functions that are only used by a function, `f`, ought to be encapsulated in `f`.
- There must always be a balance between code readability and refactoring techniques like abstraction and inlining.
- Encapsulation may remove tests that cover code not covered by the tests for the function encapsulated into and, thus, requires new tests to be developed.
- Logic is a useful tool used to simplify functions.
- Speculative encapsulation may make us aware of possible simplifications.
- The same refactoring strategies may work for different functions that refer to the same auxiliary functions.

Chapter 24
For-Loops and Pattern Matching

Abstract functions traverse data of arbitrary size to compute a value. For example, `fact` (from Sect. 81) traverses the integers in $[0..n]$ to compute n! and `map` traverses a list to compute a value. In essence, they *iterate* through the elements contained in an instance of data of arbitrary size. Every time a function that traverses data of arbitrary size is written a conditional expression is needed. This repetition suggests an abstraction is needed. In ISL+, this abstraction is provided by *for-loops*. A `for`-loop generates the sequences of values to be iterated over and combines the values obtained from evaluating an expression (known as its body) to return a value. They allow programmers to dispense with the coding of conditional expressions. In addition, they allow programmers to iterate over multiple pieces of data.

The conditionals written to process data of arbitrary size distinguish between the subtypes of a type and use selector functions to access the components of any compound subtype. For example, to process a list a conditional expression is used to distinguish between an `empty`- and a `cons`-list. If the given list is a `cons`-list, the selector functions `first` and `rest` are used to access its components. This is done every time a list-processing function is written and an abstraction is needed to avoid the repetition. A similar situation arises when several functions to process a given defined structure are written. For example, a function to process a `posn` uses the selectors `posn-x` and `posn-y`. In ISL+, a `match`-expression provides programmers with an abstraction to eliminate this repetitive practice. A `match`-expression dispatches on the type of the data and may introduce local variables to capture the values in a compound piece of data. The use of such expressions can also significantly improve code readability as done by `local`-expressions in Sect. 121.2. A `match`-expression allows programmers to dispense with writing a `local`-expression for this purpose. Determining a data type to introduce local variables or control program evaluation is called *pattern matching*.

This chapter explores problem solving and program design using `for`-loops and pattern matching. Neither of these increases our computational power. We can compute anything that is possible without them. That is, these are abstractions to make program development easier and increase readability. In order to use them you must

© The Author(s), under exclusive license to Springer Nature Switzerland AG 2022
M. T. Morazán, *Animated Problem Solving*, Texts in Computer Science,
https://doi.org/10.1007/978-3-030-85091-3_24

require the 2htdp/abstraction teachpack. That is, the following must appear in your program before any code:

```
(require 2htdp/abstraction)
```

133 For-Loops

For-loops come in two general varieties in ISL+: those that extend the variables in scope for the body of the for-loop and those that extend the variables in scope for the body and each subsequent variable introduced by the for-loop. The first we shall call for-loops and the second we shall call for*-loops. Both varieties require *comprehension clauses* that declare local variables and create the values iterated over.

133.1 for-loops

ISL+ offers 6 different for-loops with the following syntax:

```
expr ::= (for/list      (clause⁺) expr)
     ::= (for/and       (clause⁺) expr)
     ::= (for/or        (clause⁺) expr)
     ::= (for/sum       (clause⁺) expr)
     ::= (for/product   (clause⁺) expr)
     ::= (for/string    (clause⁺) expr)
clause ::= [variable expr]
```

A for-loop has a keyword identifying the type of loop, one or more comprehension clauses, and an expression for the loop's body. A comprehension clause declares a variable the sequence of values to iterate over. For each iteration step the variable takes on the next value in the sequence. The scope of a comprehension variable is the body of the for-loop. For each value a comprehension variable takes on the body of the for-loop is evaluated. The type of for-loop used defines how the values obtained from evaluating the loop's body are combined:

for/list	conses all the values of type X
for/and	ands all the Booleans
for/or	ors all the Booleans
for/sum	adds all the numbers
for/product	multiplies all the numbers
for/string	appends all the strings

The body of the loop must always evaluate to a value of the expected type. Otherwise, an error is thrown. For example, the body of a for/string must always evaluate to a string and the body of a for/and must always evaluate to a Boolean.

A comprehension clause declares a variable that shadows previous declarations of the same variable. In addition, it generates the values the variable iterates over. The type and value of the embedded expression determine the values generated as follows:

List   The elements of the given list from the first to the last element
Natural number   The integers in [0..n-1], where n is the given natural number
String   The substrings of length 1 from left to right of the given string

For example, the comprehension [i (build-list 4 (λ (x) x))] means that i is used to iterate over the list elements 0, 1, 2, and 3 and the comprehension [s "dog"] means that s is used to iterate over the substrings of length one: "d," "o," and "g."

Consider the list mapping function from Sect. 116.5:

```
;; <X Y> (X → Y) (listof X) → (listof Y)
;; Purpose: Return the values from applying the given function
;;          to the given list's elements
(define (map-f f a-lox)
  (if (empty? a-lox)
      '()
      (cons (f (first a-lox))
            (map-f f (rest a-lox)))))
```

This function distinguishes between the subtypes of a list and uses list selector functions to access the components of a non-empty list as it is traversed. Further observe that it returns a list. It returns the empty list when the given list is empty. Otherwise, it conses all the results obtained from applying f to the first list element. This makes it an ideal candidate for refactoring using for/list. The body of the for-loop must only specify what do with each of the values in the loop. In this case, apply the given f to it. This results in the following refactored function:

```
;; <X Y> (X → Y) (listof X) → (listof Y)
;; Purpose: Return the values from applying the given function
;;          to the given list's elements
(define (map-f f a-lox)
  (for/list ([an-x a-lox])
    (f an-x)))
```

The scope of an-x is the body of the loop. The loop conses the results of applying f to each element of a-lox. Take time to appreciate what has been achieved. The need to type the if-expression, the returned empty list, the cons application expression, and the recursive call is eliminated. These elements all exist but remain hidden inside the implementation of for/list. More importantly, perhaps, the above function tells us that anything implemented using map can also be implemented using a for/list loop. Consider, for example, the function to move a list of shots from Sect. 130.3:

```
;; los → los
;; Purpose: To move the given list of shots
(define (move-los a-los)
  (map (lambda (a-shot)
         (cond [(eq? a-shot NO-SHOT) a-shot]
               [(= (posn-y a-shot) MIN-IMG-Y) NO-SHOT]
               [else (make-posn
                       (posn-x a-shot)
                       (sub1 (posn-y a-shot)))]))
       a-los))
```

This function may be refactored to use a for-loop as follows:

```
(define (move-los a-los)
  (for/list ([a-shot a-los])
    (cond [(eq? a-shot NO-SHOT) a-shot]
          [(= (posn-y a-shot) MIN-IMG-Y) NO-SHOT]
          [else (make-posn
                  (posn-x a-shot)
                  (sub1 (posn-y a-shot)))])))
```

Observe that the body of the for-loop is the same as the body of the λ-expression in the previous implementation.

Loops in ISL+ may traverse multiple values of arbitrary size at the same time. At each iteration step the next value in each of the sequences created is used to evaluate the body of the loop. The loop stops when the end of any sequence is reached. Whatever remains of the other sequences is ignored. Consider, for example, the following function from Sect. 111:

```
;; (listof num) (listof num) → (listof num)
;; Purpose: Return a list with the products of corresponding
;;          elements in the given lists
;; Assumption: The given lists are of the same length
(define (mlist L1 L2)
  (if (empty? L1)
      '()
      (cons (* (first L1) (first L2))
            (mlist (rest L1) (rest L2)))))
```

Observe that both lists are simultaneously traversed. To refactor this function using a for-loop two comprehensions are needed: one for each list. The body of the loop simply has to multiply the corresponding elements as the values are iterated over. The resulting function is

```
(define (mlist L1 L2)
  (for/list ([v1 L1] [v2 L2])
    (* v1 v2)))
```

How do you feel about the result? Do you find it more elegant? Feeling comfortable with loops is a matter of practice, but you can see that they do offer the opportunity to dispense with the need to use a conditional expression to distinguish among subtypes and to use selector functions.

Consider writing a predicate to determine if all the elements of a given list of numbers are less than a given threshold. There are several options you may choose from to design this function: use structural recursion on a list of numbers, use andmap, or use a for/and loop. Perhaps, the first thing that comes to mind is to iterate through the values of the list. For each value in the list the result obtained from testing if it is less than the given threshold is anded with the result obtained from processing the rest of the list. This problem analysis suggests using a for/and loop.

The following sample instances of a (listof number) are used to develop the sample expressions using a for/and loop below:

```
;; Sample instances of lon
(define L0 '())
(define L1 '(89 33 77 56 12 8 7))
(define L2 '(8  31 37 44 12 2 4))


;; Sample expressions for all-lt
(define L0-VAL (for/and ([v L0]) (< v 887)))
(define L1-VAL (for/and ([v L1]) (< v 100)))
(define L2-VAL (for/and ([v L2]) (< v 20)))
```

Observe that all sample instances of a lon are processed the same way. The comprehension builds the sequence of values to be iterated over and, therefore, the loop is indifferent to the subtype of list it is processing.

Abstracting over the sample expressions yields the following function:

```
;; all-lt: (listof number) number → boolean
;; Purpose: Determine if numbers given list are < given number
(define (all-lt L threshold)
  (for/and ([v L])
    (< v threshold)))
```

To complete the steps of the design recipe the following tests are used:

```
;; Tests using sample computations for all-lt
(check-expect (all-lt L0 887) L0-VAL)
(check-expect (all-lt L1 100) L1-VAL)
(check-expect (all-lt L2 20)  L2-VAL)

;; Tests using sample values for all-lt
(check-expect (all-lt '() 5)             #true)
(check-expect (all-lt (list -1 2 -3) 0)  #false)
(check-expect (all-lt (list 3 -8 -4) 10) #true)
```

This completes the design of the function. You ought to run the tests and confirm that they all pass.

** **Ex. 302** — Using a for-loop, design and implement a function that takes as input a list of strings and that returns a list containing their lengths.

*** **Ex. 303** — Using a for-loop, design and implement a function to compute n!.

*** **Ex. 304** — Using a for-loop, design and implement a function that adds the corresponding elements of 4 lists of numbers.

** **Ex. 305** — Using a for-loop, design and implement a predicate to determine if all the numbers in a list of numbers are divisible by 3.

** **Ex. 306** — Using a for-loop, design and implement a predicate to determine if any image in a list of images has more than 10,000 pixels.

** **Ex. 307** — Using a for-loop, design and implement a function that takes as input a string containing only letters and that returns the string in all lower case.

*** **Ex. 308** — Using a for-loop, design and implement a function that takes a list of symbols as input and that returns a list of symbols in which every 'a in the given list is replaced with a 'z.

133.2 for*-loops

The second kind of ISL+ loop, for*-loop, has similar syntax and the same 6 varieties as for-loops. The syntax only varies by the use of a *:

```
expr ::= (for*/list     (clause⁺) expr)
     ::= (for*/and      (clause⁺) expr)
     ::= (for*/or       (clause⁺) expr)
     ::= (for*/sum      (clause⁺) expr)
     ::= (for*/product (clause⁺) expr)
     ::= (for*/string   (clause⁺) expr)
```

The difference with for-loops is the scope of the comprehension variables. While in a for-loop the scope of a comprehension variable is the loop's body, in a for*-loop the scope of a comprehension variable is the remaining comprehension clauses and the loop's body. In addition, the sequences of values are iterated over differently. For example, for every value taken on by the first comprehension variable the second sequence of values is iterated over and for every value taken on by the second comprehension variable the third sequence of values is iterated. This pattern is repeated for each subsequent comprehension. Observe that there is no difference between a for-loop and a for*-loop if there is only one comprehension clause.

Consider, for example, the problem of computing the cross-product of two lists. The cross-product of two lists, L1 and L2, is all pairs, (a b), where a is a member of L1 and b is a member of L2. For instance, the cross-product of '(a b) and '(7 8 9) is

```
'((a 7) (a 8) (a 9)
  (b 7) (b 8) (b 9))
```

In this list every value in '(a b) is paired with every value in '(7 8 9). How can such a list be created? It is straightforward to see that all the values in the first list must be iterated over. What needs to be done for each of these values? Given that each of these values must be matched with every value in the second list, we can see that the values in the second list must be iterated over to form the needed pairs. All of the pairs must be consed together to create the needed list. This suggests using a for*/list. The body of the loop creates a pair by listing the current value of the first given list with the current value of the second list.

To satisfy the next step of the design recipe we define the following sample lists:

```
;; Sample instances of (listof X)
(define L0 '())
(define L1 '(i j c d))
(define L2 '(7 6 3))
```

These sample lists are used to write sample expressions for the function that we shall call cross-product. The sample expressions ought to cover all possible combinations of the inputs. Given that there are 2 varieties of the first input and two varieties of the second input we need 4 sample expressions (i.e., $2 \times 2 = 4$):

```
;; Sample expressions for cross-product
(define L0-L0-VAL (for*/list ([v1 L0] [v2 L0])
                    (list v1 v2)))
(define L0-L1-VAL (for*/list ([v1 L0] [v2 L1])
                    (list v1 v2)))
(define L2-L0-VAL (for*/list ([v1 L2] [v2 L0])
                    (list v1 v2)))
(define L1-L2-VAL (for*/list ([v1 L1] [v2 L2])
                    (list v1 v2)))
```

Observe that the inputs are processed using a for*/list loop and that the body of the loop creates a pair using the current values of each list being iterated over. For every value v1 in the first list the values of the second list are iterated over using v2.

Abstracting over the sample expressions yields the following function:

```
;; <X Y> (listof X) (listof Y) → (listof (list X Y))
;; Purpose: To compute the cross product of the two lists
(define (cross-product a-lox a-loy)
  (for*/list ([v1 a-lox] [v2 a-loy])
    (list v1 v2)))
```

The tests using sample computations are straightforward to write:

```
;; Tests using sample computations for cross-product
(check-expect (cross-product L0 L0) L0-L0-VAL)
(check-expect (cross-product L0 L1) L0-L1-VAL)
(check-expect (cross-product L2 L0) L2-L0-VAL)
(check-expect (cross-product L1 L2) L1-L2-VAL)
```

Writing the tests using sample values requires more care. We must have a clear understanding of the ordering of the pairs in the result. Observe that for each value in a-lox the values of a-loy are traversed. This means in the resulting list the first set of pairs corresponds to the first element of a-lox, the second set of pairs corresponds to the second element of a-lox, and so on. In the interest of readability to clearly communicate how the function works we also have these tests cover all possible combinations of the inputs as follows:

```
;; Tests using sample values for cross-product
(check-expect (cross-product '() '()) '())
(check-expect (cross-product '() '(x y z)) '())
(check-expect (cross-product '(x y z) '()) '())
(check-expect (cross-product '(a b) '(7 8 9))
              (list (list 'a 7) (list 'a 8) (list 'a 9)
                    (list 'b 7) (list 'b 8) (list 'b 9)))
```

An important realization is that the values of a comprehension may be themselves be iterated over by using subsequent comprehensions. For example, consider flattening a (listof (listof symbol)). Every element of the given list is a list of symbols and a list containing all the elements of all the sublists needs to be computed. For instance, given '((o p) (q r s t) (u)) the result is '(o p q r s t u).

How can this be accomplished? Each sublist must be processed. This may be done by iterating over the elements of the given list. What needs to be done with each sublist? Each element of a sublist must be consed into the result. This may be accomplished by iterating through the sublist and returning each element. This analysis suggests using a for*/list loop. We can now develop sample instances of the data to process and sample expressions illustrating how to process the sample instances as follows:

```
;; Sample instances of (listof (listof symbol))
(define L0 '())
(define L1 '((a b c) (d e f g h) (i j)))

;; Sample expressions for flatten
(define L0-VAL (for*/list ([a-los L0] (a-symbol a-los))
                 a-symbol))
(define L1-VAL (for*/list ([a-los L1] (a-symbol a-los))
                 a-symbol))
```

Observe that values taken on by a-los in both sample expressions are of type (listof symbol). Each of the values in an instance of a-los is taken on by a-symbol. The body of the loop simply returns a-symbol to have it consed into the result.

Abstracting over the sample expressions yields the following function:

```
;; (listof (listof symbol)) → (listof symbol)
;; Purpose: Flatten the given (listof (listof symbol))
(define (flatten-lolos a-lolos)
  (for*/list ([a-los a-lolos] [a-symbol a-los])
    a-symbol))
```

This function is tested as follows:

```
;; Tests using sample computations for flatten-lolos
(check-expect (flatten-lolos L0) L0-VAL)
(check-expect (flatten-lolos L1) L1-VAL)

;; Tests using sample values for flatten-lolos
(check-expect (flatten-lolos '((x) (y) (z))) '(x y z))
(check-expect (flatten-lolos '((k l m n))) '(k l m n))
(check-expect (flatten-lolos '((o p) () (q r s t) (u)))
              '(o p q r s t u))
```

Observe that the tests using sample values test non-empty lists with varying lengths. Each of these lists contains lists of symbols of varying length including the empty list in the third test.

In closing the presentation on for-loops it is opportune to highlight that virtually all modern programming provide them. In some other programming languages, however, for-loops do not compute a value. Instead, for-loops are strictly a mechanism for controlling the flow of the program. Using such looping constructs may sometimes result in faster executing code. This, however, is not always true. Performance greatly depends on the optimizations done by the compiler (i.e., the program that translates a program into machine code). Experimentation and empirical data are required to determine if a speed-up is achieved.

*** **Ex. 309** — For Aliens Attack a (listof alien) and a (listof shot) are defined. Using a for*-loop, design and implement a predicate to determine if any alien has been hit by any shot.

** **Ex. 310** — Using a for*-loop, design and implement a function that given a posn in the first quadrant of the Cartesian plane generates all the posns with integer coordinates in the sub-plane defined by the origin and the given posn.

134 Pattern Matching

Whenever there is a variety in the data we have used a conditional expression to process said data. If the data is compound selector functions are used over and over again in every function. This repetition calls for an abstraction. Pattern matching is used to eliminate this type of repetition based on the type of data processed. In ISL+ pattern matching is done using a match-expression that has the following syntax:

```
expr ::= (match expr
             [pattern expr]⁺)
     ::= (match expr
             [pattern expr]⁺)
             [else expr]⁺)
pattern ::= literal
        ::= variable
        ::= (cons pattern pattern)
        ::= (structure-name pattern*)
        ::= (? predicate-name)
```

In parenthesis there is the keyword match followed by an expression. This expression is the matching expression. After the matching expression there are 1 or more *pattern stanzas*. A pattern stanza has in square brackets a pattern to match and a corresponding expression to evaluate if the pattern is matched. There is an optional else stanza that contains the default expression used when none of the patterns are matched. A match-expression looks like a cond-expression, but it checks the type of the value of the matching expression. First the matching expression is evaluated and then its value type is checked against each pattern from top to bottom. If a pattern is matched, the corresponding expression is evaluated to obtain the value of the match-expression. If none of the stanzas yield a match, then an error is thrown.

A pattern may be a constant (e.g., 3 or "hat"). There is a match if the value of the expression equals the constant. A pattern may (always) match a variable. Matching a variable means that a declaration that takes on the value of the matching expression and that shadows any previous declarations of the variable is made. The scope of the new variable is the corresponding expression in the match stanza. A pattern may also match a list that matches a pattern for the first element and a pattern for the second element. If either of these patterns is a variable, the variable takes on the corresponding value in the list. The scope of this variable is the corresponding expression and previous declarations are shadowed. A pattern may also match a structure that matches a pattern for each of its components. Any of the components may match a variable that, as before, shadows any previous declaration of the same variable and whose scope is the corresponding expression in the match stanza. Finally, a pattern may match by testing a predicate.

134.1 Illustrative Example

To make the semantics of match-expressions clear consider the program in Fig. 106. The tests are omitted from the figure and are discussed in detail below. To start consider the following tests:

```
(check-expect (f X) X-VAL)
(check-expect (f B) B-VAL)
(check-expect (f "Matthew Flatt")
              "Matched a string: Matthew Flatt")
```

The first test passes because the value of X, 42, is given as an argument to f and is matched in the first stanza of f's match-expression. The second two tests pass because they both provide f with a string. The given string does not match the numeric constant, 42, in the first stanza and is matched in the second stanza because when given to string? this predicate returns #true.

Now consider what happens for these tests:

```
(check-expect (f DIMITROVA) DIMITROVA-VAL)
(check-expect (f (make-student "Robby Findler" 'freshman 4))
              "Matched a student whose gpa is: 4")
```

For the arguments provided to f the first two stanzas fail to match because a student instance is neither the number value 42 nor a string. The third stanza signals a match because the input is a student instance. This match instantiates three (local) variables, n, y, and g, for, respectively, the given student's name, year, and gpa. The scope for these local variables is the expression in the third stanza. The student's gpa, g, is used to build the returned string.

The following tests give f a list that starts with a Boolean:

```
(check-expect (f BLST) BLST-VAL)
(check-expect
 (f '(#false))
 "Matched a list that starts with a Boolean: #false")
```

The first three stanzas in the match-expression do not detect a match. The fourth stanza, on the other hand, does detect a match because the value of a-value is a list and the first element of the list is a Boolean. A local variable is instantiated for the rest of the list, but not for the first list element. The string returned by the fourth stanza is constructed using the first list element and, therefore, the selector first must be used to access the needed value.

The fifth stanza detects a match for an arbitrary list and instantiates, B and C, two local variables, respectively, for the first list element and the rest of the list. The local variable B shadows the global declaration of B. Consider the following tests:

```
(check-expect (f NLST) NLST-VAL)
(check-expect
 (f '("P. Achten" "J. Hughes" "P. Koopman"))
 "Matched a list whose first element is: \"P. Achten\"")
```

Fig. 106 A function to illustrate the semantics of `match`-expressions

```
(require 2htdp/abstraction)
;; A student is a structure: (make-student string symbol number>=0)
(define-struct student (name year gpa))
(define X 42)
(define B "Basia Mucha")
(define DIMITROVA (make-student "Rositsa Abrasheva" 'senior 3.94))
(define BLST '(#true #true #true))
(define NLST '(1 2 3))
(define ELST '())
;; Any → string
;; Purpose: Illustrate the semantics of match-expressions
(define (f a-value)
  (match a-value
    [42 "Matched 42"]
    [(? string?) (string-append "Matched a string: " a-value)]
    [(student n y g)
     (string-append "Matched a student whose gpa is: "
                    (number->string g))]
    [(cons (? boolean?) r)
     (string-append "Matched a list that starts with a Boolean: "
                    (boolean->string (first a-value)))]
    [(cons B C)
     (format "Matched a list whose first element is: ~s" B)]
    [else "Nothing is matched."]))

;; Sample expressions for f
(define X-VAL "Matched 42")
(define B-VAL (string-append "Matched a string: " B))
(define DIMITROVA-VAL
        (string-append "Matched a student whose gpa is: "
                       (number->string (student-gpa DIMITROVA))))
(define BLST-VAL
        (string-append "Matched a list that starts with a Boolean: "
                       (boolean->string (first BLST))))
(define NLST-VAL (format "Matched a list whose first element is: ~s"
                         (first NLST)))
(define ELST-VAL "Nothing is matched.")
```

The first three stanzas do not detect a match because a-value is not 42, a string, or a student in either test. The fourth stanza does not detect a match because the given lists are of a different type: they do not have a Boolean as the first list element. For the fifth stanza, the first test instantiates B to 1 (which is not a Boolean) and C to '(2 3). The local B bound to 1 shadows the B bound to "Basia Mucha". The second test instantiates B to "P. Achten" (which is not a Boolean) and C to '("J. Hughes" "P. Koopman"). The local B, once again, shadows the B bound to "Basia Mucha". The expression in the fifth stanza uses the value of (the local) B to build the returned list.[29]

---

[29] The backslashes in the expected value of the second test is DrRacket's convention to indicate that a double quote, ", is part of the string.

Finally consider these tests:

```
(check-expect (f '())    ELST-VAL)
(check-expect (f (square 10 "solid" "green"))
                 "Nothing is matched.")
```

The value provided to f in each test is not 42, a string, a student, or a cons-list. Therefore, the first five stanzas do not detect a match and the returned string is given by the default stanza.

134.2 Refactoring Using Pattern Matching

All the abstraction techniques studied can effectively make programs shorter and easier to understand. We shall refactor the program developed in Sect. 106 to evaluate arithmetic expressions. The complete set of functions needed is displayed in Fig. 107. The first observation is that sum-lon, subt-lon, and mult-lon are all very similar because they are list-summarizing operations. This suggests refactoring using accum. The refactoring of sum-lon and mult-lon is

```
;; lon → number
;; Purpose: To sum the given lon
(define (sum-lon a-lon) (accum 0 id + a-lon))


;; lon → number    Purpose: To multiply the given lon
(define (mult-lon a-lon) (accum 1 id * a-lon))
```

The refactoring of subt-lon requires a little algebraic manipulation. Observe that (- a b c) is equivalent to (* -1 (+ (* -1 a) b c)). Furthermore, a match-expression may be used to eliminate the use of first and rest. These observations yield

```
;; lon → number throws error
;; Purpose: To subtract the given lon
(define (subt-lon a-lon)
  (match a-lon
    ['() (error "No numbers provided to -.")]
    [(cons fnum rnums)
     (* -1 (accum 0 id + (cons (* -1 fnum) rnums)))]))
```

The bodies of sum-lon and subt-lon have an expression to sum a list of numbers. To eliminate mostly repeated code we abstract to create a new sum-lon function and obtain

```
;; X → X                        Purpose: Return the given input
(define (id x) x)


;; (listof number) → number    Purpose: Sum given lon
(define (sum-lon a-lon) (accum 0 id + a-lon))


;; lon → number     Purpose: To sum the given lon
(define (sum-lon a-lon) (sum-lon a-lon))


;; lon → number throws error
;; Purpose: To subtract the given lon
(define (subt-lon a-lon)
  (match a-lon
    ['() (error "No numbers provided to -.")]
    [(cons fnum rnums)
     (* -1 (sum-lon (cons (* -1 fnum) rnums)))))
```

The new sum-lon function only takes a list of numbers as input. Along with mult-lon, these functions are only used in apply-f and may be encapsulated. Observe, however, that the bodies of subt-lon and mult-lon are easily inlined into the body of apply-f. The resulting function is displayed as part of the refactored program in Fig. 108.

We observe that eval-args is also a list-summarizing function and may be refactored to use accum:

```
;; (listof sexpr) → (listof number) throws error
;; Purpose: To evaluate the sexprs in the given list
(define (eval-args a-losexpr)
  (accum '() (λ (a-sexpr) (eval-sexpr a-sexpr)) cons args))
```

In this form it is easily inlined into eval-slist. In turn, eval-slist is now easily inlined into eval-sexpr. Inlining these functions eliminates the need to define them. Finally, a match-expression may be used in eval-sexpr to eliminate the use of first and rest. The refactored eval-sexpr is displayed in Fig. 108.

To complete the refactoring the refactored eval-sexpr, accum, and apply-f are made local inside a global eval-sexpr. The body of the local-expression calls the locally defined eval-sexpr. This completes the transformation of the program in Fig. 107 to the one in Fig. 108. Take time to appreciate how much shorter and simpler the resulting program is. Do you want to program with or without using abstraction? It is perfectly fine not to feel comfortable with all the abstractions yet. As your experience increases you will become more comfortable with abstraction.

Fig. 107 Functions for evaluating arithmetic expressions from Sect. 106

```
;; <X Y Z> Z (X → Y) (Y Z → Z) (listof X) → Z
;; Purpose: Summarize given list
(define (accum base-val ffirst comb L)
 (if (empty? L) base-val
     (comb (ffirst (first L)) (accum base-val ffirst comb (rest L)))))
;; X → X      Purpose: Return the given X
(define (id an-x) an-x)
;; (listof sexpr) → (listof number) throws error
;; Purpose: To evaluate the sexprs in the given list
(define (eval-args a-losexpr)
 (if (empty? a-losexpr) '()
     (cons (eval-sexpr (first a-losexpr)) (eval-args (rest a-losexpr)))))
;; slist → number throws error  Purpose: To evaluate the given slist
(define (eval-slist sl) (apply-f (first sl) (eval-args (rest sl))))
;; sexpr → number throws error  Purpose: To evaluate the given sexpr
(define (eval-sexpr a-sexpr)
 (cond [(number? a-sexpr) a-sexpr]
       [else (eval-slist a-sexpr)]))
;; function (listof number) → number throws error
;; Purpose: To apply the given function to the given numbers
(define (apply-f a-function a-lon)
 (cond [(eq? a-function '+) (sum-lon  a-lon)]
       [(eq? a-function '-) (subt-lon a-lon)]
       [else (mult-lon a-lon)]))
;; lon → number      Purpose: To sum the given lon
(define (sum-lon a-lon)
 (if (empty? a-lon) 0 (+ (first a-lon) (sum-lon (rest a-lon)))))
;; lon → number throws error  Purpose: To subtract the given lon
(define (subt-lon a-lon)
(if (empty? a-lon) (error "No numbers provided to -.")
    (- (first a-lon) (sum-lon (rest a-lon)))))
;; lon → number              Purpose: To multiply the given lon
(define (mult-lon a-lon)
 (if (empty? a-lon) 1 (* (first a-lon) (mult-lon (rest a-lon)))))
```

134.3 Designing Using Pattern Matching

Consider a function that consumes a list of numbers and then returns a list of the even numbers in the given list doubled. How can this problem be solved? Reason about the varieties of (listof number). If the given list is empty, then the result is the empty list because there are no numbers to process. If the given list is not empty, then we must distinguish between two types of (listof number): those that start with an even number and those that start with an odd number. In other words, we are redefining a list of numbers to be:

```
;; Data Definition
;; A (listof number) (lon) is either:
;;  1. '()
;;  2. (cons even-number lon)
;;  3. (cons odd-number  lon)
```

Fig. 108 The refactored program from Fig. 107

```
;; sexpr → number throws error
;; Purpose: To evaluate the given sexpr
(define (eval-sexpr a-sexpr)
  (local [;; <X Y Z> Z (X → Y) (Y Z → Z) (listof X) → Z
          ;; Purpose: Summarize given list
          (define (accum base-val ffirst comb a-lox)
            (match a-lox
              ['() base-val]
              [(cons x xs)
               (comb (ffirst x) (accum base-val ffirst comb xs))]))
          ;; function (listof number) → number throws error
          ;; Purpose: To apply the given function to the given numbers
          (define (apply-f a-function a-lon)
            (local [;; X → X      Purpose: Return the given input
                    (define (id x) x)
                    ;; (listof number) → number Purpose: Sum given lon
                    (define (sum-lon a-lon) (accum 0 id + a-lon))]
              (cond [(eq? a-function '+) (sum-lon a-lon)]
                    [(eq? a-function '-)
                     (match a-lon
                       ['() (error "No numbers provided to -.")]
                       [(cons fnum rnums)
                        (* -1 (sum-lon (cons (* -1 fnum) rnums)))])]
                    [else (accum 1 id * a-lon)])))
          ;; sexpr → number throws error
          ;; Purpose: Evaluate the given sexpr
          (define (eval-sexpr a-sexpr)
            (match a-sexpr
              [(cons op args)
               (apply-f
                op
                (accum '() (λ (a-sexpr) (eval-sexpr a-sexpr)) cons args))]
              [else a-sexpr]))]
    (eval-sexpr a-sexpr)))
```

If the given list starts with an even number, the double of the first number is consed to the result of recursively processing the rest of the given list. If the given list starts with an odd number, the answer is obtained by recursively processing the rest of the given list.

This problem analysis allows us to develop the following sample lists of numbers and sample expressions:

```
;; Sample instances of lon
(define ELON '())
(define LON1 '(0 1 2 3 4 5))
(define LON2 '(7 8 9))
```

```
;; Sample expressions for extract-double-evens
(define ELON-VAL '())
(define LON1-VAL (cons (* 2 (first LON1))
                       (extract-double-evens (rest LON1))))
(define LON2-VAL (extract-double-evens (rest LON2)))
```

Observe there is one sample list for each subtype of (listof number). The sample expressions are written in accordance to the problem analysis above.

The (listof number) varieties suggest that a match-expression may be used to distinguish among them. The match-expression needs one stanza for each variety. Each stanza may declare local variables instead of using the selectors first and rest. The following is an implementation of these observations:

```
;; (listof number) → (listof number)
;; Purpose: Return a list of doubled evens in the given list
(define (extract-double-evens a-lon)
  (match a-lon
    ['() '()]
    [(cons (? even?) rlon)
     (cons (* 2 (first a-lon)) (extract-double-evens rlon))]
    [(cons flon rlon) (extract-double-evens rlon)]))
```

Each variety is processed as suggested by the sample expressions. The only difference is that the local variables introduced by the match-expression are used to reference the list components. Observe that in the second stanza a variable is not declared for the first number in the list and, therefore, first is used to reference it.

Finally, the function is tested as follows:

```
;; Tests using sample computations for extract-double-evens
(check-expect (extract-double-evens ELON) ELON-VAL)
(check-expect (extract-double-evens LON1) LON1-VAL)
(check-expect (extract-double-evens LON2) LON2-VAL)

;; Tests using sample values for extract-double-evens
(check-expect (extract-double-evens '(-3 -7 -11)) '())
(check-expect (extract-double-evens '(88 10 120))
              '(176 20 240))
(check-expect (extract-double-evens '(1 2 4 8))
              '(4 8 16))
```

The tests using sample values clearly illustrate the function works when the given list contains only odd, only even, or a combination of add and even numbers.

*** **Ex. 311** — Using a match-expression refactor filter-pred from Sect. 116.6.

* **Ex. 312** — Using a match-expression write a function to compute the length of a list.

**** **Ex. 313** — Using a `match`-expression refactor `move-los` developed in Sect. 130.3.

** **Ex. 314** — Using a `match`-expression write a predicate to determine if a given list is a (`listof string`).

** **Ex. 315** — Using a `match`-expression refactor `andmap-pred` in Sect. 116.4. Do you prefer the refactored function? Why or why not?

135 What Have We Learned in This Chapter?

The important lessons of Chap. 24 are summarized as follows:

- A `for`-loop generates the sequences of values to be iterated over and combines the values obtained from evaluating its body to return a value.
- A `match`-expression dispatches on the type of the data and may introduce local variables to capture the values in a compound piece of data.
- Code readability can be greatly increased and code repetition greatly reduced using `for`-loops and `match`-expressions.
- In order to use `for`-loops and `match`-expressions an ISL+ program must require the `2htdp/abstraction` teachpack.
- A comprehension clause declares a (local) variable to iterate over the values generated from a list, a natural number, or a string.
- ISL+ offers 6 different `for`-loops with the following syntax:

```
expr ::= (for/list      (clause⁺) expr)
     ::= (for/and       (clause⁺) expr)
     ::= (for/or        (clause⁺) expr)
     ::= (for/sum       (clause⁺) expr)
     ::= (for/product   (clause⁺) expr)
     ::= (for/string    (clause⁺) expr)
clause ::= [variable <expr>]
```

- In a `for`-loop the scope of a comprehension variable is the loop's body.
- ISL+ offers 6 different `for*`-loops with the following syntax:

```
expr ::= (for*/list     (clause⁺) expr)
     ::= (for*/and      (clause⁺) expr)
     ::= (for*/or       (clause⁺) expr)
     ::= (for*/sum       (clause⁺) expr)
     ::= (for*/product  (clause⁺) expr)
     ::= (for*/string    (clause⁺) expr)
```

- In a `for*`-loop the scope of a comprehension variable is the remaining comprehension clauses and the loop's body.
- Pattern matching is used to process data based on its type.

- Pattern matching eliminates the repetitive use of selector functions by declaring (local) variables to capture the values contained in compound data.
- A match-expression that has the following syntax:

expr ::= (match expr
      [pattern expr]$^+$)
   ::= (match expr
      [pattern expr]$^+$)
      [else expr]$^+$)

pattern ::= literal
     ::= variable
     ::= (cons pattern pattern)
     ::= (structure-name pattern*)
     ::= (? predicate-name)

- Functions may be designed or refactored using for-loops or pattern matching.

Chapter 25
Interfaces and Objects

Previous chapters have explored the idea that functions are data. In Chap. 20 functions were passed as input to other functions. In Chap. 22 functions were returned as the value of function calls. This chapter explores the other side of the coin. Is data a function? Intuitively, perhaps, the immediate answer that comes to mind is an unequivocal no. A posn, for example, is not a function given that it does not compute anything. It stores two values called x and y. You cannot apply a posn to arguments. The same feels true about lists and trees. If L is a (listof X), what meaning can (L 'first) possibly have? Indeed, it may not be intuitive to think of data as a function.

This lack of intuition, however, is more than anything else a product of training. After all, has it ever been suggested in a high school Mathematics textbook that a number is a function? It turns out, however, that data can be a function. That is, data may be represented using a function. Traditionally, data is thought of separately from functions. This occurs despite the fact that whenever we create a data definition we have in mind functions that are valid on the defined data. In other words, we expect certain behavior from the data. For example, the program for Aliens Attack defines an alien. It is expected that the alien can be moved right, left, or down, that the alien may be determined to be at the right or left edge of the scene, and that the alien may be determined to be hit by a shot. It is not expected that an alien can provide its name or its distance to the origin on a Cartesian plane. It becomes clear that an instance of a type is information (i.e., zero or more values) and the functions that are valid on it.

Indeed, much of this textbook is about defining types: valid values and valid functions. A posn, for instance, is not simply x and y values. It is also the ability to extract the x value (i.e., posn-x), to extract the y value (i.e., posn-y), and to determine if something is a posn (i.e., posn?). Given a posn, the signature and purpose statement of these selectors, and this predicate, we understand the expected behavior. Furthermore, we can add new operations and their expected behavior. For example, we may add a function to compute the distance to the origin. Why, therefore, should anyone strictly think of a data definition and the operations on the defined type as two separate entities? Chap. 21 discussed encapsulating related functions. These

M. T. Morazán, *Animated Problem Solving*, Texts in Computer Science,
https://doi.org/10.1007/978-3-030-85091-3_25

functions can be the operations valid on some data type. If valid type operations are encapsulated, then there is no technical impediment to also encapsulating the values that define an instance of a type. To do so we must first learn how to define the operations valid on a type.

136 Interfaces

A data definition defines a type and in the case of compound data it also defines the type of the components. It states nothing about the valid type operations. An *interface* defines the behavior of a defined type. In other words, an interface specifies the operations that are valid on a type. Consider the problem of computing the distance to the origin for a given point on a three-dimensional plane. Following the steps of the design recipe yields the program displayed in Fig. 109. There are a few unstated assumptions in the program. First, it is assumed that there is a function to construct a 3Dposn. Second, it is assumed that there are selector functions for the components of a 3Dposn. Third, the values of x, y, z, and the selectors are stored separately from the function dist-origin. Would all this had been clear to you before reading the preceding chapters? Would you have known that there is a function 3Dposn-x to extract the x value of an instance of a 3Dposn?

In addition to defining a type, an interface is developed to define the expected behavior of a type. An interface outlines the valid operations and the returned type. For a 3Dposn the interface is:

Request x: number
Request y: number
Request z: number
Request distance: number

The interface makes it clear to any reader or user which are the valid operations on a 3Dposn. Observe that an interface says nothing about how a data type and its valid operations are implemented.

Take a moment to ponder what has just been done. The data definition and the interface explicitly relate x, y, z, 3Dposn-x, 3Dposn-y, 3Dposn-z, and dist-origin. If they are related, then we ought to be able to encapsulate them into a single package. Whenever a 3Dposn is constructed, the package returned ought to be able to perform all the operations in the interface. How can a 3Dposn instance perform many operations? How does it know what operations to perform?

To achieve this a technique called *message-passing* is used. An interface is implemented by a constructor function that returns a message-processing function. This is a curried function that receives as input a message requesting a service. For example, this function may get the message 'getx requesting the x value of the 3Dposn. An

Fig. 109 Distance to the origin program for a 3D point

```
;; A 3Dposn is a structure: (make-3Dposn number number number)
(define-struct 3Dposn (x y z))

;; Sample instances of 3Dposn
(define ORIGIN  (make-3Dposn 0 0 0))
(define A3DPOSN (make-3Dposn 2 3 5))

;; 3Dposn → number
;; Purpose: Return the distance to the origin of the given 3Dposn
(define (dist-origin a-3dposn)
  (sqrt (+ (sqr (3Dposn-x a-3dposn))
           (sqr (3Dposn-y a-3dposn))
           (sqr (3Dposn-z a-3dposn)))))

;; Sample expressions for dist-origin
(define ORIGIND  (sqrt (+ (sqr (3Dposn-x ORIGIN))
                          (sqr (3Dposn-y ORIGIN))
                          (sqr (3Dposn-z ORIGIN)))))
(define A3DPOSND (sqrt (+ (sqr (3Dposn-x A3DPOSN))
                          (sqr (3Dposn-y A3DPOSN))
                          (sqr (3Dposn-z A3DPOSN)))))

;; Tests using sample computations for dist-origin
(check-within (dist-origin ORIGIN)  ORIGIND  0.01)
(check-within (dist-origin A3DPOSN) A3DPOSND 0.01)

;; Tests using sample values for dist-origin
(check-within (dist-origin (make-3Dposn 10 20 30))  37.42 0.01)
```

interface, therefore, must specify the messages used to request a service. We can now refine the 3Dposn interface to be:

```
'getx:  number
'gety:  number
'getz:  number
'd2o:   number
```

Observe that there is a unique message (in this case a symbol) associated with each service. The idea is that the message-processing function determines what value to compute by examining the message it gets as input. Observe that embedded in the interface definition is a data definition for a `message`. A message is an enumeration type: either `'getx`, `'gety`, `'getz`, or `'d2o`.

A constructor function that implements an interface is called a *class*. A class encapsulates the values of and the operations on a type. It defines a constructor for instances of a type. The value returned by a class is called an *object*. An object is an instance of an interface and knows how to perform all the services in the interface using message-passing. The 3Dposn class is displayed in Fig. 110. The class takes as input 3 numbers and returns a 3Dposn. It is named `make-3Dposn` to easily identify its role as a constructor for 3Dposns. Its body is a `local`-expression that defines an

Fig. 110 Interface implementation for 3Dposn

```
(require 2htdp/abstraction)

;; number number number → 3Dposn  Purpose: Return a 3Dposn object
(define (make-3Dposn x y z)
  (local [;; 3Dposn → number Purpose: Return distance to origin
          (define (dist-origin x y z) (sqrt (+ (sqr x) (sqr y) (sqr z))))
          ;; message → 3Dposn service throws error
          ;; Purpose: To manage messages for a 3Dposn
          (define (manager m)
            (match m
              ['getx x]
              ['gety y]
              ['getz z]
              ['d2o  (dist-origin x y z)]
              [else (error (string-append "Unknown message to 3Dposn: "
                                          (symbol->string m)))]))]
    manager))
;; Sample 3Dposn objects
(define ORIGIN  (make-3Dposn 0 0 0))
(define A3DPOSN (make-3Dposn 2 3 5))

;; Tests using sample computations for 3Dposn
(check-within (ORIGIN  'getx) 0    0.01)
(check-within (A3DPOSN 'gety) 3    0.01)
(check-within (ORIGIN  'getz) 0    0.01)
(check-within (A3DPOSN 'd2o)  6.16 0.01)

;; Tests using sample values for 3Dposn
(check-within ((make-3Dposn 10 20 30) 'd2o)
              37.42 0.01)
(check-error (A3DPOSN 'move-r)
             "Unknown message to 3Dposn: move-r")
```

auxiliary function for any value that needs to be computed (in this case only distance to origin) and the message-processing function called `manager`. The `manager` takes as input a message and returns (the value of) a service defined in the interface. The body of `manager` is a cond-expression to distinguish the message varieties. If a service requires no computation, a value is directly returned. If computation is required (like computing the distance to the origin), a local function is called. In this case, `manager` is a guarded function that throws an error. It is also an object given that it knows how to compute all the services in the interface and, therefore, the `local`-expression returns it.

Testing interfaces requires defining one or more objects and writing tests to check services are correctly provided. In Fig. 110 two 3Dposn objects are defined. The tests check the result obtained from passing each message to an object. For example, the x coordinate of `ORIGIN` is obtained using `(ORIGIN 'getx)`—passing the message `'getx` to `ORIGIN`. The expected value is 0. Finally, the tests using sample values use inlined uses of the constructor to test services and errors.

A 3Dposn, which is thought of as data, is a function. Specifically, it is an instance of the curried function `manager` (i.e., an object) that is specialized for the values of x, y, z given to `make-3Dposn`. For `ORIGIN` it is an 3Dposn object in which x = y = z = 0. For `A3DPOSN` it is an 3Dposn object in which x = 2, y = 3, and z = 5. Just like functions can be data, we see that data can be functions.

136.1 Improving the Human Interface

Message-passing may reduce the readability of the code. For example, does (`A3DPOSN 'd20`) communicate to others that this expression represents `A3DPOSN`'s distance to the origin? Unless you are intimately familiar with the message-passing protocol it is likely that this expression is meaningless. Furthermore, it is unlikely that any programmer (including yourself) will permanently remember the message-passing protocol in the near and far future. This will make it unnecessarily more difficult to refine the program.

To mitigate this problem `wrapper functions` for the services provided by an interface may be written. A wrapper function hides the details of the implementation. In this case, it hides the details of message-passing. The idea is to allow programmers to use 3Dposns without forcing them to know how they are implemented (much like you do not know how posns are implemented in `ISL+`). A wrapper function is needed for each service in the interface. It takes as input an object (and any additional inputs if any) and its body applies the interface to the appropriate message. Wrapper functions are designed following the steps of the design recipe.

Figure 111 displays the wrapper functions for 3Dposn. Adding this code to the one displayed in Fig. 110 allows programmers to use a nicer version of the defined interface. Instead of explicitly using message-passing, they can use the wrapper functions. Observe that now programmers have the same interface as the one used in Fig. 109. Writing wrapper functions does not provide a programmer with new computational powers, but it is an abstraction that liberates a programmer from the details of a message-passing protocol.

136.2 Services that Require More Input

After an interface is implemented, it may be necessary to add more services. This means expanding the message-processing function and, if necessary, design (local) auxiliary functions. If a value may be computed using only the information stored in an object, then adding a service is no different than what was done for `dist-origin` for 3Dposn. For example, adding a service to determine if a given 3Dposn object is on the x-axis may be done by comparing the x value to 0.

Fig. 111 Wrapper functions for 3Dposn

```
;; 3Dposn → number
;; Purpose: Return the x of the given 3Dposn
(define (3Dposn-x a-3dposn) (a-3dposn 'getx))

;; Sample expressions for 3Dposn-x
(define ORIGINX (ORIGIN 'getx))    (define A3DPOSNX (A3DPOSN 'getx))

;; Tests using sample computations and values for 3Dposn-x
(check-within (3Dposn-x ORIGIN)  ORIGINX  0.01)
(check-within (3Dposn-x A3DPOSN) A3DPOSNX 0.01)
(check-within (3Dposn-x (make-3Dposn 10 20 30)) 10 0.01)

;; 3Dposn → number
;; Purpose: Return the y of the given 3Dposn
(define (3Dposn-y a-3dposn) (a-3dposn 'gety))

;; Sample expressions for 3Dposn-y
(define ORIGINY (ORIGIN 'gety))    (define A3DPOSNY (A3DPOSN 'gety))

;; Tests using sample computations and values for 3Dposn-y
(check-within (3Dposn-y ORIGIN)  ORIGINY  0.01)
(check-within (3Dposn-y A3DPOSN) A3DPOSNY 0.01)
(check-within (3Dposn-y (make-3Dposn 10 20 30)) 20 0.01)

;; 3Dposn → number
;; Purpose: Return the z of the given 3Dposn
(define (3Dposn-z a-3dposn) (a-3dposn 'getz))

;; Sample expressions for 3Dposn-z
(define ORIGINZ (ORIGIN 'getz))    (define A3DPOSNZ (A3DPOSN 'getz))

;; Tests using sample computations and values for 3Dposn-z
(check-within (3Dposn-z ORIGIN)  ORIGINZ  0.01)
(check-within (3Dposn-z A3DPOSN) A3DPOSNZ 0.01)
(check-within (3Dposn-z (make-3Dposn 10 20 30)) 30 0.01)

;; 3Dposn → number
;; Purpose: Return distance to origin of given 3Dposn
(define (dist-origin a-3dposn) (a-3dposn 'd20))

;; Sample expressions for dist-origin
(define ORIGIND (ORIGIN 'd20))    (define A3DPOSND (A3DPOSN 'd20))

;; Tests using sample computations and values for dist-origin
(check-within (dist-origin ORIGIN)  ORIGIND  0.01)
(check-within (dist-origin A3DPOSN) A3DPOSND 0.01)
(check-within (dist-origin (make-3Dposn 10 20 30)) 37.42 0.01)
```

If a service requires further input, the answer cannot be computed using only the values stored in an object. That is, the object providing the service (usually referred to as this) needs information beyond that which it stores. For instance, consider adding a service that computes the distance to a given 3Dposn object. In addition to this object another 3Dposn object is needed. This other object is unknown when the interface is implemented and, therefore, cannot be provided as input. It is similar to receiving a message. When the interface is written, there is no way to know which messages will actually be received as input. The solution for messages is to make a curried function that consumes the extra input (i.e., a message). The same design tactic may be employed to add services that require extra input. The interface must return a function that consumes the extra input.

To illustrate the technique let us add a service to compute the distance of this 3Dposn to a given 3Dposn. The first step is to update the interface as follows:

```
'getx   number
'gety   number
'getz   number
'd2o    number
'd2p    3Dposn → number
```

The data definition of a message is expanded to include 'd2p for the new distance-computing service. Given that extra input is needed, the interface returns a function that consumes the extra input, a 3Dposn, and that returns a number for the distance between this and the given 3Dposn.

The next step is to refine the manager function to include the new service. This means adding a stanza to the condition for the new service as follows:

```
;; message → 3Dposn service throws error
;; Purpose: To manage messages for a 3Dposn
(define (manager m)
  (match m
    ['getx x]
    ['gety y]
    ['getz z]
    ['d2o  (dist-origin x y z)]
    ['d2p  distance]
    [else (error (string-append "Unknown message to 3Dposn: "
                                (symbol->string m)))]))
```

The new stanza matches the new message and returns the distance function (yet to be written). The distance function must satisfy the return type specified in the interface definition.

Now, the distance function is designed and implemented. Keep in mind that this is a local function inside the 3Dposn class. Therefore, this function has in scope all the variables declared in the class. This is where the power of currying is exploited. The previous inputs (x, y, and z) are used to compute the distance to the 3Dposn received as input. After following the steps of the design recipe the following local function is added to the 3Dposn class:

```
;; 3Dpson arrow number
;; Purpose: Compute the distance from this to the given 3Dposn
(define (distance a-3dposn)
  (sqrt (+ (sqr (- x (3Dposn-x a-3dposn)))
           (sqr (- y (3Dposn-y a-3dposn)))
           (sqr (- z (3Dposn-z a-3dposn)))))))
```

Observe that this function uses the coordinates of this and of the given 3Dposn to compute the distance.

The final step is to develop a wrapper function for the new distance service. As before, this is done following the steps of the design recipe. The resulting function is

```
(define B3DPOSN (make-3Dposn 1 1 1))


;; 3Dposn 3Dposn → number
;; Purpose: Return the distance between the given 3Dposns
(define (3Dposn-distance p1 p2) ((p1 'd2p) p2))


;; Sample expressions for 3Dposn-distance
(define ORIGINDP  ((ORIGIN  'd2p) ORIGIN))
(define A3DPOSNDP ((A3DPOSN 'd2p) B3DPOSN))


;; Tests using sample computations 3Dposn-distance
(check-within (3Dposn-distance ORIGIN ORIGIN)
              ORIGINDP
              0.01)
(check-within (3Dposn-distance A3DPOSN B3DPOSN)
              A3DPOSNDP
              0.01)


;; Tests using sample values for 3Dposn-distance
(check-within (3Dposn-distance (make-3Dposn 10 20 30)
                               (make-3Dposn 2  3   4))
              32.07
              0.01)
```

A new 3Dposn instance is defined to facilitate writing tests. The sample expressions apply a first 3Dposn object to the message 'd2p. This returns the object's distance function. This function is applied to a second 3Dposn to compute the distance. The function is obtained by abstracting over the sample expressions. The tests are developed as always using sample computations and sample values.

137 A Design Recipe for Interfaces

The systematic steps to design the implementation of an interface may now be enumerated. The design recipe for an interface is:

1. Identify the values that must be stored and the services that must be provided.
2. Develop an interface data definition and a data definition for messages.
3. Develop a function template for the class that consumes the values that must be stored and whose body is a `local`-expression returning the message-processing function.
4. Specialize the signature, purpose, class header, and message-processing function.
5. Write and make local the auxiliary functions needed by the message-passing function.
6. Write and test a wrapper function for each service.

The first step is problem analysis. It asks you to identify the information that specializes each object and the services that an object must provide. For every piece of information identified there must be a parameter. The services must include a selector for each piece of information that specializes an object. The second step asks you to develop an interface data definition and a message data definition. There must be a message for each service identified in Step 1.

The third step asks for the development of a function template for the class. Its parameters correspond to the values identified in Step 1 to specialize an object. The name of the class is also the name of the constructor. The function's body is a `local`-expression to encapsulate all needed functions that returns the message-processing function. The fourth step has you develop the definition template for local message-passing function. This function must contain a conditional that processes a message as defined in Step 2. The fifth step asks you to develop all the auxiliary functions needed by the message-processing function and make them local. Each auxiliary function is developed using the design recipe.

The sixth step has you write a wrapper function for each service in the interface developed in Step 2. These functions take as input the object that is providing the service and the extra input, if any, required. The body of each wrapper function applies the object providing the service to the appropriate message. If extra input is needed, the function returned by the object is applied to the extra input.

---

* **Ex. 316** — Following the steps of the design recipe for interfaces, design and implement an interface for `posn`. The services offered by a `posn` are accessing the x and y coordinates.

*** **Ex. 317** — Following the steps of the design recipe for interfaces, design and implement an interface for `alien` as defined for Aliens Attack 5.

**** **Ex. 318** — Following the steps of the design recipe for interfaces, design and implement an interface for `car`. A car has three characteristics: gas tank size in liters, maximum speed in kilometers per hour, and kilometers per liter.

In addition to accessing its components, the services offered include maximum distance that may be traveled in kilometers, maximum distance that may be traveled in miles, and the number of liters used to travel a given distance in kilometers.

*** **Ex. 319** — The 3Dposn implementation has code repetition in dist-origin and distance. Refactor the 3Dposn code to eliminate this repetition.

** **Ex. 320** — Add two 3Dposn services one to move the x, y, and z coordinates by some given amounts and one to determine if this is close to a given 3Dposn. A 3Dposn is close if the distance to it is less than or equal to 2.

138 Interfaces and Union Types

Designing interfaces for data with variety requires individually reasoning about each variety. This should not come as a surprise given that individually reasoning about each variety is how functions to process a union type are designed. Consider the functions developed in Sect. 72 to compute the length and the sum of a list of quizzes:

```
;; A quiz grade (qg) is a number in [0..100]

;; A list of quiz grades (loq) is a (listof qg)

;; loq → number
;; Purpose: To compute the length of the given loq
(define (length-loq a-loq)
  (if (empty? a-loq)
      0
      (+ 1 (length-loq (rest a-loq)))))

;; loq → number
;; Purpose: To compute the sum of the given loq
(define (sum-loq a-loq)
  (if (empty? a-loq)
      0
      (+ (first a-loq) (sum-loq (rest a-loq)))))
```

Observe that a loq is a union type that has two varieties: empty and non-empty. For this reason every function that processes a loq has (repeatedly) a conditional expression just like length-loq and sum-loq. To write the conditional expression each data variety is individually reasoned about. That is, an answer is formulated for the empty list and an answer is formulated for the non-empty list.

Consider the implications of both varieties of loq offering services. The empty loq knows how to compute its length and sum. The non-empty loq knows how to compute its length and sum. This means that a conditional expression is not needed because a given list, regardless of its variety, knows how to compute its length and sum. This is called polymorphic dispatch. Polymorphic dispatch, in essence, is the automatic process of selecting which implementation of an operation to use. It means that programmers may dispense writing a conditional expression to process a union type. To achieve this, the code that provides the answer for one variety must be separated from the code that provides the answer for another variety. For instance, the code to compute the length of an empty loq must be separated from the code to compute the length of a non-empty loq. In fact, this must be done for every service that a loq offers.

How is this separation of code and conditional expression elimination achieved for a union type? For each subtype there must be a class that encapsulates the code for that subtype. Observe that each subtype must offer the same services. That is, all varieties have a common interface. Each class only implements the services for the subtype it is written for. For instance, the empty loq needs to return 0 for its length and 0 for its sum. The non-empty loq needs to return 1 plus the length of the rest of the list for its length and the first quiz plus the sum of the rest of the quizzes for its sum.

139 An Abbreviated (listof X) Interface

To illustrate interface design for data with variety, an abbreviated version of (listof X) is implemented. Abbreviated means that this implementation shall not contain all the functions associated with lists in ISL+. This implementation shall only include the familiar empty?, first, rest, cons, and map. In addition, it includes the ability to transform any list implemented using our interface into an ISL+ list.

The steps of the design recipe are outlined. The first three steps guide the rest of the design. Carefully outlining these steps greatly facilitates the remaining steps.

139.1 Step 1: Values and Services

Two classes are required: one for the empty (listof X) and one for the non-empty (listof X). The empty (listof X) needs to store no values. The non-empty (listof X) needs to store two values: an X for the first element of the list and a (listof X) for the rest of the elements of the list.

The following services are offered by a (listof X):

- Determine if the list is the empty list.
- Access the first element of the list.
- Access the rest of the list.
- Add a new element to the front of this list.

- Apply a function to every element of the list and return a list of the results.
- Transform this list into an ISL+ list.

139.2 Step 2: Interface and Message Definitions

Based on the services outlined in Step 1, 6 return types and 6 message varieties need to be defined. These may be defined simultaneously in the definition of an interface. Observe that empty? and the transformation into an ISL+ list return a value with no need for further input. The services first or rest either return a value or throw an error with no need for further input. An error is thrown if the first element or rest of the elements are requested from the empty list. Finally, adding an element to the front of the list or mapping a function requires further input. This means that these services must return a function to consume this input.

In order not to confuse ISL+ lists with lists created using the interface developed here, they are denoted differently. ISL+ lists are denoted as (listof X) and (listof Y). Lists created using the interface developed are denoted, respectively, as listofx and listofy.

The interface for a listofx is

```
;; A listofx is an interface offering
;;   'empty:  Boolean
;;   'first:  X throws error
;;    'rest:  listofx throws error
;;    'cons:  X → listofx
;;     'map:  (X → Y) → listofy
;;   '2Rlst:  (listof X)
```

A message is one of the 6 symbols listed in the interface. Determining if this list is empty returns a Boolean. Accessing the first element of this list returns a value of type X or throws an error. Accessing the rest of this list returns a listofx or throws an error. Adding a value to the front of this list returns a function that consumes a value of type X and that returns a listofx. Mapping a function onto this list returns a function that consumes a function of type (X →Y) to map a single list element and that returns a listofy. Finally, converting this returns an ISL+ (listof X).

139.3 Step 3: Class Function Template

There are a few things known about what needs to be done to implement a class for listofx. These include the need for a local message-processing function, a local function to add an element to the front of this, and a function to map a given function onto this list. In addition, it is known that wrapper functions and tests

covering both subtypes are needed for each service. The class template captures all
of these and as a result is quite long. Do not let its length intimidate you. Developing
such a detailed class template makes the next steps of the design recipe much easier.
It is a good time investment to develop a detailed class template. The class template
for listofx is

```
;; ... → listofx
;; Purpose: Return a ... listofx object
(define (class-for-listofx ...)
  (local
    [   :
    ;; X → listofx
    ;; Purpose: Add given X to the front of this list
    (define (add2front an-x) ...)
    ;; (X → Y) → (listof Y)
    ;; Purpose: Map the given function to this list
    (define (map f) ...)
    ;; message → service throws error
    ;; Purpose: Provide service for the given message
    (define (manager m)
      (match m
        ['empty? ...]
        ['first  ...]
        ['rest   ...]
        ['cons   ...]
        ['map    ...]
        ['2Rlst  ...]
        [else
          (error
            (format "Unknown list service requested: ~s" m))]))]
  manager))

;; Sample listofx objects
(define L0 ...) (define L1 ...)...

;; WRAPPER FUNCTIONS
;; listofx → Boolean
;; Purpose: Determine if given listofx is empty
(define (listofx-empty? lox-o) ...)
;; Sample expressions for listofx-empty?
(define L0E ...) (define L1E ...)...
;; Tests using sample computations for listofx-empty?
(check-expect (listofx-empty? L0) L0E)
(check-expect (listofx-empty? L1) L1E)...
;; Tests using sample values for listofx-empty?
(check-expect (listofx-empty? ...) ...)...
```

```
;; listofx → X   throws error
;; Purpose: Return first element of the given listofx
(define (listofx-first lox-o) ...)
;; Sample expressions for listofx-first
(define L1F ...)...
;; Tests using sample computations for listofx-first
(check-expect (listofx-first L1) L1F)...
;; Tests using sample values for listofx-first
(check-error  (listofx-first ...) ...)
(check-expect (listofx-first ...) ...)...

;; listofx → listofx throws error
;; Purpose: Return rest of the given listofx
(define (listofx-rest lox-o) ...)
;; Sample expressions for listofx-rest
(define L1R ...)
;; Tests using sample computations for listofx-rest
(check-expect (listofx-rest ...)) ...)...
;; Tests using sample values for listofx-rest
(check-error  (listofx-rest L0) ...)
(check-expect (listofx-rest ...) ...)...

;; <X Y> listofx (X → Y) → listofx
;; Purpose: Map given function onto the given listofx
(define (listofx-map lox-o f) ...)
;; Sample expressions for listofx-map
(define L0M ...)...(define L1M ...)
;; Tests using sample computations for listofx-map
(check-expect (listofx-map L0 ...) ...)
(check-expect (listofx-map L1 ...) ...)...
;; Tests using sample values for listofx-map
(check-expect (listofx-map ... ...) ...)...

;; listofx → Boolean
;; Purpose: Convert the given listofx to a (listof X)
(define (listofx-2Rlst lox-o) ...)
;; Sample expressions for listofx-2Rlst
(define L0RL ...)...(define L1RL ...)
;; Tests using sample computations for listofx-2Rlst
(check-expect (listofx-2Rlst L0) L0RL)
(check-expect (listofx-2Rlst L1) L1RL)...
;; Tests using sample values for listofx-2Rlst
(check-expect (listofx-2Rlst ...) ...)...
```

Observe that the template definition for the message-processing function, manager, is specialized for the message data definition developed as part of the interface in

Step 2. Furthermore, the template definition suggests making it a guarded function to signal an error when the signature is violated by a programmer. Also observe that the local-expression returns the message-processing function. The template suggests defining at least two sample listofx objects: one for each variety. In the above template it is assumed that L0 is an empty listofx object. Finally, for each wrapper function the steps of the design recipe are followed. The sample expressions and the tests using sample computations for listofx-first and listofx-rest have at least one test (not two). This is because L0 throws an error when used with these functions. The errors, as practiced in this textbook, are tested as part of the tests using sample values.

140 The Empty (listof X) Class

This section designs the class that implements the interface for the empty listofx. Steps 4–5 are outlined.

140.1 Step 4: Signature, Purpose, Class Header, and Message-Passing Function

According to the problem analysis done in Step 1 the empty listofx has no characteristics that must be stored. This means that the signature ought to be

```
;;   → listofx
```

That is, a function with no input that returns a listofx interface. Unfortunately, ISL+ does not allow functions with 0 parameters. To overcome this the class function shall have a *dummy parameter* that is never referenced. Its sole purpose is to allow for the development of the class function. This makes the signature, purpose, and class header for the empty listofx:

```
;; Z → listofx
;; Purpose: Return an empty listofx object
(define (mtList dont-care-param)
```

Z is the type of the parameter. It may be any type given that it is never used. This class returns an empty listofx object. The name of the class, mtList, is chosen to provide any reader of the code an idea of what the class implements.

The message-processing function takes as input a message as defined in Step 2. The conditional in the function definition template from Step 3 is specialized to return a value if no further input is required and a function if more input is required as outlined in the interface developed in Step 2. This function is designed to only implement the services for the empty listofx. This means that for 'empty? it must return #true, for 'first and 'rest it must throw an error, for 'cons and 'map it must return a function, and for '2Rlist it must return '(). The function may be implemented as follows:

```
;; message → service throws error
;; Purpose: Provide service for the given message
(define (manager m)
  (match m
    ['empty? #true]
    ['first  (error "first requested from the empty list")]
    ['rest   (error "rest requested from the empty list")]
    ['cons   add2front]
    ['map    map]
    ['2Rlst  '()]
    [else
     (error
       (format "Unknown list service requested: ~s" m))])))
```

Here add2front and map are two auxiliary functions (to be written) that implement the two services that require further input. This completes Step 4 of the design recipe.

140.2 Step 5: Auxiliary Functions

This class, as suggested by the class template, needs at least two auxiliary functions. The first is the function to implement the cons operation. This function must consume a value of type X and create a new non-empty listofx. To do so it must use the constructor for the other variety of listofx. This function must provide as input the given X value and this list. How do we reference this? Recall that this list is an object represented by the message-processing function. Therefore, this is the manager function. Assuming the other class is named consList, this auxiliary function is

```
;; X → listofx
;; Purpose: Add given X to the front of this list
(define (add2front an-x) (consList an-x manager))
```

The mapping function must apply the given function to every element of this list and return a listofy. There are no elements in this list. Therefore, this list must only return an empty listofy. The map function for the empty listofx class is

```
;; (X → Y) → (listof Y)
;; Purpose: Map the given function to this list
(define (map f) (mtList 'D))
```

Here 'D is a dummy value to construct an empty listofy. Given that neither of these functions requires auxiliary functions, this step of the design recipe is completed.

141 The Non-Empty (listof X) Class

We now focus on the design of the class for the non-empty `listofx`. As with the design of the empty class, steps 4–5 are outlined.

141.1 Step 4: Signature, Purpose, Class Header, and Message-Passing Function

According to the problem analysis done in Step 1 the non-empty `listofx` has two characteristics that must be stored: the first element and the rest of the elements. This means that the signature, purpose, and class header ought to be

```
;; X listofx → listofx
;; Purpose: Return a nonempty listofx object
(define (consList first rest)
```

This class returns a non-empty `listofx` object. The name of the class, `consList`, and the name of the parameters, `first` and `rest`, are chosen to provide any reader of the code an idea of what they represent.

The message-processing function takes the same input and serves the same purpose as in the empty `listofx` class. That is, this function is designed to only implement the services for the non-empty `listofx`. This means that for `'empty?` it must return `#false`, for `'first` it must return `first`, for `'rest` it must return `rest`, for `'cons` it must return `add2front`, for `'map` it must return `map`, and for `'2Rlist` it must return the consing of `first` and the conversion of `rest`. The function may be implemented as follows:

```
;; message → service throws error
;; Purpose: Provide service for the given message
(define (manager m)
  (match m
    ['empty? #false]
    ['first  first]
    ['rest   rest]
    ['cons   add2front]
    ['map    map]
    ['2Rlst  (cons first (rest '2Rlst))]
    [else
     (error
       (format "Unknown list service requested: ~s" m))]))
```

As in the empty `listofx` class, `add2front` and `map` are two auxiliary functions (to be written) that implement the two services that require further input. Pay close attention to the value returned for `'2Rlst`. Observe that `this`, call it L, is converted with the expression `(L '2Rlst)`. The rest of L is recursively processed using `(rest`

'2Rlst). The only difference is that there is no need to write a conditional expression thanks to polymorphic dispatch. Remember that rest is a listofx object and it knows how to convert its value regardless of the list subtype that it is.

This completes Step 4 of the design recipe. Take your time to understand and appreciate that we have structural recursion without a conditional expression. Together the stanzas for '2Rlst in the empty and non-empty classes are, in essence, the same code you write as when writing a recursive function. It is simply split among the classes for each subtype. The code is written differently using message-passing, but the design is the same.

141.2 Step 5: Auxiliary Functions

As the empty listofx class, this class needs two auxiliary functions: add2front and map. The add2front function must consume a value of type X and create a new non-empty listofx. To do so it must use the constructor for a non-empty listofx using the given value and this. Using the constructor for a non-empty listofx sounds like a recursive call and it is, but remember that the constructor returns a curried function. There is no recursive traversal here. The recursive call has a single step that returns an object. Therefore, it is safe to call consList. The function is implemented the same way as in the empty listofx class:

```
;; X → listofx
;; Purpose: Add given X to the front of this list
(define (add2front an-x) (consList an-x manager))
```

If you are thinking that such repetition calls for an abstraction, you are correct. To abstract away from a class you need to implement an abstract class. An abstract class contains all the common code among the classes for different subtypes. We will not delve into abstract classes in this textbook, but you shall learn about them in an object-oriented programming class.

The mapping function, as expected, must apply the given function to every element of this list and return a listofy. To do so it must recursively process the rest of this. The recursive call is implemented using polymorphic dispatch (just as the converting service). The map function for the non-empty listofx class is

```
;; (X → Y) → (listof Y)
;; Purpose: Map the given function to this list
(define (map f) (consList (f first) ((rest 'map) f)))
```

Observe that ((rest 'map) f) is requesting a service from rest. Specifically, it is requesting its mapping function to provide f to it. Once again, no conditional is required for this recursive process because rest knows how to map a function to its elements regardless of the listofx subtype that it is. Given that neither of these functions requires auxiliary functions, this step of the design recipe is completed.

142 Step 6: Wrapper Functions and Tests

This class needs 6 wrapper functions as suggested by the class function template from Step 3. Start by specializing the sample `listofx` objects. This may be done as follows:

```
;; Sample listofx objects
(define L0 (mtList 'dummyval))
(define L1 (consList
            1
            (consList
              2
              (consList
                3
                (mtList 'dummyval)))))
```

These are empty and non-empty `listofx`. These constants are used to write tests for the wrapper functions.

The wrapper functions are designed using the steps of the design recipe as suggested in the class function template. The wrapper function to determine if a given `listofx` is empty requires no further input. This part of the class function template may be specialized as follows:

```
;; listofx → Boolean
;; Purpose: Determine if the given listofx is empty
(define (listofx-empty? lox-o) (lox-o 'empty?))

;; Sample expressions for listofx-empty?
(define L0E (L0 'empty?))
(define L1E (L1 'empty?))

;; Tests using sample computations for listofx-empty?
(check-expect (listofx-empty? L0) L0E)
(check-expect (listofx-empty? L1) L1E)

;; Tests using sample values for listofx-empty?
(check-expect (listofx-empty? (mtList 'dummyval)) #true)
(check-expect
  (listofx-empty? (consList 'hi (mtList 'dummyval)))
  #false)
```

The wrapper function to access the first element of a given `listofx` requires no further input. This function, however, may throw an error given that the interface for this service states that an error may be thrown. This part of the class function template may be specialized as follows:

```
;; listofx → X throws error
;; Purpose: Return first element of given list
(define (listofx-first lox-o) (lox-o 'first))

;; Sample expressions for listofx-first
(define L1F (L1 'first))

;; Tests using sample computations for listofx-first
(check-expect (listofx-first L1) L1F)

;; Tests using sample values for listofx-first
(check-error   (listofx-first L0)
               "first requested from the empty list")
(check-error   (listofx-first (mtList 'dummyval))
               "first requested from the empty list")
(check-expect
  (listofx-first (consList 'hi (mtList 'dummyval)))
  'hi)
```

Observe that the signature specifies that an error may be thrown. In addition, there is only one sample expression and it uses L1. There is no sample expression using L0 because for this operation it throws an error. Instead, L0 is used to test the error as part of the tests using sample values.

The wrapper function to access the rest of a given `listofx` requires no further input. This function, however, may throw an error as specified in the interface. This part of the class function template may be specialized as follows:

```
;; listofx → listofx throws error
;; Purpose: Return rest of given list
(define (listofx-rest lox-o) (lox-o 'rest))

;; Sample expressions for listofx-rest
(define L1R (L1 'rest))

;; Tests using sample computations for listofx-rest
(check-expect (listofx-2Rlst (listofx-rest L1)) '(2 3))

;; Tests using sample values for listofx-rest
(check-error   (listofx-rest L0)
               "rest requested from the empty list")
(check-error   (listofx-rest (mtList 'dummyval))
               "rest requested from the empty list")
```

```
(check-expect
  (listofx-2Rlst
    (listofx-rest
      (consList 'hi
                (mtList 'dummyval))))
  '())
```

Once again, observe that the signature specifies that an error may be thrown and there is only one sample expression. L0 is used to test the error as part of the tests using sample values.

The wrapper function to add a given value to the front of a given listofx requires further input. This means that this wrapper function needs to apply the function returned by the list object to the given value. In addition, recall that function equivalence is an unsolvable problem (discussed in Sect. 115). This means that the value of a listofx object cannot be tested for equality with another listofx object (they are both functions). To overcome this problem, a listofx may be converted into an ISL+ list for testing. This part of the class function template may be specialized as follows:

```
;; listofx X → listofx
;; Purpose: Add the given value to the front of the
;;          given listofx
(define (listofx-cons lox-o an-x) ((lox-o 'cons) an-x))

;; Sample expressions for listofx-cons
(define L0C ((L0 'cons) 31))
(define L1C ((L1 'cons) 0))

;; Tests using sample computations for listofx-cons
(check-expect (listofx-2Rlst (listofx-cons L0 31))
              (listofx-2Rlst L0C))
(check-expect (listofx-2Rlst (listofx-cons L1 0))
              (listofx-2Rlst L1C))

;; Tests using sample values for listofx-cons
(check-expect
  (listofx-2Rlst
    (listofx-cons (consList "hi" (mtList 'dummyval))
                  "hey"))
  '("hey" "hi"))
```

Observe that the result to any call to listofx-cons is converted into an ISL+ list to test its value.

The wrapper function to map a function onto a given listofx requires further input. This wrapper function needs to apply the function returned by the list object to the given function. As with listofx-cons, a returned listofx is converted into an ISL+ list for testing. This part of the class function template may be specialized as follows:

```
;; <X Y> listofx (X → Y) → listofy
;; Purpose: Map given function onto given list
(define (listofx-map lox-o f) ((lox-o 'map) f))

;; Sample expressions for listofx-map
(define L0M ((L0 'map) sub1))
(define L1M ((L1 'map) (λ (n) (* 2 n))))

;; Tests using sample computations for listofx-map
(check-expect (listofx-2Rlst (listofx-map L0 sub1))
              (listofx-2Rlst L0M))
(check-expect
  (listofx-2Rlst (listofx-map L1 (λ (n) (* 2 n))))
  (listofx-2Rlst L1M))

;; Tests using sample values for listofx-map
(check-expect
  (listofx-2Rlst
    (listofx-map
      (consList "hi" (mtList 'dummyval))
      string-length))
  '(2))
```

Observe that the result to any call to listofx-map is converted into an ISL+ list to test its value.

Finally, the wrapper function to convert a given listofx into an ISL+ list requires no further input. It applies the given listofx object to '2Rlst. This part of the class function template may be specialized as follows:

```
;; listofx → Boolean
;; Purpose: Convert given listofx to a ISL+ list
(define (listofx-2Rlst lox-o) (lox-o '2Rlst))

;; Sample expressions for listofx-2Rlst
(define L0RL (L0 '2Rlst))
(define L1RL (L1 '2Rlst))

;; Tests using sample computations for listofx-2Rlst
(check-expect (listofx-2Rlst L0) L0RL)
(check-expect (listofx-2Rlst L1) L1RL)
```

```
;; Tests using sample values for listofx-2Rlst
(check-expect (listofx-2Rlst (mtList 'dummyval)) '())
(check-expect (listofx-2Rlst
                    (consList 'hi (mtList 'dummyval)))
               '(hi))
```

*** **Ex. 321** — Add the service to filter a list to `listofx`.

*** **Ex. 322** — Add the services to `or-map` and `and-map` a list to `listofx`.

**** **Ex. 323** — Add a list-summarizing service to `listofx`.

***** **Ex. 324** — Design and implement an interface for (`btof X`) (introduced in Chap. 17).

***** **Ex. 325** — Design and implement an interface for natural numbers (introduced in Chap. 14).

---

143 What Have We Learned in This Chapter?

The important lessons of Chap. 25 are summarized as follows:

- Data may be a function just like a function may be data.
- An instance of a type may contain values and the operations that are valid on it.
- An interface specifies the operations that are valid on a type.
- An interface is implemented by a constructor function called a class that returns a message-processing function.
- A class encapsulates the values of and the operations on a type.
- A class defines a constructor for instances of a type.
- The value returned by a class is called an object which is an instance of an interface.
- Testing interfaces requires defining one or more objects and writing tests to check services are correctly provided.
- To improve the human interface wrapper functions hide the details of an interface implementation.
- To implement an interface for a union type there must be a class that encapsulates the code for each subtype.
- Polymorphic dispatch allows programmers to implement structural recursion without conditional expressions.
- Code is written differently when programming with objects, but the design is the same as programming without objects.
- Objects may be converted to write tests.

Part V
Distributed Programming

Chapter 26
Introduction to Distributed Programming

You are probably very familiar with distributed programming as a user. In fact, you probably use distributed programs every day. Such programs include text messaging systems, multiplayer video games, and social media apps. As a user of a distributed program you solicit services from another program (usually running on another computer). For example, you may click on a link in your social media app. The act of clicking on the link sends a message to a computer operated by the social media company requesting the contents associated with the link. In turn the social media company's computer sends your app a message with the contents of the link. This is an example of two programs cooperating to solve a problem. Program cooperation is at the heart of many modern software systems today.

Dividing a problem into several tasks and writing a program for each task that communicates with the programs for other tasks are called *distributed programming*. The tasks cooperate to solve a problem. Each task defines a *component* that is a program that solves the task. Each component itself may be divided into subtasks and may be solved using one or more computers. The components cooperate by communicating with each other using message-passing. Messages are exchanged via a network (e.g., the internet). For messages to be exchanged a *communication protocol* must be designed. A communication protocol defines the messages that may be exchanged and when messages are exchanged. For example, a text message is not sent to your friend until you hit the Enter key or the Send button. Sending a text message in this manner means you are adhering to a communication protocol: the message must be a string and the message is only sent after you hit the right button or key. There may be, of course, a variety in the messages you are allowed to send (e.g., strings, numbers, etc.). Breaking the communication protocol means that a message is not sent or is not delivered and communication fails to take place. That is, there is a breakdown in cooperation.

Messages cannot be arbitrary. That is, there are a finite number of data types that are suitable for transmission. For example, a number is suitable for transmission but a posn is unsuitable for transmission. If a component needs to send data that is unsuitable for transmission, the data must be marshaled. *Marshalling* is the process of transforming data that is unsuitable for transmission into data that is suitable

© The Author(s), under exclusive license to Springer Nature Switzerland AG 2022   583
M. T. Morazán, *Animated Problem Solving*, Texts in Computer Science,
https://doi.org/10.1007/978-3-030-85091-3_26

Fig. 112 Protocol diagram for sending m from client$_i$ to client$_j$

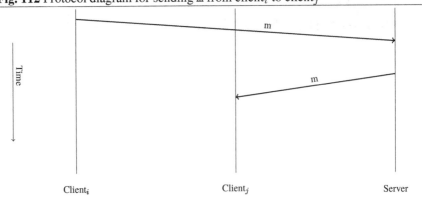

for transmission. To transmit a posn, for example, it must be marshaled into a list of two numbers for transmission. The component receiving marshaled data must unmarshal it. *Unmarshalling* is the process of reconstructing the original data from marshaled data. For example, a component receiving a marshaled posn as a list of two numbers must reconstruct the original posn. Marshalling and unmarshalling functions are inverses of each other. That is, (unmarshal (marshal x)) = x and (marshal (unmarshal message)) = message. The use of inverse functions is actually quite common in programming as mentioned in Chap. 2. You may frequently use encrypt and decrypt to protect sensitive data or compress and uncompress to reduce file size. Now, you also know about marshalling and unmarshalling data for transmission.

   A pervasively used distributed system architecture is the client–server architecture. A server is a program that provides services or coordinates the cooperation among clients. A client is a program that performs a task (usually) in cooperation with other clients to solve a problem. A client on one computer requests services from the server that typically runs on another computer. All communication between clients occurs through the server. That is, if Client$_i$ needs to send a message, m, to Client$_j$, then Client$_i$ sends m to the server and the server sends m to Client$_j$. This communication chain is part of the communication protocol. In a communication protocol there can be many communication chains for different events. For example, in a multiplayer Aliens Attack there may be a communication chain that is started when a player shoots and another that starts when a player moves the rocket. A communication protocol may be specified using protocol diagrams for different event-based communication chains. In a protocol diagram the horizontal axis represents the components and the vertical access represents time (which grows from top to bottom). Messages are represented by solid arrows from source to destination at a slight angle. The angle is used to emphasize that communication is not instantaneous. That is, time elapses as messages travel from source to destination. Dashed arrows are used to represent communication that is implemented by the API (e.g., a client registering with a server). Figure 112 displays the protocol diagram to send a message, m, from $Client_i$ to $Client_j$. Time grows from top to bottom. The first step in the communication chain is $Client_i$ sending m to the server. This is indicated in the diagram by a solid arrow from $Client_i$ to the Server. Observe that the arrow's negative slope clearly indicates that time elapses as m travels from $Client_i$ to the Server. At the Server, time elapses as m is processed before it is sent out to $Client_j$. This is indicated by the gap between the incoming arrow and the outgoing arrow at the Server. Finally, the outgoing arrow's positive slope clearly indicates that time elapses as m travels from the Server to $Client_j$. When m arrives at $Client_j$ the communication chain successfully ends.

Servers are generally described by a spectrum that goes from thin to think. A *thin server* is one that provides a minimal number of services like message broadcasting. The server itself does no or very little actual computing. A *thick server*, on the other hand, provides services that involve actual computing that directly contributes to solving a problem. For example, a server may be responsible for computing a value.

144 A Design Recipe for Distributed Programming

As you may have already deduced, distributed programming entails many characteristics that are not present when a program has a single task (e.g., like computing n!). It is important to carefully design the different components (e.g., clients and server) and the communication protocol. The magnitude of these tasks may seem overwhelming at this moment, but practicing the design and implementation of distributed programs will make you feel more comfortable. As with other topics in this textbook, there is a design recipe to help guide your development. This design recipe, however, is less prescriptive than the previously discussed design recipes. It does not tell you when to use a certain type of expression nor does it dictate what the parameters to a function must be. Instead, it guides you through the development of a distributed program assuming that you have mastered the design recipes previously studied to write functions. Each step still has a specific outcome that gets you closer to writing a program to solve a problem.

The design recipe for distributed programming is:

1. Divide the problem into components.
2. Draft data definitions for the different components.
3. Design a communication protocol.
4. Design marshalling and unmarshalling functions.
5. Design and implement the components.
6. Test your program.

Step 1 is problem analysis. It asks you to outline how the components cooperate to solve a problem. This step clearly defines the task (or tasks) carried out by a component. For example, the server may be responsible for relaying rocket movements by a player to all other players in Aliens Attack, while the clients are responsible for drawing the world. There are at least two components for every distributed application: a server and a client.

Step 2 asks you to define the types (or refine the types of an existing program) required by each component. The types required for each component are not necessarily the same. A server, for example, requires a type definition for messages that may be sent to it. A client, on the other hand, requires a possibly different type for the messages it may receive.

Step 3 asks you to develop a communication protocol. This protocol must capture all the communication chains that may occur. A communication chain is sparked by an event. For example, in multiplayer Aliens Attack a communication chain is started when a player shoots. The communication chain may be that the shot created is sent to the server and the server sends the new shot to all the other players. As part of this step you must develop data definitions for to-server messages and to-client messages. These data definitions are used to design the message-processing function for the server and for the clients.

Step 4 asks you to design marshalling and unmarshalling functions. If the data that needs to be transmitted in a message is suitable for transmission, there may be no need to develop these functions for this type of data. If the data to be transmitted is unsuitable for transmission, then a marshalling and unmarshalling function is needed to, respectively, create a message suitable for transmission and reconstruct the original data on the receiving component. Commonly, messages are tagged to easily distinguish the different varieties. This means that the need for marshalling and unmarshalling is expected for most applications.

Step 5 asks you to develop the programs for each component. This means that you need to develop at least two programs: one for the server and one for each client. The client program may or may not be the same for all clients. Nonetheless, there must be a separate program (different or copy) for each client. Observe that this means that a distributed program is written in at least two different files.

Step 6 asks you to run and test your program. As always, if any tests fail you must redesign.

145 More on the Universe API

The development of distributed programs in this textbook uses the API offered by the universe teachpack. The universe teachpack provides the functionality to develop distributed multiplayer games. Each player and the server are components. As you know, a player manages a world and is executed using a big-bang-expression. A server manages a universe (e.g., a collection of players) and is executed using a universe-expression. The players in a universe exchange messages with the server. All communication occurs through the server.

The universe teachpack provides two functions to create messages: make-package and make-bundle. The first is used by a client to create a structure that contains a (possibly new) world and a to-server message. The second is used by the universe server to create a structure that contains a (possibly new) universe, a list of mails to any of the players, and a list of worlds to be disconnected from the universe. Observe that a bundle contains an arbitrary number of mails and not an arbitrary number of to-world messages. A mail is a structure, built using make-mail, that contains the recipient player and a to-client message.

A message must be an S-expression as defined by the universe API. A universe S-expression is defined as follows:

```
A universe S-expression (sexpr) is either a:
   1. string
   2. symbol
   3. number
   4. Boolean
   5. character
   6 (listof sexpr)
```

Nothing else is suitable for transmission in a universe program. In particular observe that structures may not be transmitted. If a structure must be transmitted, you must implement marshalling and unmarshalling functions to do so.

The big-bang syntax required to run a player, as you know, specifies the handlers that update the game or render the game to the screen. If the player is part of a universe, it must also register with the server and specify a handler to process messages. To register with the host a string containing the internet address of the computer running the server is needed. The string for the internet address of your computer may be obtained by examining the value of ISL+'s LOCALHOST variable (simply type it at the prompt in the interactions window). During development and testing you can run all components on your computer by using LOCALHOST to register players with the server. For example, the run function for a player may look like this:

```
;; string → world
;; Purpose: To run the game
(define (run a-name)
  (big-bang
    INIT-WORLD
    (on-draw draw-world)
    (on-key process-key)
    (on-tick update-world)
    (stop-when game-over?)
    (register LOCALHOST)
    (on-receive process-message)
    (name a-name)))
```

There are two new big-bang clauses here. The register clause tells the universe teachpack the internet address where the server is running. If this clause contains LOCALHOST, then the server is running on your computer. If this clause contains a literal string, like "127.0.0.1", then the server is running at the computer found at that internet address. It is noteworthy that handlers that may create a new world, like process-tick, may return a world or a package. A package is returned when a message is sent to the server. Otherwise, it suffices to return a world. The world in a package becomes the next world.

Similarly, the syntax to run the universe server specifies the initial universe and the event handlers to manage events and update the universe. These events may include the arrival of a new message, a registration request from a new world, a clock tick, and a world disconnecting from the universe. For example, the run-server function for the universe may look like this:

```
;; Z → universe
;; Purpose: Run the universe server
(define (run-server a-z)
  (universe
    initU
    (on-new add-new-world)
    (on-msg process-message)
    (on-disconnect rm-world)
    (on-tick process-tick)))
```

The function has a dummy parameter that is never used because ISL+ does not allow a function to have 0 parameters. Its sole purpose is to allow us to write a server-running function. The first expression in the universe-expression is the initial universe (which you define just like you define INIT-WORLD for a player). The on-new clause specifies the handler to process the request from a new world to join the universe. The on-msg clause specifies the handler to process arriving messages. The on-disconnect clause specifies the handler to process the departing of a world from the universe. The on-tick clause specifies the handler to process clock ticks. Of these, the initial universe and the on-new and on-msg clauses are required. Any other handlers are optional and may be used if needed by the application. The universe teachpack represents the clients connected to the server using a structure called iworld. The only characteristic of an iworld that we may access is its name using iworld-name. In order to allow programmers to write tests for server functions the teachpack has three predefined iworlds that may be used: iworld1, iworld2, and iworld3. The following are the signatures required by the universe API for the handlers specified in run-server above:

```
add-new-world: universe iworld            → bundle or universe
process-message: universe iworld message → bundle or universe
        rm-world: universe iworld            → bundle or universe
  process-tick: universe                     → bundle or universe
```

A bundle is returned when there is at least one mail to be sent to a player. The universe in the bundle becomes the next universe. If no mail needs to be sent, then it suffices for a handler to return a universe.

This syntactical set-up provides a framework to design your distributed program in a top-down manner. That is, starting from the handlers and then moving on to auxiliary functions. Be aware that the above description only highlights the features of the `universe` API that are used in this textbook. If you are interested in further details about the `universe` teachpack, you are strongly encouraged to read the `universe` documentation found in DrRacket's Help Desk.

146 A Chat Application

To illustrate the use of the design recipe and of the `universe` teachpack for distributed programming the development of a chat tool is presented. The chat tool developed is not as sophisticated as the chat tools you are probably familiar with, but it is an interesting first application to develop as you explore distributed programming. The steps of the design recipe are outlined.

146.1 The Components

The chat tool is designed to allow users to share messages with everyone that is connected to the server. A user types a string of at most length 20 and sends it to the group of connected users. The server receives a message from a user and broadcasts it to the rest of the users. There are, therefore, only two components to design: the chat client and the chat server. All clients in this application execute the same code.

The client is responsible for drawing the status of the chat displaying the latest four messages and the message partially typed by the user. The partially typed message may, of course, be empty. The client is also responsible for processing keystrokes by the user. If the user hits the Enter key when the new message is not empty, the new message is added as the last message received by the user and is sent to server for it to be broadcasted to the other users. If the user hits the Backspace key when the partially written message is not empty, then its last character is deleted. The Shift and Tab keys are ignored. Any other key is added to the message as long as the length of the new message is at most 20.

The server is responsible for adding new users to the universe. A new user is added only if her name is different from the name of every other user. When a new user is added, a message is sent to all users informing them of the name of the new user. The server is also responsible for processing the messages that arrive from the clients. For each message a new `mail` is created for every user except the sender of the message.

146.2 Data Definitions

The data definitions needed for the server and for the client may differ for some applications. In other applications they may be the same. Yet in other applications some data definitions may be shared, while others are not. Our chat application is of the third variety.

To design the client program a data definition for a text message and a world are needed. We may define a text message, tm, entered by a client as

```
(define MAX-TM-LEN 20)

;; An text message (tm) is a string of length <= MAX-TM-LEN of
;; keystrokes that does not contain a return, a backspace, a shift,
;; or a tab.
```

A constant is defined to represent the maximum length of a text message. A text message is an enumeration type. It is all strings of keystrokes that do not contain the outlined keystrokes. The world needs to track the four most recent text messages and the partially written text message. This is compound data of finite size that suggests using a structure. The world may be defined as follows:

```
;; A world is a structure: (make-world tm tm tm tm tm)
;; that contains 5 text messages from left to right:
;; partially written to fourth most recent.
(define-struct world (tm1 tm2 tm3 tm4 tm5))

;; World function template
;; world ... → ...
;; Purpose:
;; (define (f-on-world a-world)
;;    (...(world-tm1 a-world)...
;;    ...(world-tm2 a-world)...
;;    ...(world-tm3 a-world)...
;;    ...(world-tm4 a-world)...
;;    ...(world-tm5 a-world)...))
;; Sample worlds
;; (define WORLD-0 (make-world ... ... ... ... ...)) ...
;;
;; Sample expressions for f-on-world
;; (define WORLD-0-VAL ... WORLD-0 ...)
;;
;; Tests using sample computations for f-on-world
;; (check-expect (f-on-world WORLD-0 ...) WORLD-0-VAL) ...
;;
;;   Tests using sample values for f-on-world
;;   (check-expect (f-on-world (make-world ...) ...) ...) ...

;; Sample worlds
(define INIT-WORLD (make-world "" "" "" "" ""))
(define A-WORLD
        (make-world "Wanna hang?" "Good thnx" "Good and you?"
                    "Hi, how are you" "Hi"))
(define B-WORLD (make-world "12345678901234567890" "Guess a number"
                    "" "" ""))
```

Here tm1 is the partially written text message and tm5 is the fourth most recent text message. The template, as expected, outlines all the steps of the design recipe that must be completed. The sample worlds include the initial world containing all empty text messages, a world that has no empty text messages, and a world that has both empty and non-empty text messages and a full partially written message.

To design the server program a data definition for a universe is needed. The server needs to track the worlds in the universe to decide whether a new world may be connected or to create a list of mails to broadcast a message. Thus, we may define a universe as follows:

```
;; A universe is a (listof iworld)

;; Universe function template
;; universe ... → ...
;; Purpose:
;; (define (f-on-universe a-universe)
;;    (if (empty? a-universe)
;;         ...
;;         (... (first a-universe) ...
;;          ... (f-on-universe (rest a-universe)) ...)))
;; Sample universes
;; (define UNIV-0 '())
;; (define UNIV-1 ...) ...
;;
;; Sample expressions for f-on-universe
;; (define UNIV-0-VAL ... UNIV-0 ...)
;; (define UNIV-1-VAL ... UNIV-1 ...)
;;
;; Tests using sample computations for f-on-universe
;; (check-expect (f-on-universe UNIV-0 ...) UNIV-0-VAL)
;; (check-expect (f-on-universe UNIV-1 ...) UNIV-1-VAL)...
;;
;; Tests using sample values for f-on-universe
;; (check-expect (f-on-universe ... ...) ...) ...

;; ;; Sample universes
(define INIT-UNIV '())
(define A-UNIV (list iworld1 iworld2))
```

A universe is the list of iworlds connected to the server. The function template to process a universe is obtained by specializing the template for a (listof X). This means that in this application the universe is a subtype of (listof X). Therefore, abstract functions on a (listof X), like map and filter, may be used to process a universe. There are two sample universes given that there are two varieties. The sample non-empty universe is built using sample iworlds offered by the API.

Fig. 113 Protocol diagram for sending a `tm` from client$_i$

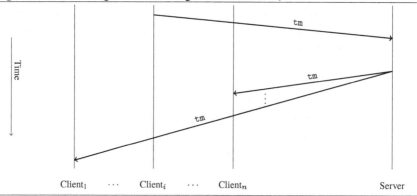

146.3 Communication Protocol

A communication chain is sparked by the keystroke `Enter`. Think carefully about what ought to happen when `Client`$_i$ sends a message. After hitting `Enter`, the partially written message is complete and must be sent to the server. Upon receiving this message, the server must broadcast it to the other users. The protocol diagram displayed in Fig. 113 illustrates this communication chain. In the diagram there are n clients and a server. The arrows indicate when messages are sent. The broadcast messages all start at the same point in the server. The vertical dots indicate that all clients get the broadcast message except `Client`$_i$ indicated by no incoming arrow to it.

Observe that there is an outgoing solid arrow from `Client`$_i$ to the `Server`. This means that `Client`$_i$ may need to marshal its message and that the `Server` might have to unmarshal the message. Given that the message, a `tm`, is suitable for transmission, marshalling and unmarshalling is not necessary. What do the solid arrows from the `Server` to `Client`$_1$ through `Client`$_n$ tell us? Essentially the same. The server and the clients, once again, do not need to marshal and unmarshal because the message is suitable for transmission.

A communication chain is also sparked when a new client joins the server. The server must broadcast a message to all the clients that a new user has joined the chat. The protocol diagram in Fig. 114 illustrates this communication chain. The dashed line from `Client`$_i$ to the server is a registration message sent to the universe system. That is, dashed lines indicate that it is not a message constructed by our code. Upon allowing the client to join the universe server, the server broadcasts the new user to all the clients in the universe. To reduce the number of message varieties we specify that this broadcast message must also be a `tm`. No marshalling or unmarshalling is necessary because the message, a `tm`, is suitable for transmission.

We can now define `to-server` and `to-client` messages as follows:

```
;; A to-server message is a tm

;; A to-client message is a tm
```

Fig. 114 Protocol diagram for a new client joining

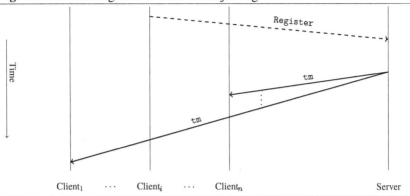

This concludes this step of the design recipe. An important lesson to remember is that a component at the beginning of a solid arrow needs the function, if any, to marshal the message and the component at the end of a solid arrow needs the function, if any, to unmarshal the message.

146.4 Marshalling and Unmarshalling

The design of the communication protocol revealed that there is only one type of to-server message and only one type of to-client message. Given that there is no variety in these types and the message is suitable for transmission, there is no need to develop marshalling and unmarshalling functions.

146.5 Component Implementation

The different components are independently designed using the protocol diagrams to guide you. The protocol diagrams need to illustrate of the types of messages that must be sent for different event-driven communication chains leading to data definitions for to-server and to-client messages.

Fig. 115 The `draw-world` handler

```
;; world → image  Purpose: To draw the given world
(define (draw-world a-world)
 (local [(define WIDTH 270) (define HEIGHT 170) (define VSPACE 10)
         (define E-SCENE (empty-scene WIDTH HEIGHT))
         ;; tm → image  Purpose: Convert the given text to an image
         (define (make-tm-img a-tm) (text a-tm 24 "brown"))
         ;;image natnum>0 image → image  Purpose:Place given tm image
         (define (place-tm img factor scn)
          (place-image img
                       (add1 (/ (image-width img) 2))
                       (* factor (+ VSPACE (/ (image-height img) 2)))
                       scn))
         ;; world → image  Purpose: To draw the given world
         (define (draw-world w)
          (local [(define IMG5 (make-tm-img (world-tm5 w)))
                  (define IMG4 (make-tm-img (world-tm4 w)))
                  (define IMG3 (make-tm-img (world-tm3 w)))
                  (define IMG2 (make-tm-img (world-tm2 w)))
                  (define IMG1 (make-tm-img (world-tm1 w)))]
            (add-line
             (place-tm IMG5 1
              (place-tm IMG4 2
               (place-tm IMG3 3
                (place-tm IMG2 4 (place-tm IMG1 6 E-SCENE)))))
             0 (* 5 (+ VSPACE (/ (image-height IMG2) 2)))
             (sub1 WIDTH) (* 5 (+ VSPACE (/ (image-height IMG2) 2)))
             "red")))]
  (draw-world a-world)))
```

146.5.1 Client

The client, according to our design, must draw the world, process keystrokes, have a (unique) name, register with the server, and process messages. The run function is

```
;; string → world
;; Purpose: Run the chat program
(define (run a-name)
  (big-bang
      INIT-WORLD
   (on-draw draw-world)
   (on-key process-key)
   (name a-name)
   (register LOCALHOST)
   (on-receive process-message)))
```

The `draw-world` function must draw the four most recent tms and the partially written tm. This can be rendered by drawing the four most recent tms above each other with the least recent on the top and most recent on the bottom. After this a red line may be drawn to visually separate them from the partially written tm at the

Fig. 116 The `draw-world` handler's tests

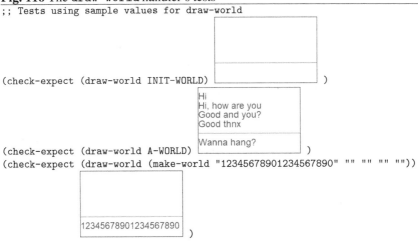

```
;; Tests using sample values for draw-world



(check-expect (draw-world INIT-WORLD)                        )

(check-expect (draw-world A-WORLD)                       )
(check-expect (draw-world (make-world "12345678901234567890" "" "" "" "")))




                                                         )
```

bottom of the scene. No messages need to be sent to the server when the world is rendered. The function to draw the world is displayed in Fig. 115 and its tests are displayed in Fig. 116. Functions to create and place tm images are encapsulated. Observe that there can only be tests using sample values because encapsulated functions may not be used to write tests.

The manner in which `process-key` processes keystrokes is exemplified by the sample expressions in Fig. 117. If the given key is Enter (i.e., `"\r"`) and the partially written tm is empty, the keystroke is ignored. Otherwise, following the protocol diagram in Fig. 113, a package is created that sends the partially written tm to the server and updates the most recently tms. If the given key is Backspace (i.e., "\b"), the keystroke is ignored if the partially written tm is the empty string. Otherwise, the last character of the partially written tm is removed. If the given key is either `"Shift"` or Tab (i.e., `"\t"`), the keystroke is ignored. Any other keystroke is added to the partially written tm if its length is less than or equal to MAX-TM-LEN and ignored otherwise. The function definition derived from the sample expressions is displayed in Fig. 118. The fact the function may need to send a message to the server is reflected in the signature that states the return value may be a world or a package. The function locally defines variables for the five tms in the given world. This avoids peppering the conditional expression with expressions using world-selectors. The tests are displayed in Fig. 117. The tests using sample values illustrate how the function is expected to behave, while the tests using sample computations illustrate that the function computes the values in the manner outlined by the sample expressions.

The remaining handler to design is `process-message`. The protocol diagrams in Figs. 113 and 114 inform us that the only message that a client receives is a tm. The received tm becomes the most recently received message and the other messages are moved to the next oldest slots. The fourth most recent message is discarded to

Fig. 117 The `process-key` handler sample expressions and tests

```
;; Sample expressions for process-key
(define INITW-RET   INIT-WORLD)
(define AW-RET      (make-package
                     (make-world "" (world-tm1 A-WORLD) (world-tm2 A-WORLD)
                                 (world-tm3 A-WORLD)    (world-tm4 A-WORLD))
                     (world-tm1 A-WORLD)))
(define INITW-BACK INIT-WORLD)
(define AW-BACK    (make-world
                    (substring (world-tm1 A-WORLD)
                               0
                               (sub1 (string-length (world-tm1 A-WORLD))))
                    (world-tm2 A-WORLD) (world-tm3 A-WORLD)
                    (world-tm4 A-WORLD) (world-tm5 A-WORLD)))
(define AW-SHIFT   A-WORLD)
(define AW-TAB     A-WORLD)
(define BW-M       B-WORLD)
(define INITW-A    (make-world (string-append (world-tm1 INIT-WORLD) "A")
                               "" "" "" ""))

;; Tests using sample computations for process-key
(check-expect (process-key INIT-WORLD "\r") INITW-RET)
(check-expect (process-key A-WORLD "\r")    AW-RET)
(check-expect (process-key INIT-WORLD "\b") INITW-BACK)
(check-expect (process-key A-WORLD "\b")    AW-BACK)
(check-expect (process-key A-WORLD "shift") AW-SHIFT)
(check-expect (process-key A-WORLD "\t")    AW-TAB)
(check-expect (process-key B-WORLD "M")     BW-M)
(check-expect (process-key INIT-WORLD "A")  INITW-A)

;; Tests using sample values for process-key
(check-expect (process-key (make-world "" "B" "A" "" "") "C")
              (make-world "C" "B" "A" "" ""))
(check-expect (process-key (make-world "" "B" "A" "" "") "\r")
              (make-world "" "B" "A" "" ""))
(check-expect (process-key (make-world "C" "B" "A" "" "") "\b")
              (make-world "" "B" "A" "" ""))
```

make room for the new `tm`. The message-processing handler may be implemented as follows:

```
;; world message → world
;; Purpose: Process the given message
(define (process-message a-world a-message)
  (make-world (world-tm1 a-world)
              a-message
              (world-tm2 a-world)
              (world-tm3 a-world)
              (world-tm4 a-world)))
```

Fig. 118 The process-key function definition

```
;; world key → world or package
;; Purpose: Return next world after the given keystroke
(define (process-key a-world a-key)
  (local [(define tm1 (world-tm1 a-world))
          (define tm2 (world-tm2 a-world))
          (define tm3 (world-tm3 a-world))
          (define tm4 (world-tm4 a-world))
          (define tm5 (world-tm5 a-world))]
    (cond [(string=? a-key "\r")
           (if (string=? tm1 "") a-world
               (make-package (make-world "" tm1 tm2 tm3 tm4) tm1))]
          [(string=? a-key "\b")
           (if (string=? tm1 "") a-world
               (make-world (substring tm1 0 (sub1 (string-length tm1)))
                           tm2 tm3 tm4 tm5))]
          [(or (string=? a-key "shift") (string=? a-key "\t")) a-world]
          [else (if (= (string-length tm1) MAX-TM-LEN) a-world
                    (make-world (string-append tm1 a-key)
                                tm2 tm3 tm4 tm5))])))
```

```
;; Sample expressions for process-message
(define IWM (make-world (world-tm1 INIT-WORLD)
                        "It's me"
                        (world-tm2 INIT-WORLD)
                        (world-tm3 INIT-WORLD)
                        (world-tm4 INIT-WORLD)))
(define BWM (make-world (world-tm1 B-WORLD)
                        "I think so!"
                        (world-tm2 B-WORLD)
                        (world-tm3 B-WORLD)
                        (world-tm4 B-WORLD)))

;; Tests using sample computations for process-message
(check-expect (process-message INIT-WORLD "It's me")  IWM)
(check-expect (process-message B-WORLD "I think so!") BWM)

;; Tests using sample computations for process-message
(check-expect
  (process-message
    (make-world "What d" "You and I?" "" "" "")
               "No way")
  (make-world "What d" "No way" "You and I?" "" ""))
```

Observe that the sample expressions and the test using a sample value illustrate that the newly arriving tm becomes the new world's most recent message. They also illustrate that the partially written tm remains unchanged when a new message arrives.

Fig. 119 Sample expressions and tests for adding a world handler

```
;; Sample expressions for add-new-world
(define ADD-INITU
        (make-bundle (list iworld1)
                     (map
                      (λ (iw)
                       (make-mail iw (string-append (iworld-name iworld3)
                                                    " has joined")))
                      INIT-UNIV)
                     '()))
(define ADD-AUNIV
        (make-bundle (list iworld3 iworld1 iworld2)
                     (map
                      (λ (iw)
                       (make-mail iw (string-append (iworld-name iworld3)
                                                    " has joined")))
                      A-UNIV)
                     '()))

(define ADD-REPEAT A-UNIV)

;; Tests using sample computations for add-new-world
(check-expect (add-new-world INIT-UNIV iworld1) ADD-INITU)
(check-expect (add-new-world A-UNIV iworld3)    ADD-AUNIV)
(check-expect (add-new-world A-UNIV iworld1)    ADD-REPEAT)

;; Tests using sample values for add-new-world
(check-expect (add-new-world (list iworld1) iworld2)
              (make-bundle (list iworld2 iworld1)
                           (list (make-mail iworld1 "iworld2 has joined"))
                           '()))
```

Given that there are no auxiliary functions needed and that all the required handlers are implemented, the design of the client code is done. Run the tests and verify that they all pass. At this point do not call the run function because there is no server for the client to connect to. Once you are satisfied that the tests pass, save two or more copies of the program in the same directory. Each copy will be a different component when executed.

146.5.2 Server

According to our design the server must process new clients attempting to register and must process messages. To add a new iworld to the server the name of the incoming iworld must be different from the name of any iworld already in the server. If it is not, the given world is not added and the universe remains unchanged. This is illustrated by the third sample expression in Fig. 119 that simply is the value of the given universe. If the name of the arriving iworld is different, then it is added to the universe. This is illustrated by the first and second sample expressions in Fig. 119.

Fig. 120 The handler to add a new world to the universe

```
;; universe iworld → bundle  Purpose: Add the given world to the universe
;; ASSUMPTION: The name of the new iworld is a string
(define (add-new-world a-universe an-iworld)
  (if (member? (iworld-name an-iworld) (map iworld-name a-universe))
      a-universe
      (local
        [(define new-univ (cons an-iworld a-universe))
         (define new-mails
                 (map
                  (λ (iw)
                    (make-mail
                     iw
                     (string-append (iworld-name an-iworld) " has joined")))
                  a-universe))]
        (make-bundle new-univ new-mails '()))))
```

Observe that the outgoing arrows from the server in Fig. 114 are implemented using map to create a mail for each iworld in the universe. The created mails have a tm informing the recipient of the new client that has joined the chat. In the first sample expression the incoming iworld is added to an empty universe. In the second sample expression the incoming iworld is added to the front of a non-empty universe. In both cases no worlds are disconnected from the universe and, therefore, the third argument to make-bundle is '(). The tests illustrate that the function correctly computes the values of the sample expressions and illustrate the creation of a bundle using concrete values. Abstracting over the sample expressions yields the function displayed in Fig. 120.

The incoming arrows to the server in the protocol diagrams in Figs. 113 and 114 inform us that the server only receives messages containing tms. The handler for processing messages, therefore, only needs to forward an incoming message to all the worlds except the sender as illustrated in Fig. 113. To achieve this the universe must be filtered to exclude the iworld that sent the message and mails must be created for the remaining iworlds. This is illustrated by the sample expressions in Fig. 121. Locally a list of mails is created using filter and map. The body of the local-expression creates a bundle with an unchanged universe, the new mails, and an empty list of iworlds to disconnect. It may seem silly to write a sample expression using an empty universe (i.e., INIT-UNIV) because there are no iworlds that could have sent the message. Although this observation is correct, do not forget that the goal is to validate the function for all universe subtypes. Therefore, a test using the empty universe must be included. Abstracting over the sample expressions yields the server's process-message function.

This completes the design of the server. Run the tests to make sure they all pass.

Fig. 121 The universe's handler to process a message

```
;; universe iworld message → bundle
;; Purpose: To process the given message from the given world
(define (process-message a-univ an-iw a-mess)
  (local [(define new-mails (map (λ (iw) (make-mail iw a-mess))
                                 (filter
                                  (λ (iw)
                                    (not (equal? (iworld-name an-iw)
                                                 (iworld-name iw))))
                                  a-univ)))]
    (make-bundle a-univ new-mails '())))


;; Sample Expressions for process-message
(define AUNIV-MESS
  (local [(define new-mails
            (map (λ (iw) (make-mail iw "Hi!"))
                 (filter (λ (iw) (not (equal? (iworld-name iworld2)
                                              (iworld-name iw))))
                         A-UNIV)))]
    (make-bundle A-UNIV new-mails '())))

(define IUNIV-MESS
  (local [(define new-mails
            (map (λ (iw) (make-mail iw "Hi!"))
                 (filter (λ (iw) (not (equal? (iworld-name iworld2)
                                              (iworld-name iw))))
                         INIT-UNIV)))]
    (make-bundle INIT-UNIV new-mails '())))

;; Tests using sample computations for process-message
(check-expect (process-message A-UNIV iworld2 "Hi!")    AUNIV-MESS)
(check-expect (process-message INIT-UNIV iworld2 "Hi!") IUNIV-MESS)

;; Tests using sample values for process-message
(check-expect (process-message (list iworld2 iworld3) iworld3 "OK")
              (make-bundle (list iworld2 iworld3)
                           (list (make-mail iworld2 "OK"))
                           '()))
```

146.6 Running the Chat Tool

To run the chat tool on your machine first, run the server and then run one or more clients. Type messages in each of the clients and see how the messages sent appear in the other clients. Figure 122 displays a snapshot of a chat session with two clients. The first client to join is *Marco* that gets a message when *Francisco* joins. Both clients in the snapshot have partially written messages that only they can see because they have not sent yet. The window in the middle is the server window. In it you can see all the server events like clients joining, messages received, and messages sent.

Fig. 122 A snapshot of the chat tool running on LOCALHOST

Once you are fairly sure that the chat tool is working, you may now use it to chat with your fellow classmates. Pick a classmate to run the server and get their internet address. All clients need to substitute LOCALHOST with a string containing the internet address of the classmate running the server. Once all clients are ready have the chosen classmate run the server and a client. Once the server is running call the run function and chat away!

** Ex. 326 — Chat tools are susceptible to security breaches or misuse. In our chat tool, for example, a joining client may have a name that is too long. Redesign the tool reject clients with names that are too long and send such clients a tm informing them.

*** Ex. 327 — The chat tool does not display the name of the sender of the message. Redesign the chat tool to display the name of the sender and the message all in one line. You may want to increase the maximum length of a tm for this.

***** Ex. 328 — Redesign the chat tool to allow users to send emojis like a smiley or a heart. Note that an emoji is an image and images are not suitable for transmission.

---

147 What Have We Learned in This Chapter?

The important lessons of Chap. 26 are summarized as follows:

- Distributing programming is ubiquitous in modern society.
- Dividing a problem into several tasks and writing a program for each task that communicates with the programs for other tasks is called distributed programming.
- In distributed programming components cooperate with each other to solve a problem using message-passing.

- A communication protocol defines the messages that may be exchanged in a communication chain sparked by an event. The design of this protocol is part of distributed programming.
- If necessary, data is marshaled by a sending component to make it suitable for transmission.
- If necessary, a component receiving a message unmarshals it to reconstruct the original data.
- Marshalling and unmarshalling are an example of the common practice of using inverse functions in programming.
- A pervasively used distributed system architecture is the client–server architecture. A server provides services and a client requests services using message-passing.
- A communication protocol is partly specified using protocol diagrams for different event-based communication chains.
- In a protocol diagram, a component at the beginning of a solid arrow needs the function, if any, to marshal the message and the component at the end of a solid arrow needs the function, if any, to unmarshal the message.
- A thin server is one that provides a minimal number of services or very little computing.
- A thick server provides services that involve computing that directly contribute to solving a problem.
- The design recipe for distributed programming is:

  1. Divide the problem into components.
  2. Draft data definitions for the different components.
  3. Design a communication protocol.
  4. Design marshalling and unmarshalling functions.
  5. Design and implement the components.
  6. Test your program.

- The universe teachpack provides the functionality to develop distributed multiplayer games.

Chapter 27
Aliens Attack Version 6

Our next goal is to refine Aliens Attack to allow for multiple players. The game is used to explore how to design a distributed program using both a thin and a thick server. First, however, this chapter explores a single-player game refinement that makes incorporating multiple players easier. The goal is to have all the `world`-related data definitions needed for multiple players in place and implemented for a single-player game. This new implementation of Aliens Attack will serve as the base code to design a multiple player game. To a player the game will look exactly the same as before. That is, no new features are added to the game. All that is refined is the implementation of the existing game.

The refinement is inspired in the expected changes that are needed for a multiplayer game. Consider the snapshot of multiplayer Aliens Attack displayed in Fig. 123. Take your time to think about what changes are needed and what elements remain the same in the `world` data definition. One difference is that the game has multiple `rockets`. The rest of the elements remain the same. That is, there are still multiple `aliens`, a `direction`, and multiple `shots`. Our initial task, therefore, is clear: define a `world` that can have multiple rockets. In this version of the game the number of players remains at 1 and, therefore, there is no need for a server, a communication protocol, and all the other necessary features for a distributed program.

148 Refining the `world` Data Definition

The world data definition needs to change from having a rocket to having multiple rockets that are all allies in repelling the invading alien army. It may be tempting to simply change the `world` data definition to have allies instead of a single rocket. We need, however, to be careful and perform a more detailed problem analysis. Think about how a player ought to start the game. Should a player start, as in the single-player game, with a world that has a full army of aliens moving in some hardwired direction with no shots? This is likely to be fine for the first player that joins the game. How about the players that join afterwards? These players cannot start with a world

M. T. Morazán, *Animated Problem Solving*, Texts in Computer Science,
https://doi.org/10.1007/978-3-030-85091-3_27

Fig. 123 Multiple-player Aliens attack

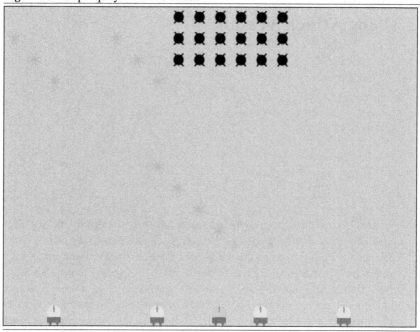

that has a full army of aliens and no shots because the first player may have already started shooting and neutralizing invaders. This means that the starting `world` for a player must be provided by the server. For the first player, it will be what is called `INIT-WORLD` in the single-player game. For the other players, it must be the state of the game when they join.

The above analysis allows us to take a top-down approach to refining the `world` data definition. It informs us that there must be variety in the `world` data definition. When a player joins the game, her `world` must be uninitialized and wait for the server to provide the value of the `world`. After the server provides this value, the `world` becomes a structure. We may now define the `world` type as follows:

```
;; A world is either
;;   1. 'uninitialized
;;   2. a structure: (make-world lor loa dir los)
(define-struct world (allies aliens dir shots))
```

Observe that `world` is now a union type with two varieties. Furthermore, the second variety is a structure that contains a `lor`, instead of `rocket`, to represent the allies. The template for a function on a world is:

```
;; TEMPLATE FOR FUNCTIONS ON A WORLD
;; world ... → ...
;; Purpose:
```

```
;; (define (f-on-world w ...)
;;   (if (eq? a-world 'uninitialized)
;;       ...
;;       (... (world-allies w)... (world-aliens w)
;;            ... (world-dir w)... (world-shots w))))
;;
;; ;; Sample instances of world
;; (define WORLD1 'uninitialized)
;; (define WORLD2 (make-world ... ... ... ...))
;;
;; ;; Sample expressions for f-on-world
;; (define WORLD1-VAL ... WORLD1 ...)
;; (define WORLD2-VAL ... WORLD2 ...) ...
;;
;; ;; Tests using sample computations for f-on-world
;; (check-expect (f-on-world WORLD1 ...) WORLD1-VAL)
;; (check-expect (f-on-world WORLD2 ...) WORLD2-VAL) ...
;;
;; ;; Tests using sample values for f-on-world
;; (check-expect (f-on-world ... ...) ... ) ...
```

This new world function template informs us that the refined functions that process a world must now contain a conditional in the body of the function. In addition, there must be at least two sample worlds, two sample expressions, and two tests using sample computations. This is the road map that guides the refinements of the game's handlers. It is also noteworthy that the tests using sample values must now construct worlds based on the new data definition.

The next step is to define lor. Given that the number of allies is not known in advance, it is data of arbitrary size. The natural choice that comes to mind is a list. We define lor as follows:

```
;; An lor is a (listof ally)
```

The template for a lor is given by specializing the template for a (listof X) with X = ally.

Can ally be replaced with rocket to complete the data definition refinements? This requires further problem analysis. In the game each player is expected to control their own rocket. Assume that an ally is simply a rocket. Consider the player, P_i, moving her rocket. Which rocket in P_i's lor ought to be moved? If there is only one rocket in the list, the answer is trivial. What if there are multiple rockets? How does the program decide which to move? Clearly, P_i wants to move her rocket and not another player's rocket. This means that an ally cannot simply be a rocket because we need to distinguish which player owns each rocket. To do so each ally rocket is associated with the name of the world that "owns" it. An ally is, therefore, defined as follows:

```
;; An ally is a structure, (make-ally rocket string), with
;; a player's rocket and name
(define-struct ally (rocket name))
```

With this data definition, it becomes clear which ally needs to be moved when P_i moves her rocket: the ally that has P_i's name. The template for a function on an ally is:

```
;; TEMPLATE FOR FUNCTIONS ON AN ALLY
;; ally ... → ...
;; Purpose:
;; (define (f-on-ally an-ally ...)
;;    (... (world-allies an-ally) ... (world-aliens an-ally)
;;      ... (world-dir an-ally) ... (world-shots an-ally))))
;;
;;  ;; Sample instances of ally
;;  (define ALLY1  (make-ally ... ...))
;;
;;  ;; Sample expressions for f-on-ally
;;  (define ALLY1-VAL ... ALLY1 ...) ...
;;
;;  ;; Tests using sample computations for f-on-ally
;;  (check-expect (f-on-ally ALLY1 ...) ALLY-VAL) ...
;;
;;  ;; Tests using sample values for f-on-ally
;;  (check-expect (f-on-ally ... ...) ... ) ...
```

Given that there are no further data definitions to develop, we define ally, lor, and world sample instances as follows:

```
(define MY-NAME "Yoli Ortega")

;; Sample instances of ally
(define INIT-ALLY  (make-ally INIT-ROCKET  MY-NAME))
(define INIT-ALLY2 (make-ally INIT-ROCKET2 MY-NAME))

;; Sample instances of lor
(define INIT-ALLIES  (list INIT-ALLY))
(define INIT-ALLIES2 (list INIT-ALLY2))

(define INIT-WORLD  (make-world INIT-ALLIES  INIT-LOA
                                INIT-DIR     INIT-LOS))
(define INIT-WORLD2 (make-world INIT-ALLIES2 (list INIT-ALIEN2)
                                DIR2         (list SHOT2)))
```

```
(define WORLD3 (make-world (list (make-ally 7 MY-NAME))
                           (list (make-posn 3 3))
                           'right
                           (list (make-posn 3 3))))
(define UNINIT-WORLD 'uninitialized)
```

A constant is defined for the world name and it is used to create ally instances. The initial ally contains the player's rocket and the initial lor only contains this initial ally. This initial lor is used to build the initial world. The other constants used to build this world are unchanged from Aliens Attack version 5 (in Chap. 23). The initial world in this version of the game is not uninitialized because the goal is to refine the single-player game to use the data definitions that allow multiple player support.

This is reflected in the new definition of the run function:

```
; string → world
; Purpose: To run the game
(define (run a-name)
  (local [(define TICK-RATE 1/4)]
    (big-bang
      INIT-WORLD
      [on-draw draw-world]
      [name MY-NAME]
      [on-key process-key]
      [on-tick process-tick TICK-RATE]
      [stop-when game-over? draw-last-world])))
```

The world argument to big-bang is not 'uninitialized. Further observe that this function now has a dummy parameter, a-name, that is never used. The name associated with the world is now defined by the constant MY-NAME. In this manner, the name associated with the world is made the same as the name associated with this world's rocket.

The following sections outline the refinements of the handlers. These sections describe the end result and do not outline the entire development process. That is, they present the final encapsulated functions and not the full development using all the steps of the design recipe. As you read, remember that all auxiliary functions were developed and tested before being made local to the appropriate handler.

149 The draw-world Refinement

The draw-world handler from Aliens Attack version 5 has the following structure:

```
;; world → scene
;; Purpose: To draw the world in E-SCENE
(define (draw-world a-world)
  (local [...]
    (draw-world a-world)))
```

According to the template for functions on a `world`, a conditional expression is
needed to distinguish among the `world` varieties. This conditional may be placed in
the body of the `local`-expression or in the body of the local `draw-world` function.
We shall take the first option to keep changes to local functions to a minimum.
We may, therefore, refactor the sample expressions to distinguish among the `world`
varieties as follows:

```
;; Sample expressions for draw-world
(define WORLD-SCN1  (if (eq? INIT-WORLD UNINIT-WORLD)
                        E-SCENE
                        (draw-world INIT-WORLD)))

(define WORLD-SCN2  (if (eq? UNINIT-WORLD UNINIT-WORLD)
                        E-SCENE
                        (draw-world UNINIT-WORLD)))
```

The sample expressions are valid because there is a local function, `draw-world`,
by the same name that draws the `world` when it is a structure. Therefore, after
abstracting over the sample expressions, the first refinement of this handler is:

```
;; world → scene
;; Purpose: To draw the world in E-SCENE
(define (draw-world a-world)
  (local [...]
    (if (eq? a-world UNINIT-WORLD)
        E-SCENE
        (draw-world a-world))))
```

Observe that the local `draw-world` function is only called when the given `world`
is a structure. That is, there is now an assumption made about the type of `world`
given to the local `draw-world` function. Also observe that E-SCENE is used in the
sample expressions. This means that it can no longer be local to `draw-world`. The
following definitions are moved to the global level in order for them to be in scope
for the sample expressions:

```
(define E-SCENE-COLOR S'pink)
(define E-SCENE
        (empty-scene E-SCENE-W E-SCENE-H E-SCENE-COLOR))
```

The new local `draw-world` function requires small refinements:

```
;; world → scene
;; Purpose: To draw the world in E-SCENE
;; ASSUMPTION: The given world is a structure
(define (draw-world a-world)
  (draw-los (world-shots a-world)
            (draw-loa (world-aliens a-world)
                      (draw-allies (world-allies a-world)
                                   E-SCENE))))
```

Observe that the assumption is made explicit for the benefit of any reader of the code. In addition, an auxiliary function to draw the allies is needed. The allies are drawn in the empty scene just like the rocket is drawn in Aliens Attack version 5.

The design of a local function `draw-allies` uses `draw-lox-maker` developed in Sect. 125. This function may be used to create a function to draw the allies as follows:

```
;; lor scene → scene
;; Purpose: Draw the given allies in the given scene
(define draw-allies
  (draw-lox-maker (λ (an-ally scn)
                    (if (string=? (ally-name an-ally) MY-NAME)
                        (draw-rocket (ally-rocket an-ally) scn)
                        (draw-ally   (ally-rocket an-ally)
                                     scn)))))
```

The function provided as input to `draw-lox-maker` draws an ally by distinguishing between the ally representing the world's rocket and the rest of the allies. The world's rocket is drawn using the existing `draw-rocket` function. The other allies must be drawn differently so that the player can easily see her rocket. This may be accomplished by implementing a new local function, `draw-ally`, that uses a different rocket image than that used by `draw-rocket` as follows:

```
;; rocket scene → scene
;; Purpose: To draw the rocket in the given scene
(define (draw-ally a-rocket a-scene)
  (draw-ci ROCKET-IMG2 a-rocket ROCKET-Y a-scene))
```

This means that we now have two functions, `draw-rocket` and `draw-ally`, that are almost identical. To eliminate the code repetition we may abstract over the functions to create a curried function that returns a rocket-drawing function that is specialized using the rocket image used. This results in the following local functions:

```
;; image → (rocket scene → scene)
;; Purpose: Create a rocket drawing function
(define (draw-ally-maker rocket-img)
  (local [;; rocket scene → scene
          ;; Purpose: To draw the rocket in the given scene
          (define (draw-r a-rocket a-scene)
            (draw-ci rocket-img a-rocket ROCKET-Y a-scene))]
    draw-r))

;; rocket scene → scene
;; Purpose: To draw the rocket in the given scene
(define draw-rocket (draw-ally-maker ROCKET-IMG))

;; rocket scene → scene
;; Purpose: To draw the rocket in the given scene
(define draw-ally (draw-ally-maker ROCKET-IMG2))
```

Both `draw-rocket` and `draw-ally` are refactored to use `draw-ally-maker`. Finally, `ROCKET-IMG2` is a locally defined variable in `draw-world`. The following are all the new local constant definitions used to create it:

```
(define FUSELAGE-COLOR2 'gold)
(define FUSELAGE2 (mk-fuselage-img FUSELAGE-COLOR2))
(define ROCKET-MAIN2 (mk-rocket-main-img WINDOW
                                         FUSELAGE2
                                         BOOSTER))
(define ROCKET-IMG2 (mk-rocket-ci ROCKET-MAIN2 NACELLE))
```

You may, of course, feel free to personalize your game by designing your own rocket images using colors of your choice.

The final step is to refine the tests for `draw-world` as follows:

```
;; Tests using sample computations for draw-world
(check-expect (draw-world INIT-WORLD)   WORLD-SCN1)
(check-expect (draw-world UNINIT-WORLD) WORLD-SCN2)

;; Tests using sample computations for draw-world
;; Added NO-SHOT to fully test draw-shot
(check-expect (draw-world (make-world (list INIT-ALLY)
                                      (list INIT-ALIEN2)
                                      DIR2
                                      (list SHOT2 NO-SHOT)))
```

```
)
```

A test to draw the uninitialized `world` is added. The test using `INIT-WORLD` remains unchanged. The test using a sample value is refactored to draw a world that has an `lor`.

150 The `process-key` Refinement

The `process-key` handler from Aliens Attack version 5 has the following structure:

```
;; world key → world
;; Purpose: Process a key event to return next world
(define (process-key a-world a-key)
  (local [...]
    (process-key a-world a-key)))
```

As suggested by the new template for functions on a world, a conditional expression is needed to process an instance of the new world data definition. We can immediately update the sample expressions to illustrate the use of such a conditional expression:

```
;; Sample expressions for process-key
(define KEY-RVAL (if (eq? INIT-WORLD UNINIT-WORLD)
                     INIT-WORLD
                     (process-key INIT-WORLD "right")))
(define KEY-LVAL (if (eq? INIT-WORLD UNINIT-WORLD)
                     INIT-WORLD
                     (process-key INIT-WORLD "left")))
(define KEY-SVAL (if (eq? INIT-WORLD UNINIT-WORLD)
                     INIT-WORLD
                     (process-key INIT-WORLD " ")))
(define KEY-SVAL2 (if (eq? INIT-WORLD2 UNINIT-WORLD)
                      INIT-WORLD2
                      (process-key INIT-WORLD2 " ")))
(define KEY-OVAL (if (eq? INIT-WORLD2 UNINIT-WORLD)
                     INIT-WORLD2
                     (process-key INIT-WORLD2 "m")))
(define KEY-NAOA (if (eq? UNINIT-WORLD UNINIT-WORLD)
                     UNINIT-WORLD
                     (process-key UNINIT-WORLD " ")))
```

Once again, such sample expressions can only be written because process-key has a local function with the same name. Observe that process-key is only called when the world is a structure. Abstraction over the sample expressions yields a handler with the following structure:

```
;; world key → world
;; Purpose: Process a key event to return next world
(define (process-key a-world a-key)
  (local [...]
    (if (eq? a-world UNINIT-WORLD)
        a-world
        (process-key a-world a-key))))
```

The tests using sample computations do not need to be updated. The tests using sample values, on the other hand, do need to be updated to properly construct world instances. These instances only have the player's rocket in the list of allies and are refined as follows:

```
;; Tests using sample values for process-key
(check-expect (process-key
                (make-world
                  (list (make-ally
                          (sub1 MAX-CHARS-HORIZONTAL)
                          MY-NAME))
                   INIT-LOA
                   'right
                   INIT-LOS)
                 "right")
                (make-world
                  (list (make-ally
                          (sub1 MAX-CHARS-HORIZONTAL)
                          MY-NAME))
                   INIT-LOA
                   'right
                   INIT-LOS))
(check-expect (process-key
                (make-world (list (make-ally 0 MY-NAME))
                            INIT-LOA
                            'left
                            INIT-LOS)
                 "left")
                (make-world (list (make-ally 0 MY-NAME))
                            INIT-LOA
                            'left
                            INIT-LOS))
(check-expect (process-key
                (make-world (list (make-ally 0 MY-NAME))
                            INIT-LOA
                            'left
                            INIT-LOS)
                 "o")
                (make-world (list (make-ally 0 MY-NAME))
                            INIT-LOA
                            'left
                            INIT-LOS))
(check-expect (process-key INIT-WORLD2 ";") INIT-WORLD2)
(check-expect (process-key (make-world
                            (list (make-ally 0 MY-NAME))
                            INIT-LOA
                            'left
                            INIT-LOS)
                 " ")
```

```
                    (make-world (list (make-ally 0 MY-NAME))
                                INIT-LOA
                                'left
                                (cons (make-posn 0 MAX-IMG-Y) '())))
(check-expect (process-key (make-world
                                (list (make-ally 0 MY-NAME))
                                INIT-LOA
                                'left
                                (cons SHOT2 '()))
                           "left")
              (make-world (list (make-ally 0 MY-NAME))
                          INIT-LOA
                          'left
                          (cons SHOT2 '())))
```

The local function `process-key` processes a world and, therefore, must be
refined to use the new `world` data definition. If the player moves her rocket, then
the ally that must be moved is the one that has the player's `MY-NAME`. If the player
shoots, then the `image-x` coordinate for the new shot is the player's rocket `image-x`
coordinate. The function is updated as follows:

```
;; world key → world
;; Purpose: Process a key event to return next world
;; ASSUMPTION: The given world is a structure
(define (process-key a-world a-key)
 (cond [(key=? a-key "right")
        (make-world (move-ally-right MY-NAME
                                     (world-allies a-world))
                    (world-aliens a-world)
                    (world-dir a-world)
                    (world-shots a-world))]
       [(key=? a-key "left")
        (make-world (move-ally-left  MY-NAME
                                     (world-allies a-world))
                    (world-aliens a-world)
                    (world-dir a-world)
                    (world-shots a-world))]
       [(key=? a-key " ")
        (make-world (world-allies a-world)
                    (world-aliens a-world)
                    (world-dir a-world)
                    (cons (process-shooting
                            (ally-rocket
                             (get-ally MY-NAME
                                       (world-allies a-world))))
                          (world-shots a-world)))]
       [else a-world]))
```

The assumption that the world is a structure is made explicit. Observe that three new auxiliary functions are needed: move-ally-right, move-ally-left, and get-ally.

Let us start with get-ally. This function must extract the ally that has MY-NAME in it. If this function works, then the signature for process-shooting is satisfied by the above function. The extraction of the correct ally may be done using filter as follows:

```
;; string lor → ally
;; Purpose: Extract ally with given name
;; ASSUMPTIONS: There is a single ally with given name
(define (get-ally a-name a-lor)
  (first (filter (λ (an-ally)
                   (string=? a-name (ally-name an-ally)))
                 a-lor)))
```

Observe that it is assumed that there is a single ally with the given name in the given lor. This means that the list returned by filter contains a single ally and all that is needed to extract the ally using first. The function given to filter compares the name given to get-ally with the name of a given ally. Remember that this function was first designed and tested before being made local to process-key.

The functions to move the player's rocket are virtually the same. They only vary by the function used to move the player's rocket: move-rckt-right or move-rckt-left. This suggests creating a curried function to create specialized ally-moving functions. The input to this function is a rocket-moving function and is implemented as follows:

```
;; (rocket → rocket) → (string lor → lor)
;; Purpose: Make an ally-moving function
(define (make-ally-mover move-rckt)
  (λ (a-name a-lor)
    (map (λ (an-ally)
           (if (string=? a-name (ally-name an-ally))
               (make-ally (move-rckt (ally-rocket an-ally))
                          (ally-name an-ally))
               an-ally))
         a-lor)))
```

The returned function takes as input a name and an lor. The given lor is traversed using map. The function given to map compares the name given to the returned function with the name of the ally in the given lor. If they match a new ally is constructed using the rocket-moving function used to specialize the ally-moving function. Otherwise, the ally from the given lor is unchanged. The ally-moving functions are implemented as follows:

```
;; string lor → lor
;; Purpose: Move ally with given name right
(define move-ally-right (make-ally-mover move-rckt-right))
```

```
;; string lor → lor
;; Purpose: Move ally with given name left
(define move-ally-left (make-ally-mover move-rckt-left))
```

151 The `process-tick` Refinement

As with the previous handlers, `process-tick` must be refined using the new `world` data definition. The sample expressions may be refined to be:

```
;; Sample expressions for process-tick
(define AFTER-TICK-WORLD1  (if (eq? INIT-WORLD UNINIT-WORLD)
                               INIT-WORLD
                               (process-tick INIT-WORLD)))

(define AFTER-TICK-WORLD2  (if (eq? INIT-WORLD2 UNINIT-WORLD)
                               INIT-WORLD2
                               (process-tick INIT-WORLD2)))

(define AFTER-TICK-UNINITW  (if (eq? UNINIT-WORLD UNINIT-WORLD)
                                UNINIT-WORLD
                                (process-tick UNINIT-WORLD)))
```

As with `process-key`, writing such expressions only works because `process-tick` has a local function with the same name. Abstracting over the sample expression yields a new `process-tick` with the following structure:

```
;; world → world
;; Purpose: Create a new world after a clock tick
(define (process-tick a-world)
  (local [...]
    (if (eq? a-world UNINIT-WORLD)
        a-world
        (process-tick a-world))))
```

The tests using sample values are also updated to conform to the new `world` data definition. They now create `world` sample instances with an `lor`:

```
(check-expect
  (process-tick (make-world
                  (list (make-ally INIT-ROCKET MY-NAME))
                  (cons (make-posn 1 5) '())
                  'left
                  INIT-LOS))
```

```
          (make-world (list (make-ally INIT-ROCKET MY-NAME))
                      (cons (make-posn MIN-IMG-X 5) '())
                      'down
                      INIT-LOS))

(check-expect
  (process-tick (make-world
                  (list (make-ally INIT-ROCKET MY-NAME))
                  (list (make-posn 2 5))
                  'left
                  (list (make-posn 1 6) NO-SHOT)))
  (make-world  (list (make-ally INIT-ROCKET MY-NAME))
               '()
               'left
               '()))

(check-expect
  (process-tick (make-world
                  (list (make-ally INIT-ROCKET2 MY-NAME))
                  (list (make-posn
                          (- MAX-CHARS-HORIZONTAL 2)
                          10))
                  'right
                  (list SHOT2)))
  (make-world (list (make-ally INIT-ROCKET2 MY-NAME))
              (cons (make-posn MAX-IMG-X 10) '())
              'down
              (list (make-posn (posn-x SHOT2)
                               (sub1 (posn-y SHOT2))))))

(check-expect
  (process-tick (make-world
                  (list (make-ally INIT-ROCKET2 MY-NAME))
                  (list (make-posn MAX-IMG-X 2))
                  'down
                  (list (make-posn 15 6))))
  (make-world (list (make-ally INIT-ROCKET2 MY-NAME))
              (list (make-posn MAX-IMG-X 3))
              'left
              (list (make-posn 15 5))))

(check-expect
  (process-tick (make-world
                  (list (make-ally INIT-ROCKET2 MY-NAME))
                  (list (make-posn MIN-IMG-X 2))
                  'down
                  (cons (make-posn 2 MIN-IMG-Y) '()))))
```

```
(make-world (list (make-ally INIT-ROCKET2 MY-NAME))
            (list (make-posn MIN-IMG-X 3))
            'right
            '()))
```

The local `process-tick` function must also be updated given that it produces a `world`. This function does not process the given `world`. Therefore, its refinement only needs to use the proper selector for the allies. The refined function is:

```
;; world → world
;; Purpose: Create a new world after a clock tick
;; ASSUMPTION: The given world is a structure
(define (process-tick a-world)
  (make-world
    (world-allies a-world)
    (remove-hit-aliens (move-loa (world-aliens a-world)
                                 (world-dir a-world))
                       (move-los (world-shots a-world)))
    (new-dir-after-tick (move-loa (world-aliens a-world)
                                  (world-dir a-world))
                        (world-dir a-world))
    (remove-shots (move-los (world-shots a-world))
                  (move-loa (world-aliens a-world)
                            (world-dir a-world)))))
```

Once again the assumption that the given `world` is a structure is made explicit for the benefit of any reader of the code.

152 The game-over? Refinement

The `game-over?` predicate must return `#false`, as before, when the given `world`'s list of `aliens` is empty or when any of the `aliens` has reached earth. In addition, it must return `#false` if the given `world` is uninitialized. This problem analysis allows the refinement of the sample expressions to be:

```
(define GAME-OVER1 (and (not (eq? INIT-WORLD2 UNINIT-WORLD))
                        (or (ormap
                              (λ (an-alien)
                                (= (posn-y an-alien)
                                   MAX-IMG-Y))
                              (world-aliens INIT-WORLD2))
                            (empty? (world-aliens INIT-WORLD2)))))
```

```
(define GAME-OVER2 (and (not (eq? WORLD3 UNINIT-WORLD))
                        (or (ormap
                              (λ (an-alien)
                                (= (posn-y an-alien)
                                   MAX-IMG-Y))
                              (world-aliens WORLD3))
                            (empty? (world-aliens WORLD3)))))

(define GAME-NOT-OVER (and (not (eq? INIT-WORLD
                                     UNINIT-WORLD))
                          (or (ormap
                                (λ (an-alien)
                                  (= (posn-y an-alien)
                                     MAX-IMG-Y))
                                (world-aliens INIT-WORLD))
                              (empty?
                               (world-aliens INIT-WORLD)))))

(define GAME-NOT-DONE (and (not (eq? UNINIT-WORLD
                                     UNINIT-WORLD))
                          (or (ormap
                                (λ (an-alien)
                                  (= (posn-y an-alien)
                                     MAX-IMG-Y))
                                (world-aliens UNINIT-WORLD))
                              (empty?
                               (world-aliens UNINIT-WORLD)))))
```

Abstracting over the sample expressions yields the refined handler:

```
;; world → Boolean
;; Purpose: Detect if the game is over
(define (game-over? a-world)
  (and (not (eq? a-world UNINIT-WORLD))
       (or (ormap (λ (an-alien)
                    (= (posn-y an-alien) MAX-IMG-Y))
                  (world-aliens a-world))
           (empty? (world-aliens a-world)))))
```

Once again, the tests using sample values must be updated to construct worlds that have a lor. They now become:

```
;; Tests using sample values for game-over?
(check-expect (game-over?
                (make-world (list (make-ally 8 MY-NAME))
                            (list (make-posn 0 3))
                            'right
                            NO-SHOT))
              #false)
```

```
(check-expect (game-over?
                (make-world (list (make-ally 8 MY-NAME))
                            (list (make-posn 0 MAX-IMG-Y))
                            'right
                            (list (make-posn 12 11))))
              #true)
(check-expect (game-over?
                (make-world (list (make-ally 8 MY-NAME))
                            (list (make-posn 0 5))
                            'right
                            (list (make-posn 0 5))))
              #false)
```

This completes the needed refinements. Make sure that all the tests pass and play the game. This refinement is the one that is used to create different implementations of a multiplayer game.

---

* **Ex. 329 —** Refactor `draw-ally-maker` to use a λ-expression instead of a `local`-expression.

**** **Ex. 330 —** Change the data definition of the world to include a timer. The timer is a natural number and is used to control how often the player can shoot. The player may shoot when the timer is 0. When a player shoots the new `world` constructed has a nonzero timer. At every clock tick the timer is decremented, and the player must wait until the timer reaches 0 to shoot again.

---

153 What Have We Learned in This Chapter?

The important lessons of Chap. 27 are summarized as follows:

- Sometimes it is possible to refine data definitions and corresponding code before introducing design elements that are specific to distributed programming.
- A change in data representation in a program does not change the interface with the user.
- When refining a sequential program into a distributed program, it may help simplify the task to first get the sequential program working with the expected data representation for the distributed version of the program.
- During a refinement problem analysis must be performed for the functions that process or return instances of a refined type (or, if you prefer, a refined data definition).

- When a data definition is refined, sample expressions and tests using sample values for functions that process or produce instances of the refined data definition must also be refined.
- Data definition refinements may create the need for new data definitions and new auxiliary functions.

Chapter 28
Aliens Attack Version 7

This chapter refines Aliens Attack 6 into a multiplayer game. Although the design and implementation of a distributed multiplayer game may seem overwhelming remember that the design recipe for distributed programming helps you manage the complexity of its development. The design recipe divides the design into several smaller and manageable steps. Collectively these steps lead to a distributed program that is readable to others.

Each section outlines a step of the design recipe. Take time to understand how the different steps are interrelated. Remember that the steps build on each other. Therefore, it is important to understand a step before proceeding to the next step.

154 Components

In Aliens Attack 6 a player's program draws the game, detects when the game is over, and updates the game by processing key events, clock ticks, and messages from the server. An intuitive design idea for a multiplayer game is to have each player be a component that performs the same tasks. In addition, each player component sends a message to a server when a player induced change occurs. A message is sent to the server when the player shoots or moves the rocket. A message is received from the server when it joins the game and when another player shoots, moves it rocket, arrives, or departs.

The server receives messages from a player, manages the joining of new players, and manages the departure of players. When a message arrives from a player, $Player_i$, the server broadcasts the message to the other players. When a player joins the game, the server provides it with its starting world and broadcast a message to all players that they have a new ally. The starting world depends on when $Player_i$ arrives. If $Player_i$ is the first player to join, the server provides it with the initial world. If $Player_i$ is not the first player to join, then the server requests the world from an existing player and sends it to $Player_i$. In order to properly select recipients of messages, each player component must have a distinct name. The server rejects

© The Author(s), under exclusive license to Springer Nature Switzerland AG 2022
M. T. Morazán, *Animated Problem Solving*, Texts in Computer Science,
https://doi.org/10.1007/978-3-030-85091-3_28

Fig. 124 The components of Aliens attack version 7

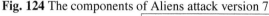

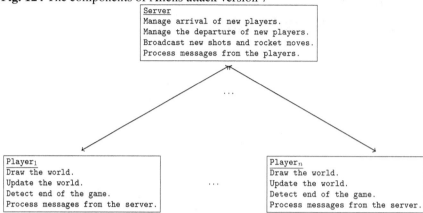

any new player that has a name already associated with an existing player. When a player departs the game, the server sends a message to all the other players to remove the corresponding `ally`.

Figure 124 visually summarizes the design idea with n players. There are n+1 components: each player and the server. The players and the server exchange messages to advance the game. Observe that the server is restricted to managing arriving and departing players and to broadcasting changes made to the game by any player. It does not perform any task to update the state of the game. That is, this design is for a thin server. Finally, keep in mind that each player and the server is a separate file. Therefore, a game with n players has n+1 programs running. Each component is written in a separate file.

155 Data Definitions

In order to send messages to specific players, the server needs to track the players in the game. Given that each player is represented as an `iworld` in our API the universe is defined as follows:

```
;; A universe is a (listof iworld), where each iworld
;; has a unique name

;; Sample instances of universe
(define INIT-UNIV '())
(define A-UNIV    (list iworld1 iworld2))
```

The sample universes illustrate each variety. The non-empty sample `universe` uses a subset of the sample `iworld`s provided by the API. Observe that each `iworld` in A-UNIV has a unique name. The comments and code above go in the server program.

Fig. 125 Protocol diagram for a `Player`$_i$ shooting

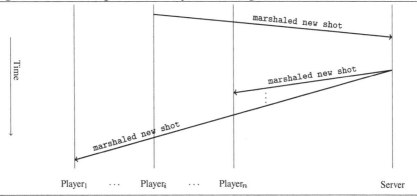

The data definitions for the `world` are defined in Sect. 148. The only detail that we highlight is that each player must have a unique value for its `MY-NAME` constant. This is the value used to give the world a name in the `big-bang` expression and is used by the server to distinguish the `iworlds` it tracks.

156 Communication Protocol

The communication chains are sparked by game-changing events that must be communicated to one or more players. Think carefully about what events cause a change in the game that must be communicated to the players. On a player's side a communication chain is sparked when the player shoots or the player moves her rocket given that either a new shot or a new `ally` is created. A communication chain is not sparked when the clock ticks. Although with every clock tick the state of the game changes, such a change occurs automatically in all the players. Thus, there is nothing to communicate. On the server side a communication chain is sparked when a player joins or leaves the game given that the allies gain or lose an `ally`.

156.1 Player-Sparked Communication Chains

When a player shoots a new `shot` is created. This `shot` does not exist for the other players. Therefore, the new `shot` must be communicated to the other players. Figure 125 displays the communication protocol diagram for the communication chain generated by `Player`$_i$ shooting. When `Player`$_i$ shoots, the marshaled new shot is sent to the server. Upon receiving the message, the server broadcasts it to the rest of the players. Take note that the new `shot` is not communicated back to `Player`$_i$ given that the new `shot` already exists in `Player`$_i$'s `world`. This diagram informs

Fig. 126 Communication protocol diagram for a `Player`$_i$ moving her rocket

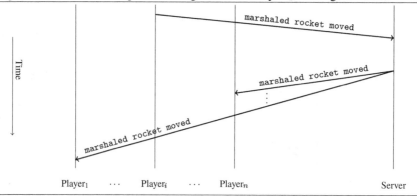

us that a marshaled new `shot` message is both a to-server and a to-player message
given that such a message may be an incoming message for both the server and the
players.

When a player moves her rocket, a new `ally` is created containing the new rocket.
This new `ally` does not exist for the other players. Therefore, the new `ally` must be
communicated to the other players. Figure 126 displays the communication protocol
diagram for the communication chain generated by `Player`$_i$ moving her `rocket`.
When `Player`$_i$ moves the rocket, the marshaled new `ally` is sent to the server.
Upon receiving the message, the server broadcasts it to the rest of the players. This
diagram informs us that a marshaled rocket moved message is both a to-server and
a to-player message.

156.2 Server-Sparked Communication Chains

When a player leaves the game (e.g., they lose their internet connection or close
the game's window), the other players lose an `ally`. The server must inform the
remaining players to remove from their `world` the `ally` that left the game. Fig. 127
displays the communication protocol diagram for the communication chain generated
by `Player`$_i$ leaving the game. When `Player`$_i$ leaves the server gets a message (that is
not generated by our distributed program) indicating that `Player`$_i$ has disconnected
from the server. The server broadcast a message to remove an `ally` to all the
remaining players. This diagram informs us that a marshaled remove `ally` message
is a to-player message.

There are two cases that need to be distinguished when a player tries to join the
game. The first case is when the universe is empty. That is, the player is the first to join
the game. Figure 128 displays the protocol diagram for the sparked communication
chain. The server gets an `API`-generated message that a new component wants to
join. If the server accepts the new player, it sends a marshaled start world message

Fig. 127 Communication protocol diagram for a `Player`ᵢ leaving the game

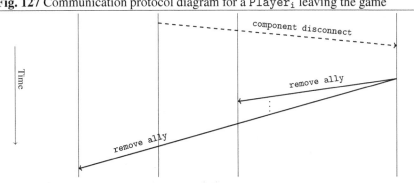

Fig. 128 Communication protocol diagram for `Player`ᵢ joining an empty universe

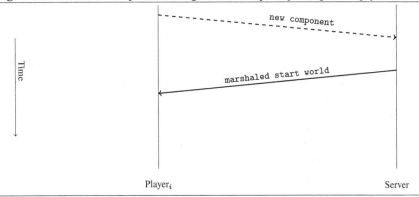

to the player. This protocol diagram informs us the marshaled start world message is a to-player message.

The second case is when a player joins a non-empty universe. Figure 129 displays the communication protocol diagram for the sparked communication chain. The server gets an API-generated new component message. If the player is admitted, the server must send out several messages. It sends a marshaled new ally message to all the players in the universe and a marshaled message to any player (in Fig. 129 it is `Player`₁) requesting the value of the `world`. Observe that in Fig. 129 all these messages originate at the same point. This is because all these messages are sent out when the new player is admitted to the game. A player, upon receiving a world request message, sends a marshaled world back message to the server. When the server receives a world back message, it sends a start world message to the player that just joined the game. This protocol diagram informs us that a marshaled world back message is a to-server message. It further informs us that a marshaled add ally message, a marshaled send world message, and a marshaled start world message are to-player messages.

Fig. 129 Communication protocol diagram for `Player`$_i$ joining a non-empty universe

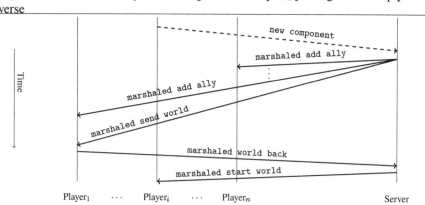

156.3 Message Data Definitions

Armed with the knowledge of the message types that need to be exchanged, to-player message and to-server message data definitions must be developed. According to our communication protocol, there are six varieties of to-player messages. Think about what each to-player message must contain. Given that an `ally` is unsuitable for transmission, a rocket move message must contain a marshaled `ally`. Similarly, a new ally message must contain a marshaled `ally`. A new shot message must contain a marshaled `shot` given that a `shot` is unsuitable for transmission. A remove ally message must contain the name of the `ally` that must be removed. A send world message must contain the name of the (new) `ally` that the value of the `world` is intended for. Finally, a start message must contain a marshaled `world`.

156.3.1 Marshaled Data Definition

The marshaled data is defined as follows:

```
;; A marshaled ally (mr) is a (list image-x string)
;; A marshaled alien (ma) is a (list image-x image-y)
;; A marshaled shot (ms) is either
;;    1. (list image-x image-y)
;;    2. 'no-shot
;; A marshaled world (mw) is a (list (listof mr)
;;                                   (listof ma)
;;                                   direction
;;                                   (listof ms))
```

Observe that the marshaled varieties of data contain structure data suitable for transmission. There is variety in `ms` because there is variety in `shot`. A `mw` itself contains marshaled allies, marshaled aliens, and marshaled shots. Based on the data definitions, we may develop function templates and sample instances of marshaled data as follows:

```
#| ;; Sample instances of mr
   (define  MR1 ...) ...
   ;; Sample expressions for f-on-mr
   (define MR1-VAL ...) ...
   ;; mr ... → ...
   ;; Purpose:
   (define (f-on-mr an-mr ...)
     (local [(define rocket (first an-mr))
             (define name   (second an-mr))]
       ...))
   ;; Tests using sample computations for f-on-mr
   (check-expect (f-on-mr MR1 ...) MR1-VAL) ...
   ;; Tests using sample values for f-on-mr
   (check-expect (f-on-mr ... ...) ...) ...

   ;; Sample instances of ma
   (define MA1 ...) ...
   ;; Sample expressions for f-on-ma
   (define MA1-VAL ...) ...
   ;; ma ... → ...
   ;; Purpose:
   (define (f-on-ma an-ma ...)
     (local [(define img-x (first an-ma))
             (define img-y (second an-ma))]
       ...))
   ;; Tests using sample computations for f-on-ma
   (check-expect (f-on-ma MA1 ...) MA1-VAL) ...
   ;; Tests using sample values for f-on-ma
   (check-expect (f-on-ma ... ...) ...) ...

   ;; Sample instances of ms
   (define MS1 ...) ...
   ;; Sample expressions for f-on-ms
   (define MS1-VAL ...) ...
   ;; ms ... → ...
   ;; Purpose:
   (define (f-on-ms an-ms ...)
     (if (list? ms)
         (local [(define img-x (first an-ms))
                 (define img-y (second an-ms))]
           ...)
         an-ms ...))
```

```
;; Tests using sample computations for f-on-ms
(check-expect (f-on-ms MS1 ...) MS1-VAL) ...
;; Tests using sample values for f-on-ms
(check-expect (f-on-ms ... ...) ...) ...

;; Sample instances of mw
(define MW1 ...) ...
;; Sample expressions for f-on-mw
(define MW1-VAL ...) ...
;; mw ... → ...
;; Purpose:
(define (f-on-mw an-mw ...)
  (local [(define lomr (first an-ms))
          (define loma (second an-ms))
          (define dir  (third an-ms))
          (define loms (fourth an-ms))]
    ...))
;; Tests using sample computations for f-on-mw
(check-expect (f-on-mw MW1 ...) MW1-VAL) ...
;; Tests using sample values for f-on-mw
(check-expect (f-on-mw ... ...) ...) ...
|#
(define MR1     '(10 "iworld1"))
(define MR2     '(8  "iworld3"))
(define MR3     `(11 ,MY-NAME))
(define MALLY1  (list 10 "Rolando"))
(define MALLY2  (list 10 "Margarita"))
(define MA      '(14 3))
(define MALIEN1 (list 0 7))
(define MALIEN2 (list 9 4))
(define MS1     NO-SHOT)
(define MS2     '(2  2))
(define MSHOT1  NO-SHOT)
(define MSHOT2 (list 11 9))
(define MLOS   '((2 2)))
(define MW     '(((7 "iworld1") (3 "iworld2"))
                 ((15 2))
                 left
                 ((8 5) (7 2))))
(define MWORLD1 (list (list (list 16 "Cristian")
                            (list 7  "Laura")
                            (list 6  "Walter"))
                      (list (list 13 4)
                            (list 11 11))
                      'right
```

```
                              (list (list 2   3)
                                    (list 12 8)
                                    (list 5   14))))
  (define MWORLD2 (list (list (list 0 "Marce")
                              (list 8 "Chaty")
                              (list 4 "Maggie")
                              (list 2 "Christy"))
                        '()
                        'right
                        '()))
```

Observe that the templates above are more sophisticated than those developed in the beginning parts of this textbook. They use a local-expression to define the different components of a message instead of littering the function body with multiple uses of list selectors that may carry no meaning for readers trying to understand the design. The larger than usual sample instances are to facilitate test writing.

156.3.2 To-Player Message Data Definition

Given the data definitions for marshaled data, a to-player message is defined as follows:

```
;; A to-player message (tpm) is either
;; 1. (list 'rckt-move  ma)
;; 2. (list 'new-shot   ms)
;; 3. (list 'new-ally   ma)
;; 4. (list 'rm-ally     string)
;; 5. (list 'send-world string)
;; 6. (cons 'start      mw)
```

Each tpm has a unique tag to identify it and the appropriate data that is marshaled if necessary. The template for a function on a tpm and sample tpm instances are defined as follows:

```
#| TEMPLATE FOR A FUNCTION on a tpm
   ;; Sample instances of tpm
   (define  ST-MSG ...)
   (define  MA-MSG ...)
   (define  NS-MSG ...)
   (define  NA-MSG ...)
   (define  RM-MSG ...)
   (define  SW-MSG ...) ...
   ;; Sample expressions for f-on-tpm
   (define  ST-MSG-VAL ...)
   (define  MA-MSG-VAL ...)
   (define  NS-MSG-VAL ...)
```

```
(define  NA-MSG-VAL ...)
(define  RM-MSG-VAL ...)
(define  SW-MSG-VAL ...) ...
;; tpm ... → ...
;; Purpose:
(define (f-on-tpm a-tpm ...)
  (local [(define tag (first a-tpm))]
    (cond [(eq? tag 'rckt-move)
           (local [(define ally (unmarshal-ally
                                  (second a-tpm)))]
             ...)]
          [(eq? tag 'new-shot)
           (if (list? (second a-tpm))
               (local [(define shot (unmarshal-shot
                                      (second a-tpm)))]
                 (if (eq? shot NO-SHOT)
                     ...
                     ...))))]
          [(eq? tag 'new-ally)
           (local [(define ally (unmarshal-ally
                                  (second a-tpm)))]
             ...)]
          [(eq? tag 'rm-ally)
           (local [(define name (second a-tpm))]
             ...)]
          [(eq? tag 'send-world)
           (local [(define name (second a-tpm))]
             ...)]
          [(eq? tag 'start)
           (local [(define world (unmarshal-world
                                   (rest a-tpm)))
                   (define allies (world-allies world))
                   (define aliens (world-aliens world))
                   (define dir    (world-dir world))
                   (define shots  (world-shots world))]
             ...)]
          [else
           (error (format "Unknown message tag received: ~s"
                          (first msg)))])))
;; Tests using sample computations for f-on-tpm
(check-expect (f-on-tpm ST-MSG ...) ST-MSG-VAL)
(check-expect (f-on-tpm MA-MSG ...) MA-MSG-VAL)
(check-expect (f-on-tpm NS-MSG ...) NS-MSG-VAL)
(check-expect (f-on-tpm NA-MSG ...) NA-MSG-VAL)
(check-expect (f-on-tpm RM-MSG ...) RM-MSG-VAL)
```

```
  (check-expect (f-on-tpm SW-MSG ...) SW-MSG-VAL) ...
  ;; Tests using sample values for f-on-tpm
  (check-expect (f-on-tpm ... ...) ...) ...
|#
    (define RM-MSG  (list 'rckt-move   MR2))
    (define RM-MSG2 (list 'rckt-move   MR3))
    (define NS-MSG  (list 'new-shot    MS1))
    (define NS-MSG2 (list 'new-shot    MS2))
    (define NA-MSG  (list 'new-ally    MR2))
    (define RA-MSG  (list 'rm-ally     "world1"))
    (define RA-MSG2 (list 'rm-ally     "Margarita"))
    (define SW-MSG  (list 'send-world  "world2"))
    (define SW-MSG2  (list 'send-world "Fernando"))
    (define ST-MSG  (cons 'start       MW))
```

Observe that each stanza uses a local-expression to capture the components of
the given tpm. Furthermore, the template suggests unmarshalling the marshaled
components and defining local variables for their values. For instance, the ally
marshaled in a new ally message is unmarshaled and locally defined.

156.3.3 To-Server Message Data Definition

According to our communication protocol, there are three varieties of to-server
messages. Two of these varieties, a rocket move message and a new shot message,
are also tpms. Think about what the third variety, a world back message, needs to
contain. It must contain a marshaled world. It must also contain the destination of
the marshaled world. That is, the name of the player that is awaiting to start playing.
A to-server message is defined as follows:

```
  ;; A to-server message (tsm) is either
  ;;  1. (list 'rckt-move ma)
  ;;  2. (list 'new-shot  ms)
  ;;  3. (cons 'world-back (cons string mw))
```

The template for a function on a tsm is:

```
#| TEMPLATE FOR FUNCTIONS ON A tsm
   ;; Sample instances of tsm
   (define TSM1 ...)
   (define TSM2 ...)
   (define TSM3 ...) ...
   ;; Sample expressions for f-on-tsm
   (define TSM1-VAL ...)
   (define TSM2-VAL ...)
   (define TSM3-VAL ...) ...
   ;; tsm ... → ...
```

```
;; Purpose:
(define (f-on-tsm a-tsm ...)
  (local [(define tag (first a-tsm))]
    (cond [(eq? tag 'rckt-move) ...]
          [(eq? tag 'new-shot)   ...]
          [(eq? tag 'world-back) ...]
          [else
            (error
              (format "Unknown to-server message type: ~s"
                tag))])))
;; Sample expressions for f-on-tsm
(define TSM1-VAL ...)
(define TSM2-VAL ...)
(define TSM3-VAL ...) ...
;; Tests using sample computations for f-on-tsm
(check-expect (f-on-tsm TSM1 ...) TSM1-VAL)
(check-expect (f-on-tsm TSM2 ...) TSM2-VAL)
(check-expect (f-on-tsm TSM3 ...) TSM3-VAL) ...
;; Tests using sample values for f-on-tsm
(check-expect (f-on-tsm ... ...) ...) ...
|#
```

This template, unlike the template for functions on a tpm, does not suggest unmarshalling the components in a given tsm. This is because our design is for a thin server that is expected to do little more than broadcast the messages it receives. It has no need to unmarshal the components because it does not process them.

The sample instances for tsms are mostly straight-forward to write because they contain the same types of marshaled values in them as tpms. We may write sample values as follows:

```
;; Sample instances of tsm
(define SRM-MSG RM-MSG)
(define SNS-MSG NS-MSG)
(define SWB-MSG (cons 'world-back (cons "iworld2" MW)))
```

157 Marshalling and Unmarshalling

Marshalling and unmarshalling, respectively, make data unfit for transmission into data that is fit for transmission and back. In Sect. 156.3.1 four varieties of marshaled data are defined explicitly: marshaled ally (mr), marshaled alien (ma), marshaled shot (ms), and marshaled world (mw). Using the generic data definition for (listof X) a list of mr, a list of ma, and a list of ms are also defined as part of an mw. We shall develop marshalling and unmarshalling functions for each of these types.

Consider marshalling and unmarshalling an ally. To marshal an ally, you need an ally as input and you need to output an mr. The mr is constructed by accessing the components of the given `ally`. The marshalling function is obtained by specializing the template for functions on an `ally` as follows:

```
;; Sample expressions for marshal-ally
(define M-ALLY1 (list (ally-rocket INIT-ALLY)
                      (ally-name INIT-ALLY)))
(define M-ALLY2 (list (ally-rocket INIT-ALLY2)
                      (ally-name INIT-ALLY2)))


;; ally → mr
;; Purpose: Marshal the given ally
(define (marshal-ally an-ally)
  (list (ally-rocket an-ally) (ally-name an-ally)))


;; Tests using sample computations for marshal-ally
(check-expect (marshal-ally  INIT-ALLY)  M-ALLY1)
(check-expect (marshal-ally  INIT-ALLY2) M-ALLY2)


;; Tests using sample values for marshal-ally
(check-expect (marshal-ally  (make-ally 12 "Cordula"))
              (list 12 "Cordula"))
```

The unmarshalling function must take as input an `mr` and return an `ally`. The function is obtained by specializing the template for functions on an `mr` as follows:

```
;; Sample expressions for unmarshal-ally
(define UALLY1 (make-ally (first  MALLY1)
                          (second MALLY1)))
(define UALLY2 (make-ally (first  MALLY2)
                          (second MALLY2)))


;; mr → ally
;; Purpose: Unmarshal the given marshaled ally
(define (unmarshal-ally ma)
  (local [(define rocket (first ma))
          (define name   (second ma))]
    (make-ally rocket name)))


;; Tests using sample computations for unmarshal-ally
(check-expect (unmarshal-ally MALLY1) UALLY1)
(check-expect (unmarshal-ally MALLY2) UALLY2)


;; Tests using sample values for unmarshal-ally
(check-expect (unmarshal-ally (list 12 "Cordula"))
              (make-ally 12 "Cordula"))
```

Observe that the tests using sample values for both functions illustrate that they are inverses of each other.

Consider marshalling and unmarshalling an `alien`. To marshal an `alien` you need an `alien` as input and you need to output an `ma`. The `ma` is constructed by accessing the components of the given `alien`. The marshalling function is obtained by specializing the template for functions on an `alien` as follows:

```
;; Sample expressions for marshal-alien
(define MINIT-ALIEN2 (list (posn-x INIT-ALIEN2)
                           (posn-y INIT-ALIEN2)))


;; alien → ma
;; Purpose: Marshal the given alien
(define (marshal-alien an-alien)
  (list (posn-x an-alien) (posn-y an-alien)))


;; Tests using sample computations for marshal-alien
(check-expect (marshal-alien INIT-ALIEN2) MINIT-ALIEN2)


;; Tests using sample values for unmarshal-alien
(check-expect (marshal-alien (make-posn 7 2)) (list 7 2))
```

The unmarshalling function must take as input an `ma` and return an `alien`. The function is obtained by specializing the template for functions on an `ma` as follows:

```
;; Sample expressions for unmarshal-alien
(define UALIEN2 (make-posn (first MINIT-ALIEN2)
                           (second MINIT-ALIEN2)))


;; ma → alien
;; Purpose: Unmarshal the given marshaled alien
(define (unmarshal-alien ma)
  (local [(define img-x (first ma))
          (define img-y (second ma))]
    (make-posn img-x img-y)))


;; Tests using sample computations for unmarshal-alien
(check-expect (unmarshal-alien MINIT-ALIEN2) UALIEN2)


;; Tests using sample values for unmarshal-alien
(check-expect (unmarshal-alien (list 7 2)) (make-posn 7 2))
```

Observe that the tests using sample values for both functions illustrate that they are inverses of each other.

Consider marshalling and unmarshalling a `shot`. To marshal a `shot` you need a `shot` as input and you need to output an `ms`. The `ms` is constructed by accessing the components of the given `shot` if it is a structure. Otherwise, there is no need to transform the `shot` because it is fit for transmission. The marshalling function is obtained by specializing the template for functions on an `shot` as follows:

```
;; Sample expressions for marshal-shot
(define M-NO-SHOT NO-SHOT)
(define M-SHOT2   (list (posn-x SHOT2) (posn-y SHOT2)))


;; shot → ms
;; Purpose: Marshal the given shot
(define (marshal-shot a-shot)
  (if (eq? a-shot NO-SHOT)
      NO-SHOT
      (list (posn-x a-shot) (posn-y a-shot))))


;; Tests using sample computations for marshal-shot
(check-expect (marshal-shot NO-SHOT) M-NO-SHOT)
(check-expect (marshal-shot SHOT2)   M-SHOT2)


;; Tests using sample values for marshal-shot
(check-expect (marshal-shot (make-posn 2 2)) (list 2 2))
```

The unmarshalling function must take as input an ms and return an shot. The function is obtained by specializing the template for functions on an ms as follows:

```
;; Sample expressions for unmarshal-shot
(define USHOT1 NO-SHOT)
(define USHOT2 (make-posn (first MSHOT2) (second MSHOT2)))


;; ms → shot
;; Purpose: Unmarshal the given marshaled shot
(define (unmarshal-shot ms)
  (if (list? ms)
      (local [(define img-x (first ms))
              (define img-y (second ms))]
        (make-posn img-x img-y))
      ms))


;; Tests using sample computations for unmarshal-shot
(check-expect (unmarshal-shot NO-SHOT) USHOT1)
(check-expect (unmarshal-shot MSHOT2) USHOT2)


;; Tests using sample values for unmarshal-shot
(check-expect (unmarshal-shot (list 2 2)) (make-posn 2 2))
```

Observe that the tests using sample values for both functions illustrate that they are inverses of each other.

Consider marshalling and unmarshalling a world. To marshal a world you need a world as input and you need to output an mw. The mw is constructed by accessing the components of the given world. What if the given world is uninitialized? How can an uninitialized world be marshaled? Indeed, attempting to do so would be an error. We can, however, assume that the given world is always structure because only a player in the game may receive a message to send the world. If a player receives such a message, then its world is initialized. The marshalling function is obtained by specializing the template for functions on an world as follows:

```
;; Sample expressions for marshal-world
(define MWORLD3 (list (map marshal-ally
                            (world-allies INIT-WORLD))
                      (map marshal-alien
                            (world-aliens INIT-WORLD))
                      (world-dir INIT-WORLD)
                      (map marshal-shot
                            (world-shots INIT-WORLD)))))

(define MWORLD4 (list (map marshal-ally
                            (world-allies INIT-WORLD2))
                      (map marshal-alien
                            (world-aliens INIT-WORLD2))
                      (world-dir INIT-WORLD2)
                      (map marshal-shot
                            (world-shots INIT-WORLD2)))))

;; world → mw
;; Purpose: Marshal the given world
;; ASSUMPTION: The given world is a structure
(define (marshal-world a-world)
  (list (map marshal-ally  (world-allies a-world))
        (map marshal-alien (world-aliens a-world))
        (world-dir a-world)
        (map marshal-shot (world-shots a-world)))))

;; Tests using sample computations for marshal-world
(check-expect (marshal-world INIT-WORLD)  MWORLD3)
(check-expect (marshal-world INIT-WORLD2) MWORLD4)

;; Tests using sample values for marshal-world
(check-expect
  (marshal-world (make-world (list (make-ally 5 "Luis")
                                   (make-ally 8 "Cova"))
                             (list (make-posn  2 17))
                             "left"
                             '()))
  (list (list (list 5 "Luis")
              (list 8 "Cova"))
        (list (list  2 17))
        "left"
        '()))
```

Observe that the assumption is explicitly stated for any reader of the code, thus, explaining why the definition lacks a conditional expression to distinguish among world varieties. In addition, observe that the code, using map, to create the marshaled lists of mr, ma, and ms is inlined instead of creating separate functions. The unmarshalling function must take as input an mw and return a world. The function is obtained by specializing the template for functions on an mw as follows:

```
;; Sample expressions for unmarshal-world
(define UWORLD1 (make-world
                   (map unmarshal-ally  (first MWORLD1))
                   (map unmarshal-alien (second MWORLD1))
                   (third MWORLD1)
                   (map unmarshal-shot (fourth MWORLD1))))


;; mw → world
;; Purpose: Unmarshal the given world
(define (unmarshal-world mw)
  (local [(define lomr (first mw))
          (define loma (second mw))
          (define dir  (third mw))
          (define loms (fourth mw))]
    (make-world (map unmarshal-ally  lomr)
                (map unmarshal-alien loma)
                dir
                (map unmarshal-shot loms))))


;; Sample expressions for unmarshal-world
(define UWORLD1 (make-world
                   (map unmarshal-ally  (first MWORLD1))
                   (map unmarshal-alien (second MWORLD1))
                   (third MWORLD1)
                   (map unmarshal-shot (fourth MWORLD1))))


(define UWORLD2 (make-world
                   (map unmarshal-ally  (first MWORLD2))
                   (map unmarshal-alien (second MWORLD2))
                   (third MWORLD2)
                   (map unmarshal-shot (fourth MWORLD2))))


;; Tests using sample computations for unmarshal-world
(check-expect (unmarshal-world MWORLD1) UWORLD1)
(check-expect (unmarshal-world MWORLD2) UWORLD2)
```

```
;; Tests using sample values for unmarshal-world
(check-expect (unmarshal-world
              (list (list (list 5 "Neil")
                          (list 6 "Constance")
                          (list 7 "Madrid")
                          (list 8 "Skyler"))
                    (list (list 0 4))
                    "down"
                    '()))
              (make-world (list (make-ally 5 "Neil")
                                (make-ally 6 "Constance")
                                (make-ally 7 "Madrid")
                                (make-ally 8 "Skyler"))
                          (list (make-posn 0 4))
                          "down"
                          '())))
```

Once again, observe that the tests using sample values for both functions illustrate that they are inverses of each other.

158 Component Implementation

Component implementation refers to the refinement of existing code to make it a component of a distributed program or to the design of new components. For Aliens Attack 7 there are two goals: the refinement of the player code and the design of the server.

158.1 Player Component

The refinement of existing code to design a component involves the adoption of new data definitions and the implementation of the communication protocol. For Aliens Attack 7, all the new data definitions are associated with the communication protocol. Therefore, all code refinement focuses on functions that send messages to the server and on the function to process tpms.

158.1.1 The process-key Refinement

A function that must send messages to the server is process-key. This means that some of the player's outgoing arrows in the protocol diagrams in Figs. 125, 126, 127, 128, and 129 must be implemented by this handler. According to Fig. 125 a new shot message must be sent when the player shoots. This means that when the player

Fig. 130 Refined local `process-key` function

```
;; world key → world or package
(define (process-key a-world a-key)
  (cond [(key=? a-key "right")
         (local
           [(define nw (make-world (move-ally-right
                                     MY-NAME (world-allies a-world))
                                   (world-aliens a-world)
                                   (world-dir a-world)
                                   (world-shots a-world)))
            (define na (get-ally MY-NAME (world-allies nw)))]
           (make-package nw (list 'rckt-move (marshal-ally na))))]
        [(key=? a-key "left")
         (local
           [(define nw (make-world (move-ally-left MY-NAME
                                                   (world-allies a-world))
                                   (world-aliens a-world)
                                   (world-dir a-world)
                                   (world-shots a-world)))
            (define na (get-ally MY-NAME (world-allies nw)))]
           (make-package nw (list 'rckt-move (marshal-ally na))))]
        [(key=? a-key " ")
         (local [(define ns (process-shooting
                              (ally-rocket
                               (get-ally
                                MY-NAME (world-allies a-world)))))
                 (define nw (make-world (world-allies a-world)
                                        (world-aliens a-world)
                                        (world-dir a-world)
                                        (cons ns (world-shots a-world))))]
           (make-package nw (list 'new-shot (marshal-shot ns))))]
        [else a-world]))
```

shoots, a new `shot` is constructed using the player's `rocket` coordinate and a new `world` is constructed by adding the new `shot` to the list of `shots`. These new values are used to create a `package`. The message to the server is constructed by making a list containing the `'new-shot` tag and the marshaled new `shot`. These refinements are implemented in the third stanza of the conditional for the local `process-key` function displayed in Fig. 130.

According to Fig. 126, a rocket move message must be sent when the player moves her rocket. This means that a `package` must be constructed with a new `world` that has the updated ally for the player and a message that contains the `'rckt-move` tag and the marshaled updated `ally`. These refinements are implemented in the first two stanzas of the conditional for the local `process-key` function displayed in Fig. 130.

This completes the refinements for `process-key` code. Observe, however, that the function may return a `package` or a `world`. This means that `process-key`'s signature must also be refined. In other words, we have done more than just refactor code. The updated signature is also displayed in Fig. 130. It is also noteworthy that the only outgoing arrow from a player that still needs to be implemented is the one for a world back message in Fig. 129. All of the incoming arrows to a player, of course, still need to be implemented by the function that processes `tpms`.

158.1.2 The `process-message` Design

The function to process `tpms` is designed by specializing the template for functions
on a `tpm` and the protocol diagrams in Figs. 125, 126, 127, 128, and 129. Develop
a sample expression for each subtype of `tpm` one at a time using the expressions in
the `f-on-tpm` definition template. Consider an incoming arrow to a player with an
ally move message in Fig. 126. What needs to be done? For a `ally` move message,
a local variable is defined to capture the `ally` embedded in the message and a new
world is constructed by substituting in the list of allies. This is done, for example, as
follows:

```
(define PM-RMOVE (local [(define ally (unmarshal-ally
                                        (second RM-MSG2)))]
                   (make-world (replace-ally
                                 ally
                                 (world-allies INIT-WORLD))
                               (world-aliens INIT-WORLD)
                               (world-dir INIT-WORLD)
                               (world-shots INIT-WORLD))))
```

Note that an auxiliary function is needed to replace an `ally` in a list of allies.
Consider an incoming arrow to a player with a new shot message in Fig. 125. What
needs to be done? For a new `shot` message, a local variable is defined to capture the
`shot` embedded in the message and a new `world` is constructed by adding the new
shot to the front of the list of shots. This is done, for example, as follows:

```
(define PM-NSHOT (local [(define shot (unmarshal-shot
                                        (second NS-MSG)))]
                   (if (eq? shot NO-SHOT)
                       INIT-WORLD
                       (make-world
                         (world-allies INIT-WORLD)
                         (world-aliens INIT-WORLD)
                         (world-dir INIT-WORLD)
                         (cons shot
                               (world-shots INIT-WORLD))))))

(define PM-NSHOT2 (local [(define shot (unmarshal-shot
                                         (second NS-MSG2)))]
                    (if (eq? shot NO-SHOT)
                        INIT-WORLD
                        (make-world
                          (world-allies INIT-WORLD)
                          (world-aliens INIT-WORLD)
                          (world-dir INIT-WORLD)
                          (cons shot
                                (world-shots INIT-WORLD))))))
```

There are two sample expressions because there are two subtypes of shot. Consider an incoming arrow to a player with a new ally message in Figs. 128 and 129. What needs to be done? For both cases, a local variable needs to be defined to capture the ally embedded in the message and a new world is constructed by adding the new ally to the front of the list of allies. This is done, for example, as follows:

```
(define PM-NALLY (local [(define ally (unmarshal-ally
                                         (second NA-MSG)))]
                   (make-world
                     (cons ally (world-allies INIT-WORLD))
                     (world-aliens INIT-WORLD)
                     (world-dir INIT-WORLD)
                     (world-shots INIT-WORLD))))
```

Consider an incoming arrow to a player with a remove ally message in Fig. 127. What needs to be done? For a remove ally message, a local variable is defined to capture the ally-name embedded in the message and a new world is constructed by removing the ally from the list of allies. This is done, for example, as follows:

```
(define PM-RMALLY (local [(define name (second RA-MSG2))]
                    (make-world (remove-ally
                                  name
                                  (world-allies INIT-WORLD2))
                      (world-aliens INIT-WORLD2)
                      (world-dir INIT-WORLD2)
                      (world-shots INIT-WORLD2))))
```

Observe that an auxiliary function to remove an ally for a (listof ally) is needed. Consider an incoming arrow to a player with a send world message in Fig. 129. What needs to be done? For a send world message, a local variable is defined to capture the world-name embedded in the message and a package needs to be constructed because the outgoing arrow with world back message in Fig. 129 must be implemented. The package is constructed with the world and its marshalling. The outgoing message must also contain the proper tag and the name of the destination world. This is done, for example, as follows:

```
(define PM-SWORLD (local [(define name (second SW-MSG2))]
                    (make-package
                      WORLD3
                      (cons 'world-back
                        (cons name
                              (marshal-world WORLD3))))))
```

Finally, consider an incoming arrow to a player with a start message in Fig. 129. What needs to be done? For a start message, a local variable is defined to capture the world embedded in the message. Local variables are also defined to capture the components of the newly arrived world instance. These components are used to build a new world by adding the player's rocket to the list of allies. This is done, for example, as follows:

```
(define PM-START (local [(define world  (unmarshal-world
                                           (rest ST-MSG)))
                         (define allies (world-allies world))
                         (define aliens (world-aliens world))
                         (define dir    (world-dir world))
                         (define shots  (world-shots world))]
                   (make-world (cons INIT-ALLY allies)
                               aliens
                               dir
                               shots)))
```

Based on the sample expressions, the process-message function definition displayed in Fig. 131 is written. Observe that with this function implementation all the player's incident incoming and outgoing arrows are implemented. The only arrow incidences remained to implement are those for the server.

The final step to complete the design of process-message is to write unit tests. Writing the tests is the same as any other function. The tests using sample computations use sample instances and the values of the sample expressions. The tests using sample computations need to test that the proper error is generated when an unknown message type is provided and illustrate with explicit instances one or more worlds expected after receiving a message. The tests may be implemented as follows:

```
;; Tests using sample computations for process-message
(check-expect (process-message INIT-WORLD  RM-MSG2) PM-RMOVE)
(check-expect (process-message INIT-WORLD  NS-MSG)  PM-NSHOT)
(check-expect (process-message INIT-WORLD  NA-MSG)  PM-NALLY)
(check-expect (process-message INIT-WORLD2 RA-MSG2) PM-RMALLY)
(check-expect (process-message WORLD3      SW-MSG2) PM-SWORLD)
(check-expect (process-message INIT-WORLD  ST-MSG)  PM-START)

;; Tests using sample computations for process-message
(check-expect (process-message (make-world
                                (list (make-ally 6 "Doris"))
                                (list (make-posn 4 9))
                                "right"
                                '())
                               (list 'send-world "Don Marco"))
              (make-package
               (make-world
                (list (make-ally 6 "Doris"))
                (list (make-posn 4 9))
                "right"
                '())
               (cons
                'world-back
```

Fig. 131 The player's `process-message` function definition

```
;; world tpm → world or package  Purpose: Process given to-player message
(define (process-message  a-world a-tpm)
  (local [(define tag (first a-tpm))]
    (cond [(eq? tag 'rckt-move)
           (local [(define ally (unmarshal-ally (second a-tpm)))]
             (make-world (replace-ally ally (world-allies a-world))
                         (world-aliens a-world) (world-dir a-world)
                         (world-shots a-world)))]
          [(eq? tag 'new-shot)
           (local [(define shot (unmarshal-shot (second a-tpm)))]
             (if (eq? shot NO-SHOT) a-world
                 (make-world (world-allies a-world) (world-aliens a-world)
                             (world-dir a-world)
                             (cons shot (world-shots a-world)))))]
          [(eq? tag 'new-ally)
           (local [(define ally (unmarshal-ally (second a-tpm)))]
             (make-world (cons ally (world-allies a-world))
                         (world-aliens a-world) (world-dir a-world)
                         (world-shots a-world)))]
          [(eq? tag 'rm-ally)
           (local [(define name (second a-tpm))]
             (make-world (remove-ally name (world-allies a-world))
                         (world-aliens a-world) (world-dir a-world)
                         (world-shots a-world)))]
          [(eq? tag 'send-world)
           (local [(define name (second a-tpm))]
             (make-package a-world
                           (cons 'world-back
                                 (cons name (marshal-world a-world)))))]
          [(eq? tag 'start)
           (local [(define world (unmarshal-world (rest a-tpm)))
                   (define allies (world-allies world))
                   (define aliens (world-aliens world))
                   (define dir    (world-dir world))
                   (define shots  (world-shots world))]
             (make-world (cons INIT-ALLY allies) aliens dir shots))]
          [else (error (format "Unknown message type received: ~s"
                               (first a-tpm)))])))
```

```
                    (cons
                     "Don Marco"
                     (list (list (list 6 "Doris"))
                           (list (list 4 9))
                           "right"
                           '())))))


(check-error (process-message INIT-WORLD
                              (list 'send-w "Magna"))
             "Unknown message type received: send-w")
```

The auxiliary functions needed by process-message are straight-forward list-processing exercises. They are presented here in the interest of thoroughness. The function to remove an ally from an lor may be implemented using filter as follows:

```
;; string lor → lor
;; Purpose: Remove given ally for given list of allies
(define (remove-ally a-name a-lor)
  (filter (λ (a) (not (string=? (ally-name a) a-name)))
          a-lor))


;; Sample expressions for remove-ally
(define RM-ALLIES1 (filter (λ (a)
                             (not (string=? (ally-name a)
                                            "Quintana")))
                           INIT-ALLIES))
(define RM-ALLIES2 (filter (λ (a)
                             (not (string=? (ally-name a)
                                            "Marco")))
                           ALLIES2))


;; Tests using sample computations for remove-ally
(check-expect (remove-ally "Quintana" INIT-ALLIES) RM-ALLIES1)
(check-expect (remove-ally "Marco"    ALLIES2)      RM-ALLIES2)


;; Tests using sample values for remove-ally
(check-expect (remove-ally "Driscoll"
                           (list (make-ally 4 "Manfred")
                                 (make-ally 7 "Cordula")
                                 (make-ally 1 "Catherina")))
              (list (make-ally 4 "Manfred")
                    (make-ally 7 "Cordula")
                    (make-ally 1 "Catherina")))
(check-expect (remove-ally "Driscoll"
                           (list (make-ally 12 "Sakas")
                                 (make-ally 14 "Davila")
                                 (make-ally 11 "Driscoll")
                                 (make-ally 17 "Morazan")))
              (list (make-ally 12 "Sakas")
                    (make-ally 14 "Davila")
                    (make-ally 17 "Morazan")))
```

The function to replace an ally from an lor may be implemented using map as follows:

```
;; ally lor → lor
;; Purpose: Replace given ally in given lor
(define (replace-ally an-ally a-lor)
  (map (λ (a) (if (string=? (ally-name a) (ally-name an-ally))
                  an-ally
                  a))
       a-lor))


;; Sample expressions for replace-ally
(define RP-ALLIES1 (map (λ (a)
                          (if (string=? (ally-name a)
                                        (ally-name INIT-ALLY2))
                              INIT-ALLY2
                              a))
                        INIT-ALLIES))
(define RP-ALLIES2 (map (λ (a)
                          (if (string=? (ally-name a)
                                        (ally-name INIT-ALLY))
                              INIT-ALLY
                              a))
                        ALLIES2))


;; Tests using sample computations for replace-ally
(check-expect (replace-ally INIT-ALLY2 INIT-ALLIES) RP-ALLIES1)
(check-expect (replace-ally INIT-ALLY  ALLIES2)      RP-ALLIES2)


;; Tests using sample values for replace-ally
(check-expect (replace-ally (make-ally 5 "Manfred")
                            (list (make-ally 4 "Manfred")
                                  (make-ally 7 "Cordula")
                                  (make-ally 1 "Catherina")))
              (list (make-ally 5 "Manfred")
                    (make-ally 7 "Cordula")
                    (make-ally 1 "Catherina")))
(check-expect (replace-ally (make-ally 10 "Mirek")
                            (list (make-ally 12 "Sakas")
                                  (make-ally 14 "Davila")
                                  (make-ally 11 "Driscoll")
                                  (make-ally 17 "Morazan")))
              (list (make-ally 12 "Sakas")
                    (make-ally 14 "Davila")
                    (make-ally 11 "Driscoll")
                    (make-ally 17 "Morazan")))
```

Finally, the updated run function for the player is:

```
;; string → world
;; Purpose: To run the game
(define (run a-name)
  (local [(define TICK-RATE 1/4)]
    (big-bang
      INIT-WORLD
      [on-draw draw-world]
      [name MY-NAME]
      [on-key process-key]
      [on-tick process-tick TICK-RATE]
      [stop-when game-over? draw-last-world]
      [register LOCALHOST]
      [on-receive process-message])))
```

** **Ex. 331** — A conditional expression and local-expressions are used to implement process-message. Simplify the implementation by refactoring it to use pattern matching.

** **Ex. 332** — The unmarshalling functions are implemented using local-expressions. Simplify their implementation by refactoring them to use pattern matching.

158.2 Server Component

Our initial problem analysis states that the server receives messages from the player, manages the joining of new players, and manages the departure of players. This means that three handlers are needed. In addition, the server must broadcast messages to selected players. This means it must keep track of the players that are in the game. Based on this, we may define the universe and the run-server function as follows:

```
;; A universe is a (listof iworld), where each iworld has
;; a unique name

;; Sample instances of universe
(define INIT-UNIV '())
(define A-UNIV    (list iworld1 iworld2))

;; Z → universe
;; Purpose: Run the chat server
(define (run-server a-z)
  (universe INIT-UNIV
            (on-new        add-player)
            (on-msg        process-message)
            (on-disconnect rm-player)))
```

The defined universe instances are used to test the handlers and observe that the second sample universe is built using the sample iworld instances provided by the API.

Each of the handlers is independently designed using the data definitions and the communication protocol defined in the previous sections of this chapter. As you proceed through the design, take note of the importance of understanding the communication protocol to properly have the components cooperate.

158.2.1 The add-player Handler

This handler manages the joining of new players. If the joining player's name is not already used in the universe, it is allowed to join the game. Otherwise it is rejected. When a player is allowed to join, as outlined by Figs. 128 and 129, there are two cases. If it is the first player to join, the protocol diagram in Fig. 128 informs us that initial world must be sent to it. If it is not the first player to join, the protocol diagram in Fig. 129 informs us that the existing players must be sent a new ally message and that the first world in the universe must be sent a send world message.

Develop at least one sample expression for each of the three possibilities. To reject a player, a bundle may be created that does not change the given universe, that creates no mails, and that disconnects the player that is attempting to join the game. A sample expression for a player with a repeated name is:

```
(define RPT-ADD (make-bundle A-UNIV '() (list iworld1)))
```

Observe that A-UNIV is unchanged and there are no mails constructed. By not constructing any mails, the elements of the communication protocol that must still be implemented remain unchanged. By disconnecting the player from the server, the player's game window only displays a message stating that the universe has disappeared.

To add a player to an empty universe, a bundle is created with a universe that contains the new player, a start message with the 'start tag and the initial world marshaled, and an empty list of players to disconnect. A sample expression for this is:

```
(define EMP-ADD (make-bundle
                (cons iworld1 INIT-UNIV)
                (list (make-mail
                        iworld1
                        (cons 'start
                                (marshal-world INIT-WORLD))))
                '()))
```

Observe that the constructed mail implements the arrow from the server to $Player_i$ in Fig. 128.

To add a player to a non-empty universe, a bundle is created with a universe that contains the new player, a list of mails containing a send world message to the first player in the universe and add ally messages to the existing players, and an

Fig. 132 The server's `add-world` function definition

```
;; universe iworld → bundle
;; Purpose: Add new world to the universe
(define (add-player a-univ an-iw)
  (cond
    [(member? (iworld-name an-iw) (map iworld-name a-univ))
     (make-bundle a-univ '() (list an-iw))]
    [(empty? a-univ)
     (make-bundle
      (cons an-iw a-univ)
      (list (make-mail an-iw (cons 'start (marshal-world INIT-WORLD))))
      '())]
    [else
     (make-bundle
      (cons an-iw a-univ)
      (cons (make-mail (first a-univ)
                       (list 'send-world (iworld-name an-iw)))
            (map
             (λ (iw)
               (make-mail iw
                          (list 'new-ally
                                (list INIT-ROCKET (iworld-name an-iw)))))
             a-univ))
      '())]))
```

empty list of players to disconnect. The list new ally messages may be constructed using map to traverse the existing universe. A sample expression for this is:

```
(define NEW-ADD (make-bundle
                 (cons iworld3 A-UNIV)
                 (cons (make-mail
                        (first A-UNIV)
                        (list 'send-world
                              (iworld-name iworld3)))
                       (map
                        (λ (iw)
                          (make-mail
                           iw
                           (list 'new-ally
                                 (list
                                  INIT-ROCKET
                                  (iworld-name iworld3)))))
                        A-UNIV))
                 '()))
```

Observe that the list of emails implements the add ally and send world messages from the server in Fig. 129.

To implement the handler, the template for functions on a `universe` is specialized by abstracting over the sample expressions. The result is displayed in Fig. 132. The signature clearly states that a `bundle` is returned. Each of the three possible cases has a stanza in the conditional expression. Observe that the initial `world`, the initial `rocket`, and `marshal-world` must be defined in the server's program. You may copy the necessary definitions into the server's program.

The handler is tested as follows:

```
;; Tests using sample computations for add-player
(check-expect (add-player A-UNIV    iworld1) RPT-ADD)
(check-expect (add-player INIT-UNIV iworld1) EMP-ADD)
(check-expect (add-player A-UNIV    iworld3) NEW-ADD)


;; Tests using sample values for add-player
(check-expect
  (add-player (list iworld2 iworld3) iworld1)
  (make-bundle (list iworld1 iworld2 iworld3)
               (cons (make-mail
                      (first (list iworld2 iworld3))
                      (list 'send-world "iworld1"))
                     (map
                      (λ (iw)
                        (make-mail
                         iw
                         (list 'new-ally
                               (list INIT-ROCKET "iworld1"))))
                      (list iworld2 iworld3)))
               '()))
```

Observe that the sample `iworld`s provided by the API are extensively used in the test using sample values.

158.2.2 The `rm-player` Handler

This handler removes a player that disconnects from the universe. To do so a new universe is constructed by removing the player and, as indicated by the protocol diagram in Fig. 127, by sending a remove ally message to the remaining players. The following sample expression illustrates how this may be done:

```
(define IW1-RM (local
                 [(define new-univ
                    (filter (λ (iw)
                      (not (string=?
                            (iworld-name iw)
                            (iworld-name iworld1))))
                      A-UNIV))]
                 (make-bundle
                  new-univ
```

Fig. 133 The server's `rm-player` function definition

```
;; universe iworld → bundle
;; Purpose: Remove a player from the game
(define (rm-player a-univ an-iw)
  (local
    [(define new-univ (filter (λ (iw)
                               (not (string=? (iworld-name iw)
                                              (iworld-name an-iw))))
                             a-univ))]
    (make-bundle
     new-univ
     (map (λ (iw)
            (make-mail iw
                       (list 'rm-ally (iworld-name an-iw))))
          new-univ)
     '())))
```

```
                    (map (λ (iw)
                           (make-mail iw
                                      (list 'rm-ally
                                            (iworld-name iworld1))))
                         new-univ)
                    '())))
```

Observe that the list of mails implements the remove ally arrows in Fig. 127 and that
no players are explicitly removed from the server.

Based on the sample expression and Fig. 127, the handler's implementation is
displayed in Fig. 133. The function returns a `bundle` because messages must be sent
out. The handler is tested as follows:

```
;; Tests using sample computations for rm-player
(check-expect (rm-player A-UNIV iworld1) IW1-RM)

;; Tests using sample values for rm-player
(check-expect (rm-player (list iworld1 iworld2 iworld3)
                         iworld2)
              (make-bundle  (list iworld1 iworld3)
                            (map
                             (λ (iw)
                               (make-mail
                                iw
                                (list 'rm-ally "iworld2")))
                             (list iworld1 iworld3))
                            '()))
```

158.2.3 The `process-message` **Handler**

The `process-message` handler must process all incoming `tsm`s. According to the protocol diagrams in Figs. 125, 126, 127, 128, and 129, the server always sends out one or more messages when it receives a `tsm`. This means that this handler must return a `bundle`. To process a `tsm`, we may define local variables for the tag of the message and for the list of players that a message must be sent to. When the message is a world back message, the mailing list contains only the recipient player's `iworld`. Otherwise, it contains all the `iworld`s in the `universe` other than the player that sent the message.

Sample expressions are displayed in Fig. 134. Observe that for each the tag and the mailing list are captured in local variables. For rocket move and a new shot messages, the server broadcasts them to all the players except the sender as defined by the protocol diagrams in Figs. 126 and 125. For a world back message, the marshaled world embedded in the message is sent to the recipient embedded in the message as a start message to implement the outgoing start message arrow from the server to `Player`$_i$ in Fig. 129.

Observe that the local variables are defined the same way for all three `tsm` subtypes. Therefore, instead of repeating the same code three times, the local variables may be defined outside the conditional that distinguishes between the `tsm` subtypes as displayed in Fig. 135. Each stanza in the conditional expression creates a bundle and is obtained from abstracting away the concrete values for the `universe`, the sending `iworld`, and the `tsm` in the sample expressions. Finally, the handler is tested as follows:

```
;; Tests using sample computations for process-message
(check-expect (process-message A-UNIV iworld1 SRM-MSG) PM-RM)
(check-expect (process-message A-UNIV iworld1 SNS-MSG) PM-NS)
(check-expect (process-message A-UNIV iworld2 SWB-MSG) PM-WB)


;; Tests using sample values for process-message
(check-error (process-message A-UNIV
                              iworld2
                              '(rocket-move ((5 "iworld2"))))
             (format "Unknown message received by server: ~s."
                     ('rocket-move ((5 "iworld2")))))
```

> ** **Ex. 333** — Improve the tests using sample values for `process-message`.
>
> ** **Ex. 334** — Improve the `process-message` implementation using pattern matching.
>
> * **Ex. 335** — Explain what happens if a player with a repeated name is not disconnected from the server in `add-player`. Try it out by temporarily changing the code.

Fig. 134 Sample expressions for the server's `process-message` handler

```
(define PM-RM
  (local [(define tag (first SRM-MSG))
          (define send-list
                  (if (eq? tag 'world-back)
                      (filter
                        (λ (iw)
                          (string=? (iworld-name iw) (second SRM-MSG)))
                        A-UNIV)
                      (filter (λ (iw)
                                (not (string=? (iworld-name iw)
                                               (iworld-name iworld1))))
                              A-UNIV)))]
    (make-bundle A-UNIV
                 (map (λ (iw) (make-mail iw SRM-MSG))
                      send-list)
                 '())))
(define PM-NS
  (local [(define tag (first SNS-MSG))
          (define send-list
                  (if (eq? tag 'world-back)
                      (filter (λ (iw)
                                (string=? (iworld-name iw)
                                          (second SNS-MSG)))
                              A-UNIV)
                      (filter (λ (iw)
                                (not (string=? (iworld-name iw)
                                               (iworld-name iworld1))))
                              A-UNIV)))]
    (make-bundle A-UNIV
                 (map (λ (iw) (make-mail iw SNS-MSG)) send-list)
                 '())))
(define PM-WB
  (local [(define tag (first SWB-MSG))
          (define send-list
                  (if (eq? tag 'world-back)
                      (filter (λ (iw)
                                (string=? (iworld-name iw) (second SWB-MSG)))
                              A-UNIV)
                      (filter (λ (iw)
                                (not (string=? (iworld-name iw)
                                               (iworld-name iworld1))))
                              A-UNIV)))]
    (make-bundle A-UNIV
                 (map (λ (iw)
                        (make-mail (first send-list)
                                   (cons 'start (rest (rest SWB-MSG)))))
                      send-list)
                 '())))
```

Fig. 135 The servers process-message function definition

```
;; universe iworld tsm → bundle
;; Purpose: To process the given message from the given world
(define (process-message a-univ an-iw a-tsm)
  (local
    [(define tag (first a-tsm))
     (define send-list (if (eq? tag 'world-back)
                           (filter (λ (iw) (string=? (iworld-name iw)
                                                     (second a-tsm)))
                                   a-univ)
                           (filter
                            (λ (iw) (not (string=? (iworld-name iw)
                                                   (iworld-name an-iw))))
                            a-univ)))]
    (cond [(eq? tag 'rckt-move)
           (make-bundle a-univ
                        (map (λ (iw) (make-mail iw a-tsm)) send-list)
                        '())]
          [(eq? tag 'new-shot)
           (make-bundle a-univ
                        (map (λ (iw) (make-mail iw a-tsm)) send-list)
                        '())]
          [(eq? tag 'world-back)
           (make-bundle a-univ
                        (list (make-mail (first send-list)
                                         (cons 'start
                                               (rest (rest a-tsm)))))
                        '())]
          [else
           (error (format "Unknown message received by server: ~s."
                          a-tsm))])))
```

159 A Subtle Bug

Before proceeding make sure you have at least two copies of the player's program saved (each with a unique MY-NAME value), the players' tests and the server tests pass, and you play the game a few times. To play the game as multiple players on your machine remember to first call run-server in the server file and then run for each of the player files.

What do you notice, if anything, after playing the game a few times on your computer? If you run it enough times, you are bound to see that there is a *synchronization bug*. That is, the state of the game is different for different players. Figure 136 displays two snapshots of the same game at the same time for two different players. Figure 136a displays the game that Player$_i$ sees and Fig. 136b displays the game that Player$_j$ sees. Observe that the army of aliens is different. How is this possible? All the changes made by one player are communicated to all other players. Therefore, the game state ought to be the same for all players.

Fig. 136 Snapshot of two different players in the same game at the same time

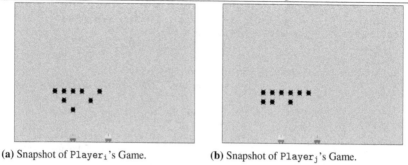

(a) Snapshot of Player$_i$'s Game.   (b) Snapshot of Player$_j$'s Game.

Fig. 137 New shot only exists in Player$_i$'s game

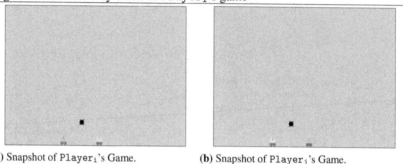

(a) Snapshot of Player$_i$'s Game.   (b) Snapshot of Player$_j$'s Game.

The problem is due to each player updating its `world` independently of the other players and to messages taking time to travel from a player to the server and then to a receiving player. Let us take a closer look at the consequences of this. Consider what happens when Player$_i$ shoots. The new `shot` is added to Player$_i$'s `world` and a new shot message is sent to the server. Player$_j$ has not yet been informed of the new `shot` by Player$_i$. The snapshots in Fig. 137, with new `shot` only existing in Player$_i$'s `world`, capture the state of the game for each player.

Let us assume that messages are very fast, and they take only one clock tick to travel from Player$_i$ to the server and then to Player$_j$. During that clock tick, the new `shot` has moved in Player$_i$'s `world`, but no movement has taken place by the copy of the shot received by Player$_j$. The two worlds are no longer synchronized. The snapshots in Fig. 138 capture the state of the game for each player.

After the following clock tick, the shot moves in both worlds. In Player$_i$'s world the shot hits the alien, but in Player$_j$'s world the shot has not reached the alien and, thus, does not hit it. The snapshots in Fig. 139 capture the state of the game for each player. This means that the `alien` is removed from Player$_i$'s `world` and is not removed from Player$_j$'s `world`. Thus, the army of `aliens` is different in these two worlds.

Fig. 138 New shot arrives at Player$_j$'s game

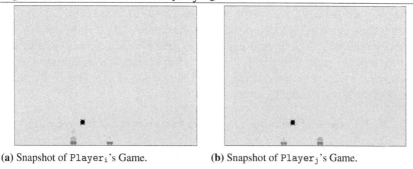

(a) Snapshot of Player$_i$'s Game.   (b) Snapshot of Player$_j$'s Game.

Fig. 139 New shot hits Alien only in Player$_i$'s game

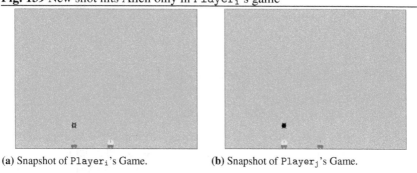

(a) Snapshot of Player$_i$'s Game.   (b) Snapshot of Player$_j$'s Game.

Synchronization bugs in distributed programming are hard to pinpoint because they do not always manifest themselves. Sometimes an application may run without seeing the bug and other times the bug is seen. There is no test we can write to protect ourselves from this potential bug. Unfortunately, it is not the only subtle distributed programming bug that may occur. Another common bug is *deadlock*. Deadlock occurs when two (or more) components are waiting for each other to perform an action. For example, two components may be waiting for each other to signal that they are ready to perform a task. Component$_i$ is waiting for Component$_j$ to signal it is ready and Component$_j$ is waiting for Component$_i$ to signal that it is ready. The two components are deadlocked waiting for a message that cannot possibly ever be sent. You will learn more about detecting and avoiding such bugs in an operating systems course or in a distributed programming course.

What can we do now to fix multiplayer Aliens Attack now? Given that the problem stems from each player making changes to its own copy of the world, the solution is to have only one component allowed to make changes to the world and all the other components get the same copy of the world whenever it is changed. The natural choice is to only allow the server to make changes to the world and in this manner maintain all the players synchronized. That is, the solution is to implement multiplayer Aliens Attack using a thick server.

Does this mean that thin servers are useless? No, it does not mean that. Thin servers are perfectly fine when clients do not need to be synchronized or when clients are automatically synchronized by the nature of the application. For example, thin servers work well for turn-based games, like Tic Tac Toe or chess, where players take turns to make changes to the game. The players are synchronized after each change. Now you have a criteria for choosing the kind of server that you ought to implement for a distributed program.

*** **Ex. 336** — Design and implement a two-player Tic Tac Toe game.

**** **Ex. 337** — Design and implement a two-player Concentration game.

***** **Ex. 338** — Design and implement a multiplayer Snakes and Ladders game.

---

160 What Have We Learned in This Chapter?

The important lessons of Chap. 28 are summarized as follows:

- Following the steps of the design recipe for distributed programming is an effective way of managing the complexity of writing distributed programs.
- Component implementation refers to the refinement of existing code to make it part of a distributed program or to the design of completely new components.
- The refinement of existing code to design a component involves the adoption of new data definitions and the implementation of the communication protocol.
- All the arrows in a communication protocol diagram must be implemented by code that sends a message from the source to the destination.
- Synchronization and deadlock are distributed programming bugs that do not always manifest themselves with every program execution.
- Thin servers are a good choice when clients do not need to be synchronized or when clients are automatically synchronized by the nature of the application.

Chapter 29
Aliens Attack Version 8

This chapter addresses the design of a multiplayer Aliens Attack using a think server. In this version of the game only one component, namely the server, is allowed to make changes to the state of the game. The players, therefore, must be carefully designed to not make changes to their local copy of the world. Players still need to have the ability to move their rocket and to shoot. When such actions are taken by a player, however, the player's program does not change the world. Instead, a message is sent to the server and the server creates a new world and sends the new world to the players. Given that the server is the only component allowed to update the world, the players cannot become unsynchronized.

The sections of this chapter outline the steps of the design recipe for distributed computing. As with the material in Chap. 28, take your time to understand how the steps are interrelated and build on each other.

161 The Components

Figure 140 outlines the components for Aliens Attack 8. The server is responsible for managing new players that connect to the server. The server does not start the game until the first player connects. If the arriving player's world has a name different from all other worlds connected to the server, then it is allowed to join the game. Otherwise, it is not allowed to join the game. The server is also responsible for managing the departure of players. As with Aliens Attack 7, the departing world must be removed from the universe and the corresponding ally must also be removed. In addition, the server is responsible for updating the world. This may occur in one of two ways: a clock tick or a message arrives from a player requesting their rocket be moved or a shot be created. Whenever the server updates the game, it sends all the players the new world.

A player component is responsible for drawing the world, processing keystrokes, detecting the end of the game, and processing messages from the server. The world is rendered and the end of the game is detected as is done in Aliens Attack 7.

© The Author(s), under exclusive license to Springer Nature Switzerland AG 2022
M. T. Morazán, *Animated Problem Solving*, Texts in Computer Science,
https://doi.org/10.1007/978-3-030-85091-3_29

Fig. 140 The components of Aliens attack version 8

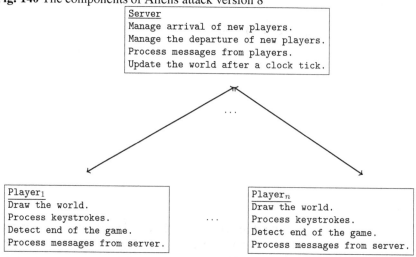

Processing keystrokes is different. When the player moves her rocket or shoots, a message is sent to the server requesting the desired change be made. Receiving a message from the server means that the server has changed the value of the `world` and the `world` embedded in the message becomes the new world.

162 Data Definitions

The data definitions for the `world` are the same as those defined in Sect. 148. That is, a world is either `'uninitialized` or is a structure that contains a list of allies (`lor`), a list of aliens (`loa`), a `direction`, and a list of shots (`los`). Remember that each player must have a constant representing a unique name. To facilitate test development, we define the following `world` sample instance in addition to those found in Sect. 148:

```
(define WORLD4 (make-world (list (make-ally 8 "iworld3")
                                 (make-ally 5 "iworld2"))
                           (list (make-posn 8 2))
                           'right
                           (list (make-posn 8 4))))
```

In order to send messages to the all players, the server needs to track the players in the game. As in Aliens Attack 7, this may be done using a list of `iworlds`. In addition the server must maintain the state of the game. Therefore, the (current) `world` must be part of the universe. Given that the universe is always a finite number of elements (i.e., two), it may be defined using a structure. The `universe`, the template for functions on a `universe`, and sample instances of `universe` are as follows:

```
;; A universe (univ) is a structure:
;;     (make-univ (listof iworld) world)
(define-struct univ (iws game))

;; Template for a function on a univ
#|  ;; Sample instances of univ
    (define UNIV1 (make-univ ... ...))

    univ ... → ...
    Purpose:
    (define (f-on-univ a-univ ...)
      (...(f-on-loiw (univ-iws a-univ))...
      ...(f-on-world (univ-world a-univ)...)))

    ;; Sample expressions for f-on-univ
    (define UNIV1-VAL ...) ...

    ;; Tests using sample computations for f-on-univ
    (check-expect (f-on-univ UNIV1 ...) UNIV1-VAL) ...

    ;; Tests using sample values for f-on-univ
    (check-expect (f-on-univ ... ...) ...) ...)  ...            |#

;; Sample instances of universe
(define INIT-UNIV  (make-univ '() UNINIT-WORLD))
(define OTHR-UNIV  (make-univ (list iworld1 iworld2) WORLD3))
(define OTHR-UNIV2 (make-univ (list iworld3 iworld2) WORLD4))
```

Observe that the initial universe, INIT-UNIV, has an empty list of iworlds and an uninitialized world. The list of iworlds is empty because no players have joined when the server starts running. The world is uninitialized because the game ought to start when the first player joins. Finally, the other two universes are defined using our API's sample iworlds to test the server's handlers.

163 Communication Protocol

As in Aliens Attack 7, there are player- and server-sparked communication chains. According to our problem analysis, player-sparked communication chains start with keystroke events when a player moves her rocket or shoots. Server-sparked communication chains start when a new player joins or departs the game and when the state of the game is updated on a clock tick.

Fig. 141 Protocol diagram for a Player$_i$ shooting

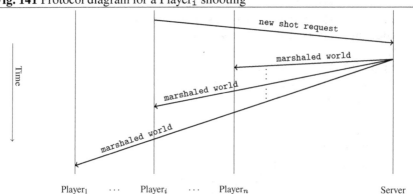

Fig. 142 Protocol diagram for a Player$_i$ moving her rocket

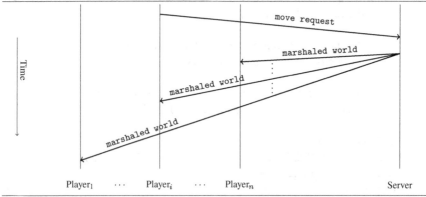

163.1 Player-Sparked Communication Chains

Consider what needs to happen when a player attempts to shoot. Recall that the player may not change the state of the game. Unlike Aliens Attack version 7, a new shot may not be added to the player's `los` and a new `shot` message must be sent to the server. Therefore, when a player shoots, a request to add a new `shot` to the `world` is sent to the server. The server processes the request to create a new `shot`, updates the `world`, and sends the new `world` to all the players. This communication chain is captured in Fig. 141. Observe that the new `world` is sent to the player, `Player`$_i$, that requested the new `shot` be created. In this manner, the shooting player receives a new `world` containing the new `shot`.

Consider what needs to happen when a player moves her rocket. Once again, a player cannot update the `ally` that contains her rocket and modify the `world`. Instead, a move request is sent to the server. The server updates the `world` and sends the new world to all the players. Figure 142 captures this communication chain. As

Fig. 143 Protocol diagram for a Player$_i$ leaving the game

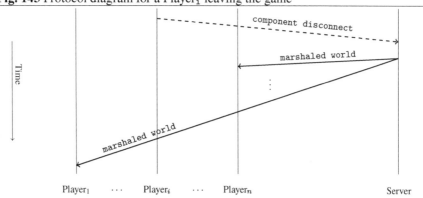

with shooting, the server sends the new `world` to the player that requested her rocket be moved.

163.2 Server-Sparked Communication Chains

Consider the communication chain that must be implemented when a player leaves the game. The server updates the `world`. The new `world` must be sent to all the players. Figure 143 captures this communication chain. Observe that when Player$_i$ leaves the game, the new `world` is sent to all the remaining players.

Consider the communication chain that is sparked when a new player is admitted to the game. The server must update the `world` to contain the new `ally`. This new `world` must be transmitted to all the players. This communication chain is captured in Fig. 144. Observe that, unlike a player joining in Aliens Attack version 7 described using multiple protocol diagrams (Figs. 128 and 129) for two different communication chains, there is a single protocol diagram for Aliens Attack 8. In terms of communication, there is no need to distinguish between a player being the first or not to join the game. Although the server may need to update the world differently in these two cases, the communication chain is the same. Regardless of how the server updates the `world`, only a marshaled `world` is sent to all the players. There is no need to request the value of the `world` from an existing player as depicted in Fig. 129.

The final server-sparked communication chain starts on a clock tick. The server updates the `world` and the new `world` is sent to all the players. Figure 145 displays the protocol diagram for a clock tick at the server. Observe that this communication chain is sparked without any player involvement. That is, it is sparked by a server event.

Fig. 144 Protocol diagram for a Player$_i$ joining the game

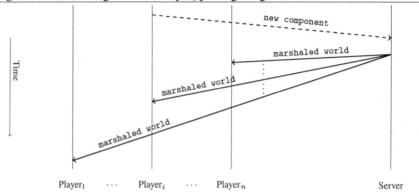

Fig. 145 Protocol diagram for a server clock tick

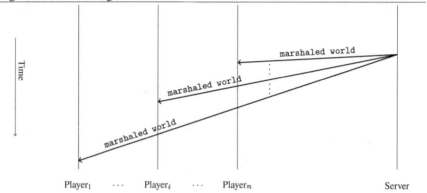

163.3 Message Data Definitions

According to the protocol diagrams in Figs. 141, 142, 143, 144 and 145, there is only one type of to-player message. Such a message contains a marshaled `world`. Given that the `world` data definition has not been changed, we use the same data definition for a marshaled world (`mw`) found in Sect. 156.3.1. We define a to-player message as follows:

```
#|   ;; A to-player message (tpm) is: (cons 'world mw)

     tpm ... → ...
     Purpose:
     (define (f-on-tpm a-tpm ...)
        (...(f-on-mw (rest a-tpm) ...)...))

     Sample instances of tpm
```

```
(define A-TPM (cons 'world ...))

Sample expressions for f-on-tpm
(define A-TPM-VAL (f-on-mw (rest A-TPM) ...))

Tests using sample for computations for f-on-mw
(check-expect (f-on-tpm A-TPM ...) A-TPM-VAL) ...

Tests using sample for values for f-on-mw
(check-expect (f-on-tpm ... ...) ...) ...        |#

;; Sample instances of tpm
(define TPM1 (cons 'world
                   (list (list (list 10 "San Martin"))
                         (list (list 5  8))
                         'right
                         (list (list 12 4)))))

(define TPM2 (cons 'world
                   (list (list (list 0 "Juarez"))
                         (list (list 5 3))
                         'right
                         (list (list 7 7)))))
```

Observe that the tag is 'world. Technically, for this version of the game it is unnecessary to have a tag, given that there is only one variety of tpm. However, it is good practice to be consistent when designing. By convention, every message is tagged. Such consistency makes it easier for others to understand the design of the code and is likely to make future refinements easier to implement.

The protocol diagrams in Figs. 141 and 142 inform us that there are two types of to-server messages. The first subtype is a new shot request. Think about what needs to be contained in such a message. The server knows what ally shot, given that it has access to the iworld that sent the message. Thus, this subtype of to-server message needs to contain nothing more than a tag. The second subtype is a move request. What content, if any, must the message contain? When a player moves her rocket, there are two options: right or left. Therefore, in addition to a tag this subtype must contain information, say the key pressed, to distinguish the direction. Based on this analysis, we may define a to-server message as follows:

```
#|  A to-server message (tsm) is either:
      1. (list 'move key)
      2. (list 'shoot)

    ;; tsm ... → ...
    ;; Purpose:
    (define (f-on-tsm a-tsm ...)
```

```
(local [(define tag (first a-tsm))]
  (cond [(eq? tag 'move)  ...]
        [(eq? tag 'shoot) ...]
        [else
          (error
            (format "Unknown to-server message type ~s"
              a-tsm))])))

;; Sample instances of tsm
(define MV-TSM ...)
(define SH-TSM ...) ...

;; Sample expressions for f-on-tsm
(define MV-TSM-VAL ...)
(define SH-TSM-VAL ...)

;; Tests using sample computations for f-on-tsm
(check-expect (f-on-tsm MV-TSM ...) MV-TSM-VAL)
(check-expect (f-on-tsm SH-TSM ...) SH-TSM-VAL) ...

;; Tests using sample values for f-on-tsm
(check-expect (f-on-tsm ... ...) ...) ...        |#

;; Sample instances of tsm
(define MV-LEFT (list 'move "left"))
(define MV-RGHT (list 'move "right"))
(define SHOOT   (list 'shoot))
```

164 Marshalling and Unmarshalling

Figures 141 142, 143, 144, and 145 inform us that the server needs to marshal a world and the players need to unmarshal a world. Given that the world data definition is unchanged from Aliens Attack version 7, the marshal-world, unmarshal-world, and auxiliary marshalling functions from Sect. 157 may be used in this version of the game. There is no need to design these functions again.

Observe that tsms only contain data that is suitable for transmission. Therefore, there is no need to implement marshalling and unmarshalling functions for these messages.

165 Component Implementation

As with Aliens Attack version 7, one of the goals is to reuse as much of the code as possible from Aliens Attack 6. Based on our problem analysis from Sect. 161, we can outline how to distribute the handlers from Aliens Attach version 6 among the player and server components of this version of the game. The player components need the following, possibly refined, handlers from Aliens Attack version 6:

1. draw-world
2. game-over? (and draw-last-world)
3. process-key

In addition, the player component needs a handler to process tpms. We can, therefore, define the run function as follows:

```
;; Z → world
;; Purpose: To run the game
(define (run a-z)
  (big-bang
    UNINIT-WORLD
    [on-draw     draw-world]
    [on-key      process-key]
    [stop-when   game-over? draw-last-world]
    [on-receive process-message]
    [name        MY-NAME]
    [register    LOCALHOST]))
```

Observe that there is not stanza for tick processing. This follows from observing that it is the server that must update the world when the clock ticks.

The server component needs the following, possibly refined, handlers from Aliens Attack version 6:

1. process-tick
2. process-key

In addition, the server component needs handlers to process tsms, to add players, and to remove players. We can, therefore, define the run-server function as follows:

```
;; Z → univ
;; Purpose: To run the server
(define (run-server a-z)
  (local [(define TICK-RATE 1/4)]
    (universe
     INIT-UNIV
     (on-tick        process-tick TICK-RATE)
     (on-msg         process-message)
     (on-new         add-player)
     (on-disconnect rm-player))))
```

Observe that `process-key` is not a handler. This is because key events do not directly affect the actions of the server. When a `tsm` is received, the server uses (a refined version of) `process-key` to update the game.

165.1 Player Component

This subsection outlines the players' handlers for Aliens Attack 8. As stated above, a goal is to reuse existing Aliens Attack version 6 code as possible. We expect a significant amount of code to be reusable because the `world` data definition is unchanged.

165.1.1 The `draw-world` and `game-over?` Handlers

Neither of these handlers change the game in Aliens attack version 6. This means that there is no need for them to be refined to send messages to the server. Furthermore, given that the `world` data definition is unchanged, there are no refinements required at all. The same holds true for the auxiliary function `draw-last-world`.

165.1.2 The `process-key` Handler

In this version of the game, the `process-key` handler may not update the game. Therefore, a refinement is needed. Think carefully about what this handler must do. As in Aliens Attack version 6, if the `world` in uninitialized then nothing needs to be done and the existing world is returned. Otherwise, the key pressed must be processed. If the key pressed is `"left"` or `"right"`, then according to the protocol diagram displayed in Fig. 142 a move request must be sent to the server. Similarly, if the key pressed is `" "`, then according to the protocol diagram displayed in Fig. 141 a new shot request must be sent to the server. In both cases, a `package` is constructed using the current `world` and the appropriate `tsm`.

Given that `process-key` is an encapsulated function, we shall explore its design by writing tests using sample values. When the player presses the right or left arrow, a package is created with the given `world` and a `'move` message containing the key pressed. Tests for the `"right"` and `"left"` key events may be written as follows:

```
;; Tests using sample values for process-key
(check-expect (process-key (make-world
                           (list (make-ally 10 MY-NAME))
                           (list (make-posn 7 2))
                           'right
                           '())
                          "right")
```

```
                        (make-package (make-world
                                       (list (make-ally 10 MY-NAME))
                                       (list (make-posn 7 2))
                                       'right
                                       '())
                                      (list 'move "right")))

(check-expect (process-key (make-world
                            (list (make-ally 10 MY-NAME))
                            (list (make-posn 7 2))
                            'right
                            '())
                           "left")
              (make-package (make-world
                             (list (make-ally 10 MY-NAME))
                             (list (make-posn 7 2))
                             'right
                             '())
                            (list 'move "left")))
```

Observe that the world given to process-key is the same as the world used to construct the package. Thus, process-key handler does not change the world. Also observe that the tsm used to construct the package contains the key pressed by the player.

When the player presses the space key, a package is created with the given world and a 'shoot message. The following test illustrates how the package is created:

```
(check-expect (process-key (make-world
                            (list (make-ally 10 MY-NAME))
                            (list (make-posn 7 2))
                            'left
                            '())
                           " ")
              (make-package (make-world
                             (list (make-ally 10 MY-NAME))
                             (list (make-posn 7 2))
                             'left
                             '())
                            (list 'shoot)))
```

Once again, observe that the world given to process-key remains unchanged. As per the tsm data definition, the shoot request message contains nothing else other than the 'shoot tag.

If any other key is pressed by the player, the world remains unchanged and no message is sent to the server. The following test illustrates that the given world is returned unchanged:

```
(check-expect (process-key (make-world
                             (list (make-ally 10 MY-NAME))
                             (list (make-posn 7 2))
                             'right
                             '())
                            "d")
              (make-world (list (make-ally 10 MY-NAME))
                          (list (make-posn 7 2))
                          'right
                          '()))
```

Based on the design idea and the tests above, the player's process-key handler is defined as follows:

```
;; world key → world or package
;; Purpose: Process a key event to return next world
(define (process-key a-world a-key)
  (local
   [;; world key → world
    ;; Purpose: Process a key event to return next world
    ;; ASSUMPTION: The given world is a structure
    (define (process-key a-world a-key)
      (cond [(or (key=? a-key "right")
                 (key=? a-key "left"))
             (make-package a-world (list 'move a-key))]
            [(key=? a-key " ")
             (make-package a-world (list 'shoot))]
            [else a-world]))]
   (if (eq? a-world UNINIT-WORLD)
       a-world
       (process-key a-world a-key))))
```

Observe that as in Aliens Attack version 6, the local process-key is only called if the world is initialized. The local process-key may return a world or a package as exemplified by the tests above. In addition, its body distinguishes between the keys that must be processed. It does not change the given world and, if necessary, creates a package.

165.1.3 The process-message Handler

This handler needs to process the single variety of tpm that has a marshaled world embedded in it. To do so, the embedded marshaled world needs to be unmarshaled. The following sample expressions illustrate how this is done:

```
;; Sample expressions for process-message
(define PM-TPM1 (unmarshal-world (rest TPM1)))
(define PM-TPM2 (unmarshal-world (rest TPM2)))
```

Observe that the `world` required as input by the API and the message's tag are not used. Abstracting over the sample expressions yields the following function:

```
;; world tpm → world
;; Purpose: Update the world with the given tpm
(define (process-message a-world a-tpm)
  (unmarshal-world (rest a-tpm)))
```

The tests using sample computations are written using sample `world`s, sample `tpm`s, and the value of the sample expressions. Tests using sample values are written using a sample `world`, and an explicit world message to illustrate that the unmarshaled `world` obtained from the embedded marshaled `world` becomes the new `world` value. The tests may be written as follows:

```
;; Tests using sample computations for process-message
(check-expect (process-message INIT-WORLD  TPM1) PM-TPM1)
(check-expect (process-message INIT-WORLD2 TPM2) PM-TPM2)

;; Tests using sample values for process-message
(check-expect (process-message WORLD3
                              (list
                               'world
                               (list (list 9 "Bolivar"))
                               (list (list 7 2))
                               'left
                               '()))
              (make-world (list (make-ally 9 "Bolivar"))
                          (list (make-posn 7 2))
                          'left
                          '()))
```

This completes the design of the player component. Make sure that the player's file has all the constants needed by the handlers and the tests. Do not forget to run the tests and verify that they pass.

165.2 Server Component

This subsection outlines the server's handlers for Aliens Attack 8. As with the player component, we shall reuse as much code as possible from Aliens Attack version 6. This reuse mostly refers to the tick handler and the auxiliary function for the message handler to process player requests.

165.2.1 The `process-tick` Handler

According to the API the tick handler must take as input a universe and return
a universe. This signature is different from the `process-tick` function from
Aliens Attack version 6 and, therefore, a new universe-processing function is needed.
Think carefully how a universe ought to be processed. If the given universe is
INIT-UNIV, it means that a player has not joined and the universe ought to remain
unchanged. Otherwise, the universe ought to be updated. The list of iworlds remains
unchanged. The game, on the other hand, needs to be updated. This may be achieved
by calling `process-tick` from Aliens Attack version 6 with the universe's game
value. This means that the `process-tick` and all its local auxiliary functions from
Aliens Attack version 6 need to be local to the server's `process-tick`. In addition,
as indicated by the protocol diagram in Fig. 145, the new world value must be sent
to all the players.

The handler is outlined as follows:

```
;; univ → bundle
;; Purpose: Create a new universe after a clock tick
(define (process-tick a-univ)

   (local [:
            ;; world → world
            ;; Purpose: Create new world after a clock tick
            ;; ASSUMPTION: The world is a structure
            (define (process-tick a-world) ... )]
     (if (equal? a-univ INIT-UNIV)
         (make-bundle a-univ '() '())
         (local [(define new-game
                         (process-tick
                          (univ-game a-univ)))]
           (make-bundle
            (make-univ (univ-iws a-univ) new-game)
            (map (λ (iw)
                   (make-mail
                    iw
                    (cons 'world
                          (marshal-world new-game))))
                 (univ-iws a-univ))
            '())))))
```

In this design the function always returns a `bundle` even when no messages are
sent to the players. The `local`-expression encapsulates `process-tick` and all its
auxiliary functions from Aliens Attack version 6. The body of the `local`-expression
distinguishes between a universe that has and that does not have at least one player.
Observe that in both cases the list of iworlds is unchanged and no iworlds are
disconnected from the universe. No mails are constructed when the game has not

started. When the game has already started, all players get the new `world` value that is locally defined (i.e., new-game).

The handler is tested in a similar fashion to testing done in previous versions of the game. That is, the tests illustrate that changes to the `aliens`, the `direction`, and the `shots` for the given `universe`'s `world` instance are correctly made and that the list of `iworlds` remains unchanged. Tests may be written as follows:

```
;; Tests using sample values for process-tick
(check-expect
  (process-tick
    (make-univ (list iworld1 iworld3)
               (make-world (list (make-ally 9 "iworld1")
                                 (make-ally 2 "iworld3"))
                           (list (make-posn 2 5))
                           'left
                           (list (make-posn 3 6) NO-SHOT))))
    (make-bundle
      (make-univ (list iworld1 iworld3)
                 (make-world (list (make-ally 9 "iworld1")
                                   (make-ally 2 "iworld3"))
                             (list (make-posn 1 5))
                             'left
                             (list (make-posn 3 5))))
      (list (make-mail iworld1
                       (list 'world
                             (list (list 9 "iworld1")
                                   (list 2 "iworld3"))
                             (list (list 1 5))
                             'left
                             (list (list 3 5))))
            (make-mail iworld3
                       (list 'world
                             (list (list 9 "iworld1")
                                   (list 2 "iworld3"))
                             (list (list 1 5))
                             'left
                             (list (list 3 5)))))
      '()))

(check-expect
  (process-tick
    (make-univ (list iworld3)
               (make-world (list (make-ally 6 "iworld3"))
                           (list (make-posn
                                  (- MAX-CHARS-HORIZONTAL 2)
```

```
                                        10))
                              'right
                              (list SHOT2))))
    (make-bundle
     (make-univ
      (list iworld3)
      (make-world (list (make-ally 6 "iworld3"))
                  (list (make-posn
                         (sub1 MAX-CHARS-HORIZONTAL)
                         10))
                  'down
                  (list (make-posn (posn-x SHOT2)
                                   (sub1 (posn-y SHOT2))))))
     (list (make-mail
            iworld3
            (list 'world
                  (list (list 6 "iworld3"))
                  (list (list (sub1 MAX-CHARS-HORIZONTAL) 10))
                  'down
                  (list (list (posn-x SHOT2)
                              (sub1 (posn-y SHOT2)))))))
      '()))
(check-expect (process-tick
                (make-univ
                 (list iworld2)
                 (make-world (list (make-ally 14 "iworld2"))
                             (list (make-posn MAX-IMG-X 2))
                             'down
                             (list (make-posn 15 6)))))
              (make-bundle
               (make-univ
                (list iworld2)
                (make-world
                 (list (make-ally 14 "iworld2"))
                 (list (make-posn MAX-IMG-X 3))
                 'left
                 (list (make-posn 15 5))))
               (list (make-mail
                      iworld2
                      (list 'world
                            (list (list 14 "iworld2"))
                            (list (list MAX-IMG-X 3))
                            'left
                            (list (list 15 5)))))
                '()))
```

```
(check-expect (process-tick
                (make-univ
                 (list iworld1)
                 (make-world (list (make-ally 3 "iworld1"))
                             (list (make-posn MIN-IMG-X 2))
                             'down
                             (list (make-posn 2 MIN-IMG-Y)))))
              (make-bundle
               (make-univ
                (list iworld1)
                (make-world
                 (list (make-ally  3 "iworld1"))
                 (list (make-posn MIN-IMG-X 3))
                 'right
                 '()))
               (list (make-mail
                      iworld1
                      (list
                       'world
                       (list (list  3 "iworld1"))
                       (list (list MIN-IMG-X 3))
                       'right
                       '()))))
               '()))
```

165.2.2 The process-message Handler

This handler is written by specializing the template for functions on a tsm. If the given tsm's tag is shoot or move, then the universe's game needs to be updated. In both cases this may be accomplished by refining process-key from Aliens Attack version 6. Think carefully about why a refinement is needed. The code for process-key always moves the ally or creates a shot for a single player. In this version of the game the server needs to do so for an arbitrary player. If process-key is made local to process-message, then the name of the iworld making the request and the universe's world value are in scope and may be used to correctly move or shoot. This means that process-key only needs the key to process as input. The key is used as expected to move an ally or to create a shot for an ally. The value returned by process-key, therefore, must be a bundle that has a univ with the new world value and the mails containing this new value for the players.

Figure 146 outlines the server's process-message handler. The signature clearly states that the handler may throw an error. This occurs when a message with an unrecognized tag is received. If the message's tag is 'shoot or 'move, then process-key

Fig. 146 The server's `process-message` handler

```
;; univ iworld tsm → bundle throws error
;; Purpose: Process the message to create new universe
;; ASSUMPTION: The given univ is not INIT-UNIV
(define (process-message a-univ an-iw a-tsm)
  (local [(define tag (first a-tsm)) (define name (iworld-name an-iw))
          (define game (univ-game a-univ))
          ;; key → bundle  Purpose: Create a bundle for player request
          (define (process-key a-key)
            (local [  ⋮
                    (define nw
                     (make-world
                      (cond [(key=? a-key "right")
                             (move-ally-right name (world-allies game))]
                            [(key=? a-key "left")
                             (move-ally-left name (world-allies game))]
                            [else (world-allies game)])
                       (world-aliens game) (world-dir game)
                       (if (key=? a-key " ")
                           (cons (process-shooting
                                   (ally-rocket (get-ally name
                                                  (world-allies game))))
                                 (world-shots game))
                           (world-shots game))))]
              (make-bundle
               (make-univ (univ-iws a-univ) nw)
                (map
                 (λ (iw)
                   (make-mail iw (cons 'world (marshal-world nw))))
                 (univ-iws a-univ))
                '())))]
    (if (or (eq? tag 'shoot) (eq? tag 'move))
        (process-key (if (eq? tag 'shoot) " "
                         (second a-tsm)))
        (error (format "Unknown to-server message type ~s" a-tsm)))))
```

is called with the key that needs to be processed. When the tag is `'move`, the needed key is extracted from the given `tsm`. The function `process-key` locally defines all the functions that were locally defined for Aliens Attack 6 (indicated by the ⋮). In addition, it locally defines `nw` for the new `world` created. This new `world` is created by processing the given key. The list of allies in this new world is computed by determining the given key's variety. Observe that `move-ally-right` and `move-ally-left` are called with `name` instead of `MY-NAME` as done in Aliens Attack version 6. This is how moving an arbitrary `ally` is achieved. The `aliens` and `direction` in the new `world` remain unchanged. The list of `shots` for the new `world` is obtained by determining if the given key is `" "`. If not, the `shots` remain unchanged. If so, a new shot is added to the game. Observe that `get-ally` is called with `name` instead of `MY-NAME` as done in Aliens Attack version 6. This is how creating a `shot` for an arbitrary `ally` is achieved. Finally, the body of the `local`-expression returns a bundle. The new `universe` is constructed using the existing list of `iworlds` and the new `world`. The list of `mails` implements all the arrows from the server to all the players in Figs. 141 and 142. No `iworlds` are disconnected from the server when a player's request is processed.

Testing the handler requires at least one test for the error thrown and one test for each `tsm` subtype. Given that functions are encapsulated, the only viable testing is using sample values. Testing the error generated is done by providing a `tsm` with an invalid tag:

```
(check-error
  (process-message OTHR-UNIV iworld2 (list 'move-left 'left))
  (format "Unknown to-server message type: ~s"
          (list 'move-left 'left)))
```

Testing the processing of a move message is done with two different `tsms`: one for each direction. The tests are written using a sample `universe` and sample `tsms`. The expected bundles illustrate that the list of `iworlds` remains unchanged and that the proper ally is moved in the proper direction. Sample tests are as follows:

```
(check-expect (process-message OTHR-UNIV iworld2 MV-LEFT)
              (make-bundle
                (make-univ (list iworld1 iworld2)
                           (make-world
                             (list (make-ally 7 "iworld1")
                                   (make-ally 8 "iworld2"))
                             (list (make-posn 3 3))
                             'right
                             (list (make-posn 1 2))))
                (list
                 (make-mail iworld1
                            (list 'world
                                  (list (list 7 "iworld1")
                                        (list 8 "iworld2"))
                                  (list (list 3 3))
                                  'right
                                  (list (list 1 2))))
                 (make-mail iworld2
                            (list 'world
                                  (list (list 7 "iworld1")
                                        (list 8 "iworld2"))
                                  (list (list 3 3))
                                  'right
                                  (list (list 1 2)))))
                '()))
```

```
(check-expect (process-message OTHR-UNIV iworld1 MV-RGHT)
              (make-bundle
               (make-univ (list iworld1 iworld2)
                          (make-world
                           (list (make-ally 8 "iworld1")
                                 (make-ally 9 "iworld2"))
                           (list (make-posn 3 3))
                           'right
                           (list (make-posn 1 2))))
                (list
                 (make-mail iworld1
                            (list 'world
                                  (list (list 8 "iworld1")
                                        (list 9 "iworld2"))
                                  (list (list 3 3))
                                  'right
                                  (list (list 1 2))))
                 (make-mail iworld2
                            (list 'world
                                  (list (list 8 "iworld1")
                                        (list 9 "iworld2"))
                                  (list (list 3 3))
                                  'right
                                  (list (list 1 2)))))
                '()))
```

Testing the processing of a shoot message illustrates that a new shot is created for
the proper ally for a given sample universe that otherwise remains unchanged. It
also illustrates that the universe's iworlds also remain unchanged. A sample test
is the following:

```
(check-expect
 (process-message OTHR-UNIV iworld1 SHOOT)
 (make-bundle
  (make-univ
   (list iworld1 iworld2)
   (make-world
    (list (make-ally 7 "iworld1") (make-ally 9 "iworld2"))
    (list (make-posn 3 3))
    'right
    (list (make-posn 7 14) (make-posn 1 2))))
  (list
   (make-mail
    iworld1
    (list
     'world
     (list (list 7 "iworld1") (list 9 "iworld2"))
     (list (list 3 3))
```

```
   'right
   (list (list 7 14) (list 1 2))))
 (make-mail
  iworld2
  (list
   'world
   (list (list 7 "iworld1") (list 9 "iworld2"))
   (list (list 3 3))
   'right
   (list (list 7 14) (list 1 2)))))
 '()))
```

165.2.3 The add-player Handler

The handler to add new players must reject iworlds that have a name that is already in use in the universe's list of iworlds. In such a case, the handler returns a bundle with an unchanged universe, an empty list of mails, and a one-iworld list to disconnect from the server that contains the iworld attempting to connect. The following sample expression illustrates the design:

```
;; Sample expressions for add-player
(define RPT-ADD (make-bundle OTHR-UNIV '() (list iworld1)))
```

OTHR-UNIV already has an iworld with the name "iworld1". The world trying to connect is rejected. If the iworld connecting does not have a name already in use, two cases must be distinguished: this is the first player that joins or it is not. If it is the first player to join, the initial world containing the ally that just joined is used to create a new universe. Otherwise, the new ally is added to the existing game. In both cases the new iworld is added to the universe's list of iworlds. According to the protocol diagram in Fig. 144, a world message must be sent to all players. The new world value containing the new ally must be marshaled to send to all the players. The following sample expressions illustrate how this may be achieved:

```
(define
 EMP-ADD
 (local
  [(define new-iws (cons iworld2 (univ-iws INIT-UNIV)))
   (define game (univ-game INIT-UNIV))
   (define new-game
           (if (equal? game UNINIT-WORLD)
               (make-world (list (make-ally
                                  INIT-ROCKET
                                  (iworld-name iworld2)))
                          INIT-LOA
                          INIT-DIR
                          INIT-LOS)
```

```
                 (make-world (cons (make-ally
                                       INIT-ROCKET
                                       (iworld-name iworld2))
                                    (world-allies game))
                              (world-aliens game)
                              (world-dir game)
                              (world-shots game))))]
   (make-bundle (make-univ new-iws new-game)
                (map (λ (iw)
                       (make-mail
                         iw
                         (cons 'world
                               (marshal-world new-game))))
                     new-iws)
                '()))))

(define
 NEW-ADD
 (local
  [(define new-iws (cons iworld3 (univ-iws OTHR-UNIV)))
   (define game (univ-game OTHR-UNIV))
   (define new-game (if (equal? game UNINIT-WORLD)
                        (make-world
                         (list (make-ally
                                   INIT-ROCKET
                                   (iworld-name iworld3)))
                         INIT-LOA
                         INIT-DIR
                         INIT-LOS)
                        (make-world
                         (cons (make-ally
                                   INIT-ROCKET
                                   (iworld-name iworld3))
                               (world-allies game))
                         (world-aliens game)
                         (world-dir game)
                         (world-shots game))))]
   (make-bundle (make-univ new-iws new-game)
                (map (λ (iw)
                       (make-mail
                         iw
                         (cons 'world
                               (marshal-world new-game))))
                     new-iws)
                '()))))
```

Local variables are defined for the new list of iworlds and for the new world value. The new list of iworlds is obtained by adding the joining iworld to the list of iworlds in the given universe. An if-expression is used to define the new world value by distinguishing whether or not the given world is the first to join. The body of the local-expression returns a bundle with the new universe and a list of mails with the marshaled new world.

Based on the sample expressions, the add-player handler is defined as follows:

```
;; universe iworld → bundle
;; Purpose: Add new world to the universe
(define (add-player a-univ an-iw)
  (if (member?
        (iworld-name an-iw)
        (map iworld-name (univ-iws a-univ)))
      (make-bundle a-univ '() (list an-iw))
      (local [(define new-iws (cons an-iw (univ-iws a-univ)))
              (define game (univ-game a-univ))
              (define new-game (if (equal? game UNINIT-WORLD)
                                   (make-world
                                    (list (make-ally
                                           INIT-ROCKET
                                           (iworld-name an-iw)))
                                    INIT-LOA
                                    INIT-DIR
                                    INIT-LOS)
                                   (make-world
                                    (cons (make-ally
                                           INIT-ROCKET
                                           (iworld-name an-iw))
                                          (world-allies game))
                                    (world-aliens game)
                                    (world-dir game)
                                    (world-shots game))))]
        (make-bundle
         (make-univ new-iws new-game)
         (map
          (λ (iw)
            (make-mail
             iw
             (cons 'world (marshal-world new-game))))
          new-iws)
         '()))))
```

The handler is tested as follows:

```
;; Tests using sample computations for add-player
(check-expect (add-player OTHR-UNIV iworld1) RPT-ADD)
```

```
(check-expect (add-player INIT-UNIV iworld2) EMP-ADD)
(check-expect (add-player OTHR-UNIV iworld3) NEW-ADD)

;; Tests using sample values for add-player
(check-expect
 (add-player (make-univ
               (list iworld2 iworld3)
               (make-world
                (list (make-ally 7 "iworld2")
                      (make-ally 9 "iworld3"))
                (list (make-posn 3 3))
                'right
                (list (make-posn 3 3))))
             iworld1)
 (make-bundle (make-univ
               (list iworld1 iworld2 iworld3)
               (make-world
                (list (make-ally 10 "iworld1")
                      (make-ally 7  "iworld2")
                      (make-ally 9  "iworld3"))
                (list (make-posn 3 3))
                'right
                (list (make-posn 3 3))))
             (map
              (λ (iw)
                (make-mail
                 iw
                 (cons
                  'world
                  (marshal-world
                   (make-world (list (make-ally 10 "iworld1")
                                     (make-ally 7  "iworld2")
                                     (make-ally 9  "iworld3"))
                               (list (make-posn 3 3))
                               'right
                               (list (make-posn 3 3)))))))
              (list iworld1 iworld2 iworld3))
             '()))
```

Observe that the test using sample values illustrates how a new player, iworld1, is
added to the universe and how all the world mails are created.

165.2.4 The `rm-player` Handler

The handler to remove a player needs to create a new `world` value by eliminating the `ally` from the disconnected `iworld` and by removing the disconnected `iworld` from the list of `iworlds`. This may be accomplished by filtering the list of allies and the list of `iworlds`. In addition, as specified by the protocol diagram in Fig. 143, the new `world` value must be sent to all the (remaining) players. The following sample expressions illustrate how this is accomplished:

```
;; Sample expressions for rm-player
(define RM-IW1 (local
                  [(define iws  (univ-iws OTHR-UNIV))
                   (define game (univ-game OTHR-UNIV))
                   (define new-iws (filter
                                      (λ (iw)
                                        (not (string=?
                                               (iworld-name iworld1)
                                               (iworld-name iw))))
                                      iws))
                   (define new-game (make-world
                                      (filter
                                       (λ (a)
                                         (not (string=?
                                                (iworld-name iworld1)
                                                (ally-name a))))
                                       (world-allies game))
                                      (world-aliens game)
                                      (world-dir game)
                                      (world-shots game)))]
                  (make-bundle (make-univ new-iws new-game)
                               (map (λ (iw)
                                      (make-mail
                                       iw
                                       (cons 'world
                                             (marshal-world
                                               new-game))))
                                    new-iws)
                               '())))

(define RM-IW2 (local [(define iws  (univ-iws OTHR-UNIV2))
                       (define game (univ-game OTHR-UNIV2))
                       (define new-iws
                         (filter
                          (λ (iw)
                            (not (string=?
                                   (iworld-name iworld2)
```

```
                              (iworld-name iw))))
                    iws))
          (define new-game
                  (make-world
                   (filter
                    (λ (a)
                     (not (string=?
                            (iworld-name iworld2)
                            (ally-name a))))
                     (world-allies game))
                     (world-aliens game)
                     (world-dir game)
                     (world-shots game)))]
          (make-bundle (make-univ new-iws new-game)
                       (map (λ (iw)
                              (make-mail
                               iw
                               (cons 'world
                                     (marshal-world
                                      new-game))))
                            new-iws)
                       '())))
```

Observe that `filter` is used to remove the disconnected `iworld` and its corresponding `ally`. The creation of the `tpms` is done using `map` and the new list of `iworld`s.

Abstracting over the sample expressions yields the function for this handler:

```
;; univ iworld → bundle
;; Purpose: Remove given iw from universe and game
;; ASSUMPTION: Given univ is not INIT-UNIV
(define (rm-player a-univ an-iw)
  (local [(define iws  (univ-iws a-univ))
          (define game (univ-game a-univ))
          (define new-iws (filter
                           (λ (iw)
                            (not (string=? (iworld-name an-iw)
                                           (iworld-name iw))))
                           iws))
          (define new-game (make-world
                            (filter
                             (λ (a)
                              (not (string=? (iworld-name an-iw)
                                             (ally-name a))))
                             (world-allies game))
                            (world-aliens game)
                            (world-dir game)
                            (world-shots game)))]
```

```
(make-bundle (make-univ new-iws new-game)
             (map (λ (iw)
                    (make-mail iw (cons 'world
                                        (marshal-world
                                         new-game))))
                  new-iws)
             '())))
```

The function is tested as follows:

```
;; Tests using sample computations for rm-player
(check-expect (rm-player OTHR-UNIV  iworld1) RM-IW1)
(check-expect (rm-player OTHR-UNIV2 iworld2) RM-IW2)

;; Tests using sample computations for rm-player
(check-expect (rm-player (make-univ
                          (list iworld3)
                          (make-world
                           (list (make-ally 8 "iworld3"))
                           '()
                           'down
                           '()))
                         iworld3)
              (make-bundle
               (make-univ
                '()
                (make-world '() '() 'down '()))
                '()
                '())))
```

Observe that the test using sample values explicitly shows everything that is removed from the `universe`.

This completes the design of Aliens Attack version 8. Make sure that you have the needed constants in the server and player files. Run the tests. Once all the tests pass, play the game on your computer. Observe that the players, unlike Aliens Attack version 7, do not become unsynchronized. This is because all players get the same game from the server.

166 A Subtle Problem

Play the game with one or two friends. Assuming your internet connection is fast enough the game ought to run smoothly. However, as the number of players increases, the game may become choppy. That is, the game becomes sluggish or momentarily stops. This may be due to *communication overhead*. Communication overhead is the proportion of time that is spent exchanging messages instead of advancing the state of the game. If communication overhead is large enough, the game becomes slow.

In distributed programming communication is necessary and, therefore, some degree of communication overhead is necessary. It is desirable, however, to keep this overhead small to make programs faster. There is no universal solution to this problem. That is, implementing a solution may or may not produce the desired result. Common approaches to reduce communication overhead are to limit the number messages exchanged and reduce the size of the messages exchanged. In Aliens Attack 8, for example, the world value is always sent to the players. This is done despite the fact that only one component of the world has changed. A different communication protocol may transmit to the players only the components that have changed. This may or may not be effective but is worth trying if communication overhead makes the game slow. The exercises have you explore the mitigation of communication overhead.

***** **Ex. 339** — Design and implement a communication protocol that only transmits to the players the parts of the world that have changed in a message. For example, when a move request is satisfied, a single `ally` is changed and nothing else changes in the game. Instead of sending the entire world to all players, only the changed `ally` may be sent. Is the resulting game noticeably faster or slower?

***** **Ex. 340** — Design and implement a communication protocol that does not send every single change to the player as they happen. Instead, the server may wait for a number of changes, n, to occur before sending a message to the players. Is the resulting game noticeably faster or slower?

167 What Have We Learned in This Chapter?

The important lessons of Chap. 29 are summarized as follows:

- Allowing only one component to change shared data (e.g., the world value) in a distributed program solves synchronization problems.
- The communication protocol for a distributed program using a thick server can be significantly simpler than the communication protocol when using a thin server.
- Components not allowed to change the value of shared data make requests to the server for changes to be made.
- Consistency in design makes it easier for others to understand the design of the code and is likely to make future refinements easier to implement.
- Code reuse is an effective way to manage the complexity of refinements.
- Communication overhead, the proportion of time that is spent exchanging messages instead of computing, may make applications slow.
- The impact of communication overhead may be mitigated by reducing the frequency and the size of messages.

Part VI
Epilogue

Chapter 30
Advice for Future Steps

Congratulations! You have reached the end of your first step into the world of problem solving and program design. There is still much more you can learn about problem solving and programming, but there is no doubt that now you have a solid foundation to continue on this journey. This journey is inevitable even for those who do not aspire to become Computer Scientists. Remember that problem solving is at the heart of many human activities.

Although the book builds on much of your background knowledge (e.g., high school algebra), you likely feel you have a different understanding now of this knowledge. The book has emphasized the use of types to organize your thoughts during the problem solving process. At the heart of this process is how elements in the real or an imaginary world are represented in a program. The chosen representation may (and should) be exploited to find solutions to problems. Remember that if you know the type of data to be processed, then you know something about what the solution to a problem may look like.

All good things must continue . . .

168 Advice for Computer Science Students

Be patient and apply the skills you have learned in the future. As your studies progress, you will discover that few textbooks on programming emphasize design. This makes it difficult sometimes to understand the programs presented. When you see such code, tease out the details. Try to formulate the steps of the design recipe to enlighten you about what the program does. This a good skill to develop given that large pieces of software evolve over years of development in which programmers come and go. Documenting the design of a program is a service that you and others will appreciate when you have to maintain code.

Where can you go from here? The most fundamental piece of advice is to read and learn more about problem solving using a computer. You will be well-served if you practice your design skills by learning about a new programming language

© The Author(s), under exclusive license to Springer Nature Switzerland AG 2022
M. T. Morazán, *Animated Problem Solving*, Texts in Computer Science,
https://doi.org/10.1007/978-3-030-85091-3_30

every semester and summer. The skills you have developed are directly applicable to solving problems using programming languages beyond BSL, BSL+, and ISL+. As you advance, you will discover abstractions that are not covered in this textbook. You are, however, well-prepared to learn about them. You will also be well-served to explore topics covered in this book in more depth, such as big-O notation (i.e., complexity), generic programming, and distributed programming. I cannot recommend strongly enough to take courses in the implementation of programming languages: truly understand the technology that is central to Computer Science.

169 Advice for Non-Computer Science Students

You may feel excited, overwhelmed, or both after completing this textbook. There is no doubt that you are a better problem solver now. The truth is that you are likely to program throughout your life. Perhaps not using a programming language as done in this textbook, but if you are problem solving then you are programming. You may write essays, diagnose a patient, or create a piece of music. What do these activities have in common with programming? They process data and are refined until you are satisfied with the result. Is this truly different than finally designing Aliens Attack 8? Do you not refine several drafts of an essay? Use the lessons you have absorbed and apply them to domains other than programming. The famous popular saying *don't reinvent the wheel* is a call for abstraction. If you think about it carefully, you will see that the steps of the design recipe are applicable to problem solving in any context.

You are now in a much better position to understand and, therefore, use software. If you use a spreadsheet, you are programming. If you adjust the settings of a thermostat, you are programming. If you are driving, you are programming. No? When you put your blinker on before turning, are you not sending a message to other drivers? If you begin to realize that problem solving and programming are fully intertwined with life, then you are now in a position to be a better problem solver.